Christmas 1984

THE HISTORY OF
THE TIMES

VOLUME I
'THE THUNDERER' IN THE MAKING
1785–1841

VOLUME II
THE TRADITION ESTABLISHED
1841–1884

VOLUME III
THE TWENTIETH CENTURY TEST
1884–1912

VOLUME IV
150th ANNIVERSARY AND BEYOND
Part I 1912–1921
Part II 1921–1948

VOLUME V
STRUGGLES IN WAR AND PEACE
1939–1966

SIR WILLIAM HALEY,
EDITOR OF *THE TIMES* 1952–1966
(Photo U.P.I.)

THE HISTORY OF
THE TIMES

VOLUME V

STRUGGLES IN WAR AND PEACE
1939–1966

by

Iverach McDonald

PUBLISHED BY TIMES BOOKS
16, GOLDEN SQUARE
LONDON
1984

Dedication
To Gwenda who since
1935 has shared all
the pleasures and the
strains of living with
The Times

British Library Cataloguing in Publication Data

McDonald, Iverach
    The History of the Times.
    Vol. 5: Struggles in War and Peace 1939–1966
    1. Times, The – History
    I. Title
    072'.1   PN 5129.L715

    ISBN 0-7230-0262-2

Typeset by
Rowland Phototypesetting Limited
Printed in Great Britain
by St Edmundsbury Press

CONTENTS

LIST OF ILLUSTRATIONS

FOREWORD

THE publication of the fifth volume of the official history of *The Times* marks the paper's two hundred year anniversary in 1985, just as the publication of the original four volume history was begun in 1931 with the object of marking the paper's 150th anniversary. We can look back on the fifty intervening years of war, turbulence and profound change in the world which it is our purpose each day to portray to our readers. In 1935 our predecessors could look back on fifty years which were just as turbulent; in 1885 the same. One can tread backwards throughout the history of *The Times* and always find the same perspective. Indeed as I approach my office each day along the corridor I am confronted by a row of portraits of my predecessors who look down on our present endeavours. There are only eleven of them. Most of them saw the paper's fortunes vary often with as much severity and unpredictability as the events narrated and examined each day in its pages. That is part of the common inheritance of editors of *The Times*. It binds us with a sense of continuity, for all the changes which have occurred both in the nature of the world we write about and in the methods we employ to produce our paper. The great strength of *The Times* has been its continuous ability to adapt to change in its environment without impairing the paper's tradition of excellence. As we approach our 200th birthday, *The Times* is once again expanding, circulation and revenue have made spectacular advances with a commensurate reduction in the paper's losses. We have emerged from a period of great change and uncertainty which will be chronicled in due course in the next volume of the official history. When that comes to be written we must hope that the quickening pace which now infects us with an expectation of sustained growth and ever greater achievement will prove to have been triumphantly vindicated.

Charles Douglas-Home
April 1984

INTRODUCTION

The main theme running through the four earlier volumes of the *History of The Times* is the triumph of the newspaper over the astonishing number of shocks and dangers which have beset it. 'The Thunderer' thrived in the storms. It was never shielded by its oft-acclaimed status as a national institution. It had to struggle for survival from the beginning, even while it was building up its own independent news service and then later while it was shaking governments by the force of its opinions. When it faltered it was chiefly in the periods when it was tempted to coast along on its hard-won reputation.

The first of its fights is described in Volume I of the *History* (1785–1841) published in 1935 to commemorate the 150th anniversary of the founding of the newspaper by the first John Walter. It was the fight to free *The Times* from the political subsidies then customary, to break the Post Office monopoly over news, and to win the paper its power in the life of the nation. That was the battle from which Thomas Barnes (editor 1817–1841) emerged to stand as the greatest journalist of the nineteenth century; in helping his own newspaper to be free and self-respecting he led the way for others. Volume II (1841–1884), published in 1939, explains the struggle to preserve the hard-won independence against all the jealous forces at Court and in government. The paper's campaign on behalf of the wounded and neglected British soldiers in the Crimean war won it fame but no immunity from outside pressures. Volume III (1884–1912), published in 1947, gives the story of the paper's survival through years of dire poverty, made worse by the damages it had to pay in the Parnell forgery case, and relieved only when the paper was bought by Northcliffe in 1908. Volume IV (1912–1948), appearing in two parts in 1952, is the chronicle of the newspaper's tribulations and progress under Northcliffe, its relative tranquillity under John Astor and John Walter IV, and its survival throughout the world wars, economic crises, and industrial upheavals of the period. Volume V, which now appears to commemorate the two hundredth anniversary of the founding of the newspaper on January 1 1785, is no less a story of struggle. It covers the years 1939–1966: years which changed the world, changed Europe, changed Britain, and changed *The Times*.

By way of preliminary it should be explained why the present volume begins by going back a little distance over ground traversed by Volume IV. In that fourth volume the late Stanley Morison and his collaborators took the story so far as 1948 because they rightly judged that the death early that year of Robert Barrington-Ward, while still editor, marked the end of one of the most memorable chapters in the newspaper's story. They gave some appraisal of Barrington-Ward's work. But Morison himself admitted in his introduction to the volume that he and his helpers could give only 'an abbreviated narrative of the principal occurrences in the office between 1939 and 1948'. The gaps have now had to be filled for many reasons, but chiefly because under Barrington-Ward *The Times* spoke out strongly, bravely, and controversially both during the Second World War and during the subsequent social revolution in Britain. To leave that period without detailed examination in the official *History* would be to leave the story of the newspaper distorted as well as incomplete. The present volume therefore begins at 1939, with a necessary look back, in the light of new evidence, at the paper's part in the Munich crisis of 1938, rehearsed here because, as is shown, the memory of it affected the editorial line in several international confrontations later.

In working on this volume the writer has had two aims chiefly in mind. The first is to be true to the title: which means to write another chapter in the history of *The Times* and not be carried away into a history of the times. That was the intention which Stanley Morison made plain nearly fifty years ago in his introductory synopsis of Volume I: 'It devotes', he wrote of the volume, 'no greater space to public affairs than is essential to explaining the growth and development of the newspaper.' The second aim derives directly from the first. The purpose is to tell the paper's story in a full and rounded way, not concentrating solely or even largely on its political opinions as presented in its leading articles, but telling also of the men and women engaged in all the many departments of a great newspaper. Over the years the news columns have had their influence no less than the leading articles.

It might be thought that the first of the two aims, avoiding general history, should not be difficult. Many of the public events that are mentioned happened within living memory; they should therefore need no re-telling. Other writers have plentifully presented the documents released from the archives of British and other governments; their contents should have similarly no need for recapitulation. Yet in practice it has been found that much of what *The Times* did can be properly explained only when the historical setting, no matter how recent, is recalled and some details of it are examined afresh. Only then can the rightness or wrongness of a given line of policy be judged or a change in policy be made intelligible. To take only one example: without some relation to the historical background the difference between the impact of *The Times* under Barrington-Ward and its later impact under Sir William Haley (editor 1952–1966) cannot be fairly assessed. Barrington-Ward was the more radical in his policies, that is true; but far more than a difference in personality or individual philosophy was involved. Britain and the world underwent many changes between the period when Barrington-Ward was editor and the period of Haley's editorship, and these changes imposed much of the change in the paper's voice.

Barrington-Ward believed that he had essentially an educative job to do in the years of the war, and in the years immediately after, when the future of Britain and of Europe was still largely a matter of deduction that often seemed nearer to guesswork. He set out to stir people to think on unaccustomed lines. He pressed the case for accepting and welcoming the welfare state, for working out a just rather than a vengeful peace, and for acknowledging the power of the Soviet Union which after its years of pre-war seclusion was appearing on the world scene like a new continent. Many of Barrington-Ward's arguments brought heavy criticism against *The Times*. They were none the less opportune, courageous, and effective; most of them have been justified in substance although occasionally their actual wording, clear and often didactic, provoked more irritation than agreement at the time among such readers as hankered for a return to the world of before the war. During Haley's years as editor Britain entered her new phase. As the welfare state was already firmly established Haley felt obliged to emphasise that a citizen had duties to fulfil as well as benefits to receive from the state. After years of heavy government spending Haley came out against the growing evils of inflation. When there was no longer any need to declare that the post-war domination by Soviet Russia over eastern Europe was inevitable (Russia had already secured such dominance for herself) he emphasised the need to strengthen the North Atlantic alliance and other defensive arrangements while still seeking east–west agreements. Barrington-Ward himself would have been influenced in his policy by the new-risen historical forces if he had lived. Certainly Haley's liberal side was to be shown in the way he assessed the force of the movement for independence in the African and Asian colonies. He supported the 'wind of change' without hesitation and

3

under him *The Times* was particularly sensitive to the problems and aspirations of the emergent countries of the third world. Such outside pressures on policy show how much more than editorial personality was involved.

Many more illustrations of the point can be made. The interplay between outside forces and editorial opinion is shown in the paper's slowly formed and then steadily held support for the European Economic Community; once again an educative influence was needed and it was strongly exerted by the paper in several series of special articles. More broadly, some of its lines, such as its argument that Communist China was not in an aggressive phase, were later to be widely accepted as self-evident; but at the time they were not so accepted, largely because China was still allied to Russia and because the rise of any new power is bound to arouse suspicions. Of particular value was the paper's emphasis on the importance of neutral groups in the world balance of power during the years when neutrality was frequently denounced as craven and immoral.

The background has also to be briefly described on the occasions when *The Times* has directly influenced events, for example, when it provoked a political storm (the 'Selwyn Lloyd affair' of 1959 comes immediately to mind) or when it went clean contrary to prevailing thought (as it did in 1963 in its sweeping attacks on the Robbins report which came out in favour of swift university expansion). General history is also invoked in the many confidential memoranda, quoted in this volume, which were written by members of the staff after talks with leading statesmen in Britain and abroad. Of particular interest are those based on conversations with Sir Anthony Eden (later Lord Avon) during the months of the Suez crisis in 1956.

None the less what follows is essentially true to the main aim of concentrating on the story of *The Times* and its works, editorial and managerial, at home and overseas. Any such attempt to give a full story of a newspaper comes up against a peculiar difficulty straight away. Much of daily journalism by its very nature does not lend itself to historiography. Presenting the news accurately day by day, being ahead of rivals with an item by twenty-four hours, carrying a brighter and fuller account of a momentous event, even advocating policies which seem novel at first but which are soon accepted as plain common sense: such exertions keep papers going. They keep journalists going. They keep the interest and loyalty of readers. But within weeks, or within a few months at most, much of it has faded into the historical background and all the enterprise and zeal of the staff are nine-tenths forgotten. What remain outstanding are the general lines of policy, the wider development of the news coverage (such as occurred under Haley), the particular news stories that stand out from the rest, the characters of members of the staff, and the varying fortunes of the newspaper itself. Such themes make up much of the present volume. I have written with the greater will about the careers and personalities of *Times* men and women in the years 1938–1966 because, having first entered Printing House Square in 1935, I have known almost every single one and have worked closely with most of them, both those on the editorial and in later years on the managerial sides.

When '*The Times* tradition' is evoked it is right to recall a succession of editors with strong views both on public affairs and on the shape and course of the paper itself. It is no less right to recall the many men and women lower down on the editorial staff who hold this tradition in their hands day by day and pass it on to their juniors. It is something that no one on the paper could escape, whether it was passed on in the inculcation of accuracy and judgment, in the need for speedy writing and prompt decision, or in the art of presenting exciting news without exaggeration. Throughout the years covered by this volume such men and women, the correspondents, reporters, critics, and sub-editors, worked anonymously. Many of their names are now very properly brought out. Some of their work has been retrieved from back numbers of *The Times*. Much of it has also been examined in the newspaper's copious and well-ordered archives which hold row after row of boxes filled with staff memoranda and letters, formal and informal, some domestic within Printing House Square, others sent from Tokyo, Brazzaville, or elsewhere. Without this disciplined array of material to draw upon the attempt to evoke the pell-mell years 1939–1966 would have been hard indeed.

During the same years *The Times*, as a commercial concern, was caught up in the struggle which afflicted all the daily newspapers in London, battered as they were with rising costs, print union power, weak management far too often, and later the surging competition from television. Especially under the editorship of William Haley and the management of Francis Mathew, *The Times* was striving to modernise itself and to expand as a condition of survival. In many ways it had to spend proportionately more on editorial content than its rivals. As a journal of record it had regularly to carry many columns of matter, such as parliamentary debates and law reports, where most other papers could pick and choose according to news value on the day. During the lean years of the Second World War newsprint rationing forced it to make one of its most painful decisions, preferring, as the present volume recounts, to cut its circulation rather than cut itself down to a size which would have left it no longer *The Times*. After the war it was the more determined to broaden itself once again into a journal of record and, with that end in view, it fought the government – and defied other newspapers – to secure the much belated ending of newsprint rationing. That was one of the paper's victories.

In those years *The Times* needed both more pages each day and more money behind it. As a journal of repute it could not make catchpenny appeals for circulation. As a newspaper for experts as well as for intelligent general readers it had to employ many specialists who could write with authority and precision. The expense of keeping such a staff mounted as *The Times*, like other newspapers, had to broaden its contents in order to withstand the competition from radio and television.

The period covered by this volume opens when the press was still the main medium for news and opinion. Even during the Second World War, when the BBC's nine o'clock news was heard on the radio each night as a voice of authority throughout the land, the habit of seeing what the papers said – seeing it in black and white – was unchecked. The years since then have shown how the heavier and always increasing challenge from television has forced all newspapers into new and in many ways diminished roles. The reply to the challenge is familiar. While the popular papers provided more entertainment the serious papers set out to offer more explanation and more pages of non-political interest. *The Times* had to meet the required outlay of expenditure out of its relatively small income and with its requirement of high quality always in mind.

It was a struggle on many fronts, and it is described in this volume as it appeared at the time in Printing House Square. Mistakes were made and are acknowledged. Some opportunities were missed; others were put off far too long. There were divided counsels over the very nature of *The Times*. Should it stay catering for the minority, particularly at Westminster and Whitehall and in the City? Or should it bend itself to modernise more quickly and appeal, as Haley sought, to the new-risen educated ranks throughout the country? This difference of view, far too seldom explored but none the less persistent within Printing House Square, contributed to the costly delay in introducing the big change of May 3 1966 when news was at last put on the front page and many other features appeared elsewhere. This change, coming at least five years late, was made only three months before Lord Thomson of Fleet began his negotiations for the purchase of The Times Publishing Company. Yet, looking back, it is right to recall that confidence within the office was generally high; the circulation was beginning to rise steadily again.

Confidence became higher still when Lord Thomson publicly promised to invest all the money which *The Times* needed for its further modernisation and expansion. That is the point at which the present narrative ends, and it would be wrong to let it be submerged by all the disputes and disappointments – as well as the substantial advances – that lay ahead and that led to the purchase of Times Newspapers Limited by Mr. Rupert Murdoch in 1981.

The years 1939–1966 were all years of struggle. Therefore they could not be gloomy. Many were heroic years. During much of the time the newspaper had too few men and women and too little money for all it sought to do. The more honour for what it did. Men and women on *The Times* are usually too busy to look back but when they do they are apt to compare their efforts with what was done for the paper by John Walter II, Thomas Barnes, and William Howard Russell. More often, being journalists, they look around to see how they are faring against their competitors in Britain and countries abroad. There is more than simple loyalty involved in saying that the period under review stands out well, whichever of the two comparisons is made.

As this volume was going to press there came the sad and unexpected news that the second Lord Astor of Hever had died after a brief illness. As Gavin Astor, John Astor's eldest son, he was deeply involved in the fortunes and the increasing financial strains of the Times Publishing Company; from 1959 he was Chairman and from 1964 co-chief proprietor; his part in the negotiations which led to the sale of the company in 1966 is described in the later chapters. His unfailing and conscientious help in the preparation of this volume was typical of his abiding concern in everything to do with *The Times*.

Iverach McDonald

I

THE NEWSPAPER AND THE MEN

T HE five and a half months which separated Hitler's invasion of Prague on March 15 1939 and his attack on Poland on September 1 were decisive for public opinion in Britain. The march into Prague made it clear beyond doubt that Hitler was not going to be halted without war, and such knowledge brought a new sense of unity in Parliament, in the City, in the constituencies, and in the newspapers.

Some few members of Parliament and some journalists still suspected throughout the summer that the Chamberlain government might try to do a deal with Germany at Poland's expense. Yet to offset such fears was the consoling thought that the government had left itself little room for manoeuvre or backsliding after giving the pledge of support to Poland on March 31 and opening the long, slow defence talks with Russia on April 15. More people came to believe that Mr. Chamberlain and Lord Halifax, his Foreign Secretary, meant what they said when declaring that future acts of aggression would be resisted.

The editorial staff of *The Times* shared that broad movement towards unity. Men in the higher ranks had been deeply and painfully divided throughout 1937, 1938, and the early months of 1939 when the paper allied itself with Neville Chamberlain's appeasement policy; but by the time the British and French governments sent their ultimatums to Hitler on September 3, after the invasion of Poland, the whole team in Printing House Square had pulled itself together as closely as any group in the country.

It may seem strange, looking back at the very deep rift in Printing House Square from 1937 to early 1939, that the healing process in the office was so easy and so complete. Two or three reasons may explain why it was so. Several of the younger men who had been most vehement against the appeasement policy had already enrolled themselves in the Territorial Army or in the Officers' Emergency Reserve; when war was imminent they left to join the armed forces, taking their convictions and their arguments with them. The older men who remained saw no point in going over all the old disagreements again. In a curious way each side

within the office – the appeasing school no less than the anti-appeasing –
was left equally sure that it was the one which had been proved right by
events; and so each side was content to rest its case.

The appeasers' argument did not lack strength. Geoffrey Dawson,[1]
the editor, Robert Barrington-Ward,[2] his deputy, and Leo Kennedy,[3]
foreign leader writer, had been the most fervent in advocating the
policy. Dawson and Barrington-Ward were the dominant forces in the
office, by reason both of their position and their personalities. When
their hopes faded and war came nearer they could claim that Chamberlain's patient and concessionary policy had demonstrated as a matter of
certainty that Hitler was not open to negotiation and was deaf to all
reasonable talk. They could also claim that the British people at home
and overseas who had been divided and uncertain were now bound
together by the knowledge that the war was forced on them by Hitler
and by Hitler alone.

The anti-appeasers in the office had the simpler and more cogent
case to sustain. At their head was the kindly and wise William Casey,[4]
the senior assistant editor, already nearing sixty and looking older with
his heavily lined face and soft white hair. He was the natural confidant
for the dissidents; he was their adviser. After the collapse of Chamberlain's policy he shared with them one mordant satisfaction at least.
Hitler, they could say, had shown himself before the world to be the
aggressor that they had for years declared him to be. There was no need
to rub that truth in now when everyone – calamitously late – had come to
see it. What mattered now was to run the paper throughout the
imminent war and help so far as they could in the national effort,
without any backward glances.

In swinging *The Times* behind the policy of appeasement Geoffrey
Dawson and Barrington-Ward were well aware that they were wielding
a potent weapon. In the 1930s British newspapers as a whole had an
enviable strength and influence. They were still the chief source of news
and comment. The printed word in a serious daily newspaper or in a
weekly still kept something of its nineteenth-century authority. Newspapers generally were only just beginning to regard broadcasting as a

---

1 Geoffrey Dawson (1874–1944). Eton; Magdalen College, Oxford. Editor of *The
Times* 1912–19 and 1922–41.
2 Robert (also known as Robin) McGowan Barrington-Ward (1891–1948).
Westminster; Balliol College, Oxford. Editor of *The Times*, 1941–1948.
3 Aubrey Leo Kennedy (1885–1965). Harrow; Magdalen College, Oxford. Leader
writer and special correspondent on *The Times* between 1911 and 1942.
4 William Francis Casey (1884–1957). Trinity College, Dublin. *The Times* editorial
staff, 1913–48; editor of *The Times*, 1948–52.

rival to them. Although the BBC wireless service was already firmly established, it took care to be neutral in its presentation of news and had not yet recruited a large reporting staff. Almost all the comments it made were evenly balanced. The revolutionary prospect of television, with its world-wide and instant coverage of events, seemed only a dream or a nightmare to newspapermen. 'The late 1930s, the last years of peace, were the golden age of newspapers in Great Britain. More newspapers reached more people than ever before, or than anywhere else in the world.'[5]

In that golden age *The Times* had its high and distinctive place. 'More than a newspaper: an institution' – the phrase was repeatedly used. Its unique standing was partly due to its own merits, partly to the semi-official status that was widely accorded to it, especially in countries abroad. No number of denials could remove the widespread assumption, highly irritating to the staff, that *The Times* was the faithful voice of whatever British government was in power at the time.

As such it was read especially closely by diplomats in London and overseas. Some of the more experienced among them might recognise that the truth was not so simple. *The Times*, they acknowledged, did not speak directly for the government; it spoke for itself; but its independent views, they noticed, generally corresponded with the thinking of influential groups in Westminster, Whitehall, the City, and the older universities. It therefore could be taken as the voice of the dominant minority in the country; sometimes in line with the government, sometimes in divergence; and where it was divergent it was (these diplomats told themselves) especially worth noting, for then it showed what kind of pressures were likely very soon to be brought against the government from within the ruling circle in the attempt to bring about a change of policy. Other diplomats and many foreign correspondents in London took the story of the direct link between *The Times* and the government quite literally, even to the point of believing that, where *The Times* took a line opposed to the government, the Cabinet ministers themselves were signalling through the columns of *The Times* that they were about to change their policy.

Geoffrey Dawson would often squirm and protest against this common view of *The Times* but he lent support to it in two ways. First, he believed that the wider interests of the country put a special responsibility on *The Times* by reason of its high prestige and influence. As a working principle the paper should be ready to give an incoming

---

5 Franklin Reid Gannon, *The British Press and Germany, 1936–1939*, p. 1.

government the benefit of the doubt and should be ready to continue that general support so long as it could in all conscience do so. Where the paper felt called upon to criticise, it should make its points in moderate and constructive terms, displaying a full knowledge and understanding of the problems facing the government. In other words – here he agreed with some of the watchful diplomats – it should write less as an outside critic and more as a judicious, informed, and independent-minded member of the governing group.

Secondly, and more decisively, Geoffrey Dawson was himself a natural member of the Establishment. Where *The Times* leading articles conformed with an official line it was not so much because Geoffrey Dawson tamely followed it as because his upbringing, background, and manner of thinking made him share the line – or sometimes anticipate it in leading articles. Being part of the Establishment in those days meant being at the top of a steep social and political pyramid. A government generally carried a prestige which its successors in the less deferential society of the 1960s and 1970s came to envy. A jibe heard throughout the appeasement period that Dawson was 'in Chamberlain's pocket' fell far short of the truth. Oliver Harvey, later Lord Harvey of Tasburgh, repeats this accusation in diary jottings which he made when private secretary to Lord Halifax in the Foreign Office. After the German invasion of Austria in March 1938, Harvey writes:

> The Press is unanimous in condemning Germany's behaviour. Even *The Times*, though reluctantly so but H. [Halifax] had spoken to Dawson who will do whatever H. tells him. (March 12 1938.)[6]

Later, on May 19 1938, Harvey records that *The Times* had a parliamentary note hinting that Anthony Eden might fairly soon be brought into the government:

> I wonder if H. is privy to this: Dawson eats out of his hand and I doubt of his putting it in (for he is no friend of A.E.'s policies) without some very high authority.[7]

Such references give no full or proper picture of Dawson's personality which is central to the story of *The Times* in the pre-war and early war years. Indeed no account of the paper in the thirties and forties can make any sense without a full assessment of the characters of the two men, Dawson and Barrington-Ward, who were dominant in Printing

---

6 *The Diplomatic Diaries of Oliver Harvey, 1937–1940*. Edited by John Harvey, p. 115.
7 *Ibid*, p. 140.

House Square. Until 1941 they worked together as editor and deputy; after 1941 Barrington-Ward was alone.

As a man Geoffrey Dawson was a much more forceful character than most contemporary accounts suggested. He had the easy habit of command, an imperturbable air about him, and the bluff manner and rugged build of a countryman; proud of his Yorkshire birth, his years at Eton (where he was a King's Scholar), Magdalen and All Souls; proud also of his years with Milner in South Africa and his appointment as editor of the Johannesburg *Star* while still a young man. In his first term as editor of *The Times*, from 1912 to 1919, he learnt by harsh experience how much mischief and frustration can be caused by proprietorial interference in an editor's work. When he was asked, after Northcliffe's death in 1922, to come back to the editor's chair he made it clear that he would return only on his own terms: he must be left entirely independent in the conduct of the paper. The new co-chief proprietors – Major J. J. Astor[8] and Mr. John Walter[9] – might remove him if they lost confidence in him: unless or until that point came they could not interfere.[10] Dawson was in a strong position to make such conditions for he was by no means anxious to return. Only a few years previously an aunt had left him a large estate at Langcliffe, Settle; he had become estates bursar at All Souls and had several other Oxford interests to occupy him.

Independence in Yorkshire, and now independence in Printing House Square, increased his natural sense of confidence. Beyond that he had the calmness of manner that comes from mastery of a craft. As an editor he worked much harder than his easy, unflurried manner suggested. He took a direct concern in most parts of the paper. He could do most things better than anyone else in the office, whether drafting leaders, or writing headings, or doing picture captions, or seizing on news and playing it up. Within the office he was an informal head, never patronising, often inviting frank criticisms of his own leader drafts; never making pettifogging suggestions to other writers; friendly to the

---

8 John Jacob Astor, 1st Baron Astor of Hever (1886–1971). Eton; New College, Oxford. Co-chief proprietor of *The Times*, 1922–66, and chairman, The Times Publishing Company, 1922–59. Conservative MP for Dover, 1922–45. First chairman, Press Council. Baron, 1956.
9 John Walter (1873–1968). Eton; Christ Church, Oxford. Entered *The Times* office, 1898; assistant correspondent, Paris; served *The Times* in Spain, The Hague and Lisbon, as well as many parts of Europe and in America on special missions; chairman, The Times Publishing Company Limited, 1910–22; co-chief proprietor, 1922–66.
10 *History of The Times*. Volume IV, p. 768 ff.

young hopefuls; given to deep, private reflexion but shying away from any long discussions of policy; becoming quickly restive at any detailed exposition of a problem by visitors or by his own experts. He preferred to go round himself from room to room to chat briefly with each leader writer in turn and even then was careful, more often than not, to stand with his hand on the open door so that he could escape the moment he chose. In his own room he had two doors: one, in front of his desk, through which a visitor would be shown into the presence; the other, behind his desk, through which Dawson could quickly disappear as soon as he thought – as he often did think – that the visitor was becoming boring.

As a general rule he seemed to think that only half a dozen leading articles a year really mattered. The rest were intellectual exercises which could instruct or entertain readers and need not take up much of his time. When, however, he had a major leader in hand he worked over and over on it. He believed that such a leader in *The Times* should not simply influence opinion; it should, and could, and often did, influence events. He would see several ministers and high officials, he would closely question the experts on his staff, and would often take up his first draft to refashion it during a day or two at Langcliffe. The result was a forceful essay, not in any way weakened because it would sometimes convey its meaning by suggestion and implication rather than bald statement. He liked to illustrate his articles with a few sly quips and with quick character portraits of the men under discussion. At its best, his writing was unpompous, sinuous, colloquial, knowledgeable, and highly persuasive.

Dawson's frequent and friendly contacts with men in high places brought him under heavy criticism from those who believed that an editor should always demonstrate his freedom from official pressures and influences. Lord Milner, on whom Dawson in his early and middle years leaned for advice, went so far as to say, 'Geoffrey's Achilles heel is his friends', meaning that they could too easily sway him. But Dawson had a brusque way of dismissing unwelcome advice or what he called 'viewy' notions, no matter how friendly the source. He was equally firm in maintaining that a good part of his job as editor lay in keeping in with the men who possessed position, power, and knowledge. He was supported in this by his unshakeable belief that, in politics and in public affairs generally, men were in the last resort more important than policies. He was on easy terms with Baldwin,[11] Neville Chamberlain,[12]

---

11 Stanley Baldwin, 1st Earl Baldwin of Bewdley (1867–1947). Prime Minister, 1923, 1924–29, 1935–37.
12 Neville Chamberlain (1869–1940). Prime Minister, 1937–40.

and Halifax,[13] and knew most of the Dominion Prime Ministers and High Commissioners exceptionally well. In the tense months of 1938–39 he was certainly influenced by Chamberlain and Halifax. But he was influenced by them chiefly in the sense that they confirmed his own thinking about the way to treat Germany. He went to them disposed to agree. With Halifax he was particularly close. Their common background of Eton, Oxford, and Yorkshire squirearchy helped to shape a common outlook between them on most matters.

Dawson's primary concern with men rather than policies could have made him wholly a pragmatist or an empiricist. In considering home affairs he was indeed largely pragmatic: a conservative who fully agreed with movements towards slow social reform, but he drew back from any radical reconstruction of the society he knew. There was nothing piecemeal, however, about his deep concern and affection for the Empire and Commonwealth during all the years – his own years – when the Commonwealth was accepted as a force in the world. He had the strategic vision of an Empire moving towards independence. This abiding concern for the world-wide Empire and Commonwealth, and his instinctive understanding of sea power did not provide him with the best equipment for evaluating the totally different problems of Europe with its nationalities and minorities, its land frontiers, its lines of jealously prized natural defences, and its easily upset equilibrium. Dawson in fact showed little awareness of the need to preserve a balance of power in Europe. It is true that, as Hitler increased Germany's armed strength in the middle and late thirties, Dawson's native shrewdness and commonsense made him advocate greater defensive strength for Britain herself. After the German armies had occupied Vienna in March 1938 Dawson had a leader recommending Britain to begin compulsory national service in ARP (air raid precautions);[14] a suggestion which, if adopted, must have led on inevitably to military conscription, not in fact introduced until a year later. Even so, he showed no awareness that Hitler's seizure of the Sudeten lands of Czechoslovakia amounted to a strategic victory that dangerously upset the military equilibrium. His approach to Europe was that of an eighteenth-century English diplomat, slightly removed, slightly impatient, not feeling compelled to become conversant with every detail of the background. His whole training and upbringing persuaded him that a reasonable argument and

---

13 Edward Frederick Lindley Wood, 1st Earl of Halifax (1881–1959). As Lord Irwin, Governor-General and Viceroy of India, 1925–31. Foreign Secretary, 1938–40. Ambassador in Washington, 1941–46.
14 *The Times*, March 15 1938. See Chapter III.

a timely concession by one power must evoke a reasonable response by the power facing it in a dispute.

Robin Barrington-Ward was a man of wholly different cast. He had a much more strongly burning sense of mission, a fiercer desire to do positive good in many fields. It was a desire shaped by his early upbringing, by a proper ambition, and by his devastating experience of fearful slaughter when he served as an officer in the First World War. Where Geoffrey Dawson appeared as basically a solitary man, in spite of all his friends, Robin Barrington-Ward was modestly conscious of being, and was widely known to be, one of five gifted brothers. They were the sons of a deeply religious inspector of schools who in his sixties – when Robin was already eighteen and a King's Scholar at Westminster – became Rector of Duloe in Cornwall, and later Canon of Truro. At Balliol, armed with the second scholarship of his career, Barrington-Ward distinguished himself far more at the Union and in editing the *Blue Book*, an undergraduate magazine, than he did in his final examinations. Afterwards he was to tell himself that he had dispersed his energies. The shock of getting a third-class degree, when a first had been foretold for him, revived in him everything that he had been taught at home about the virtues of unremitting application to work. It was a lesson he never forgot.

Before the outbreak of the First World War he put in some months in Printing House Square, first as a sub-editor, then as editor's secretary, a post then used by way of introducing likely young men to the office. Returning from France with a record of great gallantry, he went for some years to the *Observer* under J. L. Garvin, and came back to *The Times* as assistant editor in 1927. Still in his middle thirties, he had already specified in his mind the two great courses which he was determined to serve and advance. In home affairs he wished to strive as best he could to rid Britain of the areas of unemployment and poverty. He struck a blow for that cause in 1929 when he printed powerful despatches on the human and industrial predicament in the derelict areas of the North-East. He followed them up with three longer special articles and two leaders (by the labour correspondent, J. V. Radcliffe[15]) which exposed once again the waste and the misery. The series strengthened the uneasiness in the House of Commons about the whole problem and the Government was forced to appoint an Unemployment Commission.

---

15 John Vernon Radcliffe (1877–1954). After early career on provincial newspapers became Manchester correspondent of *The Times* in 1919; parliamentary correspondent, 1921; labour correspondent, 1920–21, 1923–46.

For his second cause Barrington-Ward looked across the Channel. He was determined to do all he could to prevent another war of the kind which he himself had – by 'the merest, the least deserved of flukes'[16] – survived. Knowing that war had often been caused by unrequited grievances he began by pressing for the removal of the penalties imposed last time on the defeated Germany by the Treaty of Versailles. Later he broadened this aim to cover the removal of all German grievances, and he held to this purpose steadfastly until March 1939. Until that same date in 1939 he set himself against any 'encirclement' of Germany by means of alliances, and often declared in the office that Germany was bound inevitably to have influence in eastern and south-eastern Europe. He recognised much of the evil in Hitlerism but strongly contested the opinion that a great people should be denied justice because they had fallen under a strident and tyrannous regime. 'We believe this to be a notion which plays straight into the hands of Nazism', he wrote. 'It allows the Nazi regime to found itself upon causes that are the possession of the whole German people, irrespective of view . . . I do not know what outside influence can be brought to bear for the eventual disruption or extinction of Nazism except in the removal of the causes which have created it.'[17]

From 1929 onwards Geoffrey Dawson had tended to leave most of the longer leading articles on home policy and on Europe to his deputy. Barrington-Ward was not an easy writer. Every time he picked up his pencil to do a leader he became wrestling Jacob struggling with eternal truths. Dawson left him also much of the day-to-day administration within the office and in that work Barrington-Ward went assiduously into every detail. The appointment of any new man or woman to the staff, or the approval of any article for publication, was for him an exercise in deeply considered judgment. Beyond that, he had to step forward to edit the paper when Dawson was absent, sometimes for weeks at a time; and he was always conscientious in meeting ministers, ambassadors, and officials outside Printing House Square, either in their offices or over lunch or dinner. In his own room he drove himself to the limits of his strength, his eyes burning in his lean priest-like face as he bent over his desk. He had a regular working day of twelve or fourteen hours. Sometimes it was longer. .

The result was that for years he was over-worked. The more he

---

16 B-W D, February 23 1941.
17 Letter to the Master of Balliol, October 7 1938, T.T.A. Alexander Dunlop Lindsay, Baron Lindsay of Birker (1879–1952). Master of Balliol, 1924–1949; in October 1938 was standing (unsuccessfully) as an anti-appeasement candidate in a by-election at Oxford.

over-worked, the harder he drove himself, and – as a natural consequence – he became the more firmly convinced about the correctness of
his line of policy. He was never the man to be deflected from doing the
right thing as he saw it. Both he and Geoffrey Dawson knew to the full
the workings of the political world and could shrewdly assess which
forces would prevail. The difference was that where Dawson had the
calmness of the businessman or the seasoned politician in approaching
public affairs Barrington-Ward had the inner light of the missionary.

At weekends, and occasionally of an evening, he let himself relax
with his family and his friends or in music. Then the repressed Robin in
him – a Robin of great kindness and gaiety – would emerge. To counter
his mental fatigue, he would happily go for long walks or, when the
family had a Bedfordshire cottage for some years, he would as happily
help a neighbour in his smallholding. In fact he may have made such
weekends too active; his colleagues felt that he did not always return
rested or refreshed to the office.[18]

Dawson and Barrington-Ward in fact complemented each other.
Dawson's anxiety for the safety and continuing unity of the Empire and
Commonwealth and Barrington-Ward's zeal for ensuring peace
through a timely settlement of German grievances dovetailed together
to produce the paper's European policy that encouraged the dangers to
mount far too dangerously for far too long.

In any review of that sad chapter only a few significant new points need
be added to the story (told in Volume IV of the *History of The Times*) of
how the paper sank to its low level with its leading article of September 7
1938. Most students of Munich must know by heart the chief offending
passage, published at the worst possible time when tension within
Czechoslovakia was near to breaking. After suggesting that the Sudeten
Germans might ask for more independence than Prague could tolerate,
the leader (as amended by Dawson for the later editions) continued:

> In that case it might be worth while for the Czechoslovak Govern-
> ment to consider whether they should exclude altogether the
> project, which has found favour in some quarters, of making
> Czechoslovakia a more homogeneous state by the secession of that
> fringe of alien populations who are contiguous to the nation with
> which they are united by race.

Volume IV described in detail how Dawson had come back on Septem-

---

18 For assessments of Dawson and Barrington-Ward by some former members of the
staff see Appendix A.

ber 6 from a month in Yorkshire to find the leader nearly complete, how he quickly got the writer to change parts of it, not liking them as they stood, how Casey showed his dislike of most of it when seeing it in proof, how Dawson hastily altered it again in proof, and how it finally appeared in the later editions. What Volume IV (guided by its own anonymity rules) did not say was that the first drafts, before Dawson tinkered with the article, were written by Leo Kennedy. In his own private journal Kennedy shows that in writing the leader he was guided both by the tenor of talks within the office and by the memory of two confidential remarks by the ministers most directly involved. The first remark was by Chamberlain when he told American journalists on May 10 1938 that he would not refuse the cession of the Sudeten areas to Germany; the second was by Halifax a month later when, in a letter to Dawson, he asked him not to press at that time for a plebiscite in the Sudeten areas. In his journal Kennedy goes on:

> But in that letter he added that he personally by no means ruled it [a plebiscite]out as an ultimate solution. It was this opinion of his which encouraged us [T.T.] to put forward the proposal of secession in September, when obviously Runciman's efforts were failing.[19] By that time feelings were running so high that separation without a plebiscite seemed the only solution, as Ld. Runciman himself came to agree.[20]

In short Kennedy thought that he was following government policy; but the two ministerial remarks which he quoted had been made months earlier, before tensions were stretched to the point at which a heavy public pronouncement could snap them. *The Times* was a jump ahead of the government when it made precisely such a pronouncement in its leading article on September 7.

Neither did Volume IV say how Runciman personally reacted in Prague. 'This is a black day for us', he said to a *Times* correspondent on September 7. Two blows had struck him. The Sudeten German leaders had just rejected Prague's latest offer which substantially gave them everything that they had asked for in the way of home rule; and on top of that there had come *The Times* leader. Runciman told the same correspondent during their talk that he thought his mission was now hopeless; none the less he would try, without much confidence, to get

---

19 Viscount Runciman (1870–1949), a former Liberal and Liberal National MP, and President of the Board of Trade in the governments of Asquith, MacDonald and Baldwin, had been sent to Prague in July to seek a solution between the Beneš government and the Sudeten Germans.
20 Kennedy, Private Journal, October 17 1938.

the Sudeten Germans back into the talks and he would tell the Czecho-slovak ministers that *The Times* was not the voice of the British government. He sent off a telegram of expostulation to Halifax[21] and he sent, through the correspondent, another message to Dawson. The article, he told the editor, could not have come at a worse time from his point of view.

In their diaries both Dawson and Barrington-Ward wrote that the leader had not turned out wholly as they would wish but they did not regret the substance of it. Nor did Kennedy. In his own journal he gave his own general reflexions:

> I think that Chamberlain's only mistake in the whole business was the tactical one of not saying anything about it [the idea of secession] in public before Hitler faced him with it at Berchtesgaden. Then he accepted it at once. It looked like capitulation to a dictator.[22]

It did indeed. September 7, which marked the lowest point in the paper's pre-war policy, marked also the widest division of opinion within Printing House Square. Throughout this time Casey ensured that the divisions did not become worse. There was never anything like a cabal among the dissidents. Each of them would confide in Casey who advised them all in turn to be both patient and persistent. Their main endeavour was to write their own pieces in the paper and put forward hard, factual points when talking with Dawson and Barrington-Ward.

Casey was at his desk in the evenings until about midnight. His job was to look over the proofs of leaders and news despatches, a key job in those years, although he himself used to call it a housemaid's work: 'simply sweeping up after others, my dear chap, and usually there is nothing to sweep.' No one was deceived by his irony. Armed with the proofs he would often suggest to Dawson and Barrington-Ward that they should look again at some passage in a leading article that he disliked, and sometimes he succeeded in having worthwhile changes made. He also could ensure that especially revealing news despatches from correspondents abroad were given prominently in the paper. The correspondents in the chief European centres at that time – James Holburn and Ewan Butler in Berlin, Thomas Cadett and Thomas Barman in Paris, Christopher Lumby in Rome[23] – knew that they had in Casey a sympathetic link within the office. They had no need to be in touch with him day by day. They were content to know that both Casey

---

21 *Documents on British Foreign Policy, Third Series.* Volume II, 1938, p. 271 n.
Geoffrey Dawson Diaries (GDD), September 7 1938.
22 Kennedy, *loc. cit.*
23 The working careers of these correspondents are reviewed in Chapter IV.

and G. L. Pearson,[24] the chief foreign sub-editor, were giving a proper place to despatches that demonstrated the dangers ahead.

Colin Coote,[25] one of the chief home leader writers, thought of resigning as several others were tempted to do. Outside the office Coote had supported Winston Churchill in his struggle against appeasement; and Churchill, when Coote asked his opinion about resigning, advised against, saying 'he would prefer a friend in the enemy's camp.'[26] Anthony Winn,[27] the young parliamentary correspondent, did indeed resign. Dawson had held out of the paper a note which Winn had written on Duff Cooper's resignation speech on October 3 1938 and had substituted one of his own, satirical in tone and much more critical of Duff Cooper.[28] In his letter to Dawson Winn gave the more substantial reason for his resignation: 'During the past month my deepest convictions on foreign policy have been opposed to the general line taken by the "Times" . . . My distaste for what I frankly regard as a silly and dangerous policy has been hardening for many weeks.'[29] The others who were tempted to leave decided that, given the influence of *The Times*, it was better to peg away and get a paragraph or two in *The Times* than a column elsewhere.

Dawson strongly disliked speculative pieces in the news columns, and would sometimes have them out, even though the writers had been trying to convey some useful confidential or sensitive information by hints rather than by flat statement. The paper lost some stories in that way. One such loss during the summer of 1939 was a detailed forecast, necessarily tentative and unconfirmable but (as emerged in the official announcement some weeks later) very well based, of the Hitler–Stalin pact for the division of Poland. For Dawson the report was all too much up in the air. Even so he had the true journalist's respect for hard news presented straight. His ideal newspaper, never to be realised, would have kept news and comment in separate columns or on separate pages. Staff correspondents both at home and abroad, on seeing a piece of

---

24 Geoffrey L. Pearson (1888–1981). Joined *The Times* staff 1919; foreign sub-editor, 1923; chief foreign sub-editor, 1929–50; assistant editor (night), 1950–53; retired 1953.
25 Sir Colin Reith Coote (1893–1982). Rugby; Balliol College, Oxford. Liberal MP for Isle of Ely, 1917–22. *The Times* Rome correspondent, 1922; parliamentary sketch and leader writer, 1924–42. Deputy editor, *Daily Telegraph*, 1945–50; managing editor, 1950–64. Knighted, 1962.
26 Sir Colin Coote, *Editorial*, p. 171.
27 Anthony Edmund Winn (1909–1942). Eton; Christ Church, Oxford. Lobby correspondent for *The Times*, 1938; later on editorial staff *Daily Telegraph*. Killed in action, Egypt, November 1942.
28 Alfred Duff Cooper, 1st Viscount Norwich (1890–1954). First Lord of the Admiralty, 1937–38; Minister of Information, 1940–41. Ambassador in Paris, 1944–47.
29 Winn to Dawson, October 4 1938. T.T.A.

theirs cut, would tend to suspect the editor's hand; subsequent inquiries very often showed that the cuts were made simply for reasons of space by the sub-editors.[30]

The great and immediate change brought within *The Times* by Hitler's occupation of Prague on March 15 1939 is shown in two leading articles, written within three days of each other by Barrington-Ward. In the first, published on March 13, he still defended Munich; he sustained himself by 'the knowledge that Germany had completed those demands upon her neighbours which, by their own professions, they were unable conscientiously to resist'; and he still looked ahead to further friendly talks:

> There is a readiness to confer and to cooperate with any country, under whatever Government, that is prepared to enter negotiations in the spirit of reciprocity.

In the second article, after the German troops had moved, he expressed shock, anger, and revulsion. 'No defence of any kind, no pretext of the slightest plausibility, can be offered for the violent extinction of Czech independence.' The shock was fundamental to a man who had based his policy towards Germany, even Hitler's Germany, on moral grounds. His sense of disillusionment was explicit on that point:

> The invasion, occupation and annexation of Bohemia–Moravia are notice to the world that German policy no longer seeks the protection of a moral case.[31]

From that moment until the outbreak of the war *The Times* was much firmer than it had been before when facing Hitler's Germany. It spent far less time in casting around for an easy way out of the dangers. Only once did it have a bad relapse, and it recovered from it in fairly good order. Its moment of dithering came when Neville Chamberlain, overcoming his long-harboured reluctance to see Europe 'divided into two camps', announced in the House of Commons on March 31 that Britain would give all support to Poland if Poland were attacked. Chamberlain took pride in his own wording of the pledge. Britain would give its support 'in the event of any action which clearly threatened Polish independence, and which the Polish government accordingly considered it vital to resist with their national forces.'

---

30 A fuller examination of reports about editorial 'censorship' under Dawson and Barrington-Ward is made in Appendix B.
31 *The Times*, March 16 1939.

The leading article the next day, written by Kennedy, spelled out all too clearly the inner meaning of the careful wording of the pledge:

The new obligation which this country yesterday assumed does not bind Britain to defend every inch of the present frontiers of Poland. The key word in the statement is not integrity but 'independence' . . . Mr. Chamberlain's statement involves no blind acceptance of the *status quo*.

The leading article then took even more stuffing out of the pledge:

This country has never been an advocate of the encirclement of Germany, and is not now opposed to the extension of Germany's economic activities and influence, nor to the constructive work she may yet do for Europe.[32]

Once again, as over Munich, storm broke out around Dawson's head. In the House of Commons on April 3 Churchill declared, 'There was a sinister passage in *The Times* leading article on Saturday similar to that which foreshadowed the ruin of Czechoslovakia.' Dawson showed not the least sign of misgiving. In a letter of April 4 he wrote privately:

Incidentally there was a lot of rather silly talk to the effect that *The Times* had weakened the force of the declaration by its comments. These people do not read *The Times*. What we had actually done was to point out that this declaration was not a mere pledge to respect every inch of the territorial *status quo*, but a guarantee of independence against aggression, which is a much bigger thing.[33]

Dawson's reasoning is a little hard to follow, but he was confident in the knowledge that the leader reflected the government's own view. He had met Halifax on April 3; Halifax had seen Chamberlain on the day the leader appeared, and Chamberlain had told him (said Halifax) that the leader had expressed just what he had meant.[34] Dawson also knew that Kennedy had seen Sir Alexander Cadogan,[35] the permanent head of the Foreign Office, before writing the leader. Kennedy recorded the talk and the sequel:

Great row over our leader of April 1 . . . I had seen Cadogan the day

---

32 *The Times*, April 1 1939.
33 Dawson to Stanley Washburn, an American correspondent who sent despatches to *The Times* in the First World War and remained in touch with Dawson, April 4 1939. T.T.A.
34 GDD, April 3 1938.
35 Sir Alexander George Montague Cadogan (1884–1968). Permanent Under-Secretary of State for Foreign Affairs, 1938–46.

before [Thursday] and wrote the leader entirely on the lines of our talk and of what he told me. Possibly GD and I between us put a shade too much stress on the *limitations* of the guarantee, and too little on its *implications*. But surely of all blunders the worst is to allow more to be read into a guarantee than is intended.[36]

The Polish government were none the less furious; there were hints that Colonel Joseph Beck, the Polish Foreign Minister, might not come to London as planned unless the British government repudiated *The Times's* gloss on the commitment. Chamberlain and Halifax uttered reassuring words, and a spokesman said that the Foreign Office thought some sentences in the article unfortunate, particularly the one that read, 'The key word is not integrity but "independence".' Kennedy's record sheds a little more light on the drafting both of the leader and of the government declaration:

GD put in 'not integrity' [in the leader]. I had not mentioned integrity but agreed to the insertion. In any case it was Cadogan himself who told me that the Govt. had (at first) proposed the words 'integrity and independence', and prided himself on the fact that the FO had persuaded them to drop out the word 'integrity'. I had of course reported that to GD.[37]

The repercussions broadened. Kennedy learned that the Soviet Foreign Minister, Maxim Litvinov, on hearing about the article, had informed the British Ambassador, Sir William Seeds, that it showed that Britain was not in earnest and that her guarantee was not good enough; more substantially, Moscow was deeply affronted at not being consulted over the guarantee.[38] From the Berlin Embassy, via the Foreign Office, came rumours that Hitler, 'half-crazed' at the British guarantee to Poland, was thinking of a sudden blow at the Royal Navy.[39] Kennedy had a consoling thought:

I feel that if our leader had been extra-provocative instead of extra-tranquillising, it might conceivably just have set Hit. off in his present mood. I've always said to GD – remember we're dealing with a neurotic, and it's as important to be calm as to be firm. He has quite agreed.[40]

---

36 Kennedy, Private Journal, April 4 1939.
37 *Ibid*, April 4.
38 *Ibid*, April 5.
39 Memorandum to editor from diplomatic correspondent (I McD), April 4 1939. T.T.A.
40 Kennedy, Private Journal, April 5 1939.

It is evident, looking back, that the April 1 leader neglected two large elements in the predicament. It did not recognise that, in leaving the way open for negotiations over Danzig and the Polish Corridor, it exposed Poland to Hitler's familiar technique of putting forward demands, then increasing them, and denouncing his intended victim before the world as the sole obstacle to agreement; in that way he planned to isolate the new victim (as he had isolated Czechoslovakia) and alienate it from its friends and allies.

Secondly, the article did not say (very few people at the time did say) that in giving the pledge to Poland Britain had in effect said she would go to war if one of Russia's main outer defences was attacked; the pledge was an indirect guarantee of Russia's western flank; and so Britain had lessened Russia's immediate need to come to a defensive alliance with the western powers. In the event, the uproar over the article was soon forgotten as Britain and France gave more promises of support to countries in east and south-east Europe and thereafter opened the talks with Moscow.

Dawson saw Chamberlain and Halifax several times during the desultory course of the Anglo–French negotiations with Moscow. During the early weeks he came back to the office sharing Chamberlain's view that the talks should go on but were not likely to produce anything. Nevertheless the leading articles expressed the strong desire for agreement; and the exchanges with Moscow were followed and recorded as fully as possible. James Holburn was sent to Moscow to send reports from there, and so became the first correspondent that *The Times* had stationed on a permanent basis in Moscow since the 1917 revolution. In London the News Department of the Foreign Office gave regular information, much of it secret, to members of the staff; and Ivan Maisky, the Soviet Ambassador, was ever quick to give men from *The Times*, as from other papers, his own version of Britain's laggard approaches.

Never having had much faith in the Anglo–French talks with Moscow Dawson was not alarmed when they collapsed and the Hitler–Stalin pact was announced. When the news was brought to him in his office he laughed at the thought of the two rogues getting together. He did not immediately examine the strategic consequences. Neither (to his credit) did he suggest that Britain should withdraw from its pledge to Poland on the grounds that the diplomatic upheaval had made it virtually inoperable.

The contrasting characters of Geoffrey Dawson and Robin Barrington-Ward came out in their individual responses to the outbreak of war.

24

Dawson is typically quiet, direct, and matter-of-fact both in his private diary entries and in his first leading article after the British declaration. He did not let any of his deeper thoughts appear. On September 3 he wrote in his diary simply,

WAR – I was in Printing House Square before 11 a.m. at which hour the notice to Hitler expired and heard the P.M.'s broadcast . . . Thence Coote and I were going to the House, which was to meet at 12, when the sirens went for a very prompt air raid warning and the streets were cleared and London went to ground. However we got there in time to hear the Prime Minister and Greenwood,[41] Winston and McGovern.[42]

In the leading article which he wrote that same day and which he placed second in the paper on September 4, Dawson argued the advantages of having a small War Cabinet. He wrote it in his unshakeably distinctive and artful style. Over the years he had developed to a fine art the ability to write an article in which the meaning of the whole was much greater than the sum of its words. In the September 4 article his welcome to Churchill, hitherto much distrusted in Printing House Square as being irresponsible and wild, is beautifully phrased:

Mr. Churchill comes in now, as a matter of course, because he is a man of dynamic energy, most fertile imagination, and warlike temperament. These are qualities essential in a War Cabinet. They also provide sufficient reason why Mr. Churchill was not invited to join in the Government during the period of negotiation. He himself bore witness yesterday that nothing has contributed so much to the strength of the British cause in this grave crisis as the conviction, shared with our people by the whole world, that war has been forced upon a Government completely unanimous and untiring in its pursuit of peace.

Barrington-Ward's voice and character come out no less truly in his writings during those days. To his private diary he confided his anguish of mind as his last hopes foundered:

What folly, folly, folly, this is. We shall have to fight until Hitler is put out, but that means, again, taking some sort of responsibility for the next German Government. We didn't make much of a show of it last time. An unforced evolution in Germany is what Europe needs.[43]

---

41 Arthur Greenwood (1880–1954). Minister of Health, 1929–31. Member of War Cabinet, 1940–42.
42 John McGovern. Independent Labour Party member for Shettleston, 1930–45.
43 B-W D, August 27 1939.

His leading article of September 4 (it appeared above Dawson's) is all the stronger for coming from a man who had done everything he could, driven by his conscience, to avert a war. The article very honestly goes back over those efforts:

> We have sought peace with the German people, we have given proof in word and deed of our desire for its friendship, and our quarrel today lies with its rulers and with the policy with which they have blackened the German name . . . For so long as it was possible to distinguish between the domestic and foreign policies of Nazism it was rightly contended that the future of Nazism was in the hands of the German people alone. Even the peculiar and repellent views of German authoritarianism could not shake the determination to leave German evolution in German hands.

But then came the moral revulsion and the sense of outrage:

> In the eyes of the world the calculated invention of a German–Polish crisis, the atrocity lies, and finally the fraudulent peace 'proposals' are characteristic marks of a kind of stupid and suicidal cunning which has served only to aggravate the crime which it was intended to explain and excuse . . . Self-deluded and self-doomed, the Dictator of Germany has given the British and French peoples no choice but to resist and overthrow him. Much as they loathe war, they love liberty more. The alternative that Hitlerism thrusts upon them is a surrender to organised brutality and treachery which would extinguish the last lights of freedom in Europe.

The main headlines of *The Times* that day read:

AT WAR WITH GERMANY

**BRITAIN AND FRANCE TAKE
UP THE CHALLENGE**

THE KING'S MESSAGE TO HIS PEOPLES

CABINET RECONSTRUCTED

The memory of the appeasement policy was to hang over the paper for years. Later critics were quick to bring it up when leading articles strongly supported the left wing in the Greek civil war and whenever the paper sought ways of coexistence with Stalin's Russia. But at the time Dawson and Barrington-Ward were no more wrong than the government and most of the Establishment. They shared the most serious flaw in the government's thinking – namely, the reluctance or the refusal to appreciate the need to build up a balance of power in Europe. It was this flaw that was to prove disastrous and nearly fatal for the country.

In the prevailing mood Churchill and other critics often felt like men trying to put shape into cotton wool. Behind the official reluctance to think in strategic terms lay widespread conviction that war – what we should now call conventional war – was as alien to human reason as nuclear war is now regarded as being. The determination never to risk a return to the mass slaughter in the trenches of 1914–18 was supported by the new fear of civilian annihilation from the fast developing, and still virtually untried, air weapon. The two fears combined to make many minds reject all strategic calculations as being irrelevant and dangerous when the discussion should rather be concerned with peaceful settlements. The corruptive evil and effectiveness of modern totalitarian power had yet to be generally learned. Hitler, it was thought in Printing House Square, would surely join other leaders in finding ways other than war for the solution of disputes and claims. In the meantime Britain should rearm, but cautiously, with the air of warning and deterring a would-be belligerent, without the risk of alarming him or crippling the home economy and overseas trade.

When such a background of appeasement is recalled the mistakes committed in its name become only more clearly apparent. To say, as was often said in excuse of Chamberlain at the time, that he had no option but to agree to Hitler's terms for the dismemberment of Czechoslovakia is in fact to make the most powerful condemnation of the government's policy over the years, including the slowness in rearmament and the reluctance to consider alliances until too late. Moreover, before the disparity in arms between Germany on the one side and Britain and France on the other is accepted as overwhelming proof that the Munich settlement was inevitable, the wider European picture should be considered. At least the significance of what was lost should be recalled. Munich not only removed Germany's immediate and ever-recurring fear of a war on two fronts but it neutralised a well-equipped Czechoslovak army of thirty-eight divisions – this at a time when Britain had only two divisions ready, or nearly ready, to be sent to the Continent. We sacrificed in Czechoslovakia a greater weight in armoured strength than Britain and France together had a year later, and Germany's lead in arms was growing. Britain and France had to pay dearly in 1939 and 1940 for the time they claimed to have bought in 1938.

It is profitless to be drawn into the 'ifs' of history; the exercise would have to include Stalin's watchful and cautious tactics of waiting to see how others responded before deciding his own degree of response. But what can fairly be said is that Hitler on his side was not free from anxiety as the Czechoslovak crisis mounted. For one thing he must have known, as the British government knew from the secret visitor to London, von Kleist, in August and from other sources, that General Halder, the chief of staff, and other officers were telling each other that they would oppose Hitler if he was set on war at this time. No doubt Hitler and Himmler counted on dealing with them, but it would at all events be troublesome for the regime, if not worse. As it was Hitler won his strategic gain in peaceful triumph. Out of the whole tragic business what remains without any excuse at all is the demoralising western pretence, persisted in well into 1939, that Nazi Germany's ambitions in Europe were negotiable.

The other excuse for Munich rests on the state of public opinion at the time. It may be acknowledged that Dawson was entirely right in maintaining, as he frequently did, that public opinion in Britain and the Dominions overseas was hopelessly divided during the weeks of the Munich crisis. Labour party spokesmen had for far too long proclaimed their belief in disarmament, even as dangers mounted. Many groups placed their hopes on action by the League of Nations. There would not have been unity behind a sudden call to war in 1938. Chamberlain himself and other ministers firmly based a part of their case on that public unpreparedness and they also frequently affirmed that the Dominion governments were against risking war with Germany in 1938.

The deeper question has none the less to be put: who was responsible for this lack of alertness at home and overseas in face of the growing dangers? The answer has to be found in the tone of the official telegrams going over the weeks and months from Whitehall to the Dominion capitals and in the false hopes that were sustained for too long in the leading articles of serious newspapers, led by *The Times*. Cooperation among the governments of the Commonwealth was based on the principle that freely shared information would quite naturally produce a freely shared policy. That is admirable so long as the information is sound. But when the information going out from London was mainly unalarming the Dominion governments could not be blamed for being unalarmed. In Britain itself the ministerial speeches and the *Times* leaders, read especially by people in influential positions, left the general public unprepared for the test of nerves presented by Hitler's demands over Czechoslovakia. In short, the excuse about public unpreparedness misses out the plain duty of a government and of the leading newspapers to alert public opinion when the dangers are mounting.

At bottom Dawson and Barrington-Ward were inspired by the vision – false but not ignoble – of a lasting European settlement once Germany's apparent grievances were met; and in this they were, once again, reflecting rather than leading opinion. When the outbreak of war brought about the new sense of national unity, *The Times* had a sufficiently firm and faithful following to sustain its standing and influence. Even many of the critics regarded the appeasement chapter as a single aberration, a single episode in the history of the paper. What *The Times* could not afford was another big mistake.

II

WAR AIMS UNDER DAWSON AND BARRINGTON-WARD

GEOFFREY DAWSON was editor during the first two years of the war, the years of military disaster redeemed by the Battle of Britain. Barrington-Ward was editor during the three years and nine months of the long haul that ended in victory. This contrast between the two phases, between the disaster in the one and the recovery in the other, helps to explain the different priorities in the two men's policies for the paper. Dawson's chief concern was in the conduct of the war, Barrington-Ward's in the organisation of the peace at home and abroad. But further reasons for the contrasting styles can be found in differences of age and temperament. Dawson, nearly sixty-seven when he retired in 1941, was seventeen years older than Barrington-Ward. He based himself on the lessons drawn from long experience rather than on the hopes arising from forward planning.

Experience certainly shaped Dawson's policy in the first part of the war. In the 1914–18 conflict he had constantly urged the need for a small and highly powered War Cabinet, and now once again he did what he could through the columns of the paper – and in private talks with Halifax and others – to get the right men together in a small team in Downing Street. A leading article which appeared on January 7 1941, and which urged the government to control the industrial effort more tightly and more efficiently, drew a letter the same day from Churchill, already Prime Minister for eight months:

> I have been reading your leading article today and have been wondering what it all amounts to. I wish you would let me know privately what it is you think should be done. If you could give me a few short headings I would study them with attention.[1]

Dawson sent him eight headings which combined to make the point that there was no minister with authority on the home front comparable to

1 T.T.A.

that of the Minister of Defence, with a clearly defined hierarchy dependent on him.

When he let himself look ahead to the organisation of the peace Dawson's attitude was very much like Churchill's throughout much of the war. He thought first and foremost of preserving the unity of the Empire and Commonwealth; this concern comes out in his frequent correspondence with General Smuts and other Commonwealth leaders. As for plans for the rest of the world, he was quite happy for others to speculate and expound; he thought that there was no harm and perhaps even some virtue in such forward looking. When speculating about the future of Britain he was in favour of reform, and he believed that suggestions to that end could be useful, provided that they did not become 'viewy' – his ultimate criticism of a proposal – or develop into a crusade for radically changing society. All he asked was that he himself should not be expected to pontificate in detail about the unforeseeable. The prime task, he was sure, was to see the war through.

Barrington-Ward, taking over later, was also passionately concerned in the war. Like Geoffrey Dawson he was intent on seeing a more efficient war directorate in Whitehall, and he was keen to print appraisals of strategy and articles on military training, war supplies, war industry, and allied consultations. But he was chiefly concerned in looking ahead; he believed that *The Times* could do most good in putting forward proposals for a peace settlement better than those fashioned in 1919–20 and no less strong proposals for a fairer society at home. Under him the paper's advanced, left-of-centre suggestions to those ends made their mark among wartime allies and among political parties at home. They frequently angered Churchill and other ministers. They caused Conservative members of Parliament to call *The Times* the 'threepenny *Daily Worker*'.[2] The paper's policy was in no way modified by such attacks. Being read and discussed by men and women in positions to influence national policy, the articles made their own positive contribution to the founding of the welfare state and to the recognition of Russia's new power in Europe.

Dawson's conversion in 1939 from appeasement to war-making, though it had been as deep as Barrington-Ward's, did not reveal itself in so extreme a form. His diaries for the first weeks of the war show that he two or three times discussed Hitler's so-called peace terms with Chamberlain and Halifax to see if by any chance they contained anything at all

---

2 The communist party newspaper, later to be called the *Morning Star*. It, and the popular newspapers, were then still published at one penny.

beyond propaganda, but his own distrust of Hitler was by then total, as Chamberlain's had also become. It is hard to imagine any deal which Dawson, with his fundamental scepticism and hard-headedness, could possibly endorse. On the contrary he was very soon proposing that Churchill, Chamberlain's First Lord of the Admiralty, be given charge of all the armed services. The war had been going little over a month when Dawson had a leader (October 6 1939) entitled 'War Cabinets'. The deft phrasing is distinctly his own:

> Mr. Churchill, without whom no War Cabinet would be complete, might well be allowed to range over the whole field of War, and not merely the oceans, with his fertile imagination and his inimitable powers of expression.

Even with all the slightly satirical touches – 'without whom no War Cabinet would be complete' and 'his inimitable powers of expression' – the advocacy is strong and sincere. On April 16 1940 Dawson renewed his plea for a smaller and more effective Cabinet in a leader headed 'Relief for Ministers'. At the height of the Norwegian disaster he wrote a prophetic leader (May 6) under the title, 'A warning and an opportunity', declaring that there was 'abundant room for improvement' in both the structure and the personnel of the Cabinet:

> Mr. Chamberlain's weakness has always been his devotion to his colleagues who are either failures or need a rest. . . . That Labour will be found in the ranks of the Government before the war is over is as certain as anything can possibly be. The great twin problems of man-power and supply will never be solved satisfactorily without their willing and responsible help. The setback in Norway is happily not a national disaster, but it is a warning and an opportunity.

That leading article of May 6 could not have been better timed. After two days' debate in the Commons on May 7–8, Chamberlain's hitherto huge majority fell to 81. On May 9 Chamberlain was told that Labour would not serve under him. On May 10 he resigned. On May 11 Churchill's government was announced, with Churchill not only Prime Minister but Minister of Defence. Dawson was pleased to see his hopes fulfilled with Churchill covering 'the whole field of War' but he was uneasy at the authority, inside and outside the Cabinet, Churchill bestowed upon old associates like Beaverbrook[3] and Bracken.[4] His

---

3 William Maxwell Aitken, Viscount Beaverbrook (1879–1964). Minister of Aircraft Production, 1940–41; Minister of Supply, 1941–42; Lord Privy Seal, 1943–45.
4 Brendan Bracken, Viscount Bracken (1901–58). Journalist and financier. Minister of Information, 1941–45. First Lord of the Admiralty, 1945.

diary entry for May 13 1940 has a typically detached and ironic touch about it:

> Quite a good little warlike speech from Winston and a solid vote of confidence. His new Govt. was daily enlarged by new appointments, *not* too well chosen . . . Too many friends.

By that time the German armies had invaded the Low Countries, beginning on May 10, and the Battle of France was about to open. Throughout the next few months, which brought the fall of France and the beginning of the German bombing raids on Britain, Dawson never wavered. The grimness of the news strengthened all his native doggedness, expressed in the taciturn entries in his diary each day:

> May 21. A *black* day . . . Returned to Printing House Square to find the place buzzing with the afternoon German communiqué. They had Amiens, Arras, Abbeville: the 9th Army was in dissolution: Giraud a prisoner.
>
> May 28. Blackest day yet. We heard on the wireless at 8 that Leopold [of the Belgians] had surrendered the army in the night . . . I heard Winston make a short, simple and courageous statement in the House of Commons, and then settled down again in the office with a team of leader writers . . . and a spate of fatuous and irrelevant letters to the Editor.
>
> June 10. As black a day as any yet (except May 28) and physically black, with a thick pall of hot mist over London, as dark as night.
>
> June 14. Grimmest day yet. Germans *in* Paris.
>
> June 16. Things get grimmer and grimmer.
>
> June 17. . . . Soon after midday a slip brought in to me at the office, announced that the French Army had been ordered to cease fighting. This is rather numbing and it took a bit of effort to get going again . . . [Dined with a group including] Edward H.,[5] who opined that, having touched bottom, we should now begin to rise.

These sparse entries, with no looking before or after, and without any trace of fear, were part of the stoical and unbudgable side of Dawson's character.

Dawson stayed on during all the German bombing raids[6] and the successive military disasters abroad.[7] The German invasion of Russia on

---

5 Lord Halifax, then Foreign Secretary.
6 Printing House Square during the bombing raids is described in Chapter III.
7 The coverage of the military campaigns is described in Chapter IV.

June 22 1941 brought him racing back from a weekend in All Souls to organise the leading articles and a hastily written summary of German–Soviet dealings in the past three years.

By this time his retirement from the chair had been arranged. The war had postponed it once. At the end of 1938 Dawson himself had suggested to both John Astor and John Walter that he should leave a little before or a little after his 65th birthday on October 25 1939. He followed this early warning with a long letter to Astor on April 4 1939. He was not worn out, he said; there were no difficulties within the office. 'But I have always had a horror of the sort of situation which I have seen in some other offices and businesses, where a man grows older and slower without realising it himself, and his friends are too kind to point it out to him.'[8] As his successor he suggested Barrington-Ward, who was accordingly told that he would take over by the end of 1939.

Both men had to think again when the war came and many of the staff left to join the armed forces. For nine years Dawson had had Barrington-Ward by him to take much of the load. Barrington-Ward would have no such hard-working deputy available to him when he succeeded, and he would face many other wide wartime gaps in the office. On September 22 1939 Barrington-Ward told Harold Hartley,[9] one of the directors, that he would be willing to defer his editorship if Dawson were ready to stay on beyond the end of the year – how far beyond was left indefinite. Hartley said he would have a word with John Astor. Before he could do so, however, Astor spoke to Dawson in a quite opposite sense. In his diary note for September 26 Dawson wrote:

> John was in the Office in the morning and rather surprised me by contemplating my retirement at the end of the year on the ground that B-W was looking forward to it and that the war was a great opportunity for him.

The matter was straightened out in friendly talks between Dawson and Barrington-Ward, and after further consultation with Astor, Dawson wrote to Astor:

> I think you agree that I should not give up my work here in present circumstances, and I should certainly be most reluctant to do so.

So the postponement was arranged with the utmost good will among the few at the top. The office as a whole knew nothing of Dawson's

---

8 Dawson Papers T.T.A.
9 Sir Harold Hartley (1878–1972). Dulwich; Balliol College, Oxford. GCVO, FRS. Director of The Times Publishing Company, 1936–60.

proffered retirement or its postponement. He was beginning to show his age and had neuritic pains in one leg, but his mental vigour was little abated. His bluff humour was especially good for office morale amid all the alarms in the first part of the war. Yet the uncertainty over the date of his departure became especially galling to two of Barrington-Ward's nearest associates, Stanley Morison[10] and E. H. Carr.[11] Both wished *The Times* to take the bolder line which they knew it would take under Barrington-Ward. Each of the two, in his different way, was to play a strong part in *The Times* during the next few years.

Morison, a man powerful in mind and voice, a scholar with little formal education and an untiring capacity for reading and intellectual questing, was Barrington-Ward's close friend throughout the war years and immediately afterwards. His appearance was daunting at first sight. He looked, every inch, the power behind the throne which many in Printing House Square suspected him of being and which he himself did in no way deny. His adoption of the Roman faith as a young man led him, with a convert's pride, to wear almost invariably a heavy black suit with a black tie and, very often, a black skull cap. His stoop did nothing to soften the bleak impression that strangers and chance acquaintances had of him. His friends knew another Morison: a rousing and merry companion, an eager dialectician who provoked arguments simply for the exercise of fighting them to the finish, a serious historian, a connoisseur of wine: stimulating in ideas and comments on every possible subject. It was this stimulation that Barrington-Ward valued above all in his friendship with Morison, especially in the later years when his own energies began to flag through fatigue and illness.

Morison was first and foremost a typographer, deeply interested in the history of printing. But in his mind the pedigree of printing types could not be dissociated from the pedigree of ideas for which the successive types over the centuries were the vehicle; and this led him on to the lives of the men who produced the ideas and to the theories behind the societies in which the men lived; he was captivated for a time with Marxism. When he came to *The Times* in 1929 as typographical adviser he had already published several learned monographs on print-

---

10 Stanley Morison (1889–1967). Typographical adviser to *The Times* from 1929; editor *The Times Literary Supplement*, 1945–48; retired from *The Times* 1960; edited and wrote much of *History of The Times*, Vols. I–IV, 1935–52.
11 Edward Hallett Carr (1892–1982). Merchant Taylors'; Trinity College, Cambridge. After early service with the Foreign Office, Professor of International Politics, University College of Wales, 1936–47. Contributor to *The Times* from 1937; assistant editor, 1941–46.

ing and on newspapers. It seemed right and proper that he should take over the responsibility for the first four volumes of the *History of The Times*, published successively in 1935, 1939, 1947, and 1952. Work on the volumes brought him close to Barrington-Ward, for whom the *History* was a constant source of inspiration. Nicolas Barker makes the point in his biography of Stanley Morison:[12]

The first volume of the History of *The Times* had left its mark on Barrington-Ward as well as Morison. Just as Barnes[13] after the Reform Bill had struck away from the Whig Establishment to support the Duke of Wellington, Lyndhurst and Peel, so now *The Times*, having supported the Government up to the war, should give a stronger voice to the social discontent that had grown since the depression . . . Barnes had paved the way for Peel and modern Conservatism – would a new line at *The Times* do the same for Socialism? As Barnes kept aloof from party, so should his successor.

Morison and Barrington-Ward often talked over all these matters. After Morison's flat was destroyed with all his books on September 20 1941, he went to live in Barrington-Ward's house in Regent's Park. Barrington-Ward came to refer to Morison as the Conscience of *The Times* or, with one of his deprecatory smiles, as The Sage. At the same time Morison became more and more friendly with John Astor. He gave both Barrington-Ward and Astor his hopes and fears, in writing or verbally, about the role of *The Times* in national life and about the staff which it should have to fulfil that role. He had plenty of time to learn about the most promising young men on other journals or in the Oxford and Cambridge colleges, and several men whom he introduced to Barrington-Ward were in fact appointed to the staff.

It was a highly anomalous position. Morison never had any operative post on the editorial side of *The Times* itself. Even his appointment as editor of the *Literary Supplement* – that was to come later, in 1945 – gave him no standing on the main paper itself, although before taking the new job he asked that he should act as Barrington-Ward's assistant, 'placed in charge of the editorship of the supplement', and should 'continue to keep in intimate touch with *The Times*'. These stipulations, accepted by Barrington-Ward, gave Morison the rank if not the normally accepted duties of an assistant editor. On their side Barrington-Ward and Astor, conscious of Morison's anomalous position, tended to regard him as a kind of court philosopher; to be heeded more than a

---

12 Nicolas Barker, *Stanley Morison*, p. 390.
13 Thomas Barnes (1785–1841). Editor of *The Times*, 1817–41.

court jester, by all means, but not entitled to have all his pronouncements taken seriously. This did not stop Morison's influence being
regarded with suspicion by some of the senior members of the staff;
indeed he himself boasted of discussing policy and staff matters with
Barrington-Ward. As 1941 went on he became convinced that Barrington-Ward should be given the chair without further delay.

The second man anxious for a change was E. H. Carr, whose leading
articles in *The Times* during late 1940 and 1941 had made readers aware
of a new writer of unsurpassed clarity and great force. Both Peter
Fleming,[14] struck by Carr's writing on Russia, and Dr. Tom Jones,
Lloyd George's old associate, had at different times suggested that he
should be writing for *The Times*. Barrington-Ward met him in October
1938 when Carr, having left the Foreign Office, was Professor of
International Politics at Aberystwyth. Dawson lunched with him in July
1939 and settled that he should come into Printing House Square and try
his hand on foreign leaders in September.[15] But when war came Carr
was committed to go to the Ministry of Information and he did not join
The Times officially as an assistant editor until January 1941. Already he
had written some leaders in 1940, and one of them, entitled 'Vital
Democracy', set one of the main lines which he was to follow throughout
the war. It was published on November 13 1940 and was based on
President Roosevelt's speech of two days before.

Politicians (its argument ran) had lost the confidence of ordinary
people through their inability to control the economy during the depression. They could get back that confidence only by adopting economic and social measures that would appeal to the 'little man':

> The only way to surmount the crisis of democracy is to restore to the
> 'little man' his waning faith that representative institutions really do
> play a role in his life, and do not leave him the helpless plaything of
> the vast impersonal machines of organised capital and organised
> labour.

The argument was developed and broadened three weeks later in
another of Carr's leaders which startled many readers, was much
praised at the time, and was quoted often by members of Parliament. It
was the clearest possible signal that *The Times* had a new and forceful
writer and was set on a new and forceful line of policy. It appeared on

---

14 Peter Fleming (1907–1971). Eton; Christ Church, Oxford. Author and explorer.
Contributed special foreign articles to *The Times*, 1932–36; editorial staff, 1936–39;
after war service rejoined as contributor, 1946–58; writer of fourth leaders and
occasional special correspondent.
15 GDD, July 21 1939.

December 5 1940 under the title, 'The Two Scourges'.[16] Its radical appeal may seem less startling when read by a later generation than when first it was written and read, but it remains a challenge to society, and the strength and clarity of the writing are unscathed:

The two great scourges which have most deeply touched the imagination and seared the conscience of the present generation are the scourge of war and the scourge of unemployment. For those who feel the need to look beyond the end of the present struggle, the abolition of war and the abolition of unemployment are the most urgent and imperative tasks of our civilisation.

The article then quickly developed Carr's distinctive argument. There must be a new international order with checks on the pursuit of national interests; and there must be a new social order, in which the ideals of the nineteenth century are extended from the political to the social and economic sphere. The cure for war and the cure for unemployment must go together:

So long as it remains true that war or the preparation for war is the only effective remedy for unemployment, wars will continue however cunning the machinery devised to prevent them . . . To create a new social order does not, like war, call for sacrifice of life and limb. But it does call for many of those other sacrifices of profits and luxuries, of rights and privileges, which we make unquestioningly in time of war. To formulate a social end, other than war, which will inspire such sacrifices is the cardinal problem of our time.

The article offers an excellent example of Carr's skill in slipping novel ideas into his pieces – novel ideas for *The Times* at all events – as though they were immutable truths safe from any challenge by sensible men. Dawson had no wish to challenge the ideas on this occasion. Indeed it was he, in the offhand manner which he sometimes used, who had suggested the leader. Carr later told[17] that, a few days before the leader appeared, he had gone into Dawson's room to find Lord Lothian, then ambassador in Washington, holding forth. Lothian was saying that many Americans regarded unemployment as an evil hardly less disastrous than war and they would believe more in Britain's sincerity and soundness if Britain had plans for curing unemployment after the war. Almost as an aside Dawson remarked that Carr might care to hatch

---

16 The full text of the leading article is given in Appendix C.
17 Quoted in Donald McLachlan, *In the Chair*, p. 217. Carr there got the date wrong.

something along those lines. Carr had not to be asked twice.

As more of Carr's leaders appeared Barrington-Ward rejoiced. He saw in Carr, with his broad and ruthless remedies for troubles at home and abroad, the very man he wanted. His diary records a highly congenial talk with Carr a few months before Carr joined the staff:[18]

> The Times, almost alone in the Press and certainly first, is trying to get the right 'answer to Hitler' in a statement on our plans for war and peace to show that we are fighting for a new Europe not the old – a new Britain and not the old. I wholly agree with Carr:– planned consumption, abolition of unemployment and poverty, drastic educational reform, family allowances, economic organization of the Continent, etc., but all this needs the right presentation.

While Barrington-Ward rejoiced, Dawson had increasing doubts about the presentation and the substance of the articles. Carr complained to Barrington-Ward in February 1941, only six weeks after he had joined the paper, that Dawson was making excuses for not using his articles. Barrington-Ward, the most loyal of lieutenants, was moved to make one of his rare criticisms of Dawson in his diary:[19]

> He [Carr] complains of G.D.'s 'insincerity', by which he means the rather transparent conventions that G.D. employs to stave off discussion of political or social issues. He thinks that there has been a 'change of climate' with respect to his reconstruction articles. G.D. fobs them off or doesn't use them when written. (Yet 10,000 copies have been sold of the reprint[20] of Carr's leaders and the paper has reached its circulation 'ceiling'.) He is not prepared to go on like this . . . Though I know there is great truth in all this, I begged him to remember the extent of his achievement with us up to date, to recognize that reconstruction leaders (which have already put The Times on the map) must be spaced out, and above all to exercise patience.
>
> I am much troubled and feel strongly the force of Carr's complaint. G.D. is not, I think, in real sympathy with the kind of article that Carr has been writing on home affairs, which has brought us so much credit. He does not seem to be aware that Carr is the ablest and best qualified man who has been near the paper for years. I have worked and worked to get him in, and now that he is there, I am

---

18 B-W D, July 31 1940.
19 B-W D, February 13 1941.
20 PHS pamphlet, *Planning for War and Peace*, 1940.

ready to take on (with his help and Casey's) tomorrow. I cannot stand by tamely and see him depart. I can't have G.D. queering my pitch for lack of a little imagination and perception.

According to the evidence that remains, the decisive prod in Dawson's departure was given by Stanley Morison. It would be entirely outside Barrington-Ward's character to join in any intrigue, though no doubt he spoke freely to his confidant about his fears and frustrations as well as his respect and affection for Dawson. Morison, it was said afterwards in the office, took it on himself to speak to John Astor; and this suggestion is supported by a letter which Morison wrote to a friend a year or two later. The letter is undated but was probably written in 1943:

> What I regard as a worthwhile contribution to the war effort was the change from Dawson to Bn-Ward, with E. H. Carr as Assistant Editor. The change brought others and inevitably almost meant my being invested with much 'occult' influence so that little is done with [without?] prior knowledge. Hence I am dining regularly and weekly with B-W and the others to discuss the policy of the paper and the re-arrangement of the staff. With all this I have little time to spare on my hands.[21]

Dawson himself has recorded what happened next.[22] In a memorandum he wrote for himself on September 23 1941 he recalled that he had stayed on after 1939 'with complete goodwill on the part of B-W, from whom I had no secrets throughout'. The memorandum goes on:

> But late on the night of May 5 [1941] I found the Chairman [Astor] in his room and was just parting with him when he suddenly suggested that the office seemed now to be running very smoothly, that it had been strengthened e.g. by the acquisition of Carr and the development of Iverach McDonald, and that it might be unfair to keep my duly appointed successor waiting indefinitely to step into my shoes.
>
> This rather took me aback, but I agreed at once that I ought to have thought of it sooner myself. I said I was sure that B-W. was quite capable of taking over the Editorship at any time, though the Carr–McDonald argument did not really meet the problem of his assistants and deputies at the centre.[23] Anyhow I would have a talk with him at once and see how he felt about it.
>
> This accordingly I did when I reached the Office next morning

---

21 Morison to Beatrice Warde, undated. Quoted in Barker *op. cit.* pp. 402–3.
22 Dawson papers T.T.A.
23 Both men were at that time writers rather than administrators.

. . . Nothing, of course, could have been more considerate than his [B-W's] attitude. He begged me to take my own time, said it would be a sad day for him when I left Printing House Square, suggested reconsideration in the Autumn, etc. But he left no doubt that he was prepared to take over, and I told him that in the circumstances I should not dream of lingering on the stage. I suggested the end of July as a natural breaking-point. He talked about the end of the year. In the end we agreed upon September 30, so that he might have a month's holiday with his family before settling down.

Dawson's last leading article appeared on September 8 with the title, 'Looking Ahead'. It seemed to fly a curious and awkward kite, for, out of the blue, it raised the problem of finding a successor to Churchill if a successor were suddenly required. It seemed untimely at first glance, but, given Dawson's belief in the primacy of personalities in politics, it was natural for him to be thinking of men in the government when he was himself leaving Printing House Square. Beyond that, he wished very sincerely to emphasise the unique quality of Churchill's leadership and thereby bury many past disputes:

Like no one else in sight he has the courage, the imagination, the powers of leadership which are the attributes of a great War Minister. England is fortunate indeed as she has so often been fortunate in the past, in having produced the man to fit the emergency.

Dawson edited for the last time on September 30. His entry in his diary is wholly in character, expressing none of his own deep feelings and recording in a detached, quizzical way the emotions of others:

My last day as Editor of *The Times*. I paid a brief visit to the office (in the morning) before going to the House of Commons to hear the Prime Minister review the war. A very satisfactory performance with good figures of the Atlantic battle and the air . . . and then went back to a rather emotional afternoon in Printing House Square. They insisted on my attending the Conference (which I hadn't meant to do) in order that Brodribb[24] might conclude it by delivering an unexpected funeral oration, to which I had to reply. After that Casey came and literally wept on my shoulder, and there was an equally tearful parting with Miss Dickie [his chief secretary by day]. I got home in the end rather exhausted.

---

24 Charles William Brodribb (1878–1945). St. Paul's; Trinity College, Oxford. On *The Times* from 1904; assistant editor, 1935, and special writer on many subjects.

As he left the staff felt above all that they were losing a man who, upholding the power of personality in the shaping of world events, was a big personality himself: a man soaked in politics; an untiring news gatherer from his many contacts; a pointed and often impish writer of political comment in the news columns; above all, a genial and encouraging editor for those near to him – a geniality not spoiled by his occasional gruffness or his barks of impatience when hearing something which he took to be nonsense. He was very much aware that he was one of the influential few in a society which, he assumed, generally accepted the system even though going in for moderate reforms.

Barrington-Ward's high sense of mission in approaching the editor's chair is shown in two entries in his diaries, the first a few months before he took over, the second written on the day that Astor appointed him. On February 23 1941, which was his fiftieth birthday, came the reflexion:

> My life was really forfeit in 1914 and it is the merest, the least deserved of flukes that I have survived to enjoy so much of which war robbed the pick of my contemporaries. The more reason to remember the mission which August 1914 and survival have together set men like me – namely to strive for the creation and organization of peace, above all things, and for the liberating truths at home, at whatever cost to conventional opinion.
>
> Revolution cannot do it. It is to be questioned whether revolution as such has ever achieved anything *on balance*: but evolution, active and painful evolution must. On my own humble anniversary it is well to have this old resolution sharp and clear again.

The second entry, dated May 5 1941, records his reply when Astor asked him if he was ready to take over. After some discussion about the staff who could help him, Barrington-Ward stated with great honesty the progressive social policy which he intended to pursue – a policy which, if carried into effect, would obviously enough reduce the privileges of the class to which Astor belonged:

> I went on to say that I thought it the duty and the opportunity of *The Times* to prepare for the great social changes inevitable after the war. Its function, I said, at all times is to apply common-sense, without prejudice, to issues as they arise and to gain general acceptance of novel but necessary moves by getting them rationally expounded. He most warmly agreed to all this and spoke particularly of the excellence of Carr's articles last year. All of which was good. We left it that he would see G.D. and see me again. Through-

out the talk he was his generous and understanding self.

I imparted all this later to Stanley Morison, my sole confidant, as we walked through burnt-out Holborn and battered Gray's Inn to dinner.

Very soon after taking over the chair on October 1 1941 Barrington-Ward began changing and renovating the editorial staff. He was a kind man; but he was determined to make *The Times* a new force throughout the land and throughout the western alliance; and he was quite clear in his mind that the paper would never live up to his ideals unless he surrounded himself with a corps of the most talented thinkers and writers that he could find. He had to create room for such men; and so, with varying degrees of persuasion, he led two or three of his existing colleagues to see that there was no satisfactory future for them on *The Times*. Here he was over-hasty, it would seem. The writing staff was left painfully thin. He was soon to find that it was easier to drop men than to pick up others to take their places. The result was that he had to do more work himself to fill the gaps and make up for the inexperience of several of the newcomers. None the less most of the staff changes fitted into a well-ordered plan.

One staff problem had already been solved a month after the outbreak of war when Captain Liddell Hart[25] withdrew from the paper on which he had been military correspondent for four years. It had been an increasingly tense association. Liddell Hart, possessing one of the most brilliant military minds in the country, was nothing if not individualistic. His strength lay in putting forward challenging, controversial, and often deeply disturbing views. He was often outstandingly right, sometimes he was wrong. He recognised that he frequently stepped out of line from the policy of the paper. He also recognised that such divergences could be confusing to readers when all staff writings were anonymous. But he believed that the simple ascription, 'From our Military Correspondent', was a clear enough sign that his opinions were not necessarily those of the editor or deputy editor. Neither Dawson nor Barrington-Ward could agree with him. They could not let a senior staff man write as if he were an unattached observer, especially in so thickly mine-strewn a field as national defence. They resented no less Liddell Hart's practice of giving personal advice on defence matters to Leslie Hore-Belisha, Secretary of State for War from 1937 to 1940, and to Winston Churchill, Anthony Eden, and David Lloyd George when they

---

25 Captain Basil Henry Liddell Hart (1895–1970). St. Paul's; Corpus Christi, Cambridge. Military correspondent of *The Times*, 1935–39.

were all in their different ways critics of Chamberlain's policy.

In spite of the strains Liddell Hart had many useful and challenging articles published in *The Times*: articles on the poor state of Britain's air defences and on the more efficient training and equipment of the army. These articles were picked up by members of Parliament and they helped to push the government forward into a swifter pace on rearmament.

The personal strains increased as war approached. Liddell Hart, with Dawson's support, had previously argued that Britain should send no more than a very small expeditionary force to Europe. After the dismemberment of Czechoslovakia at Munich he very sensibly revised his suggestions and wished to argue in *The Times* that Britain must now prepare an up-to-date mechanised and armoured force which could be sent to strengthen France. Such help to France was necessary, Liddell Hart pointed out, because the disruption of Czechoslovakia as an effective military force had removed from Germany her immediate fear of a war on two fronts and so would let her release more of her armed forces to prepare for action in the west. Barrington-Ward was ready to endorse Liddell Hart's plea for a more powerful expeditionary force but he was strongly against using the dismemberment of Czechoslovakia as a supporting reason. He had always disliked the French alliances that straddled Germany to find bases in central and eastern Europe, and had had a low opinion of Czech fighting potential. In any case he thought that Liddell Hart's argument went flatly against the paper's policy. The articles, written in November 1938, did not appear until February 1939 and the Czechoslovak argument was removed from them.

Curiously enough, the attitudes of Barrington-Ward and Liddell Hart were reversed when Britain gave its pledge to Poland. It was then the turn of Barrington-Ward, still bitter after Hitler's march into Prague in the middle of March, to be militant while Liddell Hart drew sharply back. Barrington-Ward accepted the pledge to Poland reluctantly but firmly and loyally. Liddell Hart, recognising that Britain and France could give no direct help to Poland if attacked, was wholly against 'this foolish, futile, and provocative guarantee', 'a staggering turn-about', 'this ill-considered gesture'.[26]

His rift with Dawson and Barrington-Ward widened when he began to suggest privately that Hitler should be encouraged to offer a negotiated peace. Dawson was irritated beyond measure:

The absurd Liddell Hart infested the office, breathing pessimism and complaining that neither his health nor his conscience would

---

26 Liddell Hart, *Memoirs*, Vol. II, p. 214.

allow him to do any work.[27]

Liddell Hart described his inner struggles at length in a letter to Dawson, written on September 7 while the battle for Poland was raging:
> All my best work for *The Times* has been done after a long period of reflexion, and has often taken several days even in the writing. And in the last year or two I have found it more necessary to think it out somewhere isolated from noise and disturbance . . . But to elucidate events of far-reaching importance on the spur of the moment is a task I should certainly be reluctant to attempt, especially when one is writing for the public directly concerned with the consequences. Indeed, as you know, I have been and am still wondering whether one is justified in attempting it at all while the fog of war remains thick.

Barrington-Ward was no less impatient than Dawson:
> LH seems to be playing for safety all round. For himself he wants to be wise after the event . . . He is a monolith of egotism and vanity.[28]

Dawson and Barrington-Ward very rarely let their feelings get on top of them in that way, even in their private diaries. They did not fully recognise how near Liddell Hart was to a break-down, but the greater pity was that *The Times*, hampered in those years by its own tight control over the expression of opinion by staff writers, was not able to give scope to one of the most original and influential military writers of modern times.

In the end both sides were glad to part, and Captain Cyril Falls[29] took Liddell Hart's place. Falls was a much less controversial writer and did not feel he had always to be commanding the strategic heights; he was conscientious in writing the kind of day-to-day tactical comments which fretted Liddell Hart, and he had a limpid narrative style. Leading generals liked him, and he maintained his calm and sound analyses of all the military threats and thrusts, as well as being, after 1946, Chichele Professor of the History of War at Oxford. On his side Barrington-Ward, recovering from the battles with Liddell Hart, was only too thankful to have a little peace on the *Times* sector of the war front.

Barrington-Ward made his own first big change on the editorial side

---

27 GDD, August 27 1939.
28 B-W D, October 2 1939.
29 Captain Cyril Bentham Falls (1888–1971). Bradfield; London University. Military correspondent of *The Times*, 1939–53.

within a month of taking over the chair. He and Leo Kennedy, senior foreign leader writer, did not always see eye to eye. Part of the trouble was that Kennedy was no less intense as a thinker than Barrington-Ward himself. Kennedy had one or two periods of absence to recover from fatigue. He wore himself down through grappling nightly with the paper's policy; he once said in anguish that whenever he wrote he felt that the chanceries of Europe were peering over his shoulder. Famous as the man who wrote the arch-appeasing leader of September 7 1938 which offered the Sudeten lands to Germany, he none the less believed that Barrington-Ward under-rated the dangers of Hitler's territorial ambitions.

In spite of such differences of policy Kennedy was greatly taken aback when he received a letter from Barrington-Ward, dated October 23 1941, suggesting that his duties be lightened within the office and he be left free to do other work outside. After further exchanges between the two men the manager, C. S. Kent,[30] wrote a letter giving Kennedy the choice between leaving on agreed terms and staying on with a small retainer instead of a salary. To the manager Kennedy replied on January 27 1942, saying that he had 'regretfully made up his mind to leave'. To Barrington-Ward on the same day he wrote, 'I feel sorry – and just a little sore – at the moment; but I hope that ultimately it will make no difference to our friendship'.[31] He was then fifty-seven and had been on *The Times* for thirty years with only a few interruptions.

Barrington-Ward next turned his attention to Colin Coote, senior leader writer on home affairs, another man of long service with the paper but also one with whom Barrington-Ward was not at ease. Once again it was partly a matter of temperament, partly a difference of policy. Coote seemed a solitary within the office, although outside it he had extensive contacts which included his informal political association with Churchill. When he joined the paper after the First World War he had behind him a fine record as an infantry officer with the Gloucesters and the distinction of having been one of the youngest members of Parliament; he was a Coalition Liberal for the Isle of Ely, 1917–22. Probably he would have been happier from the start on a paper where anonymity was not the rule, but his knowledge of the ways of Parliament and the information which he gained in frequent confidential talks with ministers gave his own recognisable imprint to his articles. When the second war came he took up some morning work at the War Office and

---

30 Christopher Shotter Kent (1887–1954). The *Standard*, 1908. Accountant on staff of Associated Newspapers, 1909. Lord Northcliffe's staff, 1917. Chief accountant *The Times*, 1921; secretary, 1922; assistant manager, 1931; manager, 1937–49.
31 T.T.A.

also, partly to meet the expense of his first wife's illness, did some broadcasting. He knew that the broadcasting would not be well seen at *The Times*. None the less he was greatly shocked to receive a letter from Barrington-Ward, dated February 1 1942:

> It has been on my conscience for a considerable time that you have not been getting the work you would wish to do for the paper. You will have seen yourself how the course of events has restricted opportunity in your accustomed field.

The letter mentioned Coote's work at the War Office and the BBC, and then suggested that 'to free you for these and other possibilities of work' he be put on a retainer of £500 a year with payment at a special rate for any work done. Like Kennedy a few days before Coote rejected the retainer. 'Naturally I refused with some indignation, and left with a handshake that was far from golden.'[32] He was then forty-eight, and he was to move on to higher posts elsewhere. From 1950 to 1964 he was managing editor of the *Daily Telegraph*.

Another man who chose, also in 1942, to leave rather than have his income and the scope of his work reduced was Dr. McNair Wilson.[33] Officially he was medical correspondent but his real service to the office was in being a splendid and rousing character. He was a man of tempestuous energy who would quickly dispose of his medical articles and then would either turn to writing his thrillers (nearly thirty of them under the name of Anthony Wynne) or seek with loud and passionate argument to enlist his colleagues into his campaigns in support of Napoleon, monarchy, and monetary reform. His influence on the work of others was disruptive and entirely good. He was sixty when he left, to be succeeded by a much younger man, Dr. Alan Moncrieff,[34] editor of *The Practitioner*.

Yet another man who, a little later, was greatly surprised and hurt by Barrington-Ward's plans was Thomas Cadett. As Paris correspondent until the fall of France he had been robustly against Munich and did not hide his distrust of Georges Bonnet, the French Foreign Minister. He was in some secret work during the first two years of the war. In April 1942 he asked Barrington-Ward about coming back to *The Times* and was dampingly told that there were no vacancies at that time: he then

---

32 Coote, *op. cit.*, p. 214.
33 Dr. Robert McNair Wilson (1882–1963). Glasgow Academy; Glasgow University. Medical correspondent of *The Times*, 1914–42.
34 Sir Alan Aird Moncrieff (1901–1971). Caterham School; MD, Middlesex Hospital. *The Times* medical correspondent, 1943–56; medical adviser to the management, 1956–60. Knighted, 1964.

joined the BBC. In 1944, in answer to a further inquiry from Cadett, Barrington-Ward gave his judgment:

> The whole outlook in and for France has been so completely revolutionized that I do not see how we can aim at any kind of continuity with our pre-war arrangements for the Paris correspondence. A new scheme of things will have to be devised and I do not see what opening it could appropriately give you . . . Indeed, I think that the fair course now will be to set you quite free in good time and to make a suitable financial arrangement with you accordingly.[35]

Cadett protested in letters both to Barrington-Ward and to John Astor about the 'most bitter blow', saying that he had been dismissed 'without any concrete explanation whatsoever'. He was afterwards to do well as Paris correspondent of the BBC for some years. His close colleague in pre-war Paris, Thomas Barman, who shared his views about Munich and had also been in war work, was told no less gently and firmly that it would be hard to fit him into *The Times* again. He too joined the BBC and became its diplomatic correspondent.

Such men left the staff under Barrington-Ward's plans of re-organisation, but advancing age claimed others. Among them were two eminently courteous and scholarly men, Harold Child and Charles Brodribb, who had their desks side by side in a book-lined room. Whenever it was said, as it often was, that being in Printing House Square was like being in the senior common room in an Oxford college, it was Child and Brodribb who came first to mind as exemplars. Child,[36] a gentle lover of books who wrote many of the best and lightest of the light leaders in the paper, began writing for *The Times Literary Supplement* in 1902 and it was only because of increasing illness that he withdrew in 1942 when he was seventy-three. The story was often told of how, by his own anonymous merit, he was picked out to contribute to the *Cambridge History of English Literature*. The Master of Peterhouse wrote to the editor of the *TLS* enclosing ten or so outstanding reviews from it; he asked to be put in touch with the authors with a view to their joining in the *History*. It turned out that all but two of the articles had been written by Child.

Brodribb, classicist and considerable poet, was an assistant editor with the special task of ensuring that all news items and all headings maintained the required standards of accuracy and good taste. He was

---

35 Barrington-Ward to Cadett, June 9 1944. T.T.A.
36 Harold Mannyngton Child (1869–1945). Winchester; Brasenose College, Oxford. Contributor to *The Times* from 1902; assistant dramatic critic, 1902–1920; special writer.

once outraged to see among the proofs a heading, 'Germans thrown back three miles'. 'They were not,' he cried. 'No one could be thrown three miles. What happened was that our men opened fire. Some of the Germans dropped down dead without further ado. The others did not like what they saw and ran away for three miles.' The abashed sub-editors admitted their mistake and substituted a new formula of classical precision and restraint. Brodribb was sixty-two when Barrington-Ward took over but he stayed on to enliven the Printing House Square team with his austere comments delivered always with the courtesy of a man who had reflected deeply. There was his judgment after some new act of aggression in Europe: 'My dear sir, the truth of the matter is: foreigners should not be trusted with firearms.' He vowed to get that wholesome sentiment into a leading article. Later, on the day that the allied armies approached the seven hills of Rome and Mussolini fled, Brodribb quickly wrote down a variant version of the mountain producing a mouse:

Parturient septem montes; nascetur ridiculus *Muss*.

Barrington-Ward was also aware that other men of long service were near retirement, and each one of them – highly expert in his own field – would leave a gap which would have to be quickly filled. Among such men were D. D. Braham,[37] the leader writer on economic and American affairs; Philip Graves,[38] with his first-hand knowledge of the Middle East and the Balkans; and J. V. Radcliffe, the labour correspondent who had a ponderous style of writing and speaking which did not mar his clear understanding and portrayal of the trade union world.

With such changes accomplished and about to come, Barrington-Ward felt free to recruit new talent. He had two aims chiefly in mind. First, for the writing of leaders and special articles he wished to bring in men who had already made a mark by their expert knowledge in their field. More than ever, *The Times* was to be a recognisable college, staffed by men with high academic qualifications that would command respect. Sir William Haley, who was to be editor from 1952 to 1966,[39]

---

37 Dudley Disraeli Braham (1875–1951). Liverpool Institute; New College, Oxford. Assistant correspondent for *The Times*, Berlin, 1899–1901; correspondent in St. Petersburg, 1901–03 and Constantinople, 1903–08; assistant and later head of the imperial and foreign department of the paper, 1912–14; rejoined *The Times* in 1929 as leader writer until retirement in 1945.

38 Philip Perceval Graves (1876–1953). Haileybury; New College, Oxford. Special and foreign correspondent for *The Times* in Egypt, Turkey, the Near East, the Balkans, India and Ireland, 1906–24; leader writer until retirement in 1946.

39 William John Haley (b. 1901). Victoria College, Jersey. Merchant marine in First World War. After service as shorthand-telephonist on *The Times* in London and

believed in recruiting good journalists – that is, men of clear mind and clear style – and training them to be experts. Barrington-Ward held that the experts could be trained into being journalists – a proposition which produced some successes for him as well as several notable failures. Secondly, he sought someone who could take from him much of the administrative burden as he had taken it from Dawson. For a time he had hopes that E. H. Carr could do it when not bent over his powerful leaders. It was soon evident, however, that Carr had no ambitions to be the administrator, and both Barrington-Ward and Stanley Morison had to cast further afield.

It was to be a long and difficult effort. Many promising men were either in the armed services or in other war work. Barrington-Ward could not secure several on whom he had set his hopes. The year 1943 and the early part of 1944 was especially difficult. Barrington-Ward, as his diaries show, had to write too many leaders himself and had too often to re-write other men's leaders. He frequently noted that he arrived late at dinners to which he was invited and then had to rush back early afterwards to the office to make further alterations in the articles. His weekends were often cut short because he could not be confident that the available writers would make the right comment on some unexpected event. Even Carr, his great support, began to need close watching and some re-writing. As late as May 1944 Barrington-Ward laments that he had much trouble with the leaders, throwing him more than usually late for his dinners and requiring him to work harder at the weekend. Not until October 1944 could he record a 'great week' for leaders; and, at last, on November 2 he could thankfully confide to his diary, 'The staff is really becoming what it should be.'

The three years of strain and over-work had tired Barrington-Ward more than he liked to admit, but he was supported by the belief that the work would now be easier. The men whom he and his associates brought in as writers had certainly the high academic qualifications which he had sought, and most of them had strongly reformist views on home and foreign affairs. They included François Lafitte,[40] Harold Stannard,[41]

Brussels, joined *Manchester Evening News* in 1922; chief sub-editor, 1925; managing editor, 1930; joint managing director Manchester Guardian and Evening News Ltd, 1939–43. Director-General BBC, 1944–52. Editor of *The Times*, 1952–66; director and chief executive, 1965–66; chairman, Times Newspapers Limited, 1967. KCMG, 1946.

40 François Lafitte (b. 1913). St. Olave's Grammar School, Southwark; Worcester College, Oxford. Political and Economic Planning, 1938–43. *The Times*, 1943–59. Professor of Social Policy and Administration, Birmingham University, 1959–80.

41 Harold Stannard (1883–1947). King Edward's School, Birmingham; Christ Church, Oxford. Joined *The Times*, 1907; frequent reviewer before returning to the staff in 1943.

Peter Utley,[42] and L. F. Rushbrook Williams.[43]

Lafitte was an extremely intelligent and painstakingly methodical young social scientist, a strong advocate of the welfare state, and a prodigious worker who several times showed that he knew more about the subject under discussion than the top officials in Whitehall who were coping with it.

Stannard was a distinguished scholar and historian, and Peter Utley, the Tory among them, a Cambridge scholar who lost his sight as a boy but who was able on most days to keep up with his colleagues and dictate a beautifully ordered leader.

Rushbrook Williams had held a university chair in India, been Foreign Minister of Patiala State in the twenties and early thirties, and was author of many scholarly books. He wrote knowledgeably and fluently on the countries of South Asia and was always sustained in spite of many disappointments by an intellectual belief in the power of reasoned argument to influence men and events.

Barrington-Ward was two and a half years in the editor's chair before he succeeded in his second aim of finding a hard-working deputy, and then he was helped once again – as *The Times* had been helped in finding E. H. Carr – by Dr. Tom Jones and Stanley Morison. They pointed to Donald Tyerman[44] who had risen swiftly from holding an academic post at Southampton to be deputy editor of the *Economist* and, during the past two years, one of the most effective men at the *Observer*. Barrington-Ward thankfully appointed him in May 1944 to be assistant editor. Tyerman was then 36. A boyhood attack of poliomyelitis had left him dependent on two heavy sticks when walking but lameness seemed only to have increased his mental energy.

No appointment could have been better for *The Times* or for Barrington-Ward at that period. Tyerman was as ready to work hard and long as Barrington-Ward himself, and much of the administrative load fell on his broad shoulders. He brought a warmth and a very genuine interest in the younger members of the staff; he recruited young men and women as they came out of the armed services, he encouraged them, he had a way of bringing out the best in them. He showed himself

---

42 Thomas Edwin (Peter) Utley (b. 1921). Corpus Christi College, Cambridge. *The Sunday Times*, 1945–47. *Observer*, 1947–48. Leader writer *The Times*, 1948–54. *Daily Telegraph*, 1964–80.
43 Laurence Frederick Rushbrook Williams (1890–1978). University College, Oxford. Leader writer *The Times*, 1944–55.
44 Donald Tyerman (1908–81). Gateshead Secondary School; Brasenose College, Oxford. Lecturer, University College, Southampton, 1930–36. Assistant and deputy editor, the *Economist*, 1937–44; deputy editor, *Observer*, 1943–44. Assistant editor, *The Times*, 1944–55. Editor of the *Economist*, 1956–65.

to be a warm and stimulating chairman whether of the formal news conferences or the less organised discussions on policy. Above all, his most valuable gift to an office that was still woefully short of staff was his ability to pack three days' work into one: a full programme of admini-stration, active supervision over the news services, and very often a long leader to write at the end. Sometimes the leader was not even the end of his day. If Barrington-Ward and Casey were away Tyerman would do their late duties, coming back to the office after the paper had gone to press at 9.15 p.m. to look over and revise the first edition.

As a writer he had strong views, as his left-inclined leaders on the Greek civil war were to show, but his dislike of any stylistic artifice made his writing at times so blunt as to be over-emphatic. His abundant energy also led him into chopping and changing other men's leaders, sometimes without any apparent compelling reason, thus chipping away at the writers' self-confidence that he himself had built up when talking to them. His power for good remained great. Within the office he got people to speak more easily about themselves and their jobs; and when he was in true form his native Yorkshireness came out in an effective, clear, down-to-earth style of thinking and writing.

Barrington-Ward secured two other men of strong assistant editor timber, but curiously enough neither of them came fully into his own until Sir William Haley arrived in 1952 and gave each of them heavier work and a more clearly established position. The first was Maurice Green.[45] He had a brilliant academic record; became editor of the *Financial News* while still a young man; was taken on by Dawson as financial and industrial editor in 1938; served in the Royal Artillery in the war; and was pulled out by Barrington-Ward in 1944 to take up his old job in the paper. But he found that the job was less satisfactory and less well-defined; he especially felt that Carr cramped the expression of his own economic views. He found some outlet in organising the special supplements, growing in importance for the paper, but he believed with justice that the best use was not being made of him.

The second man was Patrick Ryan.[46] Barrington-Ward was as proud and as happy as an angler who lands a big fish when he secured, after the

---

45 James Maurice Spurgeon Green (b. 1906). Rugby; University College, Oxford. Editor of *Financial News*, 1934–38. Financial and industrial editor, *The Times*, 1938–39 and 1944–53; assistant editor, 1953. Resigned in 1961 to go to *Daily Telegraph*; editor, 1964–74.

46 Alfred Patrick Ryan (1900–1972). Whitgift; Balliol College, Oxford. After service with the BBC, *Manchester Guardian* and *Daily Telegraph*, joined *The Times* as a special writer in 1947; assistant editor, 1948; literary editor from 1965 until retirement in 1967.

war, the man who as news editor of the BBC had built up the home news services of the corporation. Like Green, Ryan had entered journalism with a brilliant academic record behind him. He would no doubt have been glad for many reasons to stay at the BBC but he wished to get back to writing, and Barrington-Ward was looking for a man to do the major leaders on home policy and to that extent take the place of Carr. The first articles were not wholly successful. Ryan was out of practice, and he did not have time to write himself in before Barrington-Ward's death. The main work of both Green and Ryan still lay ahead.

III

THE WAR HITS PRINTING HOUSE SQUARE

T HE war hit *The Times* hard in several different ways. It struck it physically. Much of Printing House Square was wrecked by the direct hit of a heavy bomb during the night of September 24/25 1940, and at other times more than seventy fire bombs fell on the roof or in the yard. The war struck also at the paper's manpower. Out of a staff of 1570 at least 584 joined the armed forces or were taken for other national work during the course of the war. But the blow which the readers felt most acutely came with the rationing of newsprint. *The Times* had to make do with a quarter of its pre-war number of pages while still trying to present a full news service, its usual array of leading articles, and many of its features and special articles.

For three reasons *The Times* could face the prospect of air raids with something less than complete dread. First, the main part of the building was of great strength, having been built in 1874 with thick walls of Bearwood bricks, so called because they came from the Walter family estate in Berkshire. Even greater reassurance was to be found below ground, thanks to John Astor's insistence before the war that a start should then be made with the rebuilding and modernisation of the whole of Printing House Square. The work had begun with the underground machine-rooms. They were reconstructed to bear the weight and vibration of the heaviest rotary presses and support a large building above them; they might have been purpose-built to be air raid shelters. During the days and nights of the worst bombings the editorial and mechanical staffs adjourned downstairs, and there they could carry on with their work not in comfort but at any rate in reasonable safety.

Secondly, as a direct result of forward looking by Barrington-Ward and Donald McLachlan,[1] *The Times* had the best ARP – air raid

---

1 Donald Harvey McLachlan (1908–1971). City of London School; Magdalen College, Oxford. Joined *The Times* foreign department as sub-editor, 1933; twice acted as an assistant correspondent in Berlin; resigned 1935; part-time editorial work 1936–8; editor of *The Times Educational Supplement*, 1939–40. After war service in Naval Intelligence acted as special writer, 1946–47. *The Economist* editorial staff,

precaution team – of any firm in the City of London. Before the war Barrington-Ward and McLachlan wrote many cogent articles on the need to establish ARP throughout the country, and in 1937 they ensured that *The Times* set an efficient example. The members whom they enrolled in the team were keen on their work and proud of it. A government proposal during the war that *The Times* ARP should be merged with others was indignantly and successfully resisted; *The Times* kept its own team throughout the war. After some initial uneasiness, the trade unions in the office were fully ready to go on working during the raids once they were assured that ARP 'spotters' were keeping watch on the roof, day and night, and would give timely warning of imminent danger.

Thirdly, there were detailed arrangements for carrying on elsewhere if the worst happened and Printing House Square was destroyed by fire or bomb. Different plans were made to cover different crises. If only Printing House Square were knocked out and other London newspaper offices survived, *The Times* would be produced in eight-page form at the *Evening Standard* and the *News of the World*. The presses at the *News of the World* were not suitable for the actual printing but pages could be made up there and some of them could be moulded before being carried to the *Evening Standard* for printing. If, as was expected, much of London was destroyed, then *The Times* would be printed by the Northamptonshire Printing and Publishing Company Limited in its plant at Kettering. An office memorandum dated April 28 1939[2] notes that the arrangement would run for twelve months from March 1 1939 and would be terminable thereafter at six months' notice on either side. About half the editorial staff would go to Kettering, the other half would struggle on in London unless the government itself had to move. All members of the staff, editorial and mechanical, were told individually whether they were on the Kettering list or would stay on in London. On the mechanical side Kettering could provide reasonable room and capacity for producing an eight-page *Times* and a sixteen-page *Weekly Edition*. The manager of *The Times*, C. S. Kent, the assistant manager, F. P. Bishop,[3] and other men spent weeks in ensuring that the move

1947–54. Deputy editor, *Daily Telegraph*, 1954–62; first editor, *Sunday Telegraph*, 1961–66.

2 T.T.A.

3 Sir Patrick Bishop (1900–1972). Tottenham Grammar School; King's College, London. In advertising department of *The Times* before serving in the Royal Flying Corps in the First World War. Rejoined *The Times*, 1919; advertisement manager, 1928; assistant manager, 1937–45. Conservative MP, Harrow Central, 1950–64. Knighted, 1964.

could be swiftly made and that printing and distribution of the paper could be maintained from Kettering. As late as November 19 1943 Bishop recorded in greater detail some revised and updated arrangements for transmitting news, coping with different column widths, and providing living room for the staff.

In 1943 yet a third plan for emergency printing had to be worked out. The threat of German rockets and then their actual assault on London and south-eastern England required a scheme for producing the paper outside their range. An offer of help came from the *Manchester Guardian*. According to a letter from C. S. Kent to J. R. Scott, chairman of the *Guardian* and *Evening News*, the offer was first put to *The Times* by William Haley, then joint managing director of the *Guardian* company. It was gratefully taken up. F. G. Easto[4] and V. Royle,[5] having been to Manchester, reported that the facilities and accommodation there were in every way better than at Kettering, as indeed might have been supposed, given the circulation of the *Manchester Guardian* and the *Manchester Evening News*. An eight-page paper could be comfortably printed and circulated, provided that the *Weekly Edition* and the supplements were still printed at Kettering. On February 25 1944 Kent asked in a memorandum for arrangements to be speeded up:

We ought to be as prepared at Manchester as we are at Kettering . . . remembering that our policy will be to go first to Kettering for a few days, while we make the final preparations for Manchester.[6]

Happily all the plans remained plans. The bombing of London was not so catastrophic as had been expected, and the allied armies reached the launching pads in north-eastern France before the German rockets could be developed to their full number and power. But the knowledge that prepared positions were ready in the provinces, in case of need, helped the staff to carry on with greater confidence amid the bombs on London.

Throughout most of the war the staff worked on within Printing House Square in makeshift rooms that were cramped, stuffy, dark, often freezing, always uncomfortable. Most of the windows were blown out in the first heavy raids on London in August 1940. They were replaced with opaque plastic sheets which rattled with every breeze.

---

4 Frank G. Easto (1889–1970). Joined *The Times* staff, 1909. After war service returned to the paper in 1919; night liaison officer, 1926; night printer, 1937; head printer from 1938 to retirement in 1954.
5 Victor Royle (1895–1976). Joined *The Times* circulation department, 1913; circulation manager, 1952–61.
6 T.T.A.

Electric lights were reduced in power to save electricity. When the air raid sirens sounded by day many of the staff moved downstairs. By night the whole staff, editorial and mechanical, went underground, leaving only the fire watchers on the roof. In the underground workrooms the fumes from the machinery joined the tobacco smoke in using up most of the air. In the main room the editor and his secretary were in a raised glass box rather like a sea captain's bridge, reached by a steep iron staircase like a ship's companion-way. Below the editor's cabin were the heavy work benches where the sub-editors sat; and beyond them were the compositors at their machines.

When the raids continued most of the night the staff had to sleep where they could on the tables, or under them, or on camp beds. Part of a large cellar was bricked off with a blast-resistant wall to form a dormitory for those unable to get home during the night. It was filled with two-tier iron bedsteads. Each man had two blankets, and a personal sheet sleeping bag that he took home for washing. One of the sub-editors (W. R. A. Easthope)[7] vividly remembers lying in a top bunk night after night listening to the bombs and watching (from a single red electric light bulb) the shadows of rats gliding silently along overhead pipes; fortunately they were very sure-footed. Geoffrey Dawson and John Astor, if he was in the office, crept into a small cubby-hole let into the wall of the main shelter. If the All Clear sounded fairly early in the night the staff had to find their way in the black-out to their homes, mainly in the suburbs. Private cars were not yet general; in any case the fierce petrol rationing did not allow for any private motoring; and the men had to wait for the rare buses or cross Queen Victoria Street to Blackfriars station to catch an equally rare and blacked-out train. If the train reached its journey's end without being held up by bomb damage to the track the passengers called it a good night. The meagre wartime food did not make life easier, although the staff, like most other workers in the country, were helped out by off-the-ration meals in the office canteen.

Wartime restraints on the railways affected the paper more directly. The trains carrying newspaper supplies from London to the provinces were re-scheduled to run at least two hours earlier than they did before the war. *The Times* had therefore to go to press at 9.15 p.m. instead of 11.30. This meant that late news from the battle fronts and from the United States often missed the first edition altogether and had to be repeated in the early editions the next day.

---

7 William Reginald Allen Easthope (b. 1905). Joined *The Times* as home sub-editor, 1934; chief home sub-editor, 1950; editor *Weekly Review*, 1952–63; archivist, 1964–70.

Geoffrey Dawson had at least a car to ferry him about London. With many detours due to bomb damage he was able on most days to get from the office to the various places where in turn he lived: first in Sussex Place, Regent's Park, then in the Connaught Hotel, then in a flat at 24 Lowndes Square, Belgravia. He needed the car; he was on duty at all hours of the day and most of the night; and he kept up his political contacts and his social friendships over lunch and dinner almost every day. His laconic diary entries day by day show how exhausting a round it was for a man in his late sixties. August 26 1940 was an especially interesting but not unusually busy day:

To the office in the morning (Miss D.[8] had deserted me) and thence to 10 Downing St. for lunch. The Cabinet were all emerging and I was able to save an appt. w Tom Inskip[9] about Fairbridge.[10] The luncheon party was a curious quartet – Winston, the Arch,[11] Henry Strakosch[12] and I. Some little talk w. W about the Independent Companies or Commandos (storm troops) on wh. M. Burn[13] had been to see Falls and me in the morning. This partly in his Air Raid room, to wh he and I adjourned on an early afternoon warning. He was in excellent form, fit and confident, and full of Beaverbrook's achievements in production. I was in the Office by about 4; got home to dine with C.[14] and her mother: and then went back to an intolerable night of continuous air-raid. We were just going to Press when the red warning went at 9.30: missed 1st. edition trains – then 2nd: and were in the underground workrooms (w nothing to work at and the men forbidden to work) till 3.40 when we got going again. I satisfied myself that *The Times was* coming out and went home at 4.

He had been on the go for about eighteen hours. The reference to 'men forbidden to work' was to the unions' early reluctance to have men working on during air raid alerts, but a meeting the next day between the Newspaper Proprietors' Association and the unions led to an agreement

---

8 Miss Dickie, editor's day secretary, who was on leave.
9 Sir Thomas Walker Herbert Inskip (1876–1947). Held various Cabinet posts. In August 1940 was Dominions Secretary.
10 Kingsley O. Fairbridge (1885–1924). Started his first school at Pinjarra, Western Australia. Further schools opened in Australia, Canada, and Rhodesia.
11 Dr. Cosmo Gordon Lang (1864–1945). Archbishop of Canterbury, 1928–42.
12 Sir Henry Strakosch (1871–1943). Banker, friend of Churchill.
13 Michael Clive Burn (b. 1912). Winchester; New College, Oxford. Joined *The Times* staff, 1936. Returned after war service (p.o.w.) as Vienna correspondent, 1946; Balkans correspondent based at Budapest, 1948, until his resignation in 1949. Novelist, poet and playwright.
14 Cecilia, Hon. Mrs. Geoffrey Dawson. Younger daughter of Sir Arthur and Lady Lawley, later Lord and Lady Wenlock.

to let work go on. It was then that the men were assured ARP 'spotters' would give warning of imminent danger when the men could shelter until it passed. Many such warnings had to be flashed in the next days and weeks. On August 30 Dawson writes:

Our serious trouble in London began about 9 and went on till about 4 am. The paper went smoothly and after sitting about above and below I decided to take Webb[15] to his 11.19 train and went on home to bed. But not to sleep! It was a horrible night – geese cackling, planes overhead, guns, bombs, house shaking w. no doubt, remote explosions. The 2 servants came down to the drawing room in the middle of it. I stayed in bed w occasional visits to the window.

As the raids became heavier Printing House Square was often surrounded by fires, and then on the night of September 24/25, at 1.52 a.m., a big bomb fell directly on the building. During the night the ARP team on the roof had seen that the bombers' path was bringing danger closer to the office. Production had been stopped several times when emergency signals were flashed down to the building below. A spotter at No. 1 Post on the roof had the telephone in his hand telling the Control Room that he did not like the sound of a plane coming in close from the south-west when he heard the whistle of a bomb. He shouted to his two companions to duck; there was the crash; the explosion 'like the sudden opening of a blast furnace',[16] and the roar of falling masonry.

Every room at the front of the building and some of those behind were wrecked. The worst hit were the sub-editors' rooms, the messengers' room, and the library. All this was fully discovered only when dawn came. In the hours of darkness the ARP and the firemen had only their torches and hurricane lamps to help them amid the smoke, the dust, and the debris. Over three hundred men were in the building at the time; none was seriously hurt. A man who had been sleeping nearest to the point of explosion was found wandering dazedly around in his bare feet through the broken glass, politely asking others if they would kindly tell him if he was walking in the right direction for Beckenham station. John Astor was fortunate. He had been sleeping not in the shelter but in the first-floor board room which fell in bits around him. His first words to the ARP men were, 'Everyone accounted for? Good'. Dawson had returned to London from Langcliffe only on the morning before the bomb. He had gone to his camp bed below about midnight. He woke to

---

15 John Webb, editor's night secretary.
16 *When the Sirens Sounded*; an account of air raid precautions in Printing House Square 1937 to 1945. Office of *The Times*, 1949.

the bang and 'a general buzz of excitement'.[17] Both he and Astor recognised that they themselves could do little to help and went home through the rest of the bombs.

Bishop, the assistant manager, had been in charge of the building when the bomb fell; Kent, the manager, soon arrived; and they began to see what had to be done. The machine room had escaped and the paper was being printed once more only twenty minutes after the blast. Kent – who had had one hour's sleep when called from home – stayed on the job for twenty-eight hours without rest, arranging for urgent supplies of all kinds to be sent in and for repair work to be begun. Heads of department were called from home by telephone through the emergency switchboard. The mechanical superintendent[18] had his men nailing boards across windows before the day had properly dawned. Electricians came in to get the lights going again. The home news editor, Alan Pitt Robbins,[19] and Ralph Deakin,[20] the foreign news editor, were soon in touch with the news agencies to ensure that tape machines were brought in to take the place of those wrecked. The classified advertisement staff crawled among the wreckage of their room to retrieve their records. Other papers were picked up from the road outside. Builders' men began to shore up the damaged front of the building. New rooms had to be fitted up somehow for the editorial and managerial staffs; fortunately an old and empty machine room could be taken over. At all events the next day's paper was assured. Hitler's bomb was not going to make *The Times* miss publication for the first time in its history.

A few hours after the bomb the chairman received a letter from the Prime Minister. Churchill wrote:

My dear Astor,

Congratulations on the remarkable way in which *The Times* has carried on in face of all the damage and discomfort caused by the bombing of Printing House Square.

None of your readers could discover from the paper that your editorial and managerial departments have been destroyed.

The resourcefulness and adaptability of your staff are beyond praise.[21]

17 GDD, September 25 1940.
18 Edward George Shrimpton (1893–1966). Mechanical superintendent of *The Times*, 1936–59.
19 Alan Pitt Robbins (1888–1967). Joined *The Times* as a reporter in 1909; night news editor, 1914; after war service returned to editorial staff to inaugurate weekly article on the cinema; political correspondent, 1923–38; home news editor, 1938–53.
20 Ralph Deakin (1888–1952). After demobilisation from First World War joined *The Times* staff; assistant correspondent in Berlin and Paris, 1919–21; imperial and foreign news editor, 1921–52. Director of Reuters, 1941–45.
21 T.T.A.

The office would have been destroyed many times by incendiary bombs if the ARP teams had not had intensive training. All the men were taught quick and safe ways of climbing over the roofs by day and night; they were trained to cope with gas bombs as well as fires and explosions; and they manned the buildings twenty-four hours a day, seven days a week.

One of the worst raids was the last. On the night of May 10 1941 – a weekend – Printing House Square was soon surrounded by fires. Heavy bombs destroyed so many water mains that hoses were empty. *The Times* ARP men up on the roofs had to fight off not only the incendiary bombs but blazing debris which was thrown up from stricken buildings round about and which then fell down on Printing House Square. The men squeezed water from their hoses into buckets, threw sand on the flames, and stamped on the bombs with their boots. Many neighbouring buildings were not so well guarded or were less fortunate. For years afterwards the solid *Times* building overlooked derelict sites and broken walls in Queen Victoria Street and Ludgate Hill. Once again *The Times* ARP teams had saved the building when many offices in the City were destroyed.

Practically every able-bodied man who was not in the Home Guard was in the ARP service, which enrolled a total of 750 men. Over forty women were trained in the first aid section. Bishop was chairman of the organisation, and G. R. Pope[22] was the chief ARP officer. Members of the control committee were drawn from all sections of the company.

When Anthony Eden, then Secretary of State for War, made his appeal for men to join the newly formed Home Guard (then called the Local Defence Volunteers) there were some hesitations among the top men in the newspaper offices at first. Where were the men to come from? Many of the staffs had already enrolled in the ARP formations, newspapers had to be kept going almost all round the clock, and in any case most of the London papers were expecting soon to move to the provinces. But the desire to serve came strongly from the men themselves. In *The Times* more than two hundred volunteers were enrolled within a few weeks. Other newspaper offices were no less keen. In August 1940 the 5th. City of London (Press) Battalion was formed out of units from several offices. It was put on a regular military footing early in 1941. Men from the First World War were given commands. Lieu-

---

22 Sir George Pope (1902–82). Joined *Morning Post*, 1916; advertising manager, 1931. *Daily Telegraph*, 1937. *The Times* later in 1937; successively advertising manager and assistant manager; general manager, 1965–67; director, Times Newspapers Limited, 1967. Knighted, 1967.

tenant-Colonel John Astor, chairman of *The Times*, became commanding officer. Major Bishop, assistant manager, was second in command. Captain Barker, formerly manager of *The Times* Press office, became adjutant. Major Angel,[23] circulation manager, had command of 'A' Company which was the Printing House Square unit, 180-strong.

When weapons came to hand the men were given strenuous training, with several week-end camps for manoeuvres, bomb-throwing, and firing on ranges. By gradual stages, difficult to define, the battalion advanced from a purely static role and became recognised as a General Service battalion – the only complete G.S. battalion in the City of London. Colonel Astor was then appointed to take command of many other, still static, units in the City and the battalion was given direct responsibility for the military defence of the City against any infiltrating units such as parachutists. Colonel Astor had a Rolls-Royce converted into an armoured car; there was an ambulance and a mobile canteen, given through the Press Club by the citizens of Guelph, Ontario. The battalion had its intelligence, signals, and medical sections. Street fighting courses in the City were made more realistic and more useful by reason of the many wrecked buildings and many sites left derelict by the bombing. There were many regrets when the battalion had to stand down as the war came to an end.

Throughout all this time the paper was being produced without a break. Somewhat surprisingly it was never seriously short of staff. As men left in large numbers to join the armed forces *The Times* itself was page by page reduced in size as paper rationing became stricter, and the smaller issues required fewer men to bring them out. Such balanced reductions brought some slight relief in a plight that at times seemed desperate. The losses of ships in the Battle of the Atlantic cut down the imports of newsprint. The size of the paper was quickly reduced successively to 16, 14, 12 and ten pages. At the worst period *The Times* had ten pages three days a week and only eight pages on the other three days.

In March 1940 it made one of its most important, most difficult, and wisest decisions. With paper so short in supply, and likely to be shorter still, *The Times* was faced with the choice between cutting the number of pages still further and cutting the number of copies which it printed. To reduce the size of the paper would mean that it could no longer pretend to give anything like adequate space to the news services and to the features which made *The Times* what it was; it would have to cut down

---

23 Frederick Angel (1895–1970). Circulation manager, 1928–52.

the space for leading articles, letters to the editor, the parliamentary reports, and special articles of urgent public interest while hacking away still more at the home news and the war despatches. Because of its broad coverage the paper was selling every single copy it could produce. To reduce the number of copies printed would mean cutting the circulation down straight away – an idea always abhorrent to newspapermen. The private diaries of Dawson and Barrington-Ward record the many anxious talks, but neither man had any doubt in his own mind: much better keep the personality of *The Times* than provide only a shadow of it in a desire to keep up circulation. Both men knew how quickly a character can be lost. Once a newspaper's features are dropped, even for a time, it is hard to restore them. Habits fall into disuse both in the office and among the readers.

So the decision was taken to keep what could be kept of *The Times*. On March 21 1940 the paper announced that it would reduce by one-sixth the number of copies printed rather than reduce itself to a size 'which would have compelled the omission of contents which its readers rightly regarded as essential'. The circulation which had been 203,000 in 1938 was cut to 164,000. Less than three weeks later the price was raised from 2d. to 3d. Newsprint had risen from just over £11 a ton on the eve of war to £24 a ton. In 1942 the circulation had to be reduced again to 154,000, even though – as a further way of saving newsprint – the size of the paper was cut to eight pages on three days a week. By June 1943 circulation had crept up to 158,000, and it did not in fact reach its pre-war level of 203,000 until 1945 when newsprint began to come in a little more easily.

Getting out an eight-page or even a ten-page *Times* was a melancholy but exciting job. Columns of news each night had to be stripped to the bare bones. Some excellent despatches had no hope of getting into the paper at all. On some nights the whole of the home news, apart from what was on the main news page, amounted to a column. Sport and the arts looked more like postcards than newspaper features. But the essential *Times* was preserved in the leading articles, the texts of significant documents, the reports of parliamentary debates, the most informative despatches from all parts of the world, the letters to the editor. The paper also kept on its many experts – military, naval, air, political, diplomatic, scientific, medical, educational, labour, and the rest – whose news and regular analyses were more detailed on most days than appeared elsewhere.

The wisdom of the harsh decision to slash circulation rather than the paper itself was proved. In his report for the year ended June 30 1943 the manager said with great restraint, 'The demand for *The Times* greatly exceeds the maximum supply possible'. The paper began to have a rarity value which seemed to promise an upsurge in circulation when paper rationing ended. (The promise was fulfilled. Between 1945 and 1947 the circulation rose from 203,000 to 246,700.)

At the same time, contrary to many forecasts, *The Times* did well commercially in the war. So did most other newspapers. It is true that the cost of newsprint went on rising, but the increase was offset by the fewer numbers of pages printed and, in the case of *The Times*, by the cut in circulation. Staffs were smaller than before the war. Sales promotion was no longer a costly affair. Though the income on the advertising side was reduced so was the expenditure. The war which brought many appalling problems greatly simplified others. In fact several newspapers which had almost exhausted themselves in the fierce competition between the wars found respite from such out-and-out rivalry during the war. They found also that they could make money more comfortably with their smaller sizes, being less costly to produce and to distribute. They chafed less and less at the fetters of rationing and were not at all happy when *The Times* broke the system in 1956.[24]

At the beginning of the war the expectation was of losses rather than profits. In September 1939 John Astor reminded Kent that *The Times* was faced with the prospect of falling advertising revenue. He was ready to face such losses, but he suggested that, in a war in which many people would make sacrifices of every kind, there might be some reduction in the salaries paid to the staff. It was a surprising suggestion coming from a man who was both very kind and very generous even if, with his great wealth, he found it hard at times to envisage life with a family on a modest budget. Kent did not like the suggestion one bit. In his reply he pointed out that salaries could be reduced compulsorily only if requisite notice were served on each individual. Even so, there could be no reductions below the levels agreed between the Newspaper Proprietors Association and the unions. No less to the point, 'I am constantly told, as was Lints Smith,[25] that other papers pay higher salaries in various directions than *The Times*. This is probably true. It may be true with regard to sub-editors, for instance'. If a salary cut were imposed, the psychological blow would be enormous. Staff, already hit by higher taxation and long working hours, would be tempted away from Printing House Square.

---

24 See Chapter XV.
25 William Lints Smith (1876–1944). Joined the managerial staff of *The Times*, 1914; manager from 1920 until retirement in 1937.

No more was heard about the suggestion. Quite independently, both Dawson and Kent gave up part of their salaries for the duration of the war. The staff knew nothing about Astor's suggestion or the editor's and manager's action, but many in the editorial departments were increasingly worried about their generally low salaries.

In July 1941 their discontent became explosive. Leslie-Smith,[26] the deputy night editor, felt especially strongly that they must speak out. Sixty-five men on the editorial side signed a round robin which Herbert Russell,[27] the night editor, handed to Dawson on July 30. Some men, like Russell himself, did not feel aggrieved on their own account but signed the manifesto none the less, because they knew that others – mainly among the sub-editors and reporters – were miserable with anxiety. The wording was blunt:

> We know that we are the lowest paid Editorial staff in London daily journalism. We believe that, with few exceptions, our salaries would be no more than commensurate with the services we render if the present rates were raised by at least one-third.
>
> We do not undervalue our conditions of work and security. But we are concerned with the salaries on which we have to live . . . It can hardly be in the interests of the greatest newspaper in the world that many members of its staff should be dissatisfied because their remuneration falls below the Fleet Street level.

The signatories, who included several heads of department, asked Dawson to use his utmost influence with the management and the board of directors to get them more money. In particular they asked that the management should stop scaling down a salary when a post became vacant, giving the successor less money than the previous occupant had received in the post. They tactfully suggested that Dawson, with whom they said they were proud to be associated, might not himself be aware of the general low rates of pay.

Dawson received the protest with his usual calm, and urged both Astor and Kent to 'take it deliberately'. But they were both deeply shocked. Kent 'spent a sleepless night in rebutting it'[28] and sent Astor two memoranda within a few days of each other. In the first he wrote:

> Both the form and the matter of the communication from the

---

26 Leslie Horace Leslie-Smith (1895–1982). Home sub-editor on *The Times*, 1924; night editor, 1949–56; assistant to editor of Special Numbers from 1956 until retirement in 1963.
27 Herbert Spencer Russell (1884–1949). Joined *The Times* editorial staff, 1924; night editor from 1935 until retirement in 1949.
28 GDD, August 1 1941.

Editorial staff are to be deplored . . . Those who have engineered the communication have rendered a grave disservice to *The Times* in fomenting an unwarranted sense of discontent. Notwithstanding, the communication must have reasoned treatment.[29]

Kent then pointed out that the signatories had not mentioned the contributory pension scheme from which the staff benefited on retirement (the only such scheme, he said, in a London daily newspaper office at that time); nor had they acknowledged the bonuses that were paid out selectively from time to time for good work. Neither had they sufficiently emphasised the security which they enjoyed in their jobs. They had overlooked the expense of producing a paper so comprehensive as *The Times*, with its large foreign staff, its parliamentary pages, and its law reports. Other papers were spared much of this outlay. Yet, in spite of such special costs, Kent said, salaries on *The Times* – certainly for sub-editors and reporters – compared very well with the scales on all other London papers except the *Daily Express*. He may have forgotten that, less than two years before, when bringing forward arguments against Astor's suggestion that salaries could be cut, he himself had said that it was 'probably true' that other papers 'pay higher salaries in various directions than *The Times*', particularly to sub-editors. He now produced, in his second memorandum dated August 11, a detailed set of figures which showed that *The Times* came out with credit in the comparison.

The truth is that salaries on *The Times*, on both the editorial and managerial sides, were generous by the standards of the day for the men at the top but very speedily fell away and were painfully thin at the middle and lower reaches. Dawson had £8,000 a year, Kent £7,000; then came a big drop to the £2,000 a year, or slightly over, paid to their three immediate assistants. Kent displayed the rest of the scale in a memorandum written soon after the outbreak of war.[30] It shows how quickly the pyramid flattened out:

Seven salaries of £1,500–£2,000	£10,500
Five salaries at £1,250 or more	£6,650
Twenty-five at £1,000	£25,000
About 30 at £750 or more	£25,565
About 140 at £500 or more	£70,763
About 540 at £250 or more	£135,000

29 T.T.A.
30 Kent to Astor, September 21 1939. T.T.A.

On receiving the staff protest Astor asked two directors, Sir Campbell Stuart[31] and Sir Harold Hartley, to see what was wrong and to make suggestions. On August 19 they reported the strong feeling in the office that the whole system of salary-fixing was haphazard; some men received no increase for years; others got one if they asked for it, though some who asked were refused. Whether salaries on *The Times* were in general lower than elsewhere the two directors could not decide, but they were quite certain that the practice of giving selective bonuses was vicious and should be stopped. On the other hand they agreed with the manager that the staff did not sufficiently appreciate the twin value to them of job security and the pension scheme. What the two men proposed was more liaison between management and editorial staff to let the problems and finances of the paper be better understood.

Barrington-Ward, soon to sit in the editor's chair, was not at all displeased to have the matter aired in good time before he took over. He was none the less alarmed at a later suggestion that a special sub-committee of the Board should keep a constant watch over all salaries, and not simply over the higher ones. Such a watch committee, Barrington-Ward quickly saw, could undermine the position of the manager and, by extension, his own standing as editor. He made the point more than once when talking to Astor: 'It is essential to the successful conduct of the paper, both on the managerial and editorial sides, that its constitution should be scrupulously regarded.'[32] He already knew that his policy as editor would be startling to many Conservatives in Britain, and he wished no precedent for interference by the Board to be established. The idea for a special sub-committee was not pursued. In the end, after Astor and other directors had seen the chief complainants several times, men doing first-class work were better rewarded and the general level of salaries edged up.

The protest was a happening far outside *The Times* tradition and, like many breaks in tradition, it was justified. It shook the old *Times* habit of regarding money as something unfit for gentlemanly conversation. Casey used to recall that once before the war, when arguing with Brumwell[33] about pay, he said bitterly that a man on *The Times* should, it seemed, have a private income to support him, and Brumwell took the

---

31 Sir Campbell Stuart (1885–1972). Joined *The Times*, April 1919; elected to the Board the same month; deputy chairman, June 1919; managing director, 1920–24; retired from the Board in 1960.
32 B–W D, September 18 1941.
33 George Murray Brumwell (1872–1963). Manchester Grammar School; Trinity College, Oxford. Joined staff of *The Times*, 1902; sub-editor, editor's secretary, and night editor, 1908–22; assistant editor from 1922 until retirement in 1935.

jibe entirely seriously as a wise and perceptive remark. After the great protest there was less pretence.

The company had more money as the war went on. By the time it ended Kent could look back on five years of commercial success both with *The Times* itself and with the company as a whole. The paper had made a loss of £17,992 in 1940, the first year's loss in the paper's history. But then profits rose:

1941	£76,123
1942	£309,364
1943	£357,557
1944	£403,107
1945	£428,498

That was for the paper itself. For the company as a whole – The Times Publishing Company Limited – the profits were not so large; they rose from £45,000 in 1941 to £141,000 in 1945. None the less the results were satisfactory amid all the dangers and upheavals of war. While the much-contracted *Times* itself was doing well the company was still producing the *Literary* and *Educational Supplements* and its *Weekly Edition* (discontinued in 1963). From the middle of 1942 it printed miniature copies of the *Weekly Edition* for the Foreign Office and the Ministry of Information which distributed, at one time, over 12,000 copies a week. Later still miniature copies of *The Times* itself – fine production on India paper – were being distributed among allied peoples and armies.

On November 2 1942 *The Times* began setting, printing, and packing for distribution an entirely independent daily newspaper, the *Stars and Stripes*, the American army journal for US servicemen in Europe. Rooms had to be found in Printing House Square for the American editorial staff who wrote and edited the whole paper. The original contract was for a print of around 50,000 copies a day of a newspaper varying in size from four to eight pages. The project grew with the expansion of the American forces, and by 1944/5 over 318,000 copies a day were being turned out. Financing was arranged through the Lend–Lease scheme, and payment was made to *The Times* by HM Stationery Office. Within the office the Americans settled down happily with the mechanical and editorial sides. Kent would sometimes wonder whether *The Times* tradition really permitted him to print some of the livelier strip cartoons but he was reconciled by the thought that he was thereby helping the cause of allied cooperation. There were regrets on both sides when the enterprise ended on October 15 1945.

It had been a hard war for Kent, Bishop, and Pope on the management side, caught up in a hundred problems outside normal peacetime work. Before it ended the directors were already considering likely successors to Kent, who was in his fifty-ninth year by 1945. Kent had never taken his work easily, he was a methodical and careful worker, penny-wise without being ever pound-foolish. He remained on top of all the drastic changes and contingency planning forced on him by the war but the strain was apparent. When he met men or women of the paper his words were few and far between. In the little that he said when talking to editorial men he seemed to suggest that management was mainly a matter of small-digit arithmetic. It was his pursed-up manner in the office which helped to provoke the editorial protest on salaries in 1941. Yet in his manner he was often unfair to himself. He had a larger view. The true test of his management was seen in the healthy state of the company's finances when he retired in 1949.

He was one of the men who were made by Northcliffe. Like many other Northcliffe men his beginnings were modest. Born in South Kensington in 1887 he joined the old morning *Standard* in 1908 on the editorial side and then changed over to accountancy with Associated Newspapers. In 1917 there came his big chance when he went with Northcliffe to Washington with the British War Mission. In 1918 he came back to be financial controller of Northcliffe's department of propaganda to enemy countries; and in 1921, then on Northcliffe's personal staff, came to *The Times* to take charge of finance and accounts. It was a key post. When John Astor bought the greater part of the shares in the company after Northcliffe's death Kent remained on as secretary of the company and of the holding company. In 1931 he was made assistant manager under William Lints Smith, and he took over the management in 1937 when Lints Smith retired. On the day he took the chair the omens could hardly have been worse. The *Morning Post* ceased publication as a separate newspaper that very day, and there were plenty of other signs that the serious newspapers were feeling the pressure of the competition both from the popular papers and from each other. Worse assaults were to come, but Kent, in his careful way, was one of the men who ensured that *The Times* survived all the buffetings. Astor and the directors acknowledged that Kent should retire but not immediately and certainly not before a first-class successor was in sight.

For some years it seemed that Bishop was the man who would succeed. He was a man who planned a course slowly and carefully and then drove hard along it, showing exceptional mental stamina. With these qualities went a very proper ambition which took him on from one heavy job to another, some of them in the little tried fields of modern technology. There was nothing showy in his manner; the old phrase about a neat and soldierlike appearance fitted him well, provided that a deeply reflective look is added to it. He came to *The Times* as a boy of seventeen, but within a few months of joining the paper left to join the Royal Flying Corps. Back on *The Times* in 1919 in the advertising department he spent his evenings and weekends reading law, was called to the Bar by Gray's Inn in 1924, and wrote several books on the legal and ethical problems of advertising. After being appointed advertising manager in 1927 and assistant manager in 1937 he took on, as recorded earlier, much of the work with ARP and the Home Guard during the war on top of all his managerial work.

During 1944 Astor and Kent had talks with him and kept Barrington-Ward informed. Bishop had been planning ahead in his careful way and he evidently thought that it would be difficult to manage *The Times* effectively so long as the editorial and managerial sides worked, for the most part, in separate compartments. A manager must know what he is selling. Barrington-Ward, as his diary shows, was alerted to the possible dangers by the ever-vigilant Morison:

> Gave Morison dinner at the Travellers. Bishop now coming into the open. Does not wish to become Manager of *The Times* without a share in editorial policy! Wants power without responsibility, in fact. Offering his resignation with a view to joining board of *Daily Mail*. A mistaken move. The office of manager is what any man's capacity and personality make it. Status is not conferred but acquired. Limited though he is (chiefly by the ego) B. has much ability and will be a real loss. On the other hand it is a good time to bring in a new man before reconstruction begins and we have a chance to look for someone (perhaps, as Morison suggests, in the publishing trade) with real breadth in his background and outlook.

In July 1944 Bishop gave notice of his intention to resign once the German war was over. Before the year ended Astor and Kent were in touch with Frank Waters,[34] a Royal Marines lieutenant-colonel who before the war had been manager of the Scottish Office of the *Daily Express*. In January 1945 he was offered the post of assistant manager,

---

34 Frank Henry Waters (1908–1954). Loretto; Pembroke College, Cambridge. Joined *Daily Express* in 1929, and from 1934–42 was on the managerial side of *Sunday Express*, *Scottish Daily Express* and *Evening Citizen* in Glasgow. After war service, from 1945–50 he was assistant manager of *The Times*. Resigned to become manager of *News Chronicle* and *Star*.

with high salary and expenses and with the unspoken understanding that, if all went well, he would become manager when Kent left. Much was expected from the appointment. Waters was young, intelligent, knowledgeable, imaginative, and highly companionable. He was soon popular with most people in the office, managerial and editorial. He remained popular with most of them – but not, as soon became clear, with Kent. Kent's growing antipathy postponed the day of decision.[35]

35 See Chapter VII.

IV

WAR ACROSS THE WORLD

THE ease with which *The Times* changed its news coverage over from peace to war was largely due to Ralph Deakin, the foreign news editor. Deakin is one of the enigmas in the history of the paper. By 1939 he had already held his key job for eighteen years, having been appointed to it in 1921 by Northcliffe, just before Dawson came back for his second term as editor; and he was to remain foreign news editor for another thirteen years after 1939 until his sudden death in 1952. He was one of the men – every newspaper office has one or two – who do much of the work yet what they do goes unseen or is taken for granted by colleagues. He brought to the job an unceasing watch over detail, and an almost obsessive professional pride which he too often nursed within himself.

Very few on the paper knew that he spent a good part of every Friday (supposedly his day off) in sub-editing special articles. Very few knew that he would come into an empty office on a Saturday afternoon to begin sorting through the agency news tapes and thus ease the heavy work that awaited him on a Sunday, when a daily newspaper has to face the weight of two days' weekend news. He once said that he liked to lunch quickly in the office every other Thursday, and then be ready at his desk, just in case – it was the remotest possible chance – he was suddenly summoned to explain some point or other at the fortnightly directors' luncheon and meeting. (They met in what was still known as the Private House, the old home of the Walter family on one side of Printing House Square.) Deakin had many months of waiting patiently for the telephone to ring.

He wrote many warm, friendly, and helpful letters to his score of staff correspondents and to the 'stringers' – the part-time men and women correspondents – in different parts of the world. He never bothered them with the kind of request for obvious news which news editors on other papers were apt to send to their correspondents. He would say that anyone who needed such prompting was not up to the standard which *The Times* required. Men such as Sandy Inglis in India,[1]

Eric Britter also in India,[2] and Roy Curthoys in Australia,[3] whose despatches were always well judged, could be left to plan their own work most of the time. If a man was going wrong Deakin would send him letters full of understanding and guidance, and only if such letters brought no response after several months would he follow them with a final warning. His telegraphed instructions, circulated within the office for the information of assistant editors and the foreign sub-editors, were splendidly brief and clear. They varied in purport from 'Best thanks todays excellent message. *Times*' to 'Your long despatch yesterday unrequested, unwanted, unused. *Times*'. Beyond all such day-to-day routine he became absorbed in organising financial help by *The Times* for assaults on Mount Everest and other pioneering ventures.[4]

In most ways his reputation outside the office was greater than it was inside and this contrast added to the strains within him. After a few years at Lincoln Grammar School he had gone off as a young man to Vienna where he had taught English and learned the excellent German which earned him a commission in the Intelligence Corps during the First World War. The same facility in German, and his native intellect, brought him work, under Ernest Brain,[5] in reopening and reorganising the Berlin office after the war. He travelled widely thereafter both in his work and on leave. It was hardly surprising that people outside the office assumed that he was head of the whole foreign department: foreign editor, in fact. This innocent mistake touched on another sense of grievance in Deakin's mind, for Dawson had not appointed a foreign editor since the death of Dr. Harold Williams in 1928. Barrington-Ward had taken over much of the work in formulating policy in leading articles. Even so there was a gap. Two foreign leader writers – Leo Kennedy and Philip Graves – believed that they were fully qualified to fill that hole. Each was disappointed, but they had at least some compensatory satisfaction in being able to discuss policy with Dawson and more frequently with Barrington-Ward. Deakin was very rarely

---

1 Alexander Inglis (1894–1954). Herriot-Watt College, Edinburgh. Joined staff of *The Times*, 1933; correspondent in India, 1934–42; in Canada, 1943–51.

2 Eric Valentine Blakeney Britter (1906–1977). Schools in India and London School of Economics. Special correspondent of *The Times* in the Far East, 1945; Delhi correspondent, 1946–52; Tokyo, 1952–54; New York, 1954–68.

3 Roy Lancaster Curthoys (1892–1971). Editor of Melbourne *Argus* 1929–35. Chief Australia correspondent of *The Times*, 1936; retired 1957.

4 See Chapter XII.

5 Ernest Brain (1864–1928). Joined *The Times* staff 1883; successively reporter, sub-editor, editor's secretary, parliamentary correspondent, news editor, diplomatic correspondent, and correspondent in Holland, 1914; after the war in Berlin until 1920; retired 1927.

granted any such satisfaction. He was clearly expected to keep to his own field of news and 'foreign specials', which he covered admirably, although his methodical explanation of news at the regular afternoon editorial conference would too often make Dawson shuffle and mutter with impatience.

Before his energies began to fail Deakin was always at his best when faced with a large task, such as deploying men to cover the war. As no one knew what was likely to happen when war was imminent in 1939, it was decided to keep most of the main staff correspondents abroad at their posts and recruit war correspondents from among the promising younger men either in Printing House Square or in secondary posts abroad. Poland itself seemed to be taken care of: in November 1938, one month after Munich, R. O. G. Urch had been moved from Riga to Warsaw. Reginald Oliver Gilling Urch (1884–1945) had been writing on Russian affairs for *The Times* since 1922. As *The Times* would not station a man in Moscow so long as his messages were censored by the Soviet authorities, Urch was for many years placed on the wrong side of the frontier in Riga, capital of Latvia, then independent. 'Our Riga correspondent' was much derided by the left, and clearly it was a second-best arrangement. None the less Urch had served in Russia earlier, he received Soviet newspapers regularly in Riga, he listened to the Moscow radio bulletins, he had an excellent filing system, and many of his messages were much more enlightening than his critics were willing to admit at the time. He had settled in Warsaw in 1938 but, as it happened, he was due to be away on leave for some weeks in the summer of 1939.

To fill his place *The Times* sent Patrick Maitland, a young recruit on the staff who had done some writing on East European affairs.[6] It was Maitland who reported the story of Poland's collapse after that country was struck and disorganised by the new and devastatingly swift way in which the German command used tanks and bombers. After Marshal Smigly-Rydz on September 10 ordered a general retreat into south-east Poland, Maitland made his way in Urch's car to Romania. He reported from there the last stages of the Polish defeat, hastened by the Russian invasion of eastern Poland on September 17 and made final by the ending of resistance in Warsaw, reported on September 28. Maitland later went to Belgrade, his wife's home, and reported from there until in

---

6 Patrick Francis Maitland (b. 1911). Lancing; Brasenose College, Oxford. Balkans and Danubian correspondent, *The Times*, 1939–41. Unionist MP for Lanark, 1951–59; succeeded brother as 17th Earl of Lauderdale, 1968.

1941 he had once again to move from the invading German armies. He reached Lisbon in a train bringing a number of allied nationals to safety.

Urch himself was soon reporting war from Finland. After the Finnish government rejected Russian demands for bases on Finnish soil, the Soviet armies crossed the frontiers on November 30 1939. *The Times* carried daily stories of the heroic Finnish resistance from Urch and also in a series of glittering and moving despatches from Evelyn Montague, a *Manchester Guardian* staff writer whose services *The Times* shared. The eye-witness stories in *The Times* made clear not only the gallantry of the Finns but the inefficiency of the first Russian waves of attack; and they encouraged the rapidly mounting desire among MPs and others in Britain to give military support to Finland. In those days the risks of a war with Russia seemed not so great, especially in the eyes of many who believed that Russian military weakness had been exposed beyond all doubt. *The Times* was in favour of despatching supplies to Finland but not of direct military involvement. In fact the Russian armies were re-shaped, the thrusts into Finland were more efficiently directed, and on March 13 1940 the Finns had to accept the stiffened Russian terms for ending what was bound to become more and more of a one-sided war.

On the quiescent western front were two men: Robert W. Cooper[7] with the French forces and H. A. R. Philby[8] with the British. Bob Cooper was to have a proud career on *The Times*, becoming chief correspondent in Washington in 1954 and in Paris a few years later. A friendly, tall, burly man, distinguished by his deeply reflective eyes; a man slow in gait and often slow in speech, he was a writer of great power, with many passages of brilliance. His approach to writing was intuitive and ruminative rather than strictly intellectual, which meant that it took a great deal out of him. It also meant that his copy was often late and always worth waiting for.

In the early months his letters and memoranda back to the office from France are full of agonised complaints about the whims and

---

7 Robert Wright Cooper (b. 1904). Joined *The Times* staff in 1925 as a telephonist in foreign news department; after transfer to Paris in a similar capacity became sub-editor in the sporting department and Lawn Tennis correspondent, 1934; war correspondent, 1939–45; special correspondent at Nuremberg, 1945–46; correspondent in American Zone, Germany, 1946–48; then correspondent at United Nations, 1949–52; Washington, 1954–60; Paris, 1960–66. TV critic 1966 and other editorial work until retirement in 1969.
8 Harold Adrian Russell Philby (b. 1912). Westminster; Trinity College, Cambridge. *The Times* correspondent in Spain, 1937; war correspondent in France, 1939–40. Services taken over by the War Office, July 1 1940. Fled to Moscow 1963.

stupidities of the military censors, preventing him from pointing out weaknesses that he saw. When the phoney war ended with the German onslaught Cooper's despatches, so far as they could get through in all the confusion, were objective and alarming; and when he managed to reach Britain he wrote a special article, bringing out some of the lessons he could not bring out when in France. Read today it may seem to contain nothing that is especially revelatory, but at the time it was shocking: suspicions hitherto half-spoken were confirmed. After listing a number of failures, Cooper came to what he called the Maginot folly:

> Probably the greatest blunder of all was the absurd belief fostered in the public mind that the Maginot Line extended from the Channel to the Mediterranean, and here a rigid censorship was to blame.

H. A. R. Philby – Kim Philby – had been brought on to the staff by Deakin and was sent to cover the Spanish civil war from the Franco side. This he did so clearly, and apparently so fairly, that no questions at all were raised when he was posted to report on the British divisions in France when war was declared. Certainly no one suspected his communist background; some of his colleagues thought that he was, if anything, too eager in conversation to bring out Franco's good points in order to correct their own pro-Republican sympathies. He was shy in manner; his efforts to overcome his slight stammer seemed to be efforts to find the most honest word. The knowledge that his distinguished father, the Arabist St. John Philby, was coming under an official cloud in Britain made colleagues the more quick to show by their manner that they had no kind of distrust for the son. Deakin in particular had the highest hopes of his work in France. On March 9 1939 he strongly commended Philby in a letter to Ernest de Caux (1879–1960) who had been the urbanely analytical correspondent for *The Times* in Spain since 1910. During the Spanish civil war, while first James Holburn[9] and then Philby had been reporting on the Franco side, de Caux had been with the Republicans. In his letter Deakin wrote:

> He [Philby] has done very well in the face of great difficulties and is a first-class writer. If we have been at a disadvantage in recent weeks, apart from the Nationalist censorship, it has been largely due to the fact that Philby, promising as he is, has not had the journalistic experience which would teach him to overcome certain transmission

---

9 James Holburn (b. 1900). Harris Academy, Dundee; Glasgow University. Served on *Glasgow Herald*. *The Times* foreign sub-editor, 1934; later correspondent in Berlin, Spanish civil war and Moscow; Middle East correspondent, 1941; Delhi, 1943; United Nations (New York) correspondent, 1946; diplomatic correspondent, 1948–52; Middle East correspondent, 1952; resigned to edit *Glasgow Herald*, 1955–65.

difficulties. It seems desirable that he should spend some time in this office reasonably soon, learning the tricks of the trade . . .

My first desire is to get more good out of the very good Philby. I do not, of course, mean by working him harder, but through easier contacts.[10]

Ironically enough Philby wrote especially well in covering the visit which King George VI paid to his troops in France in late 1939. His true ideological feelings emerged perhaps only once. When the French armies were broken Philby wrote on June 22 1940 that some groups were none the less still keeping German units busy: 'In some respects these gallant bands recall the People's Army raised by General Chanzy after the disaster of Sedan in 1870, which succeeded in prolonging the war for several months.' Yet anyone could have expressed such populist hopes at the time, forlorn though they were bound to be. Philby seemed to have a good career ahead of him on *The Times* and there were regrets when he left to go into the secret recesses of government soon after he returned from France. When he disappeared into Russia in January 1963 and the story of his years of espionage came out, Printing House Square had no substantial evidence to offer about his character or the reasons for his actions.

Another man who described the Battle of France with good, clear strokes was Arthur Narracott[11] who was with what was called the Advanced Air Striking Force. He did not restrict himself to the aerial dog fights; he saw what was happening to the people in the villages and then, as the German armies approached, in Paris itself:

For a time people still sat about enjoying a drink and discussing the war in an atmosphere of complete calm. But when the *communiqués* told of the slow but steady German advance the exodus began in earnest. The traffic problem was further complicated by the arrival of thousands of refugees from Normandy . . . Outside one station I saw a queue at least a mile and a half long. Mingling with the taxis were cars and lorries, even horse-drawn vehicles, in which whole families and their pets had packed themselves for the journey to their new home. Some had only a faint idea of where they were going. Outside the station 50 or so perspiring gendarmes struggled to direct an ever-increasing flow of traffic. On the pavements hosts of women and children had been deposited. They sat in anxious

---

10 T.T.A.
11 Arthur Henson Narracott (1905–1967). Joined *The Times* Parliamentary staff 1938. Press officer, RAF, 1939–40. War correspondent 1940–45 with the allied air forces; air correspondent, 1945–67.

groups, surrounded by mountains of luggage. Some had even brought their canaries and their goldfish. Each train went out packed to suffocation in the stifling heat.[12]

The somewhat obscure General de Gaulle who arrived in Britain on June 17 1940 was known to two or three *Times* men who had met him. An apt character sketch of him had been given ten days earlier, on June 7, by Captain Falls when de Gaulle was called in as an adviser by Paul Reynaud, the French Prime Minister:

> He is of a type which has not a strong appeal – perhaps not a strong appeal enough – to British military students . . . Rather aggressively 'right wing', intensely theoretical, an almost fanatical apostle of the mass employment of armoured vehicles, he is also clear-minded, lucid and a man of action as well as a man of dreams and abstract ideas.[13]

To cover news coming out of Germany itself two men were sent to neutral Rotterdam: Aubrey Jones,[14] who had been in the Paris office and who was after the war to be Minister of Fuel and Power and Minister of Supply in Conservative administrations; and Archibald Gibson, who had served as a telephonist and was soon sent on to Bucharest. To watch over the tricky political situation in Belgium – especially tricky under the nervous control of King Leopold – Jerome Caminada[15] was brought back from New York. When Belgium was invaded Caminada, a South African of stalwart mind and great pertinacity, had the ill luck to be captured. Sent to the internment camp at Tost on the Polish frontier he managed, with one companion, to make the only successful escape from this camp by civilians during the war. For two years, sometimes on the run, sometimes again a prisoner, and for a time at large in Budapest, he made a continuously hazardous journey to freedom through Czechoslovakia, Hungary and Romania.

Others who were set apart for war reporting were taken from the parliamentary staff, among them Philip Ure,[16] and W. J. Prince.[17] To

---

12 *The Times*, June 14 1940.
13 *The Times*, June 7 1940.
14 Aubrey Jones (b. 1911). Served on *The Times* 1937–39 and 1947–48. Minister of Fuel and Power, 1955–57; Minister of Supply, 1957–59. Chairman, National Board for Prices and Incomes, 1965–70.
15 Jerome Charles Caminada (b. 1911). On *The Times* foreign department staff from 1938; special and staff correspondent in South East Asia, 1955; Middle East correspondent, 1960–65; foreign news editor 1965 until retirement in 1975.
16 Philip Dunbar Seymour Ure (b. 1896). *The Times* Parliamentary staff, 1928; on reporting staff from 1935; war correspondent, 1942; news department, 1945; special

the team was added Eric Phillips,[18] the deputy night news editor, and R. C. Lyle,[19] the racing correspondent. These appointments were simply the initial arrangements, taken with an eye on Europe only. The Japanese invasion of China was already being covered by Hugh Byas[20] in Tokyo and Colin McDonald[21] in Shanghai and afterwards in Chungking. Later, as Hitler's war spread and Mussolini brought Italy into it, the team of war correspondents was greatly strengthened when joined by James Holburn, the chief correspondent in Berlin who spent some months in Russia before going to the Middle East, and Christopher Lumby,[22] who had been chief correspondent in Rome and who was also sent to the Middle East.

During the strange months of waiting in late 1939 and early 1940 many warnings about the state of French morale were sent by Thomas Cadett, the chief correspondent in Paris.[23] Some of the warnings were made publicly in the paper, others privately in memoranda. In the First World War Cadett had been a subaltern in the Argyll and Sutherland Highlanders. He maintained a soldier's watchful eye on politicians, and became more than ever suspicious of several French ministers during and after Munich. He irritated the French government beyond measure

---

correspondent from 1947 until retirement in 1963.
17 William John Prince (1907–1974). Worked for *Observer* and Press Association before joining *The Times* Parliamentary staff in 1933; reporter, 1939; war correspondent with General Patton's army 1944–45; resumed as a home reporter in 1945 and joined *Daily Telegraph* in 1946.

18 Eric Edward Phillips (1892–1962). *The Times* outside contributor in 1913; staff reporter, 1921–39; after war service returned to the reporting staff in 1943 and became war correspondent with the Home Forces until 1944; reported the Second Army in North Western Europe until a motor accident in 1945; night (home) news editor and military reporter from 1946 until retirement in 1957.
19 Robert Charles Lyle (1887–1943). Felsted; Corpus Christi College, Cambridge. Joined *The Times* as sporting editor in 1919; racing correspondent from 1921; sporting editor, 1937–9; war correspondent with the Royal Navy Mediterranean Theatre, 1940–41; racing correspondent until his death.
20 Hugh Fulton Byas (1875–1945). *The Times Weekly* staff, 1909–14; Tokyo correspondent, 1926–41.
21 Colin Malcolm McDonald (1899–1982). Stewart's College, Edinburgh. Joined *The Times*, 1929; occasional correspondent in Peking from 1931; correspondent from 1937; special correspondent at Nanking, 1937; Shanghai correspondent, 1939–43.
22 Christopher Ditmar Rawson Lumby (1888–1946). Marlborough; Magdalene College, Cambridge. Foreign correspondent for *The Times* in many European centres, 1913–31; Middle East correspondent, 1931–37; correspondent in Rome, 1937–39; sent to Rotterdam at outbreak of war, 1939; war correspondent in Middle East, 1940; North Africa and Italy from 1943 until his death.
23 Thomas Tucker-Edwardes Cadett (1898–1982). Cranleigh. Joined *The Times* staff, 1924; correspondent in New York, 1927–29, and Paris, 1929–37. After war service left to join the BBC and to become its Paris correspondent.

by his outspoken mistrust of Georges Bonnet, the Foreign Minister who had been in the van of the appeasers. Some complaints from the Quai d'Orsay and others from the British Ambassador in Paris, Sir Eric Phipps, himself a fervent supporter of Munich, reached *The Times* by way of the Foreign Office towards the end of January 1939. At the same time Cadett himself wrote Dawson a long letter, dated January 31 1939, full of angry suspicion against Bonnet. On February 1 1939 Deakin wrote Dawson a memorandum:

> The Foreign Office is glad that *The Times* has urged circumspection upon Cadett *in re* Bonnet. Cadett is regarded as a most useful worker, and the coolness between him and the Ambassador, for which Cadett cannot be blamed, is regretted.

On the same day Dawson wrote Cadett a letter in his best style of diplomatic persuasion:

> Unfair as it may seem, it does really diminish your value as a detached correspondent of *The Times* if you are (or are even thought to be) involved in a personal feud with any particular French Minister.[24]

Cadett was not much deterred. He kept an even closer watch on Pierre Laval, who was to be Prime Minister during the German occupation and was to be executed after the war. In a memorandum dated October 3 1939, which Deakin circulated, Cadett wrote:

> If you have seen my published messages you will realise that I have been able to give some hint, vague and general though its terms may have been, of the peace movement now afoot. This very night I have sent off a piece, which I hope to see published, saying that for the moment the gallant little band led by Laval (I could not give his name of course) have piped down, at all events temporarily.

Cadett gave warning that the danger was by no means over:

> One Frenchman I was talking to today made a point which struck me very forcibly. He said that the French people were beginning to get *énervé* by a war in which nothing seemed to be happening (that is, on the Western Front, which is the only front in their eyes). My reply was that they must be very hard to please, for if a lot of their people had been killed they might well have raised a fuss on the lines of 'Here we are again getting killed while the British do nothing.' His answer was that the comparative lack of wholesale fighting might

---

24 T.T.A.

well make most Frenchmen feel that a war which exacted such a small toll of human life and such a big one of nervous tension and economic dislocation could hardly be utterly necessary. In other words, 'the war hasn't begun yet, really, and do we really need to start it?'

All this, of course, seems to turn me into a kind of devil's advocate, and I will therefore at once add that if properly led by their people and handled by us they will, I believe, stay the course. But I will not hide from you my belief that they will crack before we do. God grant, therefore, that the Boche cracks first.

In an even more perceptive letter to Dawson, dated the next day, October 4 1939, Cadett wrote:

As I have hinted this group, led by Laval, have been hoping to down Daladier (either in Parliament itself or in one of the Committees) on some point of policy, and set up a Government headed by the 83-year old Pétain. This is a particularly cunning move, for the old boy is greatly .respected owing to his excellent record of generalship in the last war. *But* he is among those who blame us for dragging France into war and has swallowed Laval's idea of a 'slight' slackening in Franco–British collaboration and peace negotiations on the basis of the Polish *fait accompli*, in the hope of forming a bloc with Italy and Spain to resist further German or Russian expansion . . . Laval and his movement will need watching.[25]

Cadett's warnings were borne out only too well when France was broken by the German attack on the Low Countries and France, launched on May 10 1940. Thomas Barman, the second correspondent in Paris, had already left the paper to join the political warfare department in Britain. Cadett had been joined by de Caux who, after leaving Spain, had made his home in Biarritz. De Caux, who had lived through the assault on Madrid, continued writing his despatches as the Germans approached Paris. Cadett followed the French government after it had decided on June 9 to leave Paris and he reached England to go into war work that kept him in touch with resistance movements in France. De Caux stayed on, always likely to be arrested, in southern France.

After the Battle of Britain in the summer and autumn of 1940 *The Times* was able to provide further good cheer to itself and its readers with daily reports of General Wavell's advances, begun on December 7 1940,

---

25 T.T.A.

against the Italian forces in North Africa. Lumby, remembering his years in Mussolini's Rome, took a more than professional pleasure in describing the successive blows to the dictator's pretensions. He was joined by James Holburn who was in the middle of several tank battles when the British faced both the Germans and the Italians. A long despatch which he wrote somewhere in the desert on November 23 1941, and which was printed three days later, evoked the tensions before and during the battles. He saw the tank formations going forward one morning:

> They are upon land what fighter pilots are in the air – modern versions of armoured knights – and their appearance in battle formation sends thrills of pride and fear through observers.

He watched them go past, 'with their high turrets dipping and rising as they cruised on the uneven desert surface, and their signal pennons waving.' At night the men of his group saw the lights of other tank laagers around them, quite near, but they were unable to tell whether they were German or British. Soon they knew. The shells fell about them. After the heavy fighting there was a lull but in the morning a German tank column moved up to attack a South African support group 'which turned its artillery upon them and, firing over open sights against the German tanks which came almost up to the muzzles, did a great deal of damage'. The Germans swept forward again but were counter-attacked on the flank and heavily mauled by British tanks:

> To-night, accordingly, we believe and hope that the surviving German tank force is now a modest size. But it has been a terrific battle.[26]

The desert fighting brought out writing at its simplest and best. A fine example is an article sent in by Oliver Woods, who left Printing House Square for an armoured regiment at the beginning of the war and was in the thick of many campaigns as a fighting officer. In his article he wrote about the daily waking before dawn and the scrappy breakfast, or no breakfast at all, before the enemy was first sighted:

> The German tanks look like black toads on the horizon. They creep about craftily, and nobody can afford to take chances with them, for the men of the Afrika Korps are accurate gunners and know their trade. But if, even though outnumbered, you stand and face them, they seldom come on; they have little stomach for close engagement, and, it may be added, some sound tactical reasons for avoiding it. As

---

26 *The Times*, November 26 1941.

the morning wears on shell-fire, dust, and mirage obscure the field and prompt the prayer of Achilles, 'Destroy us but destroy us in the light.' During the middle hours of the day both sides tend to draw stumps. Crews shave and brew a meal of hot tea and tinned sausage or bully, glancing warily at the occasional shell.

They all hoped each day for a quiet evening, with perhaps only a couple of Stuka raids to disturb it:

> More frequently there is an evening engagement . . . The last moments of the day are pandemonium on the Homeric scale. Right and left stretches the gun line of the British tanks, each spasmodically enveloped in its own smoke. In front lies the wreckage of derelicts, still interspersed with lurking enemy machines. The sun goes down suddenly, as red and round as an orange, partly obscured by dust and shell-bursts. Spirals of flame and black smoke mount from knocked-out tanks and petrol lorries, while ammunition trucks explode like Brock's benefit.
>
> Suddenly the man one is talking to on the wireless shouts, 'Look out, Stukas!' and the air is specked with them, 24 at a time, diving and dropping their load. Then suddenly the light fails, and all around flares go up calling the battling regiments into leaguer [laager], to take stock, rest, and lick their wounds, ready for the morrow.[27]

The widening war had to be seen strategically as well as tactically. In the spring of 1941 *The Times* gave Churchill its full support when, on February 12, he took his much contested decision to let Wavell's troops be halted just when Tripoli seemed within their range, and to divert some troops to go to the help of Greece. The Greeks had been attacked by Italy in October 1940; they had held their own until Hitler – anxious to clear up the Balkans before attacking Russia – decided to finish the Italians' work for them. To counter the new threat of a German victory the first British contingent of about 50,000 landed in Greece at the beginning of March 1941. In this case *The Times* supported Churchill's decision not so much on strategic as on moral and political grounds. Its reasoning was clear. Invasion had to be resisted wherever it could be resisted. A show of dash and courage would hearten others. Not to go to the help of a heavily threatened people would cause hopes of eventual freedom to fall in all the countries already occupied by German troops.

The forced British withdrawal after only a few weeks' foothold on the Greek mainland seemed to cause such arguments to rebound and

---

27 *The Times*, September 28 1942.

make spirits fall still lower. The division of troops had weakened the North African campaign; allied hopes were there turned to disappointment. Recent historical research even rejects the belief, once strongly held, that the problems which faced Hitler first in Greece and then in Yugoslavia (where General Simovic, the chief of the Yugoslav air force, made his anti-Axis coup on March 27) forced him to postpone his attack on Russia from May 15 1941 to June 22. This postponement, it has been held, helped to delay the German forces' arrival in front of Moscow; by the time they did arrive the unusually savage weather had set in and forced a halt which gave the Russians time to steady their front. History is seldom so simple in cause and effect. The Germans' late arrival before Moscow was undeniably costly for them, but the initial postponement has to be traced back to several causes. Probably the most that can be said about the effect of the Balkan complication on Hitler's strategy is that his need to despatch tanks, aircraft, and troops into the Balkans just as he was completing his preparations for launching the vast campaign against Russia was seriously disturbing for him. He responded decisively because he feared that the complication could be worse than in the short term it turned out to be, and (it should be remembered) he was never to be free of the tangle, especially in Yugoslavia.[28]

The German attack on Russia (June 22 1941) which surprised so many, had been foreseen on *The Times*. On May 1 1941 the newspaper published on its leader page a long article which collected together all the available evidence, much of it secret until then, about Hitler's military preparations on and near the Russian frontier. The writer of the article expected Hitler to move very soon, either by launching an invasion or – more probably, as it seemed at the time – by presenting territorial demands which Stalin, ever anxious to avoid a great war, would accept.[29]

Very soon after the German armies were thrown across the whole length of Russia's western frontiers, without giving Stalin a moment's opportunity to bargain, *The Times* recognised that it must have a man in Moscow to cover the war from the Russian side. In 1939 and for a few

---

28 Relevant arguments about the causes of the postponement of the attack on Russia, with documentation, are set out in Martin van Creveld, *Hitler's Invasion of Russia: The Balkan Clue* (Cambridge, 1974). The views of some German generals are summarised in B. H. Liddell Hart's *History of the Second World War* (London, 1970) as well as in his *The Other Side of the Hill* (London, 1951).
29 This same emphasis was given in the cautious headings: May Day at the Kremlin; Stalin's Delaying Tactics against Hitler; Two Years of Astute Manoeuvring. From Our Diplomatic Correspondent.

weeks in 1940 it had had James Holburn there; and very bleak this imperturbable Scot had found it in that uneasy time when Russia and Germany proclaimed themselves friends. There was even talk that Russia might join the war on Germany's side:

> We live here [in Moscow] in isolation, ignorance and uncertainty as to what the next day may bring forth. Our Embassy thinks Russia will not come into the war. Others think the opposite . . . Unfortunately for Correspondents, there is no chance of making a dash for the frontier here. One must go through the formalities of obtaining an exit visa, which takes days to complete. So we can only hope that the Russians will be more gracious to us than we expect them to be. Now that the censor gives us little opportunity of working, life in Moscow is appallingly dull and drab. Any correspondent who consents to be exiled here for a year or two does his newspaper an extraordinary favour.[30]

In spite of all the restrictions Holburn was able, early in September 1939, to sense that the Russians would march into eastern Poland and the Baltic states when it suited them. He sent a private message off to Printing House Square before the terms of the secret clause in the German–Soviet pact, foreshadowing the move into Poland, were known. Early in 1940 he moved to Ankara, and was back in Moscow for a few weeks in July and August when he noted a greater Russian fear of Germany and a correspondingly greater friendliness towards Britain.[31]

After Hitler's attack across the frontiers *The Times* sent Ralph Parker, who in the next few years reported both the fighting at the front and all the attendant Soviet–British–American disputes. The more he reported the more Parker seemed to take the Russian point of view. To a large extent such an exercise was his duty as a journalist accredited to an immense country that was little known, much misunderstood, hitherto largely boycotted by the western countries, and now in mortal peril. But *The Times* was soon complaining that Parker went too far in identifying himself with the Russian case.

Ralph Parker (1907–1964) was a talented man who seldom appeared to be at ease with others or, possibly, with himself. He was a deep reader and a serious linguist. After leaving Cambridge he spent some time in central and south-eastern Europe; he married a Czech wife; her death in a road accident left him painfully shocked for years. Moscow gave him some sense of stability. Russian writers, editors, and musicians accepted

---

30 Letter from Holburn to Deakin, October 2 1939. T.T.A.
31 Letter dated July 17 1940. T.T.A.

him as a friendly representative of western letters and philosophy, and he found himself given a status such as he had not had in the west. Many of his war despatches from Moscow, from Kuibyshev (the Volga town which became the diplomatic and press centre during the months of gravest danger for Russia), and from some points a little nearer the fighting front were admirably clear and vivid. He knew how to bring in a touch of sharp photographic detail to light up a story. At times this style would make him discursive. In February 1942 he suggested that, if the Soviet authorities would allow him, he should travel more to give more of his impressionistic pieces. Deakin's reply by cable was doubly dissuasive:

> Your tendency is usually over-cabling. In present world conditions quantity isn't as virtuous as crisp illumination. Politically essential that *Times* should be represented at Moscow, even though actual news reaches PHS through various wireless channels and in Urch's skilled summaries from Stockholm. Imperative to have a Moscow dateline in the paper, so as to have a Russian evaluation of front operations on broad lines, rather than record of actual operations.

Later in 1942 some of Parker's efforts could not be used. Sometimes it was because the news in them had already been covered from speedier sources. Sometimes it was because they read like leading articles. On October 25 Deakin passed on his growing misgivings to Barrington-Ward in a memorandum, saying that there was 'an ominous ring to Parker's effusions' that was 'detrimental to his service to *The Times*'. 'It looks as though he is getting the bit between his teeth.' Yet, before sending Parker another warning, Deakin was able to send two cables of warm thanks:

> Best thanks for excellent Mozhaisk article published today (December 16 1942).
>
> Congratulations on excellent Leningrad story (January 21 1943).

The warning came in a cable of March 18 1943:

> Must again remind you that effective presentation of current Russian views requires they be reported with detachment. Spoiled by too much personal advocacy.

Two months later Parker silenced all criticism for a time by securing a statement from Stalin himself that seemed to justify *The Times's* strong support of an understanding with Russia.[32] Generally in the west the

---

32 See Chapter V for a fuller examination of *Times* policy towards Stalin's Russia.

suspicions that Russia would subjugate Poland after the war had by then become deeper. On May 3 1943 Parker put two direct questions to Stalin in a letter. Back came Stalin's reply from the Kremlin under the date May 4. Translated from the Russian the reply was published in *The Times* of May 6:

Dear Mr. Parker,

On May 3 I received your two questions concerning Polish-Soviet relations. Here are my answers:

Question 1: Does the Government of the U.S.S.R. desire to see a strong and independent Poland after the defeat of Hitlerite Germany?

Answer: Unquestionably, it does.

Question 2: On what bases is it your opinion that relations between Poland and the U.S.S.R. should be established after the war?

Answer: Upon the fundamentals of solid good neighbourly relations and mutual respect, or, should the Polish people so desire – upon the bases of alliance providing for mutual assistance against the Germans as the chief enemies of the Soviet Union and Poland.

With respect,
J. Stalin

It was only the second time that Stalin, remote behind the walls of the Kremlin, had replied to a foreign correspondent's questions in that way. Every oracular phrase was examined in western foreign offices and newspaper offices. Even the most suspicious believed that he had made it harder for himself to go back on so flat and open an affirmation. For Parker, however, his success with the Stalin letter was only a brief interlude.

From time to time Barrington-Ward sent letters to Parker thanking him for his frank presentation of the Soviet view in his private letters to Printing House Square. Yet both Barrington-Ward and Deakin became more and more uneasy at Parker's support for the Russian line over Poland. Both rose in anger when Parker, having gone to see the Moscow-backed Polish authorities established on Polish territory at Lublin, broadcast his news and views over the Lublin radio and got himself quoted in the Communist *Daily Worker* in London. Much of the anger arose from a misunderstanding. With no possibility of telephoning or cabling from Lublin to London, Parker hit on the idea of broadcasting his despatches to *The Times* over the Lublin radio in the hope that someone in Britain would pick them up and pass them on to Printing House Square. Against all probabilities that is what happened one night. But Deakin was immeasurably shocked at the idea of *Times* despatches being scattered like leaves in a storm and left to be swept up by anyone at hand. On January 10 1945 Barrington-Ward sent Parker a letter:

> It has been a great surprise during the past few days to get news of activities on your part which seem altogether to outrun the purpose and limits of your mission to Lublin on behalf of *The Times* . . . It is one of the oldest rules of the paper . . . that a member of the staff should say what he has to say through the paper and not elsewhere. *The Times* takes responsibility for what appears in its own columns.

Barrington-Ward did not wish to seem ungrateful:

> I value greatly the part which you have played through your correspondence in promoting the establishment of friendly and confident relations between this country and Russia and, in particular, between this office and Moscow. But this achievement can only be jeopardised by independent activities outside the correspondence, undertaken without prior consultation with *The Times*.

Within a few weeks almost everything had been explained and almost everything had been forgiven. Parker said that he had broadcast simply to get his messages to *The Times*. On April 26 1945 Barrington-Ward wrote again to him, thanking him for three 'excellent' recent letters 'all of which I was extremely glad to get.' He continued:

> I can quite see now – and you will also have been able to see – that we were at cross purposes over your activities in Lublin.

Barrington-Ward exchanged several other friendly letters with Parker in the next eighteen months, but his uneasiness increased, as did Deakin's, at the tone of Parker's despatches. Deakin, having previously complained that Parker sent too much, now grumbled that he did not send enough. On December 12 1946 Barrington-Ward wrote a final regretful letter. Parker left the paper early in 1947 but stayed on in Moscow, where he had married a highly intelligent Russian. He reached a low point when writing on germ warfare in Korea and accusing successive British ambassadors and their staffs of anti-Soviet machinations. Later he was to find more rewarding work as the Moscow representative of the American impresario, Mr. Sol Hurok. Westerners in Moscow regularly criticised and consulted him. Except during the worst years of Stalin's rule he was able, when talking privately, to appear remarkably detached about most sides of Soviet life, and he was worth hearing. It has also to be remembered that, in his first years for

The Times in Moscow, he was often told that the paper was earnestly seeking a basis of east–west cooperation if the Russians made such cooperation possible; and he was strongly encouraged to present the Soviet attitude fully and fairly. He died in 1964, still in Moscow.

In the western theatre of war *The Times*, like other newspapers, had to prepare its coverage of the liberation of Europe both from the Mediterranean and from across the Channel. The end of the war on the Mediterranean under-belly was reported by Gerald Norman[33] and Christopher Lumby. Norman was sent to North Africa after the landings in November 1942, he was with the allied forces when they landed on France's Mediterranean shore to begin the liberation from the south, and, reaching Paris, he stayed on there to describe the rehabilitation and regeneration of France under General de Gaulle. Christopher Lumby had been on the battlefields of North Africa from the earliest days of the fighting in the Western Desert. In the Greek and Cretan campaigns he shared in the desperate rearguard actions. Illness and tiredness – he was in his late fifties – had prevented his accompanying the British armies in their victories in Tripolitania. Nothing could stop him from returning to the war to witness the final collapse of Italian Fascist power and the rolling back of the enemy forces in Italy from the Campania beach-heads northwards. On the liberation of Rome he was present at the installation of the first mayor, Prince Doria-Pampheli; Lumby recalled rowing behind him in the Magdalene College boat at Cambridge.

The last stages of the Italian campaign were to provide him with an extraordinary experience. In April 1945 the allied Fifth Army was held up below Milan. In the city Lumby had Italian friends who, he was sure, could give him news. He set off in a small car with only a young colleague, Stephen Barber of the *News Chronicle*, and a driver. He crossed about two hundred miles of German-held territory, forcing his way through all difficulties with his natural bearing of quiet command and his fluency in Italian and German. The two men reached Milan to be given a rapturous welcome by the Italian resistance fighters who had taken over the city. During the night some partisans woke them up with news that made them think they were still dreaming. Mussolini and his mistress, Clara Petacci, had been captured and killed in a village near Como. Their bodies had been brought to Milan. Would the two

---

33 George Henry Gerald Norman (b. 1907). Harrow; Balliol College, Oxford. Joined *The Times* foreign department, 1939; war correspondent in Egypt and France (southern landings), 1942–44; Paris correspondent, 1944–52; foreign news editor from 1953 until resignation in 1958 to join the BBC.

correspondents come and identify the bodies for them? (Lumby had known Mussolini when *Times* correspondent in Rome before the war; in May 1939 Mussolini had issued an order, later revoked, for his expulsion from Italy.) The two correspondents were driven to the working-class Lerato district. In *The Times* of April 30 Lumby described what they saw:

> There were the bodies heaped together in ghastly promiscuity in the open square against the same fence against which one year ago 15 partisans had been shot by their own countrymen, Italian Fascists. Mussolini's body lay across that of Petacci. In his dead hand had been placed the brass ensign of the Fascist Arditti.

Lumby returned to Army Headquarters to tell an amazed American general that the city which his soldiers were so carefully surrounding had already fallen.

For the cross-channel invasion a team of correspondents was headed by Bob Cooper, back from several arduous years in India, Burma, and the Levant. He was to be with the allied forces all the way to Berlin and until the official end of the war in Europe on May 8 1945. His despatches day by day kept their quality but, like everyone else caught up in the war, Cooper was by now feeling the strain. War correspondents do not have a regimental organisation to sustain them in their work. Beyond all the difficulties of living, Cooper felt increasingly that the authorities were helping the BBC and the American radio and newspaper correspondents to get away their despatches much more than they were helping the British press correspondents.

A fortnight after D-Day he sounded dispirited in a cable to *The Times*, dated June 21, telling Deakin that he was out day and night looking for material to send; the censorship was miles away from the house where he was dug in; there was little time for writing as light was lacking at night; he was doing his best, but the initiative must come from Printing House Square for bringing about some improvement in transmission problems. Deakin sent an understanding reply and praised him for his efforts. Cooper answered on June 30 with another heart cry:

> If these despatches are appearing in *The Times* it is in spite of public relations service that must be one of the most inept to be operated in any theatre of war. Correspondents are called for many miles from their sectors to wait hours for conferences that never take place and are regimented with an officialness that comes straight out of pantomime.

His tiredness and his frustrations vanished when he described the allied
advance on Paris, entered by General Leclerq on August 24, and the
crossing of the Rhine at Remagen on March 7 1945. He got himself on
good terms with Field Marshal Montgomery, who called him the most
soldierly of correspondents,[34] and was happy to stay on in Berlin in the
Press camp at the Hotel am Zoo. But tiredness caught up with him and
led to another explosion with Printing House Square.

It happened through a misunderstanding. In July 1945, on the eve of
the inter-allied Potsdam conference, Deakin began to wonder if Cooper
was ill as no message had been received from him for a few days. Deakin
asked the British army's public relations office in Berlin if it could
explain the silence. Cooper took the inquiry as a personal rebuke
administered through official channels. In a cable dated July 16 he said
that, following familiar practice, he had asked the *Manchester Guardian*
man to cover Sunday for him while he took a weekend off to prepare for
the allied conference. His feelings then overcame him:

> Astonished your message pubrelationwards saying youve received
> nothing from me since Wednesday. Didnt you receive Montgom-
> ery–Zhukov ceremony? . . . Would remind you I've worked
> through almost continuously since D-Day with relatively [little?]
> sympathy minimum guidance from office for what must be worlds
> low record in salaries and repeat am astonished you should now put
> me invidious position with pubrelations.

Deakin's reply sped off the next day, July 17:

> You have our fullest assurance that our inquiries reflected only
> natural and entirely sympathetic anxiety. Your continuous work
> since D-Day has been superlative and everybody here desires give
> you fullest support. Certainly didnt realise inquiry through PRO
> could be adversely interpreted. Only reason why guidance has been
> withheld is that your excellent service made it superfluous. Regret
> misunderstanding over Anderson [the *Manchester Guardian* man
> who stood in for Cooper on the Sunday] but weve no knowledge
> about him and no arrangement for pool with him. Hope this
> unreserved reassurance clears whole atmosphere wish you con-
> tinued success best regards Deakin *Times*.

Cooper remained in Germany to accomplish his greatest sustained feat
in journalism. This was his covering of the Nuremberg war crimes
tribunal from November 1945 to November 1946. Leading counsel at

---

34 In conversation with John Freeman, staff correspondent in Bonn after the war.

the trial praised his daily summaries of the long and complex hearings. More than that, they followed his reports closely and at times relied on them for quick reference as an accurate précis presented in a handy, highly readable, and illuminating manner. The astonishing thing was that no one was quite sure how Cooper did it. He did not spend long hours each day in the courtroom, though he wandered in as if by chance at crucial times. He would appear to glance through the transcripts of evidence, taking very few notes at all and even then rather impatiently. What many of his colleagues chiefly remembered was the picture of Cooper walking, deep in thought, back and forth along the corridors, occasionally shaking his head, sometimes smacking a fist into his other hand, his lips moving as he turned phrases over in his mind. Then he would slowly turn away to write his message for the day. Giving the essence of the trial each day was a prolonged effort in which Cooper seemed to absorb the evidence partly through his brain and partly through his pores; and it was all highly successful. Afterwards he wrote a Pelican paperback on the trial and settled down to a longer and fuller account of it. Unfortunately the manuscript and his notes were stolen with other things from his car in Germany, and he could not take up the work again.

War reporting in the Far East had begun eight years before Hitler invaded Poland and ten years before Japan struck at Pearl Harbor. Even if the European war is said to have really begun in 1935 when the Italian armies invaded Ethiopia, or in 1936 when Germany and Italy sent help to General Franco in the Spanish civil war, Japan had moved into Manchuria still earlier, in 1931, and had invaded China in 1932. In face of the massive invasion the Chinese government had been forced to leave Peking and take refuge in Nanking and then – while the European powers were putting off their war at the Munich conference – in Chungking. Correspondents in the Far East had not only to report a longer period of war; after Japan's vast explosion of military force in 1941 the correspondents had to try to make their daily reports build up a picture of a half-continent in upheaval. The strategic upset caused by the war in Asia was at least as great as the upset in Europe; and the social and political consequences were on many reckonings greater in Asia than in the west. In the countries liberated by the United States, Britain, and their allies in 1944–45 a natural reaction among many groups to Japan's nationalist outburst was to become strongly nationalist themselves. The old pattern of western colonialism, permanently damaged by Japan's initial blows against the western positions, had clearly no basis for survival among peoples who had been shocked into awakening.

In these years *The Times* was well served by men who knew particular countries in the region exceptionally well; and in the 1940s it was served by an outstanding young man, Ian Morrison,[35] who came to know the whole region. Japan's first moves were described with a knowledge based on long experience by Hugh Byas in Tokyo, by David Fraser[36] in Peking and by Colin McDonald in Shanghai. Several times they were joined by Peter Fleming from London and *The Times* would then have from Fleming a series of articles which served as a brief preview of one or other of his books. The last three men were all of Scottish descent, Fraser from Canada, McDonald from Australia, Fleming from Oxfordshire. Fraser, the oldest of them, had begun with *The Times* as special correspondent for the Russo–Japanese war in 1903–1905. Thereafter he was almost continually in the Middle East or in China or Japan. McDonald, fluent in Chinese, joined the paper as an occasional correspondent in Peking in 1929 and became fully established as Peking correspondent in 1937. In that year he had a double distinction: the melancholy one of being on board the American gunboat Panay when it was bombed by the Japanese, and the happier one – rare in the days of strict *Times* anonymity – of having his name put at the head of his despatch published on December 18 1937 when he wrote a direct and moving account of the outrage. He stayed in war-time China until 1943 when he retired to Australia. Hugh Byas retired from Tokyo in April 1941 when he was in his sixty-seventh year and was succeeded by the man whom he recommended, Otto D. Tolischus, of the *New York Times*. Tolischus did very well and was missing, feared dead, for some weeks after the Japanese launched their attack on the United States and Britain. But the rumour proved to be untrue.

Ian Morrison, who joined the paper after the others, had a short and wholly brilliant career on *The Times*. More than any other correspondent he understood and made known to the west the national and social ambitions of the Asia that was being fashioned in the war. Ian Morrison had the right background for such interpretative work. He was the son of the man famous as Chinese Morrison – Dr. George Ernest Morrison –

---

35 Ian F. M. Morrison (1913–1950). Winchester; Trinity College, Cambridge. Professor of English at Hokkaido University, Japan, 1935–37. Private Secretary to Sir Robert Craigie, Ambassador in Tokyo, 1937–39. Representative of the British and Chinese Corporation in Shanghai 1939–41. Deputy Director of the Far Eastern Bureau of the Ministry of Information, Singapore, 1941. Appointed war correspondent of *The Times*, 1941.

36 David Stewart Fraser (1869–1953). Special correspondent for *The Times* during the Russo–Japanese War, and in Persia, Mesopotamia, Macedonia, Siberia, Japan and Abyssinia, 1909–35; Peking correspondent, 1912–39.

who from 1897 to 1912 was correspondent for *The Times* in China and then became political adviser to the Chinese government. Born in Peking but educated in England Ian Morrison went back to the Far East and was in academic and diplomatic work in Japan before going on to represent a large concern in Shanghai. From there he wrote occasionally for *The Times*. Seeing the Japanese danger he went early in 1941 into the Ministry of Information in Singapore. Deakin then tentatively asked him if he would care, if the Japanese struck, to be war correspondent for *The Times*, based on Singapore. On December 8 1941, the day after the Japanese attack on Pearl Harbor, Deakin cabled a firm offer and Morrison accepted two days later. He was twenty-eight. His despatches during the army's retreat down the Malayan peninsula, his warnings that Singapore could not be held, and his moving accounts of the last stand and surrender of the outnumbered British troops were quoted throughout the world and brought him swiftly into the front rank of correspondents. After Singapore Morrison was in Java, reporting much the same tragic story, and then he followed the campaigns in the south-west Pacific under General MacArthur and in South-East Asia under Admiral Mountbatten. He was in danger most of the time. He reported from near to the firing lines; he shared the soldiers' life in the jungles; he was wounded more than once and was ill at times. His despatches always brought clarity and colour out of the confusion of war.[37]

The force of the Japanese strategic explosion after December 7 1941 wrecked South-East Asia and – of hardly less direct concern to Britain – threw the Indian sub-continent into new uncertainty. How would the Indian nationalists respond as the Japanese armies came nearer? Throughout much of the war these uncertainties and the whole southern Asian front were covered by two of the strongest and most dependable correspondents, James Holburn and Bob Cooper. Holburn was the more incisive in mind and style, Cooper the more intuitive and impressionistic. In Delhi Holburn watched over all the political currents and upheavals in wartime India; he reported the fighting in Burma, although he left much of the battle front to Cooper. His chief work was political, and its great value to the paper and (it may be said) to the country was demonstrated when *The Times* kept him in Delhi longer than he himself wished and when, after his move to Europe in 1944, the

---

37 Morrison's later work and his death in Korea in August 1950 are discussed in Chapter VIII.

Viceroy of India, Lord Wavell, and the India Office in London begged for his return. Deakin cabled Holburn on January 11 1945:

We are under extreme pressure to persuade you to return to Delhi for a time.

Holburn wished to stay in Europe to cover the US 9th Army, but Deakin explained that, beyond all the official desires, there was the simple fact that the paper had no staff correspondent in the whole of Asia at that time, apart from Ian Morrison in the wilds of Burma:

In such circumstances I think you will admit that there is some compensation in the keen desire that high authority has displayed to have you back.

Holburn went back with much loyalty and no illusions. He gave his thoughts in a letter to Deakin from Simla, May 9 1945:

India is proving just as tough a nut as we expected, and perhaps tougher than the gentlemen from London thought it would be. Between ourselves, I think British policy is probably twenty-five years ahead of Indian capacity to govern; but, as we are not prepared to govern ourselves, I suppose there is nothing to be done except what the Mission are trying to do.

He remained in India long enough to see the inevitability of partition in the sub-continent and left before the vast movement of the peoples and the massacres began.

Bob Cooper began his arduous time in India in 1942. For the next two years he was covering the elusive fighting beyond India's frontiers in Burma and South-East Asia. Few people, and at times no one at all, knew what was happening in the jungles. The military censors were strict, and in a letter to Deakin, dated February 19 1943, Cooper asks to be sent to another front: 'There is no real sense of urgency about the war in India. Delhi bureaucracy, with its blend of red-tape and babuism, is stifling.' He went on to bemoan the allied military shortcomings, the excessive caution of the commanders, their orthodoxy in tactics, and their preoccupation with casualties.

Deakin, however, was firm that Cooper should stay on in India and should work in harness with Holburn but be ready to move elsewhere at any moment. Three months later Cooper was able to describe the exploits of a commander – General Orde Wingate – as unorthodox and as free from excessive caution as anyone could hope for. Cooper responded to the opportunity in his best style.

Later that same year Cooper was in the Levant describing the Lebanese and Syrian bitterness against the French colonial authorities. At the beginning of 1944 he was back in South-East Asia, reporting on the advances against the Japanese but looking over his shoulder for what was likely to happen nearer home. On January 11 1944 he wrote to Barrington-Ward and had his wish fulfilled by being posted back in good time for D-Day five months later.

Looking back on *The Times* during the war the paper can take pride in its thorough coverage of the main campaigns and of the revolutionary changes which the war brought across the world. Most of the despatches stand up well to the test which hindsight can bring to them; they are written with clarity and with a deeply committed sense of objectivity.

On November 25 1944 – happily when victory was already in sight – the newspaper issued its 50,000th number. The main news headings that morning were: 'Great Battle in the Aachen Gap: Allies at Grips with Crack German Troops'. The same main news page carried messages from King George VI and Winston Churchill. The King's Secretary, Sir Alan Lascelles, wrote:

I am commanded by The King to convey to *The Times* His Majesty's congratulations on the publication of its 50,000th number.

Knowing its traditions, and the place it has won in the national life, The King is confident that the services rendered by *The Times* over a period of nearly 160 years will be as honourably and as zealously maintained in the future.

The Prime Minister wrote:

I congratulate *The Times* upon the publication of its 50,000th number. Few journals can display so notable a record or may so justly be acclaimed as an outstanding example of the virtues of a free Press. The renown of *The Times* throughout the world has for more than a century stood unassailably high. Your newspaper is one of the most powerful and respected institutions in the British Empire and I wish it a long and successful life to come.

For the occasion Barrington-Ward re-wrote the draft of a leading article written by Dermot Morrah[38] under the simple heading '50,000'. It gave

---

38 Dermot Michael Macgregor Morrah (1896–1974). Winchester; New and All Souls Colleges, Oxford. *Daily Mail* editorial staff, 1928–32. Joined *The Times* in 1932 as leader writer and assistant on *The Times History*; reported the coronations of 1937 and 1953 and covered the 1947 royal tour of South Africa for *The Times*. Editor of the *Round Table*, 1944–64. Arundel Herald Extraordinary 1953. *Daily Telegraph* 1961–67.

its own warning about the future of journalism:

It was by no accident that the first effective move in every totalitarian campaign in Europe between the wars was an onslaught on the Press and on broadcasting. Fascism and Nazism felt themselves threatened while even the most rickety vehicle of truth remained outside their power. News, like justice, had to conform to policy, and policy was the prerogative of the dictator . . . Though, before the 50,000th issue of *The Times* makes its appearance, science may well have revolutionized the mechanism by which the written word is reproduced, the fundamentals of journalism will not vary. It will still be the duty of a newspaper to hold fast to the distinction between fact and opinion and, whatever views it may hold and express, to furnish for the reader's judgment a supply of news as full and impartial as energy and good faith can make it . . . As the war draws to an end and the shadow of military necessity recedes, the immediate task will be to ensure that every encroachment of authority shall be rolled back from a field of responsibility in which, in a free community, it can have no place.

V

DEBATES AND DISPUTES
WITH CHURCHILL

BARRINGTON-WARD had the main lines of his policy clear in his mind when he took over the chair and he was soon to be driving hard along them. He had E. H. Carr at his side driving no less hard, sometimes indeed wanting to go faster and farther than Barrington-Ward, but accepting with puzzlement and patience the restraining hands of both the editor and Casey. Barrington-Ward's confidence both in his own mission and in Carr is shown in a diary entry of April 5 1942:

I am reading Carr's 'Conditions of Peace', a cogent, distinguished, independent and comprehensive effort of thought, which I find tonic. Carr is certainly a very big man, and *The Times* is lucky to have his services. I hope that we shall keep his services long enough to see the first years after the war through. I heartily agree with his approach to them. It all fits in with my own design, such as it is, for trying to create through *The Times* a central bloc of opinion agreed on a national minimum and prepared to see it through – peaceful revolution.

Inevitably, given Churchill's dominance throughout the war, *The Times* was often writing in direct or indirect criticism of the great man. The criticism was implied in the paper's constant appeals for forward thinking about the shape of British society after the war and about the organisation of peace in Europe. It was expressed more sharply in the paper's calls for a smaller War Cabinet, and in its firmly expressed belief that Churchill had too much power over the military directorate. As Barrington-Ward's diaries show, these editorials were directed both at educating public opinion and at prodding Churchill into action.

There was nothing of a personal vendetta in all this. In the editor's mind it was a debate on the highest level, an intellectual contest over the future welfare and progress of Britain. His admiration of Churchill as a war leader was much greater than his mistrust of him. None the less the mistrust was there. Basically Barrington-Ward thought that Churchill took too much on himself, leaving himself no time or inclination for thinking ahead yet being unwilling, for too long, to let others do such thinking for him. Churchill was both impatient at the criticism and sensitive to it. The private exchanges between Prime Minister and editor frequently enliven the story of *The Times* in the decisive years of the war.

Barrington-Ward had been editor only two months when he had his first lunch at No. 10 Downing Street with Churchill; a very informal and private affair; Brendan Bracken, then Minister of Information, was the only other person present. Barrington-Ward's unusually long entry in his diary for that day, December 1 1941, shows that he was well aware of Churchill's purpose in asking him to come:

I was invited, of course, as a critic – I won't say to silence criticism. But he was a little on the defensive. I was glad of the meeting, and all the more so because it was not brought about on my initiative.

His detailed account is pleasantly perceptive:

Brendan came in first. Then Winston from a War Cabinet, looking (at 67) very fresh and young and spry. He is a different man altogether from the rather bloated individual whom I last saw (close to) before the war. His cheerful, challenging – not to say truculent – look is good to see just now; but it covers up a great deal of caution, even vacillation at times. Perhaps [the look is] instinctively acquired. Anyway it is good to see, and the public thinks so too and it is the right 'face' to put on the vast responsibilities which he is discharging. A lack of the finer perceptions, no doubt! But no doubt either about vigour and purpose.

During the meal – at which the host drank 'not much by earlier standards' – Churchill seemed chiefly concerned to defend his chiefs of staff from criticisms made in *The Times* and elsewhere, and also to explain his own relations with them. The diary summarises his words:

Minister of Defence, constitutionally, must be either the Prime Minister or must hold all three defence portfolios. Described the elasticity of his system. Most often the Chiefs of Staff met without him. Sometimes he met with them, sometimes with them and their Ministers.

Barrington-Ward was left pleased but unconvinced by the conversation.

Less than a week after this talk the Japanese launched their aggression, and by the beginning of 1942 the disasters in South-East Asia and the defeats in North Africa had made many more people in Britain bitter about the government's conduct of the war. Churchill knew himself to be under heavy pressure. Leading articles in *The Times* demanding a more efficient running of the war industries were supported in two special articles by Sir William Beveridge[1] under the title 'Brakes on Production' (January 2 and 3 1942). Beveridge argued, as several industrialists were arguing, that a single Minister of Production – an appointment hitherto resisted by Churchill – should coordinate and direct the national output as a whole. The articles were discussed in the War Cabinet and Sir Edward Bridges, the secretary, was asked to obtain comments from six government departments. Churchill conceded the point, Lord Beaverbrook was appointed Minister of War Production on February 4, and he was succeeded on February 19 by Oliver Lyttelton.

A second lunch at No. 10 came soon afterwards, on March 30 1942, once again a threesome, Churchill, Brendan Bracken, and Barrington-Ward. At that time ministers had been incensed by a bitter cartoon in the *Daily Mirror* of March 6. The Home Secretary, Herbert Morrison, had already asked Barrington-Ward how the press in general would react if he invoked the Defence Regulations and gave a stern public warning to the *Mirror*; Barrington-Ward had told him that the *Mirror* did not cut 'two penn'orth of ice'; much better leave it alone. He gave the same answer when Churchill raised the matter early during their lunch together on March 30. 'If they closed down a paper with 1,800,000 circulation,' Barrington-Ward said, 'there would be widespread grousing and they would have a wolf by the ears.'

His diary record shows how Barrington-Ward took the opportunity later during the meal of pressing on the Prime Minister the need to go in for social planning for the future, not only for the sake of Britain after the war but also for the sake of building up morale during the war:

. . . Winston got on to the press generally (which he has rather on the brain). Thinks Daily Mirror, Daily Mail and Daily Herald campaigns were calculated to undermine the army. Makes no complaint of *The Times* or Manchester Guardian 'sober, reasoned criticism'. Hopes we can give him a hand from time to time to keep things steady. I said people wanted some vision of the future, some hope. British would always fight best when fighting for more than their skins.

'What do you want me to say?' I said I wouldn't offer him an offhand reply but should be prepared to draft something. 'Get it on a few sheets of paper and send it to me.' I *most* gladly undertook to do so.

---

1 William Henry Beveridge (1879–1963). Director of London School of Economics 1919–37. Master of University College, Oxford, 1937–45. Liberal MP, 1944–45. Baron, 1946.

It was then Churchill's turn to criticise by implication some of the leftist tendencies in *The Times*:

> He went on to the importance of preserving free enterprise. Nationalization of the railways – no difficulty about that. But profit was 'not an ignoble motive'. I said it was all a matter of determining where the profit motive could still usefully function and where it could not.
>
> Winston said, 'I am an old man (he didn't sound it): not like Lloyd George coming out of the last war at 56 or so. I may be 70 before this war ends.' (This was taking refuge in the view that reconstruction would be for someone else to take up in the future. He cannot see what the assurance and, in some measure, the accomplishment of it means to public confidence and war energy *now*.) 'No man has had to bear such disasters as I have.' I said the nation had taken them very well . . .
>
> Far from storming he bore my candour and listened most patiently. Not quite as fit and sparkling as at our last lunch. A very impressive person with strong limitations. His utter absence of pomposity is most engaging. He was wearing his one-piece 'siren suit'. Ate heartily.

Back in the office the editor got Carr working to draft the 'few sheets of paper' on social planning which Churchill had requested. Barrington-Ward revised the draft, Casey and other members of the staff made their suggestions. The few sheets became many and had to be pruned. In the end a not very exciting summary of *The Times's* policy was produced and sent off to Downing Street, copy to Brendan Bracken, on April 14. The editor had few illusions about the immediate impact:

> The result will be precisely nothing. That doesn't matter in so far as I have not failed to take the chance offered. It will matter greatly, however, especially to him, if Winston goes on refusing to give any lead in reconstruction.[2]

Only three days later Churchill felt called upon to answer another line of criticism in *The Times*. Leading articles that had advocated a lessening of Churchill's power over the service chiefs were supported on April 11 1942 by a signed turnover article from Sir Edward Grigg, until recently Under-Secretary for War. Grigg proposed that there should be a combined Great General Staff, subject to one condition: the chairman should be someone other than Churchill. On April 17 Churchill wrote

---

2 B-W D, April 14 1942.

what Barrington-Ward, on receiving it, called a 'vehement but good-tempered' letter. The Prime Minister pointed out that the 'proposed arrangement might only delay decisions.' When, as was all too likely, disputes arose between the chairman and the service chiefs or among the service chiefs themselves, the contentious matters would have in any case to come back to the Prime Minister or the Cabinet for decision. 'I fear I should be provided not only with solutions, but with a whole series of disputes':

> Again, have you anybody in mind? Is he to be retired or serving? Old and sagacious or young and dynamic? Who is your man? Should he belong to the Army, Navy or Air Force? It is very easy to suggest some unknown genius should be found on whom the cabinet can dump their responsibilities to win the war, and whom the Services will obey: but I think you ought to name the animal.

In Barrington-Ward's absence the Prime Minister's letter seems to have been mislaid a day or two in Printing House Square and, when it was found, Barrington-Ward rather quickly sent off a less than cogent reply. He argued that if the project of having a chief professional adviser to the Minister of Defence was right in conception, the function would make the man. 'The office would be even more than the man, in the sense that it would elicit the cooperation on which he must rely and confer not a few of the qualifications to be sought.'[3]

On April 22 Churchill replied, still saying that disputes were likely to delay proceedings, whereas under the existing arrangements he dealt directly with the responsible executive heads of the service departments who could 'give immediate effect to what is decided'. On April 23 General Ismay[4] came at Churchill's suggestion to Printing House Square to explain the existing machinery:

> I like Ismay. He is a cheerful fatalist or pessimist and gives himself no airs. But he is very much the P.M.'s A.D.C. A rambling talk. Discussed the combined general staff and the C.G.G.S. [Chief of a Great General Staff]. It comes to this. He is not really against it in principle but says it will not be possible with *this* Prime Minister. 'Winston,' Ismay says, 'wages war all day.' Alas, he does. Ismay left me with a deepened impression of how personal the whole thing is. Winston intervenes with big strategic decisions. Ismay is his personal representative at the Chiefs of Staff Committee. And so on. It is v. frightening, tested by results.

3 Letter, April 20 1942. T.T.A.
4 Hastings Lionel Ismay (1887–1965). Chief of Staff to the Minister of Defence (Churchill), 1940–45. Secretary-General of Nato, 1952–57. Baron, 1947.

Throughout all this time Barrington-Ward desired that reasoned argument, and only reasoned argument, should be used inside the War Cabinet and outside it to persuade Churchill to give up some of his control over the war machinery. He was wholly against what he regarded as a dishonest vote of censure on Churchill in the House of Commons on July 2 1942; and he was very deeply shocked when Sir Edward Grigg came to him on July 31 to ask if *The Times* would commit itself in advance to a move by Cripps against Churchill. The diary records:

He [Grigg] has been talking to Waldorf Astor and others about Winston's position and is seeing Cripps tonight. Wants Cripps to stand out for a higher professional directorate advising the War Cabinet on the conduct of the war, and for Winston's surrender of the Defence Ministry to another Minister; for a small War Cabinet in full charge and without administrative responsibilities; and for resignation if these demands are refused. Wants to offer him adequate support in that event. Can he say that *The Times* will support him? I couldn't have that. It is not for Grigg or anyone else to pledge *The Times*. Moreover, as I told him, it is useless for Cripps to act alone. He will fail and be compromised and do more harm than good. Three or four members of the War Cabinet must act together. Nor is it sound to ask any Prime Minister to give up the Ministry of Defence or, even if the office is abolished, its functions. Asquith couldn't do it in 1916. As I also told him, I have seen Cripps several times and am prepared to see him again. In the meantime the views of *The Times* are on record. All this wants careful handling if the cause is not to suffer in Germany, U.S.A., this country and elsewhere. It may be that what we all want done cannot be accomplished without the further pressure of untoward events. The first step in any case is for three or four members of the War Cabinet to agree upon sensible and practicable proposals and to present them firmly to the P.M. We can then consider the results. He [Grigg] promised to keep me in touch with his activities.[5]

It is a revealing note. No matter how strongly Barrington-Ward felt about Churchill's conduct of the war at that time, he would stand on his own and speak through *The Times* alone. Anything like a plot or a combination was obnoxious to him as a man and as editor.

The 'further pressure of untoward events', which Barrington-Ward

---

5 B-W D, July 31 1942.

thought might persuade Churchill to loosen some of his personal power made itself felt throughout the summer and autumn of 1942. No good news came from either the Pacific or North Africa, and the fearful slaughter in Russia strengthened the demands in Russia and in the West for the opening of a second front to draw off some of the German pressure on the Russian armies. Barrington-Ward and Carr were already convinced that the Soviet Union, once it had beaten back Germany, would have dominant influence throughout eastern Europe. The western allies, for the sake of world security, would have to cooperate with that new power and new presence in Europe. For his part Carr was quite clear that Russia would impose her own methods of control throughout her expanded zone, and the western powers would have also to accept that prospect. In a memorandum of January 1942 he presented his case with force and prescience:

Before the war British prestige suffered from protesting in advance against things which, when they happened, we tamely acquiesced in because we had neither the power nor the will to prevent them.

After the war Russian forces will probably march west at least as far as Berlin and dispose of Eastern Europe as they think fit. Is it conceivable that we shall have the power to interfere with them or that, even if we had the power, public opinion in this country (which, in large sections of it, shows signs of being almost fanatically pro-Russian) would allow any Government to use it . . . If we were to oppose Russian policy in Eastern Europe after the war, we should quickly re-constitute the German–Russian alliance.

We must give Russia a free hand in Eastern Europe if we wish to retain her as an ally against Germany.

Carr implicitly acknowledged that Russian methods were likely to be rough and tough, and therefore shocking to western peoples who had faith in the Atlantic Charter as a broad guide to the future. But the application of that charter had to be seen in realistic terms. Carr wrote:

We have all accepted the guiding principles of the Atlantic Charter, which provides for the maximum independence for all nations compatible with the over-riding requirements of security and well-being. But the application of these must vary. Russia will interpret them in Eastern Europe and we will in other parts of the world. For our own part we shall not quarrel with her interpretation and application of them.[6]

---

6 T.T.A.

In this memorandum Carr starkly laid down the bases of the policy *vis-à-vis* Russia which *The Times* was to follow throughout the war and for some years afterwards. The policy enraged the British government from time to time; it caused deep anguish in London among the exiled governments of the occupied peoples, and it scandalised Conservative members of Parliament. In the House of Lords on June 2 1942 Viscount Elibank denounced Carr's book, *Conditions of Peace* (which Barrington-Ward had praised in his diary two months earlier). Judging from the book, Lord Elibank said, Carr was an appeaser of the first order. He was now employed in an influential position on *The Times*, 'the most important daily newspaper and leader of opinion in this country', and was therefore a man whose views were bound to carry weight:

> Professor Carr is indeed an active danger to this country and its future in the position he holds, and if we were so foolish as to be guided by his views we should certainly lose the peace, and all our sacrifices would be in vain.[7]

Many readers of *The Times* were no less deeply upset and were hardly less vocal. With the passage of years since the Second World War, the reminder should perhaps be given that at the time the doctrine seemed shocking to many for several reasons. Readers were not only outraged at what seemed an even-tempered acquiescence in a harsh rule over others; they also found the very idea of Russia having a dominant position outside her borders both novel and repugnant. Europe was accustomed to a Russia physically confined behind the *cordon sanitaire* of the inter-war years. Carr's purpose was to show that Germany's defeat would produce a vacuum in eastern Europe which a powerful Russia would inevitably move in to fill. He wrote the more forcibly about Russia's coming place in Europe because he assumed, as many did, that the United States policy after the war would either be uncertain or be dictated by a desire for a speedy withdrawal of American forces from Europe. Above all he wished British policy to be based on a realistic appraisal of strengths in the world rather than on ideological impulses and emotional crusades.

Barrington-Ward was entirely in agreement with Carr's logic, although he would at times tone down some of its Euclidian severity in leading articles in the paper.[8] The logic of the reasoning supported him in his view that Britain must seek a basis of cooperation with Russia after the war; in *The Times* he warmly welcomed the twenty years' treaty of

---

7 *House of Lords Parliamentary Debates (Hansard)*, June 2 1942.
8 See Chapter VI.

alliance and cooperation signed between Molotov and Eden in July 1942; and he was keenly aware of the burden that Russia was carrying in the war. Such thoughts made him look forward to his long talks with Ivan Maisky, the highly intelligent Soviet ambassador in London.

The editor was struck especially by the earnestness with which Maisky, at a dinner in the embassy in July 1942, criticised the British government on two counts. First, for their timidity, as the ambassador alleged, in their running of the convoys round the North Cape with supplies to the Soviet Union; secondly, for their reluctance to open a second front in France. On the second front Barrington-Ward recorded Maisky's main points:

> Says we expect too great margin of security, are too elaborate, also that we underrate the help to be expected from France. Must we wait for special landing-craft? We could contrive the necessary surplus of shipping e.g. by passing to the defensive in the Middle East and by cutting down our ample food supplies. Our inactivity having or threatening the worst effect on Russian morale. M. argues very vigorously and cogently. I put some of the objections.[9]

The next day Barrington-Ward returned to the matter in his diary:

> Are a great opportunity and an urgent duty now being missed? Are we to sit inactive while Germany puts the Soviet out before the Americans get fully in? . . . Germany will be able to turn in force to the West and all our calculations for 1943 (joint offensive with U.S.) will be sadly out. Yet, I hear (from A.E.[10] and others) that Americans themselves rule out invasion of France this year. Couldn't they go for North Africa? I have always thought that our true offensive front.[11]

Barrington-Ward stirred up the service correspondents, Captain Falls and Admiral Thursfield,[12] to make inquiries into possibilities and the result was a long leader by Carr on July 29 arguing the case for more offensive action in the west.

Such military arguments were only a small part of the paper's persuasive efforts on behalf of closer understanding with wartime Russia. It published something like a manifesto on March 10 1943 in two

---

9 B-W D, July 22 1942.
10 Anthony Eden.
11 B-W D, July 23 1942.
12 Rear-Admiral Henry George Thursfield (1882–1963). After retirement from the Royal Navy, acted as special correspondent for *The Times* at the Fleet manoeuvres of 1934 and 1935; naval correspondent, 1936–52.

articles that appeared on the same page: an anonymous special article which was in fact written by L. B. Namier,[13] and a leading article which was one of Carr's strongest. Both writers were concerned with the bases of European security after the war; both argued that there could be no firm foundation for such security without cooperation and friendship with Soviet Russia. With great brilliance Namier exposed the mistakes and illusions of the pre-war years and demonstrated, from his reading of history, that the European continent could not be defended and stabilised without the pledged support of what he called the three extra-European empires: the American, the Russian, and the British. Certainly there could be no hope of restoring a system of alliances such as France built up after 1918 with central and east European countries. Russia would have her say in eastern Europe. 'Experience proves, most emphatically, that no Western Power, however great, can safely act on the eastern flank of Germany except in a genuine and close understanding with Russia'.

Carr's leader emphasised even more forcibly the need for Anglo–Russian partnership after the war:
> Britain has the same interest as Russia herself in active and effective Russian participation in continental affairs; for there can be no security in Western Europe unless there is also security in Eastern Europe, and security in Eastern Europe is unattainable unless it is buttressed by the military power of Russia . . . The realisation of security will depend on the joint and continuous vigilance of Britain and Russia.

Then came a splendidly characteristic Carr sentence:
> A case so clear and cogent for close co-operation between Britain and Russia after the war cannot fail to carry conviction to any open and impartial mind.

Carr had sadly to admit that not all minds reached the desired standard. Both Britain and United States, he wrote, were hesitant in recognising that Russia would enjoy the same right to judge for herself the conditions which she deemed necessary in eastern Europe for the security of her frontiers. He pressed the point home with an uncompromising sentence that was to be much quoted and which was naturally taken up with approval by the Russians:

---

13 Sir Lewis Bernstein Namier (1888–1960). Balliol College, Oxford. Professor of modern history, Manchester, 1931–53. Knighted, 1952.

If Britain's frontier is on the Rhine, it might pertinently be said – though it has in fact not been said – that Russia's frontier is on the Oder, and in the same sense.

At this point the article drew back a little by denying any implication that Russia would, or should, assail the independence of countries in eastern Europe. Russia's best interests would rather be served by neighbours who had good cause to be genuinely friendly towards her. On such friendliness she would insist; that was for sure; and she would be in a position after the war to shape the settlement on such lines consistent with her security:

> But it will make all the difference to the future of Anglo–Russian friendship whether these lines have been freely approved and welcomed by Britain in advance, or whether they are grudgingly accepted as a *fait accompli* after the victory has been won.

During much of this period Barrington-Ward had hopes of Sir Stafford Cripps, the left-wing socialist intellectual who had returned to London after his special mission as ambassador in Moscow. Cripps came back with great prestige as though he had been – as he never was – the trusted confidant of Britain's mighty new allied leader, Stalin. His prestige was greatly enhanced by a broadcast talk on February 8 1942. His contrast between what he called the 'lack of urgency' in Britain and the all-out effort in Russia – 'Every sacrifice in service and in comfort is being made by men, women and children alike' – brought a deep response from British people. Dismayed by the defeats in North Africa and South-East Asia they felt that more determination and more austerity were what was needed in Britain. 'Had our efforts in production been greater,' said Cripps, 'we should not now be retreating in North Africa.' Cripps was eager to make other broadcasts. 'He bore himself', Churchill wrote of him, 'as though he had a message to deliver'.[14] Barrington-Ward recognised a spirit near to his own, serious and forward-looking, and in a talk with Cripps in January 1942 was cheered to find that he was not averse to joining the government:

> I said I supposed he would want to enter a reformed and re-organized administration and that I wanted to see him in, but he must not expect the P.M. to part forthwith with all his stimulants, his 'necessities' – to wit, his Beaverbrooks.[15]

---

14 Churchill: *The Second World War*. Volume IV, p. 69.
15 B-W D, January 29 1942.

Churchill had in fact already assessed the wave of support behind Cripps and had offered him the Ministry of Supply – an offer which Cripps declined as it did not carry with it a seat in the War Cabinet. The worsening war news brought greater public distress. Exasperation over the inability of the navy and air force to stop the German battlecruisers Scharnhorst and Gneisenau in the Straits of Dover (February 12 1942) was merged with grief and horror at the surrender of 85,000 men in Singapore (February 15). On February 17 Barrington-Ward was told by Dr. Tom Jones that Churchill was re-shaping his Cabinet and that Cripps was likely to be brought in. On February 19, when the changes were announced, Barrington-Ward allowed himself a moment of jubilation in his diary:

> The changes are good. Beaverbrook is out altogether. Cripps is in – as Leader of the House! Attlee deputy-P.M. and Dominions Secretary. Cabinet of Ministers without, or virtually without, portfolio, except Bevin, Minister of Labour and Natl. Service. Oliver Lyttelton recalled from Cairo [to be Minister of Production]. Arthur Greenwood out. This really is a large sweep, capable of reinvigorating the conduct of the war and public confidence. Most of what *The Times* has asked for has been conceded.[16]

Less than a month later Barrington-Ward told Lord Reith,[17] according to Reith's diary,[18] that he thought that Cripps would be Prime Minister soon. ('How dreadful', Reith added when putting down his record.) But Cripps's stock was soon declining. In several talks with Barrington-Ward during the summer and autumn he complained that Churchill did not consult him, even about the business in the House of Commons where he was supposed to be Leader; and he asked Barrington-Ward several times to tell him whether he should walk out of the government. In the end Barrington-Ward suggested that Cripps should resign but, in view of pending military operations, should post-date the resignation by a month or two:

> Saw Cripps again and gave him my conclusions. He agreed with them . . . It is not the best line from his own point of view but it is a justified concession to the public interest.[19]

Cripps's indecision and some of his proposed tactics during this time

---

16 B-W D, February 19 1942.
17 John Charles Walsham Reith (1889–1971). First general manager BBC, 1922; director-general, 1927–38. Minister of Information, 1939–40. Baron, 1940.
18 *The Reith Diaries*. Edited by Charles Stuart, p. 292.
19 B-W D, October 2 1942.

appear to have shaken Barrington-Ward's high opinion of him:

I still do not know what Cripps is really worth but, in the public interest, I continue to hope he may prove a potential leader.[20]

After the victory at El Alamein in October–November 1942 Churchill – speaking from his strengthened position – told Cripps bluntly that he could either take the Ministry of Aircraft Production (outside the War Cabinet) or resign altogether. Cripps chose the Ministry, and the leading article in *The Times* of November 23, reviewing all the Cabinet changes announced the previous evening, did not blame Churchill or Cripps or anyone but, in the manner typical of Barrington-Ward, looked to the future. The argument was: if the man who had been most closely associated in the public mind with forward planning both for war and for peace was in disfavour, there was all the greater need on the part of the War Cabinet to prove to the country that such planning was not being dropped. The North African victories ought rather to be a spur to bolder and swifter planning. Decisions must be made:

if a peace policy is to be ready for launching when the tide is at the full and if civilians and soldiers alike are to know that their future and their children's future are being as fully assured as foresight, courage and organizing capacity can contrive.

In the end, when Cripps resigned from the Ministry of Aircraft Production, *The Times* was not excessive in its regrets. Events had overtaken the man.

The social changes which the paper had advocated seemed to be assured in detail by the Beveridge Plan for comprehensive health and unemployment insurance, published on December 2 1942. Barrington-Ward greeted it with a long leading article written partly by Charles Wilson[21] and partly by himself. Though reserving any detailed criticism until later, it warmly welcomed the scheme as a whole:

The prescription is for 'a British revolution' in which the experience of the past and its tested institutions as well as the creative insight of adventurous minds both have their full shares . . . The Government have been presented with an opportunity for marking this decisive epoch with a great social measure which would go far towards restoring the faith of ordinary men and women throughout the world

20 B-W D, November 20 1942.
21 Sir Charles Haynes Wilson (b. 1909). Oxford University correspondent and occasional leader writer for *The Times*, 1942–52. Vice-Chancellor, University of Leicester, 1957–61. Principal and Vice-Chancellor, University of Glasgow, 1961–76.

in the power of democracy to answer the imperious needs of a new age.[22]

This leader was the beginning of a more intense campaign. Within a week came another leader, written this time by David Owen,[23] then dividing his time between Cripps's office and Printing House Square. After demonstrating that the Beveridge proposals carried forward the traditions of British social legislation from the time of Joseph Chamberlain's Workman's Compensation Act of 1897, it argued that work had to begin straight away if the scheme was to be ready by soon after the end of the war. 'The key to the great administrative reform embodied in the Beveridge proposals is the rationalization of the social services by the centralization of authority in the hands of a Minister of Social Security'. Such a minister, *The Times* said, must be appointed forthwith. Other leading articles were soon prodding the government to make the appointment and urging more speed in discussions between ministers and the medical profession on ways of establishing the comprehensive medical service that was implied in the Beveridge Plan.

In Parliament and in political and academic groups outside Westminster the running fight between the two schools – those who maintained that all decent men would show their patriotism by getting on with the war first and foremost, and those who held that all civilised beings must plan ahead for a better and finer world – became so bitter that Churchill intervened. With some misgivings he announced a four years' plan for Britain in a broadcast speech on March 21 1943. He said quite frankly that his strong advice to everyone was still to concentrate upon the war effort. He was going against his own advice that evening, he said, and was looking at post-war issues, only in the hope of mollifying political divergences. Thereupon in very general terms he described not so much a national plan as a list of national aspirations, including full employment, a national health service, broader education, reconstruction of cities and towns, and stable prices. Churchill ended as he had begun. There was, he confessed, something unseemly and dangerous in counting up the fruits of victory while the Russians were fighting for dear life and heavy battles were going on in North Africa.

Barrington-Ward was pleased but not over-enthusiastic about the speech on first hearing. True, it was all to the good that the Prime

---

22 *The Times*, December 5 1942.
23 Sir David Kemp Owen (1904–1970). Political and Economic Planning, 1940–41. Personal assistant to Sir Stafford Cripps, 1942. Assistant Secretary-General, UN, 1946–51.

Minister should address himself for nearly forty-five minutes to domestic policy, 'on which hitherto he had not in spite of much prodding (not
least from *The Times*) said a word'. But the execution of the four years'
plan appeared to be relegated until after the war:

> Still, the broadcast is a considerable step, advocated in a tone of real
> conviction. After hearing it I warmed up Carr's leader a degree or
> two.[24]

He also took up a suggestion by S. W. Mason,[25] the parliamentary
correspondent, and had the speech re-printed as a pamphlet.

A week later, on March 29, another luncheon in Downing Street was a
most relaxed meeting. Churchill and Barrington-Ward were alone in a
basement room looking out on to the garden. Barrington-Ward's diary
records that Churchill showed no sign of his recent illness: 'pinky-fresh
in colour, hardly a wrinkle, voice firm, all his usual animation and
emphasis . . . His simplicity and lack of airs are extraordinarily engaging':

> We talked for just under an hour and a half. The main purpose,
> certainly, was to encourage aid and understanding from *The Times*,
> and the invitation itself was a recognition of the truth, plain enough
> from recent leaders, that our campaign for a full, forward coalition
> policy bore no hostility to him personally.
>
> On the contrary, he told me that he had been 'much touched'
> by several references to him lately, including one which he had
> read while he was at Algiers. But, he said, 'you can always turn
> the flank' and he hoped I should not go in for anything 'viewy'
> especially in finance I gathered. 'Remember', he said, 'that there
> are a great many Tories in the country'. I replied that anything
> he said would 'go'.

'You can always turn the flank': Churchill was to warn *The Times* about
this power on later occasions, particularly when referring to interventions by *The Times* during tough negotiations with Russia. He meant
that, given the reputation of *The Times* abroad, a leading article that
suggested, for example, a British concession during the negotiations
could encourage the other side and weaken the British government's
stand so much that it had to fall back from its prepared positions.

---

24 B-W D, March 21 1943.
25 Studley Wilson Mason (1899–1970). Parliamentary staff *The Times*, 1935–38;
parliamentary correspondent, 1938–57.

However Churchill did not press the point during a luncheon meeting when each man was explaining himself a little to the other:

'I shall come out of this war an old man. I shall be 70. I have nothing more to ask for'. He would stand on his broadcast, [proposing the four years' plan] and the Tory party would fight on that. When he turned to reconstruction he would give his whole mind to it – and admirably he would do it. (This did not sound like resignation.) I told him I was not and never had been a Socialist: I agreed with Oliver Lyttelton, in an early broadcast, that we need 'all the private and all the public enterprise that we could get.'

P.M.: 'I well remember that. I passed the broadcast beforehand. I remember inflicting a reading of it on the War Cabinet.'

Churchill rapidly reviewed the war. In general he was affectionately cynical and realistic about our Russian and American allies. Strongly in favour of full cooperation with Russia. 'I have wooed Joe Stalin as a man might woo a maid.' But also favoured confederations of smaller states. 'I do not want to be left alone in Europe with the Bear.' The two men seem to have agreed at every point, though Churchill left some of them vague, and Barrington-Ward did not drop his guard:

At 3 p.m. Maisky [Soviet Ambassador] was announced and I left. 'Come and see me at any time.' I gladly will, provided he will not think the critic an enemy. He is not the first great man and will not be the last who is galled by criticism and prefers to work in the kindly atmosphere of loyalty and approval.

He was in his 'siren suit' – what his family are said to describe as his 'rompers'. A glass of sherry followed by two or three of white wine and a couple of brandies do not conduce to my efficiency in the afternoon but make no difference to his.[26]

Certainly the luncheon did not bring about any weakening in *The Times's* campaign. In the months ahead the Churchill broadcast of March 21 was used as the basis of further prods at the government. On October 5 1943 Barrington-Ward strengthened and completed a leader written by Charles Wilson, complaining that the broadcast appeared to have been followed by no practical measures:

Either there must be a Minister of National Development with the widest powers or there must be an effective Home Affairs Committee of three or four Ministers who between them can exert their authority over the whole field of the projected reforms . . . Confi-

---

26 B-W D, March 29 1943.

dence in the Government's intentions for peace as well as for war is still the key to national unity.[27]

By 1943 the paper's campaign for a new order after the war had reached full strength. Not only leading articles but also a series of special articles pleaded the case for full employment, a comprehensive health service, and a housing programme, and put forward detailed plans for reaching the desired ends. Early in 1944 François Lafitte found his form in several acute analyses of plans for establishing the national medical service, and he became one of the country's leading experts on the working of the scheme.

Some opinion in the City hardened against *The Times* during 1943. On May 6 the parliamentary correspondent, Mason, passed on to Barrington-Ward a threat that some company advertising might be stopped in protest. On July 26 the assistant manager, F. P. Bishop, reported that three industrialists had withheld their advertisements 'on the ground,' Barrington-Ward noted, 'that we are unsympathetic to private enterprise – and have supported the Beveridge plan!' His diary note continues:

> Some of these industrialists have little idea of what we are trying to do for a peaceful future in industry when the war ends, without which the fortunes of this country may be in grave jeopardy.[28]

Barrington-Ward asked Bishop to tell one of the complainants that he could please himself where he put his advertisements but that *The Times* could not let a 'grave misrepresentation' of the paper's policy pass uncorrected.[29] *The Times* was not against private enterprise but was for social progress.

Throughout the campaign Barrington-Ward held fast to his conviction that the Cabinet had to reconstruct itself before it could reconstruct the country, and in this he had allies as well as critics. During 1943 he saw Herbert Morrison, Brendan Bracken, and other ministers to press home the arguments put forward in leading articles; and he was much cheered to find a sympathetic audience at a dinner with the Tory Reform Group, among them Quintin Hogg[30] and Peter Thorneycroft.[31]

---

27 *The Times*, October 5 1943.
28 B-W D, July 27 1943.
29 B-W D, July 29 1943.
30 Quintin Hogg (b. 1907). Minister of several government departments. Lord Chancellor, 1970. Lord Hailsham of Marylebone, 1970.
31 Peter Thorneycroft (b. 1909). Minister of several government departments, Chancellor of the Exchequer, 1957–58. Baron, 1967.

To Bracken he suggested on August 6 that Lord Woolton[32] would make a good superminister of reconstruction. At another meeting on October 15 Bracken told him that the suggestion might be taken up, and on November 11 the news was confirmed:

Brendan rang me up chaffingly about Woolton's appointment – 'The Times governing the country as usual' etc. I am delighted that it has come off.[33]

In the spring of 1944 The Times found itself caught up in one of the sudden angry disputes between Stalin and Churchill. In fact The Times had in all innocence precipitated the quarrel, which at one time seemed dangerous; Stalin threatened to stop his confidential exchanges with Churchill altogether unless their secrecy was maintained absolute. Like so many of the inter-allied wartime disputes it arose over Poland. The advance of the victorious Soviet armies towards the old Polish frontiers carried a warning to the allied leaders that they could no longer put off decisions on the future of Poland. Would Stalin hold on to the country's eastern half that had been given him in the 1939 deal with Germany? Would he insist on a communist government for the rest of the country? The Polish government, exiled in London, sent him through British channels their own proposals after discussions with British ministers. Stalin replied to these proposals in a letter to Churchill at the beginning of March.

On March 8 The Times published a long piece from McDonald, the diplomatic correspondent, who had been seeing Maisky's successor at the Soviet embassy, Fyodor Gusev, as well as talking to British and Polish officials. He wrote in part:

The Soviet Government's comments on the latest Polish proposals have now reached London. Moscow regards the proposals as inadequate, and declares once again that an understanding can be reached only if the Polish Government make changes in their membership and accept the Curzon Line as Poland's eastern frontier. When asking for changes the Moscow Government suggest that the Ministers and the high officers whom they declare to be anti-Soviet should be dropped.

On March 16 Stalin sent an angry cable to Churchill saying that the contents of secret and personal letters from him were appearing in the

---

32 Frederick James Marquis (1883–1964). Minister of Food, 1940–43; member of War Cabinet, 1943–45; Minister of Reconstruction, 1943–45; Lord President of the Council, 1945 and 1951–52. Earl Woolton, 1955.
33 B-W D, November 11 1943.

British press:

> I consider this to be a breach of secrecy. This fact makes it difficult for me to express my opinion freely. I hope that you have understood me.[34]

A little later Bracken asked McDonald to see him, told him about the angry cable, and said that the British government believed that Stalin was referring chiefly to the March 8 piece as it was the 'most authoritative and best balanced'. Churchill, he declared, was vastly annoyed at being accused of letting the news leak from British sources and intended to settle Stalin's hash by saying that it was a Soviet leak. They knew that McDonald had seen the Soviet ambassador before writing the March 8 piece, and – Bracken gave the warning – they might use this fact. When McDonald protested, saying that his talk with the Ambassador had been simply in general terms, Bracken seemed to drop the idea; but Churchill picked it up again and threw it hard at Stalin in a cable dated March 21:

> With regard to the Poles I am not to blame in any way about revealing your secret correspondence. The information was given both to the American *Herald Tribune* correspondent and to the London *Times* correspondent by the Soviet Embassy in London. In the latter case, it was given personally by Ambassador Gusev.[35]

Back came Stalin's reply on March 25. After a 'rigorous check' – knowing Stalin, one may imagine just how terrifyingly rigorous it was – he could say that neither Gusev nor any member of the embassy staff was guilty; they did not have the relevant documents, for one thing. Gusev was ready to face any kind of investigation:

> In other words, the leak came from the British not from the Soviet side . . . It appears that you have been misled as to Gusev and the Soviet embassy.[36]

The Times learned of this exchange only in the middle of April. It also learned, from the first secretary of the Soviet embassy, that the ambassador, beside himself with fury and dismay, was convinced that it was all a British plot to have him shipped back to Russia in disgrace. He was no less sure that McDonald had been sent to him as the *agent provocateur*. It was then Barrington-Ward's turn to be angry. Nothing ever roused

---

34 Public Record Office. Churchill Papers 3/355/3 T 595/4. Also in *Stalin's Correspondence with Churchill, Attlee, Roosevelt and Truman, 1941–45*, p. 210.
35 Churchill Papers. 3/355/3 T 625/4.
36 *Stalin's Correspondence*, p. 214.

him so much as a slur on *The Times* or on any member of the staff. He told Bracken that the government had wantonly ruptured relations between *The Times* and a major ally: 'This is a state of affairs which can be of no service to the national interest and is manifestly intolerable to *The Times* itself.' Unless the government acted, *The Times* would publish its own account of what really had happened.[37]

Until then Churchill, Eden, and Bracken had been hoping that the matter might be gently forgotten, although Churchill at one time thought that everyone concerned should first make affidavits for the historical record:

We really must have this skeleton properly articulated before he is put back into the cupboard.[38]

Eden and Bracken soon recognised, however, that the matter had to be put right. On May 8 they had a peace-making luncheon with Barrington-Ward and agreed to clear both Gusev of giving away secrets and McDonald of saying that he had done so. Churchill, they said, would send to Stalin a statement which *The Times* would see and approve beforehand. Naturally enough Churchill hated the thought of admitting to Stalin that his cable of March 21 had been wrong. As late as July 9 he dictated a minute consisting of the single awful sentence:

Who gave me this incorrect statement? W.S.C.[39]

It was not until Eden pressed him further that he initialled the instructions to Sir Archibald Clark Kerr on July 29 and the correction was at last passed on to Molotov in Moscow. By that time everyone was tired of an affair which had been blown up far beyond its worth. The second front had opened and was going well. Stalin was in a far better mood and was ready to forget his earlier anger which had been, as much as anything, an outburst caused by his never-resting suspicion that the western allies might not open the second front at all.

Later in that same year, 1944, Churchill and *The Times* were caught up in a much greater and fiercer dispute. The paper strongly opposed the British military intervention against the leftist forces in the Greek civil war; and this opposition enraged not only the Prime Minister but also most of the Conservative members of Parliament and very many of its own readers.

---

37 T.T.A.
38 Churchill Papers. 3/355/3 M/339 4.
39 Churchill Papers. 3/355/3 60.

Barrington-Ward's line on Greece stands out as the most controversial chapter in his editorship. Seen properly it was simply a projection of the paper's familiar ideas on organising Europe after the war. Barrington-Ward, E. H. Carr and Donald Tyerman saw Greece as the most important test case up to that time: it would show whether the British government was ready to work with the new left-wing forces that were emerging in European countries as they were liberated or whether, led by Churchill, it would go on backing military and political leaders of the old school. Greece, as *The Times* saw it, offered another and broader test. An imaginative handling of the new forces in Greece, rather than repression of them, would prove to Russia that Britain was not a reactionary, imperialist power and that proof would provide the basis for a better east–west understanding in Europe. There was also a more pressing consideration. British troops that were diverted to Greece could be better used in the war against Germany.

For such reasons *The Times* deplored Churchill's decision to send troops to support the right-wing Greek government which remained in power after the left wing had split away from the coalition patched up with British help in May and August 1944. When the fighting broke out *The Times* argued that Britain ought to press for a speedy truce, an amnesty, and early elections. In pursuing this line the paper's main fault was in being too hopeful. The trouble was that many Greek liberals, partly in reaction against British policy as they saw it, had linked themselves with EAM, the left-wing National Liberation Front in Greece. When it looked at EAM *The Times* exaggerated both the size and effectiveness of the liberal element within its ranks and minimised the strength and determination of the communists among its real leaders. Leading articles tended to equate the resistance forces in Greece with those of France, where the communist element was outweighed by the reformists and the parliamentarians. Unfortunately, what reformists there were in Greece at the time were squeezed between two extremes, right-wing (mainly royalist) and communist.

EAM had emerged from the German occupation with much political and military strength; it controlled much of the country outside Athens; and the British government believed in evidence that its communist leaders planned a full military take-over in Greece before the British forces arrived. This evidence about the planned *coup* was not taken as final in *The Times*. There was controversy over the responsibility for the first shots. Indeed Geoffrey Hoare, the correspondent in Athens, reported the beginning of the fighting on December 4 1944 with the emotive words, 'Seeds of civil war were well and truly sown by the Athens police this morning when they fired on a demonstration of children and youths'. Geoffrey Hoare was a man of experience but he knew the Middle East better than he knew the Balkans. His critics complained that he did not get about enough, was leftist in his own inclinations, and was handicapped by partial deafness. His despatches were none the less conscientiously written; they were well balanced on the whole; and he himself told a visiting British MP that they contained nothing 'which might have justified the comments of *The Times.*' Barrington-Ward thought this 'a strange statement to make and quite untrue',[40] but certainly it was the leading articles, and not the despatches, which provoked the storm against the paper.

The campaign in its columns opened with a few warnings. On December 5, the day after the first shooting, a leading article said simply that, though Britain had an interest in law and order, that interest 'must not be allowed to imply any participation in the politics of Greece.' Two days later a leader by Carr was more explicit: the 'disagreeable truth' was that British armed forces had become involved in a Greek civil war. After citing a report that the British government had forbidden any change of government in Greece at the time, it went on:

Any British Government which claimed to insist, at a time when popular elections are admittedly impossible, on this or that individual or group as alone qualified to conduct the government of a friendly nation would accept a grave responsibility which accords ill with the British tradition . . . If M. Papandreou[41] is now maintained in power by the ban of a foreign Government on any alternative, his moral authority in Greece can hardly survive; and British troops will be used, and British lives sacrificed, fighting against Greeks on behalf of a Greek Government which exists only in virtue of armed force.[42]

A third leader speedily followed on December 9, written by Tyerman and amended 'a good deal'[43] by Barrington-Ward. It emphasised the need to extricate British troops from their 'disastrous predicament' and objected to the way that Churchill, in his statement to the House on December 8, had identified EAM with communists and bandits. On the contrary, said *The Times*, EAM embraced 'the whole range of opinion from Centre to extreme Left'. The British government itself had taken Greek moderates 'into their trust' – a somewhat obscure phrase – 'and very many of these good and honest men and women are members of

---

40 B-W D, February 13 1945.
41 Georgios Papandreou (1888–1968). Greek Prime Minister, 1944.
42 *The Times*, December 7 1944.
43 B-W D, December 8 1944.

EAM.'

On December 20 another leader by Tyerman stated that British policy must make it plain that the one solution which was not, and should not be, sought was that of total victory. 'No settlement is conceivable that does not secure the assent, and the obedience, of the many-sided National Liberation Front.'

Barrington-Ward had seen Eden twice during these days for talks in which Eden indicated a little wearily that Churchill was running the Greek affair in his own way. Late on the night of December 22 Churchill rang Barrington-Ward on another matter:

Then, with no encouragement from me, he got on to Greece. Govt. desired to take a quite impartial line there, etc. etc. I said (wishing to end the conversation and let Horner [editor's chauffeur] catch his train) that what all wanted was an early conclusion of the affair. 'So do I, but not at the price of humiliating skedaddle by British troops.' . . . I said I would approach him later and we could talk then. On that, at last, he rang off.[44]

Better news came after Christmas with Churchill's and Eden's speedily arranged mission to Athens, the appointment of Archbishop Damaskinos to be Regent, and Eden's statement that he wished to see the establishment of a Greek government broadly representative of all opinion in the country, including EAM. Barrington-Ward, who had snatched a few days' rest at his Bedfordshire cottage during the holiday, was encouraged by the news. He was the more vexed on January 1 to see that Carr, in charge at Printing House Square, had published a leader which he, Carr, had written a few days before when the news was less hopeful:

I expected him to modify it but deliberately refrained from ringing him up to tell him so. No good trying to drive the car from the back seat. It was not much modified and seemed to me rather fiercer than it need have been.[45]

The leader said that progress had not gone very far; fighting was still going on, and so long as the British were fighting against one of the Greek forces they could not claim to be holding the balance impartially:

This is no question of prestige or of the pursuit of a victory for British arms. On this field, military victory spells only political defeat . . . There is no ground for pride or satisfaction in the knowledge that

---

44 B-W D, December 22 1944.
45 *Ibid*, January 1 1945.

British troops have been engaged in house-to-house fighting in a working-class suburb of Athens.

British arms, the leader went on, could without doubt secure Athens and the countryside of Attica. But would the goal of a peaceful settlement of Greek affairs have been brought one step nearer?[46]

More warnings about the build-up of anti-British bitterness in Greece were given in succeeding leaders. On January 9 an article by Tyerman argued that little consolation was to be found in the news that British troops were not to move outside Attica in pursuit of the anti-government forces; the 'supremely distasteful possibility' was emerging that British arms and supplies would nevertheless be used. Resistance might indeed be overcome with such aid:

> But at the end the civil war would remain to spring up again with the eventual withdrawal of armed British aid, and a most grave dis-service would have been rendered both to Greek peace and democ-racy and to British interests in the Balkans and the Mediterranean – and in the war against the common German enemy. These are not questions of ideology or partisanship, but of fact.

The articles were written at the time when the prestige of British arms and the nobility of British war aims alike shone brightly. *The Times* was concerned in its own mind to keep the prestige and the aims unsullied; but its many critics, angry and outraged, accused it of lack of patriotism as much as they suspected it of softness towards communism. Such feelings of outrage led to the extraordinary scene in the House of Commons on January 18 when Churchill rounded on *The Times*. The shouts of support for Churchill from the Conservative benches were no doubt especially loud because members saw that Barrington-Ward was looking down on them from the press gallery. Churchill's words were the more deeply biting for being carefully chosen:

> There is no case in my experience, certainly no case in my war experience, when a British Government has been so maligned (*loud and prolonged cheers*) and its motives so traduced in our own country by important organs of the press among our own people. That this should be done amid the perils of this war, now at its climax, has filled me with surprise and sorrow . . . How can we wonder at, still more how can we complain of, the attitude of hostile and indifferent newspapers in the United States when we have, in this country, witnessed such a melancholy exhibition as that pro-

---

46 *The Times*, January 1 1945.

vided by some of our most time-honoured and responsible journals (*loud and prolonged cheers*) and others to which such epithets would hardly apply. (*laughter*)[47]

The roar of assent in the Chamber was the first heavy shock which Barrington-Ward suffered during his term as editor. The roar was renewed when Churchill spoke of the government's difficulties being increased 'by a spirit of gay, reckless, unbridled partisanship', let loose upon those who had to bear the burden of decision. Barrington-Ward knew instantly what was behind the demonstration. The anger was not simply over Greece: it was against much of what *The Times* stood for at home and abroad. In his diary note for the day he quoted Churchill's reference to 'our most time-honoured and responsible journals':

This – a direct and obvious reference to *The Times* – immediately touched off the loudest, largest and most vicious – even savage! – cheer that I have heard in the House. It must have lasted a full minute or more. I went on with my notes and did not inspect the demonstration, but there could be no doubt that it was almost wholly Tory. There was more than Spain [Greece?] in it. It was a vent for the pent-up passions of three years, a protest against all that has, rightly or wrongly, enraged the Tories in the paper during that time.[48]

By chance it was the day of a Board luncheon at Printing House Square. During the war Parliament opened its sittings in the morning and a big speech, such as Churchill's in this case, began before lunch and was continued after. Barrington-Ward had to leave soon after hearing the attack, and at the Board lunch he met John Astor, chairman of *The Times*, who had been sitting in the Commons during all the uproar as Conservative member for Dover: the editor was naturally concerned about the chairman's reactions:

One word only with John Astor, who was in the House before lunch. I said to him, 'We had a large compliment this morning.' He smiled. This open onslaught by Winston must put a strain on the support which John gives me.

True to his character, Barrington-Ward went back to the House to hear the rest of Churchill's speech and, no less in character, he generously recorded his impressions:

---

47 *The Times*, January 19 1945.
48 B-W D, January 18 1945.

122

All Winston's speech after lunch very good. Indeed he has had a very good day. I decided on two leaders corresponding to the two halves of the speech. Asked Carr to write a good-tempered piece sustaining the right of criticism even in wartime and Morrah to tackle the rest – which they did very successfully.

Carr's long leader was a calmly balanced statement, welcoming the moves towards peace in Greece, condemning the brutalities there as strongly as Churchill had done, and giving unreserved and unswerving support to the cause of national unity in the war against Germany and Japan. It continued:

> But the unity which the coalition represents has never been, and never should be, construed as inhibiting a right of independent judgment and criticism; and the criticisms which have been addressed to some aspects of Government policy on Greece are a healthy vindication of the right of democracy to examine fully and frankly how far particular actions and particular policies are likely to contribute to the attainment of the declared national aim. Public confidence in the coalition, consistently upheld in these columns as a necessity now and for as long as national security in the fullest sense demands more than party government, depends not least upon the assurance that the Press will discharge its natural duty.

In outward appearance *The Times* seemed impervious to Churchill's strictures and the rage of most Tory MPs. Barrington-Ward none the less questioned himself and the paper's line. He was an acutely sensitive man behind the armour of his courage, and he was particularly glad to have several assurances of support during the next days and weeks. His diary records some of them:

> Two people spoke to me at the club. Victor Cunard[49] thought Winston had been 'most unfair'. Roger Cambon[50] thought Winston was in a tight corner with the British public over Greece and knew it . . . Dined with the Masseys.[51] Vincent thought Winston's sally imprudent from his point of view, suggesting intolerance.[52]
>
> Much reflexion on Thursday's event – an authoritarian symptom.[53]

---

49 Victor Cunard (1898–1960). Eton. Rome correspondent of *The Times*, 1925–27; Paris, 1928–33.
50 Roger Cambon (1882–1970). Counsellor, later Minister, French Embassy, London, 1924–40.
51 Vincent Massey (1887–1967). Canadian High Commissioner in London, 1935–46. Governor-General of Canada, 1952–59.
52 B-W D, January 19 1945.
53 *Ibid*, January 20 1945.

There came a moment of rare pleasure a few days later when Barrington-Ward met Brendan Bracken at lunch:

Not much talk about Greece, though Brendan said the Govt.'s prayer was: 'Give us peace in our *Times*, O Lord.'[54]

On that same day he was glad to have a reassuring talk with John Astor who was 'worried and puzzled by the attacks on *The Times*':

Has been re-reading the leaders and finds them quite soberly expressed, offering advice rather than censure. And that is really so . . . I feel that with care and patience T.T. will come successfully out of this stormy episode. No question of a climb-down.

Letters were pouring into Printing House Square: 'Two-fifths very friendly'.[55] More than half were 'hostile and abusive'. Barrington-Ward, still uneasy in his mind, read over all the leaders dealing with Greece again on January 31:

I am once more impressed by their balance and moderation and by the pressure we have put on the Greek left wing from the first.[56]

He was therefore well able to cope with a rumour the next day:

According to Tyerman Brendan Bracken has told Waldorf Astor that *The Times* will not be forgiven over Greece until it has climbed down! Very well. It will not be forgiven.

But in the next two sentences some small doubts recur:

Hoare has sent in two articles more or less justifying his line. I wish I could be absolutely sure of his accuracy in detail.[57]

Throughout this time Barrington-Ward kept in touch with both Eden and Brendan Bracken, and had a remarkably friendly lunch alone with Bracken on February 6. The editor did not complain about Churchill's attack – 'Ministers were entitled to defend themselves.' Equally *The Times* would defend itself, and the editor did so at length, reminding Bracken of the many times that the paper had praised Churchill, even over Greece. 'Ah,' said Bracken, 'he's very temperamental':

Then he told me that he and Max [Beaverbrook] had restrained Winston from sending me a scolding letter, with references to "Munich" too! Brendan told him, 'You can't berate an editor like

54 B-W D, January 23 1945.
55 *Ibid*, January 29 1945.
56 *Ibid*, January 31 1945.
57 *Ibid*, February 1 1945.

that. He may be wrong and I think he is but he has his point of view as you have yours. Besides you can't tackle him on "Munich". That was Geoffrey Dawson's responsibility.' 'Ah well,' said Winston (according to BB), 'he has made a better thing of *The Times* since Geoffrey Dawson went.' (I received this with no special satisfaction and exhibited none, having no desire to profit at G.D.'s supposed expense.) Further, according to Brendan, Winston was intending to say much more about *The Times* in his speech. Here Max restrained him. 'No, no,' said Max, 'look at the whole record of *The Times* and its fine work in this war. And which paper gave you the best leader on your birthday?'[58]

The Churchill papers in the Public Record Office show that the last spark to Churchill's anger expressed on January 18, was given by Carr's leader on January 1, 'Next Steps in Greece'. This was the article (quoted earlier) which perturbed Barrington-Ward himself, the one which he thought, on reading it, to be 'rather fiercer than it need have been'. Churchill dictated his draft letter the same day. He said that he was very sorry that the article 'should have darkened the pages of "The Times"' and continued:

Your article to-day sets the signal for the general attack by the extreme Left-wing forces upon the Archbishop's chances. Owing to the influence of 'The Times', I have no doubt that it will be used to the full here and still more in the United States. It will even be represented in foreign countries as the true policy of His Majesty's Government. The harm may be measureless. The dead and wounded can no doubt be counted up later on.

Considering the eminence of 'The Times', has it no responsibility? Ought not some consideration be given to a War Cabinet containing, in addition to Conservative and non-Party Ministers, three leading Socialists and the representatives of the Liberal Party? Ought all this to be brushed aside with an air of superior knowledge and, if I may say so, disregard of consequences . . . ?

If you succeed in breaking down the Archbishop, as you may well do, nothing but anarchy will exist in Attica, except insofar as it is prevented by the additional sacrifices and hard fighting of the British forces. If the question is so worked up that it comes to a Vote in the House, I have not the slightest doubt of an overwhelming majority. Therefore I ask no favours of myself or the Government.

It is only because I am convinced of your soldierly repute, of your

---

58 B-W D, February 6 1945.

patriotism and desire to see a free and peaceful democratic world not under any totalitarian rule, Nazi or Communist, that I have intruded upon you.[59]

Beaverbrook sent his first comments on the draft letter the next day, January 2:

Prime Minister
You have told me your newspaper policy was – Square or Squash. You have held to it ever since.
This letter to Barrington-Ward is a departure. It does not make any effort to 'Square' and it does not 'Squash'. Therefore I recommend against it.

Greece met Barrington-Ward almost everywhere he went in London and perhaps it was only when he had a day's break at Chichester to see the cathedral – 'a stirring place' – that he recognised how tired he was and how deeply worried he had been. 'This Greek business has taken a great deal out of me'.[60]

He was bound to ask himself whether he had forfeited, over Greece, much of the prestige and influence which *The Times* had gained, under his leadership, in its campaign for social reform. The answer is that it did lose the respect and sympathy of many moderate Conservative party members whom Barrington-Ward hoped to carry with him; it confirmed them in the doubts which were forming in their minds. It gained corresponding respect further to the left. That shift would not in itself disturb Barrington-Ward. John Astor, though deeply worried, stood by him. Editorial policy is not swayed by commercial considerations, but some of the directors must have thought that increased respect from the left was not going to advance the long-term commercial fortunes of the paper, dependent on circulation (which was rising fast) but also heavily relying on City and property advertising.

---

59 PRO. PREM 66/4 folios 472, 473, 473a.
60 B-W D, February 10 1945.

VI

BATTLES FOR THE NEW WORLD

Two brief entries in Barrington-Ward's diaries give the essence of *The Times's* policy as Britain faced the world after the war. Barrington-Ward was to conduct that policy for only two and a half more years. In that short time the storms which had gathered round the paper towards the end of the war became more acute. Never in its history was *The Times* more talked about, more attacked, more praised.

The first of the two diary entries is dated July 19 1945. Barrington-Ward was dining with Harold Macmillan.[1] The results of the first post-war election were to be announced in a week's time and Macmillan, sensing that the Conservatives had done badly, showed his fears that Labour's national welfare schemes would soften the country instead of bracing it for the hard tasks ahead. Barrington-Ward would have none of such 'diehard rubbish', as he called it in his diary that evening. In his view the welfare state would bring not only more justice but (in flat contradiction to Macmillan) more efficiency:

> The security of organised, collective self-help will foster enterprise not destroy it. The comfortable classes have always been the enterprising classes.

In the second entry, dated New Year's Day 1947, Barrington-Ward allowed himself a few and very rare words of satisfaction as he looked back on 1946 and then gave the elements of his policy for the future:

> Have finished a year which, once again, gives me unmerited cause of every kind for thankfulness. *The Times* ought to have great chances in 1947. In particular we can help by swelling the demand, which must be insistent, for production at home (*all* else hangs upon that) and by promoting a firm but realistically based understanding with Russia, without which there cannot be peace.

---

1 Harold Macmillan (b. 1894). Minister Resident, North Africa, 1942–45; Foreign Secretary, 1955; Chancellor of the Exchequer, 1955–57; Prime Minister, 1957–63; Earl of Stockton, 1984.

Throughout the war Barrington-Ward had looked forward to the coming of peace as his great opportunity for intensifying his campaign for social reform. He had hoped that the wartime coalition would stay in being long enough to put into effect the plans for welfare and reconstruction that were largely agreed in principle by the two main parties. Or, failing that, he hoped for a Conservative government led by moderate reformers such as Anthony Eden or R. A. Butler.[2] But in the first half of 1945 much had gone wrong as he saw it. He was dismayed, for a start, by the early calling of the election before even the war against Japan was over. He was the more dismayed by Churchill's rumbustious partisan electioneering:

> Read text (in advance) of Winston's broadcast. Too much Beaverbrook; distinctly cheap; Socialism and Gestapo associated; will probably lose votes.[3]

> Winston has let us all down sadly by the cheap tone which he has given to this election and presented an unworthy picture of us to foreign countries.[4]

> Today I worked at the club all the morning on a leader on the choice before the country. Difficult. How can I throw my hat up for Winston in his present temper or encourage people to vote for his Govt. without the assurance that they are going to do as well as the late coalition, or better, in fulfilment of its policy and pledges? How, again, encourage them to support ineffectual Liberalism, or to give Labour a victory which it would use for widespread nationalisation?[5]

Most unusually for him, Barrington-Ward let the questions float unanswered, both in his diary and in his leading articles. He often used to insist that a leading article must lead, but now:

> Only thing at the moment is to balance them all. I wish some kind of resumed coalition govt. were still possible – best of all for the country for the next two or three years.[6]

When Labour routed the prophets with its great electoral victory, gaining 393 seats against the Conservatives' 213, Barrington-Ward had no more doubt where *The Times* should stand. He was in favour of much that the new government was committed to do. But the paper would

---

2 Richard Austen Butler (1902–1982). Minister of Education, 1941–45; thereafter Chancellor of the Exchequer, Home Secretary, and Foreign Secretary. Baron, 1962.
3 B-W D, June 4 1945.
4 *Ibid*, July 1 1945.
5 *Ibid*, July 4 1945.
6 *Ibid*, same date.

follow its traditional practice of judging a government by its deeds; and it would also try, by pointing out that the country could not afford doctrinaire experimentation, to strengthen the moderates within the Labour party. Three days after the full weight of the Labour victory was known Barrington-Ward wrote:

> With a Labour Govt. in office – Attlee has begun well with his choice and placing of first colleagues [in the Cabinet] – *The Times*, independent but not hostile, might be, ought to be, in a good position to bring some influence to bear. I hope so. The opportunities and the risks of 1945–50 about match each other.[7]

He was to confirm this persuasive, judgmatical role more strongly over a year later in a talk with Lord Woolton, then chairman of the Conservative party. Woolton had passed on to him some Conservative complaints about the paper's line:

> I explained to him that, while it is the duty of the Opposition to oppose, it is the duty of *The Times* to get the best it can out of the Govt. of the day. The King's Govt. has to be carried on.[8]

No sentences can reveal more clearly Barrington-Ward's view of *The Times* as a special force in the conduct of public affairs, acting almost like a governor, in the sense of a balancing agent, within the political machine.

In giving general support to Labour's plans for the welfare state *The Times* pressed especially hard for the establishment of the national health service. By the end of 1944 it was already criticising the cautious approach of the British Medical Association which 'has willed almost all the ends and rejected almost all the means'.[9] Soon after Aneurin Bevan became Minister of Health a leader by François Lafitte gave reasons for not letting the preparatory discussions with the medical authorities and the local councils drag on:

> The electorate has emphatically removed one cause of uncertainty by returning a Government pledged to provide a medical service available without fee for all who wish to use it, without exclusion of the higher income groups . . . Unless the main framework of the service is firmly established in the near future, thousands of doctors will return from their war duties to conditions of insecurity; voluntary hospitals will be seriously embarrassed; and local authorities will be

---

7 *Ibid*, July 29 1945.
8 *Ibid*, December 4 1946.
9 Leading article (Lafitte), December 9 1944.

unable to plan their own services with any confidence.[10]

The Times urged each side to make concessions. It defended the doctors when Labour complained that they wished to move in and run the service by themselves, without official interference. True, the doctors ought not to demand full 'workers' control' but Labour on its side should remember that in other fields it was all in favour of 'industrial democracy'; why, then, deny that same democracy to the doctors? Yet, in spite of such admonitions to the government, there was no doubt where the paper's sympathies lay. It would not agree with the doctors' argument that any reorganisation of the medical services should be deferred until local government had been re-cast and housing and nutrition had been improved. No, said *The Times*, all the reforms should be pressed forward together. Especially during the first half of 1948 it brought on itself the renewed anger of doctors who were sure it had committed itself too soon and too far to the idea of turning doctors into servants of the state in a fully comprehensive national scheme.

One of Lafitte's leaders urging the government to put the Beveridge Plan into effect secured the inclusion of a special clause in the National Insurance Bill of 1946. Lafitte had written (November 2 1944) that rises in social benefits should not be allowed to become a matter of electoral rivalry between the political parties but should be geared to the cost of living and other objective factors, and be subject to periodic review:

> Public opinion and political pressure will force an increase in the money value of benefits in order to maintain their real value if a substantial and sustained rise in prices occurs.

James Griffiths, Minister of National Insurance in the first Attlee government, liked the idea and adopted some of the leading article's wording in his Bill.

In like fashion *The Times* gave full support to the Bill which nationalised the mines, to the Town and Country Planning Bill of 1947, and to the measure which ended casual labour at the docks. On the coming into force of the Town and Country Planning Act the paper wrote:

> The British people, almost without knowing it, are embarking upon one of the greatest experiments in the social control of their environment ever attempted by a free society. In the process they are also putting old individual liberties in trust for the common good.[11]

---

10 *The Times*, September 27 1945.
11 Leading article (Lafitte), July 1 1948.

The paper annoyed many readers by accepting the government's prolongation of food rationing and even its intensification; Barrington-Ward thought that rationing was not only necessary in itself but useful as a daily reminder that the nation was facing hard tasks in a hard world.

This was one side of the paper's policy. Churchill attacked its 'parlour socialism',[12] and many other Conservatives were irritated beyond measure at being deserted, as they thought, by their natural ally. They were astonished that *The Times* of all papers – long held to be a safe conservative institution – should treat a Labour administration for all the world as if it were a natural form of government for the country: as apt to make mistakes as other governments, perhaps, but no less entitled to have its acts judged evenly or indeed to be given on occasion the benefit of the doubt. Many Conservatives saw with amazement and chagrin that an editor of *The Times* was not letting a Labour or Socialist label on the package put him off from supporting measures of swift social reform in which he profoundly believed.

Much of the Conservative criticism was overdone. *The Times* was very far from accepting Labour measures without scrutiny. It looked at the cost and frequently asked whether the finances of specific measures had been properly assessed. It pointed out more and more strongly that the great expense of the whole social reform could be met only by increased industrial output and higher productivity. This argument, with variations, was repeated insistently:

> The purpose of the whole system is to promote national health and social economic efficiency, and there is a danger now that more attention will be given to income than to the productive sources of income. If the social plan fails to influence productivity, it will defeat its prior purposes and sap the resources from which it must be maintained.[13]

> When the ordinary man comes to reflect on the total weekly contribution required of him under the new system, it may serve as a reminder, which the Government now need to drive home in every possible way, that the price to be paid for social security is efficient productive work.[14]

> The new social services will come to claim too large a share of the national income if the citizen, in pursuit of security, leisure, and comfort, fails to understand that what he expects of society can only be secured by the enterprise, diligence, and self-discipline with

---

12 B-W D, December 19 1945.
13 Leading article (Lafitte), October 12 1945.
14 Leading article (Lafitte), January 25 1946.

which he makes his personal contribution to the enlargement of the national product.[15]

The same uneasiness about production underlay the paper's decidedly muted welcome for the government's 'first true Socialist Bill', nationalising the Bank of England:

If it lost the Bank's power to consult upon the freest terms with private banks and private industry, the State would have parted with an asset of incalculable value.[16]

In fact *The Times* throughout this period did not have any doctrinaire leanings towards nationalisation as such. Its general line, set by Tyerman, Lafitte and Duncan Burn,[17] was that the real issue was not ownership but how the industries and services could be conducted efficiently, free from political interference, and with a proper pricing policy, especially if they were organised as monopolies without competitors to keep them on their toes. The line, in short, was nationalisation if the alternative seemed worse. Such thoughts were to make it oppose the steel nationalisation Bill at the end of the Attlee period.

The Times was as fierce as any other newspaper in condemning the government's handling of the fuel crisis early in 1947. It accused the government of having put off timely measures to safeguard the stocks of coal in past months simply because such measures would have been unpopular. Such heedlessness had brought upon the country 'a degree of dislocation that not even the most savage efforts of the enemy in the recent war could impose'.[18] The same leading article said that the drastic cuts in fuel for industry and the homes should never have been allowed to become necessary:

They show plainly the improvidence of having postponed radical action, however unpopular it would have been among all parties and sections of the community, until almost too late . . . Once again it is the people of England who must take the strain.

Barrington-Ward was carrying out his promise to judge the government by its acts. Even so it has to be asked whether he did not start out by being too enthusiastic in supporting the idea of a comprehensive welfare state. The answer has to take account of the bleak conditions of the

---

15 Leading article (Lafitte), May 30 1946.
16 Leading article (Wright), October 11 1945.
17 Duncan Lyall Burn (b. 1902). Holloway County School; Christ's College, Cambridge. Industrial correspondent *The Times*, 1946–62.
18 Leading article (Tyerman), February 10 1947.

post-war period. People thought in terms of past poverty and prevailing austerity, not of an affluence which they could not foresee. Few people during the war and in the years immediately after it could foretell the upsurge in the standard of living that was to be brought about by technological invention and methods of mass production – stimulated in large part by the war itself. If the 'wages explosion' and the 'consumers' revolution' could have been foretold *The Times* would probably have questioned whether a fully national, fully comprehensive 'free' medical service was really going to be needed in an affluent society. It may also be said that Barrington-Ward, if he had lived longer, would no doubt have been less confident than he was that the provision of generous social benefits would inspire greater initiative and greater industrial production. The national experience has not supported his hopes there. A further point is that, though he gave warnings about the expense of the whole welfare scheme, he did not foresee the full weight of the bureaucratic machine that grew up to administer it. Yet the return of mass unemployment in the seventies and the early eighties gave a new relevance to *The Times* arguments in the years when the welfare state was being shaped. Barrington-Ward had to ask what was the alternative and he could find none that was not repellent to him.

For a man near the top of the Establishment he was remarkably at one with the prevalent mood of the country. He especially well understood the thoughts of the men and women in the armed forces. Hundreds of thousands who had had their lives disrupted by the war, and those who had relatives killed or wounded, had read or heard of the official promises of a new Britain and they swung between belief and disbelief in those promises. Barrington-Ward had lived through the years of disillusionment after the First World War; and he was determined – it was one of his strongest motives as an editor – to do what he could to prevent any return to the poverty and unemployment that were then widespread. He wished to avoid social and political unrest. More than that, more positively than that, he was determined that *The Times* should help in building a fairer society, with greater equality of opportunity for any boy or girl with intelligence and initiative. His home policy shook many old ideas and on balance it was right.

In the foreign field the policy of *The Times* was no less bold and provoked outcries against it even greater than those raised against its policy at home. Russia was at the heart of the storm. It was the time when the cold war was becoming the strongest force in world politics. Suspicions grew during the months of the San Francisco conference that founded the United Nations and then during the 'Big Three' Potsdam conference that registered the division of Germany; they worsened during the months when Russia was shaping eastern Europe according to her own totalitarian pattern.

Throughout this time Barrington-Ward and E. H. Carr never wavered in their main argument: that the peace of the world depended on full and trustful cooperation and friendship among what were still called the Big Three powers, the United States, Russia, and Britain – the last supported by the Commonwealth and, it was hoped, by the countries of western Europe. These powers would have the main responsibility for ensuring the peace. Each of them would inevitably have its zone of influence, openly recognised by the others – and by the rest of the world.[19]

Barrington-Ward and Carr were wholly agreed on the general strategy but Carr would often pursue the argument to its unrelenting and, in his own mind, inescapable conclusion. He was especially keen that people should understand the realities and imperatives of power in international affairs. Having once accepted the premise of great-power zones of influence he built a logical system on that premise and pursued many equally logical lines of thought from it. He was impatient with western protests against Russia's methods of imposing control in eastern Europe; impatient both because the protests were likely to be ineffective and because they would, by awakening Russian suspicions and fears of western encroachments, jeopardise the prospects of co-operation with Russia on the wider world stage. If Russian power beyond her old frontiers was to be accepted, then it should be accepted without constant niggling. He seemed to echo without dissent the famous dictum of the Treaty of Augsburg in 1555: *cujus regio, ejus religio*.

Faced with a powerful leading article from Carr, Barrington-Ward would at times – particularly if it was on a matter which had not been thoroughly discussed beforehand – spend an hour or two hours in toning it down here and there, as mentioned earlier,[20] stopping it a little short of Carr's own conclusion, and putting in a few balancing points. This was not due to timidity; he made clear his purpose, and his assessment of Carr's work as a whole, in his diary when Carr stopped full-time work for the paper in the middle of 1946:

Carr has done the paper outstanding service. I owe more than I can say to his fresh, original, powerful mind. On the whole he has played up well as one of a team and has accepted the limitations of team-work with good grace. No doubt he thinks me excessively

19 See Chapter V.
20 See Chapter V.

cautious but I am certain that his work, and the paper, have gained because he has not always been allowed to offer all the provocation that he would like! A better pen never wrote leaders for *The Times*. It made its mark immediately. What has been done could not have been done without it.[21]

To judge by the results in the paper, and the repercussions outside, the leaders were very little weakened by any such editorial trimming. Essentially they were a challenge to much of pre-war thinking. Week after week the point was made that foreign policy must be based on hard deductions from facts as they are, rather than on sentiments about what the facts ought to be:

In the situation confronting the 'Big Three' in Potsdam, therefore, 'zones of influence' already exist, were bound to exist, and will continue to exist . . . It may be that Russia recognises more frankly and more explicitly a system which English-speaking nations tend to veil from the critical eyes of a sentimental and sometimes uninformed public opinion.[22]

Britain and America had to be no less clear-sighted in the matter than Russia. They criticised Soviet repression in Poland, yet in its own way Russia was behaving as other great powers had usually behaved:

The determination of the United States that no unfriendly Government should hold the reins of power in Panama is altogether comparable to the similar determination of Russia in Poland.[23]

Like it or not, the big powers had the dominant positions and responsibilities in the world. Any attempts at the San Francisco conference to weaken such responsibilities and amend the Charter to give more rights to the smaller powers 'would be disastrous to the future of the organization as a serious factor in world politics'.[24]

Such a recognition of realities, Carr argued, must condition the kind of alliance which Britain should secure with both America and Russia; and for many reasons the greater effort had to be made to cement the alliance with Russia:

It would be the height of unwisdom to assume, for example, that an alliance of the English-speaking world, even if it were to find favour with American opinion, could form by itself the all-sufficient pillar

---

21 B-W D, July 29 1946.
22 *The Times*, May 23 1945.
23 *The Times*, July 14 1946.
24 *The Times*, April 21 1945.

of world security and render superfluous any other foundation for British policy in Europe . . . Solid and well-grounded relations between Britain and Russia are themselves complementary to Anglo–American understanding . . . With Britain and Russia on guard at their respective posts and with confidence and cooperation between them indissolubly established, the peace in Europe is secure.[25]

With remarkable foresight the same leader declared that Britain had other opportunities open to her in Europe, just across the Channel, and they 'should be seized before it is too late'. Britain should work for 'far closer forms of political and economic collaboration between Britain, France and the smaller countries of western Europe than any established in the past'. Having looked ahead to a western European community, however, the leader came back to its main point:

But the alliance between Britain and Russia provides the necessary condition without which any more limited or localised agreement would be meaningless and ineffective.

In his strong and insistent advocacy of full cooperation with Soviet Russia Barrington-Ward was influenced by Carr's brilliantly incisive mind, but it was his own policy no less. His belief in it was frequently confirmed and sustained when finding that public men and diplomatists whom he respected also believed that cooperation was possible. His diaries give summaries of far-from-despairing talks with Averell Harriman, the American special emissary, Dr. Evatt, sometime Australian foreign minister, Field-Marshal Smuts of South Africa, Sir Archibald Clark Kerr, ambassador in Moscow, John Foster Dulles, later to become American Secretary of State, Walter Lippmann, the outstanding American columnist, and even – though there was soon to be a change in his attitude – Ernest Bevin. Within Printing House Square itself very few on the foreign side opposed the basic idea of seeking cooperation with Russia, and very few believed that Russia could be denied a dominant place in eastern Europe. In office discussions William Casey and one or two others argued mainly that the difficulties in the way of Soviet–Western cooperation should be more strongly emphasised in the leading articles, that the manner in which Stalin had imposed Stalinism on eastern Europe should be acknowledged, and that full measure be taken of the solid stone wall which Molotov imported so

---

25 *The Times*, May 23 1945.

often into the conference room.[26] Above all, given the standing of *The Times* abroad, Casey expressed his dislike of the way that an over-simplified argument in a leading article would, in Churchill's phrase, 'turn the flank' of the British government during tense negotiations by admitting much of the Russian case straight away.

An example of such flank-turning appeared in October 1945. The Foreign Ministers of the United States, the Soviet Union, Britain and France had broken up one of their London conferences without coming to any agreement. Carr wrote two leading articles on successive days. The first, on October 3, pointed out that Britain and America, instead of being consistent in recognising zones of influence, had struck an attitude on Balkan affairs which seemed to imply that 'any of the three Powers may claim a right of intervention even in regions especially affecting the security of one of the others'; therein was to be found the underlying cause of the difficulties encountered during the conference. The second article, on October 4, went further in saying that it seemed inconceivable that questions of recognising or not recognising regimes within the Soviet zone 'should be allowed any longer to cloud relations between the major Powers'. The powers should negotiate on matters of prime concern and avoid 'pinpricks on what are admittedly questions of secondary importance'.

The Foreign Office felt that the British case was being given away. The very able and energetic head of the News Department, William Ridsdale,[27] wrote a minute on the day the second article appeared, suggesting that the Russians had probably been shaken by the near-unanimity of the British Press in supporting the British government's line during the negotiations. There was however one exception, wrote Ridsdale:

> The one weak patch in our position is the leader columns of 'The Times', where Professor Carr, with persistence and impartiality, continues to sabotage the policy of the Labour Government and of

---

26 In his biography of Barrington-Ward, *In the Chair*, Donald McLachlan, who was on *The Times* in the relevant period, writes: 'Coming on Printing House Square as a mature and experienced Foreign Office official, Carr had a formidable equipment of knowledge and ideas to which in the office only [Iverach] McDonald, with his detailed knowledge of what was going on from day to day in foreign affairs, could offer effective resistance. Likewise, on economic matters only Maurice Green, City Editor, could stand up to Carr. Sometimes City page comment and the leader page were in contradiction.'

27 Sir William Ridsdale (1890–1957). A former journalist who, after demobilisation in 1918, went to the Ministry of Information where the first overseas news services in morse were being developed. His main work was as head of the Foreign Office News Department, 1941–54.

its predecessors on all matters where Russia and her Eastern Bloc are concerned . . . It is I consider a matter of urgency that Mr. Barrington-Ward should be seen without delay, and should receive a straight talk upon the present issues involved, either by the Secretary of State or by the Prime Minister, otherwise 'The Times' – thanks to Professor Carr – may once again bedevil the situation.[28]

As it happened Barrington-Ward had already asked to call on Bevin for a much postponed first visit. Their discussion, when it took place on October 9, could not have been more friendly. Barrington-Ward recorded what happened after some preliminary talk:

Then he gave me an extremely frank account of proceedings at the conference, describing his open tussles with Molotov. He means to sit tight for a bit. He thinks the Russians are bargaining, trying to see how far they can go and what they can get. They have already got what they wanted out of Winston over Poland and their Western border, and he implied that they would have got still more out of Winston if he had still been there to give it. Now they are bargaining again, and he means to stand fast . . . He was most friendly and open and his forthrightness is refreshing. I am sure we have a good man for the job.[29]

Bevin was no less free and easy when Barrington-Ward met him at a Canadian luncheon party two months later:

I can't help thinking some of Bevin's views a bit naif, for immediate purposes at least, but he is without doubt a big man.[30]

They had their third meeting three months later, on March 11 1946, and it was calamitous. Six days before, Churchill had given his immediately famous speech at Fulton, Missouri, with its warnings about Soviet aggrandisement and its appeals for America and Britain to work in closer military partnership to defend their liberties. Barrington-Ward could in no way welcome the speech but the *Times* reply, in two leading articles on March 6 and March 9, was moderate in tone, chiefly asking with a well-mannered and reasonable air whether there was need for quite so much fuss about Russia's intentions in the world. The first article inquired whether it was really valid to regard western democracy and communism as irreconcilable opposites attempting to divide the earth between them. Though in many respects opposed, they surely had

---

28 Foreign Office Papers. U 8510/5559/70, folios 43–45. Public Record Office.
29 B-W D, October 9 1945.
30 *Ibid*, December 11 1945.

much to learn from each other – 'Communism in the working of political institutions, western democracy in the development of economic and social planning.' Already there existed regimes some way between the two extremes. Recognition of these points 'might well serve to mitigate on both sides some of the asperities of recent exchanges.'[31]

The second leader was a lucid presentation of what in Whitehall was often called the 'Carr line'[32] but Carr was not in the office on the Friday when it was arranged. Barrington-Ward records that before leaving for the country in the early afternoon he talked it over with Tyerman and Rushbrook Williams, and it was Rushbrook Williams who wrote it.[33] It acknowledged that several Soviet actions in Germany, northern Iran, and Manchuria had given offence but invited everyone to see the world predicament from the Soviet leaders' vantage point in a Russia that had so often and for so long faced a hostile west. 'It may be that in their eyes the actions that have inevitably perplexed and dismayed the western democracies stand as merely elementary measures of self-protection.' After going over the story of Soviet–western disputes since the war the leader said that Churchill's emphasis on an Anglo–American military understanding would be taken by Russians as confirmation of their fears, and it asked for face-to-face discussions to resolve the differences. 'If Britain and America can discover directly from the Russians how lively and natural are the fears that underlie Russian policy, they may be able to show that these fears are susceptible of ready alleviation.'[34]

It is unclear whether these two articles angered Bevin more than others that had gone before. What is beyond doubt is that Barrington-Ward was deeply shocked by the violence of the language that assailed him when he went, by appointment, to the Foreign Office. His diary takes up the story of what happened after some minor matters had been disposed of:

> Then he turned to an extraordinary attack on *The Times*. He said it had no policy. It was 'spineless'. It was 'a jellyfish'. It was neither for him nor against him. (Why should it be?) He wouldn't mind if it was either. But it was always 'balancing' – (he made the gesture of twisting his hands with outstretched fingers). (All this of course was about Russia.) . . . *The Times* did great harm. It was taken abroad for a national newspaper. He was going to tell the House of

---

31 Leading article (Carr), March 6 1946.
32 Donald McLachlan, *op. cit.* pp. 245–6, mistakenly states that Carr was the author of the leading article and quotes from it at length as an outstanding example of Carr's thought. Several in the Foreign Office made the same wrong assumption at the time.
33 T.T.A.
34 Leading article (Rushbrook Williams), March 9 1946.

Commons that it was not, and that it was pro-Russian and not pro-British. I had a lot of pink intelligentsia down there and he didn't believe I was in control. (Not intended as a compliment, I fear.)

Bevin widened the attack, first to complain that *The Times* disregarded his own policy as set out on February 21 ('Actually we had a leader on it') and secondly to bring up Greece again. Barrington-Ward reminded him that reputable Greeks had asked for the postponement of the elections before *The Times* had suggested this. 'He said, "Have you ever known a reputable Greek?" Very silly.' By this stage neither man was in a proper state for a rational talk. Barrington-Ward was taken badly off guard and upbraided himself afterwards for taking too quietly the rough and blustering assaults that were far outside his own manner of argument:

This tirade was eked out with a great deal of repetition, many of the things being said two or three times. Naturally it all took me by surprise. I had come quite unprepared for a slanging or shouting match with the Foreign Secretary. The onslaught was so crude that it was almost embarrassing for that reason alone, while the vanity and egotism of it were repellent. I kept calm – too calm, I was annoyed to think afterwards – and told him that *The Times* had a perfectly definite line, was as ready to defend British interests as anyone else, and did its best to apply reason to foreign affairs, and so on.

Like many another man after a surprise attack Barrington-Ward confided to his diary the spirited things he might have said in reply if he had thought of them in time. 'He also deserved to be told he is self-centred, touchy, and intolerant, and more also.' Yet the editor was soon being more true to himself by putting down his considered thoughts:

In truth, I suppose, some allowance should be made for a harassed Minister in an admittedly awkward situation. But my opinion of Bevin is not what it was. Vain men are always limited. He was a fool to try to tackle *The Times* in this way. It could do me no good nor him either.

Having got all this off his chest he shook hands with me twice at parting! I walked along the embankment in the cold east wind which has blown for weeks and arrived at the office having lost my voice.[35]

The row was calamitous in many ways. Barrington-Ward was the last man to be deterred by a rough scolding from what he saw as his line of

---

35 B-W D, March 11 1946.

duty. With a sense of deep responsibility he was ever-conscious of the influence and the standing of *The Times*; he was proud of the line which it had taken under his leadership in home and foreign affairs; he was used to being treated with respect. A meeting between the Foreign Secretary and the editor of *The Times* should be, he took it, something of an occasion, a meeting of minds even if it fell short of agreement. Moreover, at the time of the encounter, he had not fully recovered from the effects of two bouts of influenza during the winter. Men who saw him when he returned to the office thought him as deeply shocked as if he had been in a serious accident.

A few weeks afterwards he rode wholly successfully over what could have been a difficult short course for him within the company itself. He had every reason to be pleased with the result. He emerged with the independence of his position as editor confirmed.

Some of the directors, Conservatives to a man, had been dismayed by the paper's presentation both of Soviet Russia and of the welfare state. In theory and in customary practice Barrington-Ward's independence as editor was safely protected from them by the terms of the paper's constitution that was in effect drawn up by Geoffrey Dawson when he made his own terms for returning to Printing House Square in 1922 to be editor for the second time. An editor was to be responsible not to the whole Board but to the two chief proprietors; they appointed him and they could dismiss him; but, as mentioned in Chapter I, while he was in the chair they were to leave him to run the paper according to his own judgment. Dawson was quite explicit:

> Every Editor worth his salt must have a 'free hand' to conduct his side of the paper as he thinks best so long as he is in charge of it. The power of the Proprietors is exercised properly by the appointment and dismissal of the Editor, not by interfering with his work or doing it themselves.[36]

Naturally, in the college atmosphere of Printing House Square, proprietors and editor talked about the paper informally from time to time. John Astor, while giving Barrington-Ward his support throughout, would sometimes pass on criticisms made to him by his Conservative colleagues in the House of Commons (he sat as member for Dover). He would sometimes also, in his shy way, ask a well-directed question or two, not criticising the paper's policy on, say, the welfare state but rather as one seeking information about the likely consequences of that

---

36 Dawson memorandum, November 18 1922. T.T.A.

policy. John Walter, older in years and in the profession, was moved at times to write Barrington-Ward a remonstratory letter while still balancing himself, a little insecurely, on the convention that he was writing simply as a general reader asking for reassurance and not as a proprietor seeking to interfere. On October 25 1945 he had sent Barrington-Ward a long letter saying that for some time he had felt that *The Times* was 'over-optimistic' about Soviet Russian policy:

The Paper has steadily inculcated the idea that the men who dictate policy in Moscow are animated by the same good intentions as ourselves . . . One day there is bound to be an awakening to the truth and a reaction against the present orgy of brutality (in eastern Europe) now being perpetrated under the patronage of Soviet Russia. It would be regrettable if in days to come *The Times* should be considered to have delayed this reaction rather than to have played a significant part in anticipating it.

In his diary Barrington-Ward called it a 'silly letter' but in his reply to Walter he said with great courtesy that, though by tradition the Russians were difficult neighbours, the best evidence went to show that 'at the present time, whatever may be the case in the future, the Russians do in fact intend cooperation with the West.'

A few months later, in May–June 1946, soon after the unfortunate Bevin meeting, the grumbling among a few directors increased. They talked to John Astor. Astor, giving Barrington-Ward dinner on May 16, asked him almost casually whether he would mind meeting the directors at an informal dinner one evening soon. Barrington-Ward agreed 'perhaps a little thoughtlessly and unguardedly'. Then for some time after accepting he was 'somewhat troubled in my mind'.[37] He asked himself whether he had let himself in for a directorial inquisition and breach of the paper's constitution. Astor, while not explaining why the dinner was being held, gave a hint when saying that David Bowes-Lyon, one of the directors, was 'rather a diehard'. Bowes-Lyon,[38] a brother of Queen Elizabeth the Queen Mother, had become a director in 1939. His friendly ease of manner softened his frequent directness of speech and hid in no way the quality of his sharp, quizzical, simplifying mind. Another director, Sir Campbell Stuart, told Barrington-Ward outright that Bowes-Lyon was the man behind the dinner which (said Campbell Stuart in the first of two talks) was likely to be 'dangerous'. The dinner

---

37 B-W D, June 1 1946.
38 Sir David Bowes-Lyon (1902–1961). Merchant banker, company director and leading horticulturist. Director of The Times Publishing Company from 1939; chairman of the finance committee, June 1955.

was fixed for June 5 and Barrington-Ward set down his uneasiness in his diary:

> The person responsible for this is without doubt David Bowes-Lyon, who has no responsibility for policy at all and should have none. He has evidently been getting at John [Astor], who should have put him in his place but is apt to be a little slow at times to see or remember the editor's constitutional position . . . I am quite clear that I cannot and will not meet the Board, which for this purpose means David Lyon, for a debate on the paper's policy. My responsibility is to John and to him alone. Moreover, why should I be called upon to explain why *The Times* is following a line disapproved by some Conservatives? The general condition of the paper – revenue, circulation, and present repute – should protect me, if nothing else did, under our own roof and in our own family.[39]

Barrington-Ward was near the point of refusing to go to the dinner but, two days before it was due, he had his second talk with Campbell Stuart. After learning more about the affair he ended by being relieved. The suggestion had first been raised at an earlier directors' dinner:

> The malcontent had been David Bowes-Lyon, not unsupported by John Walter (on Russia). David apparently holds to the notion that the board controls or should control editorial policy. The rest undeceived him. John [Astor] absolutely stout and loyal throughout . . . Campbell insisted that there was no question of my being asked to come for a discussion of my policy. Merely I should be asked (by him) to give them, as a matter of interest and from the knowledge which *The Times* may be supposed to have, my view of the main course of home and foreign politics. On hearing all this I made up my mind to say no more to John and to go.[40]

When June 5 came the dinner passed off in the easiest possible way, with the directors devoting themselves purely to the pursuit of knowledge for its own sake. The diary records the crisis that did not happen:

> Went to the great dinner at Carlton House Terrace.[41] Besides John I found John Walter, David Bowes-Lyon, Campbell Stuart, Laurence Irving,[42] and Miles Graham.[43] Campbell put me a leading question

---

39 B-W D, June 1 1946.
40 *Ibid*, June 3 1946.
41 18 Carlton House Terrace, Colonel Astor's town house.
42 Laurence Henry Forster Irving (b. 1897). Director of The Times Publishing Company, 1946–62. Author, book editor and illustrator, artist, art director, film and stage producer and designer.
43 Major-General Sir Miles Graham (1895–1976). After a distinguished military staff

and we had a general talk on politics, keeping it all clear of the paper and its responsibilities, though I was glad to point out once or twice what independence in journalism means and what kind of criticism it is likely to attract. In the end it all seemed quite useful. I judged that we ended up a united party. Back very late to the office.[44]

It had all ended in a typical *Times* way. A warning had been given yet not given. The editor had faced the directors across the friendliest of dinner tables. Each side was aware of what was happening yet no one mentioned it.

Throughout these months new staffing difficulties within Printing House Square and abroad were pressing down on Barrington-Ward, and the heaviest of them was caused by Carr's wish to leave the paper. To Barrington-Ward it was a horrid blow, but by the beginning of 1946 he could regard it as not quite so crippling as it would have been two or three years earlier.

For one thing, Carr had never taken from Barrington-Ward's shoulders the weight of administrative work as Barrington-Ward had taken it from Geoffrey Dawson's.[45] On April 20 1944 Carr had written a long memorandum pointing out, very sensibly, that the editor kept to himself far too much detailed day-to-day work, administrative and editorial, which he could easily delegate to three or four others, leaving himself uncluttered for the big decisions. Barrington-Ward was curiously annoyed by the memorandum, thinking that Carr was trying to diminish his role (although editors who succeeded him found that delegation was both necessary and helpful). A month later Carr said that he at any rate wished to drop administrative work; he would confine himself to writing leaders and deputising in the editor's chair. Even this new arrangement did not wholly please either man. Barrington-Ward could never be sure that Carr's powerful and highly individual mind properly grasped the need to work within an agreed policy.

Beyond that, Carr – strong in views – could be slow in picking up news. He irritated and dismayed Barrington-Ward (away for the weekend) by not having any leading article at all when the United States opened the new era in war by dropping the first atomic bomb on Japan. The only comment carried by *The Times* on the morning of August 7

---

career in both world wars, he returned to business administration and was a director of The Times Publishing Company, 1946–62.

44 B-W D, June 5 1946.
45 See Chapter II.

1945 was a leaderish note by the diplomatic correspondent. Barrington-Ward had to face the plain truth that *The Times* had fallen behind other papers:

> Grabbed *The Times* from Bedford railway bookstall. Alas, no leader on the bomb . . . From what I heard on arrival at the office, a leader should have been manageable. I fear that Carr missed the significance of the event in the first messages. Too little journalistic imagination. At this same time Andrade[46] refused to write a special article on the ground that he knew too much and was afraid of giving something away. Got him going today and, later, got Morrah on to a leader.[47]

By this time Carr had said that he wished to withdraw wholly from the staff in order to be free for writing on a larger scale than any newspaper could provide. Morison comforted Barrington-Ward by saying again that Carr would never fit wholly within a team. None the less there were many sincere regrets when Carr left Printing House Square at the end of July 1946 to begin his many-volumed *History of Soviet Russia*. His departure was another demonstration that *The Times*, anonymous and highly centralised as it was in those days, could not allow itself the stimulus and the excitement of a columnist, even of the highest rank.

Barrington-Ward's diaries show how much time and thought he felt called upon to give to finding staff in the years immediately after the war. Finding a foreign leader writer to take the place of Carr seemed to be unexpectedly easy. Con O'Neill,[48] who had resigned from the Foreign Office over Munich and gone back during the war, joined *The Times* on May 1 1946 shortly before Carr left. During the next year, in his severely intellectual and always lucid style, he explored without any false hopes the widening rift between the Soviet Union and the western powers as the four-power conference of foreign ministers collapsed in the spring of 1947. When General George Marshall rallied the west with his plan for economic recovery, *The Times* was wholeheartedly behind the plan. O'Neill was one of the first to see that close economic

---

46 Professor Edward Neville da Costa Andrade (1887–1971). St. Dunstan's College; University College London. Scientific Adviser to Director of Scientific Research, Ministry of Supply during Second World War. Science correspondent of *The Times*, 1945–52.
47 B-W D, August 7 1945.
48 Sir Con O'Neill (b. 1912). Eton; Balliol College, Oxford. Diplomatic Service, 1936–39; resigned. Army, 1940–43. Foreign Office, 1943–46. Leader writer and special writer on foreign affairs, *The Times*, 1946–47. Returned to Foreign Office, 1947. Deputy Under-Secretary of State, Foreign and Commonwealth Office, 1969–72.

partnership must lead on to close political partnership. Yet newspaper work was not his vocation. He was never entirely happy when having to make speedy judgments without the full documentation that he had had in the Foreign Office; he left to return to Whitehall in May 1947.

For a time Barrington-Ward had hoped that Con O'Neill would be more than a leader writer for him, perhaps even a foreign editor. He had also hoped that Peter Fleming, once returned from the war, would play a big part in the paper; he even thought that if Fleming had shown only a little interest in politics, which he did not, he could have been editor one day. But Fleming had no wish to tie himself to a full-time job on the paper; he promised simply to write more of his excellent light leaders for it. For his immediate help Barrington-Ward was therefore left with two good men: Tyerman, to whom he often referred as a 'pillar of good sense and ability', and Casey, full of shrewdness and experience, 'in many ways a tower of strength but rather negative'.[49] Shortly before leaving for Canada and the United States in the autumn of 1946 Barrington-Ward discussed with these two colleagues the talent available within the office:

> Talked over staff. There is an awkward gap after the assistant editors. The four likeliest of the younger men are McDonald, O'Neill, Michael Burn and Oliver Woods. McDonald should be the first to have a chance of showing what he can do in control of proofs etc. at night.[50]

McDonald was duly told to be ready to sit in at nights while still being diplomatic correspondent. Michael Burn had returned from a German prisoner-of-war camp. After being in the foreign department as a young man before the war he had served as a commando officer and had been captured, after being nearly drowned, in the raid on St. Nazaire on March 27–28 1942. Dashing and highly intellectual, he was very much the cavalier. When the alternatives were put to him, he chose the freedom of a foreign correspondent rather than the confines of the office and was soon sent to Vienna. Austria was then occupied by the four allied powers and – thinking that here was a good part of Europe's problem in miniature – Burn set out to meet Austrian communists and as many Russians as he could, all in the effort to learn what was in their minds. His despatches did not support the black-and-white picture of the cold war; the Foreign Office, but not *The Times*, was sometimes perturbed at their tone.[51] Burn reported the Belgrade trial of Mihailo-

---

49 B-W D, December 23 1945.
50 Ibid, September 3 1946.
51 Foreign Office complaints are contained in State Papers that are indexed but not

vic, the Yugoslav Chetnik leader, and a despatch of his which appeared on July 12 1946 first used the evocative phrase – 'the gale of the world' – that was taken up and widely quoted. Burn took it down as his interpreter was translating Mihailovic's defence speech:

I wanted much, I started much, but the gale of the world carried away me and my work.

Oliver Woods[52] was another man who returned after a very gallant war record. He had fought across North Africa, up the length of Italy, and then across France into Germany, and came back with an unchanged manner that might be taken for diffidence except by those who knew him well. He was to become one of the top three on the editorial side in the later years of Sir William Haley's editorship. Barrington-Ward first put him on an all-night stint in helping the night editor but then he was given work that fitted him better as assistant diplomatic correspondent. Early in 1948 he was sent off to accompany Hilary Marquand, Paymaster-General in the Labour government, on a tour of Africa. This kindled his interest in the black continent and set him almost by chance on to the work that made his name, first as colonial correspondent, then as colonial editor.[53]

Little of this helped to solve Barrington-Ward's chief problem which was to gather one or two tough administrators around him. But several other leader writers and correspondents were recruited from outside or arrived back in the office from war service. For all the appointments Barrington-Ward kept to his plan, described in Chapter II, of choosing acknowledged experts in their fields, usually men with high academic qualifications. It was a plan which provided much stiff reading in the paper at times but produced more successes than failures. He had already won Maurice Green back to the financial and economic side. In March 1946 he brought in Duncan Burn, an authority on the steel industry and on pricing policy, to be leader-writer and industrial correspondent. Burn's writings were followed closely in Whitehall and big

---

released under the fifty years rule.

52 Oliver Frederick John Bradley Woods (1911–1972). Marlborough; New College, Oxford. Joined *The Times* in 1934; sent for a period as assistant to the Munich correspondent; at PHS he had various editorial duties, including sub-editing and work in the letters department. War service, 1939–45; MC (1943) and mentioned in despatches. Returned to *The Times* as assistant to the editor, 1945; colonial correspondent, 1948–56; colonial editor and assistant foreign editor, 1956–61; assistant editor (home), 1961–65; deputy managing editor, 1965–67; chief assistant to editor-in-chief, Times Newspapers Ltd. from 1967; chairman, steering committee, editorial methods study, 1968–69.
53 See Chapter XIV.

business. His mind was a mass of specialised information out of which he quarried weighty and many-angled paragraphs which the editor or his deputy had very often to straighten out for the benefit of the non-specialist reader without (the reviser sometimes vainly hoped) losing the main points of Burn's argument. To take the place of J. V. Radcliffe, soon to retire from being labour correspondent and leader writer, *The Times* brought in Eric Wigham,[54] a Birmingham graduate who served on northern papers before showing his true merit as labour correspondent of the *Manchester Guardian*.

In the foreign field the need for men was greater than ever in the paper's history. Broad areas of the world that had been shut by war were opened up again. Old posts had to be filled and additional posts had to be set up as new countries were emerging from out of the faltering colonial empires. As *The Times* faced this change-over from war to peace both Morison and Carr told Barrington-Ward that Deakin, the foreign news editor, who had been splendid in deploying men during the war, had not the right approach to the new age. On his side Deakin had seldom worked easily with Carr whose position and influence in the office he resented. Barrington-Ward's own doubts grew:

> Trouble with Deakin who appears to be going on leave without having provided for the representation of the paper either in Germany or, still worse, the Far East.[55]

Ten days later:

> I am horrified to find how Deakin has let our foreign service down and what fearful gaps he has tolerated in it. We have no one in Germany, no one in the Far East ready to land in Japan, no one in Norway to report the Quisling trial.

Then came the typical addendum from a man working fifteen or sixteen hours a day:

> I shall have to tackle all this.[56]

Swift moves were made across the board. Frank Hawley,[57] hastily recruited, was sent to Japan and was before long in disfavour with the

---

54 Eric Leonard Wigham (b. 1904). Ackworth and Bootham Schools; Birmingham University. Labour correspondent of *The Times*, 1946–69. Member, Royal Commission on Trade Unions and Employers' Associations, 1965–68.
55 B-W D, August 13 1945.
56 *Ibid*, August 23 1945.
57 Frank H. Hawley (1906–1961). Universities of Liverpool, Cambridge, Paris and Berlin. On staff Tokyo School of Foreign Languagues and Tokyo University of Science and Literature, 1930–39. Director of British Library and member of Ministry

American commander-in-chief, General Douglas MacArthur. Ian Morrison remained in South-East Asia to describe, with outstanding skill and deep perception, the mental and physical struggles of the peoples there as their leaders reached out for independence. The Indian sub-continent was well looked after by Bob Cooper, who returned to take James Holburn's place. He was soon to be joined by a young man, Louis Heren,[58] scarcely known then, whose intelligence, courage and drive were to win him a career which few *Times* men have equalled. Heren began work before the war as a messenger boy at the front door of Printing House Square; he was moved to the advertising department where he tried his hand at writing copy; a commission during the war brought out his talents; on his return he was taken on by the editorial department at the suggestion of George Pope, then advertisement manager, who had been greatly struck by his capability. His despatches from India, most memorably covering the massacres during the months of partition, showed a determination that became stronger in him: to make his despatches set the record straight about the deeds and misdeeds of men in authority, no matter how much he upset them. Caminada was another correspondent who covered the stormy aftermath of the war in the Far East. He was several times at risk in Malaya and Vietnam as well as earlier in Palestine, yet no correspondent worked with less fuss. He could move to a new area of disturbance and get off the first of his objective despatches from there – all with a speed and apparent ease which both hid and revealed a highly organised mind.

To Germany *The Times* sent John Buist[59] and John Freeman.[60] John

---

of Information, HM Embassy, Tokyo, 1939–41. Arrested by Japanese in December, 1941, interrogated for over a hundred days and spent more than eight months in solitary confinement. Repatriated to Britain, he worked for the BBC and Foreign Office until the end of the war. *The Times* correspondent in Tokyo, 1946–52. His reports did not always find favour with General MacArthur and questions were asked in the Commons about him in June, 1950. A devoted student of Japanese culture, he wrote a large number of articles on Japanese history, bibliography and literature.

---

58 Louis Philip Heren (b. 1919). Entered *The Times* service as a front door messenger, 1934. Transferred as office boy to the publishing department the following year. After war service rejoined publishing department, 1945; reporter, 1946; correspondent in Delhi, Middle East, Korea, Singapore and Bonn, 1947–60; Washington correspondent, 1960; American editor, 1969–70; returned to PHS as deputy editor and foreign editor in 1970; in January 1978 he became home editor while remaining deputy editor; March 1981 associate editor. Resigned October 1981. A director of Times Newspapers, 1981–82.
59 John Stewart Buist (1905–1982). Glasgow University. After early journalistic work in Dundee and as assistant to the London editor of the *Courier*, joined editorial staff of *Glasgow Herald*; 1934–39 foreign leader writer in succession to James Holburn. After war service came to *The Times* in 1945; correspondent in Germany, 1945–51;

Buist was another man who was to rise in *The Times*. He made a strong political impact, in Britain and elsewhere, with his carefully detailed despatches on the rearmament of eastern Germany. During Stalin's blockade of the city his evidence about the growing success of the allied air bridge came, day by day, as a corrective to the many doubters in London – even some in Printing House Square – who thought the bridge was too good to last. John Freeman had been a senior foreign sub-editor for many years before helping out with the leading articles during the war. In western Germany, where he married a German wife, he developed a sincere admiration for Dr. Konrad Adenauer, and his messages – much warmer in tone towards the Chancellor than many of the *Times* leading articles – helped readers to understand that the west Germans had fully committed themselves to the western side.

In Paris no men could have been more oddly or more pleasantly balanced than the two, Gerald Norman and Basil Davidson,[61] who were posted there. Though Norman would never let his private inclinations affect his work, he leaned to the right while Davidson was to the left. There were days when Norman would be listening in his room to, say, two prominent French monarchists while Davidson was talking next door no less contentedly to a group of incognito Bulgarian communists. The partnership worked well. Gerald Norman, wholly bilingual, his mother being French, had come to Paris with the southern liberating forces and stayed on to describe de Gaulle's France with the special insight of one who could think as a Frenchman, and a highly intelligent and lucid Frenchman at that. Davidson's left-wing ardour had grown in him when he was serving with Tito's partisans in wartime Yugoslavia. He seemed to carry the wartime excitement with him in other ways: he had an engaging enthusiasm about him. Like Michael Burn he would have liked to be sent either to Moscow or to report on the new regimes of eastern Europe; he had the two advantages of being an insatiable

---

Ottawa, 1951–52; NW Europe, 1954–55; returned to the foreign news department in 1956 and covered the momentous events of 1956 in Austria, Hungary and Poland; foreign news editor from 1958 until his retirement in 1964.

60 John Henry Freeman (1889–1964). Started as an editorial apprentice on the *Nottingham Express* in 1903 and followed this with journalistic work on papers in Sussex and Yorkshire. *The Times* foreign sub-editor, 1926; deputy chief sub-editor, 1935; leader writer during the war; correspondent in Paris, 1945; United Nations (New York), 1946; Berlin, 1946–49; Bonn, 1949–54; Geneva from 1954 until retirement in 1962.

---

61 Basil Risbridger Davidson (b. 1914). Editorial staff, the *Economist*, 1938–39. A correspondent for *The Times* in Paris, 1945–47; leader writer, 1947–49. Special correspondent on *New Statesman* and *Daily Herald*, 1950–57; leader writer, *Daily Mirror*, 1959–62.

political scholar and a brilliant linguist. But in 1947 he was brought back, rather unwillingly at first, to London to take over Con O'Neill's desk as leader writer.

Not the most urgent but none the less the most serious problem lay in Washington. For over twenty years Sir Willmott Lewis[62] had combined in himself all the virtues of experienced correspondent, gifted essayist, highly original character, and revered institution. Both by reason of his work and by reason of his handsome, tall, always quizzical but wholly kindly presence – with his deeply resonant voice providing a never failing background music to that presence – he was for many years the unchallenged dean of the foreign press corps in Washington. In the days before regular press conferences he frequently saw the successive Presidents for private talks, and at his own house he was a host of ambassadorial urbanity and attentiveness when entertaining senators and State Department officials.

He worked entirely according to his own rules. He reported the news with precision, usually but not always on the day it happened; his own preference was to keep it, distil it and present it perhaps a day or two late in a rarefied form with many an epigram to enliven it. He gave not the outward form but the essence. 'I pay attention', he would say, knowing that he was slightly mocking himself, 'not to the wind movements but to the *tidal* movements of political change.' Claud Cockburn,[63] who served with him before the war, used to recall Lewis's remark on a flamboyant senator: 'That man has the unique distinction of combining in his sole person *all* the disadvantages attaching to the democratic form of government'. And there was another equally pleasant observation of his: 'An atheist is a man without invisible means of support.'

One of the most steadfast of his working rules was to disregard instructions from Printing House Square – if indeed by any rare chance Printing House Square so far forgot itself as to send instructions. He would hold himself *incommunicado* for months. Something of the frustration caused is shown in a letter to him from Geoffrey Dawson, written on January 28 1935, referring to a letter written four months before:

---

62 Sir Willmott Harsant Lewis (1877–1950). Worked as a journalist in England, the Philippines, Far East (including coverage of the Boxer Rebellion and Russo–Japanese War) and USA, prior to joining the foreign department of *The Times* in 1920. Washington correspondent from 1920 until retirement in 1948.
63 Claud Cockburn (1904–81). Berkhamsted School; Keble College, Oxford; Universities of Budapest and Berlin. Correspondent for *The Times* in Berlin, 1927; Paris, 1928; New York and Washington, 1929–32. Editor, *The Week*, 1933–46; diplomatic and foreign correspondent, *Daily Worker*, 1935–46, and contributor to numerous other journals.

I wrote to you on September 26 to ask whether you would like a change of station e.g. to Paris if it could be arranged . . . I told you then that there was no urgent hurry about a decision, and I was not altogether surprised to receive no answer, though a general indication of your views would have been helpful . . . On October 10 I wrote to you again . . . Having still heard nothing from you I cabled on October 22 asking for an indication of your views on my two private letters; and on the following day I did at last receive a long and rather vague, but generally negative message, which ended however by saying 'letter follows'. For this promised letter I decided to wait.

It had not come by November 13; so I cabled you that day to ask where it was and received the answer 'Letter soon.' On December 6 it had still not reached me, and I cabled again to say so. From that time I have heard nothing whatever . . . The whole incident, as you must realize, is extremely unsatisfactory.[64]

Lewis replied a month later, February 27, in a long letter beginning, 'There is nothing to do but beat my breast and cry my culp.' But contrition did not lead to reform. Shortly before the war, when he was on leave in Britain, Dawson had another go at him, telling him to his face that originality was all very well but he really must reply to communications; at all events to letters or telegrams signed by Dawson himself. Willmott Lewis, who never forgot that he had been an actor for a short time, backed sorrowfully towards the door, and, as he backed, he drew his long hands slowly and repeatedly in two wide converging arcs towards his waistcoat. 'Your words are arrows to my heart,' he intoned. 'Arrows to my heart.' He opened the door behind him and stepped back, still gesticulating, into the shadows of the corridor, never to be seen in Printing House Square again.[65]

When the war ended Lewis was in his late sixties and was getting about Washington much less. After considering other possible successors, including Ian Morrison and Robin Cruikshank (later editor of the *News Chronicle*), Barrington-Ward picked on John Duncan Miller,[66] first mentioned to him by Geoffrey Crowther, then editor of the

---

64 T.T.A.
65 As recounted by Geoffrey Dawson and William Casey.
66 John Duncan Miller (1902–1977). Wellington; Trinity Hall, Cambridge. Director of British Information Services in Chicago, 1945–47. After a year deputising for Sir Willmott Lewis, became chief Washington correspondent of *The Times*, 1948–54. Resigned to become special representative for Europe of the International Bank for Reconstruction and Development (World Bank), 1955–68.

Economist. Miller had been much praised for his wartime work as head of the British Information Services in Chicago. He was as much a character in his way as Willmott Lewis; ever active, friendly, intuitive; willingly and incurably addicted to the American political scene. He had not done full-time journalistic work but his wife, as much caught up in politics as he was, wrote weekly articles from America for the *Economist*. The choice of Miller was another example of Barrington-Ward's refusal to be bound by routine procedures for appointments; he passed over men who thought themselves entitled to step up into a vacancy, and he cast around until he thought he had found the most knowledgeable man in the field, whether the man was a journalist or not. Miller brought both knowledge and excitement into the messages from Washington.

Throughout these busy months of 1946 and 1947 Barrington-Ward seldom had a quiet lunch or dinner to himself or with his wife, except during the short week-ends in the country. Only a few of the meals were pure relaxation. He always looked forward to dinner with his great friends, the Canadian High Commissioner, Vincent Massey, and his wife. The easy, informal talks with Massey, a Canadian diplomatist of the reflective, broad-sighted type that was to bring Canada to the fore in the world councils, were of great comfort to him. They strengthened him in the view, made plain in the leaders, that the Commonwealth and Empire must go on de-centralising in the hope that thereby a spirit of equal partnership would be strengthened. For discussions on Palestine he several times saw, without wholly agreeing with, Lewis Namier. As the Jewish claims mounted *The Times* quickly recognised that Palestine had to be divided but, like the British government itself, it had continually to adjust its views to the changing balance of forces. On India Barrington-Ward took care to have strong correspondents reporting regularly from there; and in London, where he slowly came to the view that partition of the sub-continent was inevitable, he had long talks with the successive Viceroys, Lord Wavell and Lord Mountbatten, and with Hindu and Muslim leaders. In other ways he kept up *The Times's* traditional concern with the Commonwealth.

It was an exhausting pace and colleagues began to notice a flagging in his energy. Back in October 1945 his brother Lancelot, the distinguished surgeon, had told him after examining him that he needed three months' holiday, 'which I fear is right'.[67] For all that, he went on working. At home in the country just before the new year he was feeling so much below par that when finally influenza was diagnosed it came

---

67 B-W D, October 31 1945.

almost as a relief 'since it accounted for otherwise disturbing symptoms of the past few days'.[68]

Unfortunately the influenza did not 'account for' the disturbing symptoms; it merely covered them up for a time. In the coming months his colleagues saw a more painful deterioration in him. His brisk walking pace slowed down, his shoulders stiffened, his small handwriting became minute and often difficult to decipher, he seemed to find it hard to concentrate, and was clearly forcing himself along by his unbroken will power.

---

68 B-W D, December 30 1945.

VII

NEW EDITOR, NEW MANAGER

In the years immediately after the war the four national 'quality papers' – *The Times*, the *Daily Telegraph*, the *Manchester Guardian*, and the *Financial Times* – could look forward to the next ten or fifteen years with a new confidence. Taken together the four papers were to add ten per cent to their circulation before 1955 was reached.

Partly they were helped by the unsettled state of the world. Faced with all the upheavals more people wished to have their serious news seriously presented. Some of these new readers had been led to take an interest in public affairs by the excellent educational services in the armed forces. Longer schooling gave the impetus to others. Television was not yet a powerful rival. Even though the nine o'clock news each evening on the BBC radio had become one of the main sources of news, men and women still wished to confirm with their eyes, in the papers the next morning, what they had heard the night before. Serious newspapers felt a duty to supply the printed record almost as though broadcasting did not exist. In fact the newspapers had to face only one heavy handicap – a truly heavy one – and that was the continuation of newsprint rationing, fettering the quality newspapers much more than the popular ones, and constricting *The Times* worst of all.[1]

In general the commercial prospects for *The Times* in those early post-war years were part reassuring, part troubling. It was still making the modest profits which it had made during the war. The small size of the paper, eight pages one day, ten another, reduced the expenditure on newsprint. Income had been boosted by raising the charge for advertisements from £2 to £3, and then to £4, a column inch, and the selling price had been put up to 3d. in 1942. On the debit side the price of newsprint had quadrupled from £10 a ton at the beginning of the war to £40 a ton at the end, and the newsprint rationing meant that sales of the paper were still restricted.

How this restriction held back *The Times* was seen beyond all doubt

---

1 See Chapter XV.

on September 22 1946 when the rationing was slightly eased. That night the print order – that is to say, the number of papers printed in confident expectation of sales – jumped from 233,000 to 276,000, and throughout the following weeks the actual sales kept close to the higher figure. At the end of June 1947, after the government imposed a new cut in the supply of paper, the circulation had to be pegged at 268,769 – that figure being set by working out the average circulation during the four weeks ending June 29 1947.

It was a frustrating time for all in Printing House Square, knowing that the paper could sell much more, yet those who had to make the decisions – the Board of directors, the editor, and the manager – were entirely agreed throughout those years on how the available newsprint should be allocated. They used it to publish a recognisable *Times*, one that necessarily had fewer pages but retained most of its main features, rather than going out to gain a larger circulation for a still further reduced *Times*. When, on June 5 1947, Barrington-Ward made a special application to Sir Stafford Cripps, President of the Board of Trade, he asked for more newsprint not to increase circulation but to increase the size of *The Times*. The paper felt the restrictions more keenly than others because, with so much of its space committed to long parliamentary reports, law reports, and official documentation, it had very often to leave out much distinctive writing and indeed much hard news.

The editor and manager had also to face the disagreeable knowledge that other serious newspapers were expanding. The *Daily Telegraph*, well packed with news each day, had overtaken its pre-war circulation and reached 788,000 in 1945; it was still moving ahead. In the first six months of 1949 it reached 990,281 when *The Times* was still at 262,055. Where most of the national papers were helped to cover the country by being printed in Manchester as well as in London, *The Times*, printed only in London, had to admit to itself that nine-tenths of its circulation lay within 175 miles of the capital.

Most ominously of all, its share of the national readership was dropping. In the second year of the First World War it could claim 5.56 per cent of the national readership; in the second year of the Second World War that share had dropped to 1.82 per cent, and in 1948 it had dropped still further to 1.62 per cent. Advertising in *The Times* was still buoyant in the years immediately after the war, and George Pope, in charge of advertising, could count on a revival of the lucrative company meeting columns, the property advertisements, and the situations vacant, always provided *The Times* could get more paper. But the figures about its falling share in the national readership would in the long run tend to discourage advertisements, and especially the large 'prestige' advertisements placed by the great companies to keep their names before the public.

In 1947 Colonel Astor and a few members of his Board became convinced that the manager, C. S. Kent, should leave the paper as he approached retiring age; he would be sixty-five in 1949. Kent had worked all hours during the war; throughout those years when both expenditure and income could have been chaotic he kept the accounts under control and showing a profit.[2] He had emergency plans to cover anything that might happen. His resultant tiredness showed itself in many ways. His talk became quieter, more shy, and much more cautious. He tried to keep more and more matters in his own hands. His motto was safety, and he seemed to see an unadventurous future for *The Times*, stable in circulation or growing only slightly, not competing with other papers in its payment of salaries, careful of its prestige, avoiding financial loss but not expecting large profits, and being supported by its better-paying *Educational Supplement* and other subsidiary publications. Essentially Kent saw himself as a trustee, ensuring that no harm came to the trust property – *The Times* – which Colonel Astor was holding with great pride and little profit in the national interest.

Kent's growing tiredness and sense of insecurity were shown in his treatment of the new assistant manager, Frank Waters, nearly thirty years his junior. The two men were opposites in character and in methods of work. Waters, the colonel in the Royal Marines and the international rugby player who was capped eight times for Scotland, was friendly and unembarrassed in manner. Where Kent's background was accountancy Waters had made his name by starting the Sunday edition of the *Scottish Daily Express* and buying the *Evening Citizen* for the Beaverbrook group. In the spring of 1946 Waters sent Kent a memorandum – copy to Barrington-Ward – suggesting that copies of *The Times* should be flown each day to Scotland instead of going by train. Waters supported the suggestion with several wider thoughts on how *The Times* could develop:

> Is there to be an expansion of circulation to meet the needs of the growing better-educated public? Is there to be a widening of the influence of Printing House Square, not only throughout the British Isles but all over the world – a development that can only take place provided the paper is as good as it can be made, provided the element of time-lag can be overcome, and cost of delivery to the reader be established on an equitable basis? These are questions for decision on the highest level.[3]

2 See Chapter III.
3 T.T.A.

Kent suspected that he was in the line of fire, and he shelved the memorandum. Waters had however been discussing it with Herbert Russell, the night editor, and others on the editorial side. This got back to Astor who, more than a little irritated at being kept in the dark, asked Kent to produce the memorandum:

> So on May 16 the board will have before it a recommendation on policy by the Asst. Manager with which the Manager almost totally disagrees . . . He [Kent] has fretted himself into a highly wrought state.[4]

The row ended tamely as such sudden rows in an office often do. The Board blessed the idea of air transport but sagely said that any action must await the end of newsprint rationing and the result of more inquiries into the cost and the reliability of the air services. Personal feelings were not so easily pacified. Kent, convinced that an attempt had been made to by-pass him and to undermine his authority, never forgave Waters. Some of the directors thought that Waters had spoken in the office a little too freely about his memorandum and they asked themselves again whether he was the right man to succeed Kent.

Waters stayed on until 1949 when he left to manage the *Star* and soon became the managing director of both *News Chronicle* and the *Star*. But Kent himself did not escape blame. Astor and some of the directors criticised him for sitting on Waters's luckless memorandum in the first place; and their criticism broadened. Barrington-Ward was caught in the backwash.

> Dined with J.J.A. [Astor] at 18 C.H.T. [Carlton House Terrace]. He is evidently determined to part with Kent – and he has the inflexible determination of all the Astors. Does not really like Kent. Thinks Kent never really gave Waters a fair deal (and certainly, though I don't think Waters a possible manager, Kent mishandled him), and resents what he regards as Kent's condescension to the Board.[5]

Earlier in 1947 Harold Hartley had suggested that John Astor's eldest son, Gavin,[6] should be considered as a possible managing director. Gavin Astor was then close on thirty. After serving during the war as an officer in the Life Guards he had been taken prisoner in 1944. When

---

4 B-W D, April 12 1946.
5 *Ibid*, October 22 1947.
6 Gavin Astor, 2nd Baron Astor of Hever (1918–1984). Eton; New College, Oxford. Director, The Times Publishing Company, 1952–66; chairman, 1959–66; life-president, Times Newspapers from 1967. Succeeded father, 1971.

released he was eager to learn all he could about his inheritance and spent some time in each department of *The Times*. After John Astor had almost casually mentioned the managerial proposal to Barrington-Ward,[7] the editor lost no time in going to see Hartley to point out some of the constitutional difficulties if the future chief proprietor were to be managing director as well.[8] Hartley said that he had put the idea forward chiefly to force a decision about a successor to Kent. On June 8 Astor, Hartley, and Barrington-Ward agreed that the proposal should be forgotten and that it would be far better for Gavin to learn more about the managerial side from experience on papers abroad.

Both Hartley and Barrington-Ward then suggested John Elliott, assistant manager of the Southern Railway and a former journalist, as a possible successor to Kent.[9] This idea was taken up strongly, but Kent fought back by declaring that no newcomer could learn within a few months a job which had taken him twenty-five years to learn. He suggested that George Pope and Stanley Morison be appointed assistant managers while he soldiered on as manager.[10] In the end the Elliott proposal came to nothing. On October 31 1947 the directors quickly rejected Elliott's condition that he be given a ten-year contract, and the year ended with the managerial question still wide open.

Unhappily during these same months of 1947 another and graver question arose. Barrington-Ward's health had failed so relentlessly and so distressingly that it had to be asked how long he could go on. For years he had put in a fifteen-hour or sixteen-hour day, most of it at great tension. He wrote memoranda to government ministries and letters to staff correspondents – sometimes to busybodies outside – of the kind which almost any editor a generation later would devolve more firmly upon others. He spent hours on office administration and on staff appointments.

Breakfast and the first part of the morning had him reading the other newspapers and going through *The Times* again to see what should be followed up or had been missed. The later morning was passed in the office, dealing with his own correspondence, fixing up special articles, presiding at the morning news conference attended by heads of department, and having the first talk of the day on leading articles. Lunch was seldom any break, being usually a working affair with a government minister, a leading member of the opposition, an ambassador, or two or

---

7 B-W D, May 20 1947.
8 *Ibid*, May 21 1947.
9 *Ibid*, June 8 1947.
10 *Ibid*, July 15 1947.

three colleagues. Afternoon began with his going through and choosing for publication the letters to the editor, then another news conference, another talk on leaders, and precious minutes given to one or two visitors whom he had not been able to avoid seeing. Early evening had the leaders coming to his desk, usually to be revised at speed. Dinner was once again, like lunch, almost always a working meal; even if he went for relaxation to one of his clubs he was as like as not to be set upon for some view or other expressed in *The Times*. Then back to the office at night, revising the leaders to bring them up to date in accordance with the latest news; sometimes in emergency writing a leader himself, with one eye on the racing clock; or, if it was a quiet night, he would frequently make it a busy one by dictating a letter to one or two of the correspondents abroad.

He tried to keep the weekends to himself and his family. Very often such hopes were disappointed. Especially when he was short of staff he would go back to London a day before he had planned. Or he would write a long memorandum: once it was on the lack of newsprint, another time on what the Press Council, eventually set up in 1953, should do. On top of all such work he attended meetings of deliberative committees of his old school, Westminster, and his old college, Balliol, and gave to such meetings the conscientious thought that he devoted to everything he did.

Tyerman took more of the administrative load after working himself in, and during 1947 Barrington-Ward began at last to believe that his leader writing staff was strong enough:

Some good leaders this week. Davidson has begun well. Carr [no longer on the permanent staff] has weighed in quite in the old form on the Marshall offer [of economic help to Europe], which seems more and more important. Lafitte wrote a really outstanding article on the deficiencies of the building industry. Tonight Davidson did well on the foreign affairs debate.[11]

On the debit side Casey, the wise counsellor, was often under the weather and the diary contains more complaints about Deakin's direction of the foreign news department. About this time Barrington-Ward decided to make McDonald an assistant editor who would take his turn in relieving the editor at night, although no formal announcement was made at the time.

Barrington-Ward still forced himself along, refusing to admit by any spoken word that he was ill, that his speech was slower, his walking pace

11 B-WD, June 19 1947.

without its old spring, his balance sometimes uncertain. Only in his diary did he express his impatience and his growing bewilderment. On May 6 1947 he had a thorough overhaul by a Harley Street doctor:

[He] evidently thinks I am overworked and overtired, as indeed I am – look at my tell-tale handwriting!

Other examinations were made in the following weeks:

Says I ought to go straight to bed for 3 weeks. I can't yet but will when my holiday begins. (July 22.)

Blood pressure back to near normal – 120. But I feel no real recuperation at work in spite of this marvellous holiday [at St. Margaret's Bay, Kent]. Slow and tired – handwriting difficult. These are symptoms attributed to overwork. But I think there must be some more specific cause. (Undated; August–early September.)

What he did not know was that he had Parkinson's Disease. The symptoms became plainer as the weeks went on, but the possibility was kept from him:

I am not feeling anything like 'illness' but I am slow, weak, and a little unsteady in my balance, and other symptoms persist. What can the cause be? (September 8.)

Trying to shorten my 16-hour day. (September 16.)

On November 13 John Astor, prompted by Stanley Morison in a memorandum and by others verbally, suggested to Barrington-Ward in the gentlest and most tactful of ways that he take a three months' holiday. The doctors reinforced the advice. Sir Campbell Stuart, a director of the P. & O. Line, came forward with the offer of a cabin on the Durban Castle, leaving for South Africa on January 1. True to character Barrington-Ward went on working, except for a break at Christmas, until the very eve of his departure. On his last day in London he gave lunch at the Ritz Grill to Casey and Tyerman. 'Left them my ideas about staff, etc.' In Printing House Square during the afternoon he dictated a letter to the Master of Balliol recommending L. B. Namier and E. H. Carr, in that order, for the Montague Burton chair of international relations (neither candidate was successful). He also wrote to Willmott Lewis, 'asking very gently about his plans'; and then, punctilious to the end,

Called in heads of depts. and said my farewells.[12]

---

12 *Ibid*, December 31 1947.

His colleagues hid their sad thoughts, but few of them expected to see him in the editor's chair again. He and his wife arrived in Capetown on January 17 1948 after a good rest on the outward voyage. At Durban on January 25 they met Mrs Cecilia Dawson, Geoffrey Dawson's widow, who suggested that a doctor could advise them whether they should go on up the east coast of Africa in the great heat. The doctor saw no objections and, as they moved up from port to port on board the Llangibby Castle, they had many meetings with representative men and women who took them on brief tours and gave small parties for them.

Barrington-Ward picked out a man here and there who could be useful for *The Times*. He began writing an introduction to a volume of *The Times Broadsheets* that had been distributed among the troops during the war. Almost every day he wrote down a line or two of judgment on the men and women whom they met. In the very last entry in his diary, dated Wednesday, February 11 1948, he describes being greeted at Tanga by E. F. Hitchcock, once Warden of Toynbee Hall and at that time chairman of the sisal growers' association: 'Expansive, viewy, a strong critic, unorthodox, rather original, a man of taste . . . A great upholder of the African.'

On Sunday February 29 *The Times* received a cable from Alan Neville, the local correspondent with the *Tanganyika Herald*. Barrington-Ward had died the day before on board ship in the harbour at Dar-es-Salaam. An attack of cerebral malaria brought death after only two days in bed and spared him longer torment from the Parkinson's Disease which even in its slow opening stages during the previous few months had brought him so much frustration and distress as his body began to falter and disobey his unbroken will.

On Monday March 1 his death was announced on *The Times* main news page and under the brief notice appeared a personal appreciation written by the two or three men in the office who knew him best. They were writing in haste while still shocked by the news. Though there is much to add there is nothing to take away from their assessment:

Barrington-Ward's standards, personal and professional, were high. By nature he was just, scrupulous, exact. The strict rule he applied to his subordinates he imposed upon himself. No servant of Printing House Square in the present generation has exacted more from himself in the endeavour to maintain the traditions of *The Times*. He saw his task as a mission to be fulfilled and he fulfilled it always with courage and devotion. It cannot be said that his contribution was made without effort. Rather it was made by conscious direction of the will strengthened by a native sense of duty. Barrington-Ward was a man of genuine religion. He brought to *The Times* a rare combination of talent, conscientiousness, and modesty. No Editor in a long line had given to his work greater integrity and honesty of purpose . . . He was austere yet humane; ready to forgive conduct in others that he would never have tolerated in himself.

Other points appeared in the obituary notice:

He took great pains over the contributions of his colleagues, so that little of the comment on the news that went into the paper did not bear, though invisibly, the mark of his hand.

His keen sense of the errors of Versailles, and the logical nature of his mind, led him, even after 1933, to work hard for peace; as a soldier he knew what war was and was prepared to go far to prevent a repetition of its destructiveness and wastefulness.

What can chiefly be added, in any assessment of his term as editor, was that he foresaw the social revolution at home and was determined, so far as he could, to prepare the governing classes for it. He foresaw an end to the middle-class dominance of society and industry which had shaped the Britain in which he grew up. The middle classes had to make room for the new classes as the landed classes had had to make room earlier for the middle classes. Ironically, as he saw, many of the leaders of the social revolution would come from the middle classes which would thereby be playing their familiar historical role of instigating radical social change. *The Times* was to be their guide and spokesman.

With no less strength he was determined, when turning to world affairs, to drive home the plain truth that the Soviet Union had appeared on the map like a new continent, upsetting all previous military and industrial geography. In fact both at home and abroad he was chiefly concerned to get *The Times* readers, including the ruling ranks in the country, to see that sweeping changes were crowding upon them and could not be averted. If the changes were painful that was only a further sign in his own mind that they were salutary and necessary.

Being of great goodness himself he worked in the belief that others would respond to an honest and generous approach and to reasoned argument. He was convinced that all problems were capable of a rational solution. He began most enterprises by believing the best of those he had to deal with. Perhaps he did not fully comprehend – very few people at that time did comprehend – the rapid weakening of the Commonwealth and the collapse of the British and other western empires which introduced yet another imbalance into the military scales and made the cultivation of an alliance with the United States (an idea which he supported) an urgent and entirely vital requirement. His misreading of the Greek civil war has been noted, and that was due above all to a readiness to believe in the good intentions of those who spoke as radical reformers and with a record of anti-fascist resistance behind them. Yet his policy has to be seen as a whole.

He had wished to be editor of *The Times* because, given its special position, he saw the job as a means of shaping events or, as he sometimes said, of getting things done. Any assessment comes back again and again to that sense of mission: to his steady, lonely courage in identifying and advocating the great changes that had to be made in a society that no longer fitted Britain and in an international pattern that no longer fitted the world. As he knew, the special standing of *The Times* made his advocacy the more startling and the more effective. At the same time, in using the paper so, he altered that special standing. *The Times* under him could no longer be regarded as the voice of the establishment or, as it was also called, the gazette of the ruling classes. It lost a little and it gained much. Barrington-Ward made it more exciting, more provocative, an organ for advancing ideas which at once shocked and educated its readers.

The memorial service, held at St. Paul's Cathedral on March 31, brought ample evidence of the esteem with which he was regarded as a man and as an editor. The government, the City, the universities, the newspapers and the BBC, the learned professions: all had their strong representatives in the closely packed rows on the floor of the nave.

In the spring of 1948 the two proprietors, John Astor and John Walter, were consequently faced with the need to find both a new editor and a new manager. Choosing the editor was the easier task. After all the controversies and tensions of the previous decade, covering Dawson's last years and the whole of Barrington-Ward's editorship, Astor and Walter alike considered that the office needed a respite and that the man to give that respite was William Casey, Barrington-Ward's deputy. He was appointed on April 1.

At first it was planned that he would be in the chair for little more than a year. He was close on 64; his health was not good and he made it no better by worrying about it. He himself had never wished to be editor. Only a few months before he had agreed with Barrington-Ward that he should very soon retire. He was a quiet Irishman: even, it could be said, an Irish quietist. Much of his reluctance to take a strong line, or share Barrington-Ward's fervour over some topic of the day, came from a gentle pessimism. It was almost a Tolstoyan belief that no human act could make much difference to events, and this led him to express the gravest doubts as to whether journalism was a worthwhile occupation.

One part of his work was to receive young applicants for jobs on the paper and he would sometimes startle the more promising of them out of their wits by advising them most earnestly to put all thought of newspaper work from their minds. 'Why don't you take up farming or something useful like that?'

On leaving Trinity College, Dublin, he had been called to the Irish Bar in 1909 and used to sum up his legal career in six words: 'One year, one brief, one guinea.' He had two plays produced at the Abbey Theatre, Dublin, and even then had an attitude very different from that of most proud young dramatists towards their masterpieces. During a rehearsal of one of Casey's plays an actor stumbled several times over two quite important lines. 'Oh well, if they trouble you, let's leave them out,' said Casey. 'I don't suppose they really matter.' For a brief time he was even manager of the Abbey Theatre, and the actors had to teach him how to pay them – he had not thought of that part of his duties. Yeats helped him, and carefully signed each cheque, 'Yours truly, W. B. Yeats.'[13]

Casey came to London as a writer of promise, but, after doing some reviews for *The Times Literary Supplement*, found himself in the sporting sub-editors' room at Printing House Square. Thereafter he was correspondent in Washington (1919) and in Paris for two years. From Paris he returned to London with a love and understanding of France which he later tried to oppose to the pro-German inclinations of Dawson and Barrington-Ward. After being chief foreign sub-editor he became assistant editor in 1935, with a special job of keeping an eye on the news and looking out for mistakes and libels.

There was an odd paradox about his position in those years. He was the very heart of the office; his influence and his personality spread out to every editorial department. He was the leaven of the whole. Yet in a curious way he remained detached, almost as if he was an observer and a sojourner. Remarkably enough, although never over-eager to work (he recoiled in horror once when Barrington-Ward advised him to try 'a little application'), Casey managed to keep his brain as sharp as if he exercised it daily on higher mathematics. No one could confuse his easy-going manner with sloppy mindedness. He had the gift of glancing at a column of type and straight away spotting a howler which everyone had missed. He had the same faculty for quickly detecting a false argument in a leading article, and then he would go to see Dawson or Barrington-Ward in the attempt, not always successful, to have it put right. Better still, he was an unfailing judge of men and had a deep

---

13 Story told by Casey in the office.

instinctive understanding of the play of world forces, without bothering to read all the documents or the speeches. 'I can't be doing with all that humbug. Sheer solemn levity, the greater half of it.' When he wrote a leader himself, which was rarely, it was a model of clear, direct, short-sentenced writing.

Within the office he remained, as he had been throughout the Munich crisis, the wise friend and counsellor of the younger men; and he looked the part with his silver hair, his lined and kindly face, his hooded and very blue eyes, and his gentlemanly stoop. At dinner in the spartan editorial mess he was always the dean of the college who, in a friendly and flattering way, drew out his junior colleagues, deferred to their views when they were not more than usually pretentious, and repaid them amply with his own reminiscences of life, love, the arts, and letters. Clearly, when the need for a new editor came, Casey was not simply the pilot to weather the storm. He was the man to ensure that within Printing House Square at all events there would be no storm to be weathered.

The contrast between the purposeful, often tense Barrington-Ward and the relaxed, sceptical Casey was no greater than the difference which was soon apparent between Kent and the man – Francis Mathew[14] – who was chosen to be his successor as manager. Where Kent was an accountant by training and by habit of mind, Mathew was interested first and foremost in printing. Where Kent was reserved in speech, Mathew was fluent and often boisterous. Kent was tidy and orderly in the office; Mathew during a talk had the disconcerting habit of jotting down notes on the back of an old envelope or scrap of paper which he thrust back into his pocket or into a drawer from which they were retrieved by his secretary, Freda Reed.[15] While Kent liked to see editorial men one by one quietly in his room, Mathew would drop without notice into their rooms, clutching a bunch of papers. Where Kent stood for caution, continuity, and a tidy balance sheet at the end of the year, Mathew added a love of experimentation and a strong dash of excitement to the more usual managerial qualifications which won him the job.

Stanley Morison, who had busied himself to find a manager after the discussions with John Elliott collapsed, listed those qualifications in a preliminary and persuasive memorandum to Barrington-Ward:

Francis Mathew, the Manager of the St. Clement's Press, has all the

---

14 Francis Mathew (1907–65). Downside; Grenoble University. Managing director St. Clement's Press, 1947–48; works director W. Speaight and Sons, 1946–48. Manager *The Times*, 1949–65.
15 Later employment manager; retired 1981.

abilities required for the management without any temptation to meddle with the editorial part, great as his sympathy would be with it. I think he understands enough about advertising, but his real strength is, of course, in production, labour relations, costs and finances for he understands business and would have a plan ready if the paper ran into choppy weather. Had he been protestant I would have mentioned his name earlier.[16]

On the last point Morison touched on another difference from Kent. Where Kent was a Plymouth Brother, Mathew was of an old Roman Catholic family renowned in the church and in the law. He was the son of Theobald Mathew, sometime Recorder of Margate and Maidstone and author of a number of books, both serious and half-serious, on legal subjects. He himself was educated at Downside and Grenoble, and then learned his printing at Linotype and Machinery Limited in Spain, South America, and London. He had been manager at St. Clement's Press for nine years when he was approached by *The Times*. John Astor and several of *The Times* staff had known him during the war when he was an officer in the Press Battalion of the Home Guard: an exceptionally broad-shouldered man of medium height and rather more than medium weight, a strong square face, with keen eyes peering out through heavy horn-rimmed spectacles. When he came to Printing House Square he was forty-one. He worked with Kent for some weeks, and the Board of directors approved his appointment on June 16 1949:

> On the proposition of the Chairman, seconded by Mr. John Walter, Mr. Francis Mathew was unanimously appointed Manager of The Times from from July 1st, 1949.

---

16 T.T.A.

VIII

STORMY INTERREGNUM

C ASEY was editor for four and a half years, a longer and far busier time than anyone had imagined when he was appointed. His period covered the worst crises and heaviest dangers that the world had faced since the end of the war against Germany and Japan. Throughout the Berlin blockade of 1948–49 and the Korean war of 1950–51 the never-absent question was whether the cold war could be contained within its own rough rules (one of which was that any fighting had to be kept localised) or would explode into open war across the world.

Mao Tse-tung's victory in China halfway through 1949 tilted the balance of power heavily against the west and stretched the communist block – a united block, it then seemed – the whole way across the Eurasian heartland from the Elbe to the Yangtze. National upsurges were transforming the Commonwealth and Empire; the example of India and Pakistan, independent in 1947, was soon to be followed by similar movements in other British-held territories. At home, where the first excitement and enthusiasm for the welfare state was giving way to tiredness and disillusion, the natural consequence was seen in the Conservatives' election gains in 1950 and the return of Churchill to power after the poll in 1951.

Everywhere policy had to be thought out again. The old guidelines were gone. Within the small compass of Printing House Square the re-thinking began to be carried out more and more in group discussions, largely as the consequence of two of Casey's earliest appointments. Donald Tyerman became deputy editor, first in practice and then in name; he was put much more clearly in charge of home affairs on the paper, looking after home leaders, the special articles and, at one remove, the home news. Iverach McDonald was made the assistant editor in charge of foreign affairs, with a special brief to look after the foreign leaders while leaving the news mainly to Deakin, still the foreign news editor. Both Tyerman and McDonald got away from the Dawson tradition of having tête-à-tête talks with individual leader writers. Each of them had his leader writers in his room as a group every afternoon for half an hour or so before the main editorial conference at 4.15. Tyerman also brought six or seven staff men together each week for a talk over a dinner in the old Wellington restaurant in Fleet Street. Later still he organised weekly lunches for men and women from the *Economist*, the *Observer*, and the BBC as well as from *The Times* itself. These lunches helped Tyerman to know which young men were making their mark on other papers and which of them might be interested in coming to *The Times*.

He threw himself into recruiting as men throw themselves into a sport. He never forgot that there were two sides to an appointment. He got as much genuine pleasure in finding a good post for a young man or woman of talent (and so helping forward a promising career) as in finding a young man or woman to fill a given post for the better advancement of *The Times*. Just because he went for talent first and foremost the leader writers and special writers gradually became more evenly balanced between men who were left-inclined and those who were more to the right.

In home affairs Tyerman himself, Lafitte and Wigham leaned left, but now Dermot Morrah and Peter Utley, both to the right, were joined by Henry Fairlie.[1] Fairlie was only twenty-six when he came to *The Times* in 1950 from the *Observer* and it was very soon clear, through all the anonymity of the leader columns, that a new mind was present, entirely at home in the workings of political machines. Another recruit was Peregrine Worsthorne,[2] mainly writing on foreign affairs but also on the home side. As a rather diffident young man he had applied for a job on coming down from Oxford in 1946. Told by Tyerman to go away and get himself two years' hard training somewhere else, he went to the *Glasgow Herald* and returned on the dot, two years later to the day. Such eager precision had to be rewarded. A place was found for him and he was soon showing the skill in political theory that he was to develop much further after leaving *The Times*.

On the foreign side the two newcomers who were to leave their distinctive stamp on the paper were John Pringle, who came early in the Casey period, and Teddy Hodgkin, who joined nearly at the end. Both

1 Henry Jones Fairlie (b. 1924). Highgate School; Corpus Christi College, Oxford. Editorial staff *Manchester Evening News*, 1945–48, and *Observer*, 1948–50. Editorial staff of *The Times*, 1950–54. Political journalist on staff and contributor to the *Daily Mail, Sunday Telegraph, Daily Express*, and other journals.
2 Peregrine Gerard Worsthorne (b. 1923). Stowe; Peterhouse, Cambridge; Magdalen College, Oxford. Sub-editor, *Glasgow Herald*, 1946–48. Editorial staff of *The Times*, 1948–55, with spell on Washington staff, 1952–53. *Daily Telegraph*, 1955–61; deputy editor, *Sunday Telegraph*, 1961–76; associate editor from 1976.

were *Guardian* men; both were distinguished Oxford scholars; both had served in the war; both had the light, clear, uncluttered style of writing that *The Times* was eager to encourage. Pringle[3] was thirty-five when he came straight from leader-writing in Manchester; tall, thin, dark, looking rather like Robert Louis Stevenson. He himself had all the Scottish Lowlander's respect for intellect without the Lowlander's often sardonic view of life. His mind worked quickly, casting around for a line and then following it eagerly, interrupting itself only when struck as though out of the blue – Pringle himself appeared startled – by some splendidly witty thought. He found Printing House Square and its inhabitants a constant source of puzzlement; he wondered at first if he had come into a museum:

There was no cheerful bustle of activity . . . The sub-editors looked up in hostility from their cross-words if you dared to tip-toe into their room. The reporters were tucked away out of sight in some remote part of the building. Even in my own corridor there were rooms whose occupants, so far as I knew, might have been Afghans or Chinese. Their doors never opened. I dared not knock to find out. It was rumoured that in a little cubby hole by the stairs lived an old man who wrote *The Times 100 Years Ago* from memory.

Gradually, however, as I got to know them, I discovered that Printing House Square was full of brilliant, charming and eccentric people. None was more brilliant, more charming or more eccentric than Dermot Morrah, with whom I shared a room. Dermot Morrah was a Fellow of All Souls and a fine scholar in the classics, history and mathematics . . . I remember that once, towards the end of 1949, the editor asked him to write a leader on the question, then beginning to worry the public, of whether the half-centenary should properly be celebrated at the end of the year, 1949, or at the end of the next year, 1950. Morrah strode up and down the room for half an hour with his hands clasped behind his back – he used to like to think on his feet – and then sat down at his desk and wrote a dazzling leader tracing the whole history of the controversy from the days of the early Christian Church and proving mathematically that it must, of course, be the end of 1950.[4] (The key, of course, is that the Christian Era began in A.D. 1 not A.D. 0). The leader was filled with quotations and

3 John Martin Douglas Pringle (b. 1912). Shrewsbury; Lincoln College, Oxford. Leader writer *Manchester Guardian*, 1934–39. Army, 1939–44. Assistant editor *Manchester Guardian*, 1944–48. Special writer *The Times*, 1948–52. Editor *Sydney Morning Herald*, 1952–57. Deputy editor *Observer*, 1958–63. Managing editor *Canberra Times*, 1964–65. Editor *Sydney Morning Herald*, 1965–70.
4 'Wait for it'. Leading article, December 17 1949.

delicate allusions yet I know for a fact that he never consulted a book or left the room to go to the library.[5]

Pringle had his own touch of gentle eccentricity which fitted him from the start to be a natural member of the team; and he later came to see that there was something in a remark by Henry Fairlie. Fairlie had also been puzzled at first by the air of cloistered calm, but afterwards used to say that more happened more quickly with less fuss at *The Times* than in any other place he knew. Pringle himself worked in that quick unfussy way. On July 11 1949 three of the four leaders in *The Times* were by him, and the titles show the range of his mind: 'Rebuilding Princes Street', 'The New Greek Government', and, a light essay, 'Punts and Sofas'. Sadly, after less than two years, he went down with tuberculosis. He was away for twelve months and soon after his return was invited to go to edit the *Sydney Morning Herald*. Off he went, but it was a long time before the impetus he gave to thought – especially on fitting divided Germany into Europe – stopped being felt in the office.

Teddy Hodgkin[6] was first mentioned to *The Times* by Peter Fleming who knew him on the *Spectator* where they both were working. War service had given him a close and remarkably affectionate understanding of the Middle East which he could add, by way of generous bonus, to all his other assets: a knowledge of Europe; a deep love of English literature; a rare intellectual background (his father was a Provost of Queen's College, Oxford, and his mother daughter of a Master of Balliol); and commonsense carried to an extraordinary degree with the help of the nicest sense of wit. If anyone was misled at first by Hodgkin's shy manner and soft, hesitant speech the truth would soon hit him when he saw the speed with which Hodgkin produced a beautifully turned and knowledgeable leader.

Another strong recruit was John Midgley,[7] also of the *Guardian* school, who was brought in towards the end of the Casey period. He stayed only three years in Printing House Square before going as correspondent in Germany. He was a fine German scholar, very much

---

5 John Douglas Pringle, *Have Pen, Will Travel*, pp. 56–58. Chatto & Windus.
6 Edward Christian Hodgkin (b. 1913). Eton; Balliol College, Oxford. Leader writer, *Manchester Guardian*, 1936–9. Army, 1939–45. Director, Near East Arab Broadcasting Station, 1945–7. Assistant editor, *Spectator*, 1948–52. Joined *The Times* as special writer, 1952; assistant foreign editor, 1961; foreign editor, 1965; deputy editor, 1967; associate editor, 1969–72.
7 John Midgley (b. 1911). Hulme Grammar School; Trinity College, Cambridge. Reporter, *Manchester Guardian*, 1936. Army, 1939–45. Leader writer on *The Times* 1951–54; correspondent in Bonn 1954–55. Thereafter on the *Economist*, Bonn, London, Washington.

the individualist, a quick and efficient dialectician, one of the few journalists who are as good with words when speaking as they are when writing. Like Hodgkin he brought an extra bonus with him: he had a detailed knowledge of the oil industry which was invaluable when Iraq, and then Iran under Mossadeq, claimed more control over their own oil.

Yet another newcomer, late in the Casey term, was Bobby Jessel[8] who, as defence correspondent, straddled both home and foreign affairs. He had made his name on the *Guardian*; he was making a bigger reputation for himself behind all the anonymity of *The Times*. He seemed set to be one of the great defence correspondents, but he telephoned Tyerman one day in 1954 to say quietly that he had just learned he had leukaemia and was not expected to live more than a few weeks. He died on September 28 1954.

The new diplomatic correspondent, Sandy Rendel,[9] was one of those who during the war had put their classical training to an unexpectedly practical use, serving gallantly with the partisans in Crete.

Throughout all the changes the intellectual standard remained high. Indeed it was improving. Where Barrington-Ward had one exceptional high-flier on the foreign side, E. H. Carr, Casey lost him but had a larger number of men of the *alpha* class, less controversial, less dogmatic, more willing to give credit to all sides.

The first tricky foreign problem on which *The Times* under Casey had to make up its mind came in June 1948. The news that Marshal Tito's Yugoslavia had been expelled from the eastern camp after resisting Soviet domination was bewildering at first because it went contrary to almost all the prevailing trends in eastern Europe. Only four months earlier Czechoslovakia had been taken over by the Stalinist communists. Elsewhere in the region, except perhaps in Poland, conformism was triumphant. It was not at all surprising that many in the United States and Britain, firmly believing that Yugoslavia could not stand alone, declared that it should not be given any help or support unless it came fairly and squarely over to the western camp. Talks among the foreign team in *The Times* swung the paper's line the other way.

Carr, still coming into the office occasionally at that time, brought

---

8 Robert George Jessel (1917–1954). Repton; Trinity College, Oxford. Army, 1939–45. Editorial staff, *Manchester Guardian*, 1945. Military correspondent, *Daily Express*, 1950; then deputy editor, *Daily Dispatch*, Manchester. Joined *The Times* as leader writer on defence topics, 1952; military correspondent from 1953 until his death.
9 Alexander Meadows Rendel (b. 1910). Rugby; Corpus Christi College, Oxford. Joined *The Times* as special writer on foreign affairs, 1949; diplomatic correspondent 1949 till his retirement in 1975. CBE, 1975.

out the real significance of the Yugoslav affair in a leader published on July 2. The crux of the matter was whether there could be national communism as distinct from the international communist camp, whether a communist state could exist 'without the blessing, or against the anathema, of the Kremlin.' Obviously, Carr wrote, the answer could affect the solidarity of the whole communist camp. Davidson, helped by his wartime service with Tito's partisans, testified to the strength of rugged patriotism in Yugoslavia; and the leader writers as a whole came to the view that western interests would be much better served by supporting a non-aligned communist Yugoslavia than by trying to swing it to the western camp.

Events since those years have made such a view, when recalled, appear like a glimpse of the obvious. But at the time it was novel and exciting, even though *The Times* was not alone in coming to it. In reaching it, and in shaping a line on eastern Europe as a whole, the Printing House Square foreign team was partly influenced by the thoughtful despatches of Michael Burn both from Yugoslavia and Hungary. The climax of his work came in February 1949 with his messages on the significance 'to the world and to history', as he wrote, of the trial of Cardinal Mindszenty, the Swabian peasant's son who for five years had been Prince Primate of Hungary.

On one plane the trial seemed to represent the conflict between idealist religion and materialism, but in his despatches during the four days of the trial Burn revealed another and less exalted plane. He reported that the Cardinal's reputation among the people sank heavily before the end. At the beginning of the trial Mindszenty was widely thought to be ready equally to go to the stake for his beliefs if need be or to send his enemies there if he had the chance. But after his final speech – made 'more in extenuation than in defence, certainly not in defiance' – it was being asked whether the Cardinal understood the implications of his acts or, understanding them, had ever expected or been ready in the last resort to face them. 'Such are the views being expressed here'.[10]

The despatches were widely read and quoted. In May 1949 a speaker in a public debate in London said that they were dishonest and that Burn had been told to leave *The Times* because of them. He brought an action for slander; a settlement was announced in the High Court on March 1 1950; the defendant repeated an earlier profound apology for making the groundless statements, he withdrew them completely, and agreed to pay a substantial sum by way of damages to a charity or charities of Burn's choice.[11] All Burn's work in central and eastern Europe had

10 *The Times*, February 7 1949.
11 *The Times*, March 2 1950.

been an exercise in honesty, both when he could hope for east–west understanding and when those hopes faded with the tightening of the Stalinist grip. Some years later, in the *Observer Magazine* of November 3 1974, he recalled his disillusionment and horror:

There I witnessed the enforced revolutions, attended the infamous sham trials, knew at first hand of the disappearances, the tortures, the lies, and concluded that Marxism in contemporary practice was odious; as a political theory (when I came to know more of it) manure for dictatorships and so for brutality; indispensable but inaccurate as a view of history; and inadequate as a way of life.

At the time he frankly recognised that his work was at an end. He resigned from the paper late in 1949 and came home to write his books.

In May of that same year *The Times* had another casualty in the cold war. Since 1945 Godfrey Lias[12] had been sending lucid messages on the restoration and fall of democracy in Prague. The Czechoslovak government suddenly asked the paper to withdraw him. They complained not about his messages but about some 'non-journalistic activities' which they left wholly unspecified. He had kept in touch with Czech friends who wished to leave the country. After his eventual return to London Lias was soon, like Burn, writing books.

The events in eastern Europe helped to shape and clarify *The Times's* policy on the east–west rivalry, which in those years dominated the whole field of foreign affairs. The paper's policy was based on four convictions which, though widely accepted in later years, were not at all self-evident at the time:

First, Russia was not planning a great war on the Napoleonic or Hitlerite model. Certainly Stalin would go on pushing so far as he could by other means. He would exploit all the weak areas that the west left open or half open. But all the evidence which McDonald brought back from his long visits to Russia in 1945 and 1947 – the evidence about the industrial devastation and the utter exhaustion of most of the people – strengthened the belief that Stalin would draw back the moment that he saw the risks of war were becoming too great for him.

Secondly, and even more firmly, *The Times* was convinced – there was no dissent within the office – that a balance of power must be urgently established by greater western strength and greater western

---

12 Arthur Godfrey Lias (1887–1964). St. Lawrence College, Ramsgate; King's College, Cambridge. After senior teaching posts in Egypt and India, joined the *Christian Science Monitor* as diplomatic correspondent. Correspondent for *The Times* in Prague, 1945–49; Vienna correspondent from 1949 until retirement in 1953.

unity. The lessons of the pre-war mistakes had been learned, and it was recognised that the establishment of a proper balance of power would make Stalin still more cautious.

Thirdly, it was no longer possible to sustain Barrington-Ward's early hopes of a general agreement, a general meeting of minds, with the Soviet Union. (He himself was modifying such hopes before his death.) The most that could be expected was some hard, pragmatic, well defined and toughly negotiated agreements on finite matters.

Fourthly, more broadly and rather more tentatively, each of the two world camps should acknowledge to itself – as a question not of principle but of common prudence – that the other had spheres of influence which it would be quick to defend against encroachments.

In short, amid all the ideological charges and counter-charges of the cold war, *The Times* regarded the confrontation between the two blocks chiefly as a confrontation between two groups of national states. This did not stop the paper from making periodic surveys of the political tactics of the various communist parties, but it regarded Stalin chiefly as the ruler of an empire, a ruler both ambitious and wary, more than a revolutionary ideologue.

The heaviest test of the belief that Stalin would draw back from open war came very soon with the Berlin blockade. From the earliest days of the siege *The Times* remained convinced that he was seeking a success in the city not through a direct clash of arms but through a process of siege attrition:

> The western Powers can still assume that the Russians will not deliberately push matters to the point of open military strife . . . The Russians are tightening the blockade and waiting. In their customary way they have not finally committed themselves to any single course . . . They are waiting, first to test the strength of the western response, secondly in the hope that growing unemployment and misery in the blockaded sectors will make the authorities' position untenable.[13]

In this view the writers in London were greatly helped by the daily despatches, objective and convincing, from the correspondent in the city, John Buist. He showed that the allied air lift could keep starvation away for a long time, thereby upsetting one set of Stalin's calculations. When Stalin finally called off the blockade and agreed to four-power talks on the future of Germany, it was clear that the Kremlin had been

---

13 Leading article, July 13 1948.

influenced by something more than the evidence of the western technological superiority, shown in the air lift. That evidence was in itself startling. Over 2,300,000 tons of goods had been flown by 380 aircraft in 227,264 flights. But, beyond all that, there had come the much stronger warning, shown in the new assertion of the balance of power when the North Atlantic Treaty was signed in Washington on April 4, 1949.

Like almost every other British newspaper *The Times* had welcomed every step in the revolution of American thought which led to the signing of the treaty. It had strongly advocated the first movements towards closer alliance in western Europe. As far back as April 2 1946 it gave a deliberate push to events by prominently and firmly commending a suggestion, made somewhat vaguely on an election platform by the French Prime Minister of the day, M. Gouin, that Britain and France should share an alliance together. The publication of the article so prominently in *The Times* led immediately to questions in the House of Commons; Bevin sent Oliver Harvey over to Paris to confer with some slightly surprised French officials. In the next few days the talks came to a stop as the French cabinet was divided, but the conversations were taken up again after the French general elections and led to the Anglo–French Treaty of Dunkirk, signed early in 1947 and soon to be followed by the Treaty of Brussels.[14] Bevin was nearer to seeing his old dream of western union fulfilled.

Hardly had the North Atlantic Treaty been signed than western ministers had to ask themselves a question which, forcing itself forward less than four years after the defeat of the Hitler tyranny, was disturbing and even shocking at first. Should West Germany be rearmed? Beside all the general strategic arguments for strengthening western power as a whole there was the potential need of self-defence for West Germany itself as it faced East Germany. In the autumn of 1948, in 1949, and in the first months of 1950 John Buist sent successive despatches and private memoranda confirming and amplifying earlier reports by German dissidents and others that, while West Germany was disarmed, the East German police were being reorganised and armed with field weapons as a para-military force, the so-called *Polizeibereitschaften* – 'a new Wehrmacht'.[15] The foreign leader writers in Printing House Square had many talks together on the unpleasant risk that German militarism might be revived in both Germanies alike. They came to the view that West Germany should not be rearmed until western defence as a whole

---

14 The tenor of the article on April 2 1946, written by the diplomatic correspondent, was reflected in the headings: Closer Link with France in Prospect/Britain Welcomes Proposal for Alliance/Opportunity for New Approach.
15 *The Times*, Berlin despatch, April 29 1950.

was more strongly organised both militarily and politically:

> Put another way, there could be no question of it [West German rearmament] until the Atlantic Pact and the Brussels Pact were sufficiently strong to remove any fears that the German weight might swamp the boat or, at any rate, upset the balance.[16]

The paper was no less concerned about the realities of power in the Far East, first when Mao Tse-tung's victory in China was announced in October 1949, and then when the North Koreans invaded South Korea eight months later. The leading article entitled 'The New China', published with the news of Mao's triumph, emphasised straightaway that the whole political and strategic map of Eastern Asia had been re-shaped; Mao and his men were victors in a revolution 'as great in its consequences as the Bolshevist revolution in 1917'. Indeed the effect would be greater. The Chinese communists had behind them years of practical administration such as Lenin lacked, they could learn from the 'costly blunders of the Russian revolution', they already had command over much of their huge country whereas Lenin faced a furiously mounting civil war, and they had Russia at their back as an ally where Lenin was very much alone.[17] Three days later, on October 6 1949, another long leading article followed the paper's line of encouraging practical state relationships by recommending that the new Chinese government be recognised by the British government. It based itself on the sole and simple grounds that Mao clearly exercised authority over the greater part of China:

> The purpose of recognition is severely practical . . . Recognition is not a certificate of like-mindedness or even of good conduct . . . Recognition, in short, is the acknowledgement that a new regime has, for better or worse, joined the imperfect international community.

The North Korean invasion of the south, when it was launched on June 25 1950, was immediately seen in Printing House Square to carry with it the most serious risk since 1945 of war between the powers. The risk arose precisely because one of the main rules of the cold war, and one of the main rules of traditional power relationships, was broken. The first sentences of the first leader after the invasion made the point clear:

> When the communist-led troops of northern Korea moved in force across the southern Korean border early yesterday morning they moved from a Soviet field of interest to invade an American field of

---

16 Leading article, May 24 1950.
17 *The Times*, October 3 1949.

interest . . . It is this which invests the fighting with a meaning far wider than that of a civil war. The dangers are correspondingly greater. The invasion is a deliberate challenge to American influence in the last area which remains open to it on the east Asian mainland north of Indo-China.[18]

Tyerman and McDonald were on duty that Sunday; they were confident that the United States would respond to the challenge and would have the support of most of the United Nations; the only doubt was whether the response could be speedy enough to stop the North Koreans sweeping over the whole country. In October of that same year, when the invasion had been repulsed and reversed, *The Times* repeated even more strongly its concern that spheres of interest be acknowledged as facts of international life, but this time the point was made because General MacArthur was defying Chinese warnings and was pushing his forces up to the Chinese frontier in North Korea. Successive leading articles by Rushbrook Williams and others argued that the war should be halted where it had begun, that is to say, on the frontier between North and South Korea. The western governments should make their intentions about this explicit.

When President Truman dismissed General MacArthur on April 11 1951 for conducting his own headstrong policy the paper stated that Truman was of course right a dozen times over, but the western governments themselves could not be acquitted of all blame. Their 'extraordinary silence' about what they would do as they reached or crossed the 38th parallel had 'created a vacuum which General MacArthur sought to fill'.[19]

In May and June John Pringle, returned from his illness, took up the argument. To blockade and bomb China and land Chinese nationalist forces from Taiwan, as General MacArthur proposed, would only extend the war without bringing it to an end.[20] At that time the allied forces had repulsed a new communist offensive and occupied the whole of South Korea once again:

> It would be hard to imagine a more suitable moment than the present one for attempting again to bring the Korean war to an end . . . Perhaps the most hopeful course would simply be for the Powers who have forces in Korea to offer an armistice based on the present positions of the rival armies along the 38th parallel, with a view to beginning negotiations as soon as the fighting has ceased.

---

18 *The Times*, June 26 1950.
19 *The Times*, April 12 1951.
20 Leading article (Pringle), May 12 1951.

The leader ended with a sentence which took on a more direct relevance eight or nine years later. China, the leader admitted, might refuse to talk:

> On the other hand, it should still be the policy of the western Powers to convince China, if this opportunity can be taken to end the bloody conflict, that she will have more to gain from their friendship than from dependence on Russian support.[21]

The Korean war dealt a heavy personal blow to *The Times*. Only seven weeks after its outbreak Ian Morrison was killed on August 12 1950 when his light open car struck a mine close to the fighting. He was only thirty-seven. It was a loss to the paper and a loss to the cause in which he had worked with unrivalled perception. For over nine years he had interpreted to the west the nationalist and revolutionary movements of east Asia. Few men travelled more widely or more constantly through the region. After the end of the Japanese war his headquarters were in Singapore but he was seldom there for more than a few weeks at a time. He was the friend of political leaders and administrators of all countries; they confided in him and, in return, sought and valued his opinions. They liked his modest, thoughtful and entertaining company. In the first years after the war he sent memoranda to Deakin criticising some of Rushbrook Williams's leaders for being (as he saw them when he was standing precariously in the midst of the upheavals) too hopeful. An especially sharp note of January 3 1948 questioned whether it was in the British interests to support colonial regimes; for his part he wished Indonesian nationalism to find fullest expression as a counterweight to communism. Early in 1948 he foresaw the communist victory in China, and in November 1948 he was specific in his warnings:

> My own prediction is that the Communists are going to get the whole of China – and fairly soon. There is nothing to stop them. The question is not whether they are going to come out on top, but what sort of Communists they are going to be.[22]

On the last point he had already in April 1948 given a warning against the assumption among some old China hands that nothing fundamental would change. 'China', wrote Morrison, 'will *not* always remain China'. Dynamic policies and sweeping programmes, ruthlessly pushed through, could indeed bring about deep and nation-wide changes.[23]

---

21 Leading article (Pringle), June 4 1951.
22 Memorandum to Deakin, November 19 1948, written in Singapore after tour in China. T.T.A.
23 Memorandum to Deakin from Shanghai, April 12 1948. T.T.A.

He quickly volunteered to go to the Korean war. Arriving in the days of confusion he was anxious to dispel any false hopes about the immediate fighting. The obituary notice of him published in *The Times* on August 14 1950 emphasised this last service of his:

It was typical of him that he sought out and reported all information, both good and bad, about what was happening in the areas over-run by the northern troops. He described the northern reforms; he analysed the appeals their authorisation were making; he reported their acts of brutality. He described the southerners' social and military weaknesses, and he reported their tenacity in fighting. In his last despatch to *The Times*, published on Saturday, the day of his death, he gave repeated warnings that the Americans' success at Chinju should not be overrated. It had to be seen 'in relation to the whole picture'. The northerners' attack on Pohang had exposed 'the whole weakness of the allied position in Korea'.

On August 17 1950 Ernest Bevin, the Foreign Secretary, sent Casey a letter expressing his deep regret at the news of Morrison's death:

I have never met Mr. Morrison personally, but I have read much of his work in the Times, and it was obvious to any reader that he was a brilliant and conscientious correspondent with the sense of responsibility and moral and physical courage which accorded with the highest traditions of his profession.[24]

Another volunteer, Louis Heren, took up Morrison's work in Korea by the beginning of September and, in conditions that London found hard to comprehend, coped with all the wild swings in military fortunes and the fantastic difficulties in getting the news, once it was obtained, back to London. He had to draw on all his reserves of physical and mental stamina. Communications as such did not exist near the fighting. In an article in *The Times House Journal*, dated July–September 1969, Heren gave some picture of what life was like for him:

I can remember during the battle for Seoul flying back to Japan every night to file my messages. It quickly became a routine, but remained rather tiring. One would board an empty cargo plane at Kimpo, and, squatting on the floor, type out the day's message. At the Japanese end a friendly (American) air force sergeant would put it on the wire to London, and I would go off to the officers club for a $4 steak and a drink. So far so good, but the return flights were horrible. Invariably the planes were overloaded with bombs, ammunition or petrol drums . . . One night I was about fifth or sixth in line, and watched

---

24 T.T.A.

the planes take off. Two never made it, presumably because they were overloaded or overworked. Nevertheless, the planes kept taking off and, as I watched the last plane and correspondent go up in flames at the end of the runway, that friendly air force sergeant shouted, 'Where's that Limey? He's next.'

Apart from such conflagrations, the lack of sleep was the worst part. One would get back to Kimpo, but there was no time to sleep if one was to get back to the urban battlefield in time to cover the fighting for that night's paper.

Even Heren, with his iron constitution, had to lie up in Toyo for a time in November of that same year.

By chance, only a few days before the Korean war broke out, the paper was caught up in a more direct dispute with General MacArthur. Frank Hawley, the correspondent in Tokyo, had been irritating the commander-in-chief with his occasional suggestions in his despatches that the Japanese were not all the reformed characters that the American command seemed to believe them to be. In June 1950 Hawley wrote that the Japanese government had broken the terms of the constitution by letting its police disperse a communist demonstration. He also asserted that the Japanese police were petitioning to be allowed to return their American sidearms for fear of possible reprisals against them if the communists were ever to take over in Japan. Very quickly Hawley followed this last point up with a correction showing that he had been misinformed about the sidearms but on June 8 the original version was published in the English language Tokyo newspaper, the *Nippon Times*.

On that same day General Edward M. Almond, MacArthur's chief of staff, summoned Hawley to tell him on MacArthur's instructions that his despatches were judged to have breached security and that he was *persona non grata*. The chief of the British diplomatic mission in Japan, Sir Alvary Gascoigne, had been told of MacArthur's displeasure and he was present at the Almond–Hawley meeting, chiefly to point out entirely correctly that the Foreign Office was in no way responsible for what appeared in *The Times*. When Hawley reported the uproar to London *The Times* sent him an immediate cable:

You have paper's full support. No question of withdrawal. Please continue objective reporting events in closest touch with [American] headquarters, report their information and views but dont restrict yourself to official sources only and record events in proper perspective. For information *Times* published police correction and nothing else.

In truth the paper had for some time not been happy with Hawley's work in Japan and it was to become less happy. The chief immediate effect of MacArthur's outburst was to confirm him in his post. The phrase about being *persona non grata* was forgotten. But eighteen months later Casey told Hawley by letter that he should look around for other work.

Throughout these early years after the 1939–45 war the British government faced critical decisions in three areas of the Middle East – Palestine, Egypt, and Persia. The troubles could be viewed as local and unconnected, but in their broader aspects – Arab–Israel confrontation, belligerent nationalism, oil, and Soviet penetration – they were symptoms of forces that were to interact and keep the whole region tense for at least a generation.

The Times had always felt sympathy for the concept of Zionism, but abhorred the acts of terrorism against the mandatory authorities on which the movement had increasingly relied. When, on May 15 1948, the mandate was wound up and the state of Israel proclaimed, the event aroused more regrets for the past than hopes for the future. In a long leader by Rushbrook Williams entitled 'End of a Mission' *The Times* gave a warning:

> The peoples of Palestine will now make good their independence with violence and bloodshed. It is a historic tragedy which British soldiers and administrators have striven hard and failed to stave off . . . Today's tragedy springs from the refusal of Jews and Arabs to learn that, unless they can live together amicably in the land common to them both, they cannot hope to regain the peace and prosperity conferred upon them under British rule for a generation. This they now choose to learn in the hard school of war. The British people share deeply in the sorrow and regret at this failure – for a grim time at least – of a great mission.

Two special correspondents covered the final act of British rule in Palestine and the military and political developments which followed – Jerome Caminada and Louis Heren, joined for some time by Hugh Astor[25] who was wounded in a burst of gunfire when he was with Caminada. The three men went to the area on special limited assignments. They supplemented the staff correspondent who was based in Cairo, though he was expected to cover and report on the whole area.

---

25 Hon Hugh Astor (b. 1920). Eton; New College, Oxford. Army, 1939–45. Joined *The Times*, 1947; director Times Publishing Company, 1956–67.

Underground at Printing House Square in the blitz. Clockwise left to right:
F. P. Bishop (assistant manager), Geoffrey Dawson (editor), Colonel the Hon. J. J. Astor
(co-chief proprietor), R. W. Cooper (war correspondent), Robin Barrington-Ward (assistant
editor), John Walter (co-chief proprietor).

The two war-time editors confer: Geoffrey Dawson and Robin Barrington-Ward.

September 25 1940. Printing House Square after the direct hit.

Air Raid Precautions. Colonel Astor (second from right) and a team of 'spotters' on the roof of Printing House Square.

Stanley Morison, typographical adviser.

E. H. Carr, assistant editor.

Maurice Green, financial editor, assistant editor.

Oliver Woods, colonial editor, assistant editor.

A 4.15 editorial conference, November 1949. Casey (third from the right) and his three assistant editors sit with their backs to the wall. On his right are Donald Tyerman and A. P. Ryan; on his left Iverach McDonald. Then come clockwise from the extreme right, Ralph Deakin (foreign news editor), Alan Pitt Robbins (home news editor), Leslie Leslie-Smith (night editor), Donald Holmes (chief home sub-editor), G. L. Pearson (chief foreign sub-editor), R. Wells (correspondence editor), J. Filmer (obituaries editor).

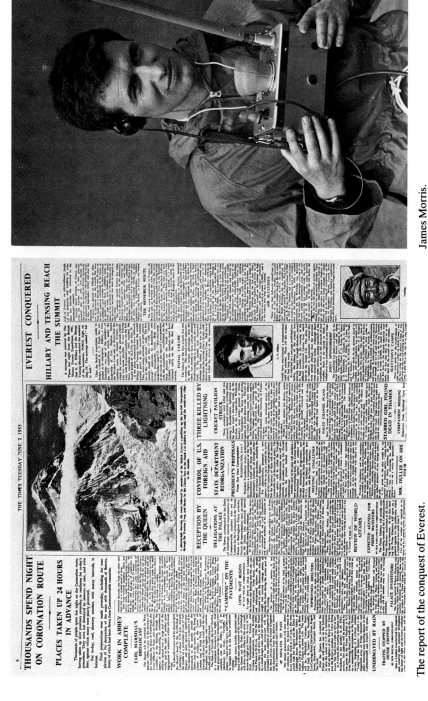

The report of the conquest of Everest.

James Morris.

R. W. Cooper: war-time France and India; Washington, Paris.

James Holburn: Moscow, Delhi, Middle East.

Ian Morrison: Far East.

Gerald Norman: North Africa, Paris, foreign news editor.

Louis Heren: India, Malaya, Bonn, Washington, foreign editor.

Sir Willmott Lewis: Washington.

J. H. Freeman: Berlin, Bonn, Geneva.

R. D. Preston: Belgrade, Vienna, Tokyo.

Dermot Morrah, special writer.

A. W. Rendel, diplomatic correspondent.

David Wood, political correspondent.

Walter James, editor, *Educational Supplement*.

1961. Old Printing House Square (on the right) goes down; new Printing House Square arises.

1962. The completed new Times offices by night against the background of floodlit St Paul's cathedral.

The first to occupy this Cairo post after the war was a regular soldier, Brigadier C. O. Quilliam. He had been introduced to Barrington-Ward by General Paget, Commander-in-Chief Middle East Forces, as one who had 'a wide knowledge of the Middle East and some of our major problems'. This was no overstatement. Quilliam, in nearly thirty years of soldiering, had spent most of his time in the Middle East theatre 'specially employed'. He spoke Turkish and some Arabic and Persian, and since 1942 had been head of the Political Intelligence Department at GHQ Middle East. In spite of some reservations by Deakin at Quilliam's lack of journalistic experience he was engaged on an experimental basis and started work in August 1945, to remain at his post for the next five and a half years.

Quilliam's training as a staff officer made it easier for him to draft confidential memoranda than news stories for publication. Indeed he was at first encouraged to do so, and the guidance which he regularly supplied to the editor and leader writers was based on a shrewd assessment of where Britain's true interests lay. In a letter dated May 2 1950, he wrote:

> I find a tendency to assume that Israel is always right and the Arabs always wrong and pigheaded – often they are, but they suffer from a burning sense of grievance which is not entirely without justification. Having lived in intimate contact with most of the present leaders of Israel, from Weizmann downwards, for some years, I have not the slightest belief in the thesis that we can appease Israel, except perhaps by the completest self-abasement. We have for years been, and will continue for years to be, public enemy No. 1 to the majority of the inhabitants of Israel . . . It is one thing to criticise – justifiably – the Arabs for their lack of realism: it is another to suggest that they can trust the Israelis or regulate their conduct on the assumption that Israel is a benevolent cooperative force in the Middle East. Israel can only exist if she weakens Arabia – and it is not certain that a weak Arabia is in British or Western interests. Nor should it be overlooked that Israeli propaganda – so often successful – is primarily directed in the Middle East to creating suspicions and ill-will between Britain and the Arab world, a propaganda we seem too easily to fall to.[26]

In fact, in spite of his background, Quilliam was very far from echoing the views of the Establishment. He repeatedly urged that British troops should be withdrawn from the centre of Cairo, where their presence

---

26 T.T.A.

after the ending of hostilities could only exacerbate nationalist feelings. This point was taken up in a leader on April 16 1946, when Rushbrook Williams commented on the composition of the delegation which the British government was sending to Cairo to negotiate a revision of the 1936 Anglo–Egyptian Treaty:

> Many Egyptians, while fully recognising that the dismantling of the enormous allied war base on Egyptian soil must take time, and that large bodies of troops cannot be evacuated overnight, regard the retention of British garrisons in such places as the Cairo Citadel and the Kasr el-Nil barracks as an indignity, only to be explained by some sinister intention on the part of Britain to continue into the years of peace the dominant position in the internal affairs of Egypt which was so ungrudgingly afforded throughout the war . . . The with-drawal of British troops from the interior of Cairo would be regarded everywhere in Egypt not as a symptom of Britain's weakness but as the kind of concession that a loyal ally may justly expect from a great and victorious friend.

When no such conciliatory gesture was made, and when five years of intermittent negotiations had ended in total breakdown, with the Nahas government tearing up the treaty, Quilliam was justified in the *post-mortem* analysis which he sent to PHS on October 15 1951:

> A reference to my past letters will show that I am not being wise after the event when I say that the Foreign Office has contributed substantially to the present mess by its lack of understanding of Egypt and its people, and its apparent disregard of Egyptian history. It started early in 1945, when a sympathetic Saadist Government asked if the Egyptian contribution to the war effort had not earned treaty revision. It was not until 1946 that we even agreed to listen to their request, and then, when negotiations did start, the Egyptian delegation – not to mention lots of British observers – got the impression that the F.O. thought it was dealing with a defeated enemy who had to be made to put its name on the dotted line.

Very soon after the war Quilliam had found the Shah of Iran inclined towards a paternalistic dictatorship, and suggested that 'in general his rather stupid behaviour is at variance with his wise talk.' It was to be on Persian soil that many of the ingredients of the Middle Eastern imbroglio – Russia, nationalism, and oil – were first to coalesce. Russia's backing for separatist movements in Azerbaijan and Kurdistan were thwarted by the firmness of the Iranian government, supported by the west, but the rise to power of Dr. Mossadeq on a wave of anti-western nationalism led to the nationalisation of the largely British owned and run oil industry.

The Times viewed this early outbreak of Middle Eastern nationalism, as it was to view many later manifestations of the same phenomenon, with a mixture of understanding and impatience. A leader by Midgley on April 30 1951 pointed out that:

Persia is a more sophisticated society than her neighbours, a relatively complex economy, an ancient and self-conscious nation . . . No true incompatibility divides the British from the Persian interests in Persian oil.

What really exasperated *The Times*, on this and on other similar occasions, was not so much the workings of xenophobia as the apparent inability of London and Washington – or rather, more particularly of their representatives on the spot – to act in harmony in a crisis. The same leader concluded that, in the oil dispute, the British and American governments had signally failed to support one another: 'A great deal can be blamed on Persian faults, but the fact remains that the two western governments primarily interested in the area have never been able to concert measures.'

A year later came an upheaval in another Middle East country which was in the long run to have a much more serious effect in Britain than did the temporary shut-down of Persia's oil. The first reactions of *The Times* to the Free Officers' *coup* in Egypt of July 23 1952 were cautious, partly because it had long been clear that the days of the monarchy were numbered. Back in April James Holburn, who had succeeded Quilliam as staff correspondent in the Middle East the year before, had warned privately: 'One has the feeling that all the stability built up since January 26 ["Black Saturday", when the mobs burned much of Cairo] could collapse in five minutes.'[27] A leader by Rushbrook Williams on July 25 took the news of the *coup* calmly:

The driving force behind the movement headed by General Neguib Mohammed [*sic*] is partly patriotism and partly professional pride. The question, as always on these dramatic military occasions, is whether power seized by these means will, in the event, be used for the good ends which have been proclaimed.

It was not until the following year that Nasser's name began to appear with any regularity in *Times* despatches, and even as late as April 16 1953 he was still described in another Rushbrook Williams leader as a

---

27 T.T.A.

man 'whose authority is second only to that of General Neguib'. A year later (February 26 1954), after Nasser had emerged on top in his struggle with Neguib, Rushbrook Williams described him as having 'the reputation of a realist, and those who know him say that he would like to strike a bargain – albeit a hard one – with this country if he can'. None the less his 'anti-British speeches' were noted and the warning was given that he might be tempted into 'chauvinistic extremes'. After the bargain over treaty revision had been struck *The Times* had no reservations in welcoming it:

> The agreement will of course have its critics in both countries. Those in Britain who see it as a surrender of prestige should consider soberly the alternatives. The Suez base in its present state has grown to be almost as much a liability as an asset.[28]

It was not long before harder language was used against Nasser.[29]

The Times's growing dislike of the Labour government's handling of affairs at home was shown especially strongly during the Argentine meat negotiations. History has let the negotiations fade into the general grey background of the years of food rationing, but at the time they stood out as a supreme illustration of the claim that Whitehall knows best. From 1946 onwards ministers believed that skilful bulk purchasing by the government would furnish a plenteous and unending supply of good-qulity meat at low prices. To hear some ministers talk, it seemed that the Argentinians would tumble over themselves to seize the opportunity. Nothing of the kind happened. Prices went up, supplies went down, rations in Britain were reduced, families complained bitterly at the quality as well as the quantity, and relations between Britain and Argentina were soured for some years as successive agreements were sought. On February 14 1948 a leader by Duncan Burn was highly critical of the first agreement:

> No one can regard with equanimity the need to buy foodstuffs from abroad at the cost of long-standing investments.

Two and a half years later Burn wrote again after the government in obstinate mood had reduced the meat ration at home rather than pay more for Argentine meat:

> The question most forcibly raised by the present dispute is whether government bulk purchase is a satisfactory means of handling trade

---

28 Leading article (Rushbrook Williams), October 20 1954.
29 See Chapter XIII.

dealing of this kind.[30]

On February 8 1951 Tyerman wrote much more strongly about the 'inexcusable miscalculations' that had brought the meat ration down to the lowest level yet endured in Britain, and he was aiming at Cripps himself, then Chancellor of the Exchequer, for Cripps still believed that he could, by tightening the British people's belts, force Argentina to bring its prices down:

> Never perhaps have the Government behaved more like Don Quixote, tilting with a fine fervour at imaginary villains and making themselves uncommonly foolish in the light of work-a-day facts . . . Now, through the haze of illusion, the outcome can be seen: practically no meat, higher not lower prices, a ridiculous outlay at home to butchers for not having more meat to sell, and a painful outcry from consumers at the high prices they have to pay for other foods to eke out the meagre ration.

Private traders, Tyerman wrote, could no doubt have done better by a process of trial and error:

> Yet even bulk buying, if it had not been led astray by austere and out-of-date notions concerning the balance of payments, could have struck a satisfactory bargain a long time ago.

Another leader by Burn on April 24 1951 rubbed in the point again. Tyerman's derogatory use of the word 'austere', inescapably coupled in the popular mind with the name of Sir Stafford Cripps (once much esteemed in *The Times*) was a clear sign in itself of the swing in the paper's thinking.

The swing was shown more heavily in the directly political leading articles as two general elections came into prospect; the first on February 23 1950 and the second on October 25 1951. As the time approached for the first both Casey and Tyerman were sure that five years in office had tired the Labour government and left it uncertain what to do next. When Tyerman wrote the leader which appeared on the morning of polling day, he rightly suggested that Labour would be returned by a small majority. His misgivings over the consequences were plain:

> The election will be remembered as the first in which the Conservatives had both a better programme and a better party machine than their Labour opponents . . . The Labour Party, clinging tenaciously

---

30 *The Times*, December 18 1950.

to the real appeal of full employment and 'fair shares', has deliberately fought a massive rearguard action, hoping to hold sufficient
ground to keep a narrow lead and simply saying in effect, with the
conservative Cavalier, 'when it is not necessary to change, it is
necessary not to change.'

Twenty months later *The Times* was more positive. When the Labour
party issued its election manifesto a leader by Fairlie pointed out that it
contained next to nothing that was both new and precise:

> A close reading reveals only one hard proposal: the Labour Govern-
> ment, it appears, are seeking a renewal of their mandate so that they
> may 'set up new auction markets in provincial towns.'[31]

Two days before the election Fairlie wrote again:

> The need for a change is unmistakable. If the vote goes against Mr.
> Attlee and his colleagues on Thursday, it will be because of the
> conviction that they have nothing further to contribute, in this
> chapter at least, to the conduct of their country's affairs at home and
> overseas . . . They can be judged by the recent facts of their
> stewardship. It is the mounting impression of indecision, delay,
> miscalculation and error that tells against them.[32]

On polling day itself there appeared yet another leader by Fairlie:

> The strongest argument for rejecting the Labour Government to-
> day is that after six testing years in office they have largely exhausted
> their capacity for creative thinking . . . From day to day they have
> still been striving to solve the problems of government with ideas
> which, precisely because they formed the basis of Labour thinking in
> the thirties, bear little relevance to the circumstances of the fifties.[33]

Casey and Tyerman – helped on the financial and economic side by
Maurice Green – had not been hasty in making up their minds. They had
praised many acts of the Labour government, particularly when it
introduced peacetime conscription, at first (in 1948) for eighteen
months' service, and then (in 1950) for two years' service. They recognised Cripps's courage in devaluing the pound in September 1949, even
while criticising the mismanagement of the economy that had made the
decision necessary. As could be expected, John Astor was easier in his

---

31 *The Times*, October 2 1951.
32 *The Times*, October 23 1951.
33 *The Times*, October 25 1951.

mind about the paper's policy under Casey. Apparently the only time that he demurred at anything was when Casey ran a leading article supporting the plan for abolishing capital punishment for a trial period. It was in Casey's very first month as editor:

> The desire to be rid of this terrible penalty, if it can be done without real danger to the community, is widely and deeply held; and this proposal offers an opportunity for a fair trial.[34]

After Astor's shy intervention, later leaders acknowledged that public opinion as a whole was probably against the proposal, but the paper none the less held to the abolitionist line.

Any general review of the Casey–Tyerman period must also pick out the way they encouraged writers, either in leading articles or in special articles, to give close and objective analyses of what was actually happening in industry or in social welfare. Two articles by Wigham reported in detail (August 25–26 1948) on a widespread mood of disappointment and disillusion in many factories where, after the proud act of nationalisation, little seemed to have changed for the man on the shop floor. In still greater detail Lafitte several times examined the working of the health service and the muddle left by the government's rent policy. Green emphasised the need to find money for the re-equipment of industry:

> There is certainly a case to be made against maintaining non-industrial building at its present level. Inevitably, if the basic industry programmes and public building are continued on the present scale, while consumption is at least maintained, the resources available for the re-equipment of the general range of intermediate and finishing industries will not be enough to safeguard the country's industrial and economic future.[35]

Such reviews in the early days of Casey's rule continued throughout his time, and they built up a strong case against the Labour administration on practical, non-ideological grounds. In general Casey was not attracted to theories and large policies as Barrington-Ward was. The cast of mind that made him respect Cripps less than Barrington-Ward had done also made him respect Churchill more warmly and more fully. Churchill noticed the difference in tone; a few days before the 1951 election he mentioned it to his doctor, Lord Moran:

---

34 Leading article (Morrah), April 14 1948.
35 *The Times*, October 16 1948.

The Times is very favourable to me, more than it has been for a long time.[36]

For all that, Casey well knew that Churchill could let himself be carried away. Once when they met at a weekend in John Astor's home, Hever Castle, Casey asked Churchill what exactly he had meant in his speech at Zurich in September 1946 on the need for European unity. Had he federation in mind, or confederation, or simply a loose association? The old warrior recoiled from such attempts to fetter his free-roving imagination. He replied at length on the opportunity that presented itself to harness and unite the creative energies of the old continent which had given so much that was precious to the world. Casey pressed him again to be precise; they had a great set-to; and at the end their fellow guests told each other that most of the points had gone to quiet, gentle Casey.

Michael Foot[37] pays a tribute, reluctantly as a politician, admiringly as an old journalist, to *The Times* in the second volume of his biography of Aneurin Bevan.[38] On July 4 1948 Bevan spoke at a great Labour rally at Bellevue, Manchester. After contrasting Labour's social programme with the memories of his own youth on the means test, he said that nothing could eradicate from his heart a 'deep burning hatred for the Tory party' that had inflicted such experiences on him. 'So far as I am concerned they are lower than vermin.' Michael Foot quotes the mild headlines of other papers before writing:

> Only one newspaper picked on the fatal word. The Times headline read: 'Mr. Bevan's "burning hatred". Attack on Tory "Vermin".' And possibly it was this nose for news of a Times sub-editor, so much more discriminating than that of his yellower rivals, which unleashed the storm.

The report appeared on the Monday. The storm gathered violence throughout the week with politicians and both dailies and Sundays seizing on the one word, vermin. Attlee sent Bevan a rebuke by letter. Bevan's fling did Labour harm for some time.

---

36 Lord Moran, *Winston Churchill: The Struggle for Survival, 1940–1965*, p. 345.
37 Michael Foot (b. 1913). Assistant editor, *Tribune*, 1937–38. Acting editor, *Evening Standard*, 1942. Managing director, *Tribune*, 1945–74. Labour MP for Ebbw Vale from 1960. Secretary of State for Employment 1974; Leader of the House of Commons 1976–79; Leader of the Labour Party 1980–83.
38 Michael Foot, *Aneurin Bevan, 1945–1960*, p. 239.

IX

END OF THE SEARCH

D URING much of Casey's term *The Times* did well as a trading company. Francis Mathew's energy was soon making itself felt. After Kent's ultra-cautious manner it was startling to have a manager who delighted to come out with the most far-fetched ideas as though they were self-evidently sound propositions. He seemed to like judging men by the degree of panic into which such ideas threw them. In fact most of the staff responded well to the stimulus and the greater informality.

Early in his years as manager he launched several ventures which helped the company, some wholly so, some with losses to offset the gains, but all stimulating. First of all he showed his training as a printer in the special excitement which he brought, with Stanley Morison's help, to introducing a new face for small type to allow more words to be set in a line. The new size of Monotype Times New Roman, Series 327, was commissioned from the Monotype Corporation and was called Claritas. It seemed a small change but had large consequences. In his enthusiasm for this space-saving Claritas type Mathew persuaded Casey and Maurice Green, then City editor, to publish in great detail and at great length on the City pages each morning the previous day's Stock Exchange dealings. Previously *The Times* had given simply each day's opening and closing prices. Mathew saw in the new plan a way of stealing some of the *Financial Times's* ammunition and stopping readers from leaving *The Times* for its City rival. He assured Casey and Green that, thanks to the new type, this new feature would not take up more than two or three columns a day. It was introduced on June 18 1951. Unfortunately it began almost immediately to eat up far more space than Mathew had imagined. When it occupied seven, eight, nine or even more columns a day it became a burden which far outweighed any advantages it brought. Worthwhile City news had often to be held out to make room for it; or, worse for other departments to bear, it spread over into space that should have gone to sports news or arts features. After Lord Thomson bought *The Times* in 1966 it reverted to the simpler and much shorter list that only gave closing prices.

Mathew had more satisfaction with the excellent device, brought in on June 15 1951, for using remote control in putting into type all the many columns of parliamentary reports. A man operated a keyboard in the Palace of Westminster; an unmanned machine in Printing House Square set the type. All the hours that had been lost in carrying a stream of reports by hand from the one place to the other were saved. *The Times* felt that it was really coming into the brave new world, tiny though the step was. Mathew had even more pleasure in the mobile printing press which he kept in the country in case Printing House Square was put out of action for any reason. The press was first seen at the British Industries Fair in April 1953. Whether the print unions would have let the press be used during a strike remained always doubtful, but the device showed at least that *The Times* believed in experiment.

Such things were infinitely small compared to Mathew's success in reaching an agreement in principle, as early as September 1950, to print the *Observer* on Saturday afternoons and evenings on the Printing House Square presses. Mathew had carefully and skilfully courted the *Observer*. Gaining the contract would mean that the *Times* presses, used six nights of the week, would be gainfully employed the seventh night. As it happened, the fast growing circulation and size of the *Observer* under David Astor's bold editorship led to delays before the project could be turned into practice. Printing House Square had to install new machinery to cope with the swollen demand and the printing did not begin until September 1958. But that first agreement of September 1950 was the start of a partnership which, bringing in substantial revenues to Printing House Square, helped *The Times* to survive in the critical years ahead.[1]

Two much larger projects were begun during Mathew's first years as manager. Both Astor and Mathew were keen to have an entirely new Printing House Square. As described in Chapter III the machine rooms downstairs had fortunately been reconstructed in time to provide the air-raid shelters during the 1939–45 war. In February 1950 preliminary plans for rebuilding all the rest – editorial, mechanical, commercial – were put before the Board of directors. It was the beginning of many years of upheaval.[2]

The second project, no less bold, was also to have long-term effects

---

1 See Chapter XV.
2 See Chapter XVII.

on the fortunes of the paper. It was the adoption and use by *The Times* of a special kind of paper that could not be classed as newsprint and was therefore outside the newsprint rationing system. This venture was to have political consequences which benefited all newspapers. The knowledge that *The Times* was developing its own independent supply of paper was a strong force in persuading government to end its newsprint rationing system in 1956.[3] By a strange ironic twist the other newspapers benefited even more than *The Times*. The others had the new freedom to use newsprint which was cheaper than the so-called mechanical paper. *The Times* had committed itself to using the dearer paper more and more.

Earlier managers, Lints Smith and Kent, had begun the talks as long ago as the thirties with the firm, Townsend Hook, which produced the so-called 'mechanical printing' paper, made from wood pulp and an unusually high proportion of chemical pulp. Mathew was authorised by the Board to take up the negotiations again very soon after he became manager. On December 1 1949 a far-reaching agreement was signed. The Times Publishing Company bound itself to use Townsend Hook paper exclusively as soon as, and for as long as, it was available in sufficient quantities to meet the needs of the paper and its supplements. Townsend Hook on their part bound themselves to enlarge their capacity until they could meet such needs. The agreement was to run for twenty-five years and be renewable after twenty. It was not until March 1956 that they could meet the full needs, but Printing House Square had been using all available supplies before then.

The disadvantages were as clear as the advantages. Reel for reel, the special paper was promised to be only five per cent dearer than the London price of newsprint. But it was of exceptional weight, which put up the cost of freightage and made the paper fifteen or so per cent dearer in all. The Board had another anxiety. How to ensure that the Townsend Hook supplies would always be ample and regular? To avert any danger the Board began to acquire shares in Townsend Hook and gradually built up a controlling interest.

Against such anxieties could be set the high quality of the paper which, especially good for the reproduction of photographs, would according to Mathew's hopes attract more 'prestige' advertisements. 'The surest way of increasing our advertising revenue,' he wrote rather too simply and cheerfully, 'would be to improve the quality of our print.' Another advantage was immediate and more tangible. In the early years of the agreement Mathew could use newsprint as well as the new

---

3 See Chapter XV.

mechanical paper. He kept all the newsprint, still tightly rationed, to be used by *The Times* itself; he was even able to increase slightly its number of pages in a week. At the same time he skilfully persuaded the government to classify all the supplements of *The Times* as periodicals, free from rationing controls. The Townsend Hook paper was consequently used not only for the usual supplements but also for three new large quarterlies that were started – the *British Colonial Review* and the *Science Review* in 1951 and the *Agricultural Review* in 1952. Each of them did well.

The Townsend Hook paper was a bold venture which brought credit to *The Times* and, it can be emphasised again, played a strong part in ending newsprint rationing. What has also to be emphasised is that the extra expense of the special paper increased the financial strains which beset the company in the sixties.

Mathew was not simply a printing manager. In 1951 he introduced an entirely new and better pension scheme for the staff. He raised some salaries in all departments, though he still left too large a gap between payments to men at or near the top and those in the middle and lower ranks. Casey was given £6000 a year when appointed, rising to £8000 in 1950, plus £2000 expenses. His assistant editors received £3000 or more, plus expenses about half of Casey's. Mathew began at £5000; he went up to £7250 after two years and he, like Casey, had £2000 expenses. His assistant managers were made roughly equal to the assistant editors at £3000. After such figures, however, there generally came a big drop to £1500. A table of payments[4] to leader writers and special writers, including assistant editors, gives some idea of the pyramid and also how salaries began to creep up between June 1946 and the financial year in which Casey left, that is, the year ended June 1953. In each case the lowest scale – 'up to £500' – covered trainees:

	June 30 1946	June 30 1953
No. of men with salaries:		
Up to £500	5	9
£500–£1000	19	9
£1000–£1500	6	13
Over £1500	2	5

---

4 The tables and figures in this chapter are all taken from T.T.A. Figures for salaries and running costs have been used sparingly because rising inflation and increased standards of living over the past thirty or forty years make them misleading more often

To put these figures in perspective it may be recalled that the minimum rate of pay for a journalist in London was £630 a year until March 1951, when it was raised to £760. In addition there was a cost of living bonus, raised from eight shillings a week in 1951 to one pound a week in May 1953. On *The Times* the chief home sub-editor was given a salary of £1050 in 1948. The night editor – the man responsible for the layout of the whole paper and also for getting it to press on time – was given a salary of £2000 in 1949.

Inflation during the years since then has made such figures seem derisory. Other papers paid more for comparable jobs, but the prestige and satisfaction of working for *The Times* were still held to offer compensatory advantages. Many men joined *The Times* as they would join an order, knowing that they were renouncing the prospect of higher pay elsewhere. (It was a sense of dedication not always shared by their wives faced with household bills.) The satisfaction in working for *The Times* showed itself no less strongly in the remarkable team spirit on the mechanical side. This spirit was brought out to the full in an emergency. A flood of news, caused by some late-night crisis in the world, had everyone going flat out to get every word of it into the next edition.Two columns of typescript could be received by the head printer within a quarter of an hour of press time; he would divide the copy up into 'takes' of a few lines for each setting machine; and the paper would still get away on time, with every word of the new copy in it, and every word corrected by proof readers who came down specially into the composing room. It was always a free and easy partnership between the editorial and the mechanical sides, such as could grow up, and be sustained, only in a small family-like organisation. Even in such a small organisation the partnership might not have survived the strains brought on by inflation and rising costs.

Francis Mathew did not escape a swift rise in costs from every side. Foreign correspondents' salaries and expenses, plus the fees for the agencies that carried foreign news, required £69,430 in 1946 and £127,654 in 1953. Other editorial departments showed similar rises. On the mechanical side the wages for the composing, reading and casting staffs came to £102,678 in 1946 and to £215,433 in 1953. The bill for newsprint trebled and for printer's ink more than doubled:

---

than not. But a general guide is given in figures supplied by the Central Statistical Office in London. The retail price index shows a pound in 1946 to be the equal of £11.66 at the beginning of 1984; the 1950 pound to equal £9.63 at the same date; the 1960 pound £6.91, and the 1965 pound £5.87.

	1946	1950	1953
Newsprint	£128,762	£208,335	£380,420
Ink	£3,763	£7,899	£9,468

To counter-balance all this the paper's revenue also rose. Money from sales and subscriptions amounted to £525,458 in 1946 and to £748,761 in 1953. This fund was helped on February 11 1952 when the price of the paper was raised from 3d. to 4d. Money from advertisements came to £702,139 in 1946 and to £1,286,776 in 1953. As trade and industry began to take up after the war George Pope, in charge of advertising, revived old lines of advertisements and opened up several healthy new ones. The columns of company-meeting reports came back and they all paid well. The big firms put in more of their quarter-page or half-page 'prestige' displays. Large advertisements for concerts, a new line for *The Times*, became a profitable and highly readable feature. Some of the smaller classified advertisements – the Situations Vacant and such like – began to appear in the larger form known as semi-display. (Ironically these semi-displays were to be greatly developed by the *Daily Telegraph*, with its much larger circulation and advertising staff, and became one of its selling assets.)

As a result of these drives *The Times* made a profit each year, but in general it was a decreasing profit in the years 1948 to 1952. The figures for these years are:

1946	1947	1948	1949	1950	1951	1952	1953
£	£	£	£	£	£	£	£
445,922	467,660	301,852	278,915	334,920	273,420	201,290	253,455

The table shows 1952, the last full year of Casey's term, as an especially disappointing year. To make it worse circulation had for some years also fallen again after rising when newsprint rationing was eased. Worse still for Printing House Square, its rivals were doing well. The circulation of the *Daily Telegraph*, packing itself with hard news and carrying a lighter burden of official and formal news than *The Times*, was rising. In 1946 *The Times* was kept by rationing to an average of 220,939 copies a day. By 1950 it had reached 254,654. In 1952 the circulation was down to 231,659 and the signs were it would fall further.

Directors and staff alike were asking what was lacking in the paper. To say that *The Times* was more badly hobbled by newsprint rationing than any other paper was true but supplied only part of the explanation for its disappointing showing. Some sections gave good value. The dangers and tensions throughout the world and the upheavals in the colonial territories made the overseas news compulsive reading. They were the years when in almost every continent British interests were directly involved and British soldiers were committed. At home the art, music and drama critics were writing more fully and more brightly again after coming out of wartime shadows. But the home news – the most tightly squeezed of any section of the paper in those years of continued rationing – had not only lost space; it had lost most of its spirit. Except for an occasional fling it played for safety day by day and kept itself to routine news.

The paper would rise splendidly to big occasions in home news and leave long troughs in between. When part of Exmoor was flooded and much of Lynmouth destroyed on a Friday–Saturday night in August 1952 Philip Ure, one of the staff reporters, was off the mark as quickly as anyone on any paper; he was soon at the right places for describing the worst havoc and meeting the right men to tell him about the work of rescue and reconstruction. He was out in the blue on his own. He himself wrote afterwards very truly: 'One of the great attractions of reporting for *The Times* is that one is allowed to use one's own judgment besides being allowed to do the job in one's own way.'[5] That was *The Times* at its best. Other examples are on the files.

In between the big occasions on the home side *The Times* would say, to its credit, that if there was no substantial news then minor matters should not be blown up out of all proportion. On the other hand this attitude often meant that news which lay just below the surface was missed or left to other papers.

Sadly, the praise given to *The Times* by the Royal Commission on the Press, in its report published in June 1949, came at the wrong time. The commission had been appointed two years earlier with Sir David Ross, a former Provost of Oriel College, Oxford (1929–47), as its chairman. Everything which it said in its report was well deserved; it was all extremely gratifying; it commended *The Times* for doing a newspaper's true job in reporting the news without bias. On the highly controversial Gravesend by-election, narrowly won by Sir Richard Acland on November 26 1947, the commission wrote:

> The treatment by the national Press of the Gravesend by-election affords an example of complete absence of objectivity. With the exception of *The Times*, all the papers reported the election from their own point of view, spotlighting the candidate they favoured and, when not ignoring, depreciating his opponent. News and views became inextricably interwoven.[6]

---

5 *House Journal*, September 1952.
6 Report of Royal Commission on the Press. Cmd. 7700. Paragraph 432.

On food rationing, which aroused much popular anger and mystification, the commission picked out *The Times* for special commendation, saying that it related the difficulties in Britain to the background of a world shortage of food. '*The Times* gave a balanced account of the support for and opposition to rationing.'[7] Similarly on housing the report found that *The Times* gave full and fair appraisals, both in the text of the news and in headlines, of the progress made in providing new homes. On the paper's coverage of the coal shortage in 1946–47 the report stated:

> The news items were detailed and balanced in tone. Absenteeism was fully reported but was not unduly emphasised.[8]

On the general appearance of newspapers the report, when discussing *The Times*, analysed more than criticised:

> The make-up of the main news page [of most papers] became more fragmented. *The Times* alone did not make more than minor concessions to this tendency. Headlines grew larger as a whole, and the main headline grew more than the rest. This tendency was noticeable even in *The Times*.[9]

In its leading article of June 30 1949, written by Ryan, *The Times* passed over the words of praise with a becoming silence and restricted itself chiefly to doubts as to whether the suggested Press Council – the chief proposal in the report – was either necessary or workable; the paper saw in the proposal a potential threat to press freedom. None the less the praise given to *The Times* in the report was welcomed in the office. The only trouble was that there had been an inevitable time lag between the commission's investigations and the publication of its findings. The tributes to the sobriety of the news columns were based on examples taken during the Barrington-Ward period when the paper was fulfilling one of the main criteria for success: it was getting itself talked about, largely by the polemical and highly controversial tone of leading articles. Coming out in the quieter year of 1949, the commission's praise, dealing chiefly with home news and comment, made the paper appear entirely worthy but rather flat. Tyerman had been doing his best to stir up the home side, but ingrained habits were slow to change.

In his autobiography John Pringle wonders why *The Times* which he knew in the Casey period was not better. He praises Casey:

---

7 *Ibid*, Appendix VII, by B. Silverman. Paragraph 448.
8 *Ibid*, Appendix VII. Paragraph 134.
9 *Ibid*, Appendix VII. Paragraph 64.

He knew exactly what *The Times* could say and could not say. When it came to policy he had very much the same shrewd feeling for what was sensible and what was nonsense. He was not an intellectual or a scholar but he had a wide knowledge of Europe and understood far better than many intellectuals and scholars how politics worked.[10]

Unfortunately, writes Pringle, Casey was appointed editor too late in his career and had stopped grappling seriously with the problems of the day:

He preferred to leave these matters to Tyerman and McDonald and only intervened when his instinct told him that they had strayed from the path of commonsense. Moreover, as time went on, he found it harder to face the detailed administrative work and constant decisions which are the lot of any editor . . . This slightly dilettante approach to his job was inevitably reflected in the paper. It was also unfair on Tyerman who often had to get the paper out for days on end without much guidance from the editor. He had the responsibility without the position.[11]

This is a recognisable but severe portrait of Casey. It underrates the extent to which his closer colleagues consulted him and were guided by him. A central influence was felt even though – as was certainly true – very little central direction was given in Casey's later months. Many excellent things were done each day. *The Times* devoted itself to providing a public service, and it was a good service. But as an organisation it had within it two large imbalances.

First there was the imbalance between the editorial and the managerial sides. Once one went below the few top men on each side, the editorial staff as a whole was of a much higher quality in educational background and in talent than the staff on the other side who had, or should have had, the vital job of promoting the financial interests of the paper. Secondly, within the editorial side, leaving aside the leader writers, there was a similar disproportion between the foreign and the home staffs. Most of the promising young men quickly applied for jobs abroad, partly for the obvious interest that such jobs offered, but partly because they saw that home news seemed to be the poor relation. Parliamentary reports, political news, law reports, and official announcements were very properly given, leaving little space for 'home specials' or even workaday home news.

---

10 Pringle, *op. cit.* pp. 52–53.
11 *Ibid*, p. 53.

In 1951 and early 1952 John Astor and one or two directors began the search for a man who could bring to the chair all the virtues that the ideal editor should have – wisdom, skill, drive – and also something extra. After the years of interregnum they saw advantages in having an editor of *The Times* who was a national figure from the beginning, a man with an established and widely recognised reputation. The decision to look outside the office came as a heavy disappointment to Tyerman. He had practically run the paper in the past months and he had found it especially wearing because he did not know, often enough, whether or not Casey would stay on in an evening, and he could not always be certain that Casey would agree with a political line taken while he was away. Casey to his credit was always easy and tactful but Tyerman was not to be envied. For years he had had the challenging but always slightly hampering job as deputy, first very largely to Barrington-Ward and then wholly to Casey.

Looking outside the office, John Astor first sounded Geoffrey Crowther who had combined much public service with his brilliant editing of the *Economist*. Crowther had however just committed himself to another long term with the *Economist*. Lord Brand, a senior director, asked Sir Oliver Franks, then ambassador in Washington, if he would answer a call, but Franks could not see himself as an editor.

In 1951 John Astor seemed to meet his biggest disappointment of all. Lord Brand, and then John Walter and Lord Brand together, approached Sir William Haley, director-general of the BBC. Haley – outstanding both as a journalist and as an administrator – appeared to have the many qualities that Printing House Square was looking for. What was more, he had first made his mark as a young man on *The Times*. After school in his native Jersey and service during the First World War as a wireless operator in the merchant navy, he had joined the foreign telephonists' room in *The Times*. His prime job was to take down despatches from the correspondents abroad. Communications from the Continent were difficult at that time, so soon after the war. Haley persuaded Lints Smith, the manager, to send him to Brussels to carry out a plan which he, Haley, had worked out with Susan Gibbons, the young secretary to B. K. Long, the foreign editor, and Hugh McGregor, foreign news editor. Miss Gibbons, then 19, as Haley was, had charge of the continental copy-takers. Their idea was that Brussels would become a centre for receiving, shortening if need be, and transmitting the continental correspondents' messages in a more order-ly way, with Susan Gibbons supervising the London end of the opera-tion. The plan worked from the start and within a few months Miss Gibbons left *The Times*; she became *Daily Mail* correspondent in

Belgium, and Haley and she were married.

Haley very soon became engrossed in the stuff of journalism as well as in its transmission. In 1922, when he was still only twenty-one, he joined the *Manchester Evening News* as sub-editor. From that time every few years brought him promotion and more varied, more responsible, and wider work. In the years 1939–43 he was not only managing director of the Manchester Guardian and Evening News Limited; he was a director of both the Press Association, coping with home news, and of Reuters, which covered foreign news. In fact he, more than anyone, reorganised the Reuters service and its foreign contracts. In 1943 he became editor-in-chief of the BBC, and within a year he was director-general. The quality of his mind then became apparent to the country and far beyond. He built up the news services; he launched the Third Programme to foster serious music, literature, and the arts; he began the Reith lectures. It seemed to Astor and others that a man who had built upon and developed the Reith tradition could build upon and develop the *Times* tradition.

Haley was attracted by the prospect but – this is where Astor met his disappointment – he felt that he could not leave the BBC in that year, 1951. The whole future of broadcasting had been thrown open by the publication of the Beveridge report on broadcasting as recently as January of that same year. The trouble lay not in the main report. Lord Beveridge and all the committee, with one exception, had come down strongly against the idea of commercial television.[12] The trouble, as Haley saw it, came from that one exception. Selwyn Lloyd,[13] already rising in the Conservative party, had put in a minority report recommending that the BBC should no longer have sole responsibility but should be given a strong competitor in a separate television service. The suggestion was in line with the Conservatives' broad attack on state monopolies as a whole.

With a general election probable soon, the BBC staff were deeply disturbed and apprehensive. Haley thought that he should stay with them until they knew what would happen, one way or another. Their fears were confirmed. In May 1952 the Conservative government, having won the election of October 1951, declared in a White Paper that it favoured 'some element of competition' in television.[14] Haley foresaw that the BBC would have to change itself and lower its standards to meet that competition. He decided to take up the still open invitation from

---

12 *Report of the Broadcasting Committee, 1949.* Cmd. 8116. paras. 171–80.
13 Selwyn Lloyd (1904–78). Secretary of State for Foreign Affairs, 1955–60; Speaker of the House of Commons, 1971–76. Baron, 1976.
14 Cmd. 8550. para. 7.

The Times.

On June 5 1952 the Board of directors was informed by John Astor and John Walter that they had appointed Haley to be editor of *The Times*. He would take over the chair on October 1. With a typical concern for method and for planning, Haley wished to have the three months before October to himself; he wanted time to think ahead to the job which he, as a journalist first and foremost, considered to be the summit of his profession.

X

HALEY: THE STYLE IS THE MAN

NORTHCLIFFE[1] used to say that *The Times* of his day had never got over the handicap of beginning life at Blackfriars on the site of an old monastery. He meant that it remained a semi-enclosed order, preserving its own canonical language and its own narrowly selective ideas about what was news. The jibe was partly true. Forty years later Beaverbrook said that Haley was turning *The Times* into a newspaper; and that was wholly true. Haley gave the paper new ambitions and new methods of working. His fourteen years in the editor's chair were years of reorganisation, moves towards modernisation, constant pressure, self-examination by the paper the whole time, intense effort for many members of the staff, and at the end the satisfaction of seeing a new *Times* that was expanding in circulation and appeal.

Haley began quietly and slowly, so slowly that men and women in the office were puzzled. His apparent diffidence did not fit in with his formidable reputation. Aged fifty-one when he arrived, and looking younger, he was at the height of his intellectual and administrative powers. All the reports from the BBC emphasized his austerity and his efficiency. The austerity was shown, it was said, in the Reith-like standards which he set for the broadcasts, in his dealings with his staff, and in his own personal way of life. The efficiency, it was added, came out in his zeal for tight budgetary discipline over every single department, his formal manner of conducting business by memorandum and carefully prepared conference, his dislike of small talk (never speaking in a lift, one heard), and his belief in keeping himself and others fully stretched. Yet, having settled in Printing House Square, he seemed quite content to spend some months in listening and learning. He told a near colleague that, once he had made some urgent appointments, he was quite prepared to let two years pass before setting about changing *The Times*.

---

1 Alfred Harmsworth, Viscount Northcliffe (1865–1922). Created *Daily Mail*; owned *The Times*, 1908–22.

He made the chief appointments swiftly. He confirmed Donald Tyerman as chief assistant editor – in effect deputy editor – with special oversight over the home side; Tyerman kept this position until he left three years later to edit the *Economist*. Haley also confirmed Patrick Ryan as an assistant editor and greatly broadened his field. It was one of Haley's most perceptive moves. He knew Ryan from their BBC days together and recognised how much there was to bring out in him. The treatment worked. After being, at times, dormant under Barrington-Ward and Casey, Ryan blossomed out. He recaptured the instincts and keenness of an all-round journalist, took charge of many of the special features and book reviews (soon to be greatly expanded),[2] and did more than anyone else under Haley to bring new subjects into the paper.

Ryan was in his early fifties when Haley came; incurably inquisitive about everything, whether it was the hidden meaning of a line in Horace, or the truth behind a nineteenth-century legal tangle involving *The Times*, or the reason why England's test captain chose to declare when he did. He was always a first-rate talker, witty, laconic, shrewd, and he wrote in the same way. His articles after his periodic visits to South Africa and Ireland – his chosen fields abroad – were always simple and outspoken. Being a sturdy patriot himself, he could recognise the patriotism in others, whether Sinn Fein or Afrikaners, and they trusted him even when he criticised them in his articles. In Printing House Square he was happily unconventional, disappearing without trace for hours if there were some books to find in the London Library or some talk to be finished at the Garrick Club. At other times he would turn up near midnight to polish off a review or would spend most of a weekend in the office when he was marked down to be off. In an office that tended to take itself over-seriously it was refreshing to see Ryan setting about a job as if he was simply doing what he wanted to do in precisely the way he wanted to do it. Younger men would cheer up when he showed them that a little commonsense could usually bring them to the nub of a problem, and they would cheer up even more when – always generous, always genuine – he hailed an article of theirs as if it were the last word on the subject. What he meant was that the article was clear, unpretentious, and free of jargon.

Haley's third appointment came when, after being in the office only a month, he made Iverach McDonald foreign editor.[3] Thereby he

---

2 See Chapter XI.
3 Iverach McDonald (b. 1908). Leeds Grammar School. Assistant editor *Yorkshire Post*, 1933. Sub-editor, *The Times* 1935; correspondent in Berlin, 1937–38 and in Prague, 1938; diplomatic correspondent, 1938; captain, General Staff, 1939–40; assistant editor, 1948; foreign editor, 1952; managing editor, 1965; associate editor, 1967–73; director, Times Newspapers, 1968–73.

revived a post which had been left unfilled for twenty-four years. When Dr. Williams,[4] then foreign editor, died in 1928 Dawson recorded in his diary that Williams was 'quite irreplaceable' and so with great logic had not replaced him. The lack was felt in the office, especially as the European crisis deepened, and it had led for some years to some heart-burning among three or four older members of the staff such as Leo Kennedy, Philip Graves and Ralph Deakin. Each of them fancied that he should be foreign editor or that he was foreign editor in all but name. When Haley came he found McDonald in charge of foreign leaders and Deakin in charge of news. He decided the more easily to unify the department because Barrington-Ward, Casey, and Mathew had all considered that Deakin, who was sixty-four when Haley came, should be asked to retire early after all his years of work that had come near to exhausting him. Casey had thought of sending him on a leisurely world tour when he could inspect and make recommendations on all *The Times* posts. In the end he was asked in the autumn of 1952 to retire at the end of March 1953, keeping his full salary until the end of the year and then taking a pension.

McDonald had already spent much of his working life abroad. When appointed foreign editor he was forty-four. He had become an assistant editor on the *Yorkshire Post* (under the anti-appeasing editor Arthur Mann) in his twenties. Most people of his generation had their views hammered into shape by the Hitler regime and by Munich. The lessons were driven home to McDonald with especial force as, after joining *The Times* in 1935, he served in Hitler's Berlin and then had agonising months in Prague and in the Czech borderlands throughout the crisis that led to the Munich surrender. He was wholly against the paper's appeasement policy, and it was he whom Runciman saw in Prague on the morning of the September 7 leader and asked to send remonstrances to Dawson.[5] Like Dr. Harold Williams, McDonald was a specialist in Russia. He had travelled in Soviet Russia three times before the war and learned Russian with tutors from Leeds University and the School of Slavonic Studies in London. As diplomatic correspondent from 1938 – broken by service in the War Office, 1939–40 – he had been in wartime Russia and North America, and had followed all the allied summit conferences during and after the war. After Casey made him assistant editor in 1948 he still did more than his fair share of travelling throughout Europe and southern Asia (neither did he forget his Scottish Highlands and their problems). One great advantage which he had on

4 Dr. Harold Williams (1876–1928). Leader writer, 1921–22; director of foreign department, 1922–28.
5 See Chapter I.

becoming foreign editor was that he knew from personal meetings most of the leading statesmen who were trying to come to a working agreement in the world.

Haley made his fourth major appointment some months later. In April 1953 he brought Maurice Green forward to be assistant editor with special charge of economic and financial affairs. As recounted in Chapter II, Green had gone into journalism before the war with a brilliant academic record at Rugby and University College, Oxford. Brendan Bracken had made him editor of the *Financial News* and Dawson took him on in 1938 with the title that he asked for – financial and industrial editor. After serving in the war as instructor in anti-aircraft artillery, he came back to his former job but found Tyerman doing much of the work and Carr laying down an economic line which Green disliked. He therefore concentrated on organising the paper's City news and views and on developing its financial and economic supplements. Like Ryan he blossomed out when Haley gave him his new appointment and, after Tyerman left in 1955, he became the chief assistant editor who was the first in the chair when Haley was away.

Green's mind worked in a highly schooled way; he wrote rapidly in classically balanced sentences; his argument usually followed a dextrous intellectual line, punctuated with expert detail, while remaining perfectly clear. But his most individualistic habit in the office was his relapse into deep silences when faced with a question, whether difficult or apparently simple. He would stare out of the window, his brows contracting with the effort at concentration, his lips opening as if on the point of utterance but then closing again. Haley used to say that he 'always enjoyed the pleasure of watching you [Green] think.'[6] John Grant, then defence correspondent, long remembered the first time that he took one of his leaders in for Green to read and pass. Green went through it without a word, then gazed out across the Thames, and went on gazing as though nerving himself for a distasteful task. Grant expected to hear that the leader was no good. Or (he thought) perhaps Green was working out the precise impact which the proposed expenditure would have on the balance of payments over the next fifteen years. Green finally spoke. 'Should we call it, "Military Muddles"?'

Anyone sitting through such silences found them hard to square with Green's great efficiency in getting through a vast amount of administrative business each day, his skill and conscientiousness as director of the paper's pension funds trust, his quick discernment in examining would-be recruits after Tyerman's departure, his speed and exact knowledge in

---

6 Farewell speech to Maurice Green, April 25 1961. T.T.A.

writing, and his stubborn battle with Haley when wishing to take on more reporters and pay them all more.[7] How much he got through each day became obvious only when he left in 1961 after being Haley's chief assistant for six years.

Another man who was quickly brought forward by Haley was Oliver Woods. As British governments spent weeks and months asking themselves whether the colonies were truly ready to govern themselves – a question that was to be swept aside by the claims from the colonies themselves – Woods's work as colonial correspondent became more intense and his journeys of inquiry became wider and more frequent.[8] He also deputised on the foreign side as a whole during the months when McDonald was in Russia or elsewhere.

Haley had hardly begun to make his first major appointments when he was suddenly confronted with the need to make another. Ralph Deakin was found dead at home on the morning of December 19 1952. Those who had been closest to him in the office were greatly shocked. They knew that he had been bitterly hurt when asked to retire a few months ahead of time. He was outraged when his work over the years was barely acknowledged in the fourth volume of the *History of The Times*, published in that same year 1952. Other disappointments were weighing on him. At the inquest on December 22–23 his widow produced a sad letter written by him. A pathologist said that he had found some barbitone *post mortem* but it was, he said, 'well within a therapeutic dose'. Later the same doctor said, 'There is no doubt there is not a gross overdose of barbitone.' Later still he said that the amount of barbiturates which he found indicated a dose of two tablets, 'which was an amount frequently used'. What the doctor discovered beyond doubt was that Deakin had advanced coronary disease:

> The coroner (Mr. W. Bentley Purchase): Is the coronary condition affected by worry or disturbance?
> The pathologist (Mr. F. E. Camps): Quite definitely; emotion plays a very big part.[9]

A verdict of death from natural causes was recorded.

Early in the new year Gerald Norman was brought from the Paris office to take Deakin's place as foreign news editor. Largely thanks to his friendliness and his neat organising sense the work of the department was brought much more closely into the general planning of the paper.

7 See Chapter XI.
8 See Chapter XIV.
9 *The Times*, December 24 1952.

Yet another change from existing practice which Haley made soon after arriving was to let Stanley Morison know very firmly that, while his views on typography would still be heeded, his observations on editorial matters would be neither sought nor welcomed. This was a blow to Morison and a relief to editorial men who had not known whether to be bewildered, suspicious, or amused by Morison's interventions. They had never been sure of his status. The nearest that anyone came to defining his titles and duties was Barrington-Ward's attempt in October 1947:

Historian, typographer-in-chief, and to carry out special duties for the editor.[10]

In carrying out those 'special duties' Morison became as close a companion and club-mate of Casey's as he had been a counsellor and friend of Barrington-Ward's. He showered comments about the paper on them both. He wrote John Astor long memoranda on the role of *The Times* and the responsibilities of its editor. Sir Campbell Stuart later stated that Morison, having been editor of the *Literary Supplement*, had sought in Casey's time to be made foreign editor of *The Times* itself and even aspired to succeed Casey as editor.[11] After being warned off by Haley he concentrated his energies in advice to Astor and Mathew and became especially close to Mathew. He was passionately devoted to *The Times* and its traditions as the earlier volumes of the *History* showed in abundance. The first trouble was that he was often over-emphatic in his chosen role as guardian of the paper's higher interests. Within Printing House Square his listeners were often too busy enjoying the cataclysmic vehemence of his manner to take in what he was saying. The deeper trouble lay in the lack of precision about what was his purview. Ill-defined duties are always disturbing in an organisation, and Haley was right to draw a line from the start.

Having appointed his chief assistants – Tyerman, Ryan and Green on the home side and McDonald on the foreign – Haley organised much of the work of the office systematically through them. From then on the old informal system, never more free and easy than under Casey, was changed into a well-stepped pyramid of command. Instead of being chiefly concerned with leading articles, each of the assistant editors was made directly responsible for all that happened, good and bad, in the department under him, and he had to run it within budgets which in the

---

10 B-W D, October 15 1947.
11 Letter from Campbell Stuart to Ryan, October 25 1969.

early years were extremely tight. To keep in touch with the main trends outside, each of them was expected to meet men and women in political and industrial life and to do regular entertaining at his club or house. Haley also encouraged them – it was an excellent idea – to take it in turns to travel on long tours of inquiry abroad. Haley also made such travels himself.

Each assistant editor was away for two or three months at a stretch every two years, not counting the journeys which McDonald frequently made to Russia and eastern Europe or the tours made by Oliver Woods as colonial editor. On his return each man would usually write a series of articles and see them reissued as a pamphlet, but the main purpose of the expeditions was simply to keep up to date with the different countries of Europe, America, Asia and Africa, and to talk privately with the heads of state and the prime ministers and other leaders. The traveller also kept the *Times* correspondents abroad in the know about events in London. The system worked well. Haley used to say that *The Times* had not only to know what was happening but also what was going to happen. The heavy expense of the long tours was a deliberate investment in knowledge that would be used over the years.

In day-to-day work within Printing House Square Haley's contacts were primarily (though not wholly) kept up through his assistant editors. Each of them, on arriving in his office about 11 a.m. every day, would find on his desk a little pile of typed memoranda. These had been dictated earlier by Haley from his home. Enid Knowles, then his principal secretary,[12] had them distributed to the men whom they most concerned. Like Northcliffe's famous memoranda thirty or forty years before, Haley's contained comments on the morning's paper, praise for good work, sharp calls for the reasons why some news item had been missed, instructions for following up news stories or for starting new subjects in the paper, inquiries about the cost of a lengthy cable, suggestions for leading articles, requests to be told how a misprint went unspotted through all editions, inquiries into a couple of minutes' delay in getting away to press the previous evening, remarks on rival newspapers, queries about an obscure line in the gardening notes, commendation for a theatre notice, puzzled words about a company mentioned on the City pages. Not a single thing in the day's paper, no matter what the page, seemed to have escaped being read and judged. Most of the memoranda in Haley's early years at *The Times* have not been kept;

---

12 Enid Knowles (b. 1928). Business manager *Sunday Times* Colour Magazine 1968; executive assistant to Sir Denis Hamilton, editor-in-chief of Times Newspapers, 1969–81; external relations executive, 1971–81; executive assistant to editor of *The Times*, 1981; resigned, 1982.

a selection from a single representative day in 1962 is given later in this volume;[13] but a few earlier ones, filed in the archives, illustrate the range and tone of the series:

To Ryan, the night editor, and the news editors:

The fact that we are going down to smaller papers tonight and succeeding nights must not be an excuse for things to be left out of the paper. We must aim at making *The Times* as comprehensive a record as we can during these days. We must try to get all the news and do a really good job of packing. That means all stories must be much shorter, concentrating on essentials. (October 29 1954.)

To McDonald:

The Foreign news this morning is very good. Hodgkin's round-up particularly strikes me as the best on the subject in this morning's papers. I think, too, Toulmin did quite a good job in Holland. And Oliver Woods's story on Malta gave us the kind of story of our own which is properly *The Times's*.

Against this one or two small points:

(1) Why, on the story giving election results in Manitoba, did we put a headline 'Liberals Return to Power in Ontario'?

(2) It is rather difficult to understand the meaning of the last paragraph in our Paris Correspondent's story 'Assembly Rejects M. Bidault'.

(3) Do you feel the late Bill Page story 'Economic Reform in East Germany' seemed rather to contradict part of your first leader, which I liked very much? (June 11 1953.)

To McDonald:

The Kampala story is better and more timely than anything anywhere else and the despatch from Belgrade is also a good piece of our own. The one weakness continues to be South Africa. Whether they are right or not the *Manchester Guardian* front page top gives a much stronger feeling of authority and decision. The general impression conveyed is that the M.G. knows what is happening while *The Times* is rather in a fog. This may not be justified. But we must do all we can in these coming weeks and months to see that *The Times* South African coverage is second to none. It may well be that the crucial stage in South Africa's relations with this country and indeed with the Commonwealth is approaching. Would you please come and talk to me about this? (November 10 1954.)

To Donald Holmes, Night Editor:

Will you please make a determined move to get more verbs into

---

13 See Appendix D.

headings. At the moment we depend far too much on ofs and ons. Page 6 is a very good (or bad) example of what I mean. 'Length of', 'Needs of', 'Finding of', and 'Deeds of'. And then in column four, one under the other are 'Talks on', 'Warning of' and 'Eden on'. They are supplemented by 'Opposition to', 'Call to', a couple of 'fors' and some 'ats' and 'bys'. Headings should be more active than this. (February 4 1957.)

Most of Haley's memoranda each day called for immediate action or reply. He expected at least an interim report to be given him after the first news conference of the day, which was held at noon. At this conference the news editors – home, foreign, industrial – and the picture editor reported on their probable schedule for the day to an assistant editor, who presided. The assistant editor thereafter went straight into Haley's room where Haley was waiting with the other assistant editors. This small inner group took final decisions, where needed, about any special news coverage and they had their first talk about the leaders to be written that evening for the next day's paper. It all meant that by mid-day or soon afterwards the next day's *Times* was beginning to be shaped so far as any daily newspaper can be shaped ahead of going to press. It was on the launching pad, with most systems Go.

Clearly much of Haley's methods of direction arose directly out of his experience in running the infinitely larger and more complex organisation at the BBC. Having to deal with most of the BBC staff through remote control he knew the value of giving instructions in black and white and he knew the equal value of calling for progress reports with the minimum of delay. Beyond all question such methods gave a healthy shock to *The Times* which at bottom still liked to work according to Geoffrey Dawson's air – a really quite deceptive air – of gentlemanly casualness.

The advantages of Haley's administrative efficiency, coupled with his energy and his flair for news, far outweighed any disadvantages, but there were times when, applied to the much smaller organisation of *The Times*, the stream of memoranda each day tended to reduce rather than stimulate initiative among the staff. The assistant editors were the least affected: they could pass many of the memoranda without further ado to their respective news editors and go back to what they liked to think were their own larger thoughts. But the news editors had promptly to drop their own projects and take up the editor's or spend valuable time in finding out why some minor things had gone wrong the night before. Some heads of department, knowing that three or four memoranda requiring action would be reaching them without fail, tended to wait to

211

be told what to do instead of planning what they should do themselves, and of course their lack of action on their own account tended to provoke a greater number of activating memoranda from the editor.

It cannot be said that the system was wrong. Haley's impact and drive were vitally necessary to *The Times* in those days. The paper became quicker off the mark than it had been. It went out to dig for news of the kind which previously it had ignored or taken from the agencies. The memoranda each day displayed an extraordinary faculty for seeing the hidden story behind a couple of obscure lines in the paper and for seeing the need to spell out a problem in, as Haley used to say, words of one syllable. It was no longer admitted that there could be dull days; the paper had to make the dull news readable.

Haley himself worked a two-man or three-man day for five days of the week. After telephoning the memoranda after breakfast he had correspondence to deal with when arriving at the office; then the noon editorial conference; a working lunch, sometimes a Board lunch followed by a directors' meeting; more correspondence in the afternoon, then the choosing of letters to the editor, a meeting on staff appointments; the afternoon editorial conference, a talk with a minister or a visiting statesman, perhaps a leading article to write or other men's leaders to vet; a quick supper, back to see the paper to press at 9.15, then rearranging the news after the first edition; at last the departure home for further close reading of the paper. His energies were as boundless as were his ambitions for the paper. The combination sometimes left weaker brethren feeling like Gideon's small band of men against the Midianites, 'faint yet pursuing'. Or even, when the pressure was really on, faint yet pursued.

The new crisp style was often shown at the main editorial news conference over which the editor presided at 4.15 p.m. or, as it became, 4.30 p.m. Each news editor presented his long list of news items for the next day. One afternoon brought the promise of photographs from an agricultural show. 'More cows?', came Haley's sharp voice. 'Are they the same cows as we had yesterday?' They did not appear the next day. At a later conference it was announced that unfortunately the Cairo correspondent could not cover a big story in Cairo as he had headed off into the desert towards Petra. Around the table there were many envious thoughts about the rose-red city, but Haley was not in the least pleased. 'What does he hope to achieve for us in Petra?', he demanded. 'I gather', said the foreign news editor, 'that he had in mind a colour piece.' 'We know the colour of Petra,' said Haley. 'Get him back'.

Another substantial way in which Haley used his assistant editors was in long and frank discussions about the future prospects for the paper. Such talks went on informally most of the time, but every few months he gathered the assistant editors more formally together, and once a year they had a grand review at a lengthy luncheon. Shortly before the first of such luncheons, which took place soon after Tyerman left, Haley tabulated the points for discussion in a long memorandum to Green, McDonald and Ryan.[14] It displays to the full his way of breaking down problems into practicable sections:

1. The purpose of Monday's lunch is to talk over the future. There is much ground to cover, so to save time I am circulating these notes. I hope, however, everyone will raise any other ideas he has.

2. Progress during the past three years has fallen roughly into three stages:
   a) Getting the staff right.
   b) Tightening up news, improving comprehensiveness, arrangement, and layout.
   c) Expansion of features.

3. Problems for the year ahead group themselves as I Particular; II General.

PARTICULAR

4. The first is the re-arrangement of Tyerman's duties. I do not propose to replace him directly. I think that provided certain easements are given we can absorb these duties between ourselves.

5. *The Times* has no need for an elaborate organisation such as the BBC's. At the same time it is useful for spheres of interest to be defined; each Assistant Editor having, as well as the general well-being and progress of the paper as a whole as his care, a special part of its activity as his special responsibility.

6. Broadly, the Foreign Editor's responsibilities should remain unchanged. He should, however, take an earlier and closer interest in the recruiting of potential foreign staff.[15] (The interviewing of other candidates must be discussed.) Green will take the home news side and general editorial production as a whole. Ryan will take all the non-news side of the paper, including all turnovers.

7. Oliver Woods has suggested to me that he might widen his scope by becoming a Personal Assistant. I do not think that he should yet abandon his colonial empire. He has usefully added to his experience by deputising for the Foreign Editor. He will do so again early next year when McDonald goes to the Far East. Are there perhaps other ways in which he can also be used?

---

14 Memorandum November 9 1955. T.T.A.
15 Recruiting had been mainly Tyerman's responsibility.

8. Editorial direction of a newspaper needs three things: Judgment, imagination, and drive. I am particularly concerned about the last. While the Management properly has its own sphere in our affairs, there is plenty of editorial management which we can do for ourselves. The more efficient we make the Editorial, the more successful the paper will be. The more money we save the more we shall have to spend.

9. We must free ourselves as much as we can for these things, and also to write. Administration is important. But journalism is above all else a writing profession. It is good for all of us to write.[16]

In the succeeding paragraphs he proposed that the staff late at night should be strengthened to remove any impression that *The Times* was 'still largely a morning paper produced the previous afternoon'; he suggested new features; and he posed the problem of how quickly *The Times* could expand without losing its character:

18. Expansion and consolidation must go hand in hand. The problem of conducting *The Times* is to preserve tradition without stagnation. While steadily seeking to do new things, we must never cease ensuring that everything *The Times* does is the best of its kind . . .

36. Its circulation is a little over 220,000. This is too near the 200,000 mark to be comfortable. Below that mark lies danger. We must seek quickly to reach safety above 250,000. Afterwards we can try to push it above 300,000. But a quarter of a million should be our immediate target.

In this chapter it is Haley's style of editing, not his actual work, that is discussed. What *The Times* did in the various fields under him is described in later pages. In his style he struck many members of the staff as being brusque and authoritarian – 'the last of the authoritarian editors', one of them was to say later. Certainly he took over the chair in the years when the freedom of the press meant essentially the freedom of a newspaper or magazine to express its opinions as a united team under the leadership of its editor. Few people would then have accepted the claim, widely made later, that freedom should mean the freedom of an individual journalist or a broadcaster to use his newspaper or the television channel to express himself as and when he wished, whether in agreement or at variance with the editor's or controller's deeply held views. Most journalists would have been puzzled if they had heard an editor's ruling being described as an act of censorship. Haley, for one,

---

16 T.T.A.

expected to run *The Times*, and did run *The Times*, as firmly as the captain ran the ships in which he served as a young man: informal at times but never leaving any doubt about who was in control.

Outside the office, too, he made sure that the editor of *The Times* was not only independent but was manifestly seen to be independent. From the start he was determined to rid people of any lingering belief that *The Times* was semi-official, mirroring the views of whatever government was in power. He had preserved the political neutrality and independence of the BBC against governmental pressures and he was on still stronger ground now in preserving the independence of a journal of opinion. To make his stand clear he did not become friends of ministers as Dawson did. He did not join the chatty clubs as Barrington-Ward had done. Though he might talk with ministers at luncheons or dinners or embassy receptions he much preferred businesslike meetings at Downing Street or elsewhere in Whitehall. He did not go either to agree or to argue, but to be put into the picture, though where he felt any kinship of spirit, as he did, for example, with Macmillan, the meetings could blossom out into relaxed exchanges in which Haley was much more than a simple questioner. Ministers knew his reputation well enough not to expect him to accept a line of policy. Even on small matters he would quickly rebuff any suggestion that *The Times* might give a favourable puff to a minister's pet project. He never believed in granting favours in the hope of receiving larger favours later. 'We do not need to go truckling to them', he would say. 'They will come running to us soon enough when they have something to say.'

How quick he was to suspect a minister of stepping over the line is best shown in a brief exchange of letters with Duncan Sandys.[17] Sandys, then Secretary of State for Commonwealth Relations, told him in a letter dated December 10 1962 that the High Commissioner of India had passed on to him some Indian complaints about a map, published in *The Times* of November 21, of the disputed frontier between India and Tibet. Indians thought the map pro-Chinese. Sandys hoped that Haley would publish some letters to redress the balance, and continued:

A Parliamentary Question about this has now been put down for answer on Wednesday and I should be grateful to have your comments before then.

The fact that Haley and Sandys had met and corresponded easily in the past did not soften the severity of Haley's reply:

---

17 Duncan Edwin Sandys (b. 1908). Diplomatic service, 1930. Held several governmental and cabinet posts. Baron, 1974.

I have received your letter of December 10. I hope we know each other well enough for me to say in all frankness that I find it and particularly the last paragraph most unusual. *The Times* has no responsibility whatsoever to Government or Parliament. If I were to go into this matter with you it would appear as if the paper had and would create a false position. Therefore I am unable to do so. Should we have any comments to make they will appear in the paper.

Sandys, on the point of leaving for the West Indies, briefly acknowledged Haley's letter, saying that he had thought it only courteous to give the editor an opportunity of making any comments before the parliamentary question came up for answer. Haley's own letter stands as the neatest and briefest statement of how he saw his role as independent editor of an independent newspaper.

That was one side, the austere side, of a man who valued rectitude in conduct among the highest of the virtues. In the columns of the paper he insisted upon precision about facts as a moral duty, and it was he who began to publish small paragraphs headed *Corrections* when errors had been made; the first such item appeared on March 6 1961. This austere side was the only one which most members of the staff saw. But others on the staff – the assistant editors and the experts of all ranks within Printing House Square – were in closer touch with the man behind all the outward manner and they found someone who could be very different.

In spite of his reputation for instant decision he would often patiently discuss a matter with one, two, or three of his experts; he had a great and genuine respect for expert knowledge; he would at times defer to expert opinion and would not make up his mind until he had reflected on the discussion. An expert whom he really trusted could set a line of policy for the paper. True, Haley would sometimes have decided views from the start and would not be moved by any amount of discussion. Sometimes there was no discussion at all. But debate happened more often than was generally supposed. With his respect for experts went another characteristic. Unlike Barrington-Ward he did not tinker with a man's leader. He might on occasion differ from a sentence or two: out they came. But he did not alter a man's style or rearrange the argument. Men wrote with more confidence as a result.

There was yet another Haley. Those who worked near to him knew the romantic in him, the man who was first determined to go into journalism by reading Philip Gibbs's *The Street of Adventure*, and the man who, never losing the sense of adventure, would delight in being in the composing room to make sure that a last-minute item of news or a last-minute change in a leader got into the paper. Beyond that, he liked quite simply to see the last of the formes being slid across to the presses in the nightly miracle of production. The few near to him also knew him when he was off parade, easy and chatting, discussing his beloved books, showing a deep thoughtfulness about families and friends, and doing many acts of kindness. Anyone's illness or misfortune brought swift and genuine sympathy. It was a pity that more could not get to know the Haley, sensitive and rather shy, that lived behind the well-schooled outward manner. Perhaps he should have given himself more time for friends. Most of his weekends seemed to be spent in his library. One Sunday afternoon, as he came into the office looking remarkably fit, he was asked what kind of a week-end he had had. 'Splendid, thanks,' he said. 'I have read seven books and reviewed four of them.' He looked as if he had just come in from two health-giving days on the moors.

Haley waited for seven months before writing his first leading article. It appeared on June 3 1953, the day after the coronation of Queen Elizabeth II. Its language was simple and stern; its central message an appeal for the nation to throw off laziness and wishful thinking and return to the old virtues of hard work, honesty, and fair dealing. It was a long leader, which Haley headed, 'And After?' The rejoicing and the holiday were over, he wrote, and the plain world had to be faced once more:

It is not a moment too soon. The British people have had a holiday from reality long enough . . . Even in a welfare State facts must be seen penny plain. Britain's economy still sways on a knife's edge. Things are better; they are a long way short of being safe against becoming worse than we have yet known them . . .

The main reason why Britain has not yet prospered sufficiently to lift herself above the safety line is that the British people as a whole have not yet had the will to prosper. Present ease is being subsidized by future penury. Yet such is the mind of the nation and the state of politics that neither Government nor Opposition dares allow itself to be disclosed fully facing the facts. A country made great by resourcefulness and energy is in many places slowly strangling itself with restrictive practices, by a placing of conveniences and comfort before efficiency and productivity, by a plain disinclination for hard work . . .

Amid the incessant and strident talk of rights the voice of duty is only half-heard. Meanness of spirit, envy, and jealousy sour too much of our national life . . . To-day it is already late, but not too late. This great nation . . . can give to the words 'Elizabethan age' a new meaning: Christian values re-established, morals reasserted, conscientiousness revived, energy renewed, and national unity restored. The Coronation ceremonies will have meant little if they do not mean this. The power is there, given the will.

This was a theme which Haley was to pursue throughout the next fourteen years. It sounded a change of tone for *The Times*. Barrington-Ward certainly believed in the maintenance of individual virtues, but in the post-war years he regarded the reform of society as the first step towards helping the individual to live more worthily, more productively, and with greater self-respect. Haley, coming along later, asked whether the cushioning by the state had gone so far that the individual was forgetting the part he or she had to play for the common good.

XI

PROGRESS ON THE HOME FRONT

'ENOUGH is enough.' In 1959 and in the early sixties the phrase became something of a political catchword which caught on because of one particular happening. That was the 'Selwyn Lloyd affair', or 'Haley's plot against the Foreign Secretary', or 'Haley's stab in the back', or, more simply and truthfully, the publication by *The Times* of a pleasant political essay on Selwyn Lloyd's future as its lead story on the morning of Monday, June 1 1959. The article, which happened to contain the 'enough' phrase, caused an uproar at Westminster and in Whitehall and was rapturously taken up by newspapers throughout Europe and North America:

'Harter Angriff auf Selwyn Lloyd': *Neue Rhein Ruhr Zeitung,* June 2.

'Fantastisk Situation om Minister Selwyn Lloyd': *Politiken,* June 2.

'British Stirred by Report of a Plan to Replace Lloyd': *New York Times,* June 3 (Amsterdam edition).

From Geneva, where Selwyn Lloyd was attending a conference on Germany, the Rhine Ruhr paper summed up by declaring that the article had 'wie eine Bombe eingeschlagen'.

The affair has a minor place in history not simply as a journalistic curiosity. It immediately became a political event in its own right. The piece had appeared in *The Times*; therefore (the assumption was) it must be official. Of more domestic concern to *The Times* in those years, the free and easy way in which the piece was written stands as a prime example of the less inhibited, less official style of writing which Haley and the assistant editors were encouraging. For all such reasons it was the most memorable incident on the home side during the first period of Haley's editorship – 1952–61, when Maurice Green was still in charge of home news and before Oliver Woods took over, 1961–66.

The writer of the article was David Wood,[1] who in 1957 had been

---

1 Gilbert David Marson Wood (b. 1914). Grantham Secondary Technical School. Reporter, *Grantham Journal*; shorthand writer, Court of Appeal; reporter, *South*

appointed political correspondent. He had some parliamentary experience and his perceptive and descriptive powers had been shown in his reporting as a correspondent during the Suez landings in 1956.[2] In January 1958 he had started a weekly essay, 'In and Out of Parliament', which let him go behind the day-to-day news and discourse on thoughts and tendencies rather than events. These essays appeared on Monday mornings. For the morning of June 1 1959 he turned to the position of Selwyn Lloyd whom Harold Macmillan had kept on as Secretary of State for Foreign Affairs when many observers had expected him to be dropped during the Cabinet reconstruction after Eden's resignation early in 1957. Normally at that time Wood's weekly article appeared on a back page, but all the routine news coming in for the paper of June 1 was painfully thin and dull. Both Haley and Ryan decided that Wood's offering should, on its merits, lead the paper unless it was overtaken (which it was not) by some harder and weightier tidings. So *The Times*, without in any way changing Wood's reflective essay-writing style, gave pride of place to the story that was to cause the storm. It began:

> We may safely accept that Mr. Macmillan has lately taken Mr. Selwyn Lloyd's arm in a paternal grip, led him to one side, and spoken from the heart. Call it the personal advice a leader offers to a favoured lieutenant, or call it the first unmistakable hint about the Prime Minister's intentions if he is summoned to form another Ministry – it makes no difference. What matters is that Mr. Macmillan has let Mr. Lloyd know that at the Foreign Office, in these troubled times, enough is enough.

The article emphasized several times that no change was to be immediate or even soon, but the strain of office could not be overlooked:

> No, a Prime Minister must not ask too much from his ministerial galley-slaves. In the Foreign Secretary's own interests, and for the sake of the service he can still give to the country and his party, a reasonable term must be set to the carrying of the burden . . . But the transposition of Mr. Selwyn Lloyd to another departmental office is still several months ahead.

Then came several paragraphs of praise for Selwyn Lloyd's work and for his courage and tenacity in recovering from the Suez venture.

Yorkshire Times. The Times parliamentary reporter, 1948–52; home news reporter and special writer, 1952–57; political correspondent, 1957–69; political editor from 1969 and European political editor from 1977; retired, 1982.

2 See Chapter XIII.

As happens with many speculative articles, all the qualifications in it were ignored by many readers. Questions were asked in Parliament; Haley was denounced for pursuing a vendetta against Selwyn Lloyd, supposedly going back to the time when Lloyd recommended the establishment of an independent television service as a rival to Haley's BBC. Emrys Hughes, the left-wing MP with a sense of humour, proposed in the House that *The Times* should be nationalised. George Wigg[3] announced that he was reporting the paper to the Press Council. The British newspapers and weeklies followed up all reactions to the story. 'Premier hunts the man with the dagger': *Daily Mail.* 'Mac Storm over "Lloyd to Go" Hint': *Daily Sketch.* 'Anger at 10, Downing Street': *Daily Mirror.* On June 6 the *New Statesman* wrote that no one could believe that '*The Times* attack on Selwyn Lloyd was an accident due to journalistic misjudgment'; in the public interest the matter must be probed to its origins and motives. On June 7 the *Observer* came nearer to the truth when it pleasantly echoed David Wood's opening words:

> We may also safely accept that *The Times* is the only paper in the world which could cause an international sensation by printing a political gossip story, such as their famous article last Monday saying the skids were under Mr. Selwyn Lloyd. The reason for this, of course, is the conviction, still widely held in this country and almost universal abroad, that *The Times* speaks for the Government of the day.

In the House of Commons Macmillan had quickly declared on June 2 that there had been no inspired statement of any kind. 'The Foreign Secretary and I,' he said, 'hope to carry on our work together for a very long time to come.' He did not, however, flatly deny the story. Indeed, while looking forward to another five years of Conservative government, he said, 'Whether we shall be able to do the full stint ourselves remains to be seen.'

There were in fact very good reasons for Macmillan's careful choice of words. The story had come direct from himself. The origins of it are shown in a little memorandum which Wood typed to Haley on May 13 1959, a fortnight before the story appeared:

> I had a few words with the PM this morning that seemed interesting. He gave the impression of being determined to turn the conversation to Selwyn Lloyd, and at one point said: 'I have told him that he must not go on as Foreign Secretary indefinitely.' Before and after this

---

3 George Wigg (1900–83). Labour MP for Dudley. Paymaster-General, 1964–67. Baron, 1967.

sentence he had much to say about the Foreign Office killing men. It killed Bevin, wrecked Anthony Eden, and got Morrison down; and 'I myself shudder every time I open a telegram'.

He praised Lloyd highly for the way he has stuck at the job. He said that being Prime Minister is like running a weekly paper – you had time to look around and collect your thoughts: being Foreign Secretary is like running a daily paper – making snap decisions hour by hour on most fateful subjects.

I had to conclude that the present series of meetings and the summit will be Selwyn's swan song.[4]

Neither Macmillan nor Selwyn Lloyd ever held the story against Wood personally. On returning from Geneva Lloyd had Wood to lunch and told him that the article had done him a world of good there. Dulles and the rest of the American delegation, still smarting from the Suez affair, had been cool towards Lloyd until the story broke. All of them came round within minutes to see him at his hotel to assure him that they would do anything they could to help him.[5] Lloyd's composure left the critics with little to shout about, and at the end of nine days Haley wrote a leader about the wonder – and about the role of *The Times* in Westminster and the country. After pointing out that the storm had been not over what *The Times* said but over what other people said it had said, Haley tried once again to dispel three closely linked ideas. One was that the paper spoke for the government of the day. The second was that it should be always especially careful what it said because many people remained convinced that it *did* speak for the government. The third was that, because of its special position, it presented news with a motive, playing politics and setting one minister against another. The theme gave him his opportunity to define the true standing and duties of *The Times*:

> *The Times* is not a Government organ . . . It is an entirely unofficial, non-party newspaper appealing to men and women of reason and good will of all kinds of opinion. It seeks to judge each issue that arises only by reference to the broad national good. It will not subordinate this judgment to the interests of one class or another.

As for the idea that the paper backed the government of the day, Haley pointed out that in a democracy any elected government that was seen to be genuinely serving the whole nation had a right to the support of

---

4 T.T.A.
5 Retrospective article in which Wood revealed for the first time in public that Macmillan was the source. *The Times*, February 2 1976.

uncommitted people of good will. In that belief *The Times* gave its backing:

> But it is a backing within clear limits. It is no more than that whatever approval or criticism seems fair shall be given whether the Government is Conservative, Labour or Liberal. It is no more than that if there can be any doubt the Government shall have the benefit of it until such time as it is clear they no longer deserve the benefit.

In reply to the other fashionable ideas Haley said that *The Times* could not hold news back because of the myth that it was semi-official; it had the duty to give information honestly. Neither could it ever work according to hidden political motives:

> These things are no part of the true function of an independent, national newspaper. Its duty is to its readers. There could be no greater affront to them than that, under the cloak of serving them, it was really pursuing some private ends, engaging in political manoeuvres, and using their attention and interest for purposes it has not disclosed.[6]

The storm had been both ridiculous and highly useful. In a remarkable way it helped to let *The Times* be seen as a wholly independent newspaper, not even demi-semi-official. Barrington-Ward's line during the Greek civil war in 1945–46 had of course been independent of the government, but that stance of independence was precisely what angered the critics in those years. It was regarded as a betrayal of the role expected of *The Times* in relation to the Churchill government and the Conservative interest. After the Selwyn Lloyd affair and other displays less was heard about what *The Times* should dutifully do and more was heard about what it was actually doing.

'In and Out of Parliament' was only one of many new features which were started on the paper with the direct aim of encouraging lighter writing and wider interests. Within four years, from March 1954 to January 1958, Haley introduced or agreed to the introduction of twenty new features, almost all of them on the home side.

The one nearest to Haley's own heart was the books page, begun on February 17 1955 and edited with splendid enthusiasm by Patrick Ryan. On this page each week, alongside the book reviews, there appeared the article by 'Oliver Edwards'. It was an essay on books, mainly of the past, very many of them Victorian. At first the work of three or four hands, it

---

6 *The Times*, June 10 1959.

became wholly Haley's after some months. All his great knowledge of literature, and especially of novels, British, Russian, French and other, came out in this weekly article. More than his knowledge, there emerged his love and his reverence for literature. The style was unforced and highly personal. Haley had taken the name Oliver Edwards from the man who, as Boswell records, confessed that he had tried to be a philosopher, 'but, I don't know how, cheerfulness was always breaking in'.[7]

Critics admitted the cheerfulness in the articles but said that Haley did not philosophise in them sufficiently; he did not give himself time to analyse and pass detailed judgment on many of the books he described and recommended each week. He in turn was hurt by some of the hostile and dismissive reviews which appeared when a selection of the articles was published as a volume, *Talking of Books*, in 1958. Many of the reviewers had missed the whole point of the exercise. Oliver Edwards was not going in for higher criticism; he was disclosing part of his inner life; he was opening a wider world of books for his readers, introducing them not so much to the great and familiar authors as to little known and mainly forgotten authors whom he had relished over the years. Academics understood that purpose very well and many of them expressed their respect and admiration for the breadth of reading and the accumulated knowledge that went into the writing of the articles. No account of the editing of *The Times* is complete if it deals only with William Haley and not with Oliver Edwards. The enthusiasms of Edwards provided an outlet and relaxation for Haley's normally tight-disciplined mind.

Among the men who took his turn at first with the Oliver Edwards articles was Iolo Williams,[8] one of the quiet, modest, scholarly, ever-inquiring men whom *The Times* liked to house. Williams had a long service with the paper. He had a naturally graceful style of writing that was entirely unforced and wrote many light leaders, drawing on his wide knowledge of English and Welsh art, literature, and culture. He did many jobs in *The Times* and in all of them he was always ready to write, almost always at short notice, on events in the cultural world.

Little behind the books page in Haley's affections was the arts page which was broadened to cover reports and criticisms of plays, operas,

---

7 Boswell's *Life of Dr. Johnson*, April 17 1778.
8 Iolo Aneurin Williams (1890–1962). Rugby; King's College, Cambridge. *The Times* museums correspondent from 1936; also travel correspondent, 1938, and leader writer. As well as a botanist, ornithologist, poet, literary critic and expert on bibliography and English water-colours, he was a student of Welsh language and culture.

concerts, recitals, painting and sculpture at home and abroad. Haley saw it doing for *The Times* what he had done for the BBC when starting the Third Programme. In John Lawrence,[9] appointed to be arts editor in 1950, he found a man with a zeal as great as his own.

It had not been without a struggle that the arts won the position in the paper which today's *Times* readers take for granted. 'Entertainments', as they were then called, were not a part of the paper that Dawson much bothered with, and though Barrington-Ward showed more interest, particularly in the annual Westminster play, by the time he became editor the cultural life of the country survived only at a very austere level. The outbreak of war had meant a temporary closure of theatres, cinemas and concert halls.

Music, being perhaps more universal in its appeal than any other of the arts, had been the first to revive. Dame Myra Hess's lunch-time concerts in the National Gallery began on October 10 1939 and lasted, five days a week, until 1945, becoming a lighthouse of hope and inspiration in the dark days of the Blitz. In spite of the closure of the Old Vic in 1940 through enemy action a revival in the theatre was not long behind. May 12 1942 saw the first night of Terence Rattigan's RAF play 'Flare Path', reviewed by A. V. Cookman,[10] who had succeeded Charles Morgan as main drama critic and who had the quick judgment of anyone who has to comment on a play with only an hour or two to do it in. He saw Peter Brook's 1950 production of 'Ring round the Moon', Christopher Fry's translation of Anouilh's 'enchanting little fairy tale', with Oliver Messel's 'exquisitely arranged winter garden' as the theatre's most conspicuous celebration of peace.

In 1956 the Royal Court theatre released the first wave of new writers, headed by John Osborne, in whom the post-war theatre found its voice. Two years later the regional theatre revival began with the opening of the Belgrade, Coventry. In 1960 Stratford gave birth to the Royal Shakespeare Company and extended its operation to the Aldwych in London. And in March 1963 Britain at last came into possession of a National Theatre. Many of these changes were pushed through by young men of the generation of Irving Wardle,[11] who

9 William Alfred John Lawrence (b. 1901). London University. *The Times* City office staff, 1919–20; advertisement and editorial clerical staff, 1923–28; reporter, with responsibility for entertainments page, 1928–39 and 1945–50; in charge of arts coverage, 1950–69.
10 Anthony Victor Cookman (1894–1962). Joined *The Times*, 1925; dramatic critic, 1943.
11 Irving Wardle (b. 1929). Bolton School; Wadham College, Oxford. Drama critic of *The Times* from 1963.

succeeded Cookman as drama critic, and his attitude towards them was one of unqualified support.

The unprecedented popularity of music in post-war Britain kept Frank Howes,[12] chief music critic since 1943, William Mann[13] and their colleagues busy with new work of unusual interest. The music of Benjamin Britten, Michael Tippett and Malcolm Arnold, and the willing audience for whatever new British composers did, created an appetite for the music of others established before 1939.

Music critics therefore found themselves dealing not only with a great deal of new music both home-made and imported, but at the same time directing their attention to unfamiliar works previously neglected in this country. The works of Mahler became popular and were followed by those of Bruckner. William Mann was fortunately equipped to deal both knowledgeably and sympathetically with such works and with the music of Schoenberg and his followers. Mann's famous study in 1963 of the Beatles' music and style broke new ground with its reference to elements in their technique with its 'chains of pandiatonic clusters', thereby showing that pop music could be as susceptible as any other to discussion in technical language.

Historically, ballet had been included among the duties of *The Times's* music critics, but its increasing popularity soon demanded specialised treatment. In 1952 the Sadler's Wells ballet became the Royal Ballet, prompting first Clive Barnes and then John Percival to contribute critical work in this field.

David Thompson[14] followed Alan Clutton-Brock[15] as art critic of *The Times* in 1956, so it fell to him to write a penetrating notice of Francis Bacon's retrospective exhibition at the Tate Gallery in May 1962: 'No other painter of our day – and for once the phrase can be left as it stands, without worrying about the word "British" – could make these five large galleries look so nearly like an exhibition by an old master, yet leave one in no doubt that here, flashed on the canvas like one of the startling news-photos of cinematic images from which the paintings so often derive, is the cry of agony of our own age, an age which has lost its faith.' Catholic in his tastes and scholarly in his judgment, Thompson allowed no exhibition that mattered to escape his pen.

---

12 Frank Howes (b. 1891). Oxford High School; St. John's College, Oxford. Joined *The Times* 1925; music critic, 1943 until retirement in 1960.
13 William Mann (b. 1924). Winchester; Magdalene College, Cambridge. Assistant music critic *The Times*, 1948–60; music critic, 1960–82.
14 David Thompson (b. 1929). Rugby; Corpus Christi College, Oxford. Art critic of *The Times*, 1956.
15 Alan Francis Clutton-Brock (1904–1976). King's College, Cambridge. Assistant to art critic, 1930. RAF 1940–45. Art critic, 1945–55.

Among the innovations on the arts pages after the war was a weekly series of articles under the heading 'Things Seen', to which William Gaunt,[16] the author of standard works on the Pre-Raphaelites, contributed several distinguished essays. Altogether the 1950s were a lively period in the arts, and in what turned out to be a timely decision John Lawrence began a series of interviews which were to become a permanent feature of the newspaper.

Laurence Kitchin,[17] a critic with several years' acting experience, was chosen to talk to prominent actors, dramatists and directors, with Athene Seyler as his first subject. Until then English actors, unlike their continental counterparts, had tended to protect the mystique of their craft by impregnable reticence, so that it was something of a breakthrough when Gielgud, for instance, revealed that he visualised printed lines when speaking verse. That elusive subjects like Callas and Ingrid Bergman agreed to be interviewed, without recourse to tape-recorder or even shorthand, was due first to the prestige of *The Times*, secondly to the understanding that no questions would be asked about private lives, and thirdly to confidence in the interviewer and his method.

Many musicians too became the subjects for interviews. Archie Camden, who had played in the Hallé orchestra under Richter when he was eighteen and served the Hallé for more than twenty years before he joined the Royal Philharmonic under Beecham, remembered his part in life as a remarkable comedy. Backhaus, interviewed in 1960, explained why in his later years he was content to play little but the music of Beethoven: only when he was satisfied with his playing of all the Beethoven sonatas, he said, would he have time to work at other music. Pablo Casals, who talked to *The Times* before a rehearsal of his oratorio 'El Pesebre', insisted on remembering his English friends, from Queen Victoria to Donald Tovey. Ashkenazy, in London and away from Russia for the first time, was working to improve his English with the aid of an interleaved Russian–English edition of King Lear. It was fascinating to know that Amy Shuard, a leading Wagnerian soprano, cherished a secret ambition to become a pantomime dame, and that Fischer-Dieskau, rehearsing 'Arabella' for Covent Garden, regarded any appearance in a Wagner role as a willing surrender to the power of a magician.

When he retired as editor in December 1966 Haley was happy to tell John Lawrence: 'You have produced something unique in daily journal-

---

16 William Gaunt (1900–80). Hull Grammar; Worcester College Oxford. Regular contributor to *The Times* from 1957; art critic and museums correspondent, 1963–70.
17 Laurence Kitchin (b. 1913). Contributor to *The Times* on theatrical subjects, 1956–62.

ism and keenly watched and admired throughout the world.' He also characteristically added: 'This has been developed with remarkable economy and at a very low cost.'

Sport, like the arts, had been another casualty of war which recovered rapidly with the return of peace to become increasingly international and so increasingly demanding on space and manpower.[18]

Among other ventures in Haley's early years in the chair were the revival (on September 26 1955) and expansion of the woman's page, the introduction of a Saturday page of mainly outdoor interests (March 17 1956), the beginning of a regular article 'Science and Medicine Today' (April 4 1956), the broadening of trade-union and industrial news by the labour correspondent, the beginning of weekly 'Architectural Notes' (April 9 1956), and the transformation of the old City news into a much wider survey of economic and industrial movements in Britain and in the leading developed countries.

Rather more distinctive and immediately popular with many readers were the Guides that were frequently produced; they were simple, factual, and clearly displayed explanations – 'in words of one syllable', Haley would say – of problems of the day, whether Middle Eastern oil (who owned it? where were all the wells?), or the TUC, or the Warsaw Pact armed forces. Along much the same lines were the no less frequent potted biographies under the self-explanatory title, 'Man in the News' or 'Woman in the News'. These guides and biographies were done by the staff, unwillingly as a general rule on the home side, very willingly by the correspondents abroad who were glad to present the personalities behind the names they so often reported.

Time and again Haley came back to the need to get more zeal and energy into the news gathering on the home side. Maurice Green fully agreed, and R. M. Dobson,[19] who had succeeded A. P. Robbins as home news editor in 1953, was lively and imaginative until failing eyesight and serious ill health weakened him. With some reason Haley grumbled that home news, especially late news, was not properly followed up. 'I think this weakness derives more from a general frame of mind than anything else.'[20] He frequently complained about dull writing and about stories that were missed or not fully exploited.

---

18 For a fuller consideration of sports coverage see Appendix E.
19 Robert Montagu Hume Dobson (1914–61). Educated privately. Reporter on west country weekly newspapers; sports sub-editor, *Morning Post*; reporter, *Daily Herald*; assistant editor, *Sporting and Dramatic News*. *The Times* parliamentary reporter, 1943–47; assistant news editor, 1947–53; home news editor, 1953–61.
20 Memorandum to heads of home departments, September 27 1955. T.T.A.

Tyerman (before he left in 1955), Green, and Dobson very often thought that Haley was demanding too much from the staff available. When he complained, as he did frequently, that the *Daily Telegraph* had got away with a news story they no less frequently reminded him that the *Telegraph* had more than twice the number of reporters ready for jobs. At the same time they were annoyed when Haley stopped them from following up stories which they thought were precisely along the desired line. He would not have any word in the paper on the arrival in July 1956 of Marilyn Monroe, then at the height of her fame; she came, as other papers proclaimed, to share the lead in a film with Laurence Olivier. A little more than a year later, on August 8 1957, the *Daily Mirror* had a leading article headed 'The Tardy "Times"', and beginning, 'Once again The Times newspaper has been tardy and timorous.' On this occasion *The Times* had not reported 'Lord Altrincham's outspoken criticisms of the Queen and the Court'. As it happened Haley was out of the office on the relevant Friday night, but he returned on the Sunday and took no public notice of the affair until Wednesday's paper. The *Mirror* ended its knock-about leader with a final punch, 'Under Sir William Haley, The Thunderer has become The Suppressor.' The jibe was ridiculously unfair but did not help the morale in the reporters' room.

In a long memorandum to Haley on February 14 1956 Green gave reasons for the low spirits at that time. The paper was losing 'its most promising men' from the home side because the ordinary reporters' pay was low and because they saw little hope of promotion. There was far too little crossing of the line between reporters who were below it and the specialist correspondents and leader writers who were above it, being better paid and better esteemed. The reporters' hopes of promotion were further dimmed, Green wrote, when they noticed an 'excessive propensity to take people into middle and higher positions from outside'. Green proposed that the dividing line should be less rigid and that, as an immediate measure, really good reporters should be paid more. They also should be given a special status, being kept primarily for big events and (in those years of strict anonymity) being granted the permanent rank and title of 'special correspondent'. Green further suggested that recruits to the reporters' room should be chosen for their native ability rather than, as happened too often in the past, for their solid dependability and experience. 'Such a system should make it more easily possible to handle the Home side in the same way as the Foreign side is handled now.'[21]

---

21 T.T.A.

Haley was slow in responding as Green wished, for he felt honour bound to keep within a tight budget.[22] Some modest increases in salary were given after further pleas by Green and Dobson. Later on, articles by the better men and women were styled, 'From a Staff Reporter', as a slight concession within the Trappist rules of self-abnegation. But for several years the reporting staff remained far too small for all that Haley wanted the paper to do.

There was much greater success in the two home editorial departments that, more obviously than any others except the leading articles themselves, made up the special personality of The Times each day. The letters to the editor had long been famous, a feature unparalleled in journalism. Geoffrey Woolley,[23] put in charge of them in 1953, developed them into being more than ever a national debating ground where archbishops and cabinet ministers, ambassadors and factory workers, admirals and wives of shopkeepers, competed for a voice. Colin Watson,[24] given charge of the obituaries in 1956, simplified the language of the articles for the benefit of the ordinary reader while keeping up the accuracy and, so far as space allowed, the completeness which made them essential reading for historians and biographers.

Woolley seemed to know about everyone in politics, the arts, and the sciences. Complaints were regularly made by aggrieved letter-writers that the editor had 'rejected' their precious contributions or had 'flatly refused to print' them. But such complaints lost whatever meaning they had as the number of letters sent in each day grew. When Woolley took over in 1953 the average number offered daily was 100 to 150. A few years later the average number was between 200 and 250, rising to 300. A national crisis always swelled the number. At the time of Suez in 1956 it reached over 400. Out of the daily inflow only twenty or so could be printed, crisis or no crisis. It was only the fittest that survived. But all the others were acknowledged, many of them with reasons why they had to be declined. Another regular complaint was that only the famous or the titled could count on their letters being published. In fact the letters printed from unknown men and women who had a valid point to make far outnumbered those from the illustrious.

---

22 See Chapter XVI.
23 Geoffrey Downing Woolley (b. 1915). Clifton; Caius College, Cambridge. Joined The Times as home sub-editor, 1939. Army, 1939–45. Assistant correspondent Washington, 1948–52; letters editor, 1953 until retirement in 1980.
24 Colin Hugh Watson (b. 1919). Gresham's School, Holt. Reporter, Isle of Ely and Wisbech Advertiser, 1938; Norfolk Chronicle, 1938–39 and Eastern Daily News, 1946–49. Army, 1939–45. Joined The Times as sub-editor, 1949–54; assistant night news editor, 1954–56; obituaries editor, 1956 until retirement in 1982.

In these and in other ways Woolley was maintaining and strengthening the old rules. No letter was ever sought from anyone; they had to be voluntary offerings. No inquirer was ever promised that a letter from him, if written, would appear. No letters from press attachés or public relations officers were knowingly printed (the rule was imposed because the number of such letters increased beyond all reason with the growth of the PR industry). No alteration was made in any letter, nor were any shortened, without reference back to the author. And – more a guide than a rule – the selection of letters on a running controversy (say, Britain's entry to the EEC) reflected not a neat fifty-fifty balance for or against the proposition but the number and weight of the letters for and against, whether four to one or ten to one, on the given day.

Watson strengthened the obituaries columns largely by forward planning. He knew, or could quickly get to know, who could best write a memoir of so-and-so which could join the hundreds of others on the files, ready for use when the day came; or, if the unexpected happened, he knew whom to ring at short notice. Memoirs of the great, whether Churchill or Eisenhower or Stalin, could take up one or two pages. Having them written was only the first stage; they had to be regularly revised and brought up to date without adding to the space thought appropriate.

The standing of *The Times* obituary columns was touchingly demonstrated one night. Haley was still at his desk when the telephone rang. 'Good evening, sir. This is Lord Woodwood's butler speaking.' Lord Woodwood (not his name) had been ill for some little time. 'Lord Woodwood presents his compliments to the editor of *The Times* and would like him to know that he does not expect to survive the night. Thank you, sir.' Haley did what he was sure Lord Woodwood had in mind. He had his obituary notice looked out from the files and sent to the printer. Before the night was out there came indeed the news of Lord Woodwood's death and the obituary appeared with the news in the paper.

Yet another department was greatly changed – and became the centre of many disputes and criticisms – after 1952. In that year Raoul Colinvaux[25] succeeded Colin Clayton[26] as legal adviser to the paper and

---

25 Raoul Percy Colinvaux (b. 1916). Mill Hill; King's College, London. Barrister-at-law. *The Times* law reporter, King's Bench Division, 1948–50; editor, *The Times* Law Reports and head of legal staff, 1951–53. Editor, Council of Law Reporting's weekly law reports, 1953–69.
26 Colin Clayton (1895–1975). Barrister-at-law. *The Times* law reporter, 1923–26; law editor, 1926–51; editor, *The Times* Law Reports, 1935–51.

editor of *The Times* law reports; within a few months he became editor of the official Law Reports as well. The unified editorship carried great prestige. Through being written only by barristers *The Times* law reports had the authority and distinction of being quotable in court as accurate records of proceedings. Lord Justice Goddard carried the privilege even further. When Clayton was about to be appointed Master of the Supreme Court in 1951 someone objected, pointing out that the post was open only to a practising barrister. Goddard put Clayton's mind at rest. 'I have clarified the rules', he told him. 'To report law for *The Times* must be being a practising barrister.'

In running the combined law reports Colinvaux had a small permanent staff and in addition he drew on the occasional services of some forty or fifty barristers during an average year. He set out to brighten the reports, encouraging his team of men and women to attract the interest of lay readers. Miss Mavis Hill and one or two others delighted to put in the quips which enlivened many a dull hearing – and it was soon noted that judges and counsel were never so sparkling as when Miss Hill was waiting in court with pencil poised. In 1962 Haley asked Colinvaux to ration the jokes more strictly while keeping the reports of interest to general readers as well as lawyers.

In the other part of his work, the leader-writing part, Colinvaux set out to expose several failings in the way the legal profession was organised and run. The climax of his campaign came with a leading article on December 10 1959. Its main argument was that all attempts at reform by the Bar Council were frustrated by the heads, the Benchers, of the several Inns of Court; but other legal practices also came under Colinvaux's attack:

> The state of the Bar is an unhappy one . . . the office inefficiency of many barristers' chambers is a disgrace to a profession. This is because they are run not by barristers but by their clerks, who are wholly untrained in modern business methods. Any act of salvage proposed by the Bar Council can, in effect, be vetoed by the Benchers or any one of the Inns of Court – notoriously unprogressive bodies. The right men are not entering the profession . . .

> Each Inn, with vast visible assets (they publish no accounts), has been contributing the derisory sum of only £600 a year to the Council. Further, it is intolerable that its efforts towards reform can be hampered by Benchers of one Inn or another . . . If the Inns fail to support the Council, reduction by Parliament of their powers becomes essential. Inquiry should be made whether they are making the most profitable use of their enormous resources, so necessary for scholarships and Council purposes.

Colinvaux was immediately accused of disloyalty to his own profession – 'There will be moaning at the Bar tonight', wrote the *Star* – and also of inaccuracies. The four Treasurers of the four Inns of Court joined in writing a long letter to *The Times* 'to correct the impressions created by the ill-informed leading article'. The Treasurers were chiefly concerned to show that the Inns of Court were exceptionally generous in caring for their students: 'From their endowments and funds many thousands of pounds in each year are disbursed in this way.' As for the annual payments direct to the Bar Council, 'the subventions in the case of each Inn now very substantially exceed "the derisory sum" which you mistakenly cite'. The Treasurers ended with a strong defence of the clerks who managed chambers.[27]

Haley had been away, and Green in charge, when the leader appeared. On his return Haley told Colinvaux not to worry and he received the Master of the Rolls, Lord Evershed, to hear his indignant complaints. 'Worse than the *Mirror*,' Evershed said.[28] Haley stuck by Colinvaux and the storm died, but many judges and counsel remained bitterly critical of Colinvaux.

In two cases of national importance *The Times* did not simply report: it stood as defendant in test cases, appearing in large measure on behalf of the whole British press. The first challenged the law of election expenses. On October 19 1951, during the run-up to the general election of that year, *The Times* published a large advertisement from the Tronoh–Malayan Tin group of companies. In part it was an anti-socialist manifesto. Did it amount to an undeclared election expense? The Crown argued that propaganda aimed at the whole country, through the medium of *The Times*, must be aimed at each several constituency in it; and that expenditure on the advertisement, not having been included in the election return of any candidate, was illegal and corrupt under the Representation of the People Act. The defence reply was that, on a correct reading of the law, not only must the expenses of the propaganda be intended to promote the election of a particular candidate but the particular candidate must also be presented to the electors in the propaganda. On February 18 1952 Mr. Justice McNair ruled in the Central Criminal Court that the defendants had no case to answer and directed the jury to acquit both the tin group of companies and *The Times*. 'Commonsense will applaud the result,' wrote *The Times* the next day.

27 *The Times*, December 14 1959.
28 Undated memorandum (c. 1970) by Colinvaux.

The second case, heard eight years later, produced the highly valuable ruling that British newspapers were protected by qualified privilege when reporting trials in duly constituted foreign courts. That is to say, fair and accurate accounts of cases of legitimate public interest and concern could be published without fear that anyone who thought himself libelled during the hearing, in arguments or utterances germane to the case, could count on being awarded damages. Mrs. Cynthia Mary Webb had complained that a report in *The Times* of September 25 1959, headed 'Hume Admits Killing Setty' and datelined 'Winterthur, Switzerland, Sept. 24', contained matter defamatory to her. After a hearing of several days in the High Court of Justice, Mr. Justice Pearson delivered a long judgment in favour of *The Times*. The proceedings in the Swiss court, producing as they did references to an earlier English hearing involving Hume, were much connected with the administration of justice in England; and this was a matter of legitimate concern and proper interest to English newspaper readers. In general, therefore, the report was privileged. Further, the sentence mainly complained of by the plaintiff was not extraneous to the issue but germane to it and so was covered by the privilege.

As a result of the hearing before Mr. Justice Pearson all British newspapers knew better where they stood when faced with tricky reports of foreign trials.

'Whatever approval or criticism seems fair.' Haley's dictum was demonstrated often in the paper both before and after his leader of June 10 1959 in which the words appeared. One of the most striking examples of criticisms of a Prime Minister had come in Haley's first years. On November 23 1954 Churchill told his constituents at Woodford that in 1945 he had sent a telegram to Field-Marshal Lord Montgomery asking him, when collecting arms from the surrendering Germans, to have them carefully stacked 'so that they could easily be issued again to the German soldiers whom we should have to work with if the Soviet advance continued'. No one on *The Times* could find any trace of such a telegram, which seemed manifestly improbable on the face of it. The records in Printing House Square showed that Churchill had indeed written messages in 1945 saying that all German arms should be preserved but only because the allies themselves might need them for their own use one day, or perhaps even quite soon, in preserving order both in France and especially in Italy. There had been no suggestion of handing them back to Nazi-trained German soldiers.

Haley and others in the office thought that the Russians, reading Churchill's speech, were bound to think that all his professions of a desire to work with them were insincere. Two days after the speech the paper came out with a leader beginning with the un-Timesy sentence:

What on earth made him say it? . . . The remark can be looked at in every way and be put to every kind of test, and in the end it is impossible to see what purpose or good it can serve at this time . . . The idea was unrealistic at the time; it is unwise to come out with it now.[29]

Lord Moran in his memoirs records that the aged Churchill read the leader, together with *Pravda's* comments, and was greatly upset:

I'm worried about this stupid mistake of mine. I was quite certain it was in my book, otherwise I would never have said what I did.

And now it seems there wasn't a telegram, after all . . . If my slip has done harm with the Russians I may pull out [of Downing Street] sooner than I intended.[30]

On December 1 the old warrior most handsomely and typically expressed his regrets in the House of Commons. He had failed, he said, to observe the rule 'which I have so often inculcated with others, "Always verify your quotations"'. *The Times* had a no less handsome leading article in reply. Churchill, however, remained troubled over the affair; and so did the many others who were anxious for him to resign. Unfortunately when he made up his mind four months later *The Times* could not pay its tribute to him on the day of his going, because for the first time in its history its record of continuous production was broken. A strike had halted it and other London newspapers.[31]

The same problem – how to keep a balance of power between the west and Russia – was at the bottom of another and much longer dispute with another Conservative government. This time the special target was Duncan Sandys, Minister of Defence, 1957–59, in the Macmillan administration. John Grant, the defence correspondent, was troubled when Sandys, with Macmillan's full concurrence, decided early in his term of office to abolish conscription; and he soon became much more alarmed. Sandys seemed to Grant to be thinking of defence too much in terms of a nuclear reply and to be neglecting the role of conventional forces. Grant argued that adequate western conventional forces could cope with, say, a hostile incursion short of an all-out attack and so might avert nuclear war over a small-scale incident.

---

29 *The Times*, November 25 1954.
30 Lord Moran; *op. cit.*, p. 612.
31 See Chapter XV.

Haley agreed with Grant and a series of sharp leading articles followed. *The Times* was in favour of keeping the nuclear deterrent for Britain but argued that any attempt to keep up with the United States in building smaller nuclear rockets was strategically useless and financially ruinous. After reading a memorandum from Grant, reporting a private talk with a high-ranking rocket enthusiast, Haley wrote:

One begins to wonder whether we intend to fight the Russians or the Americans! It is absurd for us, with our much more limited resources, to think we can match up item for item and weapon for weapon with the richest, most powerful and most productive nation the world has ever seen. The only result will be that we will do everything in a second rate fashion. It is better to be effective at one point than ineffective all along the line.[32]

Sandys, annoyed by *The Times's* criticisms, had separate arguments with both Haley and Grant. They kept to their line and, even before Sandys left the Defence Ministry in October 1959, they were relieved to find that the government acknowledged much more clearly than before the role which conventional forces had to fill. Another confidential memorandum from Grant on November 17 1959 reported (very soon after Sandys had moved) that a high-powered defence committee had 'come out decisively and unanimously against the Sandys strategy'; it recommended greater interdependence among allies in nuclear weapons and fewer attempts at independence by Britain. Haley wrote briefly back to Grant:

If the policy has changed you can take a good part of the credit for it. *The Times* has been the spearhead of this all through. It has been an excellent piece of constructive journalism.[33]

The Times could not, and did not, claim all the credit. Britain's partners in Nato had been pressing for more conventional forces within the alliance as a whole; and Britain could not afford adequate conventional forces and assorted rocketry at the same time. None the less the paper's arguments stand staunchly on record.

---

32 Haley memorandum, March 7 1956. T.T.A.
33 Haley memorandum, November 18 1959. T.T.A.

XII

EVEREST AND OTHER SUMMITS

In the middle of 1953 – the year of Stalin's death and all the world-wide speculation about a consequent thaw in Kremlin politics within Russia and without – there came the splendid interruption from Everest. Skill and chance combined to time the event brilliantly. Edmund Hillary and Sherpa Tensing climbed the peak on a day that let the news be announced by *The Times*, and be copied by other papers, on the morning of the Queen's coronation, June 2 1953.

None of the later successes on the mountain can diminish that first achievement. Everest, standing near the limits of the old British Empire, stood also at the limits of human courage and endurance. The North and South Poles had been reached but here was a third Pole, the last great prize to be gained on man's own feet. Climbing it was a national achievement; and in a minor yet special way it was a *Times* achievement. The expedition of 1953 under Colonel John Hunt was only the last of several expeditions to Everest that had been supported by *The Times*.

In particular Ralph Deakin, in his years as foreign news editor, had thrown himself whole-heartedly into the work of liaison between *The Times* and the organisers of the expeditions. There were times when the expeditions' hopes and disappointments seemed to take more out of him than anyone. He heard all the avalanches and felt all the winds as if he was on the slopes himself; many in the office felt it sad that he did not live to see the final success. Gerald Norman had to pick up all the strings from him only a few weeks before the 1953 expedition was due to leave.

Strict conditions were laid down in the agreement which *The Times* made with the Royal Geographical Society and the Alpine Club who were the joint organisers. In a letter dated January 2 1953 (addressed to L. P. Kirwan, secretary of the RGS) Francis Mathew stated that *The Times* would pay £10,000 towards the cost of the expedition. Furthermore, if the paper received more than £10,000 from the sale of rights to other papers or magazines at home or overseas it would pay all such extra sums to the organisers for the benefit of the expedition. In return it would have exclusive first rights over all news and special articles from Hunt or other members of the team.[1] From first to last it was to be a *Times* story.

That seemed fair and clear but, when Colonel Hunt came to *The Times* on February 2 for further talks, difficulties began to be seen. With the best will in the world, members of the expedition were going to have precious little time and energy to spare for writing full reports; and they were going to have even less energy for ensuring that any such reports got back to Katmandu in the total secrecy that was required. Other newspapers, it was already known, were sending special correspondents into Nepal to pick up what news they could by talking to sherpas (bearers) and others. Sir Christopher Summerhayes, the ambassador in Katmandu, had sportingly promised to send on to London, by the fastest means, all messages from the expedition, but much could happen along the long and lonely path from the mountain to the embassy. Quite plainly *The Times* ran the risk of being scooped on its own story.

It was therefore quickly decided to move Arthur Hutchinson[2] up from Delhi to Katmandu to speed on all messages addressed to *The Times*. It was also decided – a far bolder and riskier venture – to send out James Morris,[3] then a young assistant in the foreign news room, to join the expedition as a special correspondent. He was asked to push as far as he could up the middle and upper-middle slopes, organise his teams of despatch runners, and write his own despatches to supplement those of Colonel Hunt. The use of radio was thought of first, but the Nepalese government, anxious not to offend its mighty Indian and Chinese neighbours, strongly discouraged the import of radios which it could not control. Yet radio was used in the end. After Morris on his outward journey had reached Katmandu on March 25 and pressed on to Namche Bazar, he discovered there – only thirty miles from Everest – a small wireless transmitter in the hands of an Indian police post. Messages from the set could reach Katmandu and save up to twelve days of running. Morris speedily made friends with the policemen against the time when he might need them.

Having recruited his own sherpas he set off for the mountain itself

---

1 T.T.A.
2 Arthur Lockwood Hutchinson (1920–1974). Kingswood School, Bath; St. John's College, Cambridge. Foreign department, Kemsley Newspapers, 1948–49. Joined *The Times* foreign department, 1949; correspondent, Pakistan, 1950; Delhi, 1952; Rome, 1953–57. Joined BBC (Radio) editorial staff, 1957.
3 James Humphry (afterwards Jan) Morris (b. 1926). Lancing; Christ Church, Oxford. After experience in journalism in Bristol, London and Cairo, joined *The Times* sub-editorial staff, 1950; special correspondent, Canal Zone, 1951; Everest expedition, 1953; correspondent in the Middle East, 1955–56.

with two of Colonel Hunt's team, Charles Evans and Alfred Gregory. They were soon above the 15,000 foot mark:

My first experience of mountaineering proper came with the climb up the icefall into the Western Cwm, the great snow valley cut in the flank of Everest which was the highway to the summit. It would be idle to pretend that I found it easy; but the other men on the rope were some of the world's finest and friendliest climbers, and somehow they pulled me over the gaping crevasses, heaved me up the iceblocks, pushed me over the precarious makeshift bridges, and dragged me through the wilderness of crumbled snow and ice. The climate was appalling. Sometimes it was parchingly dry, and bakingly hot; sometimes cold, damp, and dreary with snowfalls. . . . At 20,000 feet and above the altitude is likely to tell quite severely on the novice climber. I found my brain a little blunted, and my natural enthusiasm dampened. I wrote less than I ought to have written, and took fewer photographs.[4]

The Hunt team's first attempt at the summit was beaten back. Hillary and Tensing were to make the second assault on May 29. As the day came nearer, Morris climbed to Camp IV, nearly 22,000 feet up at the end of the Western Cwm. On May 30 most of the team were there, watching and waiting for the two men to appear as they came down from higher slopes:

A kind of feverish hush settled on the camp when we first spotted the figures of Hillary and Tensing on the ridge high above us. Hunt, himself seriously weakened by his exploits on the final ridge a few days before, sat on a packing-case tense as a violin string. The rest of us looked through binoculars, or laid the odds, or sipped lemonade rather listlessly, or thumbed our way through the old newspapers that littered the main tent of the camp. It was, for me anyway, a decidedly pre-dentist feeling.

But I shall never, as long as I live, forget the transformation that overcame the camp when the summit party appeared and gave us the news of their victory. It was a moment so thrilling, so vibrant, that the hot tears sprang into the eyes of most of us. The day was so dazzling bright – the snow so white, the sky so blue; and the air so heavily charged with excitement; and the news, however much we expected it, was still somehow such a wonderful surprise; and it felt to all of us that we were very close to the making of history.'[5]

---

4 Article in *House Journal*, September 1953.
5 *Ibid.*

Morris immediately resolved 'in a moment of wild optimism' to get the news back to Britain in time for coronation day, little more than forty-eight hours away. It was twilight before he, stumbling and slithering, could reach Camp III, it was dusk at the icefall, and long after dark when he flopped into his tent at base camp. He typed out a brief message. In accordance with an elaborate and deliberately misleading code, arranged well beforehand, the message read:

Snow conditions bad stop advanced base abandoned May twenty-nine stop awaiting improvement stop all well

The few who had the key to the code could work out the meaning.

Snow conditions bad *stood for* Everest climbed.

Advanced base abandoned *stood for* Hillary.

Awaiting improvement *stood for* Tensing.

May twenty-nine *as sent en clair*.

All well *as sent en clair*.

Having sealed the message Morris handed one copy to a runner with instructions to leave with it at first light and deliver it to Morris's Indian friends in their radio post at Namche. A second copy he gave to another runner who was to press on to Katmandu direct with it and a rather longer despatch. Morris then slept, moved on the next day, and woke on the following morning to learn over the radio that the great news had indeed reached London and had been heard during the night by the crowds waiting in the rain for coronation day to begin. He then told his sherpas that their goddess mountain had been climbed at last. 'O.K., Sahib,' the sherpas shouted back. 'Breakfast now?'

The news reached Printing House Square one minute before the 4.15 p.m. editorial conference on June 1. William Ridsdale, head of the Foreign Office news department, telephoned to tell *The Times* that a brief message had just been received through the embassy in Katmandu. The announcement at the conference meant that much of the paper had to be happily reshaped. A little later Ridsdale rang back to ask if the Queen could be given the news straight away; it was pleasant for *The Times* to waive its copyright for the Queen on the eve of her coronation. A more difficult question was what to do in face of the certain prospect that other newspapers would lift the news as soon as they saw the first edition of *The Times* about 10 p.m. that same night. There was no question of holding the news out of the first edition; *The Times's* first duty, come what may, was to give the news to its readers whatever edition they received. After some little discussion about the expediency of making a general release of the news Haley decided the matter by saying that *The Times* had an obligation to maintain, for its part, its contract with the many newspapers in different parts of the world that had bought the syndicated service. If other papers lifted the news *The Times* could not stop them amid all the coronation excitement, but it need not give them the news on a plate with an invitation to help themselves. The other papers duly splashed the news, most of them with acknowledgements to *The Times*.

No one could remember a day when news had arrived more fortunately: a glorious present for coronation day. Senior *Times* men, watching the cheering crowds during the morning, had to shut out of their minds any nagging doubts as to whether the coded message – phrased entirely contrary to its true hidden meaning, and passed from Everest to Katmandu along so long and precarious a route – could in some impossible way have gone wrong. But double and treble confirmation of the news soon came, and Norman, who had carried most of the organising work for *The Times*, could relax. Seldom had an event brought more credit to the paper.

Two years after the Everest success Francis Mathew made an agreement[6] to provide another £10,000 for another adventurous expedition. Dr. Vivian Fuchs was to lead a Commonwealth team who during the months of November 1957 to February 1958 would cross the Antarctic continent from one side to the other, using dogs and then vehicles. At the South Pole they planned to meet Sir Edmund Hillary – the Hillary of Everest – with a New Zealand team who would have come in from the opposite side to Fuchs. Once again *The Times* secured exclusive rights for all special articles, and Mathew promised to add substantially to the £10,000 if he obtained (as indeed he did) more than that from the sale of the articles to other newspapers and magazines across the world. Safeguarding the secrecy of news was not a problem this time as it was agreed that Reuters would carry all straightforward reports of progress.

The expedition succeeded as planned. Fuchs's articles read well and were full of valuable scientific findings. Naturally enough the exploit could not make the popular impact of Everest but it had its own appeal as a hazardous and useful venture, worthy of all backing. Within the frame of the large expedition Printing House Square mounted its own one-man expedition to the South Pole. The art editor, U. V. Bogaerde,[7]

---

6 Letter to Rear-Admiral C. R. L. Parry, secretary of the Trans-Antarctic expedition committee, September 27 1955. T.T.A.
7 Ulric Van den Bogaerde (1892–1972). Joined *The Times* in 1912 as artist for special numbers; became first art editor in 1922 until his retirement in 1957.

was determined to have the Fuchs–Hillary meeting photographed at the Pole and have it sent back to London by radio, something that had not been done before. A portable radio-phone transmitter was hastily acquired. A staff photographer, Stewart Heydinger, flew to New Zealand. Hearing there that the runways at McMurdo Sound, Antarctica, were reported to be unsafe he asked, being a trained parachutist, to be allowed to drop into McMurdo from an aircraft. This was agreed, but then an aircraft landing was judged possible and Heydinger finally arrived in the American base at the South Pole with Hillary on January 18, one day before Fuchs came in with his team. Bad atmospheric conditions looked for a time like spoiling the transmission of the photographs. In the end they were sent *via* Wellington where the signal was boosted to Baldock, Hertfordshire. At 7 p.m. on January 21, two days after the meeting at the Pole, the pictures appeared on a newly installed machine in Printing House Square and were published in the paper the next day.

While the flourishes such as Everest and Antarctica were bringing in acclaim, the day-to-day work of the foreign department had to go on. Haley, McDonald and Norman, having all of them come new to the job in late 1952 or early 1953, had to give posts in different parts of the world to men whom for the most part they only partly knew. Some wrong postings were made in the first years but the staff lists[8] show how many men were in those same years picked out as being promising, were given their big chance, and were to rise high on *The Times* or elsewhere.

Louis Heren was sent to Malaya,[9] to Bonn, and later to Washington. Frank Giles,[10] who while in Rome was one of the first correspondents after the war to delve into the supposedly wholly secret politics of the Vatican, was moved to Paris. Richard Harris,[11] born in China and a Chinese speaker, correspondent first in Hong Kong and then in Malaya, was strongly encouraged to write the kind of reflective, perceptive pieces that later made his name as a China expert. James Holburn, after

---

8 T.T.A.
9 See Chapter XIV.
10 Frank Thomas Robertson Giles (b. 1919). Wellington; Brasenose College, Oxford. Joined *The Times* sub-editorial staff, 1946; assistant Paris correspondent, 1947; correspondent in Rome, 1950; Paris, 1953–60. Joined *The Sunday Times* as foreign editor, 1961; deputy editor, 1967; editor 1981–83.
11 Richard Frederick James Harris (b. 1914). Educated in China and subsequently at Taunton School. Army. Head of Information Department, British Embassy, Peking. Joined *The Times* editorial staff, 1950; correspondent in Hong Kong, 1951–53; Singapore, 1953–55; returned to Printing House Square as leader writer, 1955; deputy foreign editor, 1967, until retirement in 1979.

being diplomatic correspondent, went to Cairo and left only to become editor of the *Glasgow Herald*. James Morris, after a year on a Commonwealth fellowship in the United States, was in the Middle East before the writing of history and travel claimed him. John Buist moved from Berlin to Ottawa and was in central and northern Europe before being appointed foreign news editor in 1958. Jerome Caminada served in South-East Asia and the Middle East until he, in turn, became foreign news editor in 1965. David Holden,[12] who was murdered outside Cairo in 1977 while chief foreign correspondent of *The Sunday Times*, was first picked out to be Middle East correspondent for *The Times* in 1956.

Of the correspondents who left full service in the early fifties the one for whom there could be no substitute, no true replacement, was Louis Hinrichs.[13] He partly retired in 1952 after being correspondent in New York since 1916. Every week his Monday morning article on Wall Street quietly demonstrated his knowledge, his accuracy, his fairness. The Governor of the Bank of England, Montagu Norman, said it was 'required reading at the Bank'. Everything about Hinrichs was quiet: his New England courtesy, his Harvard breeding, his conversation that was always modest and entertaining, his manner of work. He was never famous; he would have turned and gone the other way if he had thought that he was on the road to fame; but anyone wanting to do a portrait of an old-style, deeply conscientious, steadily effective journalist could begin with Hinrichs. He went on writing his weekly column until he was eighty-seven, achieving the firmest of his ambitions, which was never to stop being a working journalist.

As it happened it was the chief correspondent in the United States, John Duncan Miller, who presented the first of Haley's big problems on the foreign side. Since 1947 Miller's work in Washington had been splendid; his love for America showed in everything he wrote. So did his passion for American politics. He not only wrote politics; he talked them and lived them. His despatches in *The Times* were widely quoted in the States and warmly commended at Washington dinner parties. He was a part of the Washington scene as Willmott Lewis had been.

He was to become too much involved. During the 1952 election

---

12 David Shipley Holden (1924–1977). Friends School, Great Ayton; Emmanuel College, Cambridge, and Northwestern University, Illinois. Joined *The Times* special numbers department, 1954; assistant correspondent, Washington, 1955; special correspondent, Middle East, 1956; roving correspondent, Africa, 1961; resigned 1961 to go to *Guardian*. *Sunday Times* from 1965 until his murder in Egypt, December 1977.
13 Louis Ernest Hinrichs (1880–1967). Private schools; Harvard. After travels in the Far East joined *The Times* in 1916 and became chief correspondent in New York in 1923.

campaign Miller's whole-hearted admiration for Adlai Stevenson's character and his dismay and anguish at General Eisenhower's platform performances were made plain in his despatches. In his desire to see Stevenson in the White House he could not let himself believe that Eisenhower could win by anything like the sweeping majority that he did in fact secure. Even before Eisenhower's victory it was being said among journalists in Washington that a Republican administration would freeze him out of the contacts normally open to a Washington correspondent. It was also being said, alternatively, that *The Times* itself would transfer Miller to a post elsewhere. These reports soon reached Printing House Square together with news that Miller had worked himself into a poor physical and nervous state.

After talks in the office Haley wrote to Miller, whom he had never met, a letter of six typed pages on January 7 1953. He told Miller that the general tenor of the criticism aroused by his election despatches was that they had led *The Times* to depart from its usual course of impartiality in reporting such matters and had made its news columns strongly partisan. Haley very fairly recognised how extraordinarily difficult it was for an English correspondent not to be affected by the passions and emotions of an American election campaign and, without labouring the point further, he went on to what in his own view was the gravamen of the criticism:

It is that, because you did become so personally imbued with an idea as to the respective merits of the two candidates, it led you unconsciously to weigh the evidence which you were reporting less dispassionately – and therefore less accurately – than you otherwise would have done. It is easy to say after the event that a movement of the American people so decisive as that which swept General Eisenhower into the White House should have been foreseen. Be that as it may, I feel that straws in the wind which tended to indicate another result became something far more than straws to you. The facts you put forward at various times in Mr. Stevenson's favour undoubtedly were facts but they had nowhere near the weight you believed or that their inclusion in your correspondence and therefore in the columns of *The Times* tended to give them.

In other words it was the evidence that *The Times* had been wrong, just as much as the belief that it had been partial, which (Haley stated) gave many of its friends in America, Democrats as well as Republicans, a feeling of criticism and disappointment. As for the future Haley assured Miller that *The Times* was not considering any early change in Washington. The real question was whether Miller himself believed that he could be as impartial and detached in judging an Eisenhower administration as he would have been in judging one under Stevenson. Haley suggested that the two of them should talk over this side of the matter when he visited Washington, as he hoped to do, within the next few weeks.[14]

Miller's reply on February 2 was equally long. While acknowledging that he had underestimated the size of Eisenhower's majority, Miller pointed out that most of the American experts had done likewise or even worse. He himself, unlike some of the experts, had believed that Eisenhower would at any rate win. In answer to the criticism that he had supported Stevenson Miller wrote that he had been deeply shocked by Eisenhower's electioneering behaviour:

> My attitude, therefore, contained much more of disgust at Eisenhower than of partiality for Stevenson – and it began to appear in the month before the Conventions, at a time when I thought that Stevenson had removed himself from the race.

Looking ahead Miller was confident:

> It will, I think, be much easier for me to be dispassionate about the Eisenhower administration, about which I have no illusions, than it might have been in a Stevenson regime, of which I might have had exaggerated hopes.

Nevertheless he said that some passages in Haley's letter perturbed him. Haley, when emphasizing the need for a *Times* man to be impartial, had referred by way of illustration to the paper's traditional role of supporting any incoming British government until that government had, by its actions, caused the paper to withdraw its support. Miller took this reference to mean that *The Times* expected a correspondent in a foreign country to give similar support to the government whose acts and policies he was reporting:

> It is, of course, simpler and infinitely more comfortable to be a public relations correspondent. But I have always taken it that my duty lay in risking discomfort if the truth demanded it.[15]

In his next letter of February 16 Haley confined himself chiefly to answering this last point and he set out very clearly his own view of a correspondent's duty and stance:

> I am afraid you have completely misread my view as to the attitude a *Times* correspondent should have to the Government of any country

---

14 T.T.A.
15 T.T.A.

he is serving. Your job is certainly to report what is happening regardless whether it reflects credit or discredit on the Government in power, and certainly no one wishes you to pull your punches. But the point is that a *Times* correspondent has to do this job professionally and with detachment. He has to be above the battle: not one of the contestants. He has to be sure that any punches he delivers are distributed wherever they are deserved, and not reserved solely for one side or the other. The point I wished to make was that the election campaign was over and, while I did not feel that even in the course of it you should have lost your detachment, it was many times more necessary now that the campaign was over for *The Times* correspondent to make reporting his first job and advocating his second.[16]

As it happened, Haley could not go over to America as he had planned. Tyerman went instead and brought back reassuring reports about Miller's health and standing in Washington. But something had changed. Miller was still unsettled by the criticisms against him. He did not find the Eisenhower regime stimulating. He was depressed by Senator McCarthy's political witch hunt which ended the careers of many men whom he most liked and respected. At bottom he was tired out after seven years of top-pressure work in Washington. In the spring of 1954 the International Bank asked him whether he could suggest a man to be their European director of public relations. He put himself forward, was quickly accepted, and 'with a feeling of sadness' resigned from the paper.[17]

Part of the truth underlying the episode goes back to the dilemma exposed by the dispute with Captain Liddell Hart sixteen years earlier. In the *Times* tradition the news staff could accommodate and welcome a strong-minded interpreter of events but not if he wrote at times more as a political columnist.

Although Korea and Vietnam brought their dangers in the early and middle fifties, and the old empires were falling apart in Africa and Asia, it was the cold war that still pressed the most heavily on Britain. Stalin's death on March 5 1953 had quickly led to what Churchill called 'the supreme event',[18] meaning a loosening of the worst rigidities of the cold war and an opportunity for the western powers to test again whether an east–west accommodation of some kind was possible.

16 T.T.A.
17 Letter from Miller to Haley, April 19 1954. T.T.A.
18 House of Commons, May 11 1953.

In the next years *The Times* joined to the full in that inquiry and put out special efforts in three fields: west, east and centre. West meant support for all the moves towards greater Atlantic and European unity. East meant objective reporting of Russia, China, and the satellite countries. Centre meant support for all sensible attempts at east–west detente and some suggestions to that end by *The Times* itself.

When looking at the west Haley was both an Atlanticist and a European – a more positive European, he soon showed, than either Barrington-Ward or Casey had been. He never had any doubts about the need to work with the United States; he summed it all up in a few sentences at the end of six articles in November 1956, after visiting the States:

Meanwhile the United States of America, working out its dream, blunders beneficently on. Of all nations, its history has a higher proportion of greatness than of baseness; of all peoples its motives are the least suspect. Its errors have been, and are, many. Its instincts have been, and are, magnificently right. We see the small debits from day to day. Let us look rather at the huge credit through the years. Amidst all the dangers that beset us we can be thankful that it is to this dynamic, humorous, impatient, impulsive, generous people there has passed the leadership of the world.[19]

Haley's positive approach to Europe had been first shown two years before in a leading article published on September 3 1954. The French Assembly had just shocked the western governments by rejecting the much too complex and much too ambitious scheme for a European army. Anthony Eden was hastily planning his rescue operations by means of visits to the main European capitals, but success could not be foreseen. In his leader Haley said that the reestablishment of German sovereignty must be the chief priority for western statesmen, but he soon came on to his main point:

The second priority should be the salvaging of the European idea. Even granting some eventual stabilizing of the opposing Powers [in the cold war], and a resultant period of 'peaceful coexistence', the west will have enough on its hands in holding off both external and internal threats to its freedom without having to cope with rising nationalisms within its own ranks. To remove all hope of a new Europe would be to destroy the most potent way of winning the new Germany . . . It would destroy the last hopes among the coming

---

19 *The Times*, November 17 1956. The six articles were reprinted as a pamphlet, 'Eisenhower's America'.

generation in many countries in the west that, however painfully and however gradually, a better, more sensible, and more stable order of things would one day replace the old.

It was a new note, even if vague in point of detail. Three weeks later, while the success of Eden's mission was still uncertain, Haley was more direct in his appeal. Britain could no longer afford, he wrote, to regard herself as only half in the debate going on in western Europe:

For morally, culturally, and geographically Britain is now a European Power . . . Britain's first allegiance is admittedly to the Commonwealth. She will also always look naturally to her great English-speaking partner across the Atlantic. But she is still the country whose guiding rule for centuries had to be that no hostile Power should establish itself in the Low Countries . . . In this jet-age of the hydrogen and the rocket bomb the whole of northern Europe is the Low Countries so far as Britain is concerned.[20]

As the leading article shows, Haley at that time was far from thinking that Europe could be Britain's sole or even chief link with the outside world. Like other *Times* men he thought of foreign policy in terms of the three 'intertwining circles', defined by Anthony Eden as the three relationships with America, with the Commonwealth, and with Europe.

Yet the emphasis on Europe was stronger than before. Haley began to stress the European relationship in years when British people as a whole would rather not hear about it. Harold Macmillan, an ardent European himself, has very fairly described the shapelessness of general thought when he became Foreign Secretary in the middle fifties. In the fourth volume of his memoirs he refers to the three famous circles and goes on:

But none of us had ever worked out in any detail how these different conceptions were to be reconciled. Indeed British opinion, both in the major political parties and in the nation itself, was hesitant about any new participation in Europe which might prove irreconcilable with other ties. In Churchill's last administration I had done my best to urge my colleagues to press forward and take the lead in the integration of Europe. But in spite of support from some of my friends – notably David Maxwell Fyfe, Peter Thorneycroft and Duncan Sandys – Churchill had been unwilling to press the issue against the hostility of the Foreign Office and the indifference of the Treasury.[21]

---

20 *The Times*, September 27 1954.
21 Harold Macmillan. Memoirs, Volume IV. *Riding the Storm*, p. 65.

Times correspondents in Europe were closely watching all the steps towards greater unity. Gerald Norman, correspondent in Paris from 1945 to 1953, had his interest in the movement awakened even before the liberation. He recognised, from a speech which General de Gaulle made to the French consultative assembly in Algiers as early as March 1944, that the general wished to have a west European community but no less firmly wished to exclude Britain from it. He had passed Britain over in silence. The speech, coming when British prestige was at its height among French people whether occupied or free, caused many members of the assembly to protest. A would-be reassuring official statement explained that the general had misread his notes; he had meant to refer to the Channel as one of the vital European highways and so, by extension, had meant to bring in Britain. This threadbare disclaimer collapsed altogether when someone close to de Gaulle told Norman that there had been no mistake, no misreading. De Gaulle, said his aide, was convinced that the prevailing mood among the British people would make them reject any membership of a European community; Britain stood apart as she had done throughout her history and she was more concerned with her own Commonwealth than with the Continent. All this was nearly twenty years before President de Gaulle's famous press conference in January 1963 when he justified his veto against British membership on the selfsame grounds. Norman sent three long despatches on the Algiers pronouncements, but in days when papers were at their wartime thinnest no place was found for them in *The Times*. Only a short Reuter summary of the speech itself was carried.

Established in Paris, Norman frequently saw Jean Monnet, then head of the French recovery plan and already one of the architects of the future European community. When the Labour government, in 1950, declined the invitation to join the Schuman Plan, which was to develop the following year into the Coal and Steel Community, Monnet asked Norman to see him urgently, read him the substance of the British note, and asked him point blank how the French government should reply. With Monnet was a Quai d'Orsay official. It was one of those times when a journalist is pulled out of his normal ambit. Evidently the two Frenchmen wished to have a quick check, from someone wholly unofficial, on whether the British ministers were right in citing British public opinion in support of their claim that no British government could enter into any compact that limited the sovereignty of parliament or weakened the Commonwealth links. In his off-the-cuff reply Norman added to the usual arguments by saying that Britain's war experiences had emphasised her separateness from the Continent. In any case her traditional policy was pragmatic and empirical rather than theoretical.

249

For that reason she would reject the proposed partnership with its supranational provisions; but for the same reason she was likely to join later if the others went ahead and manifestly made a success of it.[22] No doubt Norman's reply confirmed Monnet in an opinion on Britain's membership which he had already formed; other evidence suggests so. It remains true that both Frenchmen listened with a special intentness as Norman spoke.

The public indifference in Britain continued while the six western European countries were bringing themselves more closely together. Their conference at Messina early in June 1955 which laid the bases for their Common Market was little heeded although it was adequately reported.[23] *The Times* followed it up with a persuasive special article on June 16 1955 by Jean Monnet, 'the architect of Europe'. The signature of the Treaties of Rome, enshrining the Messina decisions, on March 25 1957, was seen to be a step towards practical politics but there was still a widespread belief in Britain that the country should hold back from Europe for two entirely contradictory reasons. If the Common Market did not work (and it had yet to prove itself), then clearly it would be a waste of time for Britain to join. If it did indeed work, then it was not the kind of thing – with all its talk of federalism – that Britain should join.

In this dilemma *The Times* did not begin a crusade. It argued in favour of a large European free trade area that would leave all questions of federalism or confederalism to be worked out in the conveniently vague future. When such an agreement between Britain and the original members of the Common Market – the famous Six – was seen to be impracticable *The Times* supported the European Free Trade Area for Britain and six of her other European neighbours. The paper maintained the hope of eventual agreement with the Six; and with that end in view it made a special point of reporting happenings within the European Economic Community.[24]

In these early years before Britain applied to join the EEC in August 1961, *The Times* – while edging towards Europe – thought of western unity first and foremost in terms of the North Atlantic Treaty Organisation. On February 26 1952 the paper had a fine leader by John Pringle entitled 'The Phantom Army'. It exposed the cheerless truth about Nato's weakness that lay behind all the easy words and robust resolutions of the assembled defence ministers. John Grant, defence correspondent after 1954, kept up the good work, pressing for more arms and

22 Memorandum: Norman to McDonald, August 29 1979. T.T.A.
23 E.g. in *The Times*, June 8 1955.
24 See Chapter XVIII.

for greater standardisation of weapons among the allies. On December 11 1957, on the eve of a meeting in Paris among all the Nato heads of government, *The Times* gave up all its leader space (except for the usual light 'fourth') to three linked leaders under the general heading, 'Can N.A.T.O. meet its challenge?' The first part emphasized that a balance of power was necessary for political reasons: 'It remains true that, while Russia and America have the power to blast each other ten times over, the launching of a great war is unlikely – and the challenge today is more political than military.' John Grant, in the second of the three leaders, broadened the point: 'The real need is not for bombs that make the biggest bang but for deterrent forces that are manifestly usable'. Duncan Burn, in the third, emphasized the need for spreading the financial and economic burdens fairly among all the partners in order to make the alliance more secure.

With the lessons of the pre-war mistakes in mind *The Times* argued for all that it was worth that the west should ensure that it had at least a balance in the weight of its arms with the eastern bloc. That did not mean, as it often said, piling on arms without limit. If a lower level could be agreed with Russia, the deterrent and reassuring effect of a balance would still be achieved and the money thus saved could be better used. Leader writers always groaned aloud when they had to enter into the higher mathematics of the disarmament debates. None the less they pursued several disarmament schemes that seemed at the time to promise some limited success.

In reporting events in eastern Europe after Stalin's death *The Times* began with the kind of ill luck that all newspapers know at one time or another. When the East Berlin riots broke out in June 1953 the Berlin correspondent, Charles Hargrove, was in London for consultation. Fortunately the paper was well covered by Reginald Peck, of the *Daily Mirror* and the Associated Press, and Hargrove was very soon back to set out the deeper meaning of this first crack in the eastern system.

Ronald Preston[25] was much luckier when the Poznan riots broke out at the end of June 1956. As east European correspondent he had always made a point of visiting the trade fairs that were regularly held, dull in themselves, none the less a forum at which ministers and officials could be met. He had a press pass for the Poznan fair when he heard, in

---

25 Sir Ronald Douglas Hildebrand Preston (b. 1916). Westminster; Trinity College, Cambridge; Ecole des Sciences Politiques, Paris. Reuter's correspondent in Belgrade, 1948–53. Deputy correspondent for *The Times* in Yugoslavia, 1948–53; correspondent in Austria and Yugoslavia, 1953–60; Tokyo correspondent, 1960–63. Diplomatic service, 1963–76.

Warsaw, the first reports of trouble; the pass opened the way to Poznan for him. His despatches brought out much of the widespread Polish frustration which lay behind the riots. Demonstrations for higher wages had led on automatically to attacks on the secret police headquarters; and in the background was the growing resentment of Polish intellectuals stifled by the regime. Looking ahead, Preston saw that a simple easing of working conditions would not be enough:

> There is also increased speculation here [Poznan] about the possible return to a position of authority of Mr. Gomulka, the former secretary of the Polish Communist Party, who was imprisoned for Titoist deviations and has recently been released. Mr. Gomulka is believed to enjoy considerable popularity among the workers, who know him as a critic of the present policies of collectivisation and over-rapid industrialization, to which many Poles attribute their present ills.[26]

It is good to be so right. Barely four months later, during the Polish October, Gomulka was brought back to full power in flat defiance of Soviet wishes and Soviet threats. Preston was in Warsaw to see it. At the same time the wave of nationalism, spreading from Poland, broke the Soviet power during the brief heroic days in Budapest and much of Hungary. In Preston's absence in Warsaw *The Times* carried vivid reports from agencies; and it had equally vivid messages from John Buist who crossed over the Austrian–Hungarian frontier several times from Vienna. He got into liberated areas and spoke to men and women who had lived through the Budapest fighting. Unhappily, though east and west alike could see the magnitude of what was happening as first Poland and then Hungary asserted its will for independence, it was only the east that could intervene. The eastern camp was shaken but not disrupted.

The future, it was evident, would depend on whether Nikita Khrushchev had the power and the ability in the long run to soften Stalin's rule both at home and within the socialist camp as a whole. To try to gauge long-term trends McDonald went back several times to the Soviet Union and eastern Europe. During the first return visit to Russia, in 1955, the contrast between Stalin's hard-frozen regime and the thaw under Khrushchev was so strong and pervasive that his descriptive articles on his return were greeted with scepticism by many in Britain. He gave plenty of warning that the changes were only marginal, nothing basic had altered; the communist party's rule had even been

---

26 *The Times*, July 2 1956.

strengthened.[27] Such warnings did not stop *Time and Tide* and *Punch* from enjoying themselves by publishing funny and wicked parodies of the articles. *Punch* scored points in its effort on June 22 1955:

Memory recalls, in particular, a visit to the salt mines at Flit in Siberia. I had been assured by the authorities, who were so helpful to me throughout my journey, that all the workers in the mines were volunteers, but I wished to find out for myself. So I asked a group of the workers if they really were volunteers. The roar of laughter with which my question was greeted still lingers. These were clearly happy men.

In 1958 McDonald went again to have long interviews with Khrushchev, Gomulka, Siroky, Prime Minister of Czechoslovakia, and other east European leaders; the talks lasted several hours each. Very little common ground between the eastern and western positions was revealed. Khrushchev did at any rate emphasize his desire for some disarmament in order to free money for raising the Soviet standard of living.[28] Gomulka, full of fear that German military strength might be revived, begged Britain to take seriously the plan – put forward at the United Nations on October 2 1957 by his foreign minister, Rapacki – for establishing a zone free from atomic weapons, and with reduced conventional weapons, covering the two Germanies, Poland, and Czechoslovakia.[29] Walter Ulbricht, the East German communist leader, showed himself totally rigid in a talk with Haley on April 22 1959. None the less, with very little hard evidence to go on, *The Times* continued its search for some working arrangements.

In the years when the western governments regularly declared that Russia had first to agree to restore German unity through free elections before they would go on to discuss arrangements for European security, *The Times* no less regularly reversed the items of agenda, putting plans for European security ahead of German unity. A united Germany was desirable in the long run, certainly, but its attainment at that time was outside the scope of practical diplomacy. The powers should therefore, *The Times* suggested, leave the question of German unity on one side and see if they could not agree on plans for partial disarmament and on other means of reducing tension in Europe. Leading articles kept up the argument for some years:

---

27 *The Times*, June 11 1955.
28 *The Times*, February 1 1958.
29 *The Times*, February 18 1958.

The probability is that Germany – and the rest of Europe – will remain divided for as far ahead as can be seen . . . When both sides are alike ridden with fear, the plan for a security pact calls for careful preparation for presentation at the right time. ('Russia's Reply': September 30 1953.)

There should in common prudence be a second plan [in addition to plans for German unity], no less well thought out, containing western proposals for regulating the peace on the basis of the continued division of Germany. By working out the reserve plan the western Ministers would not convict themselves of insincerity when putting forward their plan for German unity. They would be only like a general who organizes for success but at the same time has some prepared positions to fall back upon. ('Berlin': January 20 1954.)

On the other side the Russians can be given many guarantees. Beyond the offer to keep the whole of east Germany demilitarized, they can be assured of a strict limit on all German arms. They can be offered some 'thinning out' of all troops, western and eastern alike, across the centre of Europe. They can have a system of shared controls and inspection units to ensure that the agreed limitations and withdrawals are observed on each side. ('First Bids': July 14 1955.)

So far, the western Powers have said that there can be no European security pact unless Germany is first united. Is it not possible to have a pact on a provisional basis that in no way rules out German unity for the future? ('Three Months': October 15 1955.)

This last mild suggestion caused something of a storm. It was made as the foreign ministers of the four occupying powers were about to open another of their Geneva conferences on the future of Germany and of Europe. The Federal German Ambassador in London, knowing that Dr. Adenauer, his Chancellor, would be incensed at the article, remonstrated at the Foreign Office. *The Times* replied by setting out its views more fully:

The Foreign Office has speedily assured the German Ambassador that a suggestion in a leading article on Saturday [October 15] did not represent British official policy. Indeed it did not; it was made in full knowledge that it was not a part of official policy . . . It is, admittedly, tempting to leave matters [in Europe] as they are and to let time and restraint work out their own detente. But this thought ignores the new danger of incidents when the two parts of Germany face each other in arms across the border. Security guarantees should help to diminish such risks. The west would not give anything up. Any plan would fall to the ground if the Russians still demanded the abolition of the North Atlantic Treaty and other alliances as a 'second stage' in organizing security, or if they demanded the recognition of the East German regime. With these necessary safeguards, the suggestion is worth bearing in mind – if all else fails at Geneva. On a long view it is the persistence of tension that keeps Germany divided. ('Germany and Security': October 18 1955.)

In point of fact Harold Macmillan himself, then Foreign Secretary, was not greatly perturbed when discussing the article with Rendel on October 18. He agreed that a case could be made for saying 'that a temporary solution on the basis of a divided Germany might contribute to a relaxation of tension and that only through a relaxation could a final settlement be reached.'[30] In another talk with McDonald, still foreign editor, the next day he acknowledged that the *Times* idea was one that the Foreign Office was considering very carefully behind its stern official front at international conferences. 'Our job,' he said, 'is to keep our suggestions to ourselves, yours is to make your suggestions known.' All he asked was that any European security arrangements should not rule out German unity for the future.[31]

The Times pegged away at its policy. A typical leader dealing directly with the Rapacki plan appeared immediately after Warsaw had published a modified plan towards the end of 1958:

Once again the Poles have given the western Powers something to think about. Having taken to heart many of the weighty objections to the original Rapacki plan for having a nuclear-free zone in central Europe they have brought forward a revised version, dividing the plan into two stages . . . These can be taken as genuine efforts towards agreement. The western Powers, however, have to look at the picture as a whole . . . There may not be much hope in trying to tie the plan up directly with progress towards German unity. But at least it opens the question whether that unity is more likely to be brought about through deadlier armaments on each side or through measures of partial disarmament and relaxation. ('New Polish Lead': November 7 1958.)

Events were to show that *The Times's* order of priorities was right. By the late fifties western leaders had begun to talk less about German unity

---

30 Memorandum, Rendel to editor. T.T.A.
31 Memorandum, McDonald to editor. T.T.A.

as a prime object of policy. Most had come to be less afraid that, if they stopped preaching unity on all occasions, the Russians would outsmart them with a tempting offer to the western Germans. Their fears were less acute because Federal Germany was already closely bound up with the west. British ministers felt themselves more free to talk about plans for controlling or reducing arms in central Europe. Eden's proposals along such lines at the Geneva summit conference in the summer of 1955 were followed up by Macmillan after he became Prime Minister in January 1957. Selwyn Lloyd, Foreign Secretary under Macmillan as he had been during Eden's last months in office, was no less keen to soften the bleak east–west confrontation in the middle of Europe. Both men, much to Adenauer's irritation, gave a helpful push to the Rapacki idea when they visited the Soviet Union in February 1959; they agreed with Khrushchev that the scheme be further studied.[32]

It was a new British impetus, but a combination of half-heartedness and opposition on the part of other western partners took the steam out of it. The collapse of the Paris summit conference in May 1960, followed by bitter recriminations, seemed to close a hopeful chapter once and for all. Yet paradoxically it was the far worse dangers of the Cuba missiles crisis two years later which forced the search for détente to be started again in earnest. Though the Rapacki plan itself came to nothing, the basic idea behind it lived on in the Final Act of the Helsinki conference on European cooperation and security, concluded in August 1975, and in the talks on mutual and balanced reduction of forces in Europe.

The paper recommended a similar policy of constant inquiry and prudence when writing about the successive crises in the Far East. Its attitude was consistent: throw back aggression, strive to keep the successive conflicts localised, offer peace once the territories occupied by the aggressors had been cleared. Having urged restraint when General MacArthur was hatching his headstrong plans against China during the Korean war,[33] it urged a similar restraint during the Korean truce. On August 12 1953 a characteristic leader was headed, 'Threat or Bluster?'. It strongly criticised the sixteen governments allied in the Korean war for issuing a statement on August 7 giving dire and imprecise warnings about what they would do if the truce was broken. The sixteen governments implied that they might carry the war into China. *The Times* called the relevant sentence disingenuous, ineffective and dangerous, much more likely to deceive or alarm friends than

---

32 Anglo–Soviet communiqué, March 3 1959.
33 See Chapter VIII.

opponents. When the Chinese communist forces were shelling Quemoy and Matsu, the small offshore islands held by the Chinese Nationalist forces, *The Times* went further in its suggestions for a tacit truce between the two Chinese sides. It argued that it might be better for the Chinese Nationalists to withdraw from the small islands and put a hundred miles of blue water between mainland China and their own forces that were safely garrisoning Taiwan.

In the melancholy story of Vietnam – melancholy even before the later heavy American involvement – the paper was entirely on Eden's side in the early months of 1954 when he resisted Dulles's impulse to intervene with American forces or American bombs in the attempt to save the beleaguered French forces at Dien Bien Phu. In the western debate which later was to be called the debate between the hawks and the doves *The Times* was ranged most of the time with the doves – once the North Korean aggression had been beaten back. Largely influenced by Richard Harris it did not believe that Communist China was engaged in military aggression or even planning such aggression. It did not wish to see America and other western powers committed, in General Omar Bradley's famous phrase, to fighting 'the wrong war, at the wrong place, at the wrong time, and with the wrong enemy'.[34]

---

34 Testimony before US Senate committees on armed services and foreign relations, May 15 1951.

XIII

SUEZ

URING the twelve months before President Nasser nationalised the Suez Canal Company on July 26 1956 *The Times* had been watching, and writing about, two movements that were to have their bearing on the crisis when it came. The first was the growing conviction among many Conservatives that Anthony Eden, splendid as Foreign Secretary, was being very slow in making his mark as Prime Minister. The second was the increasing alarm among Egypt's neighbours at Nasser's emergence as spokesman for a new and aggressive brand of Arab nationalism which was finding increasingly militant support everywhere from the Persian Gulf to the Moroccan coast.

On Eden's record after his first year at No. 10 Haley came out frankly in a leader which appeared on April 5 1956, four months before the beginning of the Suez dispute. Under the slightly patronising heading, 'Running In', it posed the question whether Eden had the character for the job of being Churchill's successor. 'It is on the home front that the Prime Minister's record so far is most vulnerable'. True, the country had shown some economic and financial improvement:

> But the underlying economic weakness has not been removed. Indeed the threat to British exports is intensifying all the time . . . In the ultimate analysis British politics is still largely the story of the success or failure of character. The Prime Minister has on occasions during the past year shown unsureness of touch. There have been aberrations under strain. Most remarkable of all, even his sense of the House of Commons has occasionally deserted him . . . Whether success or failure attends his immediate efforts, Sir Anthony Eden's future depends on his remaining true to himself.

The paper's dissatisfaction with Eden's showing spread even to foreign affairs in which his touch had for years been masterly. Only three days before Nasser's *coup* against the canal it made a long complaint:

> People talk of the Russian enigma. The British Government's intentions are becoming pretty well as baffling. In many vital mat-

ters, whether it is disarmament or the Middle East or Cyprus, they have given the same uncomfortable impression – of men being slow to make up their mind and quick to change it.

The House will want to know what has happened to the Prime Minister's plans for an Arab–Israel settlement, and whether the sudden public withdrawal of the proffered aid to Egypt [for building the Aswan high dam] was independently thought out or a result of America's own decision. Information on these and other points could give a coherent picture of policy that now is so often lacking.[1]

All such misgivings over Eden's first year meant that, when the Suez crisis arose, Eden had special domestic and political reasons to prove himself the resolute leader; and *The Times* itself was ready to prod him to be firm in meeting the challenge. Certainly, for its part, the paper had left no doubts about the ambitions of Nasser as it saw them. When he officially took over from Colonel Neguib in February 1954 *The Times* had had a leading article hoping that agreement was still possible but expressing some alarm. The new ruler had made 'violently anti-British speeches'. He was reckoned to be a realist, but if his regime ran into internal difficulties 'it may be tempted into still worse chauvinistic extremes against Britain to preserve its authority.'[2] Fifteen months later the Cairo correspondent, James Morris, described the regime as 'in many ways reasonable but despotic':

The Press is ruthlessly muzzled; laws of profound effect are issued suddenly and unpredictably; foreign issues are shamefully exploited for purely political ends; and opponents of the regime are removed without ceremony. In nothing is this neo-Fascism so apparent as in the regime's propaganda services.[3]

In later years it was widely said that western countries alarmed themselves needlessly over Nasser's propaganda. This is only partly true. Admittedly in the 1950s the western world had not yet learnt to discount much of the wild and bellicose talk from some of the leaders of the Third World. But beyond all the hostile words were the hostile acts, particularly Egypt's continued raids against Israel, her refusal to allow Israeli shipping through the canal, and the various plots that were hatched within the territory of other Middle East countries. Such acts could not be written off simply as flights of compensatory self-assertion after all

---

1 Leading article (McDonald), July 23 1956.
2 Leading article (Hodgkin), February 26 1954.
3 *The Times*, May 4 1955.

the years of colonial or semi-colonial status. Even Dag Hammarskjøld, the Secretary-General of the United Nations who was very much alive to the needs and desires of the Third World, told Selwyn Lloyd in the spring of 1956 that Nasser looked like being another Hitler.[4] The dangers were felt the more deeply by many British people of the middle and older generations. They were the inheritors of an imperial sense of military geography and an experience of a Middle East in which Britain held positions of power and influence. Cutting across that region, linking Britain with India and Australasia, was the Suez trunk route.

In the 1950s Britain still had heavily manned strategic bases east of Suez. More directly, the middle and older generations had shared in, or they remembered, the North African battles of the Second World War that were fought to keep open the Mediterranean seaways and the Suez Canal itself. They knew how much of Britain's trade still passed through the canal in those years before the giant oil tankers could go regularly round the Cape. More directly still the Second World War had taught them all that Hitler's early boasts and pretensions in *Mein Kampf* were not taken seriously enough during Hitler's first years in power. They did not wish to make the same mistake over Nasser's own book, *The Philosophy of the Revolution*. The moral was clear: dangers must be acknowledged and countered when first they appeared. For *The Times* such lessons had a special force. Just because of its record before the war there was firm agreement among the staff under Haley that it would not go in for appeasement again.

When the news of Nasser's seizure of the company came over the tapes in the early evening of July 26 1956 Haley happened, most unusually for him, to be out of touch with the office. He was sailing the high seas on board John Astor's yacht. Maurice Green was in charge at Printing House Square; McDonald wrote a first leader on the *coup* for the later editions that night:

> It is a clear affront and threat to western interests, besides being a breach of undertakings which Egypt has freely given and renewed in recent years . . . They [the western governments] are faced by yet another tearing up of a contractual agreement; and this is an agreement which covers one of the world's most vital strategic and commercial waterways.

The next day McDonald went round to have a long talk with Eden at No. 10 and found him entirely calm and confident, very much in command of

---

4 Selwyn Lloyd, *Suez 1956*, p. 66.

all the moves that had to be made; attentive to detail; glad, it almost seemed, to be back on the familiar ground of a major international crisis such as he had coped with when running the Foreign Office. Speaking with the utmost frankness to someone whom he had known for twenty years, he made three main points. Added up together, they refute the suggestions of later critics that, from the very start, Eden was determined on no other course but a vengeful war against Nasser.

First, he said, Nasser's act could not be accepted; the cabinet and the chiefs of staff had agreed on that at their meeting that morning. If necessary, force would be used. Secondly, 'his [Eden's] main hope was of being able to act in full agreement with the Commonwealth and with the United States'; and, thirdly, through such cooperation there was a real chance, if Nasser would take it, of getting new and more satisfactory international arrangements established for the running of the canal. He was sending off a message on those lines to President Eisenhower:

'Dulles, as usual, is away in Peru or somewhere.' But he [Eden] was telling Eisenhower that he was not going to be drawn into the legalities of whether a country had the right to nationalise a company which was technically its own (the Suez Canal Company being nominally an Egyptian joint stock company). What he was concerned about, and what must determine British action, was the freedom of the canal. Was Nasser ready to say that he would enter into a new international agreement to safeguard the freedom of the canal, that was vital to Britain and to the whole western world?

He was warning Eisenhower that we must be ready, in the last resort, to use force to bring Nasser to his senses. He was now hoping for a speedy reply from Washington. He repeated that he hoped to get full agreement with America and France, but emphasised again we had to be ready for action, if need be.

'The question was how soon we could move,' he said. 'The military men had at first said it would take about a fortnight to perfect plans, but he had told them this was nonsense, and he must have them ready by Monday [this was the Friday]. They were sure, however, that forces could be moved quite quickly . . . We had troops in Libya and Cyprus but we might have to take some from this country . . .'

More than once Eden said that if we showed weakness in face of Nasser then all our position in the Middle East would crumble. We should be hearing of new claims against all our companies and bases. On the other hand, it was quite true that the company was outdated; it had a lot of odd people on it, and the new mercantile countries were not properly represented. There was a real chance if Nasser would take it of getting an up-to-date agreement.

Did that mean that he would accept the nationalisation of the company in return for a new canal convention to take the place of the Constantinople convention of 1888? He said, 'No.' Nasser could not be trusted with control over the canal. Too much was at stake.

Reminded of how our British generals, when we were in the canal base (evacuated the year before), said it was impossible to hold the base in peacetime if the Cairo regime was hostile, he agreed that we might have to depose Nasser, but said that the intended operation was not to occupy the base (he fully agreed it would be difficult to hold the base) but merely to secure the banks of the canal. It might be done with a division and a half:

> One question still open was whether we should appeal to the Security Council against Egypt's action. He had asked Selwyn Lloyd to look into the question, but one knew full well that taking it to the Security Council would only come up against the Soviet veto. On the other hand, he recognised that there would be much feeling in the House and country . . . Possibly the Foreign Office would find a way of making an appeal.

At the end of the talk he emphasized again that he hoped for full agreement with our allies and the Commonwealth – even with ultra-cautious India. 'It was often forgotten that a large part of India's trade came through the Suez Canal and incidentally, for what it was worth, he had heard that Nasser and Nehru had not got on too well when last they met.'[5]

It was this triple policy – negotiation if possible, cooperation with allies always, and the threat of force in the background if all else failed – which *The Times* strongly supported in the early weeks of the Suez crisis. On July 29 Haley, back in London, wrote a memorandum for guidance within the office. He said that some form of international control over the canal was necessary and that force might have to be used as a last resort. 'But every other reasonable means must be seen to have been tried first. Military considerations cannot exempt us from exhausting each one of these in turn. It is no use saying that we could not try this or that negotiation because that would have taken us too long.'[6]

Throughout the summer and autumn Haley and McDonald had many talks separately with Eden and one or two with Selwyn Lloyd;

5 Memorandum to editor, July 27 1956. T.T.A.
6 T.T.A.

McDonald and Mason saw other members of the staff at No. 10, especially the extraordinarily frank and helpful William Clark, Eden's press officer who was later to resign in protest against the final action; Oliver Woods and Rendel kept in touch throughout with Foreign Office and Commonwealth men; Cooper in Washington and Giles in Paris reported on confidential exchanges in their capitals.

Eden in his private talks more than once referred back to the western powers' failure to make a stand when Hitler marched into the Rhineland in 1936; a stand then could have been made without war, and he drew comparisons with the confrontation over Suez. He was especially glad, he said, that *The Times* was not repeating its own appeasing posture over the Rhineland. These frank talks with Eden were highly informative but had one unforeseen and unfortunate consequence within Printing House Square. Haley and McDonald were given so much secret information that they found it difficult to have the usual round-table easy talks with the leader writers as a group. Without planning it, they got into the way of discussing policy between themselves or with only Green and Woods, deputy foreign editor, brought in on occasions. Knowledgeable men such as Teddy Hodgkin and Richard Harris, most uneasy in any case at some of the paper's tougher leaders in the first weeks, felt themselves excluded from its Suez policy, although the usual discussions on all other subjects went on. With hindsight it is clear that the Suez talks within the office should have been broadened. Some of the early leaders were specifically designed to mobilize and unite public opinion in face of what the paper saw as a heavy strategic reverse, but it is more than probable that the emphasis in the first few leaders on military toughness and their vehement tone helped rather to divide and polarise opinion, certainly in Parliament and the press. The parliamentary opposition's fury with Eden, formerly their champion, grew rapidly after the first days. *The Times* and the *Guardian* – still called the *Manchester Guardian* then – fed each other for weeks with arguments to answer about the legality or illegality of Nasser's act and over the threat of using force if negotiations failed.

In the first shock after Nasser's take-over of the canal company *The Times*, anxious to support the government in the crisis and indeed fully sharing the government's view, emphasized the need for a firm stand by Britain and France, very much as Hugh Gaitskell, Leader of the Opposition,[7] emphasized it in the House of Commons on August 2. On August 1, after Haley's return, the paper published an unusually strong

---

7 Hugh Todd Naylor Gaitskell (1906–1963). Chancellor of the Exchequer 1950–51; leader of the Labour Party from 1955 until his death.

leader under the title, 'A Hinge of History'. It stated that three matters were involved, each of them vital for Britain: the safety and freedom of the canal; the security of the vast oil fields and installations in the Middle East ('Anyone who thinks that a victory for Nasser would not encourage other extremist demands against the oil fields – and against strategic bases – should confine himself to tiddleywinks or blind man's bluff.'); and, wider still, the knowledge that 'there can be no stability and confidence in the world so long as agreements can be scrapped with impunity.' The article half regretted that Britain's military withdrawal from Egypt had been total and that strong action had not been taken in immediate response to the seizure of the company. Time, it said, was now passing and international discussions were being suggested. 'The danger is that a large conference will end, as so often, in a melancholy, long, withdrawing roar. It might have been better to have had a foot in the door first.' None the less, if there was to be a conference, it must be summoned quickly and present the clearest of terms to Egypt.[8]

Two days later *The Times* amplified and explained more fully its reference to the use of force. It wrote that the government, while facing the challenge firmly, had to take care 'not to appear an aggressor, showing in fact that it was resisting an aggressor, acting in accordance with the United Nations Charter.'[9] At the same time the paper emphasized the need to shape policy in constant agreement with all interested parties, primarily the United States, France, and the Commonwealth countries. The paper's own line was by this time settled. After the first period of crisis it expected that the dispute would have to end through international agreement between the interested parties and Egypt. It was convinced that such an agreement was the more likely to be reached if the western powers, led in this case by Britain, kept up the maximum pressure. Hence its frequent references to the need to have forces mounted in readiness. Military preparations had to be made and maintained for two reasons. First a new assault on British and western interests might be launched in the region, requiring counter-action. Secondly, the oft-repeated Anglo–French threat of using military force as a last resort was a strong negotiating card in all international talks over Suez. But – a vital proviso within Printing House Square – that Anglo–French threat kept its value and cogency only for so long as it remained a threat and was not turned into action.

For some weeks Eden remained hopeful of diplomatic help and moral support from Dulles, as he was hopeful of restraint from Israel.

---

8 *The Times*, August 1 1956.
9 *The Times*, August 3 1956.

On August 3, when he talked privately with a few editors at Number 10, he showed himself encouraged both by Gaitskell's speech the day before and by Dulles's flat statement on August 1: 'A way had to be found to make Nasser disgorge what he was attempting to swallow.'[10] Eden made his relief plain to the editors, telling them:

At first, the Americans had been slow in coming along. The Mediterranean was not a direct interest of theirs, they tended to think that the Suez Canal was small compared to Panama, and of course they were busy with their elections [due November 6]. He had frankly expected Dulles to be rather negative, but Dulles began and continued very well. The talks became better after he had arrived. Undoubtedly the Americans' fear that we and the French might fly off the handle straightaway helped to bring Dulles nearer and faster to our point of view. At any rate, Dulles freely committed himself to the stand that the Canal should not be left in the sole control of Egypt and should be brought under an international authority.

Ironically enough, Eden in those early days was genuinely worried lest Israel should cause an explosion. Someone asked if the government had envisaged an early attack by Egypt on Israel by way of diversion:

Eden said that such an attack would be covered by the three-power declaration on the Middle East.[11] Even before the crisis we had prepared our plans for action. But he thought an Egyptian attack on Israel was highly unlikely. 'The boot was rather on the other foot (i.e. Israel was more likely to attack Egypt) and we were persuading Israel to be quiet. The danger of trouble chiefly arose on the Jordan–Israel frontier.'[12]

Haley, having committed himself some months earlier to a long tour in the United States, was out of the office again during the testing weeks from September 1 to October 21. A few days before he left he wrote a leader under the title, 'Escapers' Club'. Designed to keep up the pressure, it expressed his fears that the whole crisis was being comfortably shelved and would be forgotten:

Public opinion, despite what the dissidents angrily say, is remarkably firm. Of course it wants to avoid the use of force. So does everyone and we hope that no one does so more than the British

---

10 Sir Anthony Eden, *Full Circle*, p. 437.
11 The tripartite declaration of 1950, signed by Britain, France and the United States, promised action 'both within and outside the United Nations', to prevent the forcible violation of any Middle Eastern frontier or armistice line.
12 McDonald memorandum to editor, August 3 1956. T.T.A.

Government. But that is a far cry from saying that because there seems we can do little about it the best thing is to find excuses for, and forget, the whole business. Nations live by vigorous defence of their own interests . . . Doubtless it is good to have a flourishing tourist trade, to win Test matches, and to be regaled by pictures of Miss Diana Dors being pushed into a swimming pool. But nations do not live by circuses alone. The people, in their silent way, know this better than the critics. They still want Britain great.[13]

When Haley returned to London in the third week of October he found awaiting him several confidential memoranda which traced the story of the many secret dealings between the British and French governments and the fatal estrangement from the United States. These memoranda were dictated in Printing House Square immediately after the relevant talks. *The Times's* own growing emphasis on the necessity to refer the whole matter to the United Nations, as a means of getting talks with Egypt going, is reflected in the record of a conversation which Green and McDonald had with Eden on September 7. They met at No. 10 after the eighteen-nation conference had taken place in London and while Robert Menzies's[14] five-nation mission was still talking to Nasser in Cairo. The failure of the mission to Cairo already seemed all too likely, and Eden – 'very easy and relaxed' – told Green and McDonald that the government was decided to put the matter to the United Nations at some time. The two *Times* men urged him to announce the decision without delay and suggested also that he should consider calling another conference of all the interested parties. Their point was that national unity could be won again only if the government could show that its policies and actions were shaped after reference to some international forum. At the very least, in *The Times's* view, the government had to show that it was in full consultation with the United States and France. Unfortunately, while the Menzies mission was still in Cairo President Eisenhower announced at a press conference that the crisis had passed its peak and that the use of force was excluded; both Menzies and Nasser knew straight away that he need no longer listen to the five-nation mission's warnings about Anglo–French determination. No one was surprised when he turned down the proposals.

The British government, having built up military forces in Malta and Cyprus in partnership with the French, had wished Dulles to agree to referring the whole case to the United Nations. Dulles, instead of

13 *The Times*, August 27 1956.
14 Sir Robert Gordon Menzies (1894–1974). Prime Minister of Australia 1939–41 and 1949–66.

agreeing, had suddenly produced his suggestion for getting the maritime powers together to organise their own team of pilots who would willy-nilly take ships through the canal. 'After Dulles had been treading so softly,' said Eden in the talk on September 7, 'I could scarcely believe my eyes.' From a first look at it the proposal for what became known as the Canal Users' Association appeared to be far stronger than anything so far put forward by Washington.

The British Cabinet was sufficiently attracted by it to propose that it be discussed at further international talks. In the event these talks were to make little progress towards any practicable plan, but, helped by Dulles's suggestion, Britain persuaded France to agree to postpone the time limit which had been set, as detailed by Selwyn Lloyd's own account,[15] for beginning military operations if such operations were judged to be necessary.

Eden was less confident when talking privately on September 13, the second day of the clamorous debate in the Commons. 'Poor country,' he said, 'how can we do anything when the divisions are pressed so hard.' He said again that he was willing to go to the United Nations, but could not bind himself so tightly as Labour wished – though later that day he did commit himself more tightly. He told the Commons, amid the now customary uproar, that it was the government's intention, if circumstances allowed, or if there was no emergency, to refer the matter to the Security Council before using force. Amid all the fury and suspicions of the time this statement became known as the 'unfinished sentence', for Labour believed that Eden was going on to water down the commitment but could not do so amid all the shouting in the Chamber. Speaking by telephone from Chequers three days later, on September 16, Eden assured *The Times* that he had indeed finished his sentence, 'and I stand by it.'

The pleasant and unexpected respite which Eden had gained from Dulles over the Users' Association was soon to be ended with a bitter shock. For several weeks Eden and Selwyn Lloyd had been immensely patient during Dulles's twists and turns and all his legalistic arguments to justify his tactics. Even the French cabinet, more impatient than the British for direct action, had restrained themselves. But on October 2 Dulles surpassed himself with two statements at a press conference in Washington. First he destroyed his own Users' Association, saying that so far as he was aware it never had any teeth in it. Secondly there came his taunt against the colonial mentality. In the Nato area, he said, Britain, France and the United States were at one; but in areas outside,

---

15 Selwyn Lloyd, *op. cit.* pp. 134, 170–2.

'encroaching on the problem of so-called colonialism', the United States was to be found 'playing a somewhat independent role'.

At No. 10 the next morning McDonald found Eden immeasurably angry and shocked. How, Eden exclaimed, could Dulles so completely misunderstand his determination to have the canal internationally controlled as to think that he was reverting to colonialism? 'It was I who ended the "so-called colonialism" in Egypt. And look at what Britain has done all over the world in giving the colonies independence.' He was angry, too, that Dulles should have come out publicly at such a critical time to impugn the motives of an ally:

> We have leaned over backwards to go along with him. And now look. How on earth can you work with people like that? It leaves us in a quite impossible position. We can't go on like this.[16]

In the light of later events it is more than probable that it was Dulles's words on October 2, coming after all his other moves backwards and sideways, which convinced Eden into thinking that Britain and France must do as seemed best to themselves. France in fact, although this was not to be publicly known until much later, was already moving on her own account towards an agreement to supply Israel with arms sufficient for an Israeli attack on Egypt. What was clear at the time was the element of tragedy. Dulles had exploded his mine under Eden's feet just when discussions – unpromising but not entirely hopeless – were at long last about to begin between Selwyn Lloyd, Pineau, the French foreign minister, and Mahmoud Fawzi, the Egyptian foreign minister.

The last memorandum awaiting Haley when he returned on October 21 was the most startling and the most secret. For greater security McDonald wrote it by hand rather than having it typed; it was seen only by Haley and was kept out of the archives. It was written a few days after Eden and Selwyn Lloyd had returned from their talks with the French ministers on October 16 and shortly before Ben-Gurion and Moshe Dayan flew covertly to France to agree with French and British ministers on the last arrangements for intervention. On the basis of what he learned, McDonald set down in detail the essence of the still top-secret plan for the Anglo–French occupation of the canal banks, much as it was to happen and much as it was to be later revealed by Selwyn Lloyd, Pineau, Dayan, and Anthony Nutting in their memoirs.[17] Israel,

---

16 All the foregoing memoranda in this chapter from which extracts are taken are in T.T.A.

17 Selwyn Lloyd, *op. cit.*; Christian Pineau, *1956 Suez*; Moshe Dayan, *The Story of my Life*; Anthony Nutting, *No End of a Lesson*.

harassed near to breaking point by the raids and counter-raids across its borders and alarmed by Nasser's attempts to consolidate the Arab states, would strike across the Sinai peninsula; Britain and France would call on both Israel and Egypt to withdraw from the canal area; if either refused to withdraw, Britain and France would occupy points along the banks. In the memorandum McDonald expressed his own total disagreement with the manner and the timing of the projected plan of action.

When Haley was back in Printing House Square he showed himself also to be strongly opposed to the plan. Harold Macmillan and others who have written on Suez have accused *The Times* of changing sides in the affair.[18] The paper had supported Eden during August and September, they say, and then opposed him before the end. That is true; but the greater truth is that events had changed and the whole national and international background had shifted. In mid-October the Egyptian foreign minister had put forward some new proposals for further talks with Selwyn Lloyd and Pineau. *The Times* was prepared to concede that 'the result of it all [discussions at the U.N.] is that "exploratory talks" will no doubt go on with Egypt. The momentum should not be lost. Some progress has already been made.'[19] On the other side the plan for military intervention seemed, from the very start, unlikely to succeed in its political aims even if it had a short-term military success. Widespread Arab anger at an act all too clearly planned in concert with Israel had to be taken for granted; the oil pipe lines were put in danger.

Beyond such thoughts lay another. One of the soundest maxims for Britain was that strong military action could be undertaken only with the support of a united parliament, a united country, and an understanding America. In other words, no British government should commit troops in the conditions then prevailing: when the House of Commons was tearing itself apart, when the passions spread into the country at large (although support for Eden was still very strong), and when there was no assurance of American goodwill but rather the prospect of American anger and opposition.

Haley expressed his own misgivings in a letter to John Walter dated October 31, two days after the Israelis had struck and British bombs had fallen on Egyptian airfields. The time for action would have been immediately after Nasser seized the canal; but that time was long past:

---

18 See Macmillan, *Riding the Storm*, pp. 112–3; Hugh Thomas, *The Suez Affair*, pp. 63–4; *et al.*
19 *The Times*, October 15 1956.

I am afraid that the latest Suez development is rather an ill-judged business . . . The opposition is behaving disgracefully, and their desire for Britain to abdicate all responsibility and to leave everything to the Security Council which can never be effective is pusillanimous. But the fact remains that of all possible ways to go back to the Canal the Government have chosen the worst. Moreover the Prime Minister's categorical assurance – forced out of him, admittedly, but he has said it – that we will withdraw again 'immediately hostilities have ceased' leaves one baffled as to what we hope to gain from the operation.

We must hope now that the campaign is a quick success, so that there can at least be some claim of justification by results. But I am afraid the bills may be coming in, one way or another, for a long time to come.[20]

In *The Times* itself a leader on October 31 listed three reasons for deep concern: first, the lack of consultation with the United States; secondly, the all too clear testimony that the Anglo–French demand for a military-free belt along the canal was really a demand for an Egyptian unilateral withdrawal within Egyptian territory; thirdly, the predictable response among the Arab states when they asked themselves the simple question, how does the action help Israel? The Arabs were bound to say that it helped Israel in every way. The next day the paper's doubts were repeated. Israel's desire to put an end to hostile Egyptian acts was fully acknowledged:

Even so, doubts remain whether the right action has been taken now . . . Was the need for speed really so great that President Eisenhower had to hear about the Anglo–French ultimatum from Press reports.[21]

This last point was quickly reinforced in a leader by Haley, headed 'A Lack of Candour'. He quoted Churchill's remark in 1942: 'I hold it perfectly justifiable to deceive the enemy, even if at the same time your own people are for a while misled. There is one thing, however, which you must never do, and that is to mislead your ally.' Haley continued:

This is no side-issue. It is one of the most vital in the present crisis. On Britain's and America's ability to trust each other, even in disagreement, the peace of the world depends.[22]

---

20 T.T.A.
21 *The Times*, November 1 1956.
22 *The Times*, November 2 1956.

From Washington Bob Cooper described the shock and anger felt by President Eisenhower and his administration. But Cooper remained analytical; he did not join the wolf pack against Eden as did so many foreign correspondents on other papers at the time. In a despatch dated October 31, while writing that the air was thick with cries of 'perfidious Albion', he continued:

An austere view, however, has to be taken of this first flush of anger . . . Open accusations of collusion with Israel and the hot resentment felt at the lack of advance information of the Anglo–French ultimatum might have been more measured had the crisis not exploded in the last crucial days of an American election, which for the past week or more has been swept from the headlines – almost from the front pages.

Cooper wrote that the Anglo–French venture had shattered the benign suggestion, encouraged by the Republicans under Eisenhower, that the world was entering 'an era of good will'. Anglo–American relations on the official level were at a severer strain than he himself could ever remember. None the less he found some support in private conversations, and in reports coming in from outside Washington, for an action which 'would perhaps have won grudging admiration had it been taken at the onset of the Suez crisis'.

In Cairo itself both of the *Times* men, David Holden and Alan McGregor, were interned in the Semiramis Hotel with other correspondents, British and French. Holden, then in his early thirties, had been appointed Middle East correspondent only a few months before; his stormy initiation helped to bind him to the region that was to enthral him for the rest of his life. Before being interned he managed to send off a despatch – writing 'in the midst of another black-out and more desultory anti-aircraft fire' – that reported the Egyptian rejection of the Anglo–French ultimatum.[23] McGregor[24] worked mainly on the *Egyptian Gazette* and, as Holden's deputy, helped him greatly both in passing on his knowledge to him and in sending despatches to *The Times* when Holden was elsewhere in the region. Both men were released after the cease-fire, came to London, and then returned to Cairo early in 1957.

A heartening by-product for *The Times* was that David Wood, who was later to show his great skill in analysis and judgment as the paper's political editor, unmistakably displayed what was in him when sent as

23 *The Times*, October 29 1956.
24 Alan McGregor (b. 1918). Served in Egypt during 1939–45 war, joined the *Egyptian Gazette* 1951, worked for *The Times*; thereafter in Switzerland for *The Times* and BBC.

correspondent with the British landing forces. His despatches made both the news editors, home and foreign, register him in their minds as a man to bring forward when the next good job appeared. In a retrospective article in the *House Journal* (February–March 1957) he described the many built-in contradictions in the whole operation, 'at the same time brilliant and farcical'. He cited one example among many:

> I remember the paradox when, as the flagship of the destroyers that were to bombard the beach-head approached Port Said, the Admiral had me on the bridge and talked about his anxiety. He was not at all anxious about how the enemy would reply with shot and shell. What troubled him were his orders to use no armament heavier than the four inch, to limit his fire to the beach, and to give the assaulting Commandoes no support once they were among the houses . . . Troops are terribly exposed as they move in to a beach slowly in assault craft. Yet here was the Royal Navy with orders, come what may, to hit soft. Thank heaven, it turned out well. But the Admiral was a worried man until he could be sure.

In a hurried private talk at the House of Commons on November 6, a few hours before the cease-fire was announced, Harold Macmillan told McDonald that a halt was inevitable from the moment that the government knew that they were not going to have a quick success. 'It was risky from the beginning – perhaps too risky.' Now the most hopeful line was to hand over to a United Nations force. Lord Salisbury had neatly summed up the whole matter at a Cabinet meeting earlier. 'We have played every card in our hand, and we have none left.'[25] In a talk with Haley on November 22 Macmillan reverted to a similar gaming metaphor. Any further action would have meant gambling beyond Britain's resources. 'All politics, especially international politics, was a game of poker. But the golden rule of the good poker player was the moment he knew he had no more chips he gave up the game.' Macmillan liked to talk in that light way, but already, when he saw Haley, he was laying serious plans for diplomatic reconstruction. Eden was ill: there was no talk yet of his resignation, but Macmillan was already taking up once again his own personally friendly links with Eisenhower that went back to their wartime service together in North Africa.

On January 9 1957 came the news that on urgent medical advice Eden had resigned. The next day a leader by Haley recalled Eden's achievements in the nation's affairs:

> Those great services were not confined to the period before he

---

25 Memorandum, McDonald to editor. T.T.A.

entered No. 10 Downing Street. Until the fatal misjudgment that led to the Suez ultimatum the Eden Government had a good record. Uncertain in its early months, it recovered a good deal of its drive and poise with the new team of Mr. Butler leading the House and Mr. Macmillan at the Exchequer.[26]

Butler and Macmillan were the two men between whom the choice of being Eden's successor lay. Of the two *The Times* preferred Butler. In that same leader Haley acknowledged Macmillan's obvious gifts:

> Mr. Butler, on the other hand, has for long been the guide and the leader of the younger Conservatives. It is with the younger Conservatives and what they stand for that the future of the party must rest.[27]

When the choice went to Macmillan Haley gave one or two warnings. The old guard within the party, he wrote, having fought a rearguard action against the progressive social policies associated with Butler, would now be sufficiently encouraged to go on to the offensive to secure the acceptance of their views. There must be every hope that, under Macmillan, the old guard would be rebutted and rebuffed:

> The real measure of Mr. Macmillan's success will be how far he can himself fulfil these hopes. There is only a road forward for Conservatism; there is no road back. However brilliant it may be in every other direction, the degree to which the Macmillan Government succeeds in this one will depend on the degree to which it is Butlerite.[28]

Such articles bring the reminder that Haley was essentially a liberal in politics. He did not have Barrington-Ward's passionate zeal for sweeping social reform; in any case when he became editor the great post-war wave of social change had spent itself. There was less need for the editor to be the prophet who would stir the conscience of the people. But members of Parliament and others who accused Haley of being tough and reactionary over Suez could not see that his reasons for opposing Nasser's take-over were not so much imperialist and strategic as moral in origin; and so were his reasons for attacking the manner in which the British government fell in at the end with the French plan for intervention in league with the Israelis.

---

26 *The Times*, January 10 1957.
27 *The Times*, January 10 1957.
28 *The Times*, January 11 1957.

For the *Times* staff, as for many other groups throughout the country, the weeks of October and November 1956 were the most harrowing that they had lived through since Munich. Leading out from the Suez crisis itself there was the painful rift between Britain and her old ally and warm friend President Eisenhower, whose anger was manifest; and alongside the rift there was the agony of the Soviet repression of Hungary's upsurge for freedom.

The Times did not believe that the Anglo–French action at Suez gave the green light for the Soviet assault on the Hungarian people. It believed, as the later invasions of Czechoslovakia and Afghanistan were to show, that Moscow did not need any diversionary cover for its actions in areas which it claimed as its own spheres of interest; it would move, expecting protests from the west but little more. What the Anglo–French action did – coming unexpectedly so many weeks after Nasser's seizure of the canal company – was to divide and confuse western opinion when it should have been united; and it meant that Russia did not stand in conspicuous loneliness in the dock at the United Nations. Indeed many powers concentrated their attacks on the two open democracies, Britain and France, which they judged to be susceptible to pressure, rather than on Russia whose closed system made it impervious.

Neither did *The Times* at any time doubt the sincerity of Eden's motives. That some Conservatives had been grumbling against him earlier in the year was true. After Nasser's *coup* the same men, and others, said that Nasser dared to seize the canal company only because Eden had withdrawn British troops from the canal zone under the 1954 treaty with Egypt, a treaty concluded in spite of Churchill's misgivings. Later, in the international dealings during the crisis, Dulles's tactics could hardly have been more confusing, more clumsy, or worse directed. Eden – no more an island than any other man – was bound to feel some of the resultant strains. He clearly bore the signs of his deepening illness. Yet to the *Times* men with whom he talked privately throughout the summer and autumn he showed himself absorbed, to the exclusion of almost every other argument, in the strategic, political, and economic threats which he saw facing Britain and western Europe.[29]

In history the decline of a state power in the world has often shown itself gradually over a long time. For Britain, still preserving much of the prestige won by its efforts and successes in the Second World War, the decline showed itself most dramatically during the few short hours in which the government decided to call off the Suez venture under

---

29 Various memoranda, July–November 1956. T.T.A.

international pressure. It thereby acknowledged that a British government, or the British and French together, no longer had the strength to carry out an independent military venture, even one strictly limited in scope, if the United States and other allies swung against the action. Worse was to come during the ensuing weeks of diplomatic delays, frustrations, and obloquy. Every rebuff for the United Kingdom gave some British journals material for further lectures on Britain's decline and on the government's blindness in not acknowledging that decline. But it was never Haley's way to go in for repining. In his view the lessons of Suez had been driven home without need for emphasis. What mattered, as Haley wrote in his leader of January 11, was the new place that Macmillan had to win for Britain in the world. To that end the paper supported Macmillan in his determination to close the rift with the U.S.A., to explore the possibilities for Britain in the European Community, and to seek a way of living without disaster with the Soviet Union with all its neuroses, fears, and ruthlessness.

XIV

IMPERIAL TWILIGHT

SECOND only to the east–west rivalry, the upheaval within the Commonwealth and Empire took up much of the energies and attention of *The Times* throughout the fifties and early sixties. Here the paper was following its own long tradition and commitment to the imperial and then to the Commonwealth cause. For many years it had kept senior staff men in the main Dominions and in India. Now, as more colonies in Africa, Asia, and the West Indies were demanding their independence, successive news editors sent out still more men. Vast areas which before the 1939–45 war could be cheaply and, it seemed, adequately covered by an occasional staff visit began to require lengthy stays and large sums each year. Printing House Square's only regret was that it did not have a larger team and a larger budget to let it report even more fully the colonial changes which, as it knew, would affect the political balance of the whole world.

In the years immediately after the war the paper shared a good deal of Ernest Bevin's vision, which was also the view of Mackenzie King of Canada,[1] Smuts of South Africa,[2] and Fraser of New Zealand.[3] Like them *The Times* saw a new Commonwealth as a leavening force in the world, a free and effective association of different races that would be an exemplar for the United Nations and a bridge between east and west. Such a Commonwealth, several leading articles agreed, would constitute and strengthen the third of the three intertwining circles – Europe, the United States, and the Commonwealth itself – in which Britain saw itself as having an influence.

The story of how the Commonwealth ideal was battered by reality falls into four parts: the upsurge of the independence movements in the colonies themselves; the heavy fighting in Malaya, Kenya, Cyprus, and

---

1 William Lyon Mackenzie King (1874–1950). Prime Minister of Canada, 1921–30 and 1935–48.
2 Field Marshal Jan Christian Smuts (1870–1950). Prime Minister of South Africa, 1939–48.
3 Peter Fraser (1884–1950). Prime Minister of New Zealand, 1940–49.

Aden; the linked problems of South Africa and Rhodesia; and, over all, the loosening and weakening of the Commonwealth association as a whole. The account of the beginning of coloured immigration into Britain logically takes its place as a fifth strand, for the heavy tide of immigration had an impact on British thoughts about the benefits and the burdens which the new Commonwealth was bringing to Britain. The five strands require to be taken in turn.

In the story of the colonial upsurge, the work of Oliver Woods was outstanding and, for *The Times*, decisive. What he wrote in his colonial leaders and in his series of special articles, written after each of his many tours, was accepted within the office with very little question as *Times* policy. After the accidental beginning of his interest in colonial matters in 1948, when he accompanied Hilary Marquand, the Postmaster General, on an African tour,[4] he became engrossed in the whole field. Africa in particular took hold of him, though he was caught up also by the West Indies. Both areas brought out the best in him: his shrewdness, his warm sympathies, his gift of simplifying a wildly complex problem, his military-style clarity of writing with many an additional touch of colour and humour.

As he travelled his experience grew until he was second to none among writers on colonial affairs in the daily press. Many Secretaries of State for Colonial Affairs made a point of talking matters over with him while they were making up their minds on a line of policy. Throughout most of the fifties he saw much of Alan Lennox-Boyd[5] whose ideas of controlled reforms towards self-government appealed to him when first the movement got under way. But, as the pace quickened, Woods came to admire the daring and realistic policy of Iain Macleod who took Lennox-Boyd's place at the Colonial Office towards the end of 1959.

In 1956 Woods was given the titles of colonial editor and assistant foreign editor. When, in the same year, the *Colonial Review* was started as a quarterly survey he was given charge over it and over the many supplements on colonial and ex-colonial territories which *The Times* printed with its normal daily issue. He left the colonial field to take charge of home affairs in 1961, before the worst demonstrations of one-party and one-man rule appeared in some of the territories which he knew.

Some of the African militants complained that on his journeys he

---

4 See Chapter X.
5 Alan Tindal Lennox-Boyd, 1st Viscount Boyd of Merton (1904–83). Minister of State for Colonial Affairs, 1951–53; Secretary of State for the Colonies, 1954–59.

stayed too often with governors of the territories, but in fact such official stays were short and he more often put up in what hotels and rest houses there were or sometimes with Africans in their houses. It is true that he began by counting a little too much on gradual, orderly, and pro-grammatic moves towards colonial self-government and independence, as though they could be regulated by time-tables, but it was not long before he recognised that nationalism abhors any carefully staged programme; it wants instant action. He often used to say in his wry, amused kind of way that he was writing himself out of a job, meaning that more and more of the nationalist movements which he described, and largely sympathised with, were reaching their goal of independence and so narrowing his own colonial field.

At all events the understanding shown in his writings – widely read as they were in Britain and overseas – helped in its own way to ensure that the great transition to independence was made without widespread bitterness. Africans and others felt that their case was being put.

A memorandum of his, written after ten weeks of travel through Africa in 1956, shows the value of such travels and demonstrates also how much the Africa which he then saw was to change in the next twenty years. Woods had no doubt that western colonial power was 'rapidly coming to its close':

The new African continent will bear some resemblance to the Middle East, being a medley of jarring, not very viable states of varying stability.

The continent will be divided into three broad bands, Islamic in the north, pure black Christian-pagan in the centre, European-dominated in the south. Where the boundaries of these bands will be drawn is a matter for speculation. Islam is still creeping steadily south, and may, on the withdrawal of the colonial powers, resume the march southward which was interupted 150 years ago. European domination will remain up to the Zambesi, and some way beyond (E. Africa is the marginal area) for an indefinite period.

Woods was writing while the moderates among the whites were still in power in the Rhodesias; there were still some hopes that the example of a workable multi-racial federation in the Rhodesias and Nyasaland (Malawi) would eventually encourage South Africans to soften their apartheid policy. In his memorandum Woods also commented on particular regions. For example:

British West Africa: Hell-bent on self-government at varying speeds from very slow in Nigeria to break-neck in Gold Coast. British very popular but the differences between the African groups themselves are proving more phrenetic than between racial groups in other parts of Africa. All African leaders are becoming more authoritarian in outlook because they see no other means of holding things together . . . Nkrumah[6] may want to set himself up as a pan-African leader but will be challenged by French and Nigerian rivals. Apart from keeping its own house in order, this very recently evolved society will be faced with the tasks of (a) combating older-organised but still vigorous Moslem encroachment (b) trying to support its 'black brothers' against the whites in the south, as represented by the present Union [South African] government.

The memorandum contains a nugget of advance news of the kind which gave added justification to the extended travels that were regularly made by senior men on The Times:

Angola: While in Leopoldville the Belgians introduced me to a Congolese newspaper reporter whom they had sent into Portuguese territory because they found Europeans were too closely watched to find useful information. This reporter told me that he was able to contact a strong underground African nationalist movement and that it would not surprise him to see an armed revolt in five years' time.[7]

In fact the Angolan revolt broke out a few months short of five years later, in April 1961.

Malaya, Kenya, Cyprus, Aden, Rhodesia: The Times's very full reporting of the fighting in these areas required a combination of two things. First, there had to be knowledge of the background to the fighting. This was provided continuously by Woods, by his able assistants, James Bishop[8] and William Kirkman,[9] and by the paper's local correspondents. Many of these, including such men as C. J. Cowan and Rhys Meier[10] in Salisbury, G. Kinnear and E. Marsden[11] in Nairobi, and K.

---

6 Dr. Kwame Nkrumah (1900–72). Prime Minister of Gold Coast, 1952–57, of Ghana, 1957–60; President of Ghana, 1960–66.
7 Memorandum from colonial editor, December 28 1956. T.T.A.
8 James Drew Bishop (b. 1929). Haileybury; Corpus Christi College, Cambridge. Northampton Chronicle and Echo, 1953. Home sub-editor The Times, 1955; assistant colonial editor, 1957; New York, 1960; foreign news editor, 1964; features editor, 1965. Executive assistant magazine division Thomson Publications, 1970; editor Illustrated London News, 1971.
9 William Patrick Kirkman (b. 1932). Oriel College, Oxford. Reporter The Times, 1957; assistant to colonial editor, 1960; Africa correspondent, 1963–64.
10 Rhys Meier. Succeeded Colin Cowan as correspondent in Salisbury 1962.
11 Eric Marsden (b. 1926). On staff of East African Standard. The Times

Mackenzie in Nicosia, were first class journalists with an unbeatable knowledge of the territories from which they reported. The foreign pages of *The Times* owed much to its 'stringers'. Mario Modiano in Athens, for example, was a correspondent who knew everybody and whose advice was sought by all but who maintained a critical detachment even in the stormiest times. In 1961 Printing House Square's writing team was greatly strengthened by the coming of Roy Lewis from the *Economist*.[12] Secondly, there had to be rotas in war reporting by special correspondents and by the defence correspondent. Nine men were in the Congo at different times from June 1955 to March 1961: eight took turns in Cyprus over the same period.

Of all the despatches from the warring territories it was the first of them, the despatches from Louis Heren in Malaya, which provoked the fiercest storm among the British soldiers and officials. The storm was largely conducted by General (later Field Marshal) Sir Gerald Templer, who arrived in 1952 to be High Commissioner and Director of Operations in the Federation of Malaya; he succeeded Sir Henry Gurney, the High Commissioner who was murdered in the jungle the previous October. Heren had already shown what he could do in India, then in Korea,[13] and, after reaching Malaya, in his accounts of forays with British and other troops in the jungle. The troops were searching for the Chinese guerrillas – the so-called Malayan People's Anti-Japanese Army – who had taken up arms when the Malayan Federation had been established. As Heren believed that Templer and the British military authorities as a whole exaggerated the size of the task before them. He was convinced that the authorities over-estimated the number of guerrillas and he was also sure that the British, fighting intelligently, were being more successful than was admitted by the authorities. His views were confirmed when he was shown an enemy document, seized early in 1952, in which the communist leaders in effect conceded defeat. This secret document, meant to be circulated among the guerrillas in the jungle, was shown to him by General Sir Rob Lockhart, the director of operations. Heren himself records in his second volume of autobiography:[14]

---

correspondent Nairobi, 1962; staff correspondent *The Times* and *The Sunday Times* Jerusalem, 1970; Johannesburg, 1977.

12 Ernest Michael Roy Lewis (b. 1913). King Edward VI Birmingham; University College, Oxford; London School of Economics. Editor, *New Commonwealth*, 1954–55, and assistant editor, *Economist*, 1955–61. Leader writer on *The Times*, 1961–67, and resumed as leader writer in 1971.
13 See Chapter XII.
14 Louis Heren, *Growing Up on The Times*, p. 151.

It was top secret, and could not be taken from his office. I sat in an ante-room throughout a long hot afternoon reading the translation which ran to about 30,000 words. The language was unusually obscure even for such a document and the ideological jargon self-serving, but there was no doubt that the leadership had admitted defeat . . . I wrote my little scoop after promising not to reveal the source, and to my surprise it caused widespread anger rather than general jubilation. The search for the leak was as extensive as anything attempted by President Nixon's plumbers many years later. It did not matter that my report was correct. Templer was furious. From then onwards I was regarded as an enemy.

Templer complained to *The Times*, accusing Heren of distorting the news and hinting darkly at ulterior motives. Haley was new to *The Times* when the complaints arrived, but McDonald and Norman vouched for Heren, and Haley – after asking Heren for a letter explaining the situation in Malaya frankly as he saw it – wrote back to him thanking him and making it clear that, so far as *The Times* was concerned, that was the end of the affair. But Templer did not forget so quickly. Heren was soon in worse trouble. He reported on a brigade operation which Templer had mounted with the aim of capturing a supposed communist head-quarters in the jungle:

> By the end of the third or fourth day it was clear that the operation was a failure. I thought nothing more of it. For me it was just another second-rate story I was required to file, but not for Templer.[15]

When Templer happened to see Heren in Kuala Lumpur there was a brief and most unseemly row between them. Again complaints came in to *The Times* from Templer, and again they were without any effect. Shortly afterwards the Delhi post fell vacant and Heren was transferred there. But a surprise awaited anyone who thought that moving him from a colonial territory to a brand-new independent country would dull his critical faculties. It was not long before his zeal for blunt truths forced him to criticise Pandit Nehru almost as severely as he had criticised the British authorities in Malaya.

Throughout the Haley period South Africa remained impervious to criticisms by politicians and newspapers of no matter what country. Certainly *The Times* could not boast of making any dent in the National-ist front. All it could claim was to have given a reasonable coverage of

---

15 Heren, *op. cit.* p. 153.

news day by day and to have published leaders and special articles which were the more convincing because readers could see that they were written with a full understanding of why the Afrikaner leaders thought and acted as they did. The day-to-day news was handled by no fewer than thirteen local correspondents – a reminder of how fully *The Times* covered Commonwealth news. Eleven of these thirteen were on South African newspapers. They were led by D. R. D'Ewes,[16] a bilingual Rhodes Scholar, who was assistant editor on the *Cape Times*, and W. A. Bellwood,[17] the Pretoria correspondent of the Johannesburg *Star*. A third man who periodically sent news from various South African centres was Jerome Caminada, later to be foreign news editor of *The Times*. A South African commission of inquiry into the press, 1955–56, reported that these men sent factual news, very often without comment. Beyond that it predictably detected a bias in some of the correspondents' comment, when they did comment, and in some of their selection of news. The official view was bound to differ from that of an impartial observer.

Almost all of the leaders and special articles in *The Times* were the work of Patrick Ryan, taking time off from his general leader-writing and his book reviews in order to travel. He had some South African family connexions but it was probably the Irishman in him that gave him the feel of a divided country, that let him appreciate the fears of a small people facing far more heavily populated neighbours, and that at the same time gave him his hatred of discrimination or outright oppression. He described the Nationalists' fears so fairly that they rarely resented his conclusions, many times stated, that apartheid could not and should not work. Even in the days of anonymity Ryan's style of writing was unmistakable:

The ostrich is an African bird, but there are no records for success in its policy of burying its head in the sand.

What sense is there in the make-believe of declaring that the Bantus in, say, Johannesburg, born of parents and grandparents of the same origin, ought to look to chiefs in remote districts in which they have never set foot? Would it not be as sensible, say, to tell men and women of Irish origin in Glasgow that they must go back to their ancestral Tara or Connemara and settle down under the laws of Brian Boru?

16 Dudley Ridge D'Ewes (b. 1905). University of Cape Town; Keble College, Oxford. Assistant editor, *Cape Times*; *The Times* Cape Town correspondent, 1935–68.
17 W. A. Bellwood (1903–1976). Political correspondent, Johannesburg *Star*, 1929–49; chief representative in Pretoria for that newspaper, 1949–64. *The Times* Pretoria correspondent, 1950–76.

Apartheid is thus seen [by the Nationalist leaders] as the only practical Christian way of tackling the native problem. It allows, in theory, for these still largely primitive people to develop whatever latent qualities, spiritual and intellectual, they may possess . . . Conviction that despotism, benevolent and patriarchial, is the wise way of governing in this revolutionary modern world, lies at the root of the Nationalist faith. It explains why those now in power in the Union regard even the possibility of granting democratic rights to the natives as a whimsical heresy.[18]

Neither blunt criticism nor indirect persuasion had any effect on South Africa's policies. Racial discrimination also bedevilled hopes of progress in South Africa's northern neighbours. During 1952 and 1953, while the Central African Federation was being established, *The Times* gave the scheme whatever encouragement it could. A number of leading articles and special articles pointed to the advantages of linking the complementary economies of the three member states: Southern Rhodesia (later simply Rhodesia, then Zimbabwe), Northern Rhodesia (later Zambia) and Nyasaland (later Malawi). The paper trusted in the good will of men like Sir Godfrey Huggins,[19] Roy Welensky,[20] and Garfield Todd.[21] Yet it expressed its wider doubts from the beginning, knowing both the harder line of many of the white settlers and the resultant fears of the Africans who looked more and more strongly to London for protection. The titles of leading articles reveal in themselves the paper's doubts and warnings:

'Federation of Unequals' (Morrah, June 19 1952);

'Dangerous Secrecy' (Hodgkin, arguing that lack of news from the constituent talks in London added to the Africans' fears, January 19 1953);

'A Test of Faith' (Tyerman, February 6 1953);

'Good Faith in Africa' (Bishop, showing that Britain's was being doubted, November 25 1957);

'A Panic Measure' (Woods, on attempts to jettison Garfield Todd, Prime Minister of Southern Rhodesia, February 3 1958);

---

18 Last of seven special articles, *The Times*, June 2–July 22 1950.
19 Godfrey Martin Huggins, 1st Viscount Malvern (1883–1971). Prime Minister of Southern Rhodesia, 1934–53; Prime Minister of the Federation of Rhodesia and Nyasaland, 1953–56.
20 Sir Roy Welensky (b. 1907). Formed Northern Rhodesia Labour Party, 1941. Prime Minister, Federation of Rhodesia and Nyasaland, 1956–63.
21 Reginald Stephen Garfield Todd (b. 1908). Formed United Rhodesia Party, returned as leader, 1953. Prime Minister, Southern Rhodesia, 1953–58. President of New Africa Party, 1961.

'The Pot Boils Over' (Woods, on troubles spreading from Nyasa-land, March 4 1959).

The doubts and fears were soon confirmed as the moderate men to whom *The Times* looked, men of the Huggins and Welensky moulds, either resigned or were edged out of power in Salisbury. The federation broke up in 1963, and *The Times* was soon recording the beginning of the Rhodesian tragedy. In line with its overall African policy of support for black independence it gave general backing to successive British governments against Ian Smith's National Front. Haley often returned to the argument of simple arithmetic. The quarter of a million whites in Rhodesia were outnumbered sixteen to one.

None the less the reporting was as fair as correspondents could make it, and this fairness was amply vindicated in a notorious incident during Harold Macmillan's 'wind of change' tour in Africa in 1960. While Macmillan was having lunch in Ryall's Hotel, Blantyre, (Nyasaland, Malawi) on January 26, a crowd of Africans began shouting and waving hostile banners outside. Under the emergency laws their gathering was illegal. They continued until moved on by the police led by European officers; some were struck with sticks; some were pushed into police vans and driven away.

The roughness used by the police was seen differently by different correspondents. One wrote of 'a sickening spectacle', a riot provoked by senior British police officers. Women, it was stated, had their bare feet stamped upon. Other Africans were said to have been struck across their stomachs. Most of the stories agreed in blaming the police for the disorders and so for the consequent arrests. The *Daily Mail* had a leader the next day under the heading 'Police State', declaring that the picture of brutality must shame everyone; there should be an immediate inquiry.

James Bishop, for *The Times*, sent a much more restrained account. His view was that the whole demonstration had been organised in advance by the Malawi Congress Party; in his view the Africans began the trouble when they took to throwing stones and mud; the police held them back with difficulty but with restraint; he saw only one European officer use his stick about the shoulders of some Africans; some of the arrests were made necessarily roughly as some Africans struggled, but he saw no brutality. He did not criticise the police for their action.

The Reuters account, published by the *Guardian*, came near to supporting Bishop's version. Reuters apart, he was in a minority of one. This gave Francis Williams, then writing in the *New Statesman* a heavily judgmatical column on the press's work each week, the opportunity to weigh into *The Times* for all his worth. After recalling that he had

several times commented on the paper's 'odd but undoubtedly significant attitude' in its reporting of southern African affairs he quoted the
Daily Mail account of the Blantyre incident before going on:

> Every other newspaper with a special correspondent covering the
> tour reported in similar terms and with equally shocking detail –
> except *The Times* . . . The *Guardian* has no cause for satisfaction in
> the matter [having used Reuters]; but at least it has some excuse. *The
> Times* has none. It had its own special correspondent on the spot,
> and, since what happened took place with 'the whole of the interna-
> tional press corps looking on', it seems inconceivable that the full
> facts were not available in *The Times* office. If so, they were not
> passed on to its readers . . . In view of all the evidence – including
> that given in newspapers certainly as Conservative and at least as
> 'responsible' as *The Times* – if this is not partial reporting, then I do
> not know what is.

Francis Williams[22] declared also that *The Times* had played down the
exclusion of blacks from a reception given to Macmillan in Cape Town.
He concluded:

> *The Times* believes itself to be, and is thought by many to be, the
> greatest newspaper in the world and a trustworthy historical record
> of the world's news. I cannot feel that it is living up to its standards.[23]

The column attracted more attention than Williams's efforts usually
did. On his return to London Bishop wrote a long memorandum to the
editor about his reporting of the incident. He repeated that he himself
had seen no police brutality. He thought one or two officers acted
stupidly; for example, one had tried to snatch a banner. 'But in general
terms I should say that the police handled the situation firmly and
efficiently.' The memorandum went on to describe how correspondents
had exchanged their impressions very soon after the incident:

> I was disturbed to find during this that many of my colleagues were
> agreed that the whole thing could be blamed on the police. It was not
> a conclusion I had come to on what I had seen, and so I resolved to
> write strictly factually on what I had seen for myself.[24]

The government announced the appointment of a commission of inquiry under Mr. Justice Southworth. All the correspondents flew back
to Blantyre to appear before it. On February 26 Bishop gave evidence,

---

22 Francis Williams (1903–1970). Editor of *Daily Herald*, 1936–40. Baron, 1962.
23 *New Statesman*, February 6 1960.
24 Memorandum, Bishop to Haley, February 10 1960. T.T.A.

saying once again that he had seen no brutality, no whips, no bloodshed; he believed that those who were arrested deserved it as he had seen many deliberately courting arrest. On May 17 the commission published its findings. In general they supported the police and, by extension, *The Times* in its account of what had happened outside Ryall's Hotel. The commission's report included a note which Mr. Justice Southworth had made during the hearings. He had found James Bishop and René McColl, of the *Daily Express*, to be 'the most dispassionate witnesses who had given evidence up to that point.' *The Times* had a modest leader the next day, and Francis Williams handsomely withdrew most of his own criticisms.

A year later, in 1961, *The Times* was hotly accused of saying not too little but too much. John White[25] was Africa correspondent for several months. After a visit to Nkrumah's Ghana, where he had many confidential talks, he produced two special articles on the hidden economic troubles of the country and on the still more deeply hidden dismay about Nkrumah in the army and among opposition leaders.[26] The Ghana government later arrested some opposition leaders and on December 11 1961 it released a white paper justifying the arrests. It stated that certain people were plotting, through strikes, to bring about a state of chaos in the country that would lead to army intervention and the removal of the government. It accused foreign newspapers, notably *The Times*, of misrepresenting the government's measures and thus, by inference, of aiding the alleged plotters. The white paper cited White's articles, hinting that he would not have written as he did unless he had been informed by someone 'whom he believed spoke with authority'. This was a dig at some political figures whom White had seen. The white paper went on: 'The evidence shows quite clearly that the campaign conducted by *The Times*, London, is not the result of faulty knowledge of real conditions in Ghana but is inspired by a deliberate editorial policy'. In paragraph after paragraph the white paper accused the controllers of *The Times* of deliberately using 'the influence which they have on western opinion' to undermine international confidence in Ghana and in its government. 'Other newspapers took their cue from *The Times*.'[27]

---

25 John Alexander White (b. 1933). Leighton Park; Lincoln College, Oxford. Joined *The Times* staff as assistant to the special supplements editor, 1956–57; assistant letters editor, 1957–59; foreign news department, 1959; assistant correspondent, Bonn, 1959–61; correspondent in Africa, 1961; Tokyo correspondent from 1963 until his resignation in 1964.
26 *The Times*, June 13 and 14 1961.
27 *The Times*, December 11 1961.

On receiving the outburst *The Times* checked its information through the Colonial Office and elsewhere without unearthing any cause for retraction on its part. Certainly there had been no political instructions of any kind to White from Printing House Square. Some time afterwards as a sign of confidence White was promoted to Tokyo.

Covering the Mau Mau revolt in Kenya was difficult enough[28] but the war in the Congo (outside the Commonwealth) was infinitely worse. When in the Congo Bishop and Holden had very often to send off messages from remote and disorganised districts without any means of knowing whether the messages reached Printing House Square. Sometimes the messages did arrive: often they did not. For some time Holden had to cross the Congo River every evening in a crowded ferry boat, send off a message from Brazzaville in the former French Middle Congo, and then cross back again at night. All the correspondents from all papers and television services lived through the same periods of little food, little sleep, and no kind of comfort.

From the other side of Africa, in Kenya, Oliver Woods sent many private messages showing that he shared to the full the official view that Jomo Kenyatta[29] was not free from all blame in the Mau Mau revolt. Back in the office he passed on an equally strong official view that Kenyatta could never be allowed to become prime minister of Kenya; he could never be received in Buckingham Palace. In any case there came official hints that he was mortally ill. Minds changed as events changed, and Kenyatta emerged to join the company of Commonwealth leaders who graduated through prison and detention to become respected heads of state and government. *The Times* recognised that Mau Mau was more than a nationalist movement; it had evils in it that had to be suppressed. All the same, when eleven Mau Mau prisoners were killed in trouble at Hola camp on March 3 1959, *The Times* called strongly for an inquiry. 'Very sensible leader,' Harold Macmillan, still Prime Minister, wrote in his diary.[30] MPs and other newspapers were no less anxious. An inquiry was announced soon afterwards, and its carefully restrained report in July, reviewing the whole incident and thereby evoking the general Kenya dilemma, was followed by swifter government moves towards the inevitable African majority rule.

---

28 The Mau Mau uprising, 1952–56, brought deaths of 95 whites and some 10,000 Africans.
29 Jomo Kenyatta (c. 1889–1978). President, Kenya African Union 1947–52; detained by British 1952–61; minister of state for constitutional affairs, 1962; Prime Minister, 1963; President, 1964.
30 Harold Macmillan: June 11 1959. *Memoirs*, Vol. IV, *Riding the Storm*, p. 735.

During all these years *The Times* became more and more deeply concerned in the wider and more general question which it put in a leading article in 1953. The leader was on the very nature of the Commonwealth and had the title 'Light as Air, Strong as Iron':

So far, it is true, the bonds have become stronger as they have become looser. But will the process of loosening continue to vanishing point? How many republics, it is asked, can the Commonwealth contain without altering its character?[31]

The answer which the leader gave, and which *The Times* was to harden in the coming years, was that the future of the association could not depend on outward form or style. The Commonwealth had to survive on matters of conduct and substance. The chief threat to its unity would arise if a member pursued a policy, either internal or external, that put it outside the traditions of civilised conduct.

The leader writers had many discussions on this subject which threatened to become almost a metaphysical problem. Long memoranda remain in the archives. In the end leading articles came back to the view that the Commonwealth, at bottom, persisted on the self-interest of those members who still found advantages in the association. Membership increased the flow of information to each partner and helped its trade. But for how long would the advantages last? In 1956 *The Times* had three long first leaders on successive days under the general title, 'The Changed Commonwealth'. Written by Morrah, Woods and McDonald they faced the dangers ahead. The third, on June 27 1956, gave warning that two financial measures, though still some years away at that time – the free conversion of sterling into dollars and the end of discriminatory tariffs under the General Agreement on Tariffs and Trade (GATT) – would undoubtedly weaken the Commonwealth association. Britain would remain the linchpin of what was left, and as such she would have to ensure that she was strong in defence, businesslike and adaptable in exports to Commonwealth countries, and active in maintaining the exchange of government-to-government information:

At times it seems that such an exchange of views is one of the few reasonable tangible links left. It remains vital.

Four years later, after long office discussions and many talks with Commonwealth leaders, there came another series of three long first leaders, again on three successive days.[32] More than a dozen members

31 *The Times*, June 2 1953.
32 *The Times*, April 27–28–29 1960.

of the staff pooled their views before the leaders were written.[33] The articles raised the old questions and gave many of the old answers but with a stronger emphasis on the need for some common standards of conduct. Later still *The Times* came to the conclusion that the apartheid policy came under the heading of unacceptable conduct and made South Africa's continued membership untenable. For many years the paper had hoped against hope that South African policy might soften. But a long leader in November 1960 defined what in *The Times's* view was the basis of membership and what should lead to a member's exclusion. It came back once again to the question of conduct:

> If the Commonwealth is to remain a community of any purpose, its members must have some moral standards in common . . . There must be a common acceptance of the elementary rights of man, leaving no place for a political tyranny or for a member that is set on permanently refusing the opportunity of equal advance and a share in government to a race on grounds of colour.[34]

Subsequent events were to show that this code, as defined, was too ambitious and too high-minded. The code ignored the desire of successive British governments to keep on terms with the independent states of black Africa and overlook many of their faults. South Africa duly left the association but elsewhere political autocracies, and the occasional tyranny, were tolerated too long.

The newly awakened pride in the Commonwealth and Empire with which many British people emerged from the Second World War helps to explain the quiet acceptance of the first non-white immigrants into Britain. Other reasons were to be found in the strong social conscience in the country; in the hopes of industrial expansion which, it was widely thought, would require a larger labour force in Britain; and in a recognition that the West Indies and other countries had a surplus labour force ready and willing to come.

It was this last point that Oliver Woods emphasized in talks in Printing House Square. He had seen the predicament in Jamaica and other West Indian islands. Unemployment and distress were growing in step with fears about their staple exports of sugar, citrus fruits, and bananas. The islands could no longer count on the United States as an outlet for their excess labour; the warning signs from Washington were clear even before the passage of the restrictive McCarran-Walter Act in 1952. Jamaica in particular would need substantial grants from London

---

33 Memorandum, April 29 1960. T.T.A.
34 *The Times*, November 30 1960.

unless it could export some of its unemployment elsewhere, which meant to Britain. Such arguments influenced *The Times*, with its strong Commonwealth consciousness, in the years when the immigrants were too few in number to present social problems. Less credence was given within the office at the time to the other argument, privately expressed by some Treasury men and some industrialists, that the inflow of workers accustomed to low wages would help to keep all labour costs down. This argument seemed fallacious from the start because the incomers came precisely in order to get higher wages.

Like the government, and like most other journals of opinion, *The Times* did not at first see the significance of the early arrivals or the size of the future movement. Something quite normal seemed to be happening. At all events *The Times* cheerfully reported without comment the arrival of the first boatload of Jamaican immigrants on board the *Empire Windrush* in June 1948:

> Of the 492 Jamaicans who arrived at Tilbury on Monday [June 21] to seek work in this country, 236 were housed last night in Clapham South deep shelter. The remainder had friends to whom they could go with prospects of work. The men had arrived at Tilbury in the ex-troopship *Empire Windrush*. Among them are singers, students, pianists, boxers and a complete dance band. Thirty or forty of them have already volunteered to work as miners.[35]

They seemed to be a typical, carefree, sun-drenched Caribbean group. The state papers released on January 1 1979 show that Clement Attlee, Prime Minister in 1948, was puzzled by the group and asked to be told who was behind the enterprise and how long the West Indians would stay. In reply the Colonial Secretary, Arthur Creech-Jones, wrote in effect that no one had planned the arrival; it had just happened; and both the British and the Jamaican governments were trying to discourage such influxes. Some difficulties were foreseen. Three years after the first arrivals an African correspondent wrote in *The Times* about the disillusion in the minds of many who had come to Britain from West Africa and the West Indies. They believed that they were being kept out of jobs because of the colour of their skins when very often it was because they lacked skill.[36]

Another three years later, in 1954, after the incomers had swollen in numbers, *The Times* went into the whole problem more deeply and published several special articles examining the implications for Britain.

---

35 *The Times*, June 23 1948.
36 *The Times*, January 11 1951.

In two of them David Wood wrote that the first signs of a colour problem were showing in Britain. He quoted civic leaders who, in the absence of any government policy, were left coping with the housing and other stresses:

> The time has come for the Government not merely to shrug away the problem by saying that West Indians are of British nationality and must be free to come and go as the next man, but to bring immigration under some sort of control, in the interests of both white and coloured citizens.[37]

Wood emphasized that it was not basically a colour problem. Where employment and housing were good integration was easy. But where the local authorities were overwhelmed colour did come into the scene. In 1956 three special articles examined the problem again:

> Politically explosive is how one experienced social worker, not given to hyperbole, describes the domestic difficulties and frictions arising from the steady influx of West Indians . . . into this country.[38]

Having given warnings in such long special articles *The Times* was slow to support in its leading articles any move to check the number of incomers. Haley used to say that so long as Britain was the leader of a multi-racial Commonwealth it could not, without hypocrisy, stop the entry of people of different colours and races who held British passports. In essence, of course, the Commonwealth was not so much multi-racial as multi-state; each component state was not in itself a multi-racial society but was made up mainly of people of a single colour, whether white, black, or brown. As the numbers of incomers into Britain increased, and thousands came from India and Pakistan as well as from the Caribbean, the paper moved in favour of the attempts to curb immigration, but only at the source by means of bilateral agreements with the Indian, Pakistani, and Caribbean governments. Haley had several talks on the matter with Macmillan, when Prime Minister, and R. A. Butler, when Home Secretary, but he made it plain to them that *The Times* must oppose any unilateral control imposed by Britain. Even after the riots at Nottingham and Notting Hill in 1958 the paper kept this stand. It argued strongly against the Commonwealth Immigrants Bill of 1961, enacted in 1962.

On December 4 1961, a few days before the Bill was taken in committee on the floor of the House, Oliver Woods summarised in a

---

37 *The Times*, November 8 1954.
38 *The Times*, August 25 1956.

leader the paper's objections to 'this unloved baby'. By that time the Bill had attracted no fewer than 133 amendments, four new clauses, and one new schedule. Outside the House evidence suggested that nine-tenths of the British people were behind it in its main purpose. The leader acknowledged that many of those who opposed it 'would not oppose any and every Bill aimed at providing powers for some sort of control of Commonwealth immigration'. More to the point it suggested that there should be, among other provisions, an appeal tribunal to review decisions taken by immigration officers and a stipulation that the Act should be renewable annually by Parliament:

> It would be best if the Bill could be thrown out altogether. If that is not practical politics, then twelve months at a time is long enough.

The Times joined the *Tribune* in commending Hugh Gaitskell's denunciation of 'this miserable, shameful, shabby Bill'.[39] Harold Macmillan deeply resented such criticisms of the Bill and, through it, of the Home Secretary and himself. In a volume published twelve years later he wrote with some exaggeration:

> One of the leaders in this campaign was *The Times* newspaper, which exceeded itself in its self-righteous and unctuous approach. A series of leading articles followed each other week by week like an artillery bombardment, culminating on December 4 . . . It is strange how persistent has been the tradition of this great organ of the Press which has been exercising its power over successive governments for so many years.

After quoting Trollope on *The Jupiter*, the Great Thunderer, and after declaring that in times of crisis the advice of *The Times* was generally wrong and often disastrous, Macmillan reverted to the Immigrants Bill and continued:

> However, undeterred by the mistakes of his predecessors, the then occupant of the throne [Haley] discharged his thunderbolts on my colleagues and especially on myself with savage delight.[40]

Macmillan drew some comfort, he wrote, from what he calls the paper's 'bland recantation', published when he retired in 1967. Some people in 1961, *The Times* then wrote, were reluctant to believe that the restrictions in the Immigration Act were necessary. 'Since then it has become evident that they are essential'.[41]

---

39 Philip M. Williams, *Hugh Gaitskell: A Political Biography*, p. 678.
40 Harold Macmillan, *At the End of the Day*, Memoirs, Vol. VI, pp. 81–82.

In 1961, and earlier, *The Times* was indeed too slow to acknowledge the need for checks on immigration. It was wrong, but not through simple blindness. The reason for its slowness was to be found in the paper's abiding concern for the Commonwealth, the same concern which showed itself more positively in its support for unity amid all the swift changes and the emergent differences.

It was only later, as the incomers swelled still further in number with the arrival of families of men already in Britain, that *The Times* accepted the logic of Roy Hattersley's syllogism:

> Without integration, limitation is inexcusable; without limitation, integration is impossible.[42]

It was helped to accept this logic by an outstanding series of eleven articles written by Peter Evans and published in the paper in January 1965 under the title which Haley himself devised for them, 'The Dark Million'. Evans, then a reporter, had spent much of 1964 in living with immigrant families. His findings left no doubt that large parts of Britain were special areas of an unprecedented and entirely unplanned kind. Lord Gardiner, the Lord Chancellor in the Labour government, passed on the message of the eleven articles two months later when speaking in the House of Lords on March 10 1965:

> The actions, or rather the inaction, of the last two administrations mean that neither our children nor their children will ever see the England which we have been used to seeing, because for good or ill England has become a multi-racial society.

The record shows that special articles and news stories in *The Times* were on the whole stronger and clearer for some years than the leading articles. There was another reason for this initial editorial hesitancy about controls, beyond the paper's concern about relieving unemployment in the Caribbean and other Commonwealth areas. That other reason was that no one in Printing House Square was ever quite sure which department should look after immigration in the early stages. Was it a colonial matter or a home affair? Probably it was regarded as a colonial matter for too long. Successive governments, with less excuse, were much more sluggish and more deeply split in their minds over responsibility for the movement and its effects in Britain.

Much of the intensive writing in *The Times* about the Commonwealth in the ten or fifteen years after the war may seem labour in vain as

---

41 *The Times*, February 16 1967.
42 Quoted in Nicholas Deakin's *Colour, Citizenship and British Society*, p. 106.

the association has weakened. Yet something valuable in the partnership remained, and the paper's line was consistent: presenting the unwelcome facts while working hard for the continuation of the partnership, going for the spirit rather than the form, and fully recognising without any repining all the pressures for independence within the colonies.

XV

'PRESTIGE AND INDIVIDUALITY'

B Y the time Eden succeeded Churchill in 1955 most of the wartime
restrictions on trade and industry had been lifted. But not all of
them had gone. Some were kept on through governmental in-
ertia and public habit of mind. While some industrialists raged against
the residual system others came to think of it as a norm of national life, a
shield against the risks and stresses of open competition. They were not
at all eager to see the last of it go.

The Times argued against the restrictions both on political grounds
as a newspaper commenting on the state of the nation and on practical
grounds as a working company that had to pay its way and then advance.
As a newspaper it used its leader columns to protest against controls on
grounds of national efficiency. As a going concern, dealing face to face
with government ministers and other newspaper proprietors, it fought
two battles. The first battle was to have the national newspapers freed
from newsprint rationing. The second was to oppose, and finally break
out of, the compact which those same newspapers had earlier imposed
upon themselves, requiring each and every one of them to suspend
publication if any one of them was stopped by an 'unconstitutional'
labour dispute. Most of the other newspapers resisted *The Times* in
these struggles for freedom, but ultimately they gained as much out of
them as *The Times* did when success came.

The harder of the two fights was the one for freeing newsprint. Rationing was a system in which the newspapers had freely cooperated right
from the lean months of 1940. All newsprint was pooled among them
and the price of it from whatever source was equalised. The worst
feature about rationing was that each paper was limited not by the
amount of newsprint it might use but simply by the number of pages it
was allowed to print. That number of pages varied from one category of
newspaper to another; and it was fixed and changed from time to time,
after discussions with the newspapers, by the industry's own Newsprint
Supply Company Limited. As it happened the general manager of that

company from 1947 to 1957 was F. P. Bishop, who had been assistant manager of *The Times* for seven years until 1945.[1] The operation of the scheme was well explained in *The Times* early in 1954:

> At the present ration, the 1½d. daily is allowed an average of eight pages a day. The 2d. paper gets 10 pages, and a 3d. paper 12 pages. *The Times* gets 13⅓ pages – a mathematical proposition made easier by the fact that all papers can average their size over a period (at the moment 12 weeks). The size-rationing is done by authority of the Minister of Materials, in practice on the advice of the industry's 'Rationing Committee', which is closely associated with the Newsprint Supply Co., a cooperative purchasing organization jointly controlled by all the newspapers and thus representing the industry at large.[2]

With its '13⅓ pages' *The Times* would seem to have been much favoured over the rest. In fact all the quality papers suffered in their own ways, but *The Times* was the hardest hit of any. As a public duty it filled many of its columns each day with heavy and lengthy official and semi-official news: parliamentary debates, law reports, the court circular, society news, long accounts of speeches, obituaries, stock exchange dealings. It also carried the many letters to the editor and the informative leading articles, usually longer than in other dailies. Beyond that was the space – nearly half the total in the paper – that had to be given to advertisements from which three-quarters of the paper's income came. All this meant that when all the essential items had been squeezed in there was next to no room left for general news and attractive special articles.

Very different were the popular papers. Without the need to carry much official or semi-official news they had space enough for their own condensed version of the general and political news, for their sports pages, and for the chat and entertainment which their readers expected. Moreover they had another reason for being happy as things were. A return to unfettered rivalry among them would quickly mean that they were competing with each other to provide larger and larger papers, and this would come at a time when the price of newsprint had soared. £10 a ton before the war, it had risen to £66 a ton before temporarily falling to £53 a ton in 1954. Larger papers would not suit them. They got their money through sales rather than advertisements, and their optimum product was a small-size paper which sold well.

The system was unfair in very many ways. For several years *The*

---

1 See Chapter III.
2 *The Times* special article, February 8 1954.

Times chose to use its newsprint allocation to keep the number of its pages as high as it could, while deliberately cutting the circulation: as late as June 1950 it decided to cut circulation by one-eleventh in order to maintain an average 11-page paper. Later the restrictions continued to apply to a paper's number of pages even when it could get newsprint for an increased circulation. Moreover, any new paper could start up and could be allowed all the newsprint it required. Stranger still, the rationing applied only to newspapers. Periodicals, whether they used newsprint or not, were not restricted in their sizes and circulations. Local weekly newspapers and religious and sporting journals were also free. 'The whole burden of government restriction is now concentrated upon limiting the size of daily and Sunday newspapers'.[3]

The Times Board, influenced by the editor and the manager, were convinced that the system was inefficient as well as unfair. In 1949 Sir Stafford Cripps, then Chancellor of the Exchequer, had forced the industry to repudiate its Canadian contracts, and in 1952 it had to reject a large part of the Scandinavian tonnage which had been reserved to it for 1953. Naturally enough, foreign suppliers turned to markets overseas which they found more stable and rewarding. In 1954, while Britain was using up only 65 per cent of its pre-war level of newsprint, the world as a whole was consuming very much more than before. Admittedly the successive British governments had to keep a tight hold on dollars and other foreign currencies but the amount involved in much-needed purchases of newsprint for Britain from Canada and elsewhere was derisively small:

> The real price of freedom would be an additional £5m. of dollars a year in the first stage, with the possibility of a further amount, up to a maximum of another £5m. of dollars later – something, that is, between 0.8 per cent. and 1.6 per cent. on the present total dollar bill.[4]

Haley joined in the fight both in leading articles and in private memoranda to the Board. His was the leader already quoted, and it contained a typical, categorical thrust:

> It is no argument at all to say that some newspapers do not need freedom. (All should desire freedom whether they need it or not.)

He dwelt on the absurdity, then still continuing, of exporting newsprint while British newspapers were left so short:

---

3 Leading article (Haley), February 10 1954.
4 *The Times* special article, February 9 1954.

But even if the arguments against the abolition of newsprint rationing were stronger than they are, the case for freedom in the highest national interest is overwhelming. The Press – and particularly the serious Press – is being hampered in the service it should give to the nation. Restriction on information and opinion, even though it be only quantitative, cannot be justified.

In this battle *The Times* had one growing asset. Throughout 1954 it knew itself to be fighting on ever stronger ground because its supplies of its own 'non-newsprint' paper from Townsend Hook were increasing. In November 1954 John Astor saw Peter Thorneycroft, the President of the Board of Trade, to urge him to end the control of newsprint. At that time, and later, the President hoped that the newspapers would help him out of the dilemma by agreeing to a voluntary control among themselves through the Newspaper Supply Company. Some other papers were willing, but on January 13 1955 the Board of *The Times* decided to tell the President of the Board of Trade that it would oppose such a scheme; it would go over wholly to Townsend Hook paper as soon as possible, and thereafter it would not regard the government order which restricted pages as applying to *The Times*.

This was the decisive point in the dispute. Attempts were made to persuade *The Times* to fall in with the others in a voluntary scheme but the farthest it went was to empower Gavin Astor to see Peter Thorneycroft again in January 1956 and tell him that it would be ready itself to limit its pages entirely voluntarily if that would make it easier for the President to end newsprint control. *The Times* would be ready, for a year, to keep the number of its pages to a maximum of 20 or 24, plus inset supplements.

Almost total victory came at the end of 1956 when newspapers were freed at last from page rationing. After that time all that remained was a loose system of voluntary control for successive periods of six months through 1957 to the end of 1958. The rationing committee of the Newspapers Supply Company then decided that its code of rules need no longer apply and the newsprint pool which had been operated since 1940 was dispersed. That was the end of the system. From January 1 1959 – fourteen years after the end of the war – newspapers and newspaper groups could at last rely for their supplies on their own direct contracts. *The Times* could be pleased with the lead it gave in the struggle.

Some newspapers were less happy with the corollary to the scheme: simultaneously with the ending of the newsprint pool came the ending of the equalised price for newsprint and the return of normal contractual agreements, free bargaining, and the law of supply and demand. Prices rose, and *The Times* itself had to pay above the newsprint price for its Townsend Hook paper which had been a decisive lever in the argument.[5] But the fight had been worth while; it had been fought for the press's oldest cause – its own freedom.

The second struggle, over a newspaper's duty to come out or stay silent, was concerned with fundamental questions that were to be raised again, more forcefully, by *The Times* and *The Sunday Times* in 1978–79.[6] Under the shock of the general strike of 1926 all the members of the Newspaper Proprietors' Association, owners of the main London dailies, had agreed later in that same year that all their newspapers would stop publishing if any one of them was prevented by direct or unconstitutional action. The bond was renewed on October 12 1938. As the years passed *The Times* came to dislike the commitment more and more. Whatever the arguments for it in 1926 and during the war, it had quite obviously lost its power as a sanction on the workers by the fifties. It no longer carried with it its old threat of misery and want through the resultant unemployment.

In 1952 the company was advised by counsel that the bond could not in any case be enforced. On October 23 of that year the Board gave the NPA six months' notice to withdraw from the agreement. The other NPA members disliked and feared the consequences of any such break in the ranks, and *The Times* was persuaded to join in a new and slightly more flexible agreement. This signified that, if any newspaper were impeded or stopped by unconstitutional action, attempts would be made together to remove the trouble and only if these failed would all newspapers stop in support of the paper affected.

It was no mere academic problem. Labour troubles were mounting in the industry at the time. Throughout most of 1953 it looked as though the agreement would have to be invoked because of trouble, principally at the *Daily Sketch* and the *Daily Mirror*. On October 10 1954 all the London newspapers stopped publication at midnight. Full production was resumed the following day and therefore *The Times* and other papers could claim, as they had at least got their first editions out the previous night, that there had been no absolute break in their day-to-day issues.

It was a warning, though. A month later, on November 11, *The Times* Board of directors unanimously agreed that the NPA should be

---

5 See Chapter IX.
6 See Epilogue.

asked to look at the agreement once again. On January 13 1955 the manager had to report back to the Board with the news that the NPA had decided to leave the agreement unchanged. With some reluctance the directors' Board acquiesced, not wishing to break ranks. Two months later, however, all their fears were confirmed. Tensions with labour were increasing. Talks between the managements and two unions – the Amalgamated Engineering Union and the Electrical Trades Union – had broken down and a strike was called to begin on March 25. Even then the question – to publish or not to publish – was not simple to answer.

As the men on strike were maintenance men there was a possibility of producing *The Times* and other papers if men in other unions would agree. At an NPA meeting on the morning of March 25 the representatives of *The Times*, the *Daily Mail*, and the *Daily Express* said that they were ready to go ahead and publish. Four other newspapers said that they could not come out. The *Daily Mail* and the *Daily Express* thereupon said that they would not publish either, and the agreement was invoked.

The Times directors, sitting with the editor and manager, were still doubtful whether the NPA was justified and whether the strike was in fact 'unconstitutional' within the meaning of the agreement. They were also doubtful whether the bond could properly be invoked when the strike was directed not at a single paper but at the papers of the NPA as a whole. None the less when the directors met in the evening they decided to keep to their pledge with the other members and cease publication that night.

For the staff, as for the many readers who wrote in complaining, it was an unnerving decision. *The Times* had stopped publication for the first time since it was founded 170 years before. Worse still, the institution held to be unique had stopped because other papers had stopped owing to a dispute involving all of them. *The Times* did not appear again until April 21. During the blank month it missed the resignation of Winston Churchill from 10 Downing Street, it missed the budget, it had to let much other big news go by. Even though, when it finally emerged again, it gave a 10-page summary of the past weeks' events, nothing could make up for the empty days. Spirits in Printing House Square were not raised by the estimate (mentioned by Haley in an undated note to the Board, evidently written some years later)[7] that the *Manchester Guardian*, being printed out of London and therefore unaffected by the stoppage, had gained and was to hold eight to nine

---

7 T.T.A.

thousand new readers.

Once the breach was repaired Haley and Mathew wrote a long memorandum to the Board urging it to have finished with the NPA bond for good. The memorandum powerfully expressed *The Times's* opinion of its public duty and its opinion of itself as a newspaper apart from all others. In the past Haley had often fumed when other people called *The Times* a national institution; in his dismay and anger at the interruption in its course he joined with Mathew in calling it precisely that.

After giving several reasons for ending the agreement – its imprecise wording for a start, and then the evident proof that it no longer could be seen as a deterrent to strike action – the editor and manager wrote that stopping publication weakened the influence of newspapers as a whole. Their impotence had been shown up by the BBC which went on giving the news without any break. The memorandum then came to the effect on *The Times* itself:

Whatever the effect of the stoppage on the goodwill of the press as a whole has been, it can be said with some certainty that the harm done has been even greater in the case of *The Times*. *The Times* had never before voluntarily ceased publication on a normal publishing day in the whole 170 years of its existence.

The fact, moreover, that *The Times* ceased publication in common with the other newspapers has lost it prestige and individuality. *The Times* has always been considered as something apart, a national institution, a paper that was different from the *Daily Mirror*, the *Daily Mail* and the *Daily Telegraph*. More than once it was remarked during the recent strike by prominent and well informed people 'I thought *The Times* was outside all these things'.

Many generations, and many years of effort have gone to build up the idea of *The Times* as an unfailing national record. It was there for the present and it was there for posterity. Nothing should happen in the United Kingdom, the Commonwealth, or the rest of the world without its being included in *The Times* if it was at all worthy of placing on record. That *The Times* should be forced to break its tradition is bad enough – there have indeed been comments that *The Times* was never driven into silence under the General Strike:—that *The Times* should voluntarily abandon its tradition when it might by one means or another have kept going, would appear to most people unthinkable.

Haley and Mathew went on to write that *The Times*, being in a class apart, should even consider leaving the NPA rather than risk being called on to stop again. But there could be a middle way:

The Times could say that it would wish to remain a member of the N.P.A., would be a party to its wage negotiations, would take part in all the other work, but would not undertake to refrain from publishing, no matter what obstacles it might have to overcome to do so . . .

We therefore recommend to the Board that The Times should inform the Newspaper Proprietors' Association that, while it loyally stood by them in the recent strike, it can no longer subscribe to the Agreement, and it is determined in any similar event in the future to come out and serve the public to the best of its ability and with every means in its power.[8]

After a Board meeting on May 5 a letter to that effect was sent to the NPA; and the decision to withdraw from the agreement, though not from the NPA itself, was reaffirmed at another Board meeting at the end of the year. Lord Rothermere and other owners within the NPA kept trying to get The Times to think again. They believed their arguments for a united front to be strengthened by the increase in labour troubles in newspaper offices. In the end The Times reluctantly agreed to stand by the very loose 'gentleman's agreement', but emphasized that it would itself judge each emergency as it occurred and would decide then whether or not to stop printing with the others.

It had also a fall-back position. It would try, even if publication was stopped in London, to print a small 8-page edition of The Times on the mobile printing unit, which Francis Mathew was eager to use and justify, somewhere else in the country. The other NPA members liked this project no more than they liked The Times's general stance. They thought it simply a backstairs way round their proposed blockade. After some further alarms the Board of The Times declared, in a minute dated June 30 1959, that the 'gentleman's agreement' was against the public interest.

The differences surfaced more obviously in May 1960 when the production of the Daily Mirror was threatened in a dispute between labour and management on an issue related to a publication not in membership of the NPA. Once again, as George Pope explained to a meeting of the NPA Council on May 4, The Times could not commit itself in advance to stop publication. The next day Lord Rothermere wrote sorrowfully to Gavin Astor, saying that the NPA Council viewed this attitude with much concern and asked for urgent reconsideration. Astor replied on May 18. The Times, he said, was ready to make

8 T.T.A.

sacrifices for the sake of NPA solidarity but it could not bind itself to close down every time the others did; it must judge each case on its merits:

> We have always understood that the N.P.A. is a voluntary association and that all its members reserve their liberty of action. In our opinion, that right cannot be surrendered on so vital an issue just because a single member finds himself in a minority of one.[9]

As so often in its history *The Times* showed that it wished to go its own way, with all its risks, rather than have the false comfort and real danger of holding hands with others.

The risks facing *The Times* as a commercial concern were as yet hardly apparent. One large risk, however, was uncovered by Gavin Astor and his younger brother, Hugh. Gavin Astor was appointed a director on May 27 1952 and, as eldest son, was clearly intended to succeed his father as co-chief proprietor and chairman. Even before his appointment he had been inquiring about the finances and was shocked to find how little had been done to counter the impact of the death duties which would be imposed when his father died. John Astor was the major shareholder in both The Times Holding Company and The Times Publishing Company. Duties would fall heavily on both. Gavin Astor, it was apparent, would have to sell *The Times*. Very probably he would have to sell it quickly, thereby jeopardising hopes of getting a good price for it.

As soon as the danger was recognised the need for speed in remedial action was no less clearly seen. Even if John Astor were to sell or give away all his shares straight away, duties would still be imposed under the regulations of that time if he died within the next five years. The best means of reorganising the capital was exposed in necessarily lengthy and complex reports from the company's solicitors, Charles Russell and Company, and the auditors, Deloitte, Plender, Griffiths and Company. Counsel's advice was sought on how the tax authorities were likely to view the proposed scheme. In addition the final report to the Board included many suggestions from Hugh Astor's own financial adviser, C. E. M. Hardie, of the firm Dixon, Wilson, Tubbs, and Gillett. Details of the plan to be submitted to the shareholders were published in *The Times* and elsewhere on August 14 1954. Final approval was given by the Board on September 9 of that year.

The statement of August 14, copied in most British and some

---

9 T.T.A.

American papers, set out the two aims of the reorganisation:

To 'ensure the maintenance of the independence and stability of *The Times* in face of the changes which have taken place in legislation, taxation, death duties, and economic conditions'; and

To 'guard against the control of *The Times* passing out of the hands of the families of Colonel Astor and Mr. John Walter on the death of either of them'.

Before the reorganisation the holding company carried the voting shares; John Astor, as head of the Astor family interests in *The Times*, controlled nine-tenths of these and John Walter had the remaining tenth. The holding company carried £700,000 in debenture stock, £50 in £1 priority shares, £570,000 in £1 preference shares, and £10,000 in £1 ordinary shares. This holding company was dominant in the publishing company, which had £965,000 in £1 preference and ordinary shares. The reorganisation brought complex changes in the categories of shares. The holding company was wound up and its shares were distributed. The essential change was that John Astor made over his 90 per cent controlling shares to Gavin Astor; and John Walter made over his 10 per cent shares to his son John. For special reasons, however, both John Astor and John Walter kept the title of Chief Proprietor, ensuring that Astor remained chairman and that both of them were ultimately responsible for policy and for the appointment or dismissal of an editor. This arrangement seemed understandable at the time but, when it was maintained for years, even after Gavin Astor became chairman of the company, both Gavin and his brother Hugh felt that their position was weakened from the start.

In the talks leading up to the agreement John Walter, anxious to preserve the family's link with the paper which it had founded, tried hard to have his son's position made secure for the future. He proposed to John Astor an agreement under which, when Gavin Astor became chairman, John Walter would become deputy chairman and deputy proprietor with appropriate rights and duties. John Astor felt it wrong to tie Gavin's hands, and the proposal was not pursued.

In point of fact the fear which prompted the reorganisation – that John Astor and John Walter might die within five years of the transference of the shares – was happily not borne out. The shares escaped death duties as John Astor lived until 1971 and John Walter until 1968. At all events the families and company had the satisfaction of knowing that they had taken what precautions they could for the future.

Gavin Astor and his brother Hugh, who became a director in 1956, had far less success in another project that could have changed the commercial fortunes of *The Times*. That was when they proposed, after the Independent Television Authority had been established in 1954, that The Times Publishing Company should itself go into television. It should seek a licence to establish a television company or buy shares in one of the companies that were being set up in many parts of Britain. Ironically it was at this time that Roy Thomson, already owner of the *Scotsman* since 1953, was acquiring what he was later to call his 'licence to print money' through his venture in starting Scottish Television;[10] in so doing he laid the basis of his great fortune in Britain which in turn led on to his purchase of *The Times* in 1966. Curiously enough it was Thomson's lieutenant, James Coltart, who first suggested to Hugh Astor an association with television in the north-east of England.[11] Given his philosophy and background Roy Thomson had been all in favour of commercial television in Britain from the moment it started. Given its own philosophy and background *The Times* in general was against it even before it was started.

Gavin and Hugh Astor could make no headway with their arguments. Against them was their father, supported by several members of his Board. Laurence Irving, for one, speaking with his experience of the entertainment industry, told John Astor that the inevitably falling standards of television would hurt the prestige of *The Times* if the paper were in any way concerned with a commercial company. If *The Times* wished, as it should wish, to broaden its interests (Irving said) it should occupy itself with a reputable and enterprising publishing house such as Penguin Books.[12] Other directors pointed out that, financially, some television companies were not yet breaking even. 'We should be sailing in uncharted seas', said Lord Brand at the decisive Board meeting.

The Astor sons were blocked also by the explicit policy of the paper. Haley, as editor, was implacable against any connexion with commercial television. He had come to *The Times* in 1952, first because he was attracted by the job, but secondly because of the threat to his BBC posed by commercial television.[13] He felt that, in competing with its wealthy rival, the BBC which Reith and he had built up to be the envy of the world would have to cheapen itself and he wanted no part in that decline. Very soon after becoming editor he was giving his warnings in

---

10 See Lord Thomson of Fleet, *After I Was Sixty*, Chapter III.
11 Verbal communication by Hugh Astor, April 30 1980.
12 Laurence Irving recalling, in talk with A. P. Ryan on July 28 1970, his conversations with John Astor at the relevant time. T.T.A. Further details given verbally by Irving, June 7 1979.
13 See Chapter IX.

the leader columns of *The Times*. On June 17 1953, when the future structure of broadcasting was thrown open for debate by the report of the Television Advisory Committee, Haley wrote a first leader. The title, 'The Trojan Horse', set the line:

> Television is likely to be one of the most powerful social influences of the next fifty years. It should be as unthinkable to hand it over to sponsoring as it would be to give advertisers a decisive say in school curricula . . .
>
> In the effort to force sponsored television through it is being urged that American experience is no guide, that the likelihood of ill-effects is all a matter of degree, that an issue higher even than those which have been mentioned is involved – the question of freedom. In fact, American experience is a guide. Things could fall short of the worst that has happened there and still be deplorable. And when freedom is invoked, the question must be asked: Freedom to do what? Is that nobler freedom, which is the true sense of the word, more likely to come from a motive force founded on the successful selling of goods, or from a responsible public body directing television as a public service? The prospect is being held out that the British people can have both. For a time this might be true. During some hours, no doubt, the citizens of Troy believed they had preserved their inviolability and gained a horse.

On November 25 1953, after the government had made its proposals known in a White Paper,[14] Haley was stronger in his anger and scorn:

> There are people who sincerely believe that a broadcasting corporation should not have the raising of public taste as its purpose. They are convinced it is both dangerous and antipathetic to so-called democracy; the public should have nothing but what it thinks it wants and no inducement to seek anything better. There are finally those who are incensed with the 'holier than thou' attitude so often alleged against the BBC. It must be taken down a peg at all costs. But surely there are within society enough influences already at work degrading public taste to forbid adding another just for the pleasure of voting against Aristides . . . The forces egging them [the government] on want the educational purpose of broadcasting debased and vulgarity – or, at best, triviality – enthroned.

Such declarations left *The Times* no real freedom of choice. When the paper had come out so fiercely the company could hardly put its hand

---

14 Cmd. 9005.

into the till and draw profits from commercial television. In October 1957 the Board agreed – with only Hugh Astor dissenting – not to apply for a share in independent television. Gavin Astor himself was not at all happy at the decision. He accepted for the company but not for himself. In partnership with his brother Hugh and Sir Michael Balcon, he applied for control of the North-Eastern Television Company. The application did not succeed. The same team, strengthened this time by East Anglian Newspapers, then applied for a licence to run Anglia Television. The Independent Television Authority again refused the application. The disappointment was the keener because of hints that East Anglian Newspapers might be more successful if they left the Astor–Balcon team and joined with the *Manchester Guardian* in applying for a licence. The Astor brothers were left feeling that *Times* policy was the root cause of their defeat. Other newspapers did not have the same scruples as *The Times*. They did not bar themselves from the scramble for licences. They believed that if there was any money to be had they could make good use of it. This dispute over the TV franchise was symptomatic of a wider difference which developed over the role of The Times Publishing Company as a whole, with Gavin and Hugh Astor wishing the company to spread itself into new and profitable fields.

More strongly than before, *The Times* was left needing a new impetus of some kind. In spite of all the improvements under Haley circulation remained stagnant around 220,000–225,000 during the years 1953–56. Competition from other quality papers was sharpening. Worse still, *The Times's* share in the quality circulation was falling. By the second half of 1957 the circulation of the *Daily Telegraph*, at 1,116,000, showed an increase of 12½ per cent over its circulation in 1949. The *Manchester Guardian*, at 172,000, showed an increase of just over 25 per cent in the same period. On the other flank the *Financial Times*, at 84,000, had risen by no less than 40 per cent. In contrast *The Times*, although it had moved up to 235,000 by 1957, was still below its 1949 circulation of 262,000. Advertisers and their agents were becoming harder-headed and more analytical in placing their orders. They worked out the comparative cost, paper by paper, of a column-inch per thousand readers, and in such comparisons *The Times*, with its small circulation and high prestige, was seen to be expensive.

The prospect was that *The Times* itself would make little money for some years. Hugh Astor, for one, believed that the company should branch out in other interests beyond that of newspaper publishing. Beginning with the thought that managing a publishing business was very different from managing a printing business, he considered that the two could profitably be split. The printing manager would then be freer to develop other activities. In particular, he could follow up new methods of technology such as facsimile reproduction which would allow *The Times* to be printed in centres outside London. One result of Hugh Astor's persuasions was that Colin Cadell[15] was brought in as assistant manager with the idea that he should cultivate research and development – an idea that became far less precise when he was diverted to administrative work during the re-building of Printing House Square.[16] In brief, Hugh Astor argued that there could be a group of companies, under a holding company, which could pursue their own activities and provide financial security for *The Times*.

Mathew was reluctant to go so far but none the less pushed ahead on several new lines himself. He was fortunate in having the columns of classified advertisements each week in the *Educational Supplement*; it earned £54,000 in 1957 (and was to earn £251,000 in 1965, the year before the Thomson purchase). In April 1954, helped by the energetic A. W. Tucker of the managerial staff, and advised by a cartographic consultant Mathew began publishing a new five-volume edition of *The Times Atlas of the World*, a fine production that was edited by John Bartholomew, whose firm printed the maps. Within Printing House Square, having started several publications, he launched others such as the monthly *Technology*, begun in March 1957. The atlas made money, but most of the other new publications were financially disappointing.

He had bigger projects that were more successful. In 1957–58 he secured the contract for printing the *Observer* in Printing House Square, an arrangement that was within two years to bring in £750,000 a year. At the same time he persuaded the Board to buy a controlling vote in the shares of Townsend Hook, makers of the special paper used by Printing House Square in preference to newsprint.

In the late fifties the profits from most of such deals still lay ahead, and on the debit side the company was more than half committed to its rebuilding scheme at an estimated cost of £2,500,000.

That was the general background to the heavy shock – one of the heaviest since the war – which the company had to face at the end of the financial year on June 30 1957. The company finished the year with a pre-tax loss of £17,000. After tax and other adjustments the loss was nearly £50,000. On *The Times* alone the pre-tax loss was £79,000. The shock was the greater because of the run of profits in the preceding

---

15 Colin Simpson Cadell (b. 1905). Air Commodore RAF retired. Director of Signals, Air Ministry, 1944–47. Assistant general manager The Times Publishing Company, 1958–62.
16 See Chapter XVII.

years. Before tax they were:

             1948 – £388,000
             1949 – £324,000
             1950 – £345,000
             1951 – £240,000
             1952 – £118,000
             1953 – £173,000
             1954 – £286,000
             1955 – £162,000
             1956 – £323,000
             1957 – *minus* £17,000

To add to that, the prospect for the financial year ending June 30 1958 was little better. This bad news came after circulation of *The Times* had in fact risen during the Suez crisis that began on July 26 1956. Rising circulation, falling profits – it was a paradox that needs some explaining.

First of all, the trading loss in the financial year 1956–57 – covering the months of Suez and the consequent political uncertainty in Britain – shows in the clearest way how the commercial fortunes of *The Times* were affected by national emergencies and swings in the economy. Circulation rose in the summer and autumn of 1956 because more men and women turned to *The Times* as a trustworthy guide to what was happening. Advertising fell off because many industrialists and businessmen felt unable to plan ahead. Unfortunately, in hard cash, the paper could not make up from its increased sales what it lost in the withheld advertisements. The reason lay in the imbalance in its sources of income. It could never be forgotten that three-quarters of the company's total revenue came year by year from the advertisements which it carried. Since the war that revenue had been rising, but in 1956–57 it flattened out. After being £1,841,000 in 1956 (allowing for deductions for expenses and commissions) it moved up to no more than £1,848,000 in 1957. It was a rise of only £7,000 at a time when production costs rose by £197,000: from £1,996,000 in 1956 to £2,193,000 in 1957. All this threw the balance sheet badly wrong.

On the editorial side of the house the rise in circulation was seen as wholly heartening and flattering. Total circulation, which had slipped down to 218,000 in January 1956, rose to 235,000 by the end of the financial year in June 1957. Yet even this substantial rise brought its financial complications. Normally, as noted earlier, the advertisement revenue paid for most of the cost of publishing each copy of *The Times*, and allowed for some profit. But the rates charged by the company for the advertisements did not rise, and could not rise, automatically with a rise in circulation. Due and proper notice had to be given, well ahead, to the advertisers that rates were going to be increased; and until the increases took effect the company lost money on each extra copy which it printed. After the Suez crisis of July 1956 the rates were not put up until September 1957; they then rose from £8 a column inch to £9.10s. In the meantime *The Times* swung from profit to loss.

The year 1956–57 posed, more sharply than other years had done, the question that was always being discussed within Printing House Square. How could *The Times* be made strong enough to ride safely over the rises and falls in the economy? Finding the answer was becoming urgent.

The night of May 2/3 1966. First copies of the first edition of *The Times* with news on the front page. Left to right: The Hon. Gavin Astor, Henry Smith (night production manager), Fred Park (works manager), Sir William Haley, Lady Irene Astor, George Pope.

The Times – editorial conference 1966 (left to right) Sir William Haley (editor), I. McDonald (managing editor), O. Woods (deputy managing editor), F. Roberts (home news editor), J. Grant (home editor), J. Caminada (foreign news editor), J. Bishop (features editor), E. McHardy (night editor), N. Hall (pictures), O. Hickey (special writer), S. Puddefoot (editor, woman's page), K. Brookes (foreign sub editor), J. Hennessy (sports editor), W. Clarke (finance and industrial editor), D. Holmes (co-ordinating editor), A. P. Ryan (assistant editor), C. Watson (obituaries), G. Woolley (letters), A. Stovold (circulation manager), E. Russell (chief home sub editor), E. C. Hodgkin (foreign editor).

Donald Tyerman and Francis Mathew.

Henry Moore O.M. (right) explains the sundial designed by him and erected in the forecourt of the new Printing House Square building. Others in the group (left to right) The Hon. Gavin Astor, The Hon. Kenneth Thomson, Sir William Haley, Lord Llewelyn-Davies.

New ownership and old: Lord Thomson of Fleet and the Hon. Hugh Astor.

Lord Thomson of Fleet and Denis Hamilton.

Richard Harris ('Student of Asia'). Frank Giles, correspondent in Rome and Paris.

The new Board of Times Newspapers, January 1967. Left to right: Kenneth Keith, James Coltart, the Hon. K. R. Thomson, Sir Eric Roll, George Pope, Lord Robens, G. C. Rowett, Sir Donald Anderson, W. Macleod (acting secretary), Sir William Haley, Denis Hamilton, Lord Shawcross, G. C. Brunton.

The Times – noon editorial conference, summer 1967. Left to right: J. Caminada (foreign news editor), J. D. Bishop (features editor), C. Webb (home news reporter), E. C. Hodgkin (assistant editor and foreign editor), J. Hennessy (sports editor), S. Puddefoot (woman's page editor), C. Winchcombe (maps), P. Davis (deputy foreign news editor), W. Rees-Mogg (editor), I. Trewin (diary editor), M. Cudlipp (assistant editor night), J. Petty (day news editor, business news), D. Holmes (production editor), H. Stanhope (home news reporter), K. Smith (assistant pictures editor), P. Evans (head of news team).

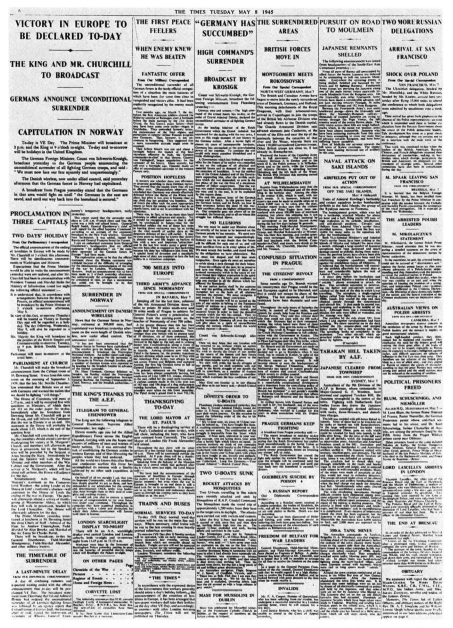

The end of the war in Europe, showing the old style main news ('bill') page before news on the front page in 1966.

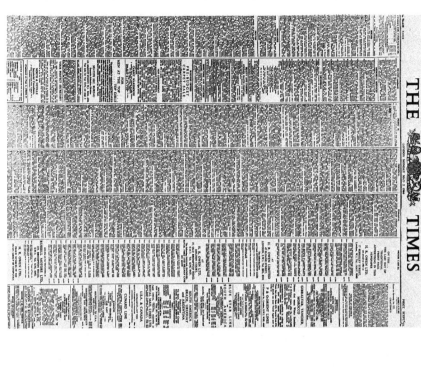

Advertisements appear on the front page for the last time, May 2 1966.

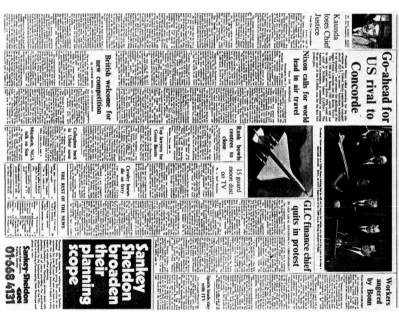

A new-look front page with eight columns, September 24 1969.

XVI

MEETING THE COMPETITION

IN the late fifties The Times Publishing Company sought in three ways to overcome its financial problems and counter the competition from other papers. It invited an inquiry from outside into methods of improving its managerial organisation; it embarked on an expensive publicity campaign; and it offered better conditions of service in order to stop a heavy drift of talented young journalists away from *The Times*.

The outside inquiry was begun at the suggestion of Gavin and Hugh Astor, supported by two more directors, Sir Harold Hartley and Sir David Bowes-Lyon. From the early fifties the two Astor brothers had warnings from their own financial advisers about the company's vulnerability. In the autumn of 1957, after the sad results of the financial year that ended the previous June, John Astor agreed that Cooper Brothers and Company, chartered accountants in the City of London, should carry out 'a review of the organisation, administration and financial position of The Times Publishing Company Limited.'[1] The Cooper representatives began the work in December. For over two months, led by the much experienced Henry Benson, they analysed many financial statements freely given them by the management. They interviewed the editor, the manager, and heads of department on both sides of the house. At the end, in February 1958, they presented a tightly written report of 199 paragraphs with seven appendices. Their warnings were urgent.

Their main argument was that the management needed reform in a number of ways which they specified. Mathew and Pope, they argued, had too much work to do. Mathew required at least two more assistant managers, and one of the new men should be young enough and able enough to be a likely successor to Mathew when the time came. Pope should drop all other work and concentrate on his main job of getting the advertisements which *The Times* so badly needed if it was to

---

1 T.T.A.

develop. In addition, the company secretary (P. E. Clarke)[2] should be in effect an assistant manager in charge of personnel. Further still, and more controversially, men of experience and knowledge should be appointed to be directors on the Board and they should concern themselves more closely than earlier directors had done in company management. 'There is no system of budgetary control in force in the company at the present time.' The accountants' department, though well staffed, tended (it was said) to produce careful details about the present rather than projections into the future.

A strong argument throughout the report was that *The Times* would not get the advertisements it needed unless the circulation was very materially increased. Could not more papers be sent to the north and west? The manager, it was noted, had been authorised by the Board to spend money on publicity. Better results were likely to be attained, the report suggested, if any further large expenditure on publicity could be postponed until it could coincide with the launching of a re-fashioned *Times*. Here the writers of the report adopted a very wide interpretation of their terms of reference. They listed several ideas for examination: news on the front page, less ponderous writing, more special features, shorter news stories, less space for leading articles. Thus organised and armed, they believed, *The Times* could set a circulation target of 400,000 within five years and 600,000 within ten.

They ended with a chilly warning:

We do not overstate the position by saying that unless there is a radical improvement, the future of 'The Times' is now in jeopardy. No business can survive for long if it makes losses and vigorous steps are necessary if profits are to be earned by the company in the future.

The immediate impact of the report among the very few who received copies – that is to say, the directors, the editor, the manager, and one or two of their lieutenants – was later described by Gavin Astor: 'If a bomb had fallen on Printing House Square it could not have caused more disturbance.'[3] Francis Mathew felt that he was being personally attacked and John Astor shared his belief that two or three directors (they had Sir Harold Hartley and Sir David Bowes-Lyon chiefly in mind) would use the report as support for the criticisms which they had already raised against Mathew.

Soon, however, there came the second and more useful result. The

2 Peter Ethelston Clarke (1916–75). Eton; King's College, Cambridge. Assistant to company secretary, The Times Publishing Company, 1951; company secretary, 1955–66; syndication department, *The Times*, 1967–69.
3 Gavin Astor, private memorandum, June 26 1978. T.T.A.

Board asked Gavin Astor to chair a small sub-committee, later known as the Cooper committee, to examine the report in detail with the manager and to put forward any proposals for managerial reform, circulation, and publicity which they thought necessary. The members under Gavin Astor were Hugh Astor, John Walter Junior, Sir Miles Graham and, when possible, Sir David Bowes-Lyon. The group met frequently and received an extraordinary number of memoranda from the managerial side. One of the very first, and one of the longest, was from Stanley Morison.[4] As historian, typographer and, more recently, unofficial adviser to Mathew, he felt himself to be *custos custodium* of *The Times's* conscience and traditions. That conscience and those traditions he thought to be assailed by Cooper Brothers. Encouraged by John Astor and Mathew, though he needed little prompting from anyone, he declared with all his rhetorical force that *The Times* was an organ of the governing class and of that class alone:

A country like Great Britain depends for its administrative efficiency upon its politically intelligent and professional men; these in turn depend upon *The Times* for the material upon which to reflect and, ultimately, act.

On May 22 Morison produced a shortened version, arguing that, as '*The Times* participates in government', it must have a unique constitution which gave special freedom to both editor and manager:

Although *The Times* can exist and even flourish without the present Directors, it can do neither without its Manager and its Editor.[5]

In playing down the role of the directors Morison did no service to Mathew at that time. In fact, as John Astor made clear in a memorandum, there was no constitutional warrant for such managerial independence. Astor recapitulated the heads of agreement which he had made with John Walter in 1922:

Outside editorial policy the conduct of the business of the Company would be the responsibility of the Chief Proprietors and directors acting as a Board . . . I am sure I have always regarded the directors as legally responsible for the Company's business.[6]

In his own early memoranda Mathew wisely kept off the constitutional point but did not conceal his indignation at some of Cooper

4 Morison to John Astor *et al*, April 1958. This memorandum is unsigned in the available copy but has marks in Morison's handwriting. T.T.A.
5 Morison memorandum, May 22 1958. T.T.A.
6 Memorandum, John Astor to the directors, July 8 1958. T.T.A.

Brothers' comments, tactfully framed though they were. In particular he picked on Cooper Brothers' approving use of the phrase 'the reading public' and on their arguments that if *The Times* had kept the share of the national daily newspaper circulation which it had in 1915 (it then had 5.56 per cent) instead of letting it fall to its 1957 level of 1.54 per cent it would have had a circulation of 890,000 in 1957:

> Their deductions are based on a fundamental misconception of the function of The Times. The Times is *not* published for 'THE READING PUBLIC', as such. It is published for a highly special-ised and unique audience . . . Every other national newspaper is projected essentially on the mass market or a section of it, as a market which has grown from 3¼ to 16 million in 43 years. Had The Times adopted a policy of seeking a share in the mass market early in the 1930s, the Morning Post might have survived to this day and taken the place of The Times as the organ of the governing class . . .

Advertisements and advertisement rates were geared to a readership among the governing class:

> The new market – THE READING PUBLIC – coming as it presumably would from the Daily Telegraph, would not command a penny above our existing advertising rates as far as advertisers were concerned. Our present rates would only be comparable with those of the Daily Telegraph on reaching a circulation of 800,000.

In other memoranda Mathew strongly defended his expenditure on publicity for the paper. True enough, he wrote, circulation went up during the Suez crisis, but it began dropping in the first days of 1957 and was resumed again only as a direct result of his publicity campaign, launched in that same month of January.

With hardly less warmth Pope defended his advertisements depart-ment. In a memorandum of May 5, and in a personal statement before Gavin Astor's Cooper committee a few days later, he showed that over the previous six years there had been steady increases in the three main classes of advertisements: classified, financial, and display. The last had gone up from 2,208 columns in 1951 to 5,392 columns in 1956. In fact it was only in classified advertisements that the *Daily Telegraph* was greatly ahead of *The Times*, carrying 170,775 inches in 1957 against the 124,192 inches in *The Times*. (These advertisements, including jobs vacant, were of course especially useful in attracting new readers for the paper.) In financial advertising the *Telegraph* carried 1,382 columns, well below the 2,380 columns in *The Times*; and in display advertising the two papers were almost exactly equal, the *Telegraph* having 5,787 columns and *The Times* 5,786. With a larger staff Pope was confident that he could bring in more classified advertisements.[7] (Gavin Astor's committee itself, in its final report, was to point out that though the rise in advertisement revenue was gratifying and highly commendable *The Times* had doubled in size during those same years and the value of the pound had halved.)

After receiving more memoranda, and having held many meetings, Gavin Astor's committee presented to the Board its own long report dated January 27 1959.[8] Hugh Astor wrote much of the draft at the end of 1958. By that time anxiety about the paper was deeper than when the Cooper report was being prepared. Although the company as a whole was showing a small profit, *The Times* newspaper itself had followed its loss of £151,000 in 1957 with another loss of approximately £130,000 in 1958.

Taking a broad look at the company the Cooper committee agreed that *The Times* was not likely to make much money until, at some distant date, it had a much larger circulation; but the committee was convinced that the company itself could be made profitable by expanding its other businesses such as printing the *Observer* (the contract had just been secured) and publishing of various kinds. Looking a little more closely, the committee accepted many of Cooper Brothers' points about methods of work in the office, the remoteness of the Board from the staff, and the aloofness of departments from each other. The committee's own recommendations may be summarised:

There should be a fresh appraisal of the contents and appearance of *The Times*, though the committee did not like the thought of news on the front page instead of the classified advertisements. Such a change would lose a regular source of advertisements and might too easily show up the lateness of news in the regional editions.

The Saturday morning issue of the paper should be enlarged and brightened, thereby drawing in more advertisements; and the *Weekly Review* should also be made brighter and more popular.

The manager should certainly be given more high-grade assistants.

To ensure closer liaison among managerial departments the manager's own discussion committee (which had already been established some months before and was made up of his principal executives) should be strengthened.

---

7 Unaddressed memorandum by Pope, May 5 1958. Also Cooper committee minutes, May 22 1958. T.T.A.
8 T.T.A.

Expenditure on publicity should be reduced until a well-prepared campaign could coincide with the launching of a re-designed *Times*.

More favourable terms for the Townsend Hook paper (dearer than newsprint) should be sought, as had been suggested by Cooper Brothers.

On February 5 1959, on a motion proposed by Gavin Astor and seconded by Lord Brand, the Board unanimously accepted the committee's report. Mathew (not a member of the Board though present at this meeting as at all others) said straight away that he could not accept some points in the report and would give his reasons in later discussions.

The editorial side had not yet been heard. It had every reason to take the Cooper report quietly. For one thing it was not in the main line of fire. For another, many of the Cooper proposals were precisely what had already been done or what were already being discussed on the editorial side. To that extent such Cooper proposals were pushing against an open door. Others were disregarded by the editorial as being irrelevant. But at the Board meeting on February 5 Haley was asked to give a memorandum under the general heading, 'How the editor sees it'. His answer was admirably designed: firm in presenting the editorial requirements, clear in setting the aims which *The Times* should have before it, conciliatory in soothing ruffled feelings, conciliatory also in suggesting that the time had come to move on from Cooper and its repercussions.

Haley said that *The Times* must have three purposes. It had to be:
(i)   A journal of record.
(ii) A daily paper which plays a useful part in the running of the country.
(iii) A balanced, interesting and entertaining paper for intelligent readers of all ages and classes.

In trying to fulfil those purposes *The Times* needed, before all else, more editorial space in the paper. How could it compete with other great newspapers of the world when it had only 14 pages on some days of the week, with perhaps six columns for home news and six for foreign? The *Neue Zürcher Zeitung* ranged between 36 and 96 pages. The *New York Times* had 217 columns as the editorial minimum (where *The Times* had 50 or 60 columns). Within such limits *The Times* could not claim to be a complete newspaper.

If a larger paper was to be the Board's first objective then the prime requirement in reaching it, said Haley, was to have more advertisements. Larger papers would mean more profitable papers because they could carry a higher proportion of advertising; and more space would allow the readers to be better informed by reports from a larger staff at home and abroad. The need at home was obvious. 'The *Daily Telegraph* has 40 general reporters in London, *The Times* 13. The *Daily Telegraph* has 20 staff in the Provinces, *The Times* 3.' The discrepancy should not be so great if *The Times* was to do its duty to its readers:

> We cannot hold our own, let alone progress, without more space. And we shall be heading for very serious trouble indeed, if circumstances force us to have less space. For that reason, I view the proposal in the Cooper Brothers' report that when papers are small the Editorial's share should be cut down in order to maintain a fixed ratio of advertising with very great alarm. *The Times* just could not fulfil its three purposes were that to happen.

Out of many other points which Haley made two in particular stand out. First, his reminder that editorial salaries should be further improved led him to speak of the challenge in salaries and in news services, coming with increasing force from the wealthy television companies; this led him to look at the imbalance of expenditure between the editorial and production sides within newspaper offices. Looking some years ahead he said:

> There is going to be a need to change the balance of newspaper expenditure. We are going to have, somehow or other, to change production methods so completely that more money can be devoted to editorial requirements. It will no longer be possible to run the editorial on 20 per cent of our total expenditure unless the turnover is greatly increased.

(Here Haley touched on the dilemma which led to the struggle fought by *The Times* and *The Sunday Times* in 1978–79.)

Secondly, Haley avoided setting any figure as the target for circulation. What mattered was not the distant goal but the continuous effort:

> Whether our ultimate sale will be 300,000, 350,000, or 500,000 is a matter that can be left to future circumstances. I would prefer us to be always after just the next 50,000.

In other words he did not seek a revolutionary change in the form or content of the newspaper, but a steady improvement and expansion.

The main achievement of the Cooper inquiry was to bring forward the need to raise standards and qualifications on the managerial side and to provide Mathew with more help. As a small outward sign of the process the simple traditional title, manager of *The Times*, disappeared and Mathew became general manager of The Times Publishing Company; the change might seem simply to be in line with the contemporary fashion for inflating titles but Gavin Astor, for one, intended it to show that the company was proposing to broaden itself. Pope became the senior assistant general manager; he was to concern himself not only with advertisements, to which Cooper Brothers would have confined him, but with publicity and circulation. Colin Cadell was appointed assistant general manager in charge of planning and development, though he found that he had to concern himself chiefly with re-building.[9] R. J. H. Pollock[10] became assistant general manager in charge of periodicals in 1963, and Theodore Cauter[11] was given charge of advertising in 1964 when Pope took on still heavier duties. At the end of 1958 Roger Harrison,[12] who had been on the staff for twelve months, was moved to the operational research department and in 1960 became head of it. Another young recruit, Rodney Fraser,[13] was appointed supplements manager in 1959 and became circulation manager in 1961. In most of these changes the incoming man had higher academic and professional qualifications than his predecessor had.

The Cooper report also led to changes in managerial methods of work. Even before the Cooper committee reported a system of tighter budgetary control was introduced after a resolution passed by the Board on July 10 1958. Monthly profit-and-loss accounts were to be produced, though Haley's point – that the editorial side could work only on an annual budget – was well taken.

Another result arose out of remarks made by Cooper Brothers on the high cost of the Townsend Hook paper used in Printing House

9 The original plan for Cadell's work is discussed in Chapter XV.

10 Ralph John Hamilton Pollock (b. 1921). Wellington; Trinity College, Cambridge. Senior managerial positions with *Readers Digest*, 1950–60; European production director *Newsweek*, 1962–63. Assistant general manager (periodicals) The Times Publishing Company, 1963–66.

11 Theodore V. Cauter (b. 1915). London School of Economics. Executive vice-president, Marplan International, 1963–64. Assistant general manager (advertising) The Times Publishing Company, 1964–65; deputy general manager, 1965–67.

12 Desmond Roger Wingate Harrison (b. 1933). Rugby; Worcester College, Oxford. The Times Publishing Company managerial staff, 1957; head of operational research department, 1960–62; head of stationery and special publications, 1962–65; promotion manager, 1966–67.

13 Rodney Ivor Fraser (1919–1974). Stowe. *Evening News*, 1946–50; *Star*, 1951–54; *Time and Tide*, 1954–56. The Times Publishing Company managerial staff, 1956; supplements manager, 1959–61; circulation manager, 1961–63; assistant general manager (circulation), 1963–64.

Square. After talks among Sir David Bowes-Lyon, Godfrey Phillips and Townsend Hook representatives the prices was reduced from 5 per cent above the London cost of newsprint to 2½ per cent above that cost. The interest on outstanding bills was also reduced.[14]

Yet another result was much broader and is harder to define. Merely by being passed round and discussed the report gave a fresh stir to the simmering problem of how *The Times* should be brought up to date. It may seem strange to later observers that the prod was not more effective at the time. The truth is that many of the suggestions bounced back off two strong conservative forces within the office: a belief that only *Times* men could know what *The Times* should do, and a still firmer belief – held by the two chief proprietors among others – that any changes should be slow and cautious. The combination of the two forces helped to build up a sense of resentment in face of Cooper. Some reforms, rather than being advanced, were held up, and the paper lost thereby. Nothing was gained by delaying for five years the start of the great push for modernisation and development.[15] They were years of intense competition among newspapers when every month counted. The Monopolies Commission in 1966 was itself puzzled by the long delay in beginning the drive within *The Times*.[16]

'Top People Take *The Times*. Do You?' The watchword became famous in the late fifties, as a result of Francis Mathew's publicity campaign. Gavin Astor's committee had endorsed Cooper Brothers' view that further expenditure should be reduced until a re-modelled *Times* appeared. Yet the publicity machine was already moving. As far back as May 10 1956 the Board had been troubled to see that, though *The Times* had become brighter and more newsy, the circulation remained stagnant at around 220,000: this was just before the Suez crisis. The Board therefore decided that the paper should advertise itself. On June 14 1956 it allocated the sum of £300,000 to be spread over three years. In fact the sum was spent in two years, and a further £100,000 was given for 1959. Mathew coordinated the campaign with his assistant managers, helped by Rodney Fraser, then rising on the managerial side, and G. H. Saxon Mills, who was in fact the campaign organiser. From January 14 1957 onwards striking posters portraying simplified figures of Top People with *The Times* under their arm appeared at strategic points in Britain. They were the work of Jean Carlu, Paris. Advertisements for *The Times* along similar lines

---

14 Minutes, Board meeting, July 10 1958.
15 See Chapter XXI.
16 See Chapter XXIII.

appeared in rival newspapers. Canvassing was done by direct mail. The *Literary* and *Educational* supplements and magazines such as *Technology* were brought into the movement. The planning was exact, the launching vigorous, and the main purpose was kept always in sight – to demonstrate that *The Times* was a newspaper which no responsible man or woman could afford to miss. In a second phase of the campaign the message was changed to appeal to a younger generation: 'Top People of Tomorrow Take *The Times*.'

The change of emphasis in the campaign was due partly to representations by Haley and others on the editorial side. They intensely disliked the snobbish Top People appeal, believing that it went clean contrary to all that they had been doing to attract a broader and younger range of readers to the paper. Haley expressed his doubts and dislike in a memorandum to Mathew on November 23 1956, a few hours after learning the details of the campaign. On January 22 1957 he told Mathew, again in a note, that his own doubts were echoed by those of many readers. He repeated this on March 10. Sharper still was a memorandum of May 23 1957:

> Don't you feel we really ought to stop and ask ourselves whether it is worth our while to go on offending people's sense of what *The Times* ought to stand for? It is rather distressing to find how many people think the less of us since the Campaign began.

The editor became reconciled to the campaign only as the Top People were demoted and the appeal was broadened. Later designs were by Beatrice Warde and the London Press Exchange. The manager himself could point to the rising circulation figures in support of his conviction that the general strategy and tactics were right. Writing to the Board in 1958, in the middle of all the stresses created by the Cooper report, he was particularly glad to record his success:

> When the Board approved in June, 1956, the expenditure of £300,000 on a publicity campaign for *The Times* the net sale figure stood at 220,700. The quarterly net sales from that date were as follows:

1956	Jul–Sept	218,400
	Oct–Dec	226,900
1957	Jan–Mar	230,800
	Apr–Jun	234,600
	Jul–Sept	235,900
	Oct–Dec	243,100
1958	Jan–Mar	247,700
	Apr–Jun	249,000 (estimated)

No other national daily newspaper can show a consistent rise in sales, quarter by quarter, over the same two years . . .

In two years home sales of The Times have risen by 30,000 copies (15%). In April/May 1956 I estimated it would cost £10 a reader and take three years to achieve this result. It was with this in mind that I asked the Board for £300,000. In fact we have reached this target in two years at a cost of £8.13s.4d a reader.[17]

At the end no one could deny that the much criticised campaign had produced results. It had passed the one unfailing test: it had got *The Times* talked about.

On the editorial side Haley and his chief lieutenants discussed every possible idea for developing the paper and meeting the competition of others. The main line of their effort is summed up in a memorandum from Haley to the foreign editor months before the Cooper inquiry was thought of:[18]

The main impression is that *The Times* is predominantly a political paper. Politics are undoubtedly important. The world has probably never been on the boil in so many places at once . . . At the same time the world is struggling to move away from any exclusive pre-occupation with politics. This is particularly true of the new generation. There is a growing interest everywhere in science, in technology, in economics, in artistic movements and so on in all lands.

The first serious newspaper which wakes up to this trend and deliberately sets out developing it, will lead the way. *The Times* should be that paper. We should make a deliberate move in that direction. Correspondents abroad should be told that we want *The Times* to report significant developments in their country as a whole, covering all the fields I have mentioned above.

In point of fact, both McDonald and Gerald Norman, the foreign news editor, had already asked correspondents many times to send precisely such non-political despatches, and the correspondents had willingly complied. It was not only the foreign side that was changing: all departments were caught up in the day-by-day drive. The pressure was great on Haley himself and those nearest to him in the office. It was one of the news editors who said that Haley, regularly working fourteen or

---

17 Memorandum, Mathew to all directors, May 30 1958. T.T.A.
18 T.T.A.

sixteen hours a day, always seemed mildly surprised that others should
wilt after twelve hours. Some slight indication of the pressure appears in
a memorandum which Haley wrote to the assistant editors on December
15 1958:

> The re-building of Printing House Square over the next three years
> has to be lived with and paid for. A general election is in the offing.
> There are also Berlin, the Common Market's effects, new tensions
> in the Middle East, and growing crisis in Africa . . . 1959 will be a
> challenging year for us. We shall be fully stretched. It is an exhilerat-
> ing prospect.[19]

All that was very true, even though those who had to read the memorandum could not quite banish the thought that taking on one exhausting
challenge after another is apt to be rather more exhilerating to the man
who leads than to the team who loyally respond behind the leader.

The pressure at the top had an unexpected and unwelcome result. It
was one of the reasons that led some of the best young men, especially
on the foreign side, to look around for other work outside *The Times*. In
talks with the foreign editor and others they frankly said that promotion
to one of the top jobs did not attract them, promising as it did the
certainty of at least twelve hours' intense work each day. That was only
one of the reasons for resignations, but it counted. As the late fifties and
early sixties brought more resignations of ill-to-spare men Haley,
Mathew, and the assistant editors had to find out and counter the causes
for the departures.

Earlier than the others had been the resignation of Peregrine
Worsthorne to join the *Daily Telegraph* in 1953. The main movement
was signalled in 1956 when James Morris – the Morris of Everest –
departed; then Frank Giles left the Paris office in 1960 to be foreign
editor of *The Sunday Times*; Gerald Norman resigned his post as foreign
news editor to join the BBC. In some ways the most startling departure
was David Holden's. With high hopes by the office he had been given
the newly created job of roving correspondent, yet within a few months,
after supremely good work in Africa, he picked up his bags in 1960 to go
off and divide his time between the *Guardian* and broadcasting. Others
to leave were Nockolds, motoring correspondent, to edit the *Motor*;
Godfrey Hodgson, Roger Toulmin (Delhi correspondent, also to join
the BBC in 1959), John Shakespeare (foreign news room who went to
the Foreign Office), John Ardagh (Paris, who went to the *Observer*),
John White (Africa correspondent, and then Tokyo, who went to the

---

19 T.T.A.

Overseas Development Institute), Christopher Johnson (to the *Financial Times*), and Jeremy Wolfenden, who was in Paris after being in the foreign news room and in 1960 joined the *Daily Telegraph*, partly because the *Telegraph* was ready to send him to Moscow; he had long hoped *The Times* would send him there. In a very different and higher category was Maurice Green's decision in 1961 to leave to become deputy editor of the *Daily Telegraph*; after several years as Haley's deputy he had little hesitation in accepting the promise of succession to Sir Colin Coote as the editor of the *Telegraph*.

The drain was no less severe in the City office. In late 1960 Haley was told by the City editor that six good men had left, or were leaving, at a time when City space had increased from 14 columns a day in 1958 to 19–21 columns. Salary scales, he said, were inadequate.[20]

Other papers took a predictable pleasure in *The Times's* losses. On March 9 1961 *Time and Tide* had a long article under the heading 'Clearing House Square'. After some quiet fun it ended on a note of advice to Haley:

Even though so many of his best horses have fled, Sir William can still do something to bolt the stable door.

As far back as 1956 Haley had told Mathew that James Morris's departure was a warning to the office. '*The Times* ought to be in a position to keep the men it wants to keep.' The traditional prestige of working for *The Times*, he said, was no longer everything for a talented young man: money and prospects also came in.[21] After this intervention by Haley some salaries moved up and men and women were allowed to broadcast more often than before, though they still had to ask permission each time to do so. But, with further resignations, the foreign editor told the editor at the end of 1960 that salaries were still too low, the anonymity rule (still enforced on all staff men) was more than ever galling, increased competition brought more offers of attractive jobs elsewhere, and other papers could afford to send more men more quickly to special assignments.[22]

After Holden resigned in December 1960 he wrote a frank letter to the foreign editor saying he did not like leaving *The Times* which he respected, but he disliked black Africa, wanted a more stable base, considered the anonymity rule was long out of date, and thought Printing House Square too tightly organised and too stuffy and formal,

---

20 Memorandum, W. M. Clarke to Haley, November 24 1960. T.T.A.
21 Memorandum, Haley to Mathew, April 16 1956. T.T.A.
22 Memorandum, McDonald to Haley, December 8 1960. T.T.A.

certainly for the younger men. Then, on a note struck by others when leaving:

> Please believe me that I am terribly grateful for the opportunities *The Times* has given me, and that I really love the damned old thing – in a way, perhaps, that I shall never love another.[23]

Haley put the case for remedial action strongly in his next half-yearly report to the Board.[24] He pointed out that while *The Times* had sent only one man (Holden himself) to cover the Congo fighting, some other papers sent five. *The Times* sent one man to Ethiopia; other papers sent three by different routes in the expectation that one at least would get through:

> This question of resources also curiously affects their attitude towards a career. The dour responsibilities and desk-bound arduousness of some of their superiors seem to them no ultimate compensation for the loss of the excitement, movement, and freedom which jobs elsewhere seem to offer. What they see in Printing House Square seems to them a poor incentive to go up the ladder.

This was plain speaking, leading to the conclusion that more money was needed to keep the best of the younger staff and maintain the pace that was being forced on *The Times*. The Board's immediate response did much to end the worst of the drain. At the January 12 Board meeting the editorial budget was increased by £75,000 or 10 per cent. The impact of this was soon felt in higher salaries, greater mobility for correspondents, and a greater feeling of confidence in Printing House Square and abroad. Staff members were also given greater freedom to have their names published, not in *The Times*, but when writing occasional articles elsewhere or giving broadcasts. The vow of poverty had gone many years before. Now the vow of silence was weakening.

The three special means by which the management sought to meet the increased competition – the Cooper inquiry, the Top People campaign, and the remedies for staff resignations – led to gains that could be clearly monitored. In the five relevant years the circulation of the paper rose from 220,700 in June 1956 to an average of 260,000 in January–June 1961. The reorganised and strengthened management produced profits at or near to £250,000 for three years in succession. Far fewer men resigned on the editorial side. Modest progress, it none the less seemed solid.

---

23 Letter from Kampala, Holden to McDonald, January 2 1961. T.T.A.
24 T.T.A.

XVII

SO FAIR A HOUSE

ABRIEF ceremony on June 8 1961, inaugurating the rebuilding of Printing House Square, marked a confident new beginning for the company. So it seemed at the time. Lord Astor of Hever[1] and John Walter IV, the two chief proprietors, tipped a little concrete into the foundations on which were to rest the light and airy buildings that were taking the place of the Victorian fortress wherein *The Times* had been printed for the past 87 years. The talk that June day was of *The Times* living long and prosperously in offices that would express the modernity for which the paper itself was striving. Yet many of the day's assumptions were soon to be upset.

Within a year of the concrete-pouring a change in the tax laws forced Lord Astor to leave Britain and live in France. Within two years the last Walter holdings in the Times Publishing Company had been sold to Gavin Astor, who had succeeded his father as chairman in 1959. Within a little more than five years *The Times* had another owner altogether in Roy Thomson,[2] and within thirteen years – ten years after the new building was completed – *The Times* had left the place and been settled next to *The Sunday Times* in Gray's Inn Road.

The decision to rebuild on the old site at Blackfriars had been taken before the war and John Astor was especially eager to complete the job when peace came. He had a strong ally in Francis Mathew who thought in 1954 that a new complex could be built for no more than £1,900,000. Lord Brand, always one of the shrewdest of the directors, believed that costs would escalate. Haley as editor was never keen on putting so much money into rebuilding, even at the lowest estimate. The existing buildings, he said more than once, could be made satisfactory at a cost of £500,000 at the outside. But no one could deny that departments, managerial as well as editorial, were scattered about the buildings in the oddest of manners, and many of them had obviously the need for more

1 John Astor was created a baron in 1956.
2 For his character and career, see Chapter XXIII.

space, more light, and generally a more modern setting for work. Printing House Square presented too much of the old-fashioned image which *The Times* as a newspaper was trying to shed.

Two large questions were decided in the fifties. First an idea of having a tall building on the Printing House square site – tall enough to have floors which could be let at a profit – came up against objections from the City Corporation. A *Times* Board meeting was told on March 22 1956 that such a building would spoil the view of St. Paul's Cathedral from the south-west.[3] The new building would have to be no more than seven storeys high. Secondly, two years later, a plan to move bodily from Printing House Square and build elsewhere had to be dropped. Mathew was at one time attracted by a site near Cannon Street railway station. But expense ruled it out. Printing House Square it would have to remain.

Thereafter plans moved forward speedily. Mr. Richard Llewelyn-Davies[4] was appointed consultant architect, to be joined by his partner John Weeks.[5] Messrs. Ellis, Clarke and Gallannough were the executive architects. Llewelyn-Davies produced his first models on October 23 1958 and on January 1959 Cadell tabled estimates of the cost: £1,970,864 in all. The cost, it was decided, would be met out of current revenue, spread over the years and helped out, if need be, by a bank overdraft.[6]

The moment that the decision to go ahead was given the snags began to be struck. For a start, the architects had to plan the construction work in a place where intensive work was going on round the clock, seven days a week; the *Observer* had to be printed as well as *The Times*. Every phase had to be carefully timed with the help of George Moore,[7] who was appointed liaison officer between the architect, the builders, and everyone else in the venture. Men and desks had to be repeatedly moved as one set of rooms was demolished at the side of them and others built.

Then it was found that the actual Printing House Square, the small area within the old complex of buildings, belonged not to *The Times* but to the City of London. Mathew had to speed off to arrange for its

---

3 Board meeting minutes, March 27 1958. T.T.A.
4 Richard Llewelyn-Davies (1912–1981). Senior partner, Llewelyn-Davies Weeks. Professor of Urban Planning, University College, London. Baron, 1963.
5 John Weeks (b. 1921). Specialist in teaching hospital design and health service planning. Co-director, Llewelyn-Davies Weeks.
6 Board meeting minutes, June 12 and October 23 1958.
7 William George Ronald Moore (b. 1907). *The Times Weekly Edition*, advertising department, 1946; advertising manager, 1949; assistant circulation manager The Times Publishing Company, 1954; administrative officer, 1959–72.

purchase. Thereupon the painful decision had to be taken to pull down the so-called Private House on the western side of the square. The house still kept much of the air which it had when the Walter family lived in it during the early years of the newspaper. Within it were the board room, the chairman's and vice-chairman's offices, and the editorial dining room. The whole house was as much a part of *Times* life as the officers' mess is part of a regiment's tradition. In the end the decision to have it down was taken with regret but with little opposition. It was in fact one of the very first buildings to go when the demolition squads moved in on March 31 1960, a few weeks before the main work began.[8]

Some departments not directly connected with the day-to-day production of the paper escaped the worst of the upheaval, being moved out to Textile House on Ludgate Hill and to other buildings. For those that remained conditions soon became worse than during the Blitz. The noise and the dust were appalling. Men and women wrote their articles, or dictated or telephoned, or shouted to make each other heard in conference, while trying wholly without success to shut their ears to the machine-gun yell of automatic drills and to the sudden crash – especially unnerving for the younger secretaries – as heavy iron balls were swung against the stoutest of the brick walls, making other walls in the building shake with the shock. The leading article in a special supplement issued at the end admitted that there had been 'a certain amount of discomfort – and much more troublesome noise than had been foreseen'. The commotion went on intermittently for two years, and then came another two years of rather less stress while the *Times* staff could watch and hear at close quarters the building of the wing which was to accommodate the *Observer*.

No issue showed any mark of the strain, so far as could be told. But what was galling for many on the editorial side was the thought that if a half, or even a quarter, of the financial cost of the new building had been put to editorial development and sales promotion *The Times* would, beyond all doubt, have made a far better showing in its news and features during the crucial years of fierce competition from other serious newspapers.

As Lord Brand and others had predicted, the original estimate of the cost was overtaken by rising prices of labour and material. Expensive new machinery was needed to cope with the demands of the fast

---

8 Messrs. Ove Arup and Partners were the consulting structural engineers, Sydney C. Gordon and Partners were the quantity surveyors, and the vast work of construction was given to a City firm established a few years before *The Times* itself; Messrs. Trollope and Colls Limited, founded in 1778. Later Professor Misha Black became design consultant, chiefly responsible for the interior.

expanding *Observer*. In his annual report for the year 1965, when the whole work was over, Gavin Astor stated that the total cost had been £4,614,000 – £3m. for the building and furniture, and £1.6m. for the new plant. The original hope that the scheme could be financed out of current revenue had rested on the assumption that profits would reach at least £500,000 a year. As the work went on, profits fell short of that target, and it had been necessary to call on Barclays Bank for a substantial overdraft. Spirits were raised, however, in 1964 when Mathew came forward with £1,114,000, made as a result of selling to the News of the World Organisation the *Times* holding in Townsend Hook, the firm which had been supplying the special paper for years. The building bill became manageable and directors congratulated Mathew on his shrewdness.

The buildings, when finished, made a handsome complex, clean in design, cream and light green in colour, the cream effect coming from a mosaic over concrete, and the broad green bands from Westmorland slate. *The Times* itself had the main building, looking out on to Queen Victoria Street from the back of the square. In the eastern wing of the complex was the *Observer* with all its editorial and managerial offices. In the western wing were the *Times* bookshop, the *New York Times* and the London offices of other foreign journals, and some of *The Times's* own supplements. It was a pleasant place for working in, but space soon began to be a problem once again. The fast-expanding financial and economic staff was moved from their old office in the heart of the City and was brought into the main body of the paper. The seventeen men and women formerly in the old City office soon became seventy as the work grew. Numbers increased in other departments, and the *Observer* too sought to expand.

The contract with the *Observer*, first to print it and then to house it, became one of the company's most profitable investments. The overtures had come from J. L. Garvin, the then editor, as far back as June–July 1939 but were not encouraged by C. S. Kent and the Board. There could be staff difficulties, Kent argued, and the public – always ready to suppose that John Astor's *Times* must have a natural political link with his brother Waldorf's *Observer* – would be further confused if the two papers were printed together. Nor was Mathew much more welcoming when the *Observer* renewed its inquiries in 1950; it was then printing 430,000 copies a week. It was not until the beginning of 1958 that Mathew advised the Board that *The Times* had enough plant to cope with the extra load of a Sunday newspaper. He added that it could even print two Sunday newspapers, each of 24 pages, if *The Times* ever decided to print its own. The *Observer*, he wrote, had asked him to take over its printing contract from July 1 1959 and had said it would like office space as well when *The Times* was rebuilt.[9] The *Observer*, recognising that some new machinery might be required, offered *The Times* an interest-free loan. Agreement to go forward was soon reached, detailed terms were arranged, and the first *Observer* to be published in Printing House Square came off the presses on the night of September 6–7 1958. The print order that night was for 716,600 copies, about three times the number for *The Times*. David Astor, son of the second Viscount, was editing the paper with brilliance and had gathered many original writers about him.[10] Seven months later the *Times* Board was informed that the *Observer* was anxious to increase its paging from 30 to 40–48 and would advance £500,000 interest free towards the cost of the necessary extra machinery. Once again the terms were arranged. In 1961 the *Observer* agreed to rent the office space set apart for it in the rebuilt Printing House Square.

For *The Times* the contract was profitable from the beginning. In 1959, the first full year, the net profit for *The Times* out of the deal was £93,588 and the profits rose as the *Observer* grew larger. In his review of 1964 Gavin Astor said: 'The Times Publishing Company depends upon the *Observer* for more than 50 per cent of its gross profits of £285,000.' He expected the *Observer* to contribute over £200,000 in 1965.[11]

The editorial staffs of the two papers seldom met except socially and individually. They never concerted policy or the presentation of news. Yet what meetings they had were entirely easy. It was a cousinly association, convenient for the *Observer*, welcome for *The Times*.

John Astor left Hever, which had always given him his happiest days, and went to live in France at the age of 76 as a result of a brief clause in Selwyn Lloyd's 1962 budget. Clause 28 of the Finance Act, as passed, imposed a liability for British estate duty on all real property owned by British subjects who died domiciled in the United Kingdom. Several people were hit by it, none more severely than the Astors. Through its impact on John Astor and on his son Gavin *The Times* was also heavily hit, for Gavin Astor after his father's departure found himself with costly new commitments and with few funds to spare for investment in *The Times* or elsewhere.

---

9 Memorandum, Mathew to Board, January 1958. T.T.A.
10 Hon. David Astor (b. 1912). Eton; Balliol College, Oxford. *Yorkshire Post*, 1936. Foreign editor, *Observer*, 1946–48; editor, 1948–75; director, *Observer*, from 1976.
11 All figures taken from annual reports by the chairman, The Times Publishing Company, 1959–65.

The blow to the family was heavy and direct because almost all the Astor wealth was, for several generations past, based on real estate in New York City. The first John Jacob Astor (1763–1848) devised his will to ensure, so far as any man could, that the fruits of the fortune he had made were passed down in turn from son to son, gaining in value. With the same ambition in mind the first Viscount Astor,[12] who left the United States to settle in Britain, made generous provision for his own two sons and daughter: Waldorf, the second Viscount;[13] John, later Baron Astor of Hever; and Pauline, the Hon. Mrs. Spender Clay. But chiefly this first Viscount created, from his American estate, settlements to be held in trust specifically for each of his grandchildren, including some as yet unborn when he died in 1919. It was a curious, leap-frogging device. His sons and his daughter could enjoy in their lifetime the income from the settlements. But they could not touch the capital. That capital could be released only as and when they themselves died, and then it was their own children – the first Viscount's grandchildren – who received the money due to them under the settlement. When the second Viscount died in 1952 his children, the Cliveden Astors, duly received their individual shares.

Until 1962 'immovable property abroad' escaped British estate duties. Successive British governments had even encouraged investment in real estate overseas. The blow for the Hever Astors in 1962, damaging from the start, became the more crippling the more it was examined. The British government was claiming the right to take 80 per cent of capital funds which had originally been created by an American in America and which were continuing to be maintained and managed by American trustees in New York. Gavin Astor flew to New York where the trustees told him that they could do nothing to help; they could not change the trust deeds. Under American law John Astor could not even dissociate himself from the settlements and renounce his income from them; the money had to go on being paid to him, like it or not. In a memorandum sent to a few friends John Astor wrote:

> My hands are tied and if I remain domiciled in this country my death will mean that almost the whole of the American property will disappear in death duties and my sons will be involved in serious financial consequences . . . I have therefore decided most reluctant-

---

12 William Waldorf Astor, 1st Viscount Astor (1848–1919). Succeeded his father as head of the Astor family and settled in Britain, becoming a naturalised British subject, 1889–90. Owner of the *Pall Mall Gazette* and *Pall Mall Magazine*, 1893; afterwards also *Observer*, 1911. Baron, 1916; Viscount, 1917.
13 Waldorf Astor, 2nd Viscount Astor (1879–1952). Eton; New College, Oxford. Unionist MP for Plymouth, 1910–19. Given control of the *Observer* by his father.

ly to take the only course open to me, namely to abandon my English domicile.[14]

Most distressing of all was the knowledge that his wife was ailing: any move would be especially sad and painful for her.[15] None the less, husband and wife left England to live in the south of France. They found a pleasant house, Terres Blanches, Pégomas, on low hills near the coast, but most of their lifelong interests were severed.

The differences between the British and French tax systems led to an ironic result. John Astor was financially better off in France. His son Gavin was left much worse off in England. He was faced with the upkeep of Hever Castle, its beautiful and highly cultivated gardens, and the estate; and he had to face it having neither the income from the American settlements, as that had still to go to his father, nor his promised share of the capital, which would come to him only at the unpredictable time of his father's death. The bulk of his own personal estate was locked up in The Times Publishing Company in which *The Times* was losing money and the other activities were combining to produce only a small profit. He opened Hever to the public in a successful venture but his financial anxieties were to persist.

John Astor's departure for France startled the *Times* staff more than anything that had happened for several years. He was to remain co-chief proprietor with John Walter, that was true, but everyone knew that the old personal link was bound to go. His decision was wholly in character: taken without any outward fuss and certainly without any thought of self-advantage. Printing House Square knew that one of the chief reasons in his mind was to ensure, so far as he could, that *The Times* as well as the family fortune was left with a solid financial base at his death. Their reflexions brought new respect and sympathy for a modest man who had always regarded his great wealth as a trust.

Without that wealth he could of course never have become owner of *The Times* but it was his own personal character that made him the ideal owner. In so many ways he regarded the paper as a very special foundation, much as he regarded the Middlesex Hospital to which he gave large sums. He did not seek for large profits from *The Times* when things were going well; neither did he grumble when there were no

---

14 Memorandum to Francis Mathew and others, September 17 1962. T.T.A.
15 Violet Mary, Lady Astor of Hever (née Elliot) (1889–1965). Third daughter of the 4th Earl of Minto, Governor General of Canada and Viceroy of India. Married first, Major Lord Charles Mercer-Nairne, killed in action; second, Captain John Jacob Astor, 1916.

profits at all. Perhaps, given his other abundant wealth, he could afford not to grumble but many other men with similar wealth would soon have been demanding higher returns. Once he was convinced, as he was in the years after the war, that larger salaries had to be paid to the staff he was in full agreement with the manager's and editor's recommendations even in the lean years.

Above all this, where he best served *The Times* was in his day-to-day observance for over forty years of his self-denying ordinance. He maintained the independence of the editor from any interference, beginning with himself. He never meddled with the policy of the paper and he made sure that other directors of the company stood back in exactly the same way. This abstinence was not always easy for him. He was against the appeasement policy before the war; members of Parliament and others were often urging him to make Dawson and Barrington-Ward change their line. He was often unhappy at the left-wing tendencies of the paper under Barrington-Ward during and immediately after the 1939–45 war. He did not share Casey's abhorrence of the death penalty. But at such times he contented himself with a mild conversational remark or an innocent-seeming question about the long-term consequences of the paper's policy at the given time. He was a shy man, but it was not shyness that held him back from blunt speaking at such times. It was loyalty to the compact which he made when first buying nine-tenths of the company's shares in 1922. The compact, often quoted, was that the editor should be left to get on with the job as he saw fit. The two chief proprietors could, if they were dissatisfied, get rid of him but while he was in the chair they could not dictate to him.

In a more particular way some of the younger and more promising members of the staff and their wives were grateful to John and Violet Astor for frequent weekends down at Hever Castle. There, in the heart of Kent, they could share for a few days in a world of style and comfort which most of them thought had ended in 1914. More to the point, they met and talked there with government ministers, ambassadors, and other men and women who were helping to steer events. Some of the staff were given longer breaks on board a motor yacht as John Astor combined his zeal for cruising with his talent for oil painting. He brought the standards and habits of an older world into his everyday life, and into his guardianship over *The Times* and the publishing company.

The other man who held the title of co-chief proprietor, John Walter, was as stalwart as John Astor in upholding the independence of the editor. He was an older man, his holding in the company was only a ninth of Astor's, and age had forced him to stop regular attendance in Printing House Square a couple of years before Astor left England.

When in his mid-eighties he was severely injured in a motor accident and was thereafter seldom able to leave his flat in Hove. Like Astor he had, in the big reorganisation of ownership in 1959, handed over his shares in the company to his son, John Walter v, or young John Walter as he was called in *The Times*.

None the less John Walter – John Walter iv or old John Walter – remained a strong influence in the higher reaches of Printing House Square right until his seclusion in Hove. At Board meetings he spoke seldom but always effectively; other directors were uneasy unless he was behind them on a given course. As one of the family who had owned *The Times* until Northcliffe bought it in 1908 he felt himself to be a special guardian of the interests and traditions of the paper, and it was not an arrogant or unworthy claim.

Like Astor, Walter was a shy man; he seemed physically and constitutionally reserved; he was serious-minded and he devoted that seriousness of purpose especially to foreign policy. By conviction he was more staunchly right-wing than Astor. Before the First World War he had been correspondent for the paper in Spain and later he held General Franco in high regard; in talks within the office he made clear his view that successive British governments and *The Times* itself should support Franco against his critics. His opinion of Stalin and of communism in general led him to remonstrate with Barrington-Ward about some of the leading articles which sought to improve relations with the Kremlin after the Second World War. There were times when his decided views seemed to be based on a society and a world structure that were wrecked in 1914–18. At other times, quite unexpectedly, his shrewd comments on contemporary men and events would disconcert anyone who was perhaps listening only half-attentively, thinking that the stiff, old-world appearance and manner represented the whole man.

His remarks and some of his memoranda within the office might seem to breach the 1922 compact on editorial independence. He was himself aware of the dilemma and, in his methodical way, he wrote himself a memorandum – apparently in 1945 or 1946 – when he was more than usually disturbed by some of Barrington-Ward's and Carr's leaders. Although addressed to the editor there seems no certainty that it was ever sent. In it Walter tried to formulate anew the correct relationship between a *Times* owner and a *Times* editor. Some phrases in it would not have been accepted by Barrington-Ward, but parts of it remain valid:

> The immemorial custom of The Paper, which has ensured its smooth working hitherto, is that in matters of public policy the Proprietor never tries to impose his views on the Editor or to encroach on his

responsibility: and that custom has a corollary, which is that the Editor takes due account of the wishes of the Proprietor. The precept suggested by Walter Bagehot as defining the relations between the King and his Prime Minister might very well be applied to the relations between the Proprietor and the Editor of The Paper, namely that the King has 'the right to be consulted, the right to encourage and the right to warn'.

In criticising any item of editorial policy there is need for circumspection. The Editor, by virtue of his office, may safely be assumed to be one of the best informed people in the country: he bases his judgment day after day and year after year upon the surest and most complete sources of information. How can any ordinary man hope to know better than that? I certainly should always be very diffident in questioning the rightness of his opinion on any matter of public interest.

At this point Walter came to his simple solution of the dilemma before him:

Any remarks I might make would have to be understood as coming from an average reader of The Times, who meets a certain number of people in the course of his avocations, and perhaps reads a few of the other papers as well as The Times. The opinion of such a man is likely to represent the view of a certain section of public opinion, and may therefore be worth considering.[16]

The extraordinary thing is that this solution worked. A senior editorial man would be bidden to take tea with Walter in his panelled room in the old private house at Printing House Square. The summons often came at five minutes' notice, usually when much of the world was in storm, and the bidden guest would find his mind torn between the trenchant leading article which he had left unfinished and his dutiful replies to Walter's questions. It was only afterwards that he realised how sharply to the point the slow and courteous questions had been and how skilfully Walter had framed them 'as coming from an average reader of The Times'.

Both John Astor and John Walter served The Times by their covenant. Sometimes one or other of them would be proved right after the event when the editor was wrong: over Munich for example. Sometimes it was the other way round. Usually the two owners seemed to agree with the editorial policy. But there was something greater than

---

16 See Chapter VI.

agreement or disagreement. By holding themselves at a distance, by genuinely respecting the craft of the men and women of Printing House Square, and by helping to keep governments and other authorities from trying to meddle, they let *The Times* find its own way forward. They let it develop what a newspaper most needs: a strong and distinct personality that comes from within the paper itself, from the paper's own editor and the staff who maintain and build on a tradition.

John Astor's departure for France and John Walter's withdrawal threw more responsibility on John Astor's two sons, Gavin and Hugh. Gavin Astor, chairman of the company since 1959, was in his mid-forties when his father left. Hugh, vice-chairman, was two years younger. Both had much of the Astor character in them. Their courtesy and outward diffidence did not hide the strong strand of determination within them. After their war service they both threw themselves into learning all sides of the Times Company business, editorial and managerial. Within Printing House Square Gavin Astor spent time in almost all the departments in turn; his brother also learned the business in the same direct way. Both travelled abroad frequently to see the correspondents at work in the field and to hear of their problems at first hand. Gavin Astor took an especially deep interest in the Commonwealth Press Union, of which he was to become chairman and president; he presided over its meetings in all continents. Soon after the war Hugh Astor served as a correspondent in the Middle East and was wounded by sniper fire in Palestine. Both brothers frequently invited members of the staff to their houses. As it was generally understood that Gavin would succeed his father Hugh consciously saw his own role as helping Gavin in all the ways that he could.

In fact the two brothers had to work closely together and help each other. They had difficulties in front of them and they took some heavy knocks; they were bitterly disappointed when the company rejected the idea of buying shares in independent television,[17] and again when the Cooper report did not make the impact for which they had hoped.[18] They felt themselves to be surrounded by older men who still regarded them first and foremost as their father's sons in need of guidance. They found this friendly and patronising attitude towards them a little hard to bear at times when some of the older men, no matter how shrewd in their own fields, had no direct experience of newspaper work or printing, especially in its new techniques. One of Gavin Astor's early

---

17 See Chapter XV.
18 See Chapter XVI.

acts was to rule that all directors over the age of seventy should retire in favour of younger men.

Even so he felt that his powers were very much restricted. He was chairman of the company from 1959 but his father, even after withdrawing to southern France, retained the title of co-chief proprietor. It was bound to be more than a courtesy title, given the habit of free-ranging discussion which had grown up between him and the directors, the editor and the manager over many years. Gavin Astor, who did not become co-chief proprietor until 1964, felt that authority and influence were often dispersed.

He faced difficulties elsewhere. He fully understood his constitutional position in regard to the editor, though equally he did not believe it should stop him from passing on to Haley the occasional complaints which came to him from outside. But he could not accept, any more than could his father, the suggestion that the manager should have an independence within the organisation similar to the editor's. Gavin Astor's conviction on this point was the stronger because of the financial plight in which he found himself after the Selwyn Lloyd budget and his father's forced departure for France. For him *The Times* had to be not simply a commitment and a responsibility but also a going concern; and both brothers wanted to have a say in making it go. Such strains seldom showed themselves. Relations within Printing House Square remained remarkably easy. All that could be felt were some underlying and counter-acting pulls among men determined to make the best of the paper and the company. The need for success was becoming more urgent.

While Printing House Square was reconstructing itself Fleet Street as a whole was suffering change and upheaval in other ways. In 1959 Roy Thomson moved on from his purchase of the *Scotsman* (1953) and his acquisition of the Scottish Television franchise (1955); he bought Kemsley Newspapers. Chief among his new group was *The Sunday Times* which quickly had the other high-class Sunday newspapers struggling to stay in the race. Other signs of the new force in journalism came in 1960 when Thomson closed two smaller Sunday newspapers of the old Kemsley group: the *Sunday Graphic* in London and the *Empire News* in Manchester. Other owners and managers were facing similar problems of rising costs and swollen mechanical staffs. October 1960 brought a heavy blow to Fleet Street when the *News Chronicle* and its evening partner, the *Star*, ceased publication. The loss of the *News Chronicle* was trebly shocking to journalists and managers alike. It had gone under in spite of having a circulation of a million and a quarter. It had a staunchly loyal Liberal and non-conformist readership. And in its news and features it filled a place midway between the quality papers and the populars. These three supports should have been strong enough to keep it above water, but they were weakened by rising costs and inefficiency.

While Fleet Street was still reading the portents Roy Thomson and Cecil King, chairman of the Mirror group, began struggling for the ownership of Odhams, the group which controlled the *Daily Herald* and the *Sunday People* as well as many magazines. When found to be in financial trouble Odhams was first offered to Thomson, but finally went to King. This struggle for possession between powerful houses, coming after the other events, spread the anxiety from Fleet Street to Westminster. Cecil King's promise to keep the Labour *Herald* going for a set number of years did little to allay the alarm about the future of newspapers.

The fear grew that Britain would have fewer newspapers owned by fewer men. In March 1961 the Macmillan government responded by appointing a royal commission under Lord Shawcross. Its main tasks were:

> to examine the economic and financial factors affecting the production and sale of newspapers, magazines and other periodicals in the United Kingdom . . . [and] to consider whether these factors tend to diminish diversity of ownership and control or the number or variety of such publications, having regard to the importance, in the public interest, of the accurate presentation of news and the free expression of opinion.[19]

The commission worked speedily and thoroughly, amassing details from dozens of press sources, and its report on September 20 1962 contained no surprises and no radical solutions for the troubles in the industry. Its main judgment, its main advice to the press, was well summed up in the title of the leading article with which Haley greeted the report: 'Physician, Heal Thyself'.[20]

After stating bluntly that the *News Chronicle* died because it was inefficient Haley agreed with the commission in believing that many, if not most, of the newspapers were inefficient and over-manned on the production side. The irony was that the newspapers were supposed to lead the nation in such matters:

> They preach efficiency for everyone else and denounce inflation. It ill befits them to be grossly overstaffed, to be continually giving way

---

19 Royal Warrant, quoted in report of the Royal Commission on the Press, 1961–62. (Cmd. 1811.)
20 *The Times*, September 20 1962.

to the highest paid manual workers in Britain, without adequate return in productivity, and to recoup by steadily raising their prices and advertising rates . . . What is needed is a thorough revolution in ideas, in methods, in materials.

Haley, ever the individualist, was characteristically less interested in the royal commission's suggestions for strengthening the Press Council and establishing a Press Amalgamations Court. 'They will not do any harm; they are not likely to do much good.' Even if they were adopted, the fundamental position would remain unchanged. 'The only men who can change it are Lord Beaverbrook, Mr. King, Lord Rothermere and Mr. Thomson.' They alone could bring about the revolution in method that was needed. They had to take on all the great complexities and risks of modernisation:

It is a job for the Press emperors. It would need rare imagination and expensive research. They would endure much travail. They would face many hazards. They would have to make life uncomfortable for themselves and others. They might suffer. In return they would have a sure place in history.

Of the four men it was the newcomer, Roy Thomson, who was to push the farthest and the most boldly with new techniques in his provincial papers. The London papers felt the stresses of competition more than at any period since before the Second World War and *The Times*, it was clear, would not be protected by any special status.

XVIII

EUROPE AMONG THE WORLD POWERS

THE *Times* was slow in convincing itself that Britain should join the European Economic Community. During the late fifties the paper, like many people then writing and speaking in Britain, was pro-European but not fervently so. It was all in favour of some close partnership with western Europe but not on the Community's terms unless those terms were amended, and not at the cost of weakening the links with the Commonwealth and the United States. In its foreign policy it still believed in the famous 'three intertwining circles' – Commonwealth, America, and Europe – although it expected the links with Europe to be strengthened.

This initial position of the paper is made plain by leading articles in the paper and by private memoranda circulated among the staff.[1] For some time the main hope in Britain was that the country might become a member provided that the Community became looser in structure and more like a free trade area, without a common external tariff. By November 1958 it became clear that any such arrangement was out of reach, largely owing to the French attitude. Maurice Green immediately wrote a first leader to which Haley gave the heading, 'France the Wrecker'.[2] Frank Giles, then chief correspondent in Paris, sent in a letter of remonstrance:

> I note with surprise and sorrow that *The Times* . . . should so completely have swallowed, hook, line and sinker, the Treasury arguments on the Free Trade Area.

The idea, said Giles, was unacceptable to any French government, as had long been clear. The French may have been tiresome and prevaricating, but the British team under Reginald Maudling had been woefully inept.[3] In a long reply, passed on to Giles, Green set out *The Times's* view at that time. It was surely wrong to speak of British

---

1 T.T.A.
2 *The Times*, November 18 1958.
3 Letter, Giles to Macdonald, November 21 1958. T.T.A.

ineptitude in negotiations when Britain could not in practice make many substantial concessions. It could not (a) impose duties on raw materials, food, or semi-manufactured goods from Commonwealth countries, (b) make its tariff reductions subject in any way to Community agreement and thereby to French veto, or (c) accept any Community authority, however vague, over monetary and fiscal policy so long as sterling was a world currency and the other European currencies were not.[4]

Within a few months Haley was in Paris where he was assured by President de Gaulle himself that the differences over the Common Market were not serious enough to spoil the 'deep and abiding' relations between the old allies, Britain and France. France, a strongly protectionist country, had made many concessions for the sake of the Community and now needed a respite, a time for digestion, before taking on more members.[5] Other French ministers spoke in a similarly unalarmist way to Haley without wholly reassuring him.

The European movement was gathering force. The six countries of the Community were not only drawing together politically; they were advancing industrially and economically at a pace which Britain could not ignore. Western Europe, it was evident, was fast returning to a position of economic power. The industrial movements were fully reported in *The Times*, particularly in the City pages to begin with. At the end of 1959 the City editor, William Clarke, visited the main financial centres on the Continent and his report removed any lingering beliefs that there was more talk than substance in the new association:

After travelling hundreds of miles on the Continent, visiting all the leading centres of industry and finance, one can feel a new impulse at work . . . The rubble of war has disappeared fast in the last two years alone. And this is as true of Rotterdam, Cologne, Hamburg and other German cities as it is of the City of London. But it is in the shopping centres of Europe that the real change can be seen. Christmas shopping reached a peak in virtually every European centre. The variety of goods in the shops of Zurich, Milan, Paris, Brussels and Amsterdam has been the rival of almost any in the western world . . . In short Europe is more prosperous than it has ever been before . . . Few will deny that Europe is now back on its feet economically for the first time in nearly 30 years.[6]

The implications for Britain – and for the United States – were not hard to draw. The accompanying rise in European gold reserves and the

4 Memorandum, November 28 1958. T.T.A.
5 Talk dated April 29 1959. T.T.A.
6 *The Times*, January 1 1960, 'Europe's Recovery'.

corresponding decline in those of the United States at Fort Knox over the late 1950s and early 1960s reflected a major shift in world economic power. They also began to be reflected in the strength of European currencies especially the Deutschmark, and the recurrent weakness of the dollar. In London these changes were seen – slowly at first – as significantly affecting Britain's relations with the members of the Common Market.

The Times shifted closer to the idea of European unity as the result of a thorough review of the paper's whole foreign policy towards the end of 1960. McDonald asked all the foreign leader writers and several of the economic and industrial writers to submit memoranda for discussion. It was an attempt to work out the main lines of global strategy and get away from a newspaper's ever-present temptation to make snap judgments on events as they occur. The memoranda were debated in a two-day conference and were then pulled together into two articles which filled all the leader space for two days.[7]

The first of the two articles, headed 'North and South', analysed the danger of the spread of communism in the third world, acknowledged that some countries would fall under the new rule, and argued that others could best be helped towards stability in practical, non-military ways through agreements on commodity prices and medium-term trade deals. The second article, headed 'East and West', took up again the *Times* line that, though no comprehensive accord with Soviet Russia was possible, there could be and should be limited treaties on hard, pragmatic matters that were capable of being monitored in order to check whether the terms were being fulfilled or not.[8] The article argued that an east–west balance of power remained necessary but could be maintained just as effectively through agreements to have a lower level of arms on each side. As a necessary part of that balance the Nato alliance had to be repaired and brought up to date.

The case for strengthening western Europe led on from this last thought. *The Times* in fact found itself arguing for a stronger and more united western Europe largely for reasons external to Europe. The paper at that time was not so much interested in building a new European entity for its own sake as concerned to remove the military and economic disunity which was a weakness in western security. The paper still hoped, a little forlornly, that agreement might be reached between the Community and the European Free Trade Association (Efta) which had been set up under British leadership in 1959 as a

7 *The Times*, November 29 and 30 1960.
8 See Chapter XII.

counter-weight to the Community.[9]

These articles of November 1960 confirmed the *Times* line throughout the early sixties. The paper still kept out of any pro-European crusade but it set out to do something more useful; that is, to explain what the Community was and what it did and to dispel so far as it could the indifference which spread out from Westminster to most parts of the land. Two long series of special articles on the rules of membership and the likely impact on Britain and her Commonwealth partners if Britain joined were re-published as pamphlets and they sold well.[10] The main weight of the argument in each pamphlet was marginally on the side of British membership in spite of all the difficulties which would be encountered before and after joining.

With the same instructional purpose in mind *The Times* appointed David Spanier[11] to be Common Market correspondent from the beginning of 1962. He was stationed in Brussels, he travelled often to Strasbourg, and there was never any doubt about his own conviction that Britain should, in the catch phrase then current, 'climb aboard the moving train that is gathering speed as it goes'. Throughout these years Rendel, the diplomatic correspondent, Europe-inclined himself, reported some of the private and intricate talks which Edward Heath was having with Commonwealth and Efta partners. Rendel was several times ahead of other papers, and the Foreign Office as regularly inquired anxiously – and in vain – about the sources of his information. In fact, he found his sources in many embassies and high commissions, and like a good journalist brought them together into the occasional long story.

When the faint hope of agreement between the Community Six and the Efta Seven vanished, the paper supported Harold Macmillan in his announcement on July 31 1961 that Britain – having consulted the Commonwealth – would seek to open negotiations for her own membership of the Community. While welcoming the move a leading article gave a warning which was to be all too well justified. Did President de Gaulle really want Britain?:

This last, indeed, is a decisive point. It is no use Britain incurring all

---

9 See Chapter XII.
10 *The Common Market*, October 1961. *Common Market and Commonwealth*, 1962.
11 David Graham Spanier (b. 1932). Charterhouse; Trinity College, Cambridge. *Yorkshire Post*, 1955–57. Joined *The Times* in 1957 as home news reporter; Common Market correspondent 1961–63; assistant City editor, 1963–64; European economic correspondent, 1964–67; economic correspondent, Washington 1968; special writer, 1969; London editor, *Europa*, 1973; diplomatic correspondent, 1974; resigned 1982.

the strains and stresses which negotiations with the Treaty of Rome Powers are bound to set up if at the end of it all France is going to make Britain's joining impossible.[12]

Macmillan told Haley later the same day that the leader was the most sensible comment he had read. By the time Heath had made his initial statement, outlining Britain's intentions in the House of Commons towards the end of November, following the submission of a secret paper to the EEC, *The Times* was ready once more to offer advice. It deplored the attempt at initial secrecy, pointing to the ludicrous situation which had arisen when Canada had asked for details and been refused: 'The best way to breed confidence is to show the greatest possible candour'. It chided Heath for saying that the government's decision had been taken 'after searching debate'. That debate was only just beginning. But to the decision itself *The Times* gave its full support. It did not hide, either from its readers or from itself, the clarifications in the political field that would still be needed. 'It is here that the water is most muddied. Nobody, not even the Six themselves, knows precisely where they are going politically.'[13] Idealism was one thing; starry eyed enthusiasm might prove to be dangerous.

For the next twelve months the debate continued in Britain and the negotiations proceeded in Brussels. In the meantime the Labour party's attitude had hardened against membership and by the time the House of Commons devoted two days to a debate on the progress of the negotiations, at the beginning of November 1962, Labour was committed to outright opposition on the terms Heath was negotiating in Brussels. *The Times* too had begun to harden its position.

On balance it was still in favour of entry but, equally, it was still against accepting entry on any terms. In a sympathetic leader on the problems faced by the Commonwealth earlier that summer, however, it had talked for the first time of 'a very strong case' for entry. This opinion was held from then on, but it did not prevent the paper from showing deep anxiety at some of the easy assumptions being made within the Conservative party about the impact on British sovereignty. It chided R. A. Butler for suggesting that the government would simply 'agree to nothing which undermines the essential powers of Parliament'. That was hardly realistic, so the paper argued. But it reserved its major criticism for Hugh Gaitskell, the leader of the opposition, who had devoted a large part of his speech at the Labour party conference at

---

12 Leading article (Haley), June 14 1961.
13 Leading article (Haley), November 28 1961.

Brighton to a demolition of the view that joining Europe would help Britain's economy. *The Times* described his speech as 'not the fair-minded economic analysis to be expected of him'. Yet throughout this period *The Times* itself, while acknowledging that the development of a market of 250 million on Britain's doorstep would be a challenge to British management and labour, still remained sceptical of the assumption that the Common Market's dynamism might be transferred overnight to Britain's ailing economy.

When President de Gaulle duly banned British membership at his press conference on January 14 1963 *The Times*, still not caught up in the European idea as such, did not lament that Britain was barred from sharing in a great political and constitutional venture. Rendel, as diplomatic correspondent, reflected more official sorrow than official anger. Macmillan himself did not take the veto tragically when Haley saw him the day after the de Gaulle press conference. The Prime Minister suspected that de Gaulle had slammed the door not because he thought that Britain – 'insular and maritime' – could never be wholly European; de Gaulle's real reason, thought Macmillan, was to be found in his desire to protect French farmers within a Community small enough for France to dominate. Macmillan hoped that the five other members of the Common Market, particularly Federal Germany, would persuade de Gaulle to let the negotiations be taken up again.

Haley himself was more concerned with the impact and response at home in Britain:

> Britain must not turn her back on Europe, or abandon for ever the idea of joining the Common Market. The immediate task is to put her own house in order . . . A fresh start is badly overdue.[14]

In a direct appeal for a lead from Macmillan – an appeal which he had already strongly urged at private meetings with the Prime Minister – Haley wrote: 'His outstanding intelligence must tell him that only radical measures will do now'. In that article Haley did not spell out precisely what radical measures were needed but within the office he often declared that he welcomed the prospect of British membership of the Community because it would face British industry with stiffer competition. Such competition would be doubly beneficial, stirring British management up to modernise its plants and jolting trade unions out of many of their comfortable restrictive practices.

The point at which Haley's interest in the European idea turned to zeal

---

14 *The Times*, January 30 1963.

can be almost exactly dated. On May 31 1963 he replied to a memorandum from the foreign editor who had summed up for him the conclusions reached at another long conference of foreign and economic leader writers. Haley wrote:

I tend to be less dispassionate about Britain's entry into Europe than the memorandum would seem to be. Admittedly we are blocked so long as de Gaulle is in power. Also we have no guarantee that whatever regime succeeds him will be less anglophobe. But it seems to me that we must be as active as we can to keep the idea of Britain joining Europe alive both here in the United Kingdom and on the Continent.

Of course the British will always hanker after remaining at the centre of the three overlapping circles that Churchill described. It begins to look more and more, however, as if they will become rather like those rings of Kipling's that 'fizz and fade'.

The Commonwealth seemed (Haley suggested) as though it could be held together only if Britain ignored many breaches of democracy and justice that were happening in some of its new members. The Atlantic alliance would remain simply a military alliance, and Britain could not hope to keep up the old 'special relationship' with the United States, given the disproportion of strength between the two countries.

On the other hand if Britain could take its place in Europe, then both politically and economically it could support its role. U.K. (53m.), Germany (54m.), France (46m.), Italy (50m.) are roughly all equals. There is no unmanageable disproportion either in their resources or their economic potentials. It is a pipe-dream to believe that the Six would accord us a moral leadership; there is no reason why we should not fully hold our own . . .

Both the Conservative and Labour parties are likely to play down Europe in the coming months. It would be an embarrassing reminder of their failure to the Tories; it would be an unwelcome hostage of fortune to Labour. It seems to me that *The Times* has a duty to be the voice that keeps the European idea alive.

Haley knew that the duty would bring in few rewards and fewer thanks. There were months when Europe seemed a goal far out of reach. After a new Labour government came into office in 1964, generally opposed to entry, Britain was occupied before all else with its own industrial and economic disappointments. On their side, too, the Six had to concentrate on their own internal developments. Here the difficulty was that virtually every proposal towards change within the Community met

French resistance. By the summer of 1965 *The Times* was convinced that the Six were being forced to 'look squarely at the possibility of failure'.[15] Ministers reached deadlock – sometimes over trade, usually over agriculture. Deadlines were set and as often as not missed. French intransigence grew until, suddenly, she withdrew her ambassador from the EEC in Brussels and created an 'empty chair' within the European Community. As it turned out this was the turning point. The shock went deep. It was followed by the personal rebuff to President de Gaulle at the hands of the French electorate and by the end of 1965 *The Times* was looking ahead with more optimism to the re-shaping of the Six's aims and developments. Throughout this period the commentators in Britain who were convinced that Britain's place was in Europe recorded only their disappointment at the disarray in Brussels. *The Times* was among those who refused to gloat. The renewal of French participation was described as 'good for the Six', and 'good for Britain too.'[16]

Slowly the European enthusiasts within the Labour government, as well as the realists, began to reconsider Britain's role in Europe and to be encouraged by the changing climate in both Paris and Brussels. The French Foreign Minister, M. Couve de Murville, seemed to add his own encouragements: 'The day when Britain decides to join the Six without reserve, she will respond to the wishes of the Europeans, because they believe that the British ought in every way to share in the destiny of the continentals'.[17] Following Labour's second election success in July 1966 the time for a new approach was again ripe, and by the autumn Harold Wilson was poised for a renewed application.

The stage was thus set for a second British assault on the EEC citadel. It was not to succeed until the beginning of 1973, but throughout this second attempt *The Times* remained faithful to the European idea, without lending its support at any cost. Behind this support was a simple economic message which had been repeated throughout the decade and had been enunciated at the beginning of the sixties:

> A Britain that becomes economically stagnant and gets into difficulties is bound to weaken the West as a whole. For Britain to go into the Common Market weak, unprepared and without her economy girded up would be to invite political as well as economic tribulation. Britain's say in world affairs can never again hope to be what it once was. But she has an important part to play. To play it she must be strong.[18]

---

15 Leading article (Davy), July 7 1965.
16 Leading article (Smith), December 30 1965.
17 *The Times*, March 17 1966.
18 Leading article (Haley), July 13 1961.

It was a theme, combining the *Times* policies on domestic economics and on Europe, that increased its warning force in the years ahead.

Over the years, as *The Times's* concern in the Common Market grew, it strengthened its correspondents in Europe. The process began with a loss. In November 1960 Frank Giles, chief correspondent in Paris for the past seven and a half years, left to join *The Sunday Times*. After being assistant correspondent for *The Times* in Paris soon after the war he had made his mark in Rome. In his four years there he had described in detail how the future of Italy was being decided in the rivalry between De Gasperi's Christian Democrats and Togliatti's very Italian Communists. More strikingly, he refused to be put off by the old myth about the 'impenetrable secrets of the Vatican'. Encouraged by Printing House Square, and helped with introductions from a leading Roman Catholic layman, a former *Times* man, Douglas Woodruff,[19] and from Archbishop David Mathew, Apostolic Delegate in British Africa and a cousin of Francis Mathew, Giles cultivated the kind of confidential, informative talks with leading Vatican officials that he had with members of state governments, notably the powerful Mgr. Montini, later to become Pope Paul VI. It was a sustained effort in tact and skill which opened up several doors long thought to be closed to newspaper men. On first being told by an official that the Vatican did not have contacts with the press Giles modestly replied that *The Times* 'wasn't quite like other newspapers' and it needed to be informed on every aspect of life and work in Italy; his argument prevailed.[20]

In Paris his despatches throughout all the country's internal upheavals and the Algerian war had, beyond all the obvious qualities of clarity and deep knowledge, a hard element of common sense. That was often their chief strength throughout the years of rumours and, so far as the Community was concerned, of extravagant hopes. They were qualities that came out again during his editing of *The Sunday Times* which began early in 1981.

The opportunity of his departure was taken to make a general post among the staff, bringing back to Europe men with previous European experience. Bob Cooper was moved, after six arduous years in New York and Washington, back to the Paris where he had worked before the war and during and after the liberation. To help him he was given Fred Emery,[21] who was to rise high and swiftly. Louis Heren was

---

19 John Douglas Woodruff (1897–1978). Downside; New College, Oxford. Editorial staff, *The Times*, 1926–38. Editor, *The Tablet*, 1936–67.
20 Letter Giles to Deakin, July 12 1950. T.T.A.
21 Fred Albert Emery (b. 1933). Bancroft's School; St. John's College, Cambridge.

promoted from Bonn to Washington. Charles Hargrove, fluent in French and German, was moved all the way from Tokyo to fill Heren's place in Bonn and already was expected to move on a few years later to his spiritual (and natal) home in Paris. In Rome there was no need for change for Peter Nichols,[22] transferred from Bonn in 1957, had soaked himself in Italian life in a way which already showed that this was going to be one of the happiest, longest and most successful correspondentships in the paper's history. Its high worth was demonstrated in his daily despatches and in several books. He became more deeply caught up in Vatican politics than even Giles had been, and was a respected expert on all church and state affairs. For many years *The Times* was content – more than content – to leave well alone in Rome. The only change which went counter to the Euro-centric moves at the time was the shift of Ronald Preston to Tokyo. It was felt he deserved a change after all the strains and stresses in central and eastern Europe. Mrs. Desa Bourne (after a second marriage she was Dessa Trevisan)[23] was moved up from Belgrade to fill Preston's central and east European post in Vienna. In yet another development of the European side of the foreign news service Kyril Tidmarsh,[24] a Research Fellow at St. Antony's College, Oxford, was brought in to write regular news features and comment in London on Soviet affairs.

The work and characters of those involved were soon seen through all the anonymity of *The Times* in those years. From the moment he arrived there Heren revelled in Washington, the open-hearted American ways, the unrivalled openings for a correspondent who was prepared for hard work, hard questioning, and hard thought; and the challenge of the daily race against the clock. A book that he was asked to write on the

---

The Times editorial staff, 1958–61; assistant correspondent in Paris 1961–63; Tokyo correspondent, 1963–67; South-East Asia correspondent, 1967–70; Washington correspondent, 1970–77; political editor, 1977; resigned, 1982. Presenter on BBC 'Panorama' programme from September 1978.

22 Peter Nichols (b. 1928). Portsmouth Grammar School; St. Edmund Hall, Oxford. Joined *The Times* special supplements, 1953; foreign news room, 1954; assistant correspondent Bonn, 1954–57; correspondent in Rome since 1957.

23 Dessa Trevisan (b. Desa Pavlovic, 1924; after first marriage was Desa Bourne; later altered spelling of first name). Belgrade University. Correspondent for *The Times* in Belgrade, 1953–60; Eastern European correspondent based in Vienna, 1960–71; based in Belgrade, 1971.

24 Kyril Ralph Tidmarsh (b. 1931). St. Paul's; Magdalen College, Oxford. On the staff of *The Times* as special writer in the foreign department, 1961–65; correspondent in Moscow, 1965–68. Resigned to become executive assistant to the Director General of the International Labour Organization.

working of the American system[25] added to his burden but also gave, through the research it required, a depth to his understanding and by extension to his despatches. On his work *The Times* received the official complaints that are traditionally made from time to time about the work of good correspondents. Those official complaints received no less traditional replies and turned more often to no less official praise as time passed.

Hargrove had for over five years in Tokyo followed and interpreted the Japan that was recovering its self-respect and gaining new strength while keeping much of the historic colour and tradition. Both the office and he himself felt that it was time for him, with his fine diplomatic sense, to be back on home ground in Europe. Like Giles he was always conscious of the special diplomatic standing of *The Times*; no correspondent had better connexions or based his despatches more firmly on tested information.

Preston was moved to Tokyo with the idea of giving him a fresh and easier field of work. For several years in eastern Europe he had lived a life which meant at best a constant fight with bureaucracy and at worst coping with deep and bitter suspicion against the western press. No correspondent was shrewder in his comments on Soviet methods of control over the region and on the outbreaks of resistance to that control. His strength as reporter at times of crisis came out at Poznan in 1956[26] and then during the Hungarian rising in the same year.

To fill the Vienna-based job Mrs. Trevisan was the obvious choice. Her schooling in politics came during the war in her native Yugoslavia, then during Tito's revolution, and throughout the Yugoslav resistance to Russia after Tito's break with the eastern camp in 1948. Her background gave her a pragmatic and clear-sighted understanding of central and east European affairs, helped also by an instinct for coming events in the region which anyone British-born found it hard to rival. She was always aware of the force of nationality behind all the ideology. In the early years when western eyes were fixed mainly on Poland and Hungary, Dessa Trevisan detected behind the scenes Romania's quiet and strong refusal to follow the Russian line in foreign and economic policies. She was one of the very first to uncover the movement. She might have been the first beyond all doubt, but an early message from her in Bucharest was held up because several in Printing House Square that night thought that it would land her in serious trouble with the Romanian authorities at that particular time; they did not wish to be

---

25 *The New American Commonwealth*, 1968.
26 See Chapter XII.

brave at her expense. Regular complaints from east European governments about her work were as regularly rebutted by *The Times*. She
herself knew, and accepted, the risks she ran: 'You have a whole system
against you and are constantly aware of it.'[27]

The Soviet Union itself had been covered by news reports from
Irving Levin, of the *Baltimore Sun*, as well as by special articles written
after staff visits. Kyril Tidmarsh came to *The Times* after having been
pulled for some years from three different sides: from St. Antony's
College where his fellowship was more than once renewed; from the
International Labour Office where he worked for four years and where
David Morse, the director general, thought especially well of him; and
from *The Times* itself where he had done the occasional leader and
special article. In January 1961 he decided to come full time to Printing
House Square to write news stories and comment under the by-line
Monitor. He was entirely bilingual in Russian and English, and politically was a former pupil of Sir Isaiah Berlin and E. H. Carr. At *The
Times* he took in Soviet newspapers and magazines; he could write more
freely than the regular Moscow correspondents, not having to fear for
his visa, and *The Times* saved the cost of keeping a flat and a car (with
indispensable chauffeur) in Moscow. The Monitor pieces, knowledgeable and careful, reported and explained the several changes among the
Soviet leaders and reviewed Russia's industrial gains and strains, but in
1965, when *The Times* was given more money for development, the
plunge was taken. Monitor moved bodily to Moscow and could then
report not only on the big events but on the bustle, the rumours, and the
frustrations of Russian everyday life. He and his American wife lived
there for three years before the ILO claimed him again.

Yet another young man at that time, Richard Davy,[28] was to develop
a deep knowledge and concern for European communist affairs. After
working as number two in Bonn and Washington he took up leader-
writing in 1961. Gradually he became caught up in the old challenge of
understanding and explaining the socialist states, and then in the greater
challenge of working out the best means for east–west coexistence. For
him it was an exercise in intellect and conscience combined. Most of his
work was to come after 1966 but long before then he was adding his own
findings to *The Times's* general policy in the years when total war and

---

27 Private letter. July 30 1978. T.T.A.
28 Richard William Davy (b. 1930). Abbotsholme; Magdalen College, Oxford;
Institut Tschulok, Zurich. *The Times* editorial staff in London, 1955–57; thereafter
assistant correspondent in Bonn and Washington, 1957–61; special writer on foreign
affairs, 1961–69; assistant editor (night), 1969–70; special writer on East European
affairs, 1970; chief foreign leader writer from 1979 until his retirement in 1984.

total peace were alike unthinkable.

The Common Market debate had raised unfamiliar problems for Britain, and in the early years of the controversy politicians and journalists alike seemed almost relieved to turn to events in the older and better known fields of British concern – the Middle East and, more broadly, great power relations.

When, on July 14 1958, it was Iraq's turn to follow Egypt's example of 1952 and have its own young officers' *coup*, *The Times* shared the general gloom about the consequences. The murders of the royal family and the experienced elder statesman, Nuri es-Said, emphasized the dangers. 'If the revolt succeeds', Hodgkin wrote as the first news was coming in, 'it will be a disaster for the west.' Extremism and instability in Iraq could quickly spread to Jordan and worsen the plight of divided Lebanon.[29] The paper had no hesitation the next day in supporting the American landings on the Lebanese beaches:

> Imagine the course of events if the United States had stood aside . . . The rebels in Lebanon would have gained fresh heart as well as new supplies of arms from across the Syrian border . . . The position of Jordan would become impossible.[30]

The landing of British troops in Jordan let *The Times* welcome the speedy and effective exercise in Anglo–American cooperation; its chief anxiety was lest America, once launched on the venture, might be tempted to go on into Iraq itself and become bogged down there. With this anxiety in mind the paper wrote that the United States and Britain should 'not only be clear about their limited objectives but make the limits clear to the world.'[31]

David Holden had succeeded Holburn and Morris as Middle East correspondent in July 1956 just in time for Nasser's nationalisation of the canal company.[32] Now, in the Lebanon crisis, he described some of the comedy that played around the serious mission of the United States marines as they moved in with their tanks and landing barges:

> What appeared to be every car in Beirut converged on the beach at Khaldi to watch them approach . . . Lunchers at the fashionable restaurant at Pigeon Rock had a fine view; most of them left their *kebabs* to take pictures and wave. Shortly before three the first landing craft moved towards the beach where bathers, reporters,

---

29 *The Times*, July 15 1958.
30 Leading article (McDonald), July 16 1958.
31 *Ibid.*
32 See Chapter XIII.

and photographers were waiting to greet them . . .

The only casualties were two light vehicles which stuck in the soft sand. They were, however, soon dragged out of the water by eager bathers. The Marines were not unnaturally surprised by the nice-looking girls reclining on the beach.

The Middle East was made steadier for a time, and the whole episode was a welcome break for the correspondents in the Arab world. Reporting had become progressively more intricate and more frustrating for them over the years. In the old days the *Times* correspondent in Cairo could do much of his work by a morning visit to the British Embassy followed by lunch at the Mohammed Ali Club – two ports of call which would give him all the political information needed for the uncensored telegraphic despatch which would reach the sub-editors' table in good time for the first edition. Later, quite apart from the difficulty of finding anything out in a government machine suspicious of all foreign questioners, there were continual problems of censorship. As Holburn reported back privately to London in 1953, a year after the Neguib–Nasser *coup*:

Under the old regime the censorship was very liberal, especially for *The Times*. But today we have a regime in which young army officers, blissful amateurs in everything except their own profession, throw their weight about in every department. Two nights ago Colonel Sadate[33] [*sic*], the Army's press chief, actually wrote into the B.B.C. correspondent's despatch what he thought the correspondent ought to say about conditions in the southern Sudan.

He added that in Syria it had become virtually impossible for foreign correspondents to work at all.

Things were easier in Israel, whose rulers were more aware of the advantages to be drawn from making the journalists' way smooth. But even there press control was subject to the exigencies of the situation. By the late fifties *The Times*, like several other papers, found that Jerusalem (or Tel Aviv) and Beirut were the easiest and most convenient centres.

Always in the background was the threat of open war once again between the Arab states and Israel. In this predicament *The Times* repeatedly urged the larger powers, led by the United States and Russia, to try to come to an agreement limiting the supply of arms to

---

33 Anwar Sadat (1918–1981). President of Egypt from Nasser's death in September 1970 until his assassination in October 1981.

both sides. It was a gallant effort, but by this time America was wholly committed to support of Israel, and Russia had swung its influence and its hopes to the side of its chosen Arab friends, so that any agreement had become out of reach.

It was the four-month period October 1962 – January 1963 that made many British people recognise, even more clearly than during the Suez crisis of 1956, how the country's strength had diminished in the world of the superpowers. Those four months brought not only the French ban on British entry into the Common Market; they also brought the Cuba missiles crisis, the Chinese armed incursion across the northern frontier hills into India, and Britain's own admission that she must drop out of missile-building and rely on American products.

In all these happenings Britain, long accustomed to influencing or directly shaping world events, was left looking on from the sidelines or found herself openly rebuffed. The lesson was the more painful because Macmillan, with his combination of shrewdness and panache, appeared for a time to have recovered for Britain some of the diplomatic ground lost at Suez. Having made friends again with the United States and joined with it in the Lebanon–Jordan landings, Macmillan instigated new east–west talks by his Soviet visit early in 1959; he did much to bring about the Paris summit conference of May 1960 and, after the Khrush-chev–Eisenhower rift over the American U-2 flights, he repaired some of the damage. His persuasive work over many months helped greatly in bringing about the nuclear test ban agreements; and Britain could still claim to possess a small and independent nuclear striking force. In public the Macwonder and the Supermac of the cartoonists did not let his style be cramped by the country's low rate of industrial production. But he knew as well as anyone that it is production which provides the substance or lack of substance in a country's foreign policy; the realist in him made him play safe when the shocks came.

Of all the crises in those years it was the fighting between China and India which let *The Times* give its clearest and most useful lead to opinion in Britain – and to many in India besides. At the time western politicians and journalists tended to declare that China had launched an all-out invasion. Some foresaw a threat to the northern Indian tea plantations and even to the Ganges valley. On *The Times* Richard Harris, with his lifelong knowledge of China, never doubted for a moment that China would retire once it had given its brief, rough warning to India. On October 12 Harris wrote that 'it would be a mistake to draw alarmist conclusions'; the Chinese were simply retaliat-ing against earlier Indian moves in the Ladakh area and they were asserting their claim across a long disputed frontier. On October 23 he suggested in another leading article that the Chinese were doing no more than demonstrate what they might do if they had a mind to it. On November 1, as concern mounted, he kept to his line:

A careful analysis of Chinese actions and statements so far does not prove that the Chinese are bent on widespread invasion.

On November 22 he was vindicated with the news that the Chinese leaders had ordered a cease-fire and a unilateral withdrawal. The affair, wrote Harris, had been bigger than what used to be called a punitive expedition, but 'that is roughly what the Chinese have been about'.[34] Harris did not justify the Chinese; they had harmed their own standing in the world. But at a time when Chinese motives were almost wholly unknown, and therefore exaggerated, it was especially useful to have *The Times* speaking calmly from knowledge.

Harris very often took an original view that began by being unpopular among many British and American officials and ended by being accepted. During the worst of the cold war and for some time afterwards, when Dulles and several other western leaders were proclaiming that neutrality was immoral, Harris steadily wrote that neutrality was inevitable and right for most states of Asia. More than that, he believed, western states would go against their own interests if they tried to change such neutrality. Living in East Asia had taught him the strength of the region's self-conscious, resistant civilisation, based on ancient culture and political tradition and persisting beneath all the modern ideological show. With the knowledge of that ancient culture Harris was confident that China would not follow the Russian pattern within its own frontiers and was not set on expanding outside them, though it would strongly resist any new incursions by others. For such reasons he had been wholly against General MacArthur's plans to carry the Korean war across the Chinese frontier.[35] Knowledge of the old cultures and traditions also made him sceptical about the supposed success of the Geneva conference of 1954 which divided Vietnam in half. The true division, he believed, lay between Laos and Cambodia on the one side (being under ancient Indian influence) and Vietnam on the other. His leading articles from 1955 onwards always presented Asia as the genuine home-made article, not as something fabricated to suit western preconceptions. They were the kind of deeply informed article that *The Times* existed to supply.

---

34 *The Times*, November 22 1962.
35 See Chapter XII.

Throughout all the weeks of uncertainty over the Indo–Chinese frontier news was sent from India by Neville Maxwell. He reported dispassionately while much of official India was excited. He got to know India well through travel in many rural areas but, partly due to his interest in Chinese motives during the frontier fighting, he became more taken up with China. That growing interest led him on in turn to academic work outside journalism.

The Cuba missiles crisis was the one single storm, beyond the others at the time, which made the British recognise their reduced size in the world. For the most part they had to look on and wait. Very few knew at the time that President Kennedy and Macmillan were having long, anxious and detailed consultations over the telephone each day; one day they spoke together three times;[36] and the respective ambassadors carried on the exchanges. But there was never much doubt that the United States, if it did decide to act in force for the removal of the Soviet offensive missiles from Fidel Castro's Cuba, would make its own unilateral decision when to do so. Louis Heren and his assistant, Nicholas Herbert,[37] reporting from Washington, made that determination as clear as the probable consequences of any such action:

> The President has chosen to see the crisis as a direct confrontation of United States and Soviet power . . . The firm belief is that as the leader of the alliance, with control of most of the nuclear power available to the west, it [the American Administration] has a right and a duty to defend itself and its allies – even to the extent of bringing about nuclear exchange.[38]

At that time it was expected that Soviet ships heading for Cuba would be intercepted by American warships:

> What happens then might well determine the future of Cuba and Berlin, if not the world.
> While few officials care to admit it even in private, they are not unaware that the nations generally, as well as the allies, may well object to their survival being decided by the two super powers.[39]

Heren reported on the stringency of the American blockade of Cuba,

---

36 Macmillan, *op. cit.* Vol. VI. Chapter VII.
37 Dennis Nicholas Herbert (Lord Hemingford) (b. 1934). Oundle; Clare College, Cambridge. *The Times* assistant correspondent in Washington, 1961–65; Middle East correspondent, 1965–68; deputy features editor, 1968–70. Editor, *Cambridge Evening News,* 1970–74; editorial director, Westminster Press, 1974.
38 Despatch from Washington, October 23 1962.
39 *Ibid.*

the other naval and military dispositions, and pressure from within Congress for an immediate invasion of the island. At the same time he showed that the President, while being wholly firm that the missiles must be taken from the island, was ready for a peaceful solution if it could achieve that end. Throughout the crisis the emphasis swung to and fro, one day bringing out the danger of war, the next the hopes of talks leading to peace. Sometimes the swings between danger and hope came hourly, and never was the five-hour difference in time between Washington and London more keenly felt as a hindrance to knowledge in London. On October 25 a sombre despatch from Heren was held out of the paper, much to his annoyance,[40] because it seemed to have been overtaken by news from Eric Britter, the United Nations correspondent in New York. Britter reported the great and sudden sense of relief in the United Nations at the news that Kennedy and Khrushchev had sent encouraging replies to an appeal by U Thant, the acting Secretary-General. In point of fact the sense of relief turned out to be somewhat excessive; the reply from Kennedy, the aggrieved party, was firmer and less conciliatory than Khrushchev's; but the subdued nature of Khrushchev's reply was itself significant, indicating a willingness to talk rather than face the near certainty of war. The Russians stopped any new shipments of missiles but evidence reaching Washington showed them still busy to make operative the missiles already in place. After a further dangerous heightening of tension came the direct contacts between Khrushchev and Kennedy, and finally the news that Khrushchev, convinced of American firmness, had decided to take all his missiles back to the Soviet Union. Heren, helped by Herbert, sent further despatches, going over the stages of the crisis, emphasizing the dangers which had been courted and averted, and drawing the lessons.

In its leading articles *The Times* had drawn attention to the potential dangers as far back as September 4. A leader by Richard Davy then said that the build-up of Soviet arms in Cuba was putting President Kennedy 'under increasing pressure to mount a full-scale invasion'. When the crisis broke another leader felt bound to recall previous American mistakes in dealing with Cuba, including the Bay of Pigs invasion fiasco eighteen months earlier, but the article stated that this time the Americans appeared to have a good case; the evidence about the missile bases on the island seemed to be hard. Still taking the crisis coolly, the article suggested that the tense dispute which obviously lay ahead might have to end with the Russians withdrawing from the Cuban bases and the Americans taking some of their missiles from Turkey and other areas

---

40 Heren, *Growing Up on The Times*, p. 283.

near the Soviet border.[41] As the dangers increased the articles swung more solidly behind Kennedy's demands for the removal of the bases in Cuba first and foremost and for close inspection of the sites thereafter:

> After Moscow's record of deception over the missiles would she honour her word not to send in more missiles?[42]

None the less the paper still regarded it as highly unlikely that the Soviet Union would knowingly press its ambitions to the point of an open clash. Here Printing House Square was guided by confidential hints from Whitehall and also by its own reading of Khrushchev's mind as shown in the long talks which staff men had had with him at different times over the years. They knew his cunning and bluster; they also knew his peasant caution. On October 29 a leading article assumed that he did not want war; the great danger always was that he might over-reach himself if not firmly resisted in time. The theme was taken up a few days later:

> Whatever else he wanted out of Cuba it is certain that Mr. Khrushchev did not want nuclear war. Faced with the risk of it he has swung right round and ordered a withdrawal . . . Being a Russian he does not use half measures. Withdrawal and courtesy take the place of threats and deliberate running of risks.[43]

President Kennedy's standing immeasurably increased after Cuba, and within minutes of his murder in Dallas on November 22 1963 every *Times* man and woman within the office, or within reach of it, was on the job of producing a paper that measured up to the man and to the shock felt throughout the world. Throughout the evening the staff members who had gone home were coming back or ringing to ask what they could do. The first news flashes came in at 7 p.m., two hours and a quarter before first-edition time. In Washington Heren began the story that was to stretch to several columns before the night was over. Herbert had set off for Dallas but turned back at Washington airport when the news of Kennedy's death was confirmed. In Printing House Square Roy Lewis, who had just finished a leader on Somalia, wrote another on Kennedy within forty-five minutes in time for the first edition. Later Haley came back from home to write a longer leader for the later editions. Colin Watson had an obituary on the stocks, about three columns long; Lewis, Hickey, and Geoffrey Smith (supposedly on holiday) added more than two columns to it. Richard Davy, who happened to be in West Germany, rang up and was asked by McDonald, in charge that night while

---

41 *The Times*, October 24 1962.
42 *The Times*, October 26 1962.
43 *The Times*, October 29 1962.

Haley concentrated on the leader, to join with Rendel in a profile on Johnson which became the 'turnover', the main special article in the paper. Pictures were swiftly changed. The heaviest work on the editorial side in London fell on the man who was constantly rearranging the paper, the night editor Tom Scott, and the chief foreign sub-editor Eric MacHardy. The printers and the photographic process men worked no less hard and willingly, combining to produce a *Times* as it should be on such an occasion.[44]

On the day before the funeral Haley said that Heren should write a full report of the day's ceremonial in the order in which it all happened, beginning with the first event of the morning and thereafter continuing hour by hour. The result the next day was an exercise in simplicity and clarity which outshone other papers' use of mechanistic devices such as 'highlights', 'new intros', and 'late night leads'. Heren began with some paragraphs on Kennedy's work, came on to Mrs. Kennedy's midnight vigil beside the coffin in the Capitol, then the long procession the next morning – 'a martial but dignified scene with none of the arrogance of militarism' – and so on hour by hour until the burial service at Arlington National Cemetery.[45]

---

44 Memorandum, November 24 1963. T.T.A.
45 *The Times*, November 26 1963.

XIX

IT *IS* A MORAL ISSUE

THE dominant theme throughout the later years of Haley's editorship is neatly presented in the heading which he gave to his most celebrated leader: 'It *is* a moral issue'.[1] The title quickly became as famous as Geoffrey Dawson's earlier gem, 'A Corridor for Camels'.[2] In 1935 Dawson's camels did as much as anything to ridicule and demolish the Hoare–Laval plan for robbing Ethiopia of large areas while offering it in return what Dawson called 'a strip of scrub' leading roadless to the sea. In 1963 Haley's title, as much as the article below it, had a similar impact in pitching *The Times* solidly against the comforting views which many in Westminster were taking about the Profumo affair. John Profumo, Secretary of State for War, resigned after confessing that he had earlier misled the House of Commons about his dealings with Miss Christine Keeler. Many MPs and others said that it was not so much a moral matter as a problem of parliamentary standards or (wrongly) of national security. Haley refused to follow such by-ways:

> Everyone has been so busy assuring the public that the affair is not one of morals, that it is time to assert that it is. Morals have been discounted too long.

Looking more broadly at many shabby strands in British society, Haley laid a large part of the blame with successive Conservative governments. Eleven years of their rule had 'brought the nation psychologically and spiritually to a low ebb':

> They declared they had the right road for Britain. They would set the people free. Change, they declared, was their ally. Nothing else, they seemed to think, mattered, compared with the assertion that the nation had never had it so good.[3] Today they are faced with a

---

1 *The Times*, June 11 1963.
2 *The Times*, December 1935.
3 'Let us be frank about it, most of our people have never had it so good.' Harold Macmillan, Conservative rally, Bedford, July 21 1957. (Macmillan used the phrase as the preface to a strong warning that the prosperity would vanish if wages, prices and

flagging economy, an uncertain future, and the end of the illusion that Britain's greatness could be measured by the so-called independence of its so-called deterrent. All this may seem far from Mr. Profumo, but his admissions could be the last straw . . .

There are plenty of earnest and serious men in the Conservative Party who know that all is not well. It is time they put first things first, stopped weighing electoral chances, and returned to the stark truths of an earlier day. Popularity by affluence is about played out, especially when it rests on so insecure a basis.[4]

He returned to the point two days later: 'This sorry business has passed from being one of politics to one of conscience.'[5]

The choice between conscience and politics was one which Haley made in several other fields. 'It *is* a moral issue' could have been the heading for many leaders which he wrote or ordered to be written. For him the crisis 'inherent in the political and economic situation of Britain is a moral one'.[6] Nowhere did the Victorian in him, often hidden behind his fervour for news and his flair for administration, show more strongly than in this unflagging habit of moral judgment.

During an office discussion at a time of some public scandal one of the men present murmured that, when writing, they should perhaps just bear in mind that there were always two sides to every question. Haley spun round at him. 'There are *not* two sides to every question. Some things are bad and cruel and ugly, and no amount of fine writing will ever make them good and kind and beautiful.'[7]

His sense of moral values was given its more direct and obvious field for exercise in 1960 when the High Court was asked to declare D. H. Lawrence's novel *Lady Chatterley's Lover* (then about to be brought out in paperback) to be obscene. The jury threw out the application. In a

---

inflation got out of hand, but it was the ebullient phrase and not the warning that was generally remembered.)

4 The full text of 'It *is* a moral issue' is given in Appendix F.
5 *The Times* leading article, June 13 1963.
6 See Chapter XX.
7 Letter, Chalfont to McDonald, August 1 1980. Haley used almost the same language in his farewell speech to the staff of *The Times* on resigning as chairman of Times Newspapers Limited, December 21 1967: 'What I am going to say now I have said before, but I believe it so deeply that I will go on saying it till I die. The truth is that there *is* a difference between right and wrong, and there *are* things that we should not be ready to compromise. There is no half-way house between honesty and dishonesty. There are things which are bad and false and ugly and no amount of argument or specious casuistry will make them good or true or beautiful. It is time for these things to be said and time for the press to say them.' *Times House Journal*, January–February 1968.

leader entitled 'A Decent Reticence'[8] Haley deplored the verdict. With all his respect for an author's craft and freedom, he none the less believed that a line had to be drawn and that Lawrence had overstepped it:

> There is no appeal against the jury's verdict. But on the grounds of decency, and taste, and even morals, it is still possible to express dissent . . . It is difficult to see where the law will now be able to make a stand . . . A great shift in what is permissible legally has been made. But not morally. Yesterday's verdict is a challenge to society to resist the changes in its manners and conduct that may follow from it. It should not be taken as an invitation to succumb.

The chief reason for Haley's strict attitude is contained in the sentence, quoted above, in which he wrote that it was difficult to know where the law could stand henceforth. He most firmly believed that many forces in society in the early sixties were pushing hard against the dykes, and that warnings by him and others had their last chance of being heard with effect before the dykes collapsed. There he was probably right, although in the event he and the others were heard but not generally heeded.

Printing House Square itself divided along predictable lines over the Chatterley case. Haley sought the views of his assistant editors who all agreed with him; they were in their middle or late fifties. Younger members of the staff said that the article was hypocritical. In Downing Street Macmillan disliked the article even more. 'The Times was awful – what has since been called a "Holier than thou" attitude, which was really nauseating.'[9] Some of the published letters to the editor made the same accusation, but most of those published and unpublished were full of praise and gratitude. Not for the first time Haley was fighting a long rearguard action.

Inflation raised questions of morality no less acutely in Haley's mind. To him money was money; it was not simply the economist's unit of exchange, something conveniently variable. A government which let the pound slide in value – or, worse still, deliberately set it sliding – was depriving the people of their earnings and their savings. In so doing the Treasury ministers were dishonouring a moral contract. He was delighted to find that Montagu Norman, Governor of the Bank of England between 1920 and 1944, had been firmly of the same mind. In reviewing Sir Henry Clay's biography of the banker Maurice Green wrote that

---

8 *The Times*, November 3 1960.
9 Macmillan, *Memoirs*, Vol. vi. p. 442. Diary entry, July 7 1963. Actually the phrase commonly used was 'Halier than thou', an obvious pun on the name Haley.

Norman regarded inflation and devaluation as forms of default; there could be no two views about it. 'Norman's moral code', wrote Green, 'was too clear to make it seem necessary to him to argue that dishonest dealing could not have good consequences.'[10] 'Excellent', cried Haley as he read a proof of the review. 'Make sure that those sentences get into the paper whatever else has to be cut.'[11]

Haley had closer relations with Macmillan than with any other Prime Minister before or after. Even so their talks were businesslike rather than relaxed. In spite of the great difference in temperament between the puritan Haley and the cavalier Macmillan, and in spite of Haley's fear that the establishment of an easy personal relationship between politician and editor was always liable to compromise the latter's integrity, there was sufficient community of interest and ideas between the two men for them to find most of their exchanges mutually profitable. Macmillan often fumed at *The Times's* moralistic strictures even while respecting Haley's rectitude and precision. Haley distrusted Macmillan's eye for political advantage and, in particular, his encouragement of the pre-election economic boom in 1959. He none the less admired the Prime Minister's historical sense, his flair, his recognition of the need for change at home and abroad. So the two men could have frank and useful discussions which, never quoted directly by Haley, allowed *The Times* to be better informed and quicker with the news than other papers on, say, Macmillan's venturesome visit to Khrushchev in Moscow in February–March 1959. They also allowed the paper to go hard in many leading articles and political notes instead of merely weighing up possibilities. Happily enough, one of Haley's last visits to Macmillan as Prime Minister was the most congenial. On February 19 1963 Macmillan noted:

> He was enthusiastic about my speech [to the Young Conservatives conference]. I was enthusiastic about his leading article. This mutual 'buttering' was agreeable and may be useful.[12]

During the months of political uncertainty after illness had forced Macmillan to resign in October 1963, *The Times* repeatedly made plain which faction and which man it wished to see in power. Its voice often went unheeded. On Macmillan's departure Haley had an article suggesting R. A. Butler as his successor, but only if Edward Heath was

---

10 *The Times*, May 2 1957.
11 See Chapter XX for a fuller discussion of *The Times's* financial and economic arguments under the Macmillan, Douglas-Home and Wilson governments.
12 Macmillan, *Ibid*, p. 397.

thought to be too young. After Sir Alec Douglas-Home was chosen for the job and had almost a year at No. 10 behind him, there was once again much speculation at Westminster and elsewhere over which party *The Times* would support before the general election which lay ahead. The *Sunday Mirror* led its issue of October 11 1964 with an across-the-page spread under the headings: 'Election exclusive. Secret fear of the Tories. Will The Times desert them on the eve of battle?' The story began:

> A shy man who now occupies an important position – Sir William Haley, Editor of The Times – is worrying the Top Tories to death this weekend.
>
> What he might do, and when he might do it, is the subject of anxious phone calls among Tory Ministers.
>
> There are rumours, disturbing to the Tories, that the august Times, pillar of The Establishment, will announce this week that 'it is time for a change' and that for the country's good Labour should win.

The scare was unnecessary. Haley had three long leaders on successive days, October 12, 13 and 14, and finally came down on the side of the Conservatives:

> It is a conclusion come to without enthusiasm. But Britain has to be governed, her economic state is serious, and these men are the better hope. Whichever party is returned, there should be the largest possible Liberal vote.[13]

As always the voters went their own way. Labour was returned with 317 seats against the Conservatives' 304. The Liberal share rose steeply to 11.2 per cent of the votes cast, but it still left them with only nine seats. In all the elections held while Haley was editor he supported the Conservatives, though more than once showing his regret that the Liberals were not strong enough to win an effective mandate. It was typical of the man that he plainly wrote what he thought ought to happen rather than what might happen.

Labour's majority of only four after the 1964 election, and the consequent fear of political instability, encouraged *The Times* to follow its tradition of giving a new government its support so long as it could in conscience do so. It made that support plain straight away.[14] A few days later, on the occasion of the Queen's Speech it wrote:

---

13 *The Times*, October 14 1964.
14 Leading article (Hickey), October 17 1964.

The speech contains a useful programme which, with one provocative exception [the re-nationalization of steel], establishes a sensible order of priorities.[15]

The paper criticised much that Labour did, and more that it did not do, but it did not regret Wilson's greatly increased majority in the House after the general election of April 1966. It had been a snap election, seldom a good thing:

Even so, in this case country and Parliament should benefit. The previous tight-rope walking may have been invigorating to Mr. Wilson but to precious few others.[16]

Henceforward Wilson had the power to tackle the dire economic dangers facing the country, provided he was ready to use that power and provided his left wing let him do so.

Below the prime-ministerial level the relations between Conservatives and *The Times* were often strained. David Wood, the political correspondent, was a natural target for criticism from MPs enraged by his fine skill in presenting startling and highly confidential news as though he had drawn it out of a private soliloquy of his own. Early in 1962 John Morrison, chairman of the Conservative MPs' 1922 Committee, warned Wood that he would complain to Gavin and Hugh Astor over his disclosures about the committee's private meetings. Wood told Morrison that timely disclosure was the job of any lobby correspondent.[17] Later Wood was given dark reminders that there was such a thing as parliamentary privilege. Haley assured him of absolute support.[18] On July 23 1963 Gavin Astor saw three officers of the committee, John Morrison (later Lord Margadale), Sir Tufton Beamish, and Sir Charles Mott-Radcliffe. They made another and stronger protest against a *Times* report about a committee meeting held at an especially delicate time when Macmillan's leadership was under question,[19] though *The Times* did not mention this particular matter then. In point of fact the report was written not by Wood but by George Clark, his assistant. Gavin Astor passed the complaint on to Haley. Haley immediately said that Morrison had made an unconstitutional approach; he alone as editor was responsible for what appeared in *The Times* and he would

---

15 Leading article (Woods), November 4 1964.
16 Leading article (Woods), April 4 1966.
17 Memorandum, Wood to Haley, February 13 1962. T.T.A.
18 Memorandum, Haley to Wood, March 12 1962. T.T.A.
19 *The Times*, July 16 1963.

resist any pressures from outside.[20] On other occasions City men as well as MPs, annoyed by pieces in the paper, complained to Gavin Astor, but such approaches – going straight to the man on top and therefore likely to be effective, as was thought by those making the protests – were always resented and firmly rebuffed by Haley.

David Wood weathered all the storms which took on new strength after Harold Wilson entered No. 10. Wilson believed that he was being personally attacked by Wood who, Wilson knew, had liked and respected Hugh Gaitskell. Wood believed that Wilson wished to use the lobby group, greatly enlarged in the preceding years, as a ready-to-hand political instrument. Wood's suspicion was shared by Wilson's Cabinet colleague, Richard Crossman. In his diaries Crossman notes (February 18 1965) that Wood had reproduced in *The Times* the substance of a minute which Crossman had written to Wilson complaining about a speech by Lord Cromer, then Governor of the Bank of England. Clearly the minute had been given to Wood in an off-the-record briefing:

> This is typical of Harold's handling of politics. He still thinks he can settle problems just by talking to the press.[21]

For all that, Wood's independence led to a worsening of relations and he found that he no longer received invitations to the so-called 'inner lobby' briefings, made to a small and trusted group within the larger group. He got all the news in other ways. In the autumn of 1966 Wilson told Lord Thomson of Fleet, whose purchase of *The Times* was about to be confirmed by the Monopolies Commission, that the first thing Thomson should do on acquiring the newspaper ought to be to get rid of David Wood.[22] Denis Hamilton, who was to be the chief-executive of the new company, and William Rees-Mogg, who was to be editor of *The Times*,[23] were present at the same Chequers dinner. They did not think for a moment of taking the advice.

When Maurice Green left *The Times* early in 1961 Haley had no hesitation in calling Oliver Woods back from a tour in Africa and making him assistant editor with a special brief to revitalise the home news. The Board of directors had just increased the editorial budget by £75,000 and much of that sum, Haley decided, was to go into the home

---

20 Note by Oliver Woods, undated but evidently July 1963. T.T.A.
21 Richard Crossman, *Diaries of a Cabinet Minister*, Vol. I: *Minister of Housing*, p. 161.
22 James Margach, *The Abuse of Power*, p. 145.
23 See Chapter XXIII.

side for long-overdue development. Haley's directive to Woods was broad in terms and in scope. The home side of *The Times* should be freed from negative inhibitions and move to a position of frankness and courage. *The Times* should be a truly national paper, aimed at all age groups and written in a correspondingly lively and aware language and style. It should explore new fields of interest and challenge:

> As society's interests change and develop, so must the national coverage of *The Times* also change. *This is the most important and exciting task of all, and the most difficult.*

Woods's appointment was wholly successful. Green, as Haley's deputy, had been caught up too much in daily and nightly administration. For the next few years it was Ryan and McDonald who mainly sat in the chair when Haley was away. Ryan was also given charge of the arts features, the books page, the woman's page, and the many special articles. All this left Woods much freer to look after the home news, special investigations, and the staffing on the home side. He soon picked a strong executive in John Grant who, after five years as defence correspondent, became home news editor. The two made an excellent team. Woods's eager and speculative approach to a new subject was well supported by Grant's hard northern mind – a mind in which his native Lancashire was reinforced by the disciplines of Balliol.

Together they organised two long series of articles which, appearing on the home news pages, produced substantial and positive evidence about two areas of public opinion which had been almost unknown territory for government and intelligentsia alike. The first series, entitled 'The Pulse of Britain',[24] was suggested at much the same time by both Haley and Brian Priestley, the Birmingham correspondent.[25] The ten articles, written by Priestley, described what different classes of people in different parts of the country were thinking about Britain's role as the empire dissolved, as Europe was beckoning, and as new technology was making the great powers greater while the poor countries became poorer. The second was the series of eleven articles already referred to written by Peter Evans[26] after he had spent six months in

---

24 *The Times*, February 3–15 1964.
25 Brian Priestley (b. 1930). King Edward's, Birmingham; Birmingham University. *Walsall Observer*, 1952–54; *Cannock Courier*, 1954–55; *Birmingham Mail*, 1955–60. Midland correspondent for *The Times*, 1960–68.
26 Peter Stanley Evans (b. 1932). Marling School, Stroud. *Stroud News*, 1949–55; *The Citizen*, Gloucester, 1955–58; *Liverpool Daily Post and Echo*, 1958–59. *The Times* home news reporter, 1959–66; head of the news team, 1967–68; home news editor, 1968–69; race relations correspondent, 1969–70; home affairs correspondent from 1970.

several cities where he lived with coloured immigrants. Haley's title for the series, 'The Dark Million',[27] had the right suggestion of the unknown and the potentially dangerous about it, and the articles themselves provided the information which many people were deliberately keeping out of their minds.[28]

To fill Grant's place as defence correspondent Haley was prepared to go against his normal and oft-declared practice; he agreed to appoint an expert who until then had no working knowledge of journalism. Alun Gwynne Jones was in his early forties, a lieutenant-colonel in the War Office. After school in Wales he served with the South Wales Borderers in India and Malaya during the Second World War and in Malaya afterwards.[29] Memories of the difficulties which *The Times* had with Colonel C. à C. Repington, military correspondent from 1905 to 1918, and with Captain Liddell Hart before the 1939–45 war, increased all the initial arguments against appointing a professional soldier. But Haley saw Gwynne Jones, liked the way he thought and talked, decided to take the risk, and within a few weeks saw that Gwynne Jones was quickly learning to write with the clarity, speed, and conciseness which journalism imposes. The newcomer recognised on his side that all the specialised knowledge in the world is no good unless it can be put into the short, clear sentences that can be read in the train or aircraft. He kept up all his contacts with high-ranking officers, he visited units in several fields, he appeared on television, and wrote several series of articles apart from his daily writings.

One major change in policy was made in the paper as a result of his persuasion. John Grant, while believing that Duncan Sandys as Secretary of State for Defence staked too much on the nuclear deterrent, was none the less convinced that Britain should keep her own bomb. She was unlikely ever to use it, true enough; but possession of it would save her from being blackmailed by the nuclear threat of others, say, in the Middle East.[30] Gwynne Jones thought that a British bomb had no credibility as a deterrent, would never be used independently of America, and was generally a waste of money. He and Haley probed the matter together in many long talks. Gwynne Jones clinched his argument in a long memorandum, saying that the choice for Britain was between Nato as it was and a European third force which would weaken

---

27 *The Times*, January 11–30 1965.
28 See Chapter XIV.
29 Alun Arthur Gwynne Jones (b. 1919). West Monmouth School; Bristol University. Army, 1938–61, *The Times* defence correspondent, 1961–64. Minister of State, Foreign Office, 1964–70. Baron Chalfont, 1964.
30 Leading article (Grant), June 23 1960.

and disrupt the western alliance:

I conclude therefore that the most desirable line for future British defence policy is to accept the indivisibility of western defence and the commitment of America to the defence of Europe;

to retire gracefully from the nuclear race when the present bomber force with its British weapons becomes obsolete;

and to concentrate on building up strong conventional defence forces, if necessary returning to compulsory military service.[31]

Grant, who had long advocated greater conventional forces, was still against giving up the bomb entirely, but Haley's mind was made up:

I have read Mr. Gwynne Jones' memorandum on the independent deterrent. Fundamentally I am in agreement with it.[32]

The manner of Gwynne Jones's departure from the paper in the autumn of 1964 provided his own most startling news story. Harold Wilson had evidently been following his writings in *The Times*, both directly on service matters and more broadly on disarmament. After the Labour electoral victory in October 1964 Wilson asked Gwynne Jones to see him and, out of the blue, invited him to be Minister of State at the Foreign Office with a special concern over disarmament and with a seat in the House of Lords. Gwynne Jones had a long talk with Haley, who reminded him that in politics a man can be dropped as quickly as he is taken up. He also might find that he had less influence on government policy than he had as an independent commentator. Gwynne Jones could not resist the new challenge; he decided to go out and meet it, much to the regret of his colleagues in Printing House Square. Several *Times* men had in the past become government ministers but Gwynne Jones beat them all in speed when making the change.

As his successor Haley and Woods chose a younger man, Charles Douglas-Home,[33] a nephew of the Conservative leader. He had served in the Royal Scots Greys and, after some time on the *Daily Express* in Glasgow and then as a writer on defence, science, and medicine in London, he was on the point of going to the United States as *Express* correspondent when *The Times* made him its offer. Like Gwynne Jones he had the most excellent contacts, military and political. He concerned himself less than Grant and Gwynne Jones with details of weaponry; he

---

31 Memorandum, Gwynne Jones to Woods, December 19 1962. T.T.A.
32 Memorandum, Haley to Woods, December 20 1962. T.T.A.
33 Charles Cospatrick Douglas-Home (b. 1937). Eton. ADC to Governor of Kenya, 1958. Defence correspondent, *The Times*, 1965–70; features editor, 1970–73; home editor, 1973–78; foreign editor, 1978–81, deputy editor, 1981–82; editor, 1982.

looked at the strategic picture and where Gwynne Jones had made giving up the bomb his main argument Douglas-Home thought it right to explore another field, advocating the withdrawal of British forces from east of Suez, except for Hong Kong.

Under Haley as under Barrington-Ward and Dawson *The Times* had a special concern in school and university education. Its most original and, to many, most surprising effort was to mount in December 1963 an all-out attack on almost the whole concept of the Robbins report on higher education. This onslaught, startling though it was, was only the culmination of a steady policy developed over many years: expansion of education, certainly, but not on too broad a front, not with the certain prospect of lowering quality, and not at the cost of neglecting techno-logical schooling.

During the war the emphasis had been on expansion. *The Times* had given its blessing, with hardly a critical note, to the government papers and discussions leading up to the Butler Education Act of 1944. Its leaders were then written largely by Harold Dent[34] who was made acting editor of the *Educational Supplement* in 1940 and produced it almost single-handed during the war years. In 1946 he fell ill, possibly through over-work, and at the beginning of 1947 Walter James[35] was appointed deputy editor of the *Supplement* with responsibility for occasional educational leaders in *The Times* itself. Unlike Dent, who had much school teaching behind him, James was not an educationalist. He had been writing leaders for the *Manchester Guardian* on many subjects, ending with the Hiroshima bomb and the Nuremberg war trials. But he was a friend of Eric James, later Lord James of Rusholme and at that time High Master of Manchester Grammar School and the leading defender of selective secondary education. Eric James's de-clared aim was that Manchester Grammar School should continue to provide for able working-class boys of south-east Lancashire as good an academic education as their richer contemporaries enjoyed at Winches-ter (where Eric James himself had taught science). It was the cause of equal opportunity in this sense that *The Times* pursued throughout the

---

34 Harold Collett Dent (b. 1894). Editor of *The Times Educational Supplement*, 1940; retired 1951; educational correspondent of *The Times*, 1952; resigned in 1955 to become Professor of Education and director of the Institute of Education at Sheffield University.
35 Arthur Walter James (b. 1912). Uckfield Grammar School; Keble and Magdalen Colleges, Oxford. *Manchester Guardian* editorial staff, 1937–46. Chief assistant to the editor, *The Times Educational Supplement*, 1947; deputy editor, 1948–51; editor, 1952–69; editor, *Technology*, 1957–60. Reader in journalism, University of Canterbury, New Zealand, 1971–74. Principal, St. Catharine's, Windsor, since 1974.

controversy that was to be aroused over comprehensive schools.

The 1950s and 1960s were a time of rising educational expenditure, interrupted by financial cutbacks from successive governments. *The Times* went on backing the Butler Act throughout, though in 1953 it commented that 'too much is being attempted and too little is being well done',[36] and it put its weight behind drives for a higher school age, smaller classes, nursery education, and more television and books in the class-rooms. But, in line with Haley's general policy, it showed a special and consistent concern for better technological and technical education and for raising the standard of industrial recruitment.

In this it was very much the voice of a minority at that time, and one that was little heard. (Thirty years later the Finniston report of 1980 on engineering was to make many of the points the paper was urging in the early 1950s.) The paper none the less threw itself into Lord Cherwell's[37] campaign to create 'at least one institution of university rank devoted primarily to the teaching and study of technology,' which led to the special development of Imperial College,[38] and wove into its many arguments for producing more engineers another favourite theme – that they, as well as everyone in higher education, should be more broadly educated.

It was Sir David Eccles[39] who put steam behind technical training with his 1956 programme of expansion. *The Times* gave its enthusiastic support not only in its leader columns but also more practically (it hoped) by launching in 1957 the monthly magazine *Technology* to record and help forward the new movement. This second venture failed within three years. It had its faults, but some part of the blame lay in the lack of public attention to the news of manufacturing industry, still the source of Britain's wealth and welfare.

Side by side with the development of technology Haley and Walter James were intent to preserve, so far as their words counted, the independence of universities against governmental and official interference. The theory that the University Grants Committee could stand as a buffer between the universities and government appealed to Haley. He fought a rearguard action in the early fifties against the claim of the Public Accounts Committee to have the right to inspect the universities' books:

No elected assembly, and no Government, can determine in detail

---

36 Leading article (James), December 18 1953.
37 Frederick Alexander Lindemann, Baron Cherwell (1886–1957). Chemist and physicist. Personal assistant to Churchill 1940–41.
38 Leading article (James), June 21 1952.
39 David McAdam Eccles, Viscount Eccles (b. 1904). Minister of Education 1954–57.

the proper objects of scholarly expenditure; it is beyond their competence.[40]

Yet the PAC had its way before the end of the decade.

It was the paper's fierce desire to help to preserve the independence and special character of the universities which led it to make its full-scale, head-on attack in 1963 against the Robbins report[41] on university expansion.[42] The report called for a trebling of student numbers by 1980. In spite of the cost it was warmly welcomed by the two main political parties and by the universities as a whole, though one or two voices questioned it on grounds of practicability. Great hopes were still held of higher education, for it was seen as a prime means for overcoming economic decline as well as a way of meeting the expected demand for university places generated by the secondary school expansion of the previous decade.

Haley and his advisers talked over the matter many times and the decision to mount the attack – one of the most cogent in the newspaper's history – was finally taken at a small special conference in the editor's room, with Oliver Woods, Owen Hickey[43] (who was to do the writing) and Walter James. It was not to be a mere critical stand, but a root and branch onslaught. At the meeting Haley settled for three first leaders on successive days, December 4, 5 and 6 1963.

The main argument pressed was that an expansion of the size and pace recommended would cause the universities to be 'transformed, not just in size and number, but in character, aims and emphasis as well.' The case was not against an extension of higher education in general, but against putting all eggs in the university basket:

Is the degree of autonomy which is necessary for the proper functioning of universities compatible with their integration into the public educational system as general post-secondary providers?

The articles went further, however, than the question of academic freedom. The Robbins report ran counter to the paper's post-war concern for technological and technical education at all levels. Had not

---

40 Leading article (James), August 6 1953.
41 *Higher Education. Report of the Committee appointed by the Prime Minister under the Chairmanship of Lord Robbins 1961–63.* Cmd. 2154.
42 Lionel Charles Robbins (1898–1984). Professor of Economics, London School of Economics, 1929–61. Chairman, *Financial Times*, 1961–70. Chairman, committee on higher education, 1961–64. Baron, 1959.
43 Thomas James Owen Hickey (b. 1924). Clifton; Magdalen College, Oxford. Army, 1940–45. Editorial staff, *The Times Educational Supplement*, 1949–54; special writer *The Times*, 1954–69; chief leader writer (home) from 1969; associate editor from 1972.

the large financial claims for academic education at universities over-looked the need to make proper provision 'for the training of craftsmen and technicians,' and indeed for 'the education of Newsom's[44] school leavers, the average and the below?' In sum, Robbins 'recommends a degree of inflation of the universities which they are unlikely to be able to sustain without devaluation,' an inflation which in the long run could be achieved only at the expense of all other sides of education, especially of those needed new institutions in the technical field for which *The Times* had campaigned steadily.

The three leaders stood up well to the test of time. Along the same line of thought the paper opposed movements to get rid of the public schools which catered for the sons and daughters of the well-to-do. Under Barrington-Ward *The Times* had very properly urged the need to spread social and educational benefits more widely, and broaden the base of the social and economic pyramid. Under Haley it did not dispute such aims but, while pursuing them, it pointed out the need to maintain the quality of an elite that, constantly replenished from below, could give leadership to the country in all fields – political, economic, cultural, educational.

At one point its pursuit of excellence led it into a misjudgment. In a leader, recording the consensus within the office, it dismissed as a gimmick the proposal for having the Open University, then styled the University of the Air,[45] and so it failed to bless the birth of an institution which manifestly brought higher learning to many who would otherwise have missed it.

By way of pleasant footnote, the paper achieved a small and finite triumph – always welcome to journalists – when it was the means of saving St. David's College, Lampeter. In 1955 St. David's, set in rural Wales, a perfect neo-Gothic copy of an Oxford college, ante-dating all the civic universities, was faced with extinction. The University Grants Committee told it that it could not be put on the list for grants because its degrees were not up to scratch. *The Times* embraced its cause in two articles[46] which produced a number of letters to the editor from its external examiners, all distinguished members of other universities, who testified that the Lampeter degrees awarded on their marks were well up to the standards of those given in their own institutions. For the UGC to question such evidence would have amounted to a vote of no confidence in the academic establishment as a whole, and in the end

---

44 The Newsom report, *Half our Future. A Report of the Central Advisory Council for Education (England)*, appeared in 1963.
45 *The Times*, April 3 1965.
46 Special article, February 8; leading article, February 19 1955.

Lampeter was put on the grants list, attached to the University of Wales. The college, which had laboured manfully in its own cause, made no secret of its debt to Printing House Square.

Owen Hickey, who wrote the three-headed attack on the Robbins report, was one of the men who gave *The Times* its special character for the simple reason that he could never disguise his own very special character. It emerged, through all the anonymity, in every paragraph he wrote. He had a mind of clinical precision, a donnish wit which would suddenly sparkle in the most serious of leaders, a daunting dialectical force in policy discussions (a force made more impressive by his head of prematurely white hair), and all the Irishman's sense of rightness and comfort when being agin' the government, whether national or local or – one suspected at times – editorial. He would disappear at regular intervals to look after a farm in the middle of Ireland not directly linked to any telephone. Certainly neither Lord Acton nor Lord Ashburton had anything to teach him on the need to expose and diminish the evils of corruptive and ever-increasing official power. For many years Hickey made such diminution of power his chief mission, while of course writing on many other subjects. He adhered to the Church of Rome and was never better than when demonstrating, for the readers' benefit, the strengths and the weaknesses in a papal pronouncement. Nearer home he and Geoffrey Smith,[47] a later arrival on the staff, were ever ready to prolong an editorial conference while they worked out with growing alarm the full dangers likely to flow from a proposed change in the laws of cricket.

Hickey and Smith were to be the mainstay of the home leader writing team. Each had been through a proven training ground for *Times* writers with the *Educational Supplement* or in the obituaries department. Smith developed a fine political sense, tracing all the shifts at Westminster while being ready to drop it all and write with little forewarning on something utterly different.

One task remained always on Woods's and Grant's desks. That was to bring up the level of talent in the home reporters' room to somewhere near the level among the specialist writers and the foreign correspondents. It was work without end, because many of the high flyers were speedily spotted on the radar screens of news editors in other journals and were enticed away. (Some of the flyers, having departed, applied

---

47 Geoffrey Peter Smith (b. 1930). Edinburgh University. *The Times* obituaries department, 1961; special writer, 1965; home leader writer, 1967; columnist, 1983.

hardly less speedily to come back to *The Times*.) Others were lost to the reporters' room on becoming specialist writers on *The Times* themselves. The four reporters whom Oliver Woods, during his early months in the job,[48] rated as outstanding all moved on: T. Windsor Davies to be parliamentary sketch writer and then leader writer,[49] Hugh Noyes to be diarist and the parliamentary sketch writer,[50] Geoffrey Charles to be motoring correspondent,[51] and Hugh Cochrane, Scottish correspondent,[52] to another paper. Five others rated highly also moved on at various times: David Leitch,[53] David Spanier, John Greig, Margaret Allen, Brian Priestley. Yet the level certainly rose amid all the changes. Philip Howard[54] in particular was a man whose light, amusing, and graceful style began to break through all the bonds of anonymity from the day he was recruited in 1964.

Another task was to ensure the right administrative staff both in the home news room (in charge of the reporters and coordination of the specialists' work) and at the home sub-editors' table. Frank Roberts, calm and apparently unhurried, was an excellent deputy to John Grant; and he in turn was supported by Cyril Bainbridge[55] and Arthur Reed,[56] who joined in 1961. To overcome an evident weakness in following up

48 Memorandum, Woods to Haley, June 1 1961. T.T.A.
49 Thomas Windsor Davies (b. 1930). Newport High School. *Keighley News* and *Yorkshire Observer*, 1951–57. *The Times* parliamentary reporter, 1957–59; home news reporter, 1960–61; parliamentary sketch writer, 1961–63; leader writer, 1963–67. Resigned to join *Daily Telegraph*.
50 Hugh Calverly Eric Noyes (b. 1928). Cate School, California; Princeton University. *Wiltshire Gazette*, 1954–56; *North Western Evening Mail*, 1956–58. *The Times* home news reporter, 1958–66; diary reporter, 1966–67; parliamentary correspondent from 1967. Resigned 1982.
51 Geoffrey David Charles (b. 1925). Ealing Central School; Pitman's College. *Middlesex Advertiser and County Gazette*, 1942–47; *Middlesex County Times-Gazette*, 1947–50; *Press Association, parliamentary staff*, 1950–52. *The Times* parliamentary reporter, 1952–59; home news reporter, 1959–61; motoring correspondent, 1962–70.
52 Hugh Graham Cochrane (b. 1932). Hyndland Senior Secondary School. *Kilmarnock Standard*, 1952–55; *Scotsman*, 1956–60. *The Times* staff correspondent in Scotland, 1960–68.
53 David Paul Leitch (b. 1937). Merchant Taylor's; St. John's College, Cambridge. *The Times* home news reporter, 1961–63. *Sunday Times* editorial staff, 1963–72.
54 Philip Nicholas Charles Howard (b. 1933). Eton; Trinity College, Oxford. Joined staff of *The Times* as home news reporter, 1964; literary editor from 1979.
55 Cyril Bainbridge (b. 1928). Negus College, Bradford. Press Association, 1954–62. *The Times* home news reporter, 1963–67; deputy news editor, 1967–69; regional news editor, 1969–77; managing news editor 1977–82. Assistant managing editor '82.
56 Arthur Laurence Reed (b. 1928). John Ruskin Grammar School, Croydon. *Surrey Times*, 1945–53. Press Association, 1955–59. *The Times* parliamentary reporter, 1959–60; home news reporter, 1961–65; deputy home news editor, 1965–67; air correspondent 1967–82.

late stories Colin Wilson[57] was made news editor at night, later followed by Brian Packham,[58] the result was seen in the appearance of many more late-night or early-morning stories in *The Times* at breakfast.

There were disappointments. Haley, after driving the team forward, would sometimes brake hard. After the Vassall spy trial Grant was 'bitterly disappointed' when Haley killed 'an informative and important piece' on Vassal's private life; the story had taken 'a week's real hard digging by Mr. Leitch'.[59] In reply Haley wrote that, while it was right to start the project, no one could ever foretell how a piece would shape out in the end: 'And the way the story did turn out meant that it would have seemed to the majority of our readers out of keeping with the paper's character.'[60]

Grant and Haley were facing the ever-present dilemma: at what point in the process of brightening *The Times* did polishing stop and spoiling begin? Part of the answer is that Haley, while intent to get all the hard news, was happier when the paper was following up exciting new developments in science and the arts than when delving into the kind of personal tangles which other papers carried.

The specialist writers themselves were given more help and more space. Eric Wigham, appointed labour correspondent in 1946, had an integrity in him which came out in all his reports on the faults, ambitions and frustrations among managers and trade unionists alike. A quiet man, keeping always something of his Quaker schooling, he preferred to explain rather than pontificate, and his explanations at the height of many a dispute were especially useful in years when 'union power' and 'crisis management' were developing as problems to be reckoned with. Wigham's standing with both sides was officially acknowledged in 1965 when he was asked to sit on the royal commission on trade unions and employers' associations.

Wigham's line was sometimes gentler than Haley's or that of other writers on home affairs who emphasized the need for efficiency and innovation. Time and again leading articles were impatient with restrictive practices on the shop floor and with resistance to change, whether in

---

57 Colin Perkins Wilson (b. 1931). South Leeds Commercial College. *The Times* home news reporter, 1966; assistant home news editor, 1967; home news editor (night), 1970; head of intelligence department from 1981.
58 Brian Fiveash Packham (b. 1916). *The Times* editorial messenger, 1932; reporter, 1951; assistant home news editor (night), 1964; home news editor (night), 1967; syndication department, 1970; resigned 1981.
59 Letter, Grant to Haley, October 23 1962.
60 Letter, Haley to Grant, October 25 1962.

industry or on the railways. Several writers – David Wood, Windsor Davies, and Michael Baily,[61] the excellent transport correspondent – gave warm support to the Beeching proposals (1963–65) for closing many railway lines, although the writers pointed out that a simple profit-and-loss account could not be the sole basis for deciding whether a line should stay open or go. In 1963 Baily accepted the logic of the Buchanan report on urban traffic: cities simply could not accommodate the cars and drivers that wished to enter them; for far too long the authorities had been trying to solve traffic problems on the cheap, producing industrial slums and suburban sprawls:

> A society affluent enough to spend £900m. a year on new road vehicles is affluent enough to spend far more than £100m. on new roads.'[62]

More of the writing on local government affairs began to be done by Norman Fowler[63] who came to Printing House Square in 1961. Some years later he was to follow Gwynne Jones's example and become a government minister, although he made the change far less abruptly, and whereas Gwynne Jones sat on the Labour side in the Lords Fowler was an active Conservative from his Cambridge days. On *The Times* he argued for efficiency in the fields in which he was to work when in government office: local government, police pay and status, and more housing. Housing in turn merged with the work of the architectural correspondent, J. M. (afterwards Sir James) Richards.[64] Through him, and often through the eager pen of Patrick Ryan, *The Times* gave its support to the most modern of building designs and to projects which elsewhere were greeted with dismay. Far better, ran the paper's argument, to have bold new designs than watered-down imitations of old styles. That was true (to take only one example) of the rebuilt Coventry Cathedral:

> Truth is being set over and above materialism. Coventry has not turned her back on a long tradition of civic self-respect.

---

61 Michael Fawcett Baily (b. 1924). St. Bede's Grammar School; Merton College, Oxford. *Harrogate Herald*, 1947–51; *Nottingham Guardian*, 1951–54. *The Times* shipping correspondent, 1954–60; transport correspondent from 1960.
62 Leading article (Baily), November 28 1963.
63 Norman Fowler (b. 1938). King Edward vi School, Chelmsford; Trinity Hall, Cambridge. Joined *The Times* staff 1961; special correspondent and leader writer, 1962; home affairs correspondent, 1966–70; reported Middle East war 1967. Minister of Transport 1979; Secretary of State for Social Services 1983.
64 James Richards (b. 1907). Gresham's School, Holt. *The Times* architectural correspondent, 1947–71. Editor *Architectural Review*, 1937–71. Professor of architecture, Leeds University, 1957–59. Knighted, 1972.

XX

THE UNENDING CRISIS

THE most substantial single change in British newspapers, if their contents before the Second World War are compared with what they offered in the fifties and sixties, was in the vast growth of economic and industrial news and comment in their pages. The reason is plain enough. Newspapers were giving their own professional response to the unending economic anxieties and crises which dominated national life. A falling pound, adverse balances of payments year by year, poor rates of industrial production, strikes, inflation, further falls in the pound, further failures in production, heavy wage demands: all such symptoms of the national illness set politicians and journalists seeking for the underlying causes and the cures.

Within *The Times* there was not much disagreement about the diagnosis. Most of the causes could be traced back to the war. Fundamentally Britain ended the war with large sterling debts – the so-called sterling balances – held initially by India, Egypt, and several Commonwealth countries in Africa and elsewhere. They totalled £4,000 million in 1946. Though they later changed hands, the total remained largely unchanged for the next two and a half decades, and led to pressure on the pound (because so many holders were able to sell) whenever Britain's balance of payments or inflation rate seemed to be deteriorating. At the same time Britain had to bear the formidable loss, through wartime sales, of many of her foreign assets which before the war had been a painless means of helping to maintain a healthy export–import balance.

Britain would have to work harder to earn her keep, but that thought immediately led on to other consequences of the war which were less tangible. The victory, achieved after the massive mobilisation in armed services and factories, had left the British people more tired than many of them acknowledged; they were ready for some easing in their weekly work. The beginning of the technological revolution (itself stimulated by the war) was soon to set off a process of chain reaction: the explosion in durable consumer goods provoked the swiftly rising demands for wages to pay for the new goods and services on offer. The inevitable consumer boom backfired all too often, and for one reason above all. Britain, needing imports if it was to eat and live at all, was especially hard hit by the rise in world prices. By the fifties the stop-go-stop pattern in the national economy was painful and familiar. The economy would expand, causing imports to increase, causing a deficit in the balance of payments, causing a run on the pound, causing a clamp-down on the national economy – until a Chancellor of the Exchequer judged it safe or expedient to set the cycle rolling again.

Before The Times could formulate and offer anything like a detailed coverage of such trends, or work out its own policy towards them, it had to reorganise and enlarge what used to be called the City office. Before the Second World War the City staff seemed for most of the time a tiny world to itself, shut away in a street a few yards from the Bank of England, rarely visiting Printing House Square, and scarcely ever visited by anyone from Printing House Square. It had prestige. It had authority. Its words were closely read in the City. Before and after the Second World War Maurice Green had the right idea of expanding the work when taking the broader title of financial and industrial editor.[1] Closer liaison was achieved, but even when William Clarke[2] was appointed City editor in 1957 his early visits to Printing House Square, especially his calls on Haley, were formal, courteous affairs. In later years he recalled the ritual of tea. 'It was almost as if I had come from a fiefdom at the ends of the earth. I soon realised that, subconsciously at least, I was being treated like a far-flung correspondent. How different life was later, when I had been absorbed into the twelve o'clock leader conference, my views sought and listened to with respect daily, and I was contributing as many leaders as anyone else. There were more kicks and no tea, but The Times had once again moved with the times.'[3]

The conversion of the old City news into a much wider display of financial, economic, and industrial features was carried out by William Clarke himself and Ansell Egerton.[4] Both had been on the paper for less

1 See Chapter X.
2 William Malpas Clarke (b. 1922). Audenshaw Grammar School; Manchester University. *Manchester Guardian*, 1948–55. *The Times*, assistant City editor, 1955–57; City editor, 1957–62; financial and industrial editor, 1962–66. Editor of, and later consultant to, the *Banker* and the director of the Committee on Invisible Exports, 1966.
3 Memorandum to McDonald, September 1980. T.T.A.
4 Reginald Ansell Day Egerton (b. 1926). Eton; Melbourne University; Oriel College, Oxford. Lecturer in economics, Queen's University, Belfast, 1950–56. *The Times* assistant financial editor, 1956–57; assistant City editor, 1957–62; City editor, 1962–66; economics editor, 1966–67; assistant editor (executive), 1967–68.

than two years when Clarke was made City editor and Egerton became his chief assistant. Both believed that financial and economic news meant far too much for the nation to be hidden away at the back of the paper. They provided many stories for the main news pages. Many of their leading articles were as much political as economic. In fact they changed and broadened *The Times* much as British embassies abroad were being changed and broadened to cope with trade and industry, and they had the full support of Haley and Green. The change was urgently needed. The *Financial Times* and the *Daily Telegraph* had been beating *The Times* day by day in their financial and industrial news; they gave more of such news and they were very often better informed than *The Times*.

Between 1956 and 1960 the City office slowly came to terms with the new demands on its resources. At home take-over bids became major news stories. *Times* readers were shocked to find even Harrods at risk. Sterling crises pushed the stories well beyond London to encompass what was going on in Washington as well as New York, in Brussels as well as Paris, Zurich and Frankfurt. Overseas it was essential to cover politico-economic talks about the so-called Six and Seven, the embryo Common Market and the embryo European Free Trade Association. Fundamentally these talks were about politics: in essence they discussed detailed economic, agricultural and financial topics. And while all this was going on, a remarkable transformation was taking place on *The Times's* own doorstep. Quietly London's banks were beginning to bid for surplus dollars throughout Western Europe. It was the start of the vast Euro-currency market, which was to transform the world's financing of economic development over the next three decades and to support London's marked recovery in world financial affairs.[5]

Against this background *The Times* City office extended its overall financial coverage; introduced the new Times industrial share index; widened its reports of industrial developments; started its regular list of top 300[6] industrial companies; and set up a small network of financial correspondents in other centres, such as Zurich, Paris, Frankfurt, Milan, Brussels, Amsterdam and New York. Above all the City office was gradually brought closer to the mainstream of policy making in Printing House Square. By 1962 Clarke had been appointed financial and industrial editor, and had become the regular economic leader writer. Egerton succeeded him as City editor. The City office then

---

5 According to the 1972 Supplement to the Oxford English Dictionary the first recorded reference to the 'Euro-dollar market' was in *The Times* financial review of October 24 1960.
6 Later it became *The Times 1000*.

moved physically into the new building in Printing House Square. The integration was complete.

Clarke and Egerton had hardly settled into their jobs when their department and Haley himself were brought into the famous 'Bank rate leak', which provoked one of the Labour Opposition's storms over next to nothing. On September 19 1957 the Bank of England raised what used to be called Bank rate, later the minimum lending rate, to 7 per cent. In those days any move whether up or down was rare, startling, and portentous. Almost immediately after the Bank had announced the change Harold Wilson and some other Labour MPs worked themselves up with demands to be told whether someone either in the Bank or the Treasury had whispered beforehand to some brokers or journalists. Wilson was going on the fact there there had indeed been some rather puzzling eve-of-announcement selling in the gilt-edged market and there had been some newspaper speculation. On September 18, the day before the news was official, *The Times* carried a report by Charles D. Lloyd, one of the most experienced men in the City office, saying that some unexpected selling had 'prompted talk of currency or Bank rate moves'. On September 20, the day after the announcement, Lloyd referred to the 'inspired selling' of September 18. He meant simply that some people had had a happy brain-wave, but Labour seized on the word 'inspired'. Other newspapers carried similar reports at the time.

Labour's protests were so persistent that the Macmillan government stated on November 14 that a tribunal of inquiry had been appointed under Lord Justice Park. Haley was among the 132 witnesses called upon to give evidence before it. On November 18, in a letter to the Treasury Solicitor, Sir Harold Kent, Haley explained how Lloyd's pieces came to be written, not on any foreknowledge of any kind but on a shrewd reading of the mood of the City. In a personal statement Haley further said that he saw the Chancellor of the Exchequer, Peter Thorneycroft, on the day before the announcement; Thorneycroft told him – as he told other editors in turn on the same day – something about some of the coming changes but nothing at all about Bank rate. (Haley returned to Printing House Square so little impressed by Thorneycroft's words that he said to Maurice Green, 'If this is all the government are going to do, God help us.') Other witnesses gave similar evidence. On January 21 1958 the tribunal made known its unanimous conclusion: there was 'no justification for allegations that information about the raising of the Bank rate was improperly disclosed to any person'. The non-event was over, but because of it much time had been wasted in *The Times* and very many other offices. Politicians are often slow to believe that a good journalist is capable of working not through a tip-off but through reading the signs and drawing his own conclusions from them.

It was not the only such episode. Even while the Bank rate tribunal was taking evidence, another City crisis was appearing and was promising to split the City down the middle and raise personal emotions to a rare pitch. This was the battle for British Aluminium. It began as a simple take-over bid by Tube Investments and the American-based Reynolds Metal for British Aluminium. It ended as a campaign against the American share in the bid by the largest roll-call of City merchant banks for years, with *The Times* taking a clear international view, refusing to support the large City consortium, and with the City editor under attack by the doyen of the merchant bankers, Olaf Hambro.

Even an attempt by the Governor of the Bank of England, Mr. Cameron (later Lord) Cobbold, to intercede to facilitate a truce in the take-over battle proved fruitless. By the beginning of 1959 the battle lines had been drawn, with Hambros, Lazards, Benson Lonsdale, Brown Shipley, Robert Fleming, Guiness Mahon, Samuel Montagu, Morgan Grenfell, M. Samuel, Edward de Stein, and Whitehall Trust on the side of British Aluminium; and Warburgs and Helbert Wegg and Schroders on the side of Tube Investments and Reynolds. Only Rothschilds, Kleinworts, and Barings appeared to be neutral. The struggle grew increasingly bitter and soon spread to the stock market, where Tube Investments and Reynolds eventually acquired sufficient British Aluminium shares to secure control.

The sequel for the press in general and for *The Times* itself was healthy and revealing. Olaf Hambro, Chairman of Hambros Bank and a leading supporter of British Aluminium, wrote a strong letter to *The Times*[7] contrasting the silent support of virtually every merchant bank in the City with the critical attitude of the press. 'It is very unclear,' he wrote, 'why the majority of the City Editors of the press seemed to be against City opinion and openly wrote in favour of the take-over bid.' And he made it clear privately (as he had done earlier) that the City editor of *The Times* had been a prime irritant. The episode was a major element in reminding the City that it still lived in an international environment and that it could not necessarily count on a subservient press in its day-to-day activities.

Both the Bank rate tribunal and the British Aluminium take-over pushed City affairs onto the main news. There they joined the more frequent stories on the continuing sterling crises which had erupted for

---

7 *The Times*, January 12 1959.

the first time in 1946 after the premature attempt to establish the convertibility of sterling (making it freely exchangeable into US dollars and other leading currencies). The same weakness manifested itself thereafter almost every other year, with the two main parties contributing their own solutions. The Labour government of 1946–51 had nationalised the Bank of England and Britain's basic industries, coal, steel, electricity, gas and railways. The Conservative governments of 1951–63 had dismantled war-time controls, abolished the remnants of rationing, denationalised steel, and reopened several of the City's financial markets. Finally, the Labour governments of 1964 and 1966, elected against a background of firm promises of a white-hot technological revolution, quickly introduced government planning with firm growth targets and encouraged union cooperation in an incomes policy. Yet throughout the decade, Britain's growth rate remained persistently below that of western Europe and sterling crises seemed, if anything, to grow in intensity, culminating in some of the heaviest foreign borrowings in the mid-1960s and to the devaluation of the pound in November 1967.

Throughout these crises *The Times* continued to analyse and comment on the economic plight of the country. It took an apolitical and moral attitude from the outset. It had become convinced that neither Conservative nor Labour governments had the true solution, and, above all, that neither party had a leader with the ability (or desire) to remould the national will.

The decline in the domestic value of the pound was at the heart of the matter. Macmillan for some time was influenced by Keynesian, expansionist thoughts on economics. He was not against some modest, controlled inflation. Several times he grumbled to Haley when *The Times* published charts, as it regularly did, showing the decline in the pound's value. As early as April 10 1957 he told Haley that he hoped *The Times* would not 'do that kind of thing' too often; such charts did no good. Had anyone proved that inflation, which had been going on for two or three hundred years, had done any real harm? To reverse the process would be to go back to the unemployment of the thirties. Haley said that inflation reduced the incentive to save and so to work, and it was getting out of hand. At later meetings Macmillan himself betrayed doubts about the convenience of inflation, which was then rising more dangerously, due mainly (he believed) to excessive wage demands.

Haley went on exposing the evil over the years. Within the office he frequently said to colleagues, 'The most pressing domestic political problem of our time is how inflation is to be controlled in a democracy'. On April 1 1957 he had a leader with no heading to it at all but simply a single thick black line which slanted down from top left to bottom right of the heading space and thus graphically represented the descent of the pound. The article asked Macmillan and his ministers once again to show not financial wizardry so much as moral stamina in resisting political temptations to take an easy path:

They have seriously to ask themselves whether this is not the time to have courage to countenance a stand being made . . . Otherwise the day will come when we shall no longer be talking of the £'s decline but of its collapse.'

Nine months later there came the same note. At a time of financial stringency Peter Thorneycroft, Chancellor of the Exchequer, and two of his Treasury lieutenants (Enoch Powell[8] and Nigel Birch[9]) resigned rather than agree with Cabinet colleagues who begged the Chancellor to let government expenditure rise marginally. News of Macmillan's acceptance of their resignations came out late in the evening of January 6 1958. Haley got Maurice Green to write a first leader for the later editions. A characteristic Haley heading – 'Flinching' – summed up the argument which followed:

So Macmillan has not, in the end, supported his courageous Chancellor of the Exchequer. All those who have felt that the battle for Britain's economic security is still in the balance must have hoped that that support would be forthcoming. But, as it was not, Mr. Thorneycroft had no choice but to resign . . . If ever there was a point at which the Treasury team had to stand on a matter of principle, this was it.[10]

The policy of *The Times* throughout this period was to support any politician who showed signs of choosing bravely and taking action. It supported Selwyn Lloyd in his initial stance on taking on the task of the Chancellor, dubbing one of his early speeches 'admirably frank, forthright and courageous'. But it quickly put the country's economic problem in perspective. 'It is as well to say now that the task is beyond him. It is beyond any Chancellor of the Exchequer. No matter what the measures may be they will not, on their own, cure the deep-seated ills of the British economy. Nothing short of an effort by the whole nation can

---

8 Enoch Powell (b. 1912). Financial Secretary to the Treasury, 1957–58; Minister of Health, 1960–63.
9 Nigel Birch (1906–1981). Secretary of State for Air, 1955–57; Economic Secretary to the Treasury, 1957–58.
10 *The Times*, January 7 1958.

do that.'[11] Two weeks later the same theme was developed:

Britain's economy has been sick for years. The malady has outstayed all too many Chancellors. They come; they apply their nostrums at some feverish moment; they declare the patient will now recover; they go. Before the public have had time to know much about their successor the trouble starts all over again. This is the sixth economic crisis a British Government has had to deal with since the war . . . Every British Government since the war has funked the consequences of really fighting inflation. It is hard to believe that at long last Britain has come to the turning point.[12]

It was an accurate, if scarcely difficult, conclusion; and it was soon confirmed. Within two years another crisis had loomed, following the exclusion of Britain from the Common Market. In February 1963 *The Times* was again setting out as simply as it could what it regarded as the aim of official policy:

The answer is a morally healthy, efficient Britain, innovating and exporting to its fullest capacity, a leader in the unending battle to feed, educate and enrich the deprived nations of the world . . . If the House of Commons is to get to the heart of the matter today it will have to acknowledge that the crisis inherent in the political and economic situation of Britain is a moral one.[13]

The emphasis was thus placed equally on efficiency and morality. As the Conservative government came towards the end of its decade of dominance, the moral tone was to be heard increasingly in the paper's comments on financial and economic affairs as it was on other national trends. 'Everything depends on the sincerity of the politicians' belief that inflation is an evil. Some do not believe this.' Efficiency was not overlooked, however. The Resale Prices Bill, under which Edward Heath[14] promised to dismantle the long-held acceptance of resale price maintenance, whereby manufacturers could insist on levels of retail prices to the detriment of competition, came to be the testing ground of the government's economic determination. The original Bill was full of good intentions. Resale price maintenance was to be illegal and exceptions would be dealt with by a judicial tribunal. But, as the Bill progressed through Parliament and as manufacturers and other commercial interests perceived the threats to their profitable habits, press-

---

11 Leading article (Haley), July 13 1961.
12 Leading article (Haley), July 26 1961.
13 Leading article (Haley), February 11 1963.
14 Edward Richard Heath (b. 1916). Prime Minister, 1970–74.

ures on the government increased and the watering down began. *The Times*, detecting that Heath was in danger of being undermined by political pressures – even within the Cabinet – kept up its insistence for reform. 'Not enough bite' was its final verdict.[15]

A few weeks later in 1964, as wage claims by the busmen, the postmen, the electricity workers and others threatened to give another painful push to domestic prices, *The Times* was again taking up the cudgels (and its chart):

> The fact remains that the 1938 £1 was worth 11s.10d. in 1946, Labour's first year of power; it was worth 8s.11d. when the Conservatives took over in 1951; and was worth 6s.6d. last year. The £ chart which was published in *The Times* just before Budget Day is a shocking record of political and economic failure.[16]

Soon *The Times* was pressing the point home to the newly elected Labour government. That Harold Wilson's cabinet ministers were no less concerned at *The Times's* simple chart analysis was displayed in a telephone call one afternoon, from the Chancellor of the Exchequer, James Callaghan, to William Clarke, in an effort to dissuade the paper from publishing the inflation chart the following day. He was fearful that in the current state of the exchange markets its appearance could cost the gold reserves a significant amount. *The Times* considered its responsibilities and, on the instructions of the editor, told the Treasury that the chart would be appearing the following day as planned. Callaghan's call was not the only evidence of a sensitivity in the Treasury and Bank of England at leaders and reports in *The Times* which it was feared might damage the pound. A wrong word in *The Times* on a Friday could, it was said, cost the Exchequer £20 million over a weekend in efforts to support the pound. All such pleas were considered and set aside in Printing House Square; they simply served to underline the sensitivity of the pound and the weakness of the British economy rather than any irresponsibility of *The Times*.

Soon the new Labour government in the autumn of 1964, with its 'paper-thin majority', was plunged into a new round of sterling crises, the first largely of its own making. It had inherited a large and growing balance of payments deficit; it had proceeded to exaggerate it for its own political reasons; and it had then compounded its own difficulties by delaying monetary action. When it did act, it decided to impose an import surcharge which simply succeeded in annoying almost all its friends in Europe. It was the start of another series of economic

15 Leading article (Clarke), February 26 1964.
16 Leading article (Haley), April 20 1964.

difficulties which were to continue until the devaluation of the pound in November 1967.

The Times continued to call for fundamental treatment. On November 26 1964 a leading article by Haley complained once again that no government over the past twenty years had imposed efficiency or curbed uneconomic wage demands: 'Much of British management lacks initiative and much of British labour is inert'. At the beginning of 1965 it had one of its shortest first leaders on record – eleven lines in italics – with a simple message: 'Nineteen sixty four was a year of words. The only hope for Britain is that 1965 shall be a year of deeds.'[17] It was not. Nor was 1966. And in the March of that year, as the next election approached, *The Times* once again set out what it saw as the state of the nation, this time in a remarkable list of reasons explaining 'Why the £ is weak'. It gave 26 separate reasons and ended:

. . . because for twenty years leadership has been lacking; soft words have been substituted for hard facts; exhortation has never been followed by deeds; rights have come before responsibilities; the national philosophy has been all take and no give;

. . . because the world knows that, however slow the descent, the abyss is still at the end of the road.

The pound could be strong if the British people had the ears to hear, the eyes to see and the will to recover their native sense and energy. They had done it time and again in wars; why can they not do it just once in peace? This is what the general election should be about.[18]

The Labour government won the election and was quickly in the throes of yet another sterling crisis and again *The Times* was putting the issue in perspective, not throwing the whole of the blame on to successive governments. 'Britain's solution can in the long run depend on no one but herself. What *The Times* has been saying for many years is at last becoming accepted. The only solution to Britain's problem lies in the will of its people. Even the British Government can do only so much'.[19]

Throughout the years *The Times* did not merely scold. Its warnings were amply justified but it also emphasized what it called (February 2 1965) the three keys to a change of fortune: modernization, competition, and control:

Modernization without competition will in the long run stultify itself . . . Competition without modernization is hardly possible. And

---

17 Leading article (Haley), January 1 1965.
18 Leading article (Haley), March 10 1966.
19 Leading article (Haley), July 30 1966.

every country has had to learn that economic miracles turn out to have been hoaxes if the Government is not master of the economy as a whole.

Haley was nearing the end of his long campaign for financial probity, industrial advance, and self-discipline at work. On no matters did he feel more strongly. Yet he was addressing himself to a changing society, a significant part of which was 'permissive' not only in social habits but, by extension, in attitudes to work and to the old idea of industrial progress as a worthwhile aim in itself. The trade unions were blamed for extravagant wage claims, but behind the unions was the broader force of the consumers' revolution, as it was to be called: the working assumption that old luxuries – holidays in the sun, cars, television, labour-saving household goods – were present indispensables. The society which was emerging was not one to heed calls for discipline and austerity. That is one reason why the line pursued by *The Times* for so long did not win speedy and broad popularity.

While the departments in the main body of *The Times* – home, foreign, industrial, arts – were being drawn together in a closer team, the several supplements were pursuing their own ways. In effect they were almost wholly autonomous. The *Literary Supplement*, was the oldest and most renowned of them. Its founder, Sir Bruce Richmond, who had edited the *Supplement* for thirty-five years, was succeeded in 1937 by D. L. Murray. Murray, long on the staff, had hoped to go on writing his historical romances, but once he became editor he joined in an endeavour to broaden the *Supplement's* appeal. From next Saturday, said *The Times* of April 25 1938, '*The Times Literary Supplement* will appear in a new and enlarged form and will include a number of fresh features designed to meet the changing needs of modern readers'. More and larger illustrations were promised – and 'the high quality of the reproduction will render them especially attractive to the eye'. But the new dispensation was little short of a disaster, falling lamentably between half-hearted popularization and informed, scholarly guidance to world literature. The quality of the reviews never fell beneath tolerable standards, but the dichotomy caused circulation to slide. The sales graph was reaching dangerously low levels when the war came and sent it down to an all-time low.

Paradoxically, the war saw the *TLS* through its most dangerous hour. Paper rationing meant that daily newspapers had to jettison their book pages and – which was important – a good deal of their book advertising. The *TLS* thus became almost the only medium giving adequate coverage to books at a time when they were the perfect antidote to the blackout, sitting in shelters and tedious waiting for battles.

But inside *The Times* office there was some dissatisfaction with the way that Murray was running the *TLS* (in any event he had announced his intention of leaving to continue his novels after the war's end), and a plain-dealing verbal skirmish was fought between Stanley Morison and Murray, when the latter discovered that Charles Morgan had been sounded out by Morison about taking over the *TLS*.

Murray discovered this through a chance meeting with Morgan in the street when he was greeted by 'Hallo, David, I didn't know you were giving up the *TLS*'. Morgan, however, did not want the job. A temporary truce was then called and Murray continued his work, publishing in the meantime 'Menander's Mirror', a weekly series of reflective articles written by Morgan as Menander. (In one of these his spelling of Baudelaire as Beaudelaire managed to escape all proof readers' eyes and earned him a magisterial rebuke from T. S. Eliot.)

Early in 1945, with the allied victory beyond doubt, Murray resigned and was succeeded in February by Morison. To some people this appointment was all the more surprising because Morison had been an active member of the pre-war reformist committee and had advised behind the scenes on various *TLS* features which were to distinguish the new version from the old.

Morison, given a free hand to restore the journal's authority and standing, promptly threw out most of his own and other so-called reforms. Away went the pictures and ephemera like the 'literary' crossword puzzle (he never even printed the solution to the last published puzzle) and in again came the long authoritative front-page article and more concentration on serious subjects, until Morison could say with some satisfaction, 'I've made the *Supplement* difficult to read again.' Be that as it may, during the two years of Morison's stewardship the circulation of the *TLS* showed an increase.

Morison's holding operation – he was anxious to relinquish the *TLS* once it was on the right road and return to his *History of the Times* and to his typographical work with the Monotype Corporation and the Cambridge University Press – came to an end in 1947 when Alan Pryce-Jones,[20] appointed assistant editor at Morison's instigation a few months earlier, took control.

At this time the end of paper-rationing was in sight and with it

20 Alan Payan Pryce-Jones (b. 1906). Eton; Magdalen College, Oxford. Army 1939–45. Joined *The Times* staff, 1946; assistant editor *TLS*, 1947–48; editor, 1948–59.

greater freedom of competition, not only between publishers themselves, but also between the *TLS* and various other newspapers and journals anxious to reclaim a share of the publishers' advertising cake.

Pryce-Jones's task, then, was to guide the *TLS* through the postwar period and, without sacrificing any of its traditional standards, to meet and match the challenge of change. This he was admirably equipped to do. Versatile, unusually widely read in French and German as well as in English, with a deep and lively knowledge of the arts, especially music, Pryce-Jones retained the established experts, but introduced into the *TLS* some of the most able of early post-war critics and a good deal of original poetry. He appointed Anthony Powell fiction editor and widened the scope of the reviewing of the foreign books, always an important part of the *TLS's* function. The *TLS* enjoyed a considerable circulation and prestige abroad – at one count it was circulated, however minutely, in eighty-seven countries. Pryce-Jones it was, too, who initiated the practice of publishing special issues more concerned with the adequate presentation of particular themes than with the amount of extra revenue they brought in. His totally modern outlook dispelled any notion that the *TLS* was in danger of becoming a literary anachronism.

He was also an excellent ambassador for British books – and the *TLS*. He had an insatiable curiosity about the creative talents and cultures of other lands and this took him quite often to foreign parts. In the end, to no one's surprise within the office, he accepted a job abroad. The Ford Foundation in New York offered him wide scope in its humanities and arts programme, and he gave up the *TLS* in July 1959.

He had already left Arthur Crook[21] and Kathleen Dowding,[22] his two chief assistants, to get on with the job of editing the *Supplement* while he was abroad. Arthur Crook, who had been on the staff since a very young man and was soaked in *TLS* traditions, was appointed editor. He was wholly at one with Haley in keeping all the book reviews anonymous but that rule did not prevent him from securing the most eminent scholars or the most experienced specialists, from devoting days of work and lengthy research into an article which might be perhaps be less than a thousand words. Deducing, from tricks of style or quirks of mind, who had written such-and-such a review was a weekend pastime at many a senior common room. An author whose book was given a favourable notice in the *TLS* knew that it had passed the stiffest test; it had the stamp of merit.

---

21 Arthur Crook (b. 1912). Holloway County School. Joined staff of *The Times* as messenger, 1926; assistant editor *TLS*, 1941–59; editor, 1959–74.
22 Kathleen May Dowding (Nixon). Joined *TLS*, 1945; assistant editor, 1948–55.

An influence different from that of the *TLS*, an influence more closely directed in aim and much more concerned with current affairs, was exercised each week by the *Educational Supplement*. It had zest, it was controversial, it was always ready to go against official fashions in educational theory; and it got its individuality largely from its two forceful editors, Harold Collett Dent (1940–52) and Walter James (1952–69).

The two men differed in style and in several of their policies. Dent was an idealistic egalitarian educationalist and this raised doubts in certain minds on the main paper. He would have gone a long way with Helvétius who, back in the middle of the eighteenth century, said 'Education can do everything'. The pragmatism of Printing House Square never allowed it to believe that anything could do everything. But Dent made the *Supplement* wholly educational where previously it had carried some pages of supposedly general interest. After leaving the chair he remained faithful to the cause. He became educational correspondent to *The Times* until he left for a professorship of education at Sheffield University.

Where Dent was first and foremost an educator James was a professional journalist. Dent was devoted to the subject, James to its presentation, although his opinions were strongly based.

On a strictly materialistic view *The Times Educational Supplement* provided a post-war success story of Printing House Square. It doubled its circulation, reaching 90,000 by 1966, and increased its revenue many times over. By the 1960s it was making a substantial contribution to the company's finances. Admittedly it was favoured by the expansion of education in the country as a whole. The 1944 Act brought many more schools and more teachers. It meant more buildings, more furniture, more teaching posts to be filled – and, by extension, many more advertisements for a paper like the *Educational Supplement*. The paper was fortunate in having an energetic advertising manager in Frank Derry. It was helped by having the national tide running its way. True enough; yet in that same post-war period its main weekly competitors saw their circulation fall.

It was often said that people bought the *Supplement* largely for the job advertisements. The editorial staff were suitably chastened, but they also accepted the jibe as an added challenge to them. True or not, it provided another reason for them to make education readable, clear, and attractive, with perhaps a little sugaring added on occasion. A prime mover in this throughout was Miss L. M. Bennett, a Wren officer taken on by Dent after the war; she became art editor, presiding over the much increased use of pictures and the cartoons which developed thick and fast after 1960. Over the years, as the paper enlarged itself, educational news and views became interspersed with the features associated with a general weekly review, especially on the side of the arts.

The assumption was made that many teachers were cultivated men and women, not well paid enough to buy a clutch of periodicals over the weekend and so likely to be grateful if their professional journal stood in for them. It was a policy that lightened the pages with the first writings of young critics who later found success elsewhere – Peter Heyworth, Andrew Porter, and David Cairns, for instance, on music and opera, Irving Wardle on the West End theatre and John Russell Taylor on television, Peter Brinson on ballet, and John Pearson and Sue Puddefoot on the new films. There was a column called 'The World at Large', in which the younger leader writers of *The Times* sought to divert the teacher from the classroom to the affairs of the great world. It was a plot to make a paper that was basically educational more entertaining to its readers as well as to the staff who wrote it.

In its policy the *Supplement* under James was profoundly antipathetic to the strong trend towards equality in education at whatever cost to quality. It so found itself in lively conflict at times with the Department of Education and almost invariably with the National Union of Teachers and the later extinct Association of Education Committees who acted, it often seemed, as though they had been constituted to direct between themselves the national system of education.

The educational sphere is always apt to be influenced over much by theory and emotion, and James liked from time to time to inject into the scene some new and relevant facts. The *Supplement* engaged Peter Townsend, a young man then at the start of his career, to make a factual survey of the contentious field of teacher supply, and in 1952 printed two articles by Professor P. E. Vernon on the effect of coaching on scores which fatally undermined the confidence felt until then in scholastic IQ testing and were something of a high water mark in the controversy. Later, in 1965, valuable light was thrown on the admission of boys from the maintained system to the public boarding schools by a series based on tape-recorded interviews with local authority bursars who had gone to Winchester, Eton and Rugby and, ten years after leaving these schools, were out in the world. It was the first attempt to find out how boys from state schools got on in public schools. The remembered experiences of those recorded were not as rosy as some might have hoped and expected; the head of one of the schools described them as 'faintly depressing'.

The *Supplement* tended to be on the side of the small against the big.

The grammar school was upheld against the comprehensive throughout the long and bitter controversy, and necessarily the secondary modern school too whose achievements, when in good hands, were too often forgotten. When the large National Union of Teachers tried to prevent the small National Association of Schoolmasters from being represented on the Burnham salaries committee, the *Supplement* espoused the NAS cause which eventually triumphed in 1966.

The paper was often denounced for being reactionary, but no one could ever say that it refused its own space to its most virulent critics. Writers of letters to the editor were sometimes less urbane and measured than their counterparts on *The Times*; they were invariably published in full. In the news columns it was a matter of honour to publish the speeches and statements of those on the extremist other side of the argument, and their views were invited in feature articles as well. The theory behind this keeping of open house could be grandiloquently expressed as *magna est veritas et praevalebit*, but there was a lower journalistic sense that a blazing row in your pages was good for business.

There was a less controversial area – perhaps so because the country had not grasped its vital importance – to which the *Educational Supplement* gave a lot of attention. In 1950 appeared a series entitled 'The Case for a Technical University', later republished in booklet form, and among the contributors were Lord Cherwell and James R. Killian, then President of the Massachusetts Institute of Technology. The heading on one of the articles, 'Britain's Weakness in Applied Science', became a continuing theme in the paper. The argument in the series was for the founding of a technological university in Britain, but the paper's concern was no less for the training of craftsmen, apprentices, and technicians. As already mentioned an opportunity came in 1956 when Sir David Eccles, as Minister of Education, initiated the large expansion of the technical colleges for which he is chiefly remembered. It was then that *The Times* decided to launch, in 1957, its monthly, *Technology*.

Another more enduring venture was made in 1965, in a Scottish edition of the *Educational Supplement*, edited in Edinburgh. The moving spirits behind it were Leonard Buckley,[23] the deputy editor, who was always extremely ambitious for the paper, and Charles Gray,[24] a Scot on the advertising side. Buckley, a former classics master, had come on to the staff after sending in, out of the blue, some light leading articles – a new feature for the supplement but soon a regular one. Charles Gray's researches in the North established the need, if any

23 Leonard R. Buckley (b. 1911). *Times Educational Supplement*, 1951–76.
24 Charles D. S. Gray (1917–74). Advertising manager Scottish edition *Times Educational Supplement*, 1965–74.

success was to be gained, for a Scottish editor, a Scottish office, and a Scottish staff. The Scottish editor, Colin Maclean,[25] was found in the letters department of *The Times*. A graduate of Aberdeen, he showed a combination of prudence, geniality, and scholarliness greatly to the Scottish taste. An office was found in Hanover Street, Edinburgh, and from it eight pages of Scottish news and views emerged, to be sent down to London to be printed in substitution for purely English pages, the new *Educational Supplement Scotland* being sent north by train for the first time on September 17 1965.

During the whole of this period Walter James joined in *Times* policy-making rather as if he were an assistant editor of *The Times*. He served the main paper directly in another way: that is, in training young men and women who, after two years or so with him, went on to do well at *The Times*. They were carefully selected, usually straight from university. Their places in the class-lists of their final examinations, the higher the better, were first noted and then their tutors' opinions sought. They could as well have been chosen for their potential as dons. For three months, with hardly an exception, they were unreliable, careless about dates, initials, and so on; then they blossomed and began to add lustre. Many went on to become foreign correspondents of *The Times*, or transferred to other papers or television or radio – one of them, Simon Jenkins, became editor of the *Evening Standard* and, later, political editor of the *Economist*; Christopher Johnson was managing editor of the *Financial Times*; Stuart Maclure after an apprenticeship on the *Educational Supplement* came back as editor in 1969. The first of them, Owen Hickey, appointed in 1949 after a lunch in the old George Restaurant in Oxford, became deputy editor and afterwards associate editor of *The Times*. Not every one had to be a high-flying academic. It was then still possible to promote a bright girl who had proved herself as a secretary into the ranks of journalists, and some came up that way. Even as early as the 1950s, there was almost an exact balance of young men and young women. The paper drew liveliness from the youth of its staff.

Several ironic touches colour the story of *The Times Weekly*. When it had to cease publication on December 26 1963, after a long run from January 5 1877, it fell as a victim to modern technology. For generations it had seemed secure. It had been prized by Britons and others in distant parts of the world who could read in it the essence of what had appeared over the past week in *The Times*. During the South African war many

---

25 Colin George MacLean (b. 1925). Dingwall Academy; Aberdeen University. Assistant in the letters department *The Times*, 1961–65; editor Scottish edition *Educational Supplement*, 1965–77.

copies were shipped out to the British troops. For many years HM Stationery Office arranged for it to reach ships of the Royal Navy. It was a tangible link of Empire and Commonwealth.

Irony entered the story when the *Weekly* began within Printing House Square to introduce new techniques which were afterwards copied by *The Times* itself and which eventually helped to cause the *Weekly's* own demise. News by radio and the delivery of daily newspapers by air would probably have killed it in any case but the process was hastened, in particular, by the *Weekly's* own greatest technical achievement: the air edition on india paper.

This feather-weight edition began in the Second World War as a secret exploit of wartime propaganda to spread the truth about Britain in enemy-occupied countries. At the request of the Political Intelligence Department of the Foreign Office copies were photographically reduced, page by page, to 5½ in. by 8¼ in. Plates were cast, and the miniatures were printed on flatbed machines and published by The Times Publishing Company. Every word was readable, and the pictures were admirable.

Copies were dropped over enemy-occupied territory and were eagerly passed round. They were valued because they contained no propaganda as such, but were a faithful miniature replica of the standard *Weekly*. The circulation was approximately 13,000. Later the Ministry of Information ordered copies primarily for Latin America, and others for press attachés abroad for local distribution and for large British firms for their agents abroad. The miniatures were produced fortnightly from April 22 1942 until June 3 1945, and then weekly until January 30 1946.

The success stimulated Printing House Square to work on producing full-size india paper issues of *The Times* on the rotary presses, which had not been designed for anything so thin. Full-size air editions were eventually produced both for *The Times* and the *Weekly*. Thereupon many readers began to switch from the *Weekly* to the daily.

Its circulation peak was reached in 1946 with 59,000 copies a week, including those to the loyal postal subscribers. But sales fell as members of the armed forces were withdrawn from overseas, and the Stationery Office cancelled supplies for ships of the Royal Navy. By 1951 circulation had fallen to just below 30,000. A management investigation blamed four causes: sales behind the Iron Curtain had become impossible; *The Times* air edition had grown; *The Times* news service was widely used abroad; the BBC took matter from *The Times* for foreign broadcasts. The layout of the *Weekly* was also criticised as dull and old-fashioned.

Richard Grierson, who had been editor since October 1948, retired late in 1951, and Reginald Easthope, chief home sub-editor of *The Times*, was appointed to revitalise the *Weekly* while 'preserving its essential character'. The first new number went to press on the first day of January, with magazine-like makeup, new-style headlines, specially-written features, even a fresh title – *The Times Weekly Review*, No. 1, with a compact page size. The contents were broadened and brightened in many ways. At the end of the year the circulation had gone up to 33,000 and the paper had settled down in its new format. But although it was lively and liked, the circulation again began to ease off as British officials returned home from emergent countries and representatives abroad of British companies took to the airmail edition of *The Times*, often provided for them by their firms. As *The Times* airmail circulation grew that of the *Weekly* sagged.

Advertising revenue was also a problem. The *Weekly* did not attract consumer goods advertising because it could not offer a concentrated market but a scattered one, even though world-wide. Prestige advertising was shrinking. With reluctance the Board of directors decided in the summer of 1963 to close the *Weekly*: the last number was dated December 26 1963. It still had a postal subscription list of some 10,000 out of a circulation of about 20,000. It was attractive, and it had prestige and pleasant tradition behind it. But it had no means of catching up with a swiftly advancing world.

XXI

NEWS ON THE FRONT PAGE

IN retrospect the early sixties stand out as the heroic years for the serious British newspapers. They were the years of striving, development, progress; harder years than they had in the 'golden age' of the late thirties, but still years of hope. As a class the serious newspapers were doing better than the mass-appeal papers and far better than those in between which tried to be serious and popular at one and the same time. The disappearance in October 1960 of the *News Chronicle*, middle of the road politically as it was middle of the market commercially, and the sale of the *Daily Herald* to the Mirror Group three months later had shown the dangers in the centre of the line. Rivalry from television, fiercer inter-paper competition, and increasing costs brought the total daily circulation of national newspapers, serious and popular combined, down from the 16,983,000 which they could claim in January–June 1956 to 15,831,000 in the same months of 1964 – a drop of over a million. Yet within the total drop there were gains as well as losses. For all their cultivation of mass appeal, the popular papers dropped 1,144,000 in daily sales during the period whereas the daily sale of the serious papers, taken altogether, increased by 466,000.

It was a well-merited increase. The *Guardian* showed its new spirit of enterprise when it began printing in London in 1960. The *Financial Times* was developing more and more into a paper for the businessmen who had political, literary, and artistic interests.[1] The *Daily Telegraph* was extending its formidable news service, especially in domestic matters, and its new companion, the *Sunday Telegraph*, was covering the exposed right flank of politics at the weekend. *The Sunday Times*, bought by Roy Thomson in 1959 and edited by Denis Hamilton, was pushing out the boundaries of journalism, especially with its investigatory teams of reporters, its in-depth surveys of national and world problems, and its generous and extensive serialisation of memoirs by prominent soldiers and politicians.[2] Under David Astor the *Observer*,

1 See Chapter XXII.
2 See Chapter XXII.

always intelligent, always politically challenging, was swiftly increasing its circulation.

In most ways *The Times* shared in this upsurge of serious journalism. Certainly the early sixties were the heroic years for it. Exhausting effort had brought results in its quicker news-gathering and wider range of features. In the late fifties more readers had taken to it, many of them having had their curiosity stirred, or their ambitions flattered, by the 'Top People' advertising campaign.[3] In early 1960, when the paper serialised its extracts from the Suez volume of the Eden memoirs,[4] it saw its circulation rise to an average daily total of 263,355 during the first six months of 1960. Yet the curve soon dipped down again and remained down. By the second half of 1961 it was about 253,500 and nothing could move it from around that figure throughout the next few years.[5] The improvements in the paper had not caught the public eye.

As other serious papers were advancing *The Times* was demonstrating the old truth that if a man stands still he is actually moving back. Its share of the serious market (that is, the sales of serious papers) dropped from 16.2 per cent in January–June 1953 to 12.8 per cent in January–June 1964. As manufacturers and traders were aware of this fall advertisements in the paper did not increase as planned. The conviction grew that something new and radical needed to be done to *The Times*.

Tracing the reasons for its frustrating plight brought the inquirers round in a circle. *The Times* was much improved as a newspaper. It needed more pages each day in order to have more news and features and so be better still. Until it was better still it would not attract more regular readers. Until it got those new readers it would not draw in more advertisements. And until it got those added advertisements it could not afford the extra pages which it needed for the new features which would attract those extra readers.

This was the problem to which Gavin Astor as chairman, Hugh Astor as deputy chairman, Haley as editor, and Mathew as general manager, bent themselves without remission. Its persistence is shown in countless memoranda, in Board minutes, and in Gavin Astor's annual reports. In September 1959 the Board of directors agreed that one of the company's first aims should be to raise the gross profits to at least £500,000 a year. Only so could the company meet all its commitments and rebuilding requirements and allow it to provide financial security

---

3 See Chapter XVI.
4 *Full Circle*. The third volume, although the first published, of the Memoirs of Sir Anthony Eden, later the Earl of Avon.
5 Report by Rodney Fraser, assistant general manager (circulation), September 1964. T.T.A.

for *The Times* newspaper. The target was duly reached in 1959 with a profit before taxation of £505,057: the total turnover of the company was for the first time over £5m.[6] The years 1960 and 1961 were also modestly satisfactory, although in his 1961 report Gavin Astor gave the warning:

> Everything depends upon The Times Publishing Company continuing to maintain gross annual profits in excess of £½m. (after charging increased depreciation) until at least 1967 . . . Thus if The Times Publishing Company is not likely to make gross annual profits of £½m. the situation must be regarded as a virtual emergency and remedial action must be introduced forthwith.[7]

His words came home the next year, 1962, when the company had a profit of only £209,900 and *The Times* itself as a newspaper lost £136,566. What was worse, it was overtaken in circulation by the *Guardian*. Advertising revenue dropped by £189,925 or 5.91 per cent. Still worse came in 1963 with a profit of only £125,951 and a loss on *The Times* of £143,538. What kept the company going was its other, not strictly *Times*, revenue which could be divided into three roughly equal parts. The first third came from the profits of the *Educational Supplement* (over £113,000 in 1963), the second from the contract for printing the *Observer*, and the last from investments. To give the company a firmer trading basis for itself Gavin Astor, strongly supported by Hugh Astor, suggested that it should broaden and diversify itself by taking on more printing and publishing work. He came to the heart of *The Times's* problems of format and size when he asked why it was not getting more advertisements even though the editorial side was brighter than before:

> Is the layout and presentation of the paper sufficiently 'with it'? . . .
> It is an unfortunate fact that the *Daily Telegraph* at 3d. is consistently larger than *The Times* at 5d. and can therefore provide a more complete service and news coverage for its readers and advertisers.[8]

Haley had been repeatedly hammering at this point, and it was at this time that he asked for £350,000 a year more for editorial development. In 1964 the chairman had again to sound a note of acute anxiety about the paper's readership and finances:

> *The Times* has a static circulation. This spells danger; danger spells urgency . . . During the last five years, considerable alterations in content and layout and an expenditure of £¾m. on sales promotion

---

6 Gavin Astor. Annual report, 1959.
7 Gavin Astor. Annual report, 1961.
8 Gavin Astor. Annual report, 1963.

with the object of raising the circulation of *The Times* from 255,000 to over 300,000 by 1964 have in fact raised it by less than 10,000; and Home Sales have actually fallen from 235,000 in 1959 to about 230,000 in 1964.[9]

Reinforcing his argument Astor pointed out that the company had by then come to depend on the *Observer* contract for more than half its gross profits of £285,000:

More professionalism must be introduced into the Times Organisation. I am convinced that the management structure must be re-organised to provide more decentralisation, more individual profit responsibility.

This report by the chairman was given at the end of the financial year, June 1964. On September 24 Haley wrote to Mathew a memorandum which was to be decisive in bringing about the changes in the *Times* format which had for long been discussed. Exactly a year earlier the *Encyclopaedia Britannica* had made Haley its first invitation for him to go to Chicago to edit a new edition of the great work. He had then turned the offer down and, having decided to stay, he was the more determined to see that something drastic was done to modernise *The Times*.[10] Some proposed changes in the City pages, in which Mathew showed a direct concern, gave Haley his cue for his September 24 memorandum:

We must do this thing together from the start. I propose that we should form a committee of the Editor, the Manager, the Deputy Manager, and the Assistant Manager (Advertising). We should at once take in hand a *working* study of the whole future possible layout of the paper. We should start with open minds. But we must consider everything – editorial layout, typography, number of columns, effects of all these things on advertising, advertising requirements, cost of proposed changes, staffing implications, and so on . . . It should be a working committee. By that I mean its meetings should be regular, businesslike, and brief.

The committee should have a secretary to look after papers and minutes. Assistant editors might be brought in:

I think the Editor should be chairman for a number of reasons. The main one is that this is a matter primarily concerning the editorial

---

9 Gavin Astor. Annual report, 1964.
10 Verbal communication, June 1978. Haley was to accept the *Britannica* offer in 1968.

arrangements of the paper. We shall of course proceed by agreement.

The Board of directors accepted Haley's proposal on October 8 1964, and within a week the committee – called the MDE working group, MDE being short for Modernisation, Development, Expansion – had its first meeting. The key question was already clear. Almost all reforms turned on whether *The Times* would decide at last to put news on the front page. Displacing the solid columns of decorous small classified advertisements would be the one unmistakable sign that *The Times* was coming into the modern world. After many talks together Haley and his assistant editors had become wholly convinced that the contents of their brightened paper no longer fitted the staid old format. *The Times* had outgrown its clothes. True enough, regular readers liked it as it was but non-readers tended to be put off by the unchanging general appearance of the front page – proof, in their eyes, that the paper was official and stuffy. News on the front page would help to close the gap between what *The Times* actually contained and what non-readers thought it contained.

The change would necessarily bring others with it. There would have to be larger headings and a more open make-up altogether. Far beyond that, the change in appearance would make sense only if it was part of a modernising drive that would bring with it an extended news service and many new features such as a woman's page and a gossipy diary each day. To get *The Times* moving there had to be an all-round effort which Haley called Operation Breakthrough.

Such were the broad thoughts that Haley took with him into his MDE working group. To begin with Mathew was far less sure about the advantages of change. He was reluctant to do anything to upset the élitist readers who provided the solid core of the *Times* readership. Readers, he believed, were happy to be paying more for something that was special and that looked special. They liked the feeling (some confessed) that in a train they could read the contents in privacy behind the anonymity of the outer pages, front and back. They could be sure that no heading had been written to catch the eye of a potential buyer. They valued having a paper for connoisseurs. Other serious papers had fallen for news on the front page – the *Daily Telegraph* before the war, the *Manchester Guardian* in 1952, the *Scotsman* in 1957, the *Glasgow Herald* in 1958 – and had suffered no evident harm. Yet the greater the reason, it was widely said, to preserve the lone distinction of *The Times*.

In point of fact *The Times* had put news or other editorial matter on the front page several times in the past. On January 1 1785 the front page of the very first issue of the *Daily Universal Register* – *The Times's* first name – carried a two-column letter 'to the Public' from John Walter I. The battle of Trafalgar was reported on the front page on November 7 1805. On April 7 1806 the paper, supposed to have been stuffy from the start, carried front-page illustrations for a murder story. The revolution in France of 1848 was described, front page, in a special Sunday issue. The first six months of the First World War produced 19 Sunday issues, almost all with news on the front page.[11] Admittedly all these displays were exceptions. The traditionalists could still say that births, marriages, and deaths notices had first appeared in their familiar position on April 20 1854, and that these notices were news in themselves, earning their place by merit.

By February 17 1965 Haley's working group, including Mathew, had agreed in principle to have news on the front page provided that the rest of the paper could be satisfactorily arranged. The work of planning the new paper in detail was delegated to a sub-committee under McDonald, who was still foreign editor but had been drawn more into the general running of the paper. Management and editorial were represented on the sub-committee which within three weeks presented miniature *Times* dummies displaying new sequences of pages. All the members of the sub-committee agreed that the existing front page of the paper should be transferred bodily to the back page and that home and foreign news pages should follow in natural sequence from the main news on page one.

On May 13 Haley presented to the Board of directors a long report on the findings up to date of the MDE working group. Knowing that the Board had its staunch traditionalists and its doubters, Haley very fairly argued the case for and against changes in *The Times* while making his own reformatory view plain beyond doubt. After emphasizing the special standing of *The Times* as 'the most authoritative, most serious, and most important paper in Britain; many would say in Europe; some in the world', Haley said that the paper undoubtedly depended on its prestige:

Hardly anyone would deny this. At the same time, newspapers cannot survive on prestige alone. They have to be viable . . . The flow of advertising depends on the paper having enough readers to persuade advertisers that to buy space in it is worth-while.

Presenting the case for the main change, news on the front page, Haley

---

11 T.T.A.

wrote:

> News is the most important thing in the paper. The front page is where it belongs.
>
> To be odd man out is a liability if the oddness represents a false value.
>
> *The Times* is commonly accused of being old-fashioned. No other single step could so clearly and immediately bring it into the world of today. Indeed, all other steps would be ineffective without it.
>
> News on the front page of *The Times* is bound to come in the end. Its effect is needed now.

The Board had hardly given its agreement when there came a heavy and wholly unexpected shock. Francis Mathew, manager and general manager for the past sixteen years, died suddenly on May 29 1965, aged 57.

The shock to the staff was the heavier because Mathew had been very much a personal manager, working in his own forceful, individualistic way, putting less on paper than most men in a comparable position would have done, coming in the end to rely more and more on those nearest to him in the office as their quality improved yet still serving the company most by his own will and drive:

> He combined in his working career and in a remarkable degree two abilities that are not often found together. He was a master of the intricacies of the printing trade in which he had been thoroughly grounded. He had also financial acumen and a flair for handling business matters expeditiously and fruitfully. This versatility was given unity by the integrated character of the man. Mathew was all of a piece.[12]

To bring in an outsider as Mathew's successor would have been to risk losing momentum when the company was midway in the work of modernising *The Times*. Haley was heading that work; he had years of administrative work behind him in Manchester, at Broadcasting House, and in Printing House Square; he had imagination and, at sixty-four, had enviable stamina. So the solution to the problem presented itself without further inquiry. On September 9 1965 came the announcement that Haley had been appointed chief executive of the company while remaining editor of *The Times*. Pope became general manager, responsible to Haley and the Board but with wide powers in the day-

---

12 *The Times*, May 31 1965. See Chapters VII and IX for fuller reviews of Mathew's work.

to-day running of the company. T. Cauter became deputy general manager and J. Pollock assistant general manager (periodicals). The next month, in October, Haley coordinated the work of the management by setting up what he called the Clearing House Committee, a small body under him which regularly discussed all managerial and related matters.

As editor Haley planned still to preside whenever he could over the daily afternoon editorial conference and would try to send his regular morning memoranda of suggestions and admonitions. But clearly he could not carry on editing in anything like his old intensive way. There had to be someone in day-to-day charge of paper and staff. McDonald was moved up to fill the new post of managing editor, and Oliver Woods became his deputy. E. C. Hodgkin, the Middle East expert with world-wide interests, became foreign editor, and was also brought in to share with McDonald and Woods responsibility for editing the paper at night. The arrangements worked easily because the men had come to know each other well over several years.

In the intervening months, May to September, the work of planning the new *Times* was driven forward. On July 29 Haley's working group ruled against McDonald's sub-committee on a matter which greatly affected the whole paper. It decided against transferring the existing front page, with all the births, marriages, and deaths notices, to the back page as the sub-committee had proposed. Pope, with all his advertising experience behind him, prevailed in his view that the highly profitable property advertisements should be kept on the back page and that the births, marriages, and deaths should be switched to an inside page, probably page two. This change meant that the news pages could no longer be read in sequence, following straight on from page one. They had to be read, as before, outwards from the middle spread. McDonald's sub-committee (it had come to be called the Operation Breakthrough committee as its work increased) recorded its own unanimous view that the working group's decision was 'a blow to a well-designed paper'[13] but straight away set about devising a *Times* within the newly prescribed lines. It was one of the occasions when the editorial side, having secured so much of what they wanted, were ready to accept points on which management spoke as experts. The resultant page-sequence in the re-fashioned paper had its obvious flaws but they were held to be small compared to the great gain in getting news on the front page. (The sub-committee's plan for the order of pages was in fact adopted almost

---

13 Operation Breakthrough committee minute, August 3 1965. T.T.A.

bodily very soon after the Thomson purchase in 1966.)

Throughout the spring and summer the working group and its sub-committee were helped by W. Tracy, brought in as typographical adviser, and by J. Blackburn and P. Gardner, creative consultants. Later still the two groups had advice from Roger Harrison, assistant manager, William MacLeod,[14] then chief accountant, and Fred Park,[15] works manager. But throughout all the period most of the essential, practical, detailed work of shaping the new *Times* was done by Donald Holmes.[16]

Holmes was a skilled and deeply thoughtful journalist who had been night editor (the man responsible for getting the paper away each night) for eight years when in 1964 Haley asked him to do some experimenting in types and headings against the still conjectural day of change. Early in 1965 he was put full time on the re-modelling task for which all his experience and temperament fitted him. Before becoming night editor he had been successively home and foreign chief sub-editor, and in each job he had done the apparently impossible each night in a reflective, unruffled manner.

Throughout 1965 Holmes was in all the meetings of the Operation Breakthrough committee and it was he who turned the suggestions and decisions into tangible form as miniature mock-up 24-page papers. Later in 1965 and early in 1966 Holmes joined with Walter James in carrying forward the plans still further. In October 1965 Holmes was given the job of producing the first of several complete full-scale dummy papers with news on the front page and with other pages in the suggested new sequence. Beginning at midnight as soon as the London edition was available he cut up and rearranged the whole paper according to the new plan. Then the whole dummy *Times* was printed, and was ready the next day for suggestions from top editorial and managerial executives.

Apart from the actual rearrangement of the paper several decisions had to be taken. An early question was whether *The Times*, which had seven columns to the page, should fall in with other serious newspapers, and please advertisers, by having eight columns. Haley had no doubt that, for the sake of readability, it should stay with seven columns a page. (It

14 William MacLeod (b. 1924). Joined staff of The Times Publishing Company, 1958; chief accountant, 1960; company secretary, Times Newspapers Limited, 1967.
15 Frederick Stanley Park (b. 1917). Joined staff of The Times Publishing Company, 1950; deputy day printer, 1956; night production manager, 1960; works manager, 1963.
16 Arthur Donald Holmes (b. 1906). *The Times* home sub-editor, 1937; chief home sub-editor, 1947; chief sub-editor, 1952; night editor, 1956; coordinating editor, 1966 until retirement in 1971.

was another decision that was to be reversed after the Thomson purchase.)

The second arose from a delightfully characteristic *Times* controversy, pursued with all the eagerness of a senior common room argument. In the title-piece on the front page should the royal coat of arms be kept in its customary place between the *The* and the *Times*? Or should it be dropped? Some thought it would not fit in with the larger headlines of the new front page. Others thought it gave a misleadingly official air to the paper. Others – among them John Walter Senior – wished to preserve tradition and the emblem of loyalty. To this came the reply that the paper had no right to use the royal coat of arms anyway. An informal poll taken by Haley at a meeting of senior editorial staff virtually decided the matter by a small majority. A plain, uncrested title-piece was designed by B. L. Wolpe, Royal Designer to Industry, and was adopted. After the change was made the editor received a letter from Sir Anthony Wagner, Garter King of Arms, which left no room for repining:

> May I offer congratulations on the disappearance from your masthead of the representation of the Royal Arms, which so long and misleadingly suggested that *The Times* had an official character. It is to be hoped that those newspapers which still continue this eighteenth century solecism will now follow your example and drop it.[17]

A minor change, more esoteric, was made on the leader page when a new masthead was drawn by A. Campbell to go above the two columns of leading articles. The design retained the clock in the centre of the masthead but, after due discussion, the hands of the clock were changed. Previously they had pointed at six minutes past six, which in the old days had been the average time of morning publication. Now they were moved to 4.30, which throughout Fleet Street had come to be the average time of printing the last copy of the night's run.

A question of greater substance was whether the larger headings should be all in capitals or whether lower case be used. There was little doubt that lower case was the most modern usage: the only regret was that a new condensed type, designed by Tracy, could not be manufactured in time to appear in the new-model paper. Another typographical change was not likely to be consciously noted by the general reader. He or she would, it was hoped, simply find the print in most of the paper easier to read. What was done was to restore the long letters like *g* and *p*

---

17 *The Times*, May 4 1966. The crest was restored to the title-piece in July 1981, starting with the issue covering the wedding of the Prince of Wales.

to their original shape after their tails had been shortened to save space in the years of newsprint rationing. In technical terms, the type was no longer 8-point on 7½ but 8-point on 8. More generally, the appearance of the paper came to be increasingly influenced by Jeanette Collins.[18] In preparation for the change on May 3 1966 she was appointed art editor of the woman's page a few weeks ahead. Her bold lay-outs and designs were soon being used in other parts, and she was to become design editor of the whole paper.

On one of the largest questions of all – whether, while modernising itself, *The Times* should drop its anonymity rule – Haley was firm against any change. Under him as under his predecessors all staff writers and all the paper's part-time correspondents at home and abroad, wrote without their names appearing. At the most they could signal themselves as 'Our Labour Correspondent', for example, or more vaguely 'Our Special Correspondent' or 'Our Own Correspondent'. Kyril Tidmarsh's articles on Soviet affairs were headed 'By Monitor' – the nearest approach to a personal attribution.[19] Haley acknowledged that the practice of anonymity had its snags. A writer, nameless in *The Times*, could appear on television or radio and there be introduced with his name and with direct reference to the job he had on the paper. Haley also acknowledged that sometimes, particularly in the *Literary Supplement*, a writer could anonymously criticise an author and his work in a style far fiercer, and even more spiteful, than he would have done under his own name. 'Masked infighting', Haley was to write, 'can put academic, political and other reputations unfairly at stake'. That was a danger to be watched and controlled. Even so Haley still believed that the idea of *The Times* as a corporate body, speaking in its own right, gave the paper's views greater authority than any individual writer could command. Looking at the problem some years later he wrote that he remained in favour of anonymity:

> It may be that the circumstances which could hold a band of people together, each satisfied with sharing in a common purpose without individual acknowledgements, no longer exist. I still have greater respect for a view, or a review, offered me by a paper than one presented by a person. Signed writing invites exhibitionism, though it may be unconscious.[20]

---

18 Jeanette Lilian Collins (b. 1939). Art editor, woman's page, 1966; design editor *The Times*, 1970–79.
19 See Chapter XVIII.
20 Haley. Article headed *T.L.S.* in 'The American Scholar', Spring 1980. Washington, D.C.

Haley's desire to keep anonymity was confirmed by the Board on June 2 1966. (The rule was yet another which was to be abolished some months later after the Thomson purchase.)

Preparing the main new features, which were the diary and the woman's page each working day, fell mainly to Patrick Ryan and Walter James respectively. For the diary Haley remembered Harman Grisewood[21] from their BBC years together; Grisewood took up the offer, and it was he who started the feature off after several dummy runs. For the woman's page James passed on to Haley a long memorandum written by Susanne Puddefoot[22] who had done some work for James. Haley and others liked the way in which she pictured a page for citizens who happened to be women and were no less intelligent and widely interested than men. She made the page successful from the start and was especially fortunate to gain Prudence Glynn,[23] with her easy, elegant pen, as the fashion editor.

Yet another new feature for the paper was a regular cartoon. Out of many artists whose work was seen, K. Mahood – with his bold and distinctively angular political sketches – was chosen; he was given a retainer and payment for each cartoon printed. More women were joining the staff as a matter of course: Margaret Allen[24] in Business News, later to be features editor; Margaret Laing[25] in the reporters' room, later author of a biography of Edward Heath; Winifred Lodge[26] and Margaret Alexander[27] guarded and presented the higher mysteries of the court page.

When a ship is launched, or the prototype of an aircraft gathers speed on the runway, everyone concerned knows that every detail has been checked a hundred times and more. Everyone knows also the weeks of absorption beforehand, the eleventh-hour questionings which each man

---

21 Harman Joseph Grisewood (b. 1906). Ampleforth; Worcester College, Oxford. Controller of BBC Third Programme, 1948–52. Diary editor for six months in 1966.
22 Susanne Puddefoot (b. 1934). Blackpool Collegiate School; Girton College, Cambridge. Editor *The Times* woman's page, 1966–69.
23 Prudence Loveday Glynn (Lady Windlesham) (b. 1935). Fashion editor *The Times*, 1966–80.
24 Margaret Allen (b. 1933). Fallowfield Convent, Manchester; London School of Economics. Joined staff of *The Times*, 1933; assistant City editor, 1966; deputy features editor, 1971; features editor, 1973; resigned, 1981.
25 Margaret Irene Laing (b. 1935). *The Times* special supplements, 1958; home news reporter, 1959; joined staff of *The Sunday Times*, 1964.
26 Winifred Mary Catherine Lodge (b. 1907). Joined staff of *The Times* as secretary, 1929; social department, 1932; assistant on *History of The Times*, 1934; social editor, 1938–67.
27 Margaret Alexander (b. 1921). Joined staff of *The Times*, 1950; social editor, 1967.

keeps to himself, and the final moments of supreme tension and relief. All *Times* people lived through such weeks early in 1966. Many of them were there to share the final moments of launching on the night of Monday–Tuesday, May 2–3. All were keyed up as they stood closely around the stone (the steel make-up bench in the composing room) to watch the last page being locked up before it was slid away to be moulded and printed. The electric bell rang as usual: *Last page gone.*

On the editorial side everything had been rehearsed, but one thing could not be guarded against, and that was a drying up of news on the very night when news was most needed. The decision had earlier been taken not to pre-fabricate a lead story, but to go on hard news. In desperation, when the country and the world showed unruffled calm and press time was coming nearer, Rendel was asked as diplomatic correspondent to expand a story based on suggestions that the Nato headquarters might be moved to London. The one consolation for him and others was that readers were, for once, more interested in the appearance of *The Times* than in its contents.

Most of the night's burden swung to the mechanical side under Fred Park, works manager, Jock Sullivan,[28] head printer, and George Vowles,[29] who was to succeed Sullivan. They had not only to cope with the new make-up and the new order of pages; they had to print not the usual 250,000 copies of a 20-page or 24-page paper but 450,000 copies of a 32-page paper. The whole printing was done on time. Every copy was sold the next day. On May 4 400,000 copies were printed; on May 5 360,000; on May 6 355,000. As expected, the demand then declined as the novelty wore off but the solid circulation, which had been around 250,000, rose steadily by about 10,000 a month. In October Pope reported it to be 294,000. There was a breakthrough at last.

---

28 E. W. (Jock) Sullivan (b. 1903). Joined staff of The Times Publishing Company, 1929; deputy head printer, 1954; head printer, 1955–67.
29 George Henry Vowles (b. 1919). Joined staff of The Times Publishing Company, 1950; deputy head printer, 1963; head printer, 1967; composing room manager Times Newspapers, 1980–82.

XXII

RESCUE OPERATION

T HE new face and form given to *The Times* in May 1966 seemed to be highly successful. Readers who had opposed the change were soon writing in to say that they liked it. Many were sure that *The Times* had done much more than give itself a new front page, larger headings, and some new features. They were positive – such is the effect of a right frame around a picture – that the whole style of writing within the paper had been brightened and tightened. Yet none of this, and not even the rise in circulation, helped the paper's financial plight.

Ironically the very success of the face-lift had the immediate effect of making the financial balance worse. *The Times* had to bear the extra burden of what are called 'run-on costs', familiar to all newspapers that draw their revenue much more from the advertisements in their pages than from the sale of the papers themselves. After May 3 1966 the sums which *The Times* gained from its extra sales did not cover the extra expenses in newsprint, ink, and labour; and the management had to wait before it could think of putting up the advertisement rates to meet those added expenses. Many advertisers thought that the existing rates were already dear when compared to those of papers with larger circulations. With the development of marketing techniques the old vague notions of 'prestige advertising', which favoured *The Times*, counted for less than hard figures of the cost of an advertisement per inch per reader. *The Times* could still hold its own in property and company-meeting advertisements but in much other advertising it came out poorly from such assessments of returns for money. It would be able to offer competitive rates only if circulation was increased substantially.

Quite evidently the MDE exercise had to be only the beginning of a wider drive, commercial and managerial as well as editorial. No less evidently, large sums would have to be invested in such a drive for expansion. In March 1965 Haley had told the Board, when it was considering the MDE exercise, that several hundreds of thousands of pounds were needed. In August 1966 he spoke of the immediate need for £3,000,000. *The Times* did not have anything like that sum available.

The Times Publishing Company as a whole was making a small profit, but it was too small to count, and the paper itself was losing money.

Anxiety about the future was deepened by another thought. In the past there had been a largely unspoken assumption that Lord Astor of Hever would not let *The Times* sink. If need be (so it seemed to Francis Mathew and to others) Astor would put more of his money into the paper. But Gavin Astor inherited a very different world. At a time of rising taxes and rising costs it was impossible for him to share his father's easy contentment at the prospect of getting little or no return on the money that was invested in *The Times*. As for the idea of adding yet more money to the sums already invested, the answer was clear to all concerned in running the paper. The money was simply not available.

In the early and middle sixties such considerations began more and more to occupy the minds of Gavin Astor, his brother Hugh, the members of the Board, Haley (especially after he became chief executive) and the general manager, first Mathew and then Pope. Like the nation as a whole, *The Times* was confronted by an acute need for investment, although there was no immediate crisis facing the company. The new-model *Times* of May 1966 was likely to go on climbing slowly in circulation. What the paper could not do was greatly expand; and without such expansion – without the heavy investment needed to make such expansion possible – it would fall back, falter, and fail.

Gavin Astor was feeling more than the financial strain. With all his pride in the position he held, and in spite of Operation Breakthrough, he could not help being restless and increasingly uneasy. He was paying substantial interest on a bank loan which he had taken out to help him buy the Walter shares, thus making himself virtually sole owner of the company. Yet with what result? He reflected on how many of the plans which he and his brother Hugh had put forward for developing the business had been resisted – whether for going into television, or for diversifying the company's activities in other promising fields including book publishing, travel, and the promotion of exhibitions, or for speedily reorganising and modernising the structure of management along lines suggested by the Cooper report. More and more keenly he regarded his position as anomalous and anachronistic. He was later to express his dissatisfaction in carefully restrained language: 'I have come to realise that to carry the entire financial risk as Proprietor no less than the full legal responsibility as Chairman for the success or failure of the Company, without also carrying executive power, is not a satisfactory situation.'[1]

---

1 See Chapter XXIII and Appendix G.

The general predicament facing *The Times* was clear to discerning men inside the office and outside it. On February 18 1963 Godfrey Phillips,[2] one of the most influential members of the Board, waved the red warning light in a strong letter to Gavin Astor. He estimated that The Times Publishing Company's debt to Barclay's Bank would, by 1965–66, probably be near £3,500,000. A fall in profits – caused, say, by the loss of the contract for printing the *Observer* – would increase the debt. The company could raise funds by borrowing, or by selling assets, or by raising new equity. Phillips pointed out the disadvantages of each course but went in some detail into the last of the three – raising new equity by broadening the financial base of the company. He pointed out that no one in his senses would invest in the company simply and solely to make money. The only other motive for investment would be to gain a say in the editorial policy of the paper. Phillips then referred in a general way, without comment, to the idea of a closer association between *The Times* and the *Observer*.

The Times's predicament was becoming clearer to others outside the office. In that same year, 1963, Lord Drogheda on behalf of Lord Cowdray[3] mentioned to Gavin Astor the possibility of an arrangement between *The Times* and his own *Financial Times*. A little later Roy Thomson, later to be Lord Thomson of Fleet, called on John Astor in the south of France and tentatively suggested that *The Times* and his own *Sunday Times* might have some kind of association together, helping each other perhaps by way of sharing machinery and other services. Thomson had already put in a bid for the Walter shares which Gavin Astor bought instead. He was left feeling that neither the Astors nor the Walters had liked his approaches at that time. None the less he let it be known, as did Cowdray, that he was still interested. Inquiries began to come from other concerns. *The Times* also began to make its own inquiries about suitable partners, especially after Haley became chief executive in 1965. By the end of 1965 and during the spring and summer of 1966 contacts were kept up with two, three, and occasionally four concerns at one and the same time.

There was no lack of candidates. It was a period when 'quality papers' were growing in size and circulation; a period when owners, editors, and managers were outstanding in their drive and journalistic skill. The best of British journalism was at its very best. Its response to the challenge of television had been rapid and imaginative, particularly on the part of *The Sunday Times* and the *Observer*. All this meant that

2 George Godfrey Phillips (1900–1965). Managing director, Lazards. Director, The Times Publishing Company, 1953–65.
3 3rd Viscount Cowdray (b. 1910). Chairman, S. Pearson and Son Limited, 1954–77.

The Times, while taking its own part in the renaissance by reforming itself, was facing highly intelligent competition from those who were forging ahead faster. The competition came on several flanks. The *Daily Telegraph* was still pulling in readers and advertisements. The *Guardian*, under the leadership of its chairman, Laurence Scott, and its young editor, Alastair Hetherington, had advanced swiftly since beginning printing in London on September 11 1960. On another front there came a formidable and admirably planned thrust from the *Financial Times* under its managing director Lord Drogheda and its editor, Gordon Newton.[4] They had recognised that the businessmen wished to read not only City matters but general news, especially essential foreign news, when tersely presented and ably explained. He wished also to have a guide to the theatre and the arts; the paper's reviews became famous for their excellence.

In many ways the most natural associate for *The Times* was the *Observer*, being both a close neighbour and a close relative.[5] Though often differing in their policies the two papers liked both the seriousness and the quirkiness in each other. After some gentle feelers in the early spring of 1965 Haley agreed in May of that year to chair some formal talks to see if the existing landlord-tenant relationship could become a closer partnership. Gavin Astor wanted Haley to become the managing director of a combined organisation, of which he himself would be chairman. Haley did not wish to give up the editorship of *The Times* but agreed that he might become chairman of the *Times* company within the combined organisation and have an executive editor under him. David Astor would be chairman of the *Observer* company within the same united framework. The talks went on for some time but it became clear that the *Observer* needed money for development, much less than *The Times* needed but still substantial. Putting the two wants together would not get rid of them. It would merely produce a combined need of at least £4,000,000. With the best of good will on both sides little progress could be made. At one time David Astor said that he believed that a consortium of interests, including some Canadian money, could support a combined *Times–Observer* company. Nothing hard emerged, although talks continued on and off until September 1966.

Talks with the *Guardian* were briefer and less intensive. On November 2 1965 Laurence Scott saw Haley and suggested that there could be a merger of the two companies and the two papers. Gavin Astor should be chairman of the united company, Scott himself should be chief execu-

---

4 Sir Gordon Newton (b. 1907). Editor *Financial Times*, 1960–72. Knighted, 1976.
5 See Chapter XVII.

tive, and Haley should be editor. An alternative proposal was for Gavin Astor to be president and Scott chairman. Two days later Gavin Astor agreed that talks should be opened. The idea had its appeal. Both papers were moving ahead and were planning further reforms. The *Manchester Evening News*, part of Scott's company, was making money. A combined *Times–Guardian* could appeal to readers more numerous and more varied than either paper could attract on its own. It could offer first-class news coverage, more special articles, and more writing of a simple, informal style. This style had for long distinguished the *Guardian*, and *The Times* itself was cultivating it more widely in its own pages. Yet the idea never got very far. One difficulty was that there would be redundancies among the staffs. Another was over editorial policy. Talks between Haley and Hetherington during November were entirely friendly but necessarily vague. When it came to the point no one could precisely envisage a paper that combined the formality of *The Times* and the informality of the *Guardian*. Nor could anyone work out a joint editorial policy in advance except in the most general of terms. Yet another difficulty could arise with the Monopolies Commission, faced with what would in effect be the loss of one daily paper. The truth is that none of the principals really had his heart in the exercise, superficially attractive though it was. On May 31 1966 Scott wrote to Haley, saying to him that evidently no progress could be made; perhaps in the years to come changed circumstances might cause them to revive it, but unless that happened they should put it out of their minds.

By this time – May 1966 – Astor, Haley, and Pope were in the thick of negotiations with Cowdray, Drogheda, and Newton of the *Financial Times*. For some weeks the talks seemed promising. As far back as September 1961 Francis Mathew had talked in Printing House Square about a joint ownership shared by Cowdray and Astor, perhaps bringing in the *Observer*. The serious talks had begun towards the end of March 1966 when Drogheda met Kenneth Keith,[6] a member of *The Times* Board and Gavin Astor's especially close financial adviser. Drogheda asked what *The Times* would think of a union in which – to put it in an over-simplified form – the *Financial Times* would become the business section of *The Times*? This idea opened up many solid and workmanlike prospects. Each paper had much to give the other: broader general news from the one, deeper financial and industrial coverage from the other. Each paper had prestige, earned by proven professional skill and achievement. The combined paper would have

---

6 Kenneth Keith (b. 1916). Chairman Hill Samuel Group, 1970–80; Director Times Newspapers, 1967–81. Baron, 1980.

unrivalled authority in the City and in industry generally, and that authority would strengthen its voice in Westminster and abroad.

The strong hopes which each side brought to the talks in the early weeks and months were later to be recalled by Lord Drogheda, then managing director of the *Financial Times*, in his memoirs:

The estimates of costs which I worked out with George Pope of *The Times* and with the other members most closely concerned on both sides convinced me that, from the very start, the merged paper would be significantly more profitable than the *FT* alone, and I was confident that the shareholders would by no means suffer. I also believed that the new paper could achieve a degree of international importance which neither of the constituent parts could ever do on their own. In this view, I was wholeheartedly backed by William Haley, who was at first extremely excited by the possibilities; a 'meeting of two equal partners' was a phrase he used . . . The title to be preserved, all were agreed, must be *The Times*; but throughout its pages the paper would be strongly impregnated with the personality of the *FT* and we of the *FT* increasingly came to feel that we would have to be the predominant force, while preserving and embodying the best features of *The Times*. The change of emphasis undoubtedly lessened Haley's ardour.[7]

None the less Haley still thought that safeguards could be built into an eventual deal and a stronger *Times* could be fashioned out of it. On April 1 Drogheda amplified the whole proposal in talks with Gavin Astor, Haley, and Pope. On May 17, after further talks, Drogheda told Haley of two firm conditions: Cowdray should have sufficient shares in the company to give him control, and Newton should be editor. Later in the discussion Drogheda proposed that Haley should be chairman of the company and that Drogheda himself should be managing director. Haley came back to the question that was to recur many times. How would the independence of the editor be guaranteed? This vital matter was discussed the next day during a dinner which Gavin Astor gave at his London house. A newcomer to the talks at this May 18 dinner was Lord Poole[8] who was to play a decisive part in the next moves. His frank, plain dealing greatly impressed Haley and Astor.

The *Times* men were still uneasy about the degree of authority to be given to the editor of the proposed new *Times*. How could they be sure that Cowdray would carry on the Astor tradition of the constitutional

---

7 Lord Drogheda, *Double Harness*, pp. 191–2.
8 Oliver Brian Sanderson Poole (b. 1911). Director S. Pearson and Son. Baron, 1958.

monarchy? Poole affirmed that if Haley was unhappy the whole matter would be dropped. In fact two things were necessary, he said, if the deal was to go through: Newton must be editor, Haley must stay. On June 1 Haley, after talks with John Astor as well as Gavin, suggested that he himself should be both chairman and, in the American sense, publisher. That is to say, he should have general editorial oversight and responsibility. Mainly he would be in the background and would leave the editor entirely alone most of the time to get on with the work of editing. On occasion he might join in discussions on policy but his chief purpose would be to put a broad pair of shoulders between the editor and anyone, from anywhere, who was out to apply pressure on that editor.

The second cloud was heavier and could not be so easily lightened or ignored. It was directly financial. On June 9, when the *Times* Board met, Gavin Astor explained the company's financial straits. At least £2,500,000 was needed for development; he could not supply it; a bank loan would not be forthcoming so long as profits were as low as they were. Looking ahead, the death duties that would have to be paid when he died would wreck any hope that his family could keep the company intact. Haley then gave the other picture that had emerged. The *Financial Times* was making a profit of £1,360,000 a year; the Westminster Press,[9] which would be part of the proposed new organisation, had a profit of £2,500,000 a year.

The next day, June 10, Gavin Astor wrote to Poole giving the Board's understanding of the deal. There were further talks throughout the rest of June and throughout July. From the Cowdray side it was pointed out that they would be asking *Financial Times* shareholders to transfer their shares to the new company; they would have to assure those shareholders that they would be financially better off. But the loss on *The Times* in 1966 was going to be so great that they could give such assurances of early and continuing profit only if the Astor share in the new company was made very small indeed. From this it followed that Gavin Astor must expect a small sum for *The Times* and a small voice in the new company. Haley passed such warnings on to Astor and then, having completed his part of the discussions which concerned the character and editorial independence of the new *Times*, went away on August 3 for a holiday in France. He was convinced that the financial side, which was not his direct concern, would be straightened out.

While he was away everything was decisively changed. Keith and one or two others among Gavin Astor's financial advisers came to like the deal less and less the more they heard about it. Even one or two of

---

9 Westminster Press, Cowdray's substantial provincial group.

Cowdray's men said that his offer when it came was bound to disappoint Astor; one of them called it 'derisory'. From the Cowdray side Drogheda was later to describe how the offer came to be so low:

> Many hours were spent by the financial experts upon the numerous problems but the one overriding question was the valuation to be placed on *The Times* newspaper itself, because on this depended the proportion to be held by Gavin Astor of the capital of the new company combining *The Times, FT* and Westminster Press; yet, beyond a valuation of the Printing House Square plant and buildings, which could be assessed, the value of the goodwill of *The Times* itself was something no one could scientifically measure. It was possible to argue that the figure should be a purely nominal one, or even negative, because of the losses *The Times* was incurring. An indication had been conveyed to us that if Gavin Astor were to be offered a 12½ per cent or one eighth interest in the combined group he would be willing to accept. However, the financial experts advising Pearsons suggested that his proportion should be no more than 8¼ per cent . . . The truth was that Pearsons were divided over their attitude towards the merger; otherwise I feel sure that the offer would have been improved.[10]

Where Drogheda was disappointed with the low offer Gavin Astor was deeply disturbed and became increasingly anxious about the future. If Cowdray would not pay him a good price who on earth would? At this low point Keith had lunch, arranged some time beforehand, with Denis Hamilton. Hamilton was editor of the fast-expanding *Sunday Times* and the close friend, confidant, and business associate of Lord Thomson of Fleet, owner of *The Sunday Times* and many other papers in Britain and North America as well as the greater part of Scottish Television. Roy Thomson had already changed the balance of newspaper ownership in Britain. He and Hamilton together looked at newspapers with modern eyes and they had the drive and the courage to bring about long-needed and revolutionary changes in the papers they controlled. Hamilton's lunch with Keith led on swiftly to Thomson's proudest achievement in the newspaper world.

Thomson and Hamilton differed greatly in their manner and bearing: the first appearing lively, talkative, extrovert, stout, irrepressible; the second quiet, slim, appraising, reflective, courteous-voiced. Their backgrounds were wholly different. Hamilton had interests outside his work;

---

10 Drogheda, *op. cit.* p. 193.

Thomson had virtually none. Yet over the next ten years, right up until Thomson's death on August 4 1976, they were to be united in upholding and advancing *The Times*: Thomson as chief owner, Hamilton as chief executive and editor-in-chief, later as chairman of the new company, Times Newspapers Limited.

Roy Thomson was a prodigy: 'an omen, portent. Now *rare*', 'a person with some quality which excites wonder'.[11] The title of his autobiography, *After I was Sixty*, published when he was turned eighty, brings out the most extraordinary feature of his extraordinary career. His flowering, his great burst of energy and imagination, came only after he left Canada for Edinburgh when he was fifty-nine years old.

He was the great-great-grandson of a master-mason who emigrated from Dumfriesshire in 1773. Roy himself was the son of a Toronto barber and (often a prescription for a man's success) a capable, talented mother. Very early in life, inspired by romantic story books about poor boys who rose high, he set his mind on becoming a millionaire. The first attempts did not get him far. He had failures as a farmer and as a small salesman for motor supplies. He had a thin time selling radio sets. He then decided, helped by a bank loan, to buy a tiny, almost Heath-Robinson, local radio station at Timmins, Northern Ontario. He bought the *Press*, one of the two local weekly newspapers, and about a year later turned it into a daily. He bought another small radio station. The tide turned his way during the war. When the size of the larger Canadian papers was restricted, many advertisements and the incomes from them were channelled into just the kind of local paper and local radio which Thomson owned. In 1944 he was at long last out of financial danger. He went on buying papers in the United States as well as in Canada, and he went on offering to buy many more. His genius for finance began to show itself. First and foremost, he was never afraid of incurring heavy bank loans. To him they were splendid opportunities, not the burdens that lesser men would think them. 'I am as rich as my credit is limitless', he used to say.

In the early fifties there came sadness. He had become the millionaire he wished to be, but his wife died; a close business partner left him; and he failed in a bid to enter the Canadian Federal Parliament as a Tory. He was restless and depressed. At that very time, quite unexpectedly, he reaped the reward of his old practice of asking newspaper owners whether their publications might some time or other be for sale. Back in the 1940s he had inquired whether shares in the *Scotsman*, in Edinburgh, could be bought. Not put off by being firmly told that it was

---

11 Shorter Oxford English Dictionary. 3rd edition revised, Oxford 1964.

a close family business, not for sale, he kept on asking. The *Scotsman's* answer remained unchanged until April 1953. A letter then arrived from Thomson's main contact on the company board, Colin Mackinnon, asking if he was still interested in buying some shares or even becoming sole owner. Thomson's reply was emphatic. He would buy some or all of the shares. After being delayed by the Federal elections he flew to Scotland in August and within a short time, after some hard bargaining, the *Scotsman* and its evening partner, the *Edinburgh Evening Dispatch*, and the *Weekly Scotsman* were his. He borrowed £393,750 in Canada to help him in the deal.

In his memoirs he tells of his cold and sometimes hostile reception among Edinburgh society and the resentment caused by the changes he introduced into the *Scotsman*. He was the more determined to turn loss into profit, and he succeeded. By now he had recruited a man as unorthodox and as extrovert as himself, James Coltart, an accountant who after some years in business was assistant general manager of the *Scottish Daily Express* when Thomson weighed up his talents and liked them. Together, almost alone, they started Scottish Television in 1955 with a ridiculously small initial outlay. Afterwards Thomson would take a hearty pleasure in listing the names of prominent Scots who loftily refused to join him in what he later called 'a licence to print money'. The few that did make the plunge with him were repaid many times over. He himself later wrote:

> During the eight years we had an 80 per cent holding in Scottish Television until ITA forced us to reduce our holding first to 55 per cent and then to 25 per cent, our share of the company profits ran to £13m.

The next step was greater from the very start. Lord Kemsley had rebuffed several bids from Thomson to buy his *Aberdeen Press and Journal*. Suddenly in 1959 Kemsley offered him the whole of his nationwide group of newspapers, *The Sunday Times* chief among them. When Thomson protested that he had not the money Kemsley briefly told him to get his financial advisers, S. G. Warburg's, in touch with Lionel Fraser of Helbert Wagg's. 'They'll work something out together.' What they worked out was a brilliant and vastly complex financial deal, leaving Thomson to seek a bank loan of £3,000,000 to cover the balance of the cash payment to Kemsley for his own shares in the Kemsley Group. The loan was swiftly given in Scotland, the deal was completed, and Thomson emerged in complete control of the new Kemsley Newspapers/Scottish Television group. He moved to London, having become one of the big four newspaper owners in Britain.

His time of great expansion was only beginning. Seven years later, after he had vastly extended his commercial field – in printing and book publishing, Thomson Holidays, yellow-pages telephone directories, large holdings in North Sea oil, and other enterprises in many lands – *The Times* assessed the significance of the man and his work. On August 5 1976, the morning after his death, the first leading article was devoted to him:

> He was obviously in his own field a genius; the business achievement cannot quite be paralleled and is unlikely ever to be paralleled. Indeed the exceptional ability that he had as a businessman helped to set free his quality of personal warmth. You do not need to take a hard or cynical approach to business if you happen to be ten times better at doing business than anyone else around . . .
>
> The principles of his life were those taught by a poor childhood in the 1890s in what was still a pioneer's country . . . He practised the principles of a pioneer, hard work, loyalty to friends and colleagues, a strong family life, a belief in a man's responsibility for his own destiny, an impatience with outside interference, straight speaking.

The straight speaking was inseparable from the man. It was an expression of the genuine, native, unaffected simplicity that lay at the very centre of a mind that could comprehend financial deals involving millions of pounds, past, present, and future. His frankness often appalled his lieutenants. Either he was silent or he spoke the truth, quite simply because nothing else was worth speaking. He often called himself a rough-neck Canadian, and he remained of one piece. In this unshakeability he had a very useful testing time soon after reaching Britain. On first taking over the *Scotsman*, when he was cold-shouldered by most of 'east-windy, west-endy' Edinburgh, he had to decide whether to try to change himself and conform more nearly to Scottish and English upper-class ways and manners. His character decided the matter for him, and it was that staunchness and un-changeability which people respected in him, along with his warmth, his courage in taking risks, and his vision which always let him see beyond the horizon.

Publicly he made a show of regarding his newspapers simply as vehicles for profit-making. He enjoyed having attributed to him – wrongly, as it happens – the saying that editorial matter was 'just the stuff between the ads'. What is true is that he regarded the editorial content as a matter for the editor's judgment. Beyond that he saw his newspapers as responsible providers of a service to the community.

They should make money, certainly; they should expand; but not by an easy appeal which would shame both him and the journalists.

At his side in 1966 was Denis Hamilton, editorial director of the Kemsley Newspapers group since 1950 and editor of *The Sunday Times* since 1961. Other London editors and managers found themselves watching with admiration and dismay the great expansion of *The Sunday Times* during the five years of Hamilton's editorship. Hamilton's success was essentially due to his sense of strategy. He planned on a very broad field. Throughout the 1939–45 war he had been a fighting soldier, winning an immediate DSO on the field in 1944 when in command of an infantry battalion. He became one of Field Marshal Montgomery's closest friends. He brought to newspapers some of the methods and practices he had seen being applied in the war and debated in his many talks after the war with the Field Marshal. Especially he brought the working principles of forward planning, of seeing the exercise as a whole, stripping it down to its main essentials, plotting out the advance on that simplified basis, concentrating his own mind on the main plan, leaving most of the detailed elaboration to his lieutenants, devolving a great deal of responsibility onto them, letting them get on with it and report back to him when necessary. He liked to ponder over all sides of a problem, even if it meant delaying a decision, but once having seen his way ahead he kept to that road. He also brought with him another guiding principle from the army, one that is not always easy for a naturally reflective and analytical man to follow, but he did follow it: the man in command had always to appear calm and confident. Like Haley, he had started in journalism at an early age and had a full training on evening papers in Middlesbrough and Newcastle – as a reporter, sub-editor and feature writer until he was embodied as a Territorial Army officer in August 1939. He had only been demobilised one month when he was appointed chief editorial assistant to Lord Kemsley, who owned the largest British group of newspapers, including *The Sunday Times*. He believed that a quarter of an editor's week should be devoted to the training of outstanding young journalists and looking for talent.

When he took over *The Sunday Times* in 1961 he saw that it needed much more news space and many more special features; hence it had to have more pages; hence it had to have many more advertisements to support those pages; hence there had to be a strong drive for advertisements based on modern methods of market research and salesmanship. The drive, when it came, was successful; more advertisements were brought in month by month, increasing the profits as well as providing the extra pages. Hamilton felt that all this concerned him directly as editor. In an article in *Punch* on December 23 1964 he wrote:

It is absolutely necessary, today, for an editor to be actively involved in newspaper economics; the economic viability of his paper is just as much the concern of the editor as it is of the proprietor.

Still more directly, Hamilton made sure that the editorial side seized the new opportunities with news stories that dug down deeply into a subject and he recruited the best writing and critical talent in Fleet Street without disposing of a single member of the old team. He was not afraid to pay high rates for special articles by men or women who knew most, and could write most clearly, about contentious topics of the day. In particular he gave the paper the reputation for securing the advance serial rights of eagerly awaited books, mainly autobiographies such as Field-Marshal Montgomery's *Memoirs*. As the number of pages grew Hamilton divided the paper into two, with the *Weekly Review* as the second part, and then into three with the launching of the colour magazine (February 1962), then into four with the establishment of the business news section (September 1964). Thomson was the keenest of all on starting the colour magazine; he recorded that it cost him £900,000 in the first eighteen months.[12] But Hamilton laboured hard to get the formula right, one that would get away from travelogues and stately homes and would deal directly with the ambitions and problems of men and women under forty. In the end the magazine won through, the advertisers rallied to it, and it brought 200,000 new readers to the paper. The *Observer* and the *Daily Telegraph* were to follow suit.

Hamilton had reason not only to appear confident but to be so within himself. He saw the circulation of *The Sunday Times* rise from almost half a million in 1950, the year he became editorial director of Kemsley Newspapers, to a million and a half in 1966.

Hamilton's lunch with Kenneth Keith in August 1966 was not the first contact between Thomson and *The Times*. In his autobiography Thomson records that from their first days in London he and Jim Coltart began looking around for a daily newspaper to run in conjunction with *The Sunday Times*. They thought of many:

But of all the daily papers in London, clearly *The Times*, with its title, its not dissimilar approach, its supreme reputation, and the

---

12 Thomson of Fleet, *Ibid*, p. 122.

tremendous boost it would give to our reputation – and our ego – would be the best for us to link with.[13]

After having some tactical talks with Coltart and Hamilton, Thomson (as mentioned earlier in this chapter) gently and apparently informally dropped his hint to John Astor in the south of France in 1963. Might not the two papers have 'some sort of association'? According to Thomson Astor resented and rebuffed 'this innocuous approach'. 'He was reluctant to face the realities of his own position; or he didn't like my style.'[14] Undeterred, Thomson took up the idea later with Gavin Astor, without any more success. Later still he talked to Francis Mathew and Stanley Morison who were both more encouraging although neither felt that he could mention the matter to John Astor. Thomson also made occasional inquiries of Kenneth Keith who could not offer hope that Thomson's idea would come to anything.

In 1965 Denis Hamilton had meetings with Gavin Astor; he reminded Astor that The Times's circulation had been on a plateau while those of other quality papers were rising; its advertising rate per reader was becoming higher in comparison with the rate of others. What The Times needed, said Hamilton, was a transfusion of technical, marketing, and managerial skills. Later still Hamilton pursued his argument in talks with Haley and Pope. He passed on to them the benefits of his experience with The Sunday Times, and he pressed his well-based argument that the extra pages which The Times needed if it was to surge ahead could come only from a successful drive for more advertisements. Hamilton told Thomson afterwards that neither Times man made much response; the next day he received a friendly letter from Haley thanking him for his advice but indicating that The Times wished to work out its own destiny. What Hamilton could not know was that Haley, even before he became chief executive, had himself been advocating a strong advertisement drive with precisely the same objective – more editorial space – in view.

There the Times–Thomson contacts rested until the Hamilton–Keith luncheon. Keith, knowing that The Times's negotiations with Cowdray and his Financial Times were going to collapse, asked Hamilton straight away whether Thomson was still ready to make a bid. In almost the same breath Keith said that the independence of The Times had not only to be preserved but be seen to be preserved, which meant that Thomson could not be in direct control. Hamilton was a little

---

13 Thomson of Fleet, *Ibid*, p. 166.
14 *Ibid*, p. 166.

surprised by the timing of the approach but, knowing Thomson's mind, had his answers well prepared. Thomson had himself, in talks with Hamilton, suggested that in any talks with the Astors he should propose the formation of a new company into which he would put the highly successful *Sunday Times* and the Astors should put *The Times*. The Board should be made up of four Thomson-appointed members, four Astor-appointed, and four 'national directors', public men whose remit would be to watch over the continuing role of *The Times* in the life of the country. The votes of these national directors would constitute a 'blocking third': neither the Thomson nor the Astor side could get its own way unless it had the four national votes with it. Hamilton elaborated this basic idea in reply to Keith who thought it highly promising as a constitutional answer to those who thought that selling to Thomson would lead to direct control of the paper by a man who already was one of the large press barons. That massive holding, not anything in Thomson the man, was the main reason for doubt. The consensus of thought in Printing House Square had been given two years earlier when Thomson was trying to buy the *Glasgow Herald* to add to his *Scotsman*. A leading article noted that many people in Glasgow and beyond were concerned at the prospect:

> Their concern is justified. Lord Thomson of Fleet is a man to be admired. We believe he is a beneficent force in the newspaper world. But even if he were the Archangel Gabriel, we would also believe that he has quite enough papers in the United Kingdom already.[15]

After the August lunch with Keith Hamilton's immediate urgent task was to find Thomson, then somewhere in Northern Ontario:

> It took him two days to get a message to me, and that brought me running to the nearest telephone. I learned all that had been said and unhesitatingly authorized Denis to carry on until a final financial settlement had to be decided. I was back in London by the beginning of September to arrange the concluding details.[16]

Hamilton next had a dinner with Gavin Astor, assuring him of Thomson's desire to preserve and help *The Times*. Fortified with Thomson's go-ahead signal, he had another encouraging meeting with Keith over dinner on Saturday, August 20. Haley had meanwhile returned from the south of France on Thursday, August 18, expecting to learn of progress on the Cowdray front and finding instead a memorandum from Gavin

---

15 Leading article (Haley), October 6 1964.
16 Thomson of Fleet, *Ibid*, p. 170.

Astor advocating a deal with Thomson. Pope filled Haley in with details so far as he knew them, and he learned some more from Gavin Astor at lunch that day. Astor could tell him little about any proposed financial arrangements; he chiefly emphasized that his own position on *The Times*, restricted as he was in what he could do, had become intolerable. On Sunday Haley and Pope saw Keith at his flat in London. Keith told them that he had now received the Cowdray offer; it amounted to £2,100,000 for the equity shares and £700,000 for the preference shares. Keith could not recommend Astor to accept it; he also told Haley and Pope about his further talks with Hamilton and the proposed new constitution that was designed to preserve the editorial independence of *The Times*.

On each side was a sense of both urgency and gravity. Each was anxious to conclude the deal quickly, Thomson because he knew others were in the field, Astor and Haley because they had lost far too many months already in talks with prospective partners and buyers. *The Times* had had to postpone many decisions about its development and its staffing during those months. Always hanging over it was the thought of the crippling death duties to be paid if Gavin Astor were to die while sole owner. It could not afford more delay. The sense of responsibility was no less evident. Each side, the Thomson organisation as much as *The Times*, was aware that it had entered into something far bigger than a business deal. Each knew that it was dealing with a unique national newspaper which, in spite of all its protestations to the contrary, was also a unique national institution. *The Times* was tough; it had a long, sturdy, and resilient tradition to support it; it had a heavy momentum of its own which at times made it seem stronger than the staff which served it. Yet, tough as it was, it could be damaged and it could be turned on to a wrong road. Each side had this thought very much on its mind.

On *The Times* side there was something else. By now the other negotiations had either run out of steam or were moving slowly along without conviction. An inquiry which came in January 1966 from Lord Egremont – who as John Wyndham had been an honorary political secretary to Harold Macmillan when Prime Minister – was not followed up; he had thought he might lead a consortium of buyers. The prospect opened by Thomson was regarded as very nearly the last chance. The talks would show whether or not *The Times* was to be sold on anything like satisfactory terms. On his side, too, Thomson had special reasons for seeking a deal quickly while *The Times* was willing. Success would mean that he had reached the very heights in the newspaper world.

No sooner was he back from Canada than he took control; he watched over every move, down to the smallest point. Several times the hard-headed businessman waived an obvious financial advantage. Always he said that he would not go forward with the deal unless John Astor and Haley, as well as the immediate vendor Gavin Astor, were satisfied. Always he heeded the argument that the higher interests of *The Times* had to be respected. In going forward he was fulfilling a personal ambition much more than he was securing a property which might be financially profitable one day.

After Haley's return the negotiations divided in effect into two lines. Keith chiefly carried forward the financial arrangements, very often directly with Thomson himself; Haley mainly concerned himself with the constitutional safeguards. Before becoming engrossed in this new pursuit Haley most scrupulously saw David Astor to ask him whether anything further had come from the idea of the Canadian consortium, mentioned earlier in the *Times–Observer* talks. It was evident from David Astor's reply that *The Times* could not count on help from that quarter. No less scrupulously Haley warned Astor that other offers were being made. On August 23 Haley had a long exploratory talk with Hamilton, agreeing on a joint company on the understanding that the independence of the two editors was assured. The next days brought meetings at all hours by different groups dealing with different parts of the deal. Early in September Haley asked Keith to pass on word that Thomson could not be chairman or even a member of the Board as the public would immediately assume that he was running the whole business. On September 8 Keith reported back that Thomson, after being hurt and angry at being excluded, had agreed. He recognised that it was better for *The Times* to be independent than to emerge as simply the 138th paper in his group. Several men were proposed to be chairman before there was full agreement that Haley should be the man. Even then Thomson told Keith (September 8) that Haley should have the chair for only two years. Haley stuck out for three, wishing to see the new editor's independence fully consolidated before he left, and Thomson agreed on September 16.

There was also full agreement that Denis Hamilton should be the executive head of the new company; the combined title of editor-in-chief and chief executive was proposed. Chief executive was quickly accepted. Editor-in-chief led to questioning and some counter-proposals from Haley and others. There was no disagreement on the substance of the job. It was understood that Hamilton should have ultimate responsibility for long-term planning and development, he would allocate the editorial budgets, he might make senior staff appointments. In his relations with the two editors, he would be there in the background and would, in Bagehot's words, advise, encourage, and perhaps warn them. On policy he might express his own views but it would be for them to heed the advice or not as they chose. He should be the guardian of the papers' interests, the chief link with Lord Thomson and the pursestrings. All this was understood and accepted. None the less the title seemed to suggest directive power. No one however could think of any better description equally brief, and editor-in-chief it remained.

In the meantime Thomson was conducting his own financial negotiations. He was advised among others by Gordon Brunton,[17] soon to be managing director and chief executive of the Thomson Organisation, but Thomson himself attended to everything down to the smallest point. At first it was proposed that Gavin Astor should keep the buildings at Printing House Square, estimated to be worth £4,500,000. Thomson would under that scheme have been mainly buying the title and good will of *The Times*, and would have leased the buildings and the presses from Astor. Very soon there were second thoughts. The deal was made wider and more complete. Under its financial terms, signed in October, the goodwill, copyright and business of both *The Times* and *The Sunday Times* was transferred to the new Times Newspapers Limited. The Times Publishing Company also transferred to the new company its freehold property at Printing House Square, together with all plant, equipment, and other assets that were defined in the agreement. The Thomson Organisation received 850,000 'A' shares in the new company; the Times Publishing Company received 75,000 'B' shares and 75,000 'C' shares. All shares were rated at £1. In effect the Thomson Organisation held 85 per cent of the new company's stock and the Astor Foundation held 15 per cent. In addition the Times Publishing Company – in effect Gavin Astor and his children's trust – would receive from Times Newspapers Limited (a) £1,000,000 in cash within three months of purchase, (b) £1,000,000 in the form of an unsecured note payable ten years later and bearing interest at 8½ per cent a year, and (c) another sum to be decided by a complex formula based on the notional rent on the profits of the new company as they would appear in its eighth, ninth, and tenth year of operation. The payments under (a), (b) and (c) would, it was calculated, provide for a minimum sum of £2,000,000 and a maximum of £3,300,000.

On *The Times* side there were three positive reasons for going ahead. Every assurance was given about editorial independence. The

---

17 Gordon Charles Brunton (b. 1921). President of International Thomson Organisation and chief executive of the Thomson Organisation from 1968. Director Times Newspapers, 1967.

Thomson Organisation had modern managerial and marketing expertise in abundance. And Thomson and his son Kenneth promised to put
their financial resources behind the development of *The Times*, increasing its size and broadening the range of its news and features.

The last stages of the negotiations went easily, sometimes at Hill,
Samuel and Company in the City, sometimes in Thomson's own office,
sometimes at Gavin Astor's house in Lyall Street. At one point, when
the gap had been narrowed to £50,000, Thomson offered Keith to settle
the matter by the spin of a coin. Keith agreed. Thomson spun a florin,
and lost. As Keith left Thomson said he had one favour to ask of him:
'Don't let anyone think I bought it for the money. It's for the honour
and glory.'[18] Gavin Astor approved the scheme on September 22. On
September 23–24 Haley flew to Pégomas to seek John Astor's approval;
it was freely and thankfully given. Later he went to Hove to break the
news to John Walter, then turned ninety; it meant a break between *The
Times* and the Walter family after an unbroken association of 181 years,
but the old man took the tidings stoically.

There were other, more official, calls to make. On September 26
Haley was at 10, Downing Street, having arranged some little time
before to have one of his general talks with the Prime Minister. As it
was, much of the conversation was on the proposed deal. Haley
emphasized the continued independence of both *The Times* and *The
Sunday Times*. He wished Harold Wilson to know of such assurances in
advance of any move to refer the merger to the Monopolies Commission. Wilson thought that the proposed arrangements were 'most
ingenious' and he gave his good wishes. Haley, sometimes accompanied
by Lord Sherfield,[19] also saw the *ex officio* Trustees of *The Times*,
appointed in 1924 for the single purpose of approving or disapproving
any transfer of the controlling shares of The Times Publishing Company. A strict reading of the text of the deed of 1924 suggested that the
proposed merger did not come within their terms of reference,[20] but
simple courtesy demanded that they be told; their own duties were
about to lapse with the appointment of the 'national directors' on the
new Board. Haley and Sherfield in turn saw the Lord Chief Justice; Sir
Maurice Parsons, Deputy Governor of the Bank of England (the
Governor being abroad); and the President of the Institute of Chartered
Accountants. (Professor Blackett, President of the Royal Society at the
time, had declined to serve as trustee.) Haley also drove to Oxford to

18 Verbal communication, April 7 1981.
19 Roger Mellor Makins (Lord Sherfield) (b. 1904). Ambassador in Washington,
1953–56. Director of The Times Publishing Company, 1964–67.
20 See *History of The Times*, Vol. IV. pp. 790–91.

see John Sparrow, Warden of All Souls. All the serving trustees gave their approval in principle.

The first version of the agreement, arranging for the merger and the new company but not yet bringing in the sale of Printing House Square was initialled on September 30. Gavin Astor had cheerfully entertained Lord Thomson and the other chief negotiators the night before. On October 1 *The Times* announced in agreed terms the news that henceforth it and *The Sunday Times* were to be owned and published by the new company:

> The object of the new company will be to publish *The Times* and *The Sunday Times* as independent and non-party newspapers, having regard only for the national interest. Both papers will be vigorously developed.

The Times also published a statement from Lord Thomson:

> I regard this opportunity to assist in the development of these two great newspapers as the greatest privilege of my life. National newspapers today cannot survive in isolation – they need exceptional skills and research of all kinds . . . I am a great admirer of *The Times* and its special position throughout the world will now be safeguarded for all time, as well as its commercial prosperity . . . All my life I have believed in the independence of editors and the new editor-in-chief of the company has been guaranteed absolute freedom from interference. He will direct the papers in the best interests of the country.

In a leading article on the same day, under the heading, 'A Natural Marriage', Haley went over the reasons which had made *The Times* seek a partnership: the knowledge that death duties would force a sale if Gavin Astor died with things as they were then, the rise in taxation which made it no longer possible for a rich man to support a serious paper through bad times, and the need for a broader base of finance and expertise:

> The first thing to be stressed about the announcement now made is that its sole purpose is to ensure for as far ahead as can be foreseen the independence of both papers . . . Both are old, well-established, internationally famous newspapers, respected for their standards and traditions. Whatever Britain's place in the world may be ultimately, her influence and interests can be enhanced by the strength and reputation of her journals of record and opinion. *The Times* and *The Sunday Times* should together be able to render improved services to their readers in Britain.

428

XXIII

THE NEW START

THROUGHOUT the summer the staff in Printing House Square had heard nothing but the faintest of rumours about any negotiations with anyone. They had been absorbed by the May 3 renovation in the paper itself and had been cheered by the consequent rise in circulation. *The Times*, they felt, was winning through. The greater was their shock on learning of the revolution in ownership: they had lost their easy constitutional monarchy and been thrust into the modern, competitive world under new management which promised from the start to employ every modern resource of technology, market research, and sales promotion. The official talk of a simple merger between *The Times* and *The Sunday Times* did not obscure the power and wealth of the Thomson Organisation that were clearly apparent. Obviously great changes were to come. There was some uneasiness among the staffs of both *The Times* and *The Sunday Times*. On *The Times* many dismally expected that some of the brighter and more aggressive journalists would be transferred from *The Sunday Times* to be over their heads in Printing House Square. On their side the staff on *The Sunday Times* were no better pleased with the prospect of losing some of their best men and women.

Four things helped to lessen the uneasiness in Printing House Square. First, Haley very frankly explained to all the heads of department why the change was necessary and why the Thomson deal offered by far the best hope of saving and developing *The Times*. Secondly, Denis Hamilton, going round to meet the men and women on the paper, reassured them by his quiet manner of a man absorbing his new surroundings; several times he said he had been struck by the evident excellence of the editorial staff. Thirdly, there was the thought that *The Times* had often in the past shown a gift for absorbing changes and drawing the best out of them while keeping its essential character. Fourthly, the progress of the paper since the May 3 remodelling took away any sense of defeat in the minds of most *Times* journalists; they could at least go into the new arrangements with drums beating; they had shown what they could do.

On his side Lord Thomson discovered at the very moment of his triumph that he had to pass through a searching test which at first he found bitter. The Prime Minister, acting through the Board of Trade, referred the proposed deal to the Monopolies Commission in the following terms:

Whereas the Board of Trade have this day received an application for their consent under section 8 of the Monopolies and Mergers Act 1965 to the transfer of 'The Times' and 'The Sunday Times' newspapers to a newspaper proprietor: And whereas, by virtue of section 8(1) of the said Act, the Board may not give such consent until they have received a report on the matter from the Monopolies Commission;

Now, therefore, the Board of Trade, in pursuance of section 8(3) of the said Act, hereby refer to the Monopolies Commission for investigation and report the matter of the proposed transfer of the said newspapers.

Dated 30th September 1966.[1]

The commission was required under section 8(3) of the Act to make its report within three months from the date of reference. Mr. A. W. Roskill, QC, was appointed chairman. The members under him were Lord Annan, Provost of University College, London; Mr. Brian Davidson, a director of the Bristol Aeroplane Company and a member of Gloucestershire County Council; Professor B. S. Yamey, holding the chair of economics at University College, London; Lord Francis-Williams, former editor of the *Daily Herald* and spokesman at 10, Downing Street; Mr. W. E. Jones, former president of the National Union of Mineworkers; Mr. Edgar Richards, stockbroker, and Mr. Donald Tyerman, who had recently left the editor's chair at the *Economist* and had before that been assistant editor at *The Times* itself.[2]

It was an able and well-balanced team which began work immediately after its appointment and held twenty hearings in all. From *The Times* it heard and questioned Gavin Astor, William Haley, and George Pope. From the Thomson Organisation it heard Lord Thomson himself, his son Kenneth, Denis Hamilton, James Coltart, and Gordon Brunton; it saw them first on October 27 and then questioned most of them again a month later. It also saw the controllers of the *Observer* and the

1 The Monopolies Commission, The Times Newspaper and The Sunday Times Newspaper. A report on the proposed transfer to a newspaper proprietor. Appendix 1.
2 See Chapter II.

Guardian. It received written evidence from proprietors' associations, trade unions, newspapers of different kinds, weeklies, and private individuals. Its report, signed on December 15 (with one dissenting voice from Brian Davidson) had authority from the House of Commons on December 20 to be printed and was published on December 21.

Having begun work the members of the commission decided in the best academic tradition to define what it was exactly that they were considering – namely, the nature of *The Times* itself. After hearing much conflicting evidence, varying from the myth that *The Times* was an official organ and the mouthpiece of the government to the hard-headed belief that it was a newspaper like any other, the members concluded:

> We do not accept that the role of the Times is in any way special. Its prestige and the authority with which it speaks should depend entirely on the quality of the newspaper itself. By this criterion it deserves a high reputation. Although we do not consider that the Times has any right to be accorded a special status or unique role, we recognise that it occupies a position of importance and that its loss would be a serious matter, as indeed would be the loss of any of the quality newspapers with which it competes.
>
> It is valued for two qualities. The first is the nature and range of its news reporting . . . The other quality which the Times has is freedom to express opinions on great issues of the day without regard to popularity or to political or other pressures. The Times is not unique in this, but there are few newspapers whose editors are completely free to express forthright views uncoloured by special or sectional interests. (Paragraphs 158 and 199.)

The next question to be considered – taking the questions in logical order, not necessarily in the order in which they arose during the hearings – was why *The Times* had been seeking a buyer during the past few months. The commission accepted all the arguments advanced by Gavin Astor, Haley, and Pope; the members recognized the lack of capital for development; they saw that the increase in circulation since the change of make-up in May would cause financial losses until the advertisement rates could be increased. Yet they remained puzzled. Why had the May improvements not been made months or years earlier? And what was the reason for haste in selling now? The report reflects the members' puzzlement:

> Some witnesses expressed the view that the Times Publishing Company could have avoided its present difficulties if the problem of increasing the circulation of the Time had been tackled energetically some years ago. We see no reason to disagree. Indeed, we find it

surprising that the company found it urgently necessary to look for
rescue by a change of ownership at this particular stage. On the face
of it the company's financial prospects do not appear desperate . . .
We do not regard the figures that we have been given as demonstrating that there can be no hope of restoring profitability within a period
of years; within a year or so the company should reap the benefit of
the higher circulation already achieved and it should then be better
placed to make further progress. (Paragraph 150.)

At this point the commission seemed to underestimate the need for
large sums of capital for development. It also seemed to make light of
the plain fact that Gavin Astor did not have such large sums available
and could no longer contemplate having few or no returns on the money
invested in *The Times*. Haley as chief executive knew that he could get
no money for further investment from that source. That was the
predicament. The commission came nearer to this heart of the matter,
later in the same paragraph, when it recognised the paper's urgent need
for modern management (not to be secured without a substantial outlay
in salaries) and also when it noted a lack of confidence within the higher
direction of the company. In making these points the commission
repeated its sense of surprise that forward moves were not made earlier;
by inference, when Francis Mathew was manager:

The most pressing need is probably for good management, skilled in
marketing, which could make a determined and well directed effort
to get the greatest advantage from the higher circulation which is
already being achieved and which could be raised further. But we
feel some surprise that, on the one hand, the need for more effective
marketing and the likelihood of losses for a period were not sufficiently foreseen before the recent costly effort to increase circulation was undertaken; and that, on the other hand, having undertaken this effort the company should have found it necessary to give
up the struggle so soon. Nevertheless it is plain that the company no
longer has confidence in its own ability to carry on successfully, and
this in itself makes change desirable. Furthermore the present
outlook for business is causing a reduction in newspaper advertising
which, if it continued, could seriously upset the finances of any
newspaper. (Paragraph 150.)

With these thoughts in mind the members examined all the offers which
had been made for *The Times* and came to the conclusion that the
Thomson offer not only won the round but also promised the most
advantages to the paper. They had however to satisfy themselves on two

432

matters. The first was whether Lord Thomson's offer to subsidize *The Times* either from *The Sunday Times's* profits or from his own funds raised the spectre of unfair competition, even to the extent of threatening the existence of other papers. The members speedily disposed of this argument. They recognized that using the profits from one branch of a company to support a weaker branch was common commercial practice, even in the newspaper world. Besides that, any measure at all which helped *The Times* to advance and expand was bound to increase competition with other papers.

The second matter was much more substantial and took up far more time. It was the question of Lord Thomson's character and motives, no less, and it was this which caused his initial resentment. Even nine years later, when he came to write his memoirs, he could live through his anger once again:

In many ways it was farcical to suggest that this commission would serve any useful purpose. We were the only people who could save *The Times*. Whatever Lord Astor might think about my not being on the board, and whatever device we might adopt to give the new company a respectable public image, there was no doubt the people who could save the newspaper itself were the highly skilled marketing, advertising and editorial men who belonged to the Thomson Organisation and would have the full use of the organisation's resources and services.

What *The Times* had lacked had been precisely the skills and expertise which 'only we could give to the paper':

So it was really silly that these good men of the commission should be required to spend so much time investigating us to see if we would 'do'. For this, explicitly, was their commission: they had to seek out whether the arrangements we would be making for 'their' paper would be commendable in the tradition of *The Times*, whether we had appointed or would appoint the right kind of men to run it, and whether we would guarantee it its independent voice.

It was as if, at the end of my working life, I was being put on trial by the decision of the English Establishment to see whether I and my money were worthy of their trust to the extent of being allowed to take care of their leading Establishment paper, the paper that the 'top people' read.[3]

Thomson felt the more aggrieved because he knew, as others did, that

---

3 Lord Thomson of Fleet. *op. cit.* pp. 172–73.

the Monopolies Commission was not being called on to consider a new monopoly. The figures showed that plainly enough. According to the Thomson reckonings, the International Publishing Corporation (IPC), commonly known as the Mirror Group, held 36.8 per cent of the national and provincial paper circulation, Lord Beaverbrook had 18.1 per cent, Associated Newspapers had 10.9 per cent. The Thomson Organisation, with *The Times* added, would have only 6.5 per cent. If the quality papers alone were considered, Thomson had 40 per cent of the Sunday circulation and would have, with the addition of *The Times*, only 12 per cent of the daily circulation.[4] The commission put some of the figures slightly higher, calculating that the Thomson Organisation had 44 per cent of the quality Sundays and would have 13 per cent of the national quality dailies. None the less, after considering whether the deal would mean that one man or one company would have too much influence on public opinion, the commission concluded that there were 'factors which suggest that the present proposal need not be regarded as a matter for serious concern'.

On his side Lord Thomson recovered much of his good humour as the hearings went on. He recognized that the long series of searching questions were based on something more than uneasiness or suspicion; they were a tribute to the special standing of the institution which now was to be his. The members of the commission were out to ensure, so far as any outside authority could, that the unique position of the man who edited *The Times*, free from any outside interference, should be preserved. But the hearings had also a significance extending beyond *The Times*. Every proprietor and every editor could learn much from them. The subject under discussion was the nature of a free and self-respecting press.

Certainly when Lord Thomson answered the questions he spoke his mind, simply and directly, revealing his character and his determination in a way that the commission could not mistake:

Not once but many times I told them that I was only taking on *The Times* because I reckoned its rescue and restoration to health would be a worthy object and perhaps a fitting object for a man who had made a fortune out of newspapers. I knew, I said, that I was going to lose a lot of money before *The Times* became viable again, and if it ever did become a profitable concern, it would very likely never repay the big sums, the millions, we would have to invest in it. We knew that, my son and I, yet we were prepared to devote a large amount of our private fortune to that end. There was no question

---

4 Thomson of Fleet. *Ibid*, p. 177.

about that. Kenneth was as keen as I was, now that we saw we had been given the chance to save *The Times* and to take it under the wing of our organisation . . .

The financial arrangement was that in the first place *The Times* losses would be shouldered by the *Sunday Times*. If the *Sunday Times* were to make too little profit in any one year to cover those losses, then my son and I would forgo enough of the dividends which would be due to us on our 78 per cent holding of Thomson Organisation shares. This would leave the outside shareholders of the organisation untouched. To make this a foolproof arrangement, Thomson Scottish Associates, a company which derived its income wholly from Thomson Organisation and from which my son and I got our private fortune in Britain, gave an official company guarantee to cover *The Times* losses.[5]

Later still he said that they were putting no limit to the money they were ready to put into the paper:

We could afford this one impulse of generosity, this one extravagance. The transcript says that I added, 'I would not do that ordinarily.' This was surely a choice understatement.

We expected to lose over a million in the first year, and we told the commission that we might have to provide five million before we could pull *The Times* into a position of viability.[6]

Thomson's tone hardened at one point during his second appearance. Questions about whether *The Times* would really be independent were being pressed hard; there was some talk of laying down safeguards of guarantees. In the end he gave a quiet and very firm warning, quoted in the transcript:

This is the most difficult task that we have ever accepted. It is going to be a very big job to carry it through. We cannot do it, we will never accomplish it, if there are any handicaps placed in our way. As a matter of fact, if there are, I will not even undertake it, because it would be a hopeless proposition. I hope that, in any recommendations you make, you will have that in mind.[7]

On this basic question of the continued independence of *The Times* the commission (always with the exception of the dissenting voice) soon saw

---

5 *Ibid*, pp. 173–4.
6 *Ibid*, p. 175.
7 *Ibid*, pp. 177–78.

that they could only accept the word of Lord Thomson and his son and the assurances given by Denis Hamilton. The Thomson Organisation was bound to hold the purse strings, and everyone would be aware of it. During the negotiations The Times Publishing Company, though relying mainly on Lord Thomson's own assurances, had gained extra comfort by the creation of a new company – Times Newspapers Limited – separate from the Thomson Organisation and also by the appointment of four national figures who would sit as watchdogs on the Board of directors. The members of the commission were less hopeful about the efficacy of such safeguards:

> We share the doubts expressed by most of the witnesses with whom we discussed the matter whether any reliance could be placed on such safeguards. The creation of a separate company does not alter the fact that the Times and the Sunday Times would be owned, as to 85 per cent, by The Thomson Organisation. The four national figures would be a minority of the board with no powers effective in the last resort against the representatives of The Thomson Organisation . . . At best therefore we regard the inclusion of four national figures on the board as no more than a declaration of good intent by The Thomson Organisation designed to reassure the public.

It was a severe comment, but in making it the commission used in an almost dismissive way a phrase that was the key to the whole deal. That was the declaration 'of good intent' by the Thomson Organisation. Far more than anything else it was this good intent, many times expressed, which finally carried the day before the Monopolies Commission. The members had many questions to ask about the freedom of *The Times* and *The Sunday Times* from proprietorial and commercial pressures in the future. They had as many questions to ask about the independence of the two editors in running their two papers. No steel-bound guarantees could be given by way of answer. There could only be the most solemn assurances, supported by references to Lord Thomson's oft-demonstrated practice in letting his editors get on with their jobs.

In particular the commission sought answers to three anxieties in their minds. Would *The Times* and *The Sunday Times* be required to speak with the same voice, once they were part of the same administration? Could the two editors be really independent when they were to have an editor-in-chief, Denis Hamilton, above them? Would either editor be free to criticise, if he wished, other activities of the vast Thomson Organisation in different parts of the world?

The two first questions were answered together, as the commission recorded in its report:

Mr. Hamilton assured us that the two editors would be responsible for the editorial opinions of the two newspapers, and that they would be free to put forward opposing views. He also assured us that he would make it clear to the editors on appointment that they would be expected to take full responsibility for the editorial policy of their papers; indeed he did not think that editors of suitable quality could be recruited on any other basis . . .

In his oral evidence Lord Thomson gave us his views on editorial relationships: 'Denis Hamilton and I have worked together since I appointed him editor of the Sunday Times in 1961, and we frequently talk together. I have views on various questions and I make sure he knows them, but I never see them in the paper unless he agrees with them . . . I think there must be an editor of the Times and there must be an editor of the Sunday Times and I think they both must make their own decisions, as Mr. Hamilton has said, in the final analysis. I think they need a lot of help and assistance and advice, and I think if they are the type of people that I hope they will be they will want to seek advice as Mr. Hamilton seeks it from me occasionally, but he does not observe it unless he sees fit to carry it out. I believe that he will be a tower of strength to these editors . . . They need help and he is a sort of director, editorial manager for the paper. As well, of course, he is going to be chief executive, but he is the sort of director who will lend tremendous assistance.

Sir William Haley, as chairman designate of Times Newspapers, assured us that it would be his intention that the two editors should retain their independence. He told us that he would regard the establishment of the independence of the editors as his major task during his three years as chairman.[8]

In answer to the third question – whether any criticism of the Thomson Organisation could ever appear in *The Times* and *The Sunday Times* – Lord Thomson said that each editor 'would be entirely free to express that comment, and in doing so would have the complete protection of Denis Hamilton.'[9]

When coming to the point of approval or disapproval of the deal the commission members recognised that there could be no final certainty about the future of *The Times*. They believed that if it came under the control of the Thomson Organisation commercial considerations would play a greater part than they had in the past.[10] They thought that the title

---

8 The Monopolies Commission. *op. cit.* paras 86–88.
9 Thomson of Fleet. *op. cit.* p. 177.
10 The Monopolies Commission. *op. cit.* para. 182.

of editor-in-chief was likely to be confusing to many and they regretted that it had ever been conferred, but they accepted that a change straightaway would be inadvisable. More to the point, they agreed that it was both desirable and essential that one man 'should have the executive authority to allocate resources between the two newspapers and to develop such common services as might be thought necessary'. Even more to the point, 'we are satisfied that there is reasonable assurance the editors of the Times and the Sunday Times would be given full and independent responsibility for the opinions expressed in their papers'.[11]

In their final paragraphs seven out of the eight members referred back to the apprehensions they had heard before giving their judgment:

But in the light of The Thomson Organisation's assurances about its intentions for the paper's management, as recorded in this report, we think that there is every prospect that the survival of the Times would be assured, that the public would continue to be offered a good, and in some respects an improved, newspaper, and moreover that in matters of editorial opinion there is reasonable assurance that it would continue to speak with a separate voice. It would no longer be the same voice or the same Times as in the past, and it is important that it should be recognised, both at home and abroad, that it would have no claim to any special role or status; but we do not regard that as contrary to the public interest. The combination of the Times and the Sunday Times, backed by the commercial strength of The Thomson Organisation, would present formidable competition to the other quality newspapers, some of which already face a difficult future. But we consider that neither this increase in competitive strength nor the increase in concentration of newspaper ownership which would result from the proposed transfer is, of itself, cause for concern.

Taking into account all the relevant circumstances and having regard to the need for accurate presentation of news and free expression of opinion we conclude that the proposed transfer of the Times and the Sunday Times to a newspaper proprietor may be expected not to operate against the public interest.[12]

In his note of dissent Brian Davidson considered that the step in the direction of monopoly control of the quality nationals was more significant than his colleagues thought. If the *Financial Times* was excluded

---

11 The Monopolies Commission. *op. cit.* para. 181.
12 *Ibid*, paras. 182–83.

because of its specialist character there were only six quality nationals, that is, week-days and Sundays. After the transfer the Thomson Organisation would control one in three as against the one in six which it had so far. Furthermore, while he fully accepted the assurances given by Lord Thomson and Denis Hamilton, neither of the two men could bind a body corporate 'whose future views and policies may well differ from those of its present directors'. So, while the proposed transfer had much to commend it immediately, he could not avoid the conclusion that it might operate against the public interest.

Davidson therefore suggested that both the Thomson Organisation and Times Newspapers Limited, when incorporated, should give formal undertakings that they accepted as binding the assurances already given about preserving the separate identities of the two papers and the independence of their editors.[13]

This suggestion from the dissenting member had an immediate and positive result. On December 16 – the day after the majority report and the dissenting note were signed – Denis Hamilton and James Coltart were called urgently to the Board of Trade. There they were asked to give, on behalf of the Thomson Organisation, written assurances such as Davidson had proposed. The request might seem unnecessary as Lord Thomson and others had already given the assurances when appearing before the commission. But Douglas Jay, as President of the Board of Trade, wished to strengthen himself when facing a House of Commons which he suspected would be uneasy at the deal; he wished to produce hard evidence that the assurances came not only from the Thomson family but from the Thomson Organisation as a whole. For their part Hamilton and Coltart willingly repeated, in writing, the Thomson Organisation's assurances on editorial independence for *The Times* and *The Sunday Times*.[14]

On December 21 Douglas Jay reported to the Commons the Monopolies Commission's main conclusion, as he put it, 'that the proposed transfer may not be expected to operate against the public interest'. 'I accept their conclusion, and have accordingly given my consent to the proposed transfer.'

---

13 *Ibid*, paras. 186–89.
14 The actual text of the letter was: 'During the enquiries by the Monopolies Commission into the proposed Transfer of The Times newspaper, Lord Thomson gave certain assurances to the Commission about the preservation of the separate identities of The Times and The Sunday Times, and about the maintenance of the independence of their editors.

'I am now writing to affirm, on behalf of The Thomson Organisation Limited, the assurances given by Lord Thomson personally to the Commission.'

Members had many questions to ask. All agreed that the dangers which faced *The Times* faced other newspapers too. Conservatives blamed restrictive practices within the printing unions, Labour members blamed monopolistic tendencies. One or two of the socialists proposed that *The Times* and perhaps other papers should be brought under public control or be run by the BBC. Douglas Jay had to answer many inquiries about the nature of the written assurances which, very early on in his statement, he had announced. His most specific reply was to Sir Derek Walker-Smith (Conservative):

The original assurances were given personally by Lord Thomson to the commission. Renewed and stronger assurances were given by the Thomson Organisation to myself, and they are clearly morally binding on that organisation. What I said was that I would do all in my power to see that they are carried out, and I have no reason to believe that they will not be carried out.

After further exchanges John Mendelson (Labour) tried to move the adjournment of the House to discuss 'a matter of definite, urgent public importance' but the Speaker ruled against him. This left Douglas Jay with the most telling word on the Thomson plan 'to ensure that *The Times* can carry on'. 'The commission had three months to consider this,' he said, 'and no other practical way was in sight.'

While counting nothing as certain until it happened, the main principals in the deal – Lord Thomson himself and Denis Hamilton, Gavin Astor and William Haley, with their advisers – were ready to get their plans moving as soon as the commission gave its favourable report. On December 22 *The Times* carried, with the news from the commission, a joint statement from the two sides to the deal. It announced that *The Times* and *The Sunday Times* would be transferred to their new company, Times Newspapers Limited, at the turn of the year. It confirmed that Gavin Astor would be president for life of the new company and it made known the membership of the new Board of directors, twelve in number:

Sir William Haley, chairman, representing Mr. Gavin Astor.

Mr. Kenneth Thomson, deputy chairman, representing the Thomson Organisation.

Lord Shawcross, the lawyer, banker, and chairman of the royal commission on the press (1961–62); and Sir Donald Anderson, chairman of P & O: both of them national directors appointed by Mr. Gavin Astor.

Lord Robens, chairman of the National Coal Board, and Sir Eric

Roll, UK delegate in many high-powered international financial and economic negotiations: both national directors appointed by the Thomson Organisation.

Mr. James Coltart and Mr. Gordon Brunton, managing director of the Thomson Organisation, both representing the Thomson Organisation.

Mr. Kenneth Keith, representing Mr. Gavin Astor.

Mr. Denis Hamilton, editor-in-chief and chief executive.

Mr. Geoffrey Rowett, general manager, having been managing director of *The Sunday Times*.

Mr. George Pope, deputy general manager while remaining general manager of *The Times*.

The joint statement continued:

Sir William Haley is relinquishing the editorship of *The Times* from January 1 1967 on appointment as chairman of the new company.

Mr. Denis Hamilton is relinquishing the editorship of *The Sunday Times* on appointment as editor-in-chief and chief executive of Times Newspapers Ltd.

The names of the new editors of the two papers will be announced in due course after the board of directors have appointed them. In the meantime Mr. Iverach McDonald (at present managing editor) will be in charge of *The Times*, and Mr. William Rees-Mogg (at present deputy editor) will be in charge of *The Sunday Times*.

The composition of the Board of directors, fitting in both old and new, seemed as complex as a jigsaw. In fact, as was soon to be proved, the key appointment was that of Denis Hamilton; he was the guiding force of the new organization.

In their report the members of the Monopolies Commission confessed themselves baffled, as was mentioned earlier in this chapter, by two matters that lay at the very heart of *The Times's* predicament. 'We see no reason to disagree,' they wrote, with those witnesses who believed 'that the Times Publishing Company could have avoided its present difficulties if the problem of increasing the circulation had been tackled energetically some years ago'. Why in fact did the MDE effort – the drive for modernization, development, and expansion – begin so late after the danger lights had begun to flash? Secondly, 'we find it surprising that the company found it urgently necessary to look for rescue at this particular stage' just after the promising launch of the expansion programme. What precipitated the sale precisely at that time?

The delay in beginning the drive for modernization is indeed hard to defend when the repeated warnings about the company's financial vulnerability are recalled. Gavin and Hugh Astor had found their long-felt anxieties confirmed by their own financial advisers well before Cooper Brothers expressed their opinion early in 1958 that without radical improvement 'the future of "The Times" is now in jeopardy'. February 1963 brought the grave assessment from Godfrey Phillips, showing himself again to be one of the ablest of the directors. Yet it was not until September 24 1964, more than six years after the Cooper report, that Haley as editor wrote to Mathew as manager proposing that they set up the MDE committee as an urgent matter.

Much had of course been done in between times. Earlier chapters of this volume have told of the strengthening of the management team and Haley's broadening of the usefulness and appeal of the paper itself. Yet the real advance was put off. Most of the reasons for the delay are to be found in the long-unchanged structure of the company and in the personalities at the top. John Astor saw himself as the trustee of a public institution far more than as co-chief proprietor of a company competing with other companies; he was the confidant of the editor and the manager, and remained so even after he ceased to be chairman and after he left Britain in October 1962 to live in the south of France; the fact that in making his painful move he was thinking of deflecting death duties from *The Times* as well as from the family fortunes created another bond between him and those who were conducting the company in London. Gavin and Hugh Astor, however, were left feeling that they had neither the power nor the influence which they wished to have as chairman and vice-chairman of the company. Like them, the other directors were also non-executive, some of them being little more than occasional observers of the company's affairs. The result was that much authority was effectively exercised by the editor and the manager. This remained true even though Gavin Astor held informal working lunch and dinner parties for directors, editor, and general manager, and set up a chairman's committee which met weekly to keep him informed of progress on all fronts.

The pattern of authority seemed straightforward and entirely right on the editorial side. The whole strength and influence of *The Times* have rested on the independence of its editor, free from interference by either the proprietor or the manager. This condition of service, formally written down in 1922, has often been quoted. Haley further ensured such independence by the force of his character and also by taking such precautions as always keeping within his editorial budget each year.

Such a precaution removed any excuse for questions in his field by the management. The corollary was that he did not seek to interfere with the management. Almost the only exception came in 1957 when he urged Mathew three times to drop the Top People advertising campaign, and he intervened then only because the whole campaign presented an image of the paper from which Haley was trying to escape. Generally the two men were on remarkably good personal terms, respecting each other's sphere. But nothing to do with *The Times* was ever simple.

If the division of labour had been less strict they would have had more opportunity to discuss within the office the all-round development of the paper and see where they differed as they looked ahead. Some differences there were. Haley sought to broaden the interests of the paper and expand its circulation by improving the quality of the product. He was sure that excellence would be the best selling asset.[15] Mathew, to judge by his talk in the office, imagined a *Times* that would appeal chiefly to the City, Westminster, and a small directive elite; it would necessarily have a small circulation.[16] Mathew's picture of such a *Times* (it cannot be dismissed lightly) explains in part why he was slow to fall in with the idea of putting news on the front page. Such differences of view were not brought into the foreground; but – though no firm evidence can be adduced – they were almost certainly among the reasons for the delay in launching the combined editorial–managerial exercise in modernization and expansion. With rather more certainty it can be said that planning and carrying out the re-building of Printing House Square in the late fifties and early sixties took up time, money, and mental energy which could, part of it at least, have gone into planning and providing for future development. A small concern such as *The Times* then was, no matter how hard-working and devoted, has not many extra man-hours to spare. As it was, Haley and the other reformers had to undertake an intense exercise in persuasion before they could hope to have big changes accepted. John Astor and John Walter were as always courteous but for a long time reluctant to have the changes. Some among the senior staffs had to be moved from anxiety to enthusiasm. It was a process that took too long.

On the second question – why sell at that particular time? – Gavin Astor gave many of the answers in his remarkably frank personal message to the staff soon after the sale. He wrote both of the financial straits of the company and of his own frustrations, shared very largely by

---

15 See Chapter X.
16 See Chapter XVI.

his brother Hugh. He looked back on the recent history of the paper, including the years in the early 1960s when *The Times* was standing still while other quality papers advanced, and the last big effort at modernization and progress in the spring of 1966. The effort, successful so far as it went, revealed both what could be done to develop the paper in the future and how much investment would be needed to do it. Astor had thought, when buying the Walter shares in 1962, to add to his own preponderant holdings and give him one hundred per cent ownership, that he could serve as a bridge until such time as the paper made profits:

> But this bridging operation was costing me a lot of money which I was only able to provide by heavy borrowing. This in itself was an expensive operation and was rapidly eroding my liquid capital.
>
> How much longer was the 'bridge' going to be? There was no sign of the end of it: and I could not wait much longer . . .
>
> It was becoming more and more urgent for *The Times* and for my family to extricate themselves from the increasingly vulnerable financial entanglement in which they both found themselves.

Astor touched on the sense of frustration which he came to feel as a sole owner who had little effective voice in the running of the concern although he had often argued that the company's activities should be spread out along money-making lines. He was indeed 'intensely proud' of his inheritance:

> But to be private owner of a 'National Institution', whose Editor is answerable only to non-executive Proprietors and whose General Manager is answerable to a non-executive Chairman and Board, and which is inhibited in its commercial enterprise by voluntary and statutory restrictions, is an anachronism today. The new scheme recognises that the age when proprietors could successfully run their newspapers as a sideline is fading into an age where the survival and prosperity of newspapers depend upon brilliant commercial and professional management.

He referred back to his own happy relations with the editor and the general manager:

> Yet I have come to realise that to carry the entire financial risk as Proprietor no less than the full legal responsibility as Chairman for the success or failure of the Company, without also carrying executive power, is not a satisfactory situation.

Astor ended with a declaration of full confidence in the new regime for *The Times* and *The Sunday Times*.[17]

His frustration built up as he saw himself in a world where money had to bring in good returns while he lacked the authority, so long as his father was alive, to put into practice the plans – such as diversifying the activities of the company – which he and his brother saw as means of bringing in such returns. His father, Haley and Mathew considered several of these plans to be against the best interests and traditions of *The Times*. Partly the differences arose from the differences in age. So long as John Astor lived, and kept his position as co-chief proprietor, it was natural that he should continue the old familiar habit of confidential talks with Haley, Mathew, and one or two of the directors. It was no less natural for his sons to feel that these older men were more in tune with each other's own ideas than with the plans and hopes put forward by the sons themselves. The 'lack of confidence' which the Monopolies Commission noted could in part be applied at times to relations at the top. Gavin Astor felt it all especially keenly: the lack of influence, as he saw it, no less than the financial drag upon him. So he resolved to lighten his burden, provided that a fair deal could be arranged for *The Times*. He thought, as Haley thought, that such a deal could be worked out with Lord Cowdray and the *Financial Times*, but then with very little warning came one of his worst moments when Cowdray made his 'derisory' offer. The bad moment was also a decisive one for Astor. He was ready, as never before, to listen to the Thomson offer.

Thomson could afford to offer, with many self-denying safeguards, an independent regime for *The Times* because he could draw on the income and huge profits from the many highly diversified concerns which he had built up. Gavin Astor was painfully aware of the contrast between the positions of the two men, Thomson and himself. 'Thomson', he recalled later, 'was not hampered by the peculiar inhibitions which had grown into traditions of Printing House Square and which my father [John Astor] wished to see preserved at all costs and against the more contemporary inclinations of Hugh and myself. But what was even more important, Thomson had the capital and the cash flow necessary to implement and support these changes.'[18] He would remember in particular how Thomson secured the licence for Scottish Television in the period when The Times Publishing Company rejected the two brothers' wish for it to enter the television field.

Other journals and periodicals were quick to give their opinions about the sale. The self-denying, self-effacing role that was expected of an

---

17 The text of the personal message is given in Appendix G.
18 Personal communication, October 3 1983.

owner of *The Times* was examined by the *Economist* on October 8 1966. Neatly paraphrasing Lord Thomson's well known quip it headed its long leading article 'A Licence to Lose Money?' and it went on to give the most perceptive of all the journalistic comment on *Times* affairs during that autumn. Against all conventional wisdom it thought that *The Times* might have fared better on the management side if John Astor, proprietor for so long, had interfered and prodded more than he did:

> The Astors have behaved more like trustees than active owners, and the result has been some lack of dynamising force on the marketing and other business sides of the paper. There are some tough eggs in Fleet Street who take this merger as a recognition that family non-management (for however good a reason) can in some sense be as much a mistake as the most meddling kind of family management.

The *Economist* had little doubt that Thomson would sink a great deal of money into *The Times* in the hope of eventual profitability, but it asked whether *The Times* would be as ready in the future as in the past to take an unfashionable or awkward line in policy. (The *Economist's* fears there were not borne out.) Its most encouraging passage came where it wrote that *The Times*, and indeed quality newspapers as a whole, had much less influence than previously on politics, but they 'can have a wider influence than ever on actual policies'. If that seemed paradoxical, the explanation was that such papers can provide, and should provide, a serious and continuous intellectual argument over all the issues of the day. How they did this differed from practice in the past. They did it as much through the special articles by their experts as through their leader columns, and these special articles themselves were often the result of long office discussions in which ideas were thoroughly discussed. The individual political whims of proprietors or editors counted for less. With a remarkably accurate analysis of how *The Times* would develop the *Economist* wrote:

> What a quality newspaper does now include is a staff of thirty or forty people, most of them with first or top second class university degrees, whose job is to throw out ideas; and it is by now a common experience of those who have worked on them that many ideas, which go down well when first mooted at an editorial conference of such a newspaper, tend to go down equally well when they are thrown in the newspaper's published columns before – for example – the civil service, which also consists of a very similar group of people mostly with first and top second class university degrees. It is these offerings and arguments which are apt to pass, surprisingly often, into the eventual law or policy of England.

So the prime objective of the new editor of *The Times*, said the *Economist*, must be to show that the paper could exercise a full flexibility of intellectual freedom, a willingness to explore all ideas on their merits:

> Otherwise, although a newspaper called *The Times* may have been saved, something of value to the country may still have been lost.

Of other weeklies and journals the *Glasgow Herald* came out most strongly against the merger. Remembering how it had itself fought off a Thomson bid only two years earlier, it wrote, 'Dismay and disquiet will greet the announcement'. In the *Sunday Telegraph* of October 2 Peregrine Worsthorne described the news as 'another rather sad sign of the times' and asked whether the paper would, under new ownership, keep its cutting edge, its definable character, and its respect for more than passing cultural and intellectual fashions. But in the main the news was accepted as inevitable and even hopeful, both for the simple reason that Printing House Square needed money and commercial expertise. In the *New Statesman* of October 7 Tom Baistow wrote that the decline of *The Times* was due not to editorial defects but to commercial and managerial weakness. Most commentators expected that the *Guardian* would be the first paper to feel the impact of competition from a more aggressive *Times*, yet the *Guardian* itself was generous in its welcome for the Monopolies Commission's approval of the deal: 'So Lord Thomson is free to go ahead. Good luck to him.' On the very subject of competition the *Guardian* quoted the commission's view that the consequences of the transfer would not of themselves kill any newspaper that would otherwise survive:

> This is a fair statement. We accept it and agree with it . . . We are endeavouring to resolve our difficulties on our own. We believe that, given union cooperation, we shall succeed. As we said three months ago, we hope long to continue in friendly rivalry with *The Times*.

The Times gave its own view on December 22 in a leader by Haley. Characteristically he placed the paper's problems in the national setting without any special pleading for the paper itself. The commission's insistence that *The Times* could claim no special status, but must stand or fall on its merits as a newspaper, was very much to his liking. He went on to knock down any idea that the government or any public corporation like the BBC could help *The Times* or any other serious journal. His argument at this point was to gain extra force in later years when the proposals were revived:

> The economics of newspaper publishing in Britain do cause concern

at present. The only way the Government can help is by getting the country healthily prosperous and on an even keel, and by restraining the morbid phobia some of its followers have against advertising. For the rest, the press's salvation must depend on the newspapers themselves. The status of journalists is not as high as it ought to be. They must serve the community more responsibly. The industry is not an efficient one. It must make itself efficient. The unions are among the least enlightened. Somehow or other, however painful the process, they must be brought to see the light. Methods of production all along the line are all too often antiquated and absurdly expensive. They must be revolutionized and cheapened. There is a need for new men, new materials, and new methods.

We hope that *The Times* and *The Sunday Times* under their new ownership will play their part in this process.

Within Printing House Square itself, once the initial shock was over, the staff as a whole felt more hope than despondency as they looked ahead. After feeling the sense of loneliness that surrounds people caught up in a crisis they were reassured by the evidence that the future of *The Times* was a matter of broad national concern. At the very time of radical change they were themselves more than usually aware of the strength of unbroken custom within Printing House Square. Without talking about it much, or only in matter-of-fact terms, they came back to the thought that their daily working practice could not be built up or shattered overnight; it was something compact and tenacious that had absorbed and profited by many changes in the past. It had kept the essential character of the paper among all the developments of style and format and the broadening range of features each day. The leading articles, the letters to the editor, the special despatches from home and abroad, the harmless necessary quota of official and social news, the striving to write exactly what was happening and to present it without exaggeration, the expression of opinion without party or other influence: these were among the contributions which the old team could bring with them into the new regime.

EPILOGUE

THE end of the Astor era and the beginning of the Thomson era mark the chosen and appropriate point at which this volume of the history was to end. To try to continue the narrative into more recent years would have been a mistake. Such an attempt was made in Volume IV, but with so many actors still alive, and so many of their actions still a matter of controversy, it was bound to be inadequate. Only a part of the story could be told, and it has therefore been necessary to go over the ground again in greater detail and with greater candour in the early chapters of this volume.

However, so much was to happen to *The Times* in the two decades between Lord Thomson's purchase of the paper and the bicentenary of its foundation that there would seem to be room for a brief interim report to round off the story. It must be emphasized that the following pages do not, like the previous chapters, make use of archive material, and are in no way intended to pre-empt the work or direct the judgment of whoever may eventually be entrusted with writing Volume VI of the *History of The Times*. They are a quick sketch, not a full-length portrait. A detailed chronology of events between 1966 and 1984 may be found at the end of this chapter.

The years since 1966 have been difficult and stormy ones for newspapers in Britain. In addition to the familiar struggle for circulation and profits they faced in this period an increasing battle on two fronts – with other methods of communication, particularly television, and with the print unions.

It has been explained earlier[1] how newspapers, particularly 'quality' newspapers, could in 1945 look at their post-war position with a good deal of confidence. Certainly the war had greatly encouraged the habit of listening to radio broadcasts, but this complemented rather than conflicted with the habit of reading newspapers. Even the expansion of

---

1 See Chapter VII.

television in the fifties and early sixties did not at first give serious cause for alarm. But in 1967 came the introduction of colour television, and by the spring of 1974 the BBC estimated that nearly three-fifths of the population (33 million) listened to or watched at least one full news bulletin a day, while ITN's 'News at Ten' was daily commanding an audience calculated to number between 12 and 15 million. How could morning newspapers hope to find something fresh to say about stories which had already been so graphically explained to everybody the previous evening? What attraction superior to time on independent television could they offer to advertisers?

To a certain extent television and newspapers could complement each other, just as radio and newspapers had done earlier. Even though both BBC and ITV greatly increased the time devoted to news bulletins and current affairs programmes they still could not provide the detailed analysis and the considered comment which a newspaper like *The Times* could supply. As regards advertising, newspapers on the whole stood up better than had been expected to the challenge, classified advertisements in fact rising over the period, though display advertising showed some decline.

Television, however, was by no means the only form of new competition that newspapers had to face. Commercial radio began in 1973, providing another competitor for advertisers' budgets, as well as yet more news bulletins tailored to local audiences. Transistor and car radios proliferated, making it possible for anyone who wanted to get news anywhere at any time. A new development in communications, and in appearance at least a more direct rival to the national and provincial press, was the free sheets, financed entirely by advertising and distributed through the post or at supermarkets. True, their news content was not comparable to that of the established press, but their rate of growth (up 25 per cent in 1981 and 31 per cent in 1982) deserved the adjective 'revolutionary'. And rising rapidly on the horizon were new viewing techniques like Ceefax and Oracle.

To begin with, however, these new developments seemed to pose no real threat to the emerging Thomson *Times*. On January 12 1967 William Rees-Mogg[2] was appointed the paper's new editor, and he quickly showed that he was in command of the ideas, as well as of the funds, necessary for setting *The Times* off on its fresh course.

Rees-Mogg's background was not unlike Geoffrey Dawson's,

2 William Rees-Mogg (b. 1928). Charterhouse; Balliol College, Oxford. *Financial Times* 1952–60. Political and economic editor *The Sunday Times*, 1961–63; deputy editor, 1964–66; editor *The Times*, 1967–81.

Somerset rather than Yorkshire but with similar wealth and landed interest behind him. Rees-Mogg fitted in with *The Times* tradition by being not simply a man of outstanding ability but also one in startling contrast to his immediate predecessor. Barrington-Ward was the opposite of Dawson, Haley of Casey. Rees-Mogg differed in almost every way from Haley. A disparity in age was naturally to be expected; Rees-Mogg was thirty-eight when he took over from the sixty-five year old Haley. But age was the least of the differences. In methods of work Haley was the centraliser, Rees-Mogg the devolutionist. Haley looked after every detail so far as was humanly possible, Rees-Mogg left much on trust to his lieutenants. Haley worked all hours, making a point of seeing the first edition away and then going through the newly printed paper at night in the office; Rees-Mogg believed that he served the paper better by an evening's discussion or reading at home. Haley wished each *Times* to be in his own image or at any rate to bear his stamp; only a specially compelling reason would have persuaded him to publish an article by a staff man contradicting a leading article. Rees-Mogg believed as a matter of principle in letting his gifted men express their personalities and views with a minimum of interference, even though he might not always agree with a particular piece.

Rees-Mogg valued good talk and instituted regular weekly meetings in his room, with a wider attendance than the daily leader conference, over which he presided in a symbolically at ease rocking-chair. There was one meeting for *The Times* special writers and another for the staff of Business News, at which topics of the day were discussed and often – though this was not their sole purpose – some sort of editorial consensus achieved. His staff quickly came to appreciate that the new editor could express himself in print with beautiful fluency, for whereas Haley had waited seven months after becoming editor before writing his first leader Rees-Mogg had written a long leader within hours of occupying the editorial chair. The same unmistakably clear and unponderous style was for the next fourteen years to illumine a wide variety of topics in signed articles as well as in the anonymity of leading articles.

The new editor introduced himself to *Times* readers on the front page of the issue of January 13. 'I believe', he was quoted as saying, 'that *The Times* ought to be the natural main newspaper of what I call all the seriously occupied people of the country – business people, those in the universities, doctors, politicians, civil servants – and a much wider band of people than that as well . . . We certainly want it to be a newspaper with a broader area of circulation.' He elaborated his views a few days later in a leader called 'The Ideas of *The Times*'. 'Certainly,' he wrote, 'nobody can understand *The Times* who does not understand that it is an institution.' But, he went on, there had been, as he saw it, four periods of 'institutional change and development' in the history of the paper, of which the challenge faced by the present transfer of ownership was the fourth. Two principles must guide the paper he was to edit: 'The first principle was, is, and will be that of independence of judgment . . . Other papers have a duty of independence. *The Times* has a vocation to it.' The second principle was 'that of coverage . . . It is our present task to strengthen, continuously and in every possible way, the thoroughness, fairness, lucidity and comprehensiveness of our coverage.'

The new editor's position was greatly strengthened by the promise of a large injection of funds into the editorial budget. For the past few years Haley had, on his own admission, been obliged to count candle-ends. Now the Thomson purse was to be opened to ensure that *The Times's* coverage of news should in fact become 'thorough and comprehensive'. This was a prospect which, judging by the number of applications for jobs which flowed into Printing House Square, excited not just the staff there but the whole of Fleet Street.

The effects of this new transfusion of cash were quickly felt. The number of home news reporters was increased by more than a third. A 'news team' was set up, capable of providing massive and instantaneous coverage of any major event at home or abroad (though unfortunately suitable occasions for the team's deployment were slow to materialise, the wreck of the tanker Torrey Canyon off the Scillies and the civil war in Angola being rare examples of its working as it should). The foreign department was rewarded with three new staff appointments, in South America, Japan and South Africa, as well as by subscription to Agence France Presse, which at that time meant that *The Times* had access to virtually the only western staff correspondent in Peking.[3]

The objective of the Business News, in a significantly larger space than the former City columns, was to present economic and industrial news in addition to financial and stock market coverage. As well as Anthony Vice[4] as editor, Derek Harris was brought from *The Sunday Times* to be responsible for production; George Pulay,[5] a *Times* man,

---

3 Five years later, in October 1972, following Lord Thomson's visit to China, *The Times* was for the first time since 1936 to have its own resident staff man in Peking in the person of David Bonavia, a Chinese scholar as well as an experienced newspaper man who had earlier that year been thrown out of Moscow where his contacts with dissident elements had given offense to the authorities.

4 Anthony Vice (b. 1930). Hymers College, Hull; Queen's College, Oxford. Joined *The Sunday Times*, 1964; editor *The Times Business News*, 1967–71.

5 George Pulay (1923–1981). Joined *The Times* as assistant City editor, 1962; City editor 1966; resigned, 1968.

remained as City editor. A number of journalists were recruited from the daily and weekly press, and two from Whitehall: Peter Jay[6] came from the Treasury as economics editor and Hugh Stephenson[7] from the Foreign Service. Stephenson became editor when Vice left in 1970 to join Rothschilds, the bankers, Peter Jay going to an even more illustrious billet in Washington.

An early date, April 1967, was set for the launch of Business News, and good progress was made, with *The Times* pioneering in Fleet Street the computer-based production of share prices. But production problems, particularly getting into the first edition a great deal of late material, much of it in figure form, proved difficult to overcome, and it soon became uneconomic to continue the publication of a separate pull-out section – the theory behind this having been that the husband would take that section to his office, leaving the main paper for his wife to read during the day.

Rees-Mogg had for long been a convinced 'European' and was determined that *The Times* should be a thoroughly European newspaper. European news was grouped together on a separate page which led the rest of the foreign news. Debates in the European parliament and cases in the European court were reported in the same way as proceedings in Westminster and the Law Courts in the Strand. In October 1973 an existing cooperation with three other leading European newspapers, *Le Monde*, *Die Welt* and *La Stampa*, blossommed into a joint monthly publication, *Europa*, with identical editorial matter and advertisements and published simultaneously in four languages.

Another step taken by the new regime, almost as revolutionary in its way as news on the front page, was the abolition of anonymity. Within a week or two Kyril Tidmarsh and Richard Harris had thrown off their *noms de plume* ('Monitor', 'Student of Asia') as had 'Our Racing Correspondent' (Michael Phillips) and 'Our Rugby Correspondent' (U. A. Titley), and many others. At first the idea was that home and foreign correspondents should only be given their by-line for pieces of exceptional importance, or when they were away from their base, or when for some other reason personal identification seemed desirable.

---

6 Peter Jay (b. 1937). Winchester; Christ Church, Oxford. Joined *The Times Business News* as economic correspondent, 1967; joint deputy editor *Business News* and economic editor *The Times*, 1968; resigned, 1977. Ambassador to the United States, 1977–79.
7 Hugh Arthur Stephenson (b. 1938). Winchester; New College, Oxford. Joined *The Times Business News* as economic writer, 1968; foreign editor, 1969; editor, 1972; resigned, 1981.

But very soon, and probably inevitably, the unsigned contribution became the exception. There can be no doubt that the change was warmly welcomed by many of those it affected.

A month or so later a series of regular columns was instituted on the left-hand centre page, facing the leader page. Louis Heren from Washington and Kyril Tidmarsh from Moscow reported each week on some aspect of life in the two super-powers; other foreign correspondents took it in turns on another day; David Wood continued to write each week on politics,[8] and on Saturday there was a column by one of the sporting staff. Each columnist had his copy adorned by his photograph, on the American model. It was a far cry from the day when members of *The Times* staff used to cut each other in the street lest they betray to the outside world their connexion with the Thunderer.

In addition Rees-Mogg recruited a number of distinguished outside contributors. Ian Trethowan and Auberon Waugh became writers of regular weekly columns, and after June 1971 Bernard Levin, who had made a brilliant reputation on the *Spectator*, the *Daily Mail* and television, produced three columns a week. Impressed by his reporting in the *Evening News* of the 1968 Democratic convention in Chicago Rees-Mogg invited Winston Churchill, grandson of the great statesman, to undertake special assignments for the paper.[9] Roger Berthoud, who had made a name for himself as editor of the *Evening Standard's* Diary, was brought in to revitalise *The Times* Diary, and Mark Boxer to provide a pocket cartoon to go with it. No part of the paper remained unaffected by the winds of Thomson change.

Some readers, it is true, felt that in its eagerness to prove that it was not fuddy-duddy and appeal to the young the new *Times* sometimes strayed into unsuitable paths. There was, for example, the occasion towards the end of 1969 when it was revealed that two *Times* reporters had for a month photographed meetings and monitored conversations between a petty criminal and three police officers who were blackmailing him. It was certainly a coup for *The Times*, but many of the popular papers felt *The Times* had no business poaching on their territories.

Judged in terms of circulation the new editorial policies were an undoubted success. When Thomson took over the daily circulation of *The Times* had been a little over 300,000; by the end of 1968 it was well

---

8 See Chapter XI.

9 During the summer of 1968, after the Russians had invaded Czechoslovakia, Winston Churchill was one of those reporting to *The Times* from inside the country. Another was Charles Douglas-Home, then defence correspondent. It is hardly surprising that the Russians, when they reflected on these two names, felt that *The Times* must after all have very close connexions with the British Establishment.

over 400,000, and a year later over 450,000. The target of half a million, which had long been talked of and dreamed about, seemed well within reach. But such rapid growth brought complications. The printing and production sides were stretched up to and beyond capacity. What struck readers most was the growing number of mistakes in a paper which had for so long made almost a fetish of accuracy. With the great volume of copy to be dealt with there was not enough time for adequate subediting, and a lot of material went into the paper without being 'read' at all. (Newspaper 'readers' checked proofs against the written copy.)

That was a change for the worse. A change for the better came with the redesigning of the paper in September 1970 'in a tighter and more classical style'. The ample lower case headlines were closed up; more space was allowed for home and foreign news, for a woman's page and for the arts. Most noticeable was a new look on the leader page. The turnover article (which had long ceased to turn over) was dropped, thus allowing three columns instead of two for leaders and four instead of three for letters to the editor.

Two years later came another change. Times New Roman, the type sponsored by Stanley Morison and in use since October 1932, was abandoned in favour of Times Europa. The reason for this was that Times New Roman did not stand up well in a newspaper now being printed at higher speeds and on inferior paper. It was adequate for the larger type (9-point), but there was 'a sharp fall in comprehensiveness and convenience' in the smaller type (8-point) in which most of the paper was printed.

But all these achievements took place against a rumbling background of industrial trouble.

One debilitating legacy to national newspapers from the post-war days of easy profits and weak management has been the exceptionally high earnings of print workers and a disposition among publishers to yield easily to threats of unofficial action. Industrial relations in Fleet Street have been notoriously bad for a generation and their improvement has been the regularly falsified hope of everyone who has attempted to set the industry on the path of modernisation.

Thus spake the Royal Commission on the Press[10] which reported in July 1977. It was not an overstatement. Seven years later industrial relations in Fleet Street have shown little or no improvement and fresh hopes for modernisation have been, in the main, just as regularly falsified.

---

10 Cmd. 6810.

The Times was to suffer from industrial disruption as much as any newspaper. In retrospect its troubles may be attributed, in part at least, to the decision to move the paper from its original site in Blackfriars to Grays Inn Road. This move, completed in July 1974, seemed a logical step since *The Times* and *The Sunday Times*, long housed in Grays Inn Road, were now sister papers, both owned by Lord Thomson. But sharing a site failed to produce any significant savings in editorial costs, while the effect on the printing and production staffs of *The Times*, where labour relations had on the whole been outstandingly good, of close contact with the staffs of *The Sunday Times*, where labour relations had on the whole been outstandingly bad, was little short of disastrous.

The first occasion since 1785 when *The Times* failed to appear in any form was in the month-long stoppage at the beginning of 1955 called by maintenance engineers and electricians which brought all national newspapers to a halt. Every year between 1968 and 1974 saw protest strikes of one sort or another affecting all nationals, but the first occasion when *The Times* was stopped because of an internal dispute was July 28 1971. More interruptions followed, with an ominous new twist on January 13 1977 when machine minders objected to four lines in a report in *The Times* of a magazine article on Fleet Street by David Astor, editor of the *Observer*, printing of the paper being consequently interrupted for three nights. Throughout 1977 and 1978 there was hardly a day without some production difficulties.

This is not the place to describe the protracted negotiations throughout the summer and autumn of 1978 which ended in the shutting down of *The Times* and *The Sunday Times* at the beginning of December. Staff and readers of *The Times* watched the date fixed for the shut-down, if there was no last-minute agreement, with a mixture of incredulity, sorrow and frustration. The last issue to appear, that of November 30 1978, contained a leading article by the editor called 'There will be an Interval'. 'It is quite certain', the leader said, 'that *The Times* will return. Indeed, there would have been much more reason to fear that *The Times* would come to an end if we had not been prepared to go through this crisis.' What made the dispute particularly galling for *The Times* was that in its origins it much more concerned *The Sunday Times*, though now, from an industrial point of view, the two papers were obliged to stand or fall together. Moreover, it came at a time when, thanks to increased sales and working economies, *The Times* was at last in a position where profitability was in sight.

Nobody really expected the stoppage to be a long one, though considerately the solution of that day's crossword was printed on another page of the paper. One letter in a column adjacent to the editor's leader was from a correspondent who wrote: 'I shall be wearing a rose in my buttonhole on that happy day after the dismal period of suspension when *The Times* will once more appear. I hope your readers will do likewise.' But roses were not going to be in season when that happy day eventually came round, almost a year later.

The shut-down cost Times Newspapers £46 million, and though an agreement between management and unions was finally hammered out in the early hours of Sunday October 21 1979 the price exacted by the unions for their return to work was a stiff one. On paper the agreement looked quite good, since it contained promises of a 15 per cent reduction in staffing, improvements in production, a disputes procedure to eliminate unofficial stoppages, and the introduction of new technology. Unfortunately the agreement did not stick. The same old complaints resurfaced, leading to the same cycle of disruption, particularly on *The Sunday Times*.

But it was to be *The Times* which was to have the unenviable distinction of providing quite a new example of industrial unrest. In August 1980 *The Times* journalists went on strike in pursuit of a pay rise of 21 per cent, management offering 18 per cent. The strike in fact lasted only a week, but its effect was catastrophic. 'If the strikers do not give their priority in loyalty to *The Times* – as, fortunately, a great many *Times* journalists still do – why should they expect that their readers, or indeed the proprietors of *The Times* should continue to be loyal to the paper?' That was the question asked in a leading article headed 'How to Kill a Newspaper' on August 30, the day when *The Times* reappeared.

The journalists' strike did not kill *The Times* but it was a considerable contributing factor in bringing about another change in ownership. Both the Thomsons, father and son, had taken great pride in their ownership of *The Times*, had wanted the best for it and for those who worked on it. They had spent millions of pounds of their own money on it, and rewards for most *Times* journalists had, by 1980, greatly improved since the Astor days. Yet now the journalists had bitten the hand that fed them. 'My father and I', said Lord Thomson, 'have repeatedly made it clear that our continued support for Times Newspapers was conditional on the overall cooperation of the newspaper employees, and I have sadly concluded that this cooperation will not be forthcoming under our ownership.'

Enough, Lord Thomson felt, was enough, and if anyone else was prepared to take on the thankless task of running Times Newspapers they were welcome to try. On October 22 Gordon Brunton, chief executive of the Thomson Organisation in Britain, announced that *The Times*, *The Sunday Times* and the supplements were up for sale. The Thomson Organisation would continue to finance them until March, but if no buyer had been found by then they would all be closed down. To begin with it appeared that the titles might be sold separately, and attempts were made by the two editors, William Rees-Mogg and Harold Evans, to put together independent consortiums, including members of their respective staffs, which would be in a position to make valid bids for the titles. Later, however, it was made clear that all the titles, *The Times, The Sunday Times, The Times Literary Supplement, The Times Educational Supplement* and *The Times Higher Educational Supplement*, would have to be sold together.

Several would-be purchasers appeared on the scene, but only one seemed to meet all the required conditions, and that was Rupert Murdoch of News International. Rupert Murdoch had inherited newspapers in Australia from his father, Sir Keith Murdoch, had added to them and built up a communications empire in his own country, in 1969 had acquired two of Britain's leading popular newspapers, the Sunday *News of the World* and the *Sun*, which he turned into a tabloid with the highest circulation of any newspaper in the country, and in America had bought the *New York Post* and other papers. He was forty-nine years old and the toughest entrepreneur to get his hands on *The Times* since Northcliffe.

It might have been thought that this new concentration of newspaper ownership would be referred to the Monopolies Commission, as had happened when Thomson took over, but it was not. The Secretary of State for Trade, John Biffen, declared himself satisfied that neither *The Times* nor *The Sunday Times* were 'economic as a going concern', and that in view of this, of the deadline under which the sale of the papers was being conducted, and the time which a reference to the Monopolies Commission would inevitably take, the sale should go ahead. He also took note of the guarantees on editorial freedom which Murdoch had agreed should be written into the articles of association of News International. These included: 'The Editor of each newspaper shall retain control over any political comment published in his newspaper and, in particular, shall not be subject to any restraint or inhibition in expressing opinion or in reporting news that might directly or indirectly conflict with the opinions or interest of any of the newspaper proprietors . . . Instructions to journalists shall be given only by the Editor or those to whom he has delegated authority.'

On February 17 1981 Murdoch offered Harold Evans, who had edited *The Sunday Times* for the past fourteen years, the editorship of

The Times (Rees-Mogg had let it be known that he wished to step down). He accepted. Evans was still young, an energetic crusading journalist skilled in every aspect of his profession. He quickly brought several new men into senior staff positions, though with little regard for cost, and made many changes in the style and content of the paper, that most obvious to *Times* readers being the Information Services which now occupied the bottom half of the back page. But Evans had held the job for little over a year before disagreement between proprietor and editor led to his enforced resignation. He was succeeded in the editorial chair in March 1982 by Charles Douglas-Home who had been his deputy and who had in seventeen years occupied a number of responsible positions on the paper. Now aged forty-five, Douglas-Home was six years younger than Haley and seven years older than Rees-Mogg when they had taken over the editorship. Like his most famous predecessor, Delane, he was 'a familiar figure in the hunting-field' and, also like Delane, he seemed to enter on his troubled inheritance 'with perfect serenity and self-confidence.'[11] His assessment of his responsibilities may be found in the Foreword to this volume.

E. C. Hodgkin

---

11 Sir Edward Cook, *Delane of 'The Times'*, pp. 9–10.

APPENDIX A

GEOFFREY DAWSON AND
ROBERT BARRINGTON-WARD

T HE personalities and working methods of Geoffrey Dawson and Robert Barrington-Ward have been described in several biographies and books of memoirs. The following selection of passages is taken from the writings of some of those who served on *The Times* at various dates and knew both men:

1 SIR BASIL LIDDELL HART, *Memoirs*. Volume Two. London, 1965. pp. 148–49.

In five years fairly close contact with Geoffrey Dawson – the years immediately before World War II – he seemed to me one of the most talented men I have met. His talents were so various that I was puzzled why his interests did not correspondingly cover all the main fields with which a great newspaper has to deal. For example, he never seemed to show any such strong interest in foreign affairs and defence as he did in Imperial, or Colonial, affairs.

Pondering that question, I came to feel that the explanation was perhaps that he had too many interests and activities outside his profession, for dealing with world affairs, so that he was inclined to devote too much of his time and attention to the affairs of Oxford, Eton, and his Yorkshire estate.

He was a puzzle also, in other respects – especially in his varying attitude. One day, or on one particular issue, he would talk in a most liberal-minded and progressive way. But when one proceeded on the assumption that this was his bent of mind, one was apt to be startled another day to hear him express views that seemed instinctively conservative and traditional.

There was a similar variability, or mystery, about his line and lead over the big issues of British policy in Europe. That may best be illustrated by recalling a discussion I had when lunching with several of the chief members of *The Times* staff at a time when Czechoslovakia's situation had become even more precarious than in the spring. I expressed strong criticism of *The Times* leader that morning, and was rather surprised to find that the others agreed with my criticism. So I said 'If you all share my view, who does hold the view taken in today's leader?' At that one of them replied: 'Only one man for certain – B-W. Geoffrey Dawson perhaps!' It was a very significant comment.

Barrington-Ward, too, was a man of great talents, which he canalised more effectively for a concentrated purpose than Geoffrey Dawson. It had been a delightful experience to work with anyone so considerate as well as intelligent. Thus I was all the more sad about our growing divergence of view. In argument he was always most reasonable, and wonderfully patient with my persistence in pressing points that he was not disposed to accept. But I gradually became aware that underlying his reasonableness in discussion there was an inflexible will on which argument could make no impression. When he had made up his own mind on an issue nothing would change it except his own process of thought, and if he did change it was apt to be a complete right-about turn, and result in an equally positive move in the opposite direction – it happened over the Polish guarantee the following year. His consistency, in whatever direction he took, was as marked as Geoffrey Dawson's variability.

The basic fault of both in editorial policy was, it seemed to me, that they sought to

460

make *The Times* the 'submerged half' of the Government, or the cabinet behind the Cabinet, instead of giving priority to its function as a newspaper.

2 DONALD MCLACHLAN, *In the Chair: Barrington-Ward of The Times, 1927–1948.* London, 1971. pp. 3–4 and 96–98.

Some friends of B-W think that Dawson made too great demands on him, even exploited his passionate sense of duty to the office. The diary will throw light on this; but it may be observed that deputy editors aspiring to the chair are likely to seize any opportunity of showing their stamina and capacity. B-W, who was a most loyal assistant for fourteen years, may have deferred too much to his chief's judgement; but Dawson was a formidable personality and brilliant journalist, with twenty years of editing behind him, who had stood up to and broken with Northcliffe, and then returned to the chair on his own terms. At the farewell lunch given to him in 1941 by his staff the menu offered a tribute in verse by one of his colleagues:

The glancing smile, the devastating glare,
The Jovian nod, the rapt Olympian air,
The eagle puissance, ample graciousness.

Awe in his presence was understandable.

B-W should have known from his own days with Dawson just how much a deputy can spare his chief. But this anxious wish to be personally involved in the daily creation of a newspaper is something that has to be experienced to be understood; it is a feeling like that of the doctor for his patient, of the gardener for his roses, or of the chef for the serving of the meal that he has cooked – a conviction that there are always finishing touches to be given and that only he can give them.

Dawson, with two decades of editorship behind him, had by the thirties worked his way out of this obsession. He was happy to delegate and get off to Yorkshire and, if he felt like it, stay away a bit longer than he had said he would. He could concentrate on essentials and leave himself free of anything that did not interest him. Indeed, his more relaxed approach to work could give the appearance of carelessness. B-W, on the contrary, found it difficult to shake off the hounding conscience, although there were signs towards the end of his life that he was beginning to do so as he realized he was overtaxing his strength. There was not in his case the lure and distraction of a permanent country home like Dawson's; he had country roots in Cornwall, but they were too far away to be developed. He never had a deputy as experienced, trusted and conscientious as he had been himself for Dawson.[1]

B-W was not normally a fast or easy writer, although no one could do more rapidly a late-night job of surgery or improvization. He needed the special emergency to spur him into disregard of the caution with which he approached most matters for comment. He had no use for the columnist who sees no virtue in consistency, to whom a good idea is one that startles and stirs talk, who maintains that readability is all and that one idea is as good as another. To B-W his pen was the pen of *The Times*; it must do its work with the deliberation and sense of responsibility that are attributed to the Lord Chief Justice or the Permanent Head of the Foreign Office, every sentence to be weighed. He was deeply conscious of being in the succession to Barnes and Delane, without having that sheer beefy recklessness which inspired the Victorians or the jaunty brilliance of Dawson.

These inhibitions made him not only a slow writer of his own articles but a zealous corrector of other people's work. They might fancy themselves as coiners of a phrase or masters of epithet: if B-W thought their style inappropriate to the paper he would not

---

1 Already in 1926 at the *Observer* he noted: 'The worst of it is that decisions fall to be taken towards midnight when one is most tired. Things that a fresh mind might judge rightly, a tired mind often does not. Then worry follows in the train of errors and fatigue.'

hesitate to change it – as he had a right to do. All this took time. To judge from his diaries he found special satisfaction in such work: there are frequent references to having to do a lot of work on this or that man's leader.

On this evidence alone of the working day at Printing House Square, it is fair to say that here was a man doomed to take too much out of himself. Brought on to *The Times* as a writer, he accepted from Dawson more and more administrative work in the day without giving up the writing at night. It is hard to blame him: this was the way to the editorship, to become indispensable. Far from giving up writing to become an editor, he regarded writing as a prime function of editing. That is to say, he believed that the leading articles and comment of the paper must bear the stamp of the office even when the personality of the writer was as strong as that of E. H. Carr or Basil Liddell Hart. Here, perhaps, is to be found the explanation for that sense of strain day by day as B.W. records the rapid shift of his mind from papers to people, from people to ideas, from concept to detail, from detail to sub-editing, from tactics to strategy and back again. One wonders how he found time to think. The answer is that thinking was done in those leisure hours of the weekend when he should have been resting and relaxing.

3 THOMAS BARMAN, *Diplomatic Correspondent*. London, 1968. pp. 58, 61 and 62.

I am more than ever convinced that Dawson's basic fault was not so much that he held certain views on foreign policy, but that he thought of himself as a statesman rather and as a journalist. The two are incompatible . . . Dawson's pursuit of appeasement as a consistent policy, often through the suppression of news that militated against that policy, violated what must remain the basic principle of good journalism. It therefore diminished the reputation of *The Times* at a time when its influence was sorely needed.

In all this, Barrington-Ward was as rigorous as Dawson ever was. But he was more difficult to deal with: where Dawson had all the normal man's healthy laziness and might thus from time to time let things slip, Barrington-Ward was extremely hardworking and did not miss anything; where Dawson would take a man-of-the-world view of things, Barrington-Ward was conscientious to a degree; where Dawson was at times slapdash, as in the matter of the leading article on the Sudetenland, Barrington-Ward was infuriatingly painstaking. In slightly different circumstances he might have been a non-conformist Doctor of Divinity with pacifist leanings. His pacifism was rooted in his experiences in the First World War. His bravery earned him both the DSO and the MC; but he could not forget the horror of it all, and was willing to pay almost any price to save the coming generation from the fate that had overtaken his.

The effect of his views on editorial policy was more damaging than Dawson's because they were more deeply felt, and were the product of great moral strivings.

The Times was a house divided against itself. There were those who by conviction were completely on the Editor's side . . . There were others, W. F. Casey, D. D. Braham (one of the principal leader writers) and Iverach McDonald (then Diplomatic Correspondent) who held diametrically opposite views on the question of the government's appeasement policy, and who did their best to get them into the paper in spite of Dawson. McDonald was so upset at times that he could be heard muttering to himself words of Old Testament vengeance as he came out of the office.

4 COLIN R. COOTE, *Editorial*. London, 1965. pp. 168 and 170.

Geoffrey Dawson's attitude was entirely dictated by two facts. He knew that the Dominions were passionately pacifist, and the ruling passion in his life was to keep the Commonwealth together. Secondly, he was the intimate friend of Baldwin and of Halifax; and Baldwin had been frightened into pacificism by the East Fulham election . . .

The atmosphere in the office was quite horrible; and even more when Dawson was away and Barrington-Ward was deputizing for him. There was another instance of a man acting entirely out of character. We had been contemporaries at Oxford, where he had done brilliantly. He had won the DSO and MC in the war. Yet when Hitler invaded the Rhineland [1936] and I rushed hopefully in his room expecting that this breaking of the Fuhrer's own pledges would be castigated, I found him writing a leader himself entitled 'A Chance to Rebuild'. In reply to my protests he uneasily rejoined, 'I fear we must continue our dusty and undistinguished way.' Strange language for the erstwhile Thunderer!!

5 DOUGLAS WOODRUFF, *Times Remembered: Golden prewar days at the old Printing House Square*. Article in *The Times*, May 2 1977, in which Woodruff describes his first meetings with Geoffrey Dawson in 1926.

At Printing House Square I was ushered in by Miss Dickie, the gentle, white-haired day secretary who had come to *The Times* from Lambeth Palace. I did not know this about her, or it might have prepared me, for when I first saw Geoffrey Dawson he immediately reminded me of Thomas Cranmer, the oval face, rather small mouth, but above all the large, dark, unfriendly eyes which looked as though they could very easily glare, but he had a better complexion than the portrait, and as soon as he began to talk the impression of unfriendliness was quickly wiped out, for he had indeed a marked gift for immediately establishing a warm relationship . . .

When I saw him again he came at once to brass tacks. I could see that he had liked my articles [which Dawson had asked for] and he wanted more. How about becoming a journalist? I thought I should like it very much, but said I ought to tell him I did not consider myself a Conservative. To this he said no more did he. *The Times* looked at every question on its merits, and it was the beauty of a large newspaper that no one need ever be asked to write anything against his own convictions . . .

The easy, free hand is also illustrated by a letter he wrote to Max Beerbohm, who sent him a cutting from *The Times* in September, 1929, headed 'Heirs to the Victorians', with a second line, 'Mr. Belloc on British Literature'. Max was horrified at the adjective, but Dawson, explained:

My dear Max Beerbohm,

It was delightful to see your handwriting even on the subject of 'British Literature'. I was absent, I hasten to say, or hope I should have spotted it. For it isn't funk that does it, nor yet Imperial sentiment, but the solid phalanx of Scots sub-editors that dominates this and every other newspaper office. No other race can stand the strain and they must have their fling sometime.

'They must have their fling' expresses very well Dawson's philosophy of editing in a relaxed and easy-going way.

6 DEREK HUDSON, *Writing between the Lines: an Autobiography*. High Hill Press Ltd., 1965. pp. 154–166.

Many have said that Dawson made too much use of the 'Old Boy' network, and of what later *Times* advertisements have trumpeted as the world of 'Top People' (how Dawson would have destested that gambit, by the way! He hated to see even the bare exhortation *'Read The Times'* on a blank wall). One answer is that Dawson's chief interest lay in the prestige and advancement of *The Times*; it was his duty no less than his pleasure to cultivate the acquaintance of the influential figures of the time (many of them Etonians and Oxford men); he did so with great success, and *The Times* benefited accordingly. Would it have been better if he had cast his net more widely and had been more flexible in his views? I believe it would, but to say this is to postulate a different Dawson. Was there a vein of almost boyish over-confidence in which he imposed, to the point of obstinacy, the conservative views and prejudices of a patriotic, right-living, Empire-conscious but insular governing class? This could be argued. Dawson was not indeed a man of perfect wisdom; but then, as I have already emphasized, he was human, and he had his loyalties . . .

Both men worked extremely hard. Of the two, Dawson had the better health and the stronger nerves. At Printing House Square Dawson was still the country squire whose natural tenacity and resilience combined with a dash of cavalier frivolity enabled him to keep on top of the job. B-W. (as Barrington-Ward was always known) appeared relatively a puritan governed by his conscience to an unusual degree: he never spared himself, and his thin clear-cut features reflected the strain . . .

The face I got to know so well in later years was finely moulded to the point of severity. B-W. had gone bald early in life. His mouth tended to set in a thin straight line, yet there was a lurking humour at its corners. B-W.'s eyes were memorable – they were serious eyes, with a hint of suffering and reproach behind them; they looked searchingly into the eyes of those with whom he talked, as if to test them and to exhort them to aim at his own high standards. Lacking Dawson's freedom from self-consciousness, he made up for it in moral earnestness. Considering with care each point that was put to him, he gave firm and decided answers . . .

The Times leaders of December 1944 and January 1945 were long, 'reasonable', idealistic, carefully argued; but they were also more than a little self-righteous, unrealistic, and obstinate. Excellent as it is for a newspaper editor to show himself independent of Ministers, as B-W. did, a policy of independence, especially when pursued in wartime on limited information, carries with it as many dangers of error as a policy of giving general support to the Government. If a Radical Tory, as B-W. has been termed, grasps the wrong end of the stick, he can hold on to it more firmly than anybody. Many members of *The Times'* editorial staff became increasingly gloomy and exasperated as the long series of articles on the Greek question continued; they were greatly relieved when the course of events removed the embarrassing subject from the leader page.

His colleagues' affection for B-W. nevertheless remained constant. That affection was offered to the finely tuned spirit of a man who gave his very utmost to the paper – more indeed than could have been expected of him.

APPENDIX B

'SUPPRESSION OF NEWS'

OBJECTIVE testimony gives little support to the common charge that Dawson and Barrington-Ward stopped any news that they did not like from going into the paper. Both had a respect for hard news, no matter how much it went against their policy. *The Times* carried such news day by day. In fact, what evidence there is goes to show that Dawson was not thinking of news at all when he wrote the two letters, both dated May 23 1937, which have often been held up against him. (*Vide: History*, Vol. IV, p. 907; Gannon, *The British Press and Germany, 1936–1939*, p. 114; and Donald McLachlan, *In the Chair*, pp. 131, 282.) In the first, to H. G. Daniels, who had returned temporarily as special correspondent in the Berlin office, Dawson's words were:

> But it would interest me to know precisely what it is in *The Times* that has produced this antagonism in Germany. I do my utmost, night after night, to keep out of the paper anything that might hurt their susceptibilities. I can really think of nothing that has been printed now for many months past which they could possibly take exception to as unfair comment. No doubt they were annoyed by Steer's first story on the bombing of Guernica, but its essential accuracy has never been disputed, and there has not been any attempt here to rub it in or to harp upon it. I should be more grateful than I can say for any explanation and guidance, for I have always been convinced that the peace of the world depends more than anything else on our getting into reasonable relations with Germany.

In the second letter, sent to his old friend Lord Lothian, Dawson wrote in similar terms, but expanded the second sentence to read: 'I spend my nights . . . dropping in little things which are intended to soothe them'. This secondary claim can be easily explained. Dawson was especially referring, as an earlier letter to Daniels makes clear, to two articles published shortly before: the first expressed sympathy on the loss of the German airship Hindenburg, wrecked at New York only a few days before, the second gave a welcome to Field-Marshal von Blomberg, the German War Minister, as German representative at the Coronation service at Westminster Abbey on May 12. But the main claim that he tried 'to keep out of the paper anything that might hurt their susceptibilities' defies a wholly convincing explanation. As it stands it is nonsensical. It is contradicted by the fact that Norman Ebbutt, the chief staff correspondent in Berlin, was thrown out of Germany barely three months later simply and solely because of the lengthy, detailed and informative despatches, highly damaging to Hitler's peaceful pretensions and his boasts of unity within Germany, that had regularly appeared in the columns of *The Times*. Their appearance day after day cannot be reconciled with Dawson's professed efforts 'night after night'.

Some years later Donald McLachlan, when working on his biography of Barrington-Ward, *In the Chair*, asked surviving members of the staff if they could recall any censorship of hard news from abroad by either Dawson or Barrington-Ward, and not one of them could remember such a case. The explanation of the letters is probably as follows. Dawson had not only his respect for hard news. He had no less a respect for the old (and never entirely workable) convention that news and comment should not be mixed. News should be kept for the news columns and all comments should be confined to the leader columns or special articles. He disliked having in the news columns anything which he would call 'waffle' or 'idle speculation' and he would want these passages removed. Sometimes, it is true, the 'speculation' that was removed would include passages which seemed to others to be simple logical deduction from given facts.[1] Ebbutt complained of excisions from time to time, but the cuts were usually made in his despatches not by the editor but by sub-editors (who prepare all copy for the printer) and they were made not on any grounds of policy but because this courageous correspondent wrote often at too great length, at times obscurely, and occasionally very late. The cuts were made to ensure clarity in meaning and speed in printing.

In a letter dated April 29 1978, addressed to Gordon Phillips, archivist of *The Times*, Geoffrey L. Pearson, who was chief foreign sub-editor for many years, wrote:

I am happy now to repeat that never, to my knowledge, did Dawson censor any despatch from Ebbutt or any other correspondent in Berlin. It would have been impossible for him to alter a message from Berlin – or anywhere else – without my being aware of it, for it would have been essential that any alteration he made should pass through my hands. (I may explain that he received typed duplicates of all telephoned foreign messages, as others in the office did.) I am absolutely certain about this. As I, like other members of the staff, did not like the appeasement policy at all, I have all the more reason for remembering this.

I knew Norman Ebbutt quite well. He was an old colleague, and always came in to see me when he visited London; and he never complained that any messages of his had been censored. I am sure he would have done if they had been. He did complain about his despatches being cut, by us subs. Cut, yes, but censored, no. His messages were frequently too long; and when he became a correspondent he forgot all he had learned as a sub about space restrictions.

---

1 See p. 20.

APPENDIX C

THE TWO SCOURGES

Text of leading article (Carr), December 5 1940.

T HE great twin scourges which have most deeply touched the imagination and seared the conscience of the present generation are the scourge of war and the scourge of unemployment. For those who feel the need to look beyond the end of the present struggle, the abolition of war and the abolition of unemployment are the most urgent and imperative tasks of our civilization. It is natural, but it may be unwise, to express them in this negative form. They can be realized only through positive and constructive action. To abolish war means to create an international order in which good faith will be observed, and in which the unchecked pursuit of national interest will be tempered by consciousness of loyalty to some wider community. To abolish unemployment means to create a social order in which the ideals of the nineteenth century democracy are extended from the political to the social and economic sphere – in which liberty will imply not so much freedom from interference as a chance for all; equality, not only equal access to the polling booth and the court of law, but equal access to the more restricted field of social and economic opportunity; fraternity, not the mere formal recognition of common citizenship, but a lively sense of common responsibility for the well being of the least fortunate.

In the nineteen-twenties a series of bold – indeed over-confident – attempts were made to abolish war. They failed either because, like the Kellogg Pact, they remained purely negative, or because, like the League of Nations, they lacked the support of power on a world-wide scale and sought salvation in the barren accumulation of legal instruments and rules of procedure. The spirit of a constructive international order was lacking. Within the framework of a British Commonwealth of Nations Great Britain has long been acutely sensitive to the needs and interests of her sister nations; and in her relations to those parts of the Empire not yet ripe for full self-government she is progressively substituting the principles of responsibility and trusteeship for that of exploitation. The whole structure of Imperial unity rests on the assumption that the national interests of the United Kingdom will not be asserted beyond the point at which they become seriously incompatible with those of her partners in the Commonwealth.

Internationally, on the other hand, British policy – equally with that of other countries – has almost completely failed to develop this spirit. Much has been said of the need to sacrifice a mystical attribute called sovereignty. But abstractions are dangerous when they serve to mask concrete realities. The sacrifices required are of something more tangible than sovereignty. No British statesman has hitherto had the courage to oppose a policy advocated by British industrialists or British workers on the ground of the injury which it will inflict on the industries of France or Belgium or Germany, or to reject a measure designed to favour British agriculture because it would spell ruin to the Danish farmer. Yet there is little doubt that we shall fail to achieve any effective international order, or any alternative to the horror of recurrent war, until we witness some fundamental change, generally and reciprocally among the nations, in the scale of values. The problem of collective security is not so much whether men are prepared to sacrifice their lives for other countries, but whether they are prepared to sacrifice some of their profits and some of their wages to promote a common welfare in which they will eventually share.

A like change of values is an equally essential condition of the cure of unemployment. Perhaps the fundamental cause of our failure after 1919 was that, in attempting to create a new international order, we ignored the needs of a new social order. The social and economic foundations on which the political structure of 1919 was so light-heartedly erected were crumbling in ruins. Social and economic stresses were the revolutionary force which swept away the work of the peace-makers – the good and bad together. The connexion between unemployment and war was not fortuitous. Seven million unemployed brought Hitler to power. He rewarded them by finding them employment in preparation for war. Today millions of workers in more than one country are learning the dangerous lesson that nothing creates regular and well-paid employment, and makes labour a scarce and valued commodity, so certainly as war. So long as it remains true that war or preparation for war is the only effective remedy for unemployment, wars will continue however cunning the machinery devised to prevent them. Any new international order will be still-born so long as this cancer is not eradicated from the social system.

Put in these terms, the problem of unemployment becomes simple for those who have the courage to face its implications. There is no formula, no specific, for the abolition of unemployment any more than there is for the abolition of war. It is a problem less of means than of ends. It can be solved (or transformed, as at the present moment, into a technical problem of fitting supply to demand) when we recognize in time of peace a social purpose as compulsive and as worthy of sacrifice as the purposes of war. In 1940 the manufacturer foregoes profits, the worker foregoes trade union restrictions on conditions of employment, the consumer foregoes luxuries and lends to the Government to finance expenditure for which no material return is asked or expected. In 1930 a small fraction of these sacrifices would have sufficed to arrest the unemployment crisis of the ensuing years, and, at the same time, to bring to the countries now involved in war better housing, more ample nutrition, better education, and more amenities for the leisure of the masses. These sacrifices were not made because they were not called for by any political leader; they were not called for because the lesson had not yet been learned. There is no longer any reason for failure to understand. To create the new social order does not, like war, call for sacrifice of life and limb. But it does call for many of those other sacrifices of profits and luxuries, of rights and privileges, which we make unquestioningly in time of war. To formulate a social end, other than war, which will inspire such sacrifices is the cardinal problem of our time.

The greatest obstacle to the realization of this need is the fact that we still live in the afterglow of nineteenth century splendour, when prosperity seemed within the reach of almost all and sacrifices were demanded of few. Gradually we came to understand that this prosperity was the product of conditions which are gone beyond recall – expanding frontiers, expanding populations, freedom of movement for men and capital, and quick profits in undeveloped countries oversea. Then for a time, as profits became precarious, slogans like 'Make the foreigner pay' and 'Soak the rich' seemed to offer a cheap way out. Now we know that there is no such easy road, that prosperity can be regained only by new policies adapted to new and sterner conditions, that we must plan for peace as consciously and deliberately, and with the same common readiness for sacrifice, as we now plan for war. It must not be said that we are more ready to risk our lives than our vested interests, or that peace – unlike war – holds no purpose worthy of sacrifice of things we prize for a greater common good. The British people will shrink from no sacrifice for a purpose in which it believes. In war it has gladly accepted – indeed demanded – leadership which asks for sacrifice from all. The planning of peace calls for a leader who will have the courage and the vision to make the same appeal.

APPENDIX D

HALEY'S MEMORANDA

A SELECTION of from one day's output of Sir William Haley's memoranda to his staff, drawn from the files in *The Times* archives, gives some indication of the range and the care for detail which characterised them. The date was March 7 1962. Haley had then been editor between nine and ten years:

To all heads of department:
We have a good all-round paper this morning. The awkward space on page 3 has been well used. The picture on page 4 is the focal point for the best news story on the page. The Arts Page has plenty of contrast in its material and is well laid out; the only point to be made is that the Liverpool double column heading at the foot of the page is too large for the story it covers. The new Parliamentary layout is settling down quite well and is now being more competently handled. I am still not satisfied with the 'House of Lords' and 'House of Commons' lines but I am waiting on Mr. Harling for some improvement of this. The Accrington Stanley story makes a new kind of lead for the home pages. The collection and selection of the news of these three pages is a good round-up in general. . . .

The Rhodesian story and picture makes a very good show on page 10. The whole thing is alive with a minimum of display. Our Salisbury correspondent's despatch on Welensky's speech is the best I can find. I think we want to keep a close eye on our Common Market stories. This morning's just gets by but it is rather diffuse. . . . The Bill Page was greatly improved by moving the lead over to Captain Powers. The two home tops on the page are well worth their place. The page rather runs into the sands in the south east quarter; it would have been better if there had been a stipped story across two or three columns down the bottom to hold it up.

The leaders are an interesting collection and the letters remain, with the obits, the two departments in which *The Times* has no rival anywhere. The City notes cover a good deal of land and water, and the supporting notes in the other columns throughout the City pages continue to be lively. I now find I cannot afford to miss it on any day. On the other hand the City pictures continue to be disappointing. I do not know how many objects we have depicted hung from how many cranes, nor does the drilling picture look very different from any other drilling picture one has seen in the past. With the whole world of industry both here and on the continent to go at – as well as occasionally America – there must surely be more interesting subjects than these. The back page pictures are moderate. The top one of the trawler does complete a curiously open air feeling that this morning's issue has throughout. But maybe that's the spring!

Financial Editor:
How is the graph of Government expenditure coming along, please?

Home Editor:
Our Defence Correspondent's Bill Page story this morning is another valuable

piece. He goes from strength to strength.

The Manager:
I expect you will have seen the front page picture and story in the *Guardian* this morning about the transatlantic T.T. test. Why did the *New York Times* do this with the *Guardian* and not with *The Times*?

Arts Editor:
I was pleased to see the drawing on the Arts Page this morning. It is some time since we had one of these.

Arts Editor:
The second paragraph of the King Richard III notice has no bearing on the first. It just does not make sense. Is the whole paragraph misplaced?

Home Editor:
Page 8 column 4 'extra ministers at Cabinet meeting'. Our political correspondent says that 'Mr. Butler presided at in the absence of Mr. Macmillan, who had not returned from Leicester where he fulfilled an engagement on Monday night.' The word 'spoke' would have been much shorter and stronger than 'fulfilled an engagement'. This is a small matter but we should encourage all our writers to remember that the shortest words are generally the best.

Home Editor:
The Petersfield story is nicely written.

Foreign Editor:
Mrs. Bourne's [Dessa Trevisan's] piece about the Djilas magazine story is excellent. This is the kind of thing she does better than anyone else.

Home Editor:
We have completely missed the news aspect of the Wolfson Drage deal this morning. One has to read the rather technical (and where it is, this is quite proper) piece on the City pages to find out exactly what has happened so far as the Wolfson Foundation is concerned. Other papers, including the *Financial Times*, have seized on the news aspect of this and pulled it out. It was right to do so because the Wolfson benefactions are a matter of general interest. I am afraid that the liaison between Room 1 and the City office is not yet as good as it might be. Even though perfection must await the new building we must do all we can to avoid misses like this in the meantime.

Some days would bring more suggestions for following up news, or for having a leader on such and such a topic, or for inquiries why *The Times* had missed a story which other papers had carried that day. (Hard pressed news editors, anxious to get on with the coming day's news, would often bewail the time which they had to spend on a *post mortem*.) But the above selection is typical of the general tone.

A memorandum of about the same time is doubly pleasant, both for the praise it carries and for the illustration of Haley's wide reading which he was not slow to apply to the work of the paper from day to day. It is dated March 27 1962:

Mr. Emery's despatch on the Algiers shooting yesterday is a mature and firm piece of work. He is fair, objective, and clear. The despatch is one of the main [most?] useful pieces of reporting we have had for a long time. Reading the despatch, the episode reminded me more and more of the famous December 1851 'massacre' in the streets of Paris, which F. A. Simpson made one of the centre pieces of his great history. The parallel, even as to who fired first, civilians or soldiers, is remarkable.

Yet another may be given again taken from the same period. It displays Haley's close concern for all money matters and his care to have all the effects of any threatened change carefully worked out. It is to the foreign editor, dated February 8 1962:

Commonwealth Press Rate
As you probably know the Commonwealth Communications Board have told the bodies concerned that the proper Commonwealth press rate should now be 3d. a word. Negotiations to maintain the penny rate are now beginning and there will be political representations if they fail. Meanwhile I have had the effect worked out for *The Times* for the year 1961. The figures were as follows:

Africa	£4,485
India and Pakistan	1,956
Hong Kong	126
Singapore	109
Rangoon	75
Australasia	705
West Indies	161
Canada	2,350
Other places	124
	£10,091

In other words each penny that was added to the Commonwealth press rate would cost us £10,000 a year. This is a useful figure to bear in mind.

APPENDIX E

SPORTS COVERAGE IN WAR AND PEACE

THE outbreak of war in September 1939 meant that football pitches were turned into parade grounds, race courses into transit camps, golf courses became tank ranges, and the sports pages of *The Times*, which during the 1930s had luxuriated in good print, spacious presentation and leisurely accounts of the day's play, shrank in the national cause. An occasional contest in aid of Red Cross funds brought relief, but of the Cup Final, the Boat Race, the Open golf championship, of Wimbledon, Lords, Henley or Cowes there was no trace.

A racing correspondent of non-combatant age was engaged to cover the few meetings that were allowed. On the day of the invasion of Normandy, June 6 1944, before the news had appeared in the papers, the correspondent had the satisfaction of tipping the winner of the Coronation Stakes to be run during a one-day meeting, beginning at 11.30, at Newmarket under whose stands troops had previously been stationed. The day after, when news of the landings broke, sports coverage was down to less than half a column, all of it devoted to that meeting, except for the notice of a cricket match to be played, one-day of course, between the Fire Service and the Metropolitan Police. Even Bernard Darwin, whose eagerly awaited Saturday column on golf had survived the outbreak of war, and who had shown such ability to write about anything or nothing in particular, had been reduced to silence.

The war left an indirect mark on sport, broadening the public's taste, breaking down international barriers – foes were after a brief but decent interval forgiven at that level – and producing improved means of communication and travel. The European Cup in football was started in 1956, and in the twenty years after hostilities ceased international cricket grew fast. In 1952 Pakistan played their first Test series of cricket; the West Indies became a formidable side as distinct from an attractive one with a few gifted individual players.

The first sports correspondent to be sent abroad in this field was R. B. 'Beau' Vincent, a former sports editor; he was also a fresh and vivid writer who could assimilate, while conversing, the smallest detail which might escape the notice of a more serious and silent spectator. John Woodcock took over the job full time in 1954 and went on every major tour thereafter, combining in his reports much of the pre-war atmosphere with the occasional note of asperity which changing conditions came to require.

In one sense sport has always been international. For years the Centre Court had rung with foreign-sounding names; Henley had attracted crews from far afield, and at least every other year American golfers landed to compete in our championships. But the tendency had been for the players to come to the correspondents; correspondents had not generally gone to them, and the recital of their achievements in their own countries was left to the agencies.

Twenty years later the emphasis was much stronger on going to find top international sport wherever it might be, and it would have been stronger still if the need for economy had not imposed a brake. Exactly twenty years after D-Day, on June 6 1964, the rugby football correspondent was recording from New Plymouth the exploits of the British

Lions against the All Blacks, the yachting correspondent was in Amsterdam, and the motor racing correspondent, Harold Nockolds, found himself as far afield as Indianapolis.

A shining exception to that early insularity had been the visit paid by Bernard Darwin in 1922 to the United States when he accompanied the first Walker Cup team. He provided a good example of a sports writer being expert as a performer in his own field. Not only did he take part in that golf match when the British captain fell ill, but he twice reached the semi-finals of the Amateur championship. Others writing just before or after the Second World War were also good practitioners. Geoffrey Green who started contributing articles in the 1930s, had been a Corinthian-Casual until a damaged knee-cap ended his career on the football field. John Board who wrote on equestrianism and polo was an expert horseman. In 1948 Richard Burnell, the rowing correspondent, won a gold medal at the Olympics in the double sculls with B. H. T. Bushnell; and another gold medallist, Thomas Dow Richardson, was the skating correspondent.

They were specialists, but they were for the most part also versatile. This was in particular true of Richard Hill, who had opened the batting for Winchester with D. R. Jardine, but who later became an acknowledged expert on all forms of racket sports, winning among other distinctions the MCC Silver Racket competition for real tennis. It was during one such contest that in a match against the Rev. Arthur Buxton he lost the first two sets and left the court thinking that the contest was over. On being persuaded that it was not, he returned politely to the court and won the next three sets. Even Darwin, very much a one-sport man in practice, reported on university athletics sometimes until, in his own words, he was sacked for gross partiality, while through thick and thin his fourth leaders provided an indication of his facility as an essayist.

Such characters did not, of course, lack resourcefulness and adaptability. Hill, caught late one evening returning from Wimbledon, wrote his piece strap-hanging on the underground back to Blackfriars, using the back of a fellow strap-hanger for his desk. On another occasion, finding himself at dusk in a telephone kiosk from which the bulb had been removed, he got through a box and a half of matches providing himself with enough light to read what he had written. Such as these would have survived with as much honour as their successors; what could not hope to survive in the straitened circumstances at the beginning of the second half of the century was the relaxed and expansive mood of the articles which had been the strength of the sports pages before the war.

An incident about that time illustrates the gap that was opening between the old and the new. During the national shooting championships at Bisley two men in the butts were injured, one fatally. No mention was made of this in *The Times* next day, and when the sports editor upbraided the rifle shooting correspondent for not making any reference to it, he received a reply that deserves to be regarded as a landmark in reporting: he did not feel, said the correspondent, that to have done so would have been in the best interests of rifle shooting. The dilemma is familiar to any journalist: the need to reconcile the duty to produce an honest report with the desire not to damage those contacts on which a special knowledge of his sport may in part depend. But in the mood of the time, with a wider public becoming critical generally of sport as it came to rely increasingly on commercial interests, sport could no longer remain a sheltered subject.

Television was beginning to play a major part in not only changing public attitudes toward sport but also in affecting the style of newspaper reporting. The first Test series in cricket to receive television coverage was the Australian tour of Britain in 1948. Football soon followed; golf and other less 'captive sports' lagged behind, but in 1957 the closing scenes of the Open golf championship were televised for the first time. As this development began to turn a vast audience into armchair critics, bringing personalities in sport into direct confrontation with the spectator, a new challenge was thrown out

473

to the writer. The public began to feel more interested in the player as a personality than in his technique and the run of play. Feature articles, which had hitherto been rare or non-existent, began to make regular appearances; sports journalism was entering the age of the 'quote'.

Darwin, in one of his last visits to an Open championship, in 1951, gave a good example of changing attitudes. After Max Faulkner's victory the press interviewed him in a room. Darwin was present but after a few minutes started to leave the room and was heard to mutter that what his readers wanted to know was not what Faulkner thought of his victory but what Darwin thought of Faulkner. Darwin was succeeded in 1953 by Peter Ryde, who also was not only a graceful writer on that sport but also the author of many of the most engaging fourth leaders in the post-Darwin era.

Darwin's remark sums up the changing attitude towards sports writing. It was a wide difference but one that a few managed to cross with seeming effortlessness. Green provided an outstanding example in a career on *The Times* which extended over forty years. His writing had seemed well suited to the comparatively benign atmosphere of before the war. His overall knowledge of games was such that he was at one time or another cricket, football, and tennis correspondent. He even had a brief spell as sports editor after the sudden death of Oliver Beaumont who had watched over sport during the war and then taken it into a new era, as gentle and as dedicated as anyone who ever held the post.

Before him R. C. 'Bob' Lyle had also briefly filled the post and had managed at the same time to indulge his real love by carrying on as racing correspondent. But in those days the pace was slower; the telephone rang less often, and the first edition did not go to press till 11.30. What Green saw ahead of him in 1954 when he was offered the job was an increasing amount of administrative work, and the lure of the outdoors proved too strong. He was succeeded by John Hennessy, promoted from the sub-editorial desk, sufficiently robust and resolute to withstand the pressures of the editorial chair for twenty years.

Green had taken over the duties of football correspondent in 1946, and his first engagement on the Continent came four years later when he was sent to Rome to cover a match. This engagement was followed by another in Switzerland, and searching inquiries were made into the total cost of the two-week trip. It amounted to £151 and since subsequent trips were sanctioned at increasing cost, it must have been considered money well spent. Indeed it was. His style of writing was individual, exploring sometimes the realms of fantasy to a degree that would have been less easily tolerated if he had not shown such a grasp of the subject. Like Darwin, though in different ways which included a strong mixture of metaphors, he broke down the barriers of anonymity which, though increasingly under review, still prevailed.

Television was responsible, unwittingly, for the growth of a new hazard for writers: evening starting-times made possible by the advent of flood-lighting. Not every sport was amenable to such treatment but football was an exception. Ad-libbing of material late at night was always held to be an occupational hazard for a boxing correspondent, as portrayed by ringside commentaries on fights in Hollywood films. Neil Allen, who was appointed to the post in succession to O. L. 'Ginger' Owen, was surely at the age of 22 one of the youngest sporting appointments; about three-quarters of the fights he covered were reported 'off the cuff' late at night. But in football this was a new hazard and one that had to be frequently faced, especially in connexion with the European Cup. Green cleared that hurdle undismayed, relaying from a darkened arena in some Balkan capital by means of a borrowed telephone, and wearing perhaps the notorious shaggy-dog coat presented to him by a hotel manager in Sofia, a thousand-word report backed only by a half-page of notes.

Communications were improving; the days of the cabled message were fading although the Melbourne Olympics of 1956, the first of six covered by Allen in his capacity as athletics correspondent, was sent entirely by cable; the telephone was not once used. Also fading was the train news parcel, although the skating correspondent in

1959, Dennis Bird, remembers the difficulty he had in getting the guard to accept his copy at Nottingham, sent overnight on a Saturday because the paper at that time did not accept phoned copy on a Sunday.

APPENDIX F

'IT *IS* A MORAL ISSUE'

Text of the leading article by Haley, June 11 1963.

WHETHER the fact that Mr. Profumo resigned early in the Whitsun recess was fortuitous or not it was fortunate for the Government. Eleven days were interposed before the reassembling of Parliament. That is a lot of time to give so able a politician as Mr. Macmillan. He can at any rate seek to come to terms with his own party before he is set upon by the Opposition. How far can he do this? Much will depend on how many Conservative MPs are dismayed by the event itself and the state of affairs revealed, and how many are angry primarily because of its effect on the party's already decaying fortunes. The will to stay in office is strong. It is part of the fervour of politics to believe that almost anything is more tolerable than to see the other side in power. Short of that, the number of future Crown Princes who would welcome Mr. Butler's taking over must be small. At sixty he would be more than a stopgap. The instinct for self-preservation, for the retention of both place and potentialities, will be strong.

Such calculations are not cynical. They are realistic. They reflect the mood of a large section of the public that ought to know better. Mr. Harold Wilson also is a shrewd politician and his immediate reaction was to stress that Labour's concern was about security, not about morals. (It will be interesting to see how he can deploy his attack on the Government's security arrangements without the question of Mr. Profumo's morals coming in.) Everyone has been so busy assuring the public that the affair is not one of morals, that it is time to assert that it is. Morals have been discounted too long. A judge may be justified in reminding a jury 'This is not a court of morals'. The same exemption cannot be allowed public opinion, without rot setting in and all standards suffering in the long run. The British are not by and large an immoral nation but through their pathetic fear of being called smug they make themselves out to be one.

No one would wish the security aspects of the matter to be ignored. There is no danger of this. Many questions have already been aired about it in public and they touch the Prime Minister both as the Minister ultimately responsible for the security services and as the head of an administration the conduct of one of whose members has been questioned. Yesterday it was revealed that before he went on his holiday, and before the House rose, Mr. Macmillan asked the Lord Chancellor to conduct an inquiry into the security side of the affair. (Why this should have been kept secret for five days after the announcement of Mr. Profumo's resignation is yet another thing to be explained.) The outcome must at latest be told to the House of Commons in next Monday's debate. Beforehand the point must be stressed that even if the Prime Minister confirms what has so far been accepted, that there was no security risk, and even if the Opposition force a vote and for one reason or another the Government gets its usual majority, that will not be the end of the business. For the Conservative Party – and, it is to be hoped, for the nation – things can never be quite the same again.

The hope must be that they will become better. There is plenty of room for this. However multifarious and ingenious the causes to which the Conservative Central

Office ascribe the desperate state of the party's present fortunes as shown by the opinion polls, the overriding reason is that eleven years of Conservative rule have brought the nation psychologically and spiritually to a low ebb. The Conservatives came to power a few months before the present reign opened. They have been in office so far throughout the whole of it. The ardent hopes and eager expectations that attended its beginning have been belied. They gibed at austerity, and in all truth the British people deserved some easement after their historic and heroic exertions, although history is never a nicely balanced business of rewards and penalties. They declared they had the right road for Britain. They would set the people free. Change, they declared, was their ally. Nothing else, they seemed later to think, mattered, compared with the assertion that the nation had never had it so good. Today they are faced with a flagging economy, an uncertain future, and the end of the illusion that Britain's greatness could be measured by the so-called independence of its so-called deterrent. All this may seem far from Mr. Profumo, but his admissions could be the last straw. It remains strange that not a single member of the Government resigned when the affair broke in March and he did not himself resign.

What the Conservatives need now, and what they have needed ever since Churchill was in his heyday, is courage. One of the paradoxes of modern war is that defeat is more likely to restore a nation's fibre than victory. There is no hiding place from the tidal wave of overthrow and disaster. All too dangerously comfortable is the slow, insidious, almost imperceptible but inexorable ebb tide. Appeal after appeal has been made to immediate self-interest. The professional politicians will assert that these have worked. Has not the pendulum been stopped? Have not the Conservatives won three elections in a row? Granting that politics is mainly the pursuit of power, this is not its only purpose. The Prime Minister and his colleagues can cling together and be still there a year hence. They will have to do more than that to justify themselves.

Whether in the next few days some heads fall or none, damage has been done. It may be a caricature for the *Washington Post* to say that 'a picture of widespread decadence beneath the glitter of a large segment of stiff lipped society is emerging'. But the essence of caricature is to exaggerate real traits. There are plenty of earnest and serious men in the Conservative Party who know that all is not well. It is time they put first things first, stopped weighing electoral chances, and returned to the stark truths of an earlier day. Popularity by affluence is about played out, especially when it rests on so insecure a basis. Even if the call had metaphorically to be for 'blood, sweat, and tears' instead of to the fleshpots they might be surprised by the result. The British are always at their best when they are braced.

APPENDIX G

TIMES CHANGE

A personal message from Mr. Gavin Astor to each member of the staff of The Times Publishing Company

FOR five generations of the Walter family, one of Lord Northcliffe and two generations of Astors, THE TIMES has prospered as a small family business. But THE TIMES has now grown into a much larger enterprise, and it has moved into a world of far greater competition and more restrictive legislation.

Years ago THE TIMES could afford to boast of its 'splendid isolation'. But in today's world, isolation spells gradual extinction.

The worthy aim that THE TIMES must not as far as reasonably possible be used for 'personal ambition or commercial profit' – while no doubt quite realistic in the 1920's – was having an inhibiting effect upon the Company's growth in the 1950's and the 1960's. For to be strong and influential, THE TIMES like any other newspaper must be commercially successful. Its name, its history and traditions, and its prestige are not enough to keep it in business. Without profits it can have no prestige.

It was clear even during the middle 'fifties that THE TIMES was entering a period of hard competition as commercial television, instant communications, and mass circulation newspapers increased in influence and attracted an ever larger share of advertizing revenue.

As long ago as 1958, the Board had felt it necessary to ask an independent firm of Chartered Accountants to examine and advise upon the whole financial and administrative composition of The Times Publishing Company which exists to serve THE TIMES. Several ways of re-organizing, developing and expanding the Company's activities, and also of modernizing THE TIMES itself, were suggested by Cooper Brothers' Report. But there was such opposition to the Report in Printing House Square at the time that seven years elapsed before some of its most vital recommendations could be implemented.

In 1958 it was decided to proceed with the rebuilding of Printing House Square for which purpose a fund had already been accumulated and borrowing facilities arranged with Barclays Bank. There was however, an urgent necessity for continuing to maintain minimum gross annual profits of £½m. The Company was successful in achieving these profits until the end of 1961 by which time the July 'Little Budget' of Selwyn Lloyd began to make itself felt.

Percentage of profit to turnover of The Times Publishing Company fell from 10.7% in 1960 to 3.4% in 1965, and percentage of profit to funds employed from 17.3% to 3.8% during the same period. THE TIMES circulation share of the market fell from 14.7% in 1960 to 12.7% in 1965. The number of readers per copy dropped from 4.5 in 1960 to 3.5 in 1965. Home sales gradually dropped from 239,600 in 1960 to 228,300 in 1965.

There is no standing still in newspapers. They either progress or they die. THE TIMES was not only standing still but others were overtaking it. It was becoming imperative to restore the health of the paper; and the best way to do this was to ensure that it was better than any of its competitors so that it would attract readers as well as advertizers.

At last a committee under Sir William Haley's Chairmanship was formed to study modernization, development and expansion. It reported to the Board in May 1965. The changes which it proposed were accepted only if they seemed likely to contribute towards an increased circulation – not as the result of a crash programme, but by a gradual process and continuing operation, and without damaging but rather enriching the character of the paper.

With the appointment in September 1965 of a Chief Executive, and with the improved composition of the Board of Directors the stage was already set for a complete reorganization of the management and of the capital structure of The Times Publishing Company; and by the end of 1965 plans were being formulated for carrying out a more expansive policy to develop the main areas of the Company's activities, to diversify into others, and to stimulate job opportunities, promotion prospects and profit responsibility. Meanwhile a new look for THE TIMES was being designed.

On May 3 1966 the redesigned paper was launched. With its keener selection and sense of news and its more extensive coverage, it broke through many outworn conventions and traditions. It opened the door to items and features of more topical and wide-ranging interests for which there would have been no accommodation before. Sales had risen by 20% at the end of the first six months. But even at 300,000 the circulation still falls short of what it should and could be, and is still below the target which in 1959 the Board intended, after considerable expenditure, should be achieved by the end of 1964.

It was recognized that the successful achievement of the various objectives which were essential for strengthening the political and social influence of THE TIMES, would require an immediate infusion of management and marketing skills, would cost at least £2½m. over the next five years, and would absorb most if not all of the anticipated annual profits until 1970. This extra £2½m. development expenditure would be exclusive of any increased annual operating costs; and indeed the newsprint and wage increases expected in 1967 would alone be likely to absorb the entire trading profit of the Company for next year. It was recognized also that even by 1970 THE TIMES standing alone would be on a vulnerably narrow base, and that it would be necessary to invest still more development capital during the 1970–80 decade.

For some time my own finances have been inextricably interwoven with those of The Times Publishing Company. The situation has been aggravated firstly by recent legislation which added to my family commitments, and secondly by my decision a few years ago to acquire the Walter shares thus giving me virtually 100% control of the Company.

I did this as an act of faith, which I still have, in the continuing and growing prosperity of THE TIMES. I saw myself as a 'bridge' pending such time as the Company was running sufficiently profitably to make the Preference shares marketable, and to attract a partner or partners to share the equity with me. As the sole owner I would be in a strong position from which to negotiate the most advantageous arrangement both for The Times Publishing Company and for my family. But this bridging operation was costing me a lot of money which I was only able to provide by heavy borrowing. This in itself was an expensive operation and was rapidly eroding my liquid capital.

How much longer was the 'bridge' going to be? There was no sign of the end of it; and I could not wait much longer.

I had already taken what steps I could to try and protect The Times Publishing Company from the impact of estate duties; but my financial advizers still showed that the property could not possibly be retained in the family in the event of my untimely death.

It was becoming more and more urgent for THE TIMES and for my family to extricate themselves from the increasingly vulnerable financial entanglement in which they both found themselves.

Three courses seemed to be open to me:–

a to continue in the honour and privilege of sole ownership while THE TIMES remains vulnerable to a forced sale at any moment and gradually declines and wilts through lack of development capital;
b to sell out completely;
c to seek a suitable partnership.

Following discussions during the summer between myself, my Father and my colleagues on the Board, it was agreed that under all the circumstances the ownership of THE TIMES newspaper and of the Company should be reconstituted on favourable terms now rather than that they should continue to be exposed to the contingent liability of estate duties on my death, and to the uncertainty and risk of a forced sale at any moment for the highest price obtainable, perhaps to an undesirable purchaser. Such a prospect could not possibly be in the best long term interests of THE TIMES as a 'National Institution', or of the Staff who serve it. The situation was one which had to be tolerated until wholly satisfactory alternatives could be found, and it would be irresponsible of me not to recognize this fact and prepare to meet it.

Accordingly I reached the conclusion in the summer of 1966, and reported to the Board of The Times Publishing Company that I must seek a partnership which would:
a consolidate the financial strength of The Times Publishing Company;
b eliminate so far as possible the continuing and crippling vulnerability to THE TIMES of death duty liabilities;
c enhance the position of THE TIMES as one of the most authoritative and influential newspapers in the world;
d maintain the principles and traditions for which THE TIMES has so long stood;
e protect the welfare of the staff and the rights of the Pensioners;
f preserve the mutual goodwill and interdependence between THE TIMES and THE OBSERVER;
g provide liquidity to the unrealizable assets of the Astor Estate at present locked up in The Times Publishing Company.

A most ingenious scheme has been worked out which should achieve all of these objectives. It will take about ten years before the whole operation is finally completed, and apart from minor adjustments and the repayment of preference shares I will not receive any very substantial cash repayment. My present 98% interest in THE TIMES will simply become a 15% share of an immensely richer business. But this 15% participation will be put into the control of a perpetuating charitable trust. I am happy to think however that as Life President of the new Company I shall be able to maintain a close link with Printing House Square.

There has been some speculation on the price which Printing House Square might fetch as a building. Such speculation is idle. To render THE TIMES homeless by a sale of the building would have destroyed THE TIMES: and the building was an essential part of the dowry without which the marriage necessary to save THE TIMES would not have been possible.

Some time after the announcement that THE TIMES and the SUNDAY TIMES proposed to merge into a new joint newspaper Company, other people came forward with the idea that they could make a rival bid. But of course THE TIMES was not up for auction. Indeed this was the very thing which we were striving to avoid and prevent.

I am intensely proud of my inheritance and inevitably I am sorry to see the end of a long era in the history of THE TIMES. It is a unique property. But to be the private owner of a 'National Institution', whose editor is answerable only to non-executive proprietors and whose General Manager is answerable to a non-executive Chairman and Board, and which is inhibited in its commercial enterprise by voluntary and statutory restrictions, is an anachronism today. The new scheme recognizes that the age when proprietors could successfully run their newspapers as a sideline is fading into an age where the survival and prosperity of newspapers depend upon brilliant commercial and professional management.

It has been well said that a man can have influence without power, or power without

480

security. I hope I may have had some influence. Rightly or wrongly I have never sought power. As Proprietor and non-executive Chairman I have been able to evolve over the years a happy working relationship and a mutual confidence between myself and the Editor and the General Manager. Yet I have come to realize that to carry the entire financial risk as Proprietor no less than the full legal responsibility as Chairman for the success or failure of the Company, without also carrying executive power, is not a satisfactory situation.

So now the merger of THE TIMES and the SUNDAY TIMES into a new company called Times Newspapers Ltd. will concentrate the responsibility and the power where it should be – with the Board.

The scheme provides for the appointment of a new independent Editor of THE TIMES while retaining the wisdom and experience of Sir William Haley as Chairman of the new joint Company for a period of three years. By that time the traditional standards and principles of THE TIMES should have been firmly incorporated with those of the SUNDAY TIMES.

No doubt commercial considerations will play a greater part in running THE TIMES than they have done in the past. But it will continue to be essential to the quality and character of THE TIMES that editorial comment and the treatment of news shall not be inspired by personal, political, or commercial pressure. This means that editors must continue to be free to pursue an honestly considered policy – even a policy which could put the paper at commercial risk, perhaps by supporting the unpopular side in some great national controversy.

Both I and Lord Thomson and Lord Thomson's son realize very well that there is something much more important at stake than the financial security of these two great newspapers. The editorial independence of THE TIMES and of the SUNDAY TIMES must go on.

With Sir William Haley as the first Chairman of the new well balanced Board, with Mr. Denis Hamilton as Editor-in-Chief, with two independent editors yet to be appointed, and with Lord Thomson's assurance that the full resources of the Thomson Organisation will be available to the new joint newspaper Company, it would seem that THE TIMES and the SUNDAY TIMES are heading for a bright future.

May they prosper and flourish!

Gavin Astor

December 1966

APPENDIX H

OBITUARY NOTICES

I N March 5 1976 *The Times Literary Supplement* published a long review by Alan Bell of a large volume containing selections from obituary notices which had appeared in *The Times* in the years 1961 to 1970. Some passages from the review, indicating the breadth and quality of the obituaries, are given here:

Some 1,500 obituary notices have been chosen, occupying 868 three-column pages of ample size. The final eighty-one pages contain a full index of all the obituaries, short notices and tributes which appeared in the decade. Sated by the main text (which between T and V had an air of the Huntingdonshire cabmen about it, though it picked up later), I have not given the index any detailed attention. It would be possible to debate individual inclusions endlessly, but one-and-a-third million words provide a sufficiently representative coverage of the main obituaries published.

These do not of course represent *The Times* obituaries as a whole, where the peculiarly naive short accounts of lesser industrialists or Masters of Fox Hounds give an occasional charm to the Court page of a morning. There are none of these tributes here in which 'a friend writes', sometimes to add major facts or striking indications of character, but often taking refuge in quotations like 'he was a very parfit gentil knight' which recall the formularies of doggerel available for In Memoriam notices in provincial newspaper offices. And did I not see something beginning 'His many friends will be aggrieved to learn of the death of . . .' not long ago, about the time that someone was reported in *The Times* as saying at his inquest that the late Dominic Elwes 'like many extroverts had a depressing [for depressive] side to his character'? Sir Robert Lusty wrote recently of Walter Hutchinson, the publisher, that 'when he died, he was accorded one of the harshest obituaries ever to appear in *The Bookseller*, and no word arrived from any source to deny its truth'. It was not so with Sir Denys Lowson, who was treated to some harsh but just strictures in *The Times* last year, after which one counted the days before a supplementary tribute appeared. 'The evil', a friend inevitably concluded his remonstrance, 'that men do lives after them; the good is oft interred with their bones.'

The Times obituaries have a peculiar mystique and a well-deserved authority. Comparison with death notices in some other papers, compounded out of standard reference books and the night-editor's memory (there are a few of these here too, assembled from cuttings files when *The Times* was taken short) shows the generally high standard. Anonymity is very carefully preserved, but where authorship becomes known one can usually admire the enterprise which has commissioned a notice for stock from such an appropriate hand. Even the knowledge that William Plomer wrote parts of his own obituary (the introduction to his *Autobiography* has some passages interesting to those who preserved the cutting) displays a curious suitability. The stock of material awaiting publication is apparently secure against interference by the living: rumours that Stanley Morison influenced – perhaps even wrote – his own while in a position of eminence at Printing House Square are, on investigation, quite unfounded. Anonymity is sometimes in jeopardy: the paper once found itself understocked with dons and too many were commissioned – counter-commissioned – at once. There was a good deal of contrived conversation in the United University Club, which rustled to the sounds of furtive note-taking on prep schools and wives' maiden names as the answers came from both sides of the dinner tables.

Reading so many obituaries in a month is highly instructive, partly for a wealth of diverting fact: the conferment on (Bishop) Askwith of The Stall of Grantham Borealis in Sarum Cathedral, we learn, 'seemed to indicate that he was destined to high preferment'; the wrestler George Hackenschmidt's publishing in retirement *Man and Cosmic Antagonism to Mind and Spirit*; or the pianist Western Brother ending his life 'a far cry from the glamorous microphone or stage years – he took over a sweet and tobacco kiosk at Weybridge station'. More importantly, an overwhelming evenness of tone can be detected. I often recalled Charles Augustus Fortescue: 'In public life, he always tried/to take a judgment broad and wide;/in private none was more than he/renowned for quiet courtesy./He rose at once in his career,/and long before his fortieth year/had wedded Fifi, only child/of Bunyan first Lord Alberfylde.' Seen time and again, even the usual phrases about marriage begin to look odd. 'There were no children of the marriage' comes to provoke suspicions of many elsewhere; used of bishops, the thought is an entertaining one. Other marriages mentioned in passing – T. S. Eliot's first, Somerset Maugham's, Augustus John's ('John was twice married', *tout court*, in a notice published at a very low point in his reputation) – surely merited a sentence or two of explanation.

Many conventions of necrological form and style have of course to be observed in preparing the obituaries. Conventions of tone are also necessary when publication must take place while the funeral meats are baking – sometimes, indeed, while the inquest is preparing. Assessments of character which show a proper reserve at the time of death may look pusillanimous when seen collectively a decade or two later. Full-blooded opinions are all the more welcome, particularly when they are stylishly conveyed – for example, Air Chief Marshal Sir Philip Joubert, who 'was never hampered by the cares of the introvert; his life was full and he knew his own mind', or Admiral Sir Michael Le Fanu who was 'a sailor's sailor who fought pedantry and protocol and took pride in his victory over both'. It is refreshing to read of H. G. Bartholomew of the *Daily Mirror* that he was

> volatile in temperament and audacious in action. If his interests were not cultured, he lacked neither ideas nor the ruthlessness to put them into effect. If he was not an easy man to work with, he had the more priceless asset of energy, and energy untrammelled by inhibitions.

Those two doubtful *ifs* can be forgiven for the near-frankness of the judgment.

Antithesis is one of the conventions of the obituarist's art of the *suggestio veri*, and not merely in the vague and paradoxical attempt at (for example) E. M. W. Tillyard's character – 'As a man he was at once frank and reserved, simple and subtle.' There is, it seems, a rule of the *but*. Sir Arthur Dixon, a Home Office eminence, was 'a shy man; this quality at times gave him an appearance of aloofness, perhaps on occasion of rudeness. He was a difficult man to get to know intimately. But those who worked with him . . .'. The *but* is characteristic particularly of the notices of officials, though industrialists are also accorded it: Hardie of the Iron and Steel Corporation 'was known as a just but severe employer' (perhaps 'severe but just' might have been meant). Randolph Churchill merits a similar *yet*: 'Yet, however irritating, or, in certain circumstances despicable, he might appear, his intimates knew that underneath he was a sensitive, perceptive person, easily wounded, very unsure of himself, and, ultimately, lovable and affectionate.' (A magnanimous tribute, that, obviously by a friend who had much to forgive.)

One higher than *but* in the scale of epicedian hesitancy is *nevertheless*, as achieved by the distinguished public servant Sir James Grigg:

> A man of brilliant gifts, of outstanding intellectual attainments, and of strong

opinion, which he was fearless in expressing, he was not always patient of minds slower than his own. In character tenacious and argumentative, with a reserved and slightly brusque manner, he was nevertheless capable of forming deep and enduring attachments . . .

Attempts at balanced assessment are perhaps at their best when uncluttered with conjunctions, freely admitting both sides of a character – as with Dame Ivy Compton-Burnett:

Those who loved her – and they were many – must have been stupid or self-satisfied indeed if they were quite without fear of this acute observer, this high-minded judge of human behaviour; but she was as sensitive as she was acute, and her mercy was of the quality required by that Christianity in which she did not believe.

That is excellent, with just the right amount of astringency. But it is only one remove from the housemasterly sententiousness which can write of Brendan Behan: 'He exceeded his own ideal of mediocrity not through self-indulgence or through his conversation, which was sometimes no more than obstreperous or silly, but through his writing.' The landlord of The Gates of Paradise would look askance at a new customer with such an end-of-term report. Dispraise must be carefully controlled, but when kept in hand – as in the two columns of cumulative dismissal of John Steinbeck – it can be critically valuable in an obituary. Praise is even more difficult to handle; there is but a very thin line between elegy and eulogy. It may be personally true to write of Sir John Cockcroft (his entry is out of alphabetical order) that 'he was a fine scientist, one of the most reliable and upright human beings of his time, and a man of absolute good will. As a friend he was like a rock', but such lavishness puts the reader too much on his guard. . . .

The politicians are seen at their best when there are questions to be asked. Attlee's obituarist begins 'When the importance of the social revolution and the smoothness with which it was effected are set beside the surface qualities of the man who presided over it, there emerges the paradox that lurks in all assessments of his statesmanship'. Although he is nowhere near explaining the paradox at the end of the essay, it is much improved by the questioning tone. Iain Macleod's notice also asks a number of questions ('with this record of acting from conviction it must seem surprising that he earned a reputation for being devious', etc), and it successfully juggles general praises and particular blames to provide an account which might have been less satisfactory if the career had been completed with every question answered, every failing demonstrated and every hope fulfilled.

Generally speaking, however, there is little in the political parts of this volume to justify Asquith's aphorism reported by Bruce Lockhart in 1930 that 'the object of biography is to increase self-confidence; the object of obituary notices is to increase caution'.

CHRONOLOGY

1966 **September 30**
Announcement of formation of new company, 'Times
Newspapers Limited', which was to own and publish *The
Times* and *The Sunday Times*, the latter already owned by
Lord Thomson. Gavin Astor – Life President, Sir William
Haley – Chairman, Kenneth Thomson – Vice Chairman and
Denis Hamilton – Editor-in-Chief and Chairman of Executive
Committee, plus four independent national directors.

December 21
Monopolies Commission published report on the proposed
merger of *The Times* and *The Sunday Times*.

1967 **January 1**
Times Newspapers Limited takes control.

January 12
William Rees-Mogg appointed editor; Iverach McDonald
becomes associate editor.

January 13
Last fourth 'light' leader published.

January 23
By-lines begin to be used by principal staff correspondents.

April 11
Pages restyled and number of type columns increased from
seven to eight.
'Personal column' (classified advertisements) moved inside
from back page.
Business news started as separate section.

July 15
First pre-printed colour pages appear in *The Times*.

October 14
Saturday Review first appears, separate from main paper.

The Times Atlas of the World, Comprehensive Edition, first published.

December 31
Haley leaves to join *Encyclopaedia Britannica*.

1968 **January 1**
'One Hundred Years Ago' ceases and 'Twenty-five Years Ago' begins.

1969 **January 8**
First colour feature in *The Times*, Apollo 8 mission.

December 31
Royal edition of *The Times* (printed on special paper) ceases.

1970 **June 29**
Agreement between Times Newspapers Limited and Thomson Scottish Associates Limited whereby latter to publish former, profits and losses accruing to them.

July 10
The Times, first national newspaper to print from pages set by photosetter.

December 23
Business News becomes part of main paper.

1971 **January 1**
Denis Hamilton appointed Chairman TNL.
M. J. 'Duke' Hussey appointed Chief Executive/Managing Director.

October 15
Higher Educational Supplement begins.

1972 **1972**
Tutankhamun exhibition at British Museum sponsored by Times Newspapers.

October 9
Europa typeface introduced.

1973 **October 2**
Monthly survey 'Europa', an economic and business monthly newspaper, begins in conjunction with *Le Monde*, *Die Welt*, and *La Stampa*.

1974   **June 7**
Anonymity in *Times Literary Supplement* abandoned.

June 24
The Times moves from Printing House Square, Queen
Victoria Street to Gray's Inn Road.

1977   **May 11**
Special 50,000th issue.

1978   **September 11**
The Times Atlas of World History published.

November 30
Last issue of *The Times* before suspension of publication.

1979   **November 12**
The Times resumes publication.

1980   **July 1**
James Evans appointed Chairman TNL (resigned February 13
1981).

October 22
The Times is offered for sale.

1981   **February 13**
Ownership of *The Times* passes to Rupert Murdoch's News
International.

March 9
Harold Evans appointed editor of *The Times*.

June 2
The Times Information Service starts on back page.

July 30
The Times features royal wedding in colour.

1982   **March 15**
Harold Evans resigns as editor of *The Times*.

March 18
Charles Douglas-Home appointed editor of *The Times*.

May 3
The Times becomes the first national newspaper to be set
entirely by photocomposition.

August 30
Times Europa typeface replaced by Times Roman, a version
of the Times New Roman typeface designed by Stanley
Morison for *The Times* in 1932.

1983 **February 21**
First concise crossword appears.

Average daily sale of *The Times* year by year:
1966	281,817
1967	349,168
1968	408,300
1969	431,721
1970	388,406
1971	339,231
1972	340,540
1973	344,840
1974	345,399
1975	318,565
1976	309,560
1977	298,443
1978	295,864
1980	297,392
1981	289,987
1982	303,237
1983	352,804

BIBLIOGRAPHY

As for Volume IV a principal source of material for this volume of the *History* has been the archives of *The Times* (T.T.A.) now preserved in The Times Building in Grays Inn Road, London.

The files of *The Times* and of its supplements, particularly *The Times Literary Supplement* and *The Times Educational Supplement*, have of course been continuously consulted, as have all the paper's special publications in pamphlet form.

Much use has also been made of the diaries of Geoffrey Dawson (GDD) and Robin Barrington-Ward (B-WD) as well as those of A. L. Kennedy and Sir Basil Liddell Hart.

Many private memoranda to the author from past and present members of the staff have been used and will now be added to the archives.

The Public Record Office has been invaluable as a source. Papers of especial relevance are:
Churchill Papers 3/355/3 T 595/4
　　　　　　　　3/355/3 T 625/4
　　　　　　　　3/355/3 M 339/4
　　　　　　　　3/355/3 60
PREM 66/4, folios 472, 473, 473a.
Foreign Office Papers U 8510/5559/70, folios 43–45.
　　Principal government publications referred to are:
Documents on British Foreign Policy, Third Series. Volume II, 1938. London 1949.
Royal Commission on the Press 1947–1949. Cmd. 7700.
Report of the Broadcasting Committee 1949. Cmd. 8116.
White Paper. Broadcasting: Memorandum on the Report of the Broadcasting Committee 1949. Cmd. 8550.
White Paper. Broadcasting: Memorandum on Television Policy 1953. Cmd. 9005.
Report of the Royal Commission on the Press 1961–1962. Cmd. 1811.
Report of the Committee on Higher Education 1963. Cmd. 2154.
The Monopolies Commission: The Times Newspaper and The Sunday Times

Newspaper. A report on the proposed transfer to a newspaper proprietor. London HMSO 1966.

Final Report of the Royal Commission on the Press 1977. Cmd. 6810.

Avon, Earl of. *The Eden Memoirs*: Volume 1. *Facing the Dictators*, London 1962. Volume 2. *The Reckoning*, London 1965. Volume 3. *Full Circle*, London 1960.

Barker, Nicolas. *Stanley Morison*, London 1972.

Barman, Thomas. *Diplomatic Correspondent*, London 1968.

Beloff, Max and Peele, Gillian. *The Government of the United Kingdom: Political Authority in a Changing Society*, London 1980.

Birkenhead, Earl of. *Life of Lord Halifax*, London 1965.

Bullock, Alan. *The Life and Times of Ernest Bevin*: Volume 2. *1940–1945*, London 1967. Volume 3. *Foreign Secretary 1945–1951*, London 1983.

Butler, Lord. *The Art of the Possible*, London 1971.

Butler, J. R. M. *Lord Lothian*, London 1960.

Cadogan, Sir Alexander. *The Diaries of Sir Alexander Cadogan*, edited by David Dilks, London 1971.

Calvocaressi, Peter and Wint, Guy. *Total War: Causes and Courses of the Second World War*, London 1972.

Churchill, Winston Spencer. *The Second World War*. Six volumes, London 1948–1954.

Coote, Sir Colin. *Editorial*, London 1965.

Crossman, Richard. *The Diaries of a Cabinet Minister*. Volume 1. *Minister of Housing 1964–66*, London 1975.

Dayan, Moshe. *Story of my Life*, London 1975.

Deakin, Nicholas. *Colour, Citizenship and British Society*, London 1970.

Dilks, David (Editor). *Retreat from Power: Studies in Britain's Foreign Policy of the Twentieth Century*. Volume 2. *After 1939*, London 1981.

Drogheda, Earl of. *Double Harness*, London 1978.

Evans, Harold. *Good Times, Bad Times*, London 1982.

Foot, Michael. *Aneurin Bevan 1945–1960*, London 1973. *Debts of Honour*, London 1980.

Gannon, Franklin Reid. *The British Press and Germany 1936–1939*, Oxford 1971.

Gilbert, Martin. *Winston S. Churchill*. Volume V, 1922–1939, London 1976.

Harris, Kenneth. *Attlee*, London 1982.

Harvey, Oliver. *The Diplomatic Diaries of Oliver Harvey, 1937–1940*. Edited by John Harvey, London 1970. *The War Diaries of Oliver Harvey*, London 1978.

Haslam, Jonathan. *The Soviet Union and the Czechoslovakian Crisis of 1938. Journal of Contemporary History:* Volume 14, London and Beverley Hills 1979.

Heren, Louis. *Growing up on The Times*, London 1978.

Home, Lord. *The Way the Wind Blows*, London 1976.

Hutchinson, George. *The Last Edwardian at No. 10: An Impression of Harold Macmillan*, London 1980.

Ismay, Lord. *Memoirs of General the Lord Ismay*, London 1960.

Jacobs, Eric. *Stop Press*, London 1980.

Jenkins, Simon. *Newspapers: The Power and the Money*, London 1979.

Khrushchev, Nikita Sergeyevich. *Khrushchev Remembers*: Volume I, London 1971. Volume II, London 1974.

Kilmuir, Lord. *Political Adventure*, London 1964.

King, Cecil. *The Cecil King Diary, 1965–1970*, London 1972.

Kirkman, William P. *Unscrambling an Empire*, London 1966.

Kissinger, Henry. *The White House Years*, London 1979.

Lewin, Ronald. *The Chief: Field Marshal Lord Wavell, Commander-in-Chief and Viceroy, 1939–1947*, London 1980.

Liddell Hart, Sir Basil H. *History of the Second World War*, London 1970. (Pan Books Edition 1973.) *Memoirs*: Volumes I and II, London 1965.

Lloyd, Selwyn. *Suez 1956*, London 1978.

Lloyd, T. O. *Empire to Welfare State: English History 1906–1976*, Oxford (second edition) 1979.

McDonald, Iverach. *A Man of the Times*, London 1976.

McLachlan, Donald. *In the Chair: Barrington-Ward of The Times, 1927–1948*, London 1971.

Macmillan, Harold. *Memoirs* (six volumes): *Winds of Change*, London 1961. *The Blast of War*, 1967. *Tides of Fortune*, 1969. *Riding the Storm*, 1971. *Pointing the Way*, 1972. *At the End of the Day*, 1973.

Margach, James. *The Abuse of Power*, London 1978.

Marwick, Arthur. *The Explosion of British Society, 1914–1970*, London 1971.

Mastny, Vojtech. *Russia's Road to the Cold War: Diplomacy, Warfare and the Politics of Communism, 1941–1945*, New York 1979.

Middlemas, Keith. *Diplomacy of Illusion: The British Government and Germany, 1937–1939*, London 1972.

Moran, Lord. *Winston Churchill, The Struggle for Survival, 1940–65*, London 1966.

Nutting, Anthony. *No End of a Lesson: The Story of Suez*, London 1967.

O'Neill, Robert J. *The Germany Army and the Nazi Party, 1933–39*, London 1968.

Pineau, Christian. *1956 Suez*, Paris 1976.

Pringle, John Douglas. *Have Pen: Will Travel*, London 1973.

Reith, Lord. *The Reith Diaries*. Edited by Charles Stuart, London 1975.

Robbins, Keith. *Munich 1938*, London 1968.

Rowse, A. L. *All Souls and Appeasement*, London 1961.

Seymour-Ure, Colin. *The Press, Politics and the Public*, London 1968. *The Political Impact of Mass Media*, London 1974.

Sked, Alan and Cook, Chris. *Post War Britain: A Political History*, London 1979.

Soviet Ministry of Foreign Affairs. *Stalin's Correspondence with Churchill, Attlee, Roosevelt and Truman, 1941–45*, Moscow 1957. London 1958.

Stronge, Brigadier, H. C. T. (Military attache in Czechoslovakia and Yugoslavia 1936–38.) *Personal Memorandum on the morale and readiness for war of the Czechoslovak army in September 1938*, Bodleian Library, Oxford; and T.T.A.

Taylor, A. J. P. *English History 1914–1945. (The Oxford History of England.)* Oxford 1965.

Thomas, Hugh. *The Suez Affair*, London 1967.

Thomson of Fleet, Lord. *After I was Sixty*, London 1967.

Van Creveld, Martin. *Hitler's Invasion of Russia: The Balkan Clue*, Cambridge 1974.

Whale, John. *The Politics of the Media*, London 1977.

Williams, Philip M. *Hugh Gaitskell: A Political Biography*, London 1979.

Wilson, Harold. *The Labour Government, 1964–1970*, London 1971.

Woods, Oliver and Bishop, James. *The Story of The Times*, London 1983.

Wrench, John Evelyn. *Geoffrey Dawson and his Times*, London 1955.

Young, Kenneth. *Sir Alec Douglas-Home*, London 1970.

ACKNOWLEDGMENTS

THE author of this volume of the *History* has been especially fortunate in the help which he was given throughout seven years of work. Earlier volumes had to depend almost entirely on documentary evidence; only towards the end of Volume IV could the historians draw upon the recollections of some men and women who were still living at the time. For the present volume documentary evidence has been available even more abundantly and it has been extensively drawn upon, but the outstanding good fortune has come from the happy chance that very many men and women who were concerned in *The Times* during the years 1939–1966 were still alive when the volume was being prepared. All of them who were approached responded with detailed memoranda and letters or with the offer of personal meetings at which memories could be shared and information could be given. The volume can therefore depend more substantially than the earlier ones on direct recollections, subsequently checked by the archival records.

Because such personal assistance provided the happiest and in several ways the most rewarding contribution to the work it may be acknowledged first. The most sincere thanks go to:

The second Lord Astor of Hever, who had a key position for many years as chief proprietor and chairman of Times Newspapers Limited until 1966. He spoke freely and gave valuable written evidence.

His brother Hugh Astor, deputy chairman of the company. He was as helpful as his brother both on paper and in talk.

Sir William Haley, editor of *The Times* 1952–1966 and chairman of Times Newspapers Limited from 1966 to 1968. During days of talk in Jersey he threw light on many shadowy problems and gave the acute assessment of events that only he could give.

Lord Keith of Castleacre, director of The Times Publishing Company, whose expert advice was particularly useful in the writing and

493

correcting of the chapters on the sale of *The Times* in 1966. He was generous in providing documentation which clarified the negotiations at that time.

Sir George Pope, general manager of The Times Publishing Company 1965–67 and director of Times Newspapers Limited 1967–76.

Laurence Irving, director 1946–62.

Sir Denis Hamilton, chairman and editor-in-chief of Times Newspapers until 1981. He authorised the launching of this volume and, out of his deep knowledge of newspapers in general and *The Times* in particular, gave constant encouragement and salutary advice.

Lord Drogheda was most helpful in describing how the 1966 negotiations looked to him in his high position at the *Financial Times*.

David Astor was no less generous with help and advice on *The Times's* long and close relations with his own newspaper, the *Observer*.

D. C. Watt, Stevenson Professor of International History at the London School of Economics, read the whole typescript. His comments were sometimes corrective and always helpful.

Kenneth Kirkwood, Rhodes Professor of Race Relations in Oxford, provided useful comments on Chapter XIV.

Conversations with Michael Howard, Regius Professor of Modern History at Oxford, especially on the Munich period, were stimulating and profitable.

Thanks go no less warmly for similar help from very many of the author's former colleagues, among them:

The late Donald Tyerman, assistant editor 1944–55 and thereafter editor of the *Economist* 1956–65.

Maurice Green, assistant editor 1953–61 and thereafter editor of the *Daily Telegraph*, 1964–74, who guided me through several of the economic passages.

E. C. Hodgkin, leader writer, foreign editor, deputy editor and later associate editor, who helped in many ways over the years, revised the text, and prepared it for the publisher. The debt to him is very great.

Louis Heren, correspondent in many places including Washington, later deputy editor, and later still associate editor.

William Clarke, financial and industrial editor, and later director general of committee on invisible exports, to whom this volume owes much, particularly in Chapters XVIII and XX.

Lord Chalfont who as Alun Gwynne Jones was defence correspondent 1961–64 and became minister of state in the Foreign and Commonwealth Office.

Richard Harris, leader writer on Asian affairs.

John Grant, defence correspondent before Alun Gwynne Jones and then home editor, managing editor, and finally deputy editor.

Professor François Lafitte, home leader writer 1943–59, who provided much information and comment on the newspaper's social policies after the Second World War.

Arthur Crook, editor of *The Times Literary Supplement* 1959–74, who supplied relevant passages and much excellent comment.

Walter James, editor of *The Times Educational Supplement* 1952–69, who also provided relevant passages and specialised advice.

Miss Enid Knowles, principal secretary to Sir William Haley and executive assistant to Sir Denis Hamilton.

Gerald Norman, correspondent in Paris and then foreign news editor.

Donald Holmes, night editor.

Geoffrey Woolley, correspondence editor.

Colin Watson, obituaries editor.

John Lawrence, in charge of the arts pages.

Peter Ryde, sports editor.

James Holburn, foreign correspondent and diplomatic correspondent before becoming editor of the *Glasgow Herald*.

James Bishop, foreign news editor and features editor before transferring to be editor of the *Illustrated London News*.

A. M. Rendel, diplomatic correspondent throughout much of the period under review.

Robert Cooper, foreign correspondent, ending in Washington and Paris.

Sir Ronald Preston, correspondent in central and eastern Europe and in the Far East.

Mrs. Dessa Trevisan, expert on east European affairs.

William MacLeod, company secretary, Times Newspapers Limited.

Jack Lonsdale, head of the intelligence department of *The Times*, who gave instant and generous help during the work on the volume as he always did in the years when the author was a staff colleague. Nor should the pioneering work, in the intelligence department and archives, of his predecessor J. S. Maywood, a member of the staff for nearly 70 years, be forgotten.

Reginald Easthope, who was archivist of *The Times* for some years after being chief home sub-editor on the paper and editor of the *Weekly Review*, and who made many valuable suggestions from his knowledge of the paper's history.

Gordon Phillips, archivist and researcher of *The Times*, to whom the most grateful thanks were due – and expressed – every day during much of the work on the volume. His combination of zeal and scholarly care, his ability to handle large stacks of paper while still attending to important detail was of invaluable and constant help. Without him the writing of the volume would have been infinitely harder than it was. Many thanks also are due to Anne Piggott, his no less zealous successor as archivist.

Barry Winkleman, Managing Director of Times Books.

Ailsa Hudson and Robert Allen of Times Books, who gave much help in the preparation of the text for the printer.

Barbara James, who prepared the index.

In general, it may be said that where no footnote reference is given to any statement of fact in this volume the statement is made either out of the author's own knowledge or as the result of talks with former colleagues. Sometimes such talks are directly attributed, sometimes (for various reasons) not.

When help from former colleagues is cited it is right to mention with gratitude the notes which were left by the late Patrick Ryan, assistant editor and later literary editor. He had been collecting material for this volume before his death in 1972. The memoranda in his files were not many but were full of stimulating comment and sharp information. The present writer was no less grateful to a shortened history of *The Times* left in manuscript by Oliver Woods and eventually completed by James Bishop and published in 1983 (*The Story of The Times* by Oliver Woods and James Bishop).

At the head of documentary evidence that lay outside the *Times* building, and was made available, must be placed the diaries of Geoffrey Dawson, editor until 1941, and Robert Barrington-Ward, editor 1941–48. For the loan of these diaries and for permission to quote from them warm thanks are due to Mrs. William Bell, Geoffrey Dawson's daughter, and to Mark Barrington-Ward, the former editor's son. Both Mrs. Bell and Mr. Barrington-Ward made helpful comments; I was grateful to the latter for some necessary corrections. Thanks are similarly expressed to Mrs. B. H. Heddy, daughter of Leo Kennedy, foreign leader writer for many years; she lent her father's diaries and allowed quotations from them. Lady Liddell Hart was no less generous with the papers left by her husband.

On the official plane I thank the Controller of H.M. Stationery Office for permission to quote from Crown copyright documents; Gordon Phillips sought out most of the State papers from which extracts are made. I also thank Bodley's Librarian for his help and the help of his staff in providing books and newspaper files on more occasions than can be counted. To Sir William Rees-Mogg, editor of *The Times* 1967–81, to Harold Evans and Charles Douglas-Home, his successors in the chair, I am grateful for permission to quote freely from *The Times*, *The Times Literary Supplement*, *The Times Educational Supplement*, and other periodicals of the Times Publishing Company and Times Newspapers Limited.

Quotations have been taken from many volumes of memoirs, works of historiography, studies of the press, and journals other than *The Times*. The exact references are given in the appropriate footnotes. For permission to publish such quotations thanks are warmly given to: Nicolas Barker, Thomas Barman, Sir Colin Coote, David Dilks, Lord Drogheda, Michael Foot, Franklin Gannon, Martin Gilbert, John Harvey, Kenneth Harris, Lord Ismay, Simon Jenkins, William Kirkman, T. O. Lloyd, Donald McLachlan, Harold Macmillan, John Douglas Pringle, Fred Taylor, Philip M. Williams.

Finally I thank Sir Edward Pickering and Mr. M. J. Hussey for their guidance and encouragement in the later stages of the project.

INDEX

499